Prospectus for the Public Offering of Securities in Europe

The Prospectus Directive is one of several directives on financial matters intended to create a unified European market with respect to financial markets and services. The Prospectus Directive, complemented by the Prospectus Regulation, sets forth unified European rules for the content and approval of prospectuses to be made public in the event of a public offering of securities in a Member State of the European Union or the European Economic Area. It introduces a single European passport for a prospectus that has been approved by the competent authority of a Member State, permitting this prospectus to be used for the public offering of securities in other Member States without the need to obtain approval in each state.

The Prospectus Directive sets forth the general rules and requirements for the preparation, approval and distribution of prospectuses and defines the content, format and publication of the prospectus to be made available in the event of a public offering of securities or admission to trading on a regulated market. The Prospectus Regulation, which complements the Prospectus Directive, defines the minimum information that must be included in the prospectus and its related documents.

This book discusses the Prospectus Directive and the Prospectus Regulation and their implementing rules in each Member State of the European Union and the European Economic Area. It provides companies and advisors with useful insight into the legal framework and the underlying principles applicable to prospectuses for the public offering of securities and the admission of securities to trading on regulated markets in the European Union and the European Economic Area.

This book is divided into two parts. Part one analyses the Community rules laid down in the Prospectus Directive and the Prospectus Regulation. The second part contains chapters discussing the laws of each Member State, each in accordance with a common format and contributed by a practitioner from that state. The annex to this book lists the implementing legislation in each Member State.

DIRK VAN GERVEN is a Brussels partner with the Benelux law firm of NautaDutilh and a member of the Brussels and New York Bars. He has extensive experience in all areas of corporate and financial law, including securities regulation. He is in charge of continuing legal education for the Dutch-speaking Bar Association of Brussels and has published widely in the fields of corporate and financial law. Since 2003, he has been a member of the supervisory board of Belgium's Banking, Finance and Insurance Commission.

Prospectus for the Public Offering of Securities in Europe

Volume I

General Editor

DIRK VAN GERVEN

CAMBRIDGE
UNIVERSITY PRESS

CAMBRIDGE UNIVERSITY PRESS
Cambridge, New York, Melbourne, Madrid, Cape Town, Singapore,
São Paulo, Delhi

Cambridge University Press
The Edinburgh Building, Cambridge CB2 8RU, UK

Published in the United States of America by Cambridge University Press, New York

www.cambridge.org
Information on this title: www.cambridge.org/9780521880701

First published 2008

Printed in the United Kingdom at the University Press, Cambridge

A catalogue record for this publication is available from the British Library

ISBN 978-0-521-88070-1 hardback

Contents

Contributors

BELGIUM
Dirk Van Gerven
Elke Janssens
NautaDutilh

CZECH REPUBLIC
Petr Kasik
Vlastimil Pihera
Kocián Šolc Balaštík

DENMARK
Vagn Thorup
David Moalem
Kromann Reumert

ESTONIA
Raino Paron
Monika Koolmeister
Raidla & Partners

GREECE
Vassiliki Lazarakou
George Georgiou
Zepos & Yannopoulos

HUNGARY
Jacques de Servigny
Gide Loyrette Nouel

LATVIA
Dace Silava-Tomsone
Toms Sulmanis
Aigars Gozitis
Lejinś, Torgāns & Partners

LITHUANIA
Irmantas Norkus
Eva Suduiko
Norcous & Partners

LUXEMBOURG
Josée Weydert
Franck-Olivier Cera
NautaDutilh

THE NETHERLANDS
Jan Paul Franx
NautaDutilh

POLAND
Danuta Pajewska
Jakub Pietruszka
Wardyński & Partners

PORTUGAL
José Alves do Carmo
José Miguel Oliveira
Arifo Amada
Barrocas Sarmento Neves

SLOVAKIA
Michaela Jurková
Čechová & Partners

UNITED KINGDOM
Nigel Boardman
Slaughter and May

NORWAY
Solveig Fagerheim Bugge
Sverre Tyrhaug
Thommessen

Preface

When offering securities to the public or requesting the admission of securities to trading on a regulated market in the European Union, the offeror or entity requesting admission must prepare a prospectus providing information about the securities being offered and the issuer. When securities are offered to the public, national law requires that the prospectus be reviewed and approved by the national financial supervisory authority. Until recently, the rules in each Member State were quite different, meaning that deciding on which market to offer securities, or request admission to trading, required a detailed comparative study. Furthermore, a simultaneous offering in several Member States entailed the application of different rules and approval of the prospectus by several supervisory authorities. In order to unify these rules and designate a single competent authority to approve prospectuses, the Council adopted the Prospectus Directive on 4 November 2003. The deadline for transposition of this directive into national law by the Member States was 1 July 2005. All Member States, including Bulgaria and Romania, have adapted their national legislation accordingly.

The main achievements of the Prospectus Directive are without a doubt (i) harmonisation of the applicable rules; (ii) the designation of a single competent authority to approve prospectuses; and (iii) the introduction of a European passport, allowing the same prospectus to be used throughout the European Union and the European Economic Area without new approval in each Member State being required. The Prospectus Directive reflects the desire of the European Commission to create a single passport for the publication of prospectuses for the offering of securities in the EU, and is part of a broader plan to create a single market for financial services, as confirmed at the March 2000 European Council meeting in Lisbon.

A book providing a comprehensive analysis of the European legal framework and the implementing legislation in each Member State of the European Union and the European Economic Area is a useful tool for companies seeking to finance their activities by issuing securities to the public. It will also prove helpful to their advisors and intermediaries involved in the offering of securities or the admission of securities to trading on a regulated market. This book has two volumes. Part one of the first volume explains the legal framework and Community rules laid down in the Prospectus Directive and the Prospectus Regulation. The second part focuses on the rules implementing the Prospectus Directive in each Member State; the Prospectus Regulation does not require implementation as it is directly applicable in the Member States. Volume one contains reports from fifteen Member States. The remaining reports will be published in the second volume.

Finally, I would like to thank the contributors to this book, esteemed practitioners from law firms throughout Europe, all of whom are well positioned to discuss the rules applicable in their respective countries. My thanks also go to those whose names are not mentioned in the reports but whose work was essential to the success of this project, namely Katherine Raab, Bianca Porcelli and Claire Platteuw, all of whom work at NautaDutilh.

Dirk Van Gerven
Brussels, 10 January 2008

PART I

1

General provisions of Community law relating to the prospectus to be published when securities are offered to the public or admitted to trading

DIRK VAN GERVEN
NautaDutilh

I Introduction

1 European passport

1. In a single market, it should be sufficient to have a prospectus for securities offered to the public or admitted to trading approved by a single authority, even if the offering encompasses several Member States of the European Union (EU). This is what Directive 2003/71 of the European Parliament and of the Council of 4 November 2003 on the prospectus to be published when securities are offered to the public or admitted to trading (the 'Prospectus Directive' or 'Dir.'),[1] amending Directive 2001/34, seeks to achieve by granting a European passport to prospectuses approved in a Member State under legislation implementing the Prospectus Directive. The other Member States must accept such prospectuses and cannot impose additional formalities (other than a requirement to notify the prospectus in accordance with the Prospectus Directive and to translate the summary into their official language). In this respect, the requirements for preparation, approval and distribution of prospectuses have been harmonised (Art. 1(1) Dir.). As explained below, under no. 8 of this report, these rules only apply to offerings having a total value of at least €2,500,000. For smaller public offerings, there is no obligation for the Member States to harmonise their rules in keeping with the Prospectus Directive. This limitation does not apply to the admission of securities to trading on a regulated market, however.

Furthermore, the Prospectus Directive intends to eliminate differences in the methods and timetables used to verify information in the various Member States, so as to better enable investors throughout the EU to assimilate information about securities in order to make wise investment decisions. The Prospectus Directive furthermore aims to ensure investor protection and guarantee market efficiency in accordance with the high regulatory standards used in the international markets.[2]

Finally, the Prospectus Directive defines the content, format and publication of the prospectus to be made available in the event of a public offering of securities or admission to trading on a regulated market.

The basic rule is that an offer to the public of transferable securities requires a prospectus containing sufficient information to fully inform investors about the securities offered and allow them to make an informed assessment of the associated risks.[3] Prior to publication, the prospectus must be approved by the competent authority supervising the offering and admission to trading of securities in that Member State. In this way, the prospectus, together with the applicable rules on the conduct of the

[1] *Official Journal* L 345 of 31 December 2003; *see* Annex I to this book.

[2] Tenth recital to the Prospectus Directive.

[3] Nineteenth recital to the Prospectus Directive.

business, will increase investor confidence and contribute to the proper functioning and development of the securities markets.[4]

The Prospectus Directive has been drafted with the following principles in mind:[5] (1) the introduction of enhanced disclosure standards in keeping with international standards for the public offering and admission to trading of securities; (2) the introduction of a document registration system in order to ensure that key information about the issuer is updated annually; (3) the possibility to offer or admit securities to trading on the basis of a prospectus approved in the home country; (4) the concentration of responsibility in the hands of the home-country authority; and (5) exclusive use of the comitology procedure, which entailed involving Member State representatives in preparing the implementing measures. This procedure was organised in consultation with the Committee of European Securities Regulators (CESR), which issued its recommendations for possible amendments to the Prospectus Regulation (see no. 4 of this report).[6]

2 Brief history

2. The first proposal for a directive on the prospectus to be published for a public offering or admission to trading of securities dates back to 30 May 2001.[7] At that time, the European Commission expressed its desire to introduce a single passport for the publication of prospectuses for the offering of securities in the EU. This initiative formed part of a broader plan to create a single market for financial services.[8] In order to facilitate access to investment capital throughout the European Union, the question of a single European passport for issuers was thus raised at the March 2000 European Council meeting in Lisbon.[9]

The European Central Bank (ECB) supported the Commission's initiative by a favourable opinion of 16 November 2001.[10] The Economic and Social Committee rendered its opinion on 17 January 2002.[11] The

[4] Eighteenth recital to the Prospectus Directive.

[5] *See* Initial Legislative Document (COD/2001/0117) of 30 May 2001.

[6] Initial Report of the Committee of Wise Men on the Regulation of European Securities Markets of 9 November 2000, p. 25; Final Report of the Committee of Wise Men on the Regulation of European Securities Markets of 15 February 2001, 94, 104; Annex 5 to both reports sets forth the comitology procedure.

[7] *Official Journal* C 240 of 28 August 2001.

[8] This project was made a priority at the European Council meeting in Cardiff on 15 and 16 June 1998 (see no. 24 of the Presidency Conclusions) and was further developed in the Financial Services Action Plan (Commission Communication of 11 May 1999), '[i]mplementing the framework for financial markets' (COM(1999) 232 final; www.europa.eu).

[9] No. 21 of the Presidency Conclusions of the European Council meeting in Lisbon of 23 and 24 March 2000. [10] *Official Journal* C 344 of 6 December 2001.

[11] *Ibid.*, C 80 of 3 April 2002.

European Parliament proposed sixty-five amendments, which resulted in an Amended Proposal for a Directive of the European Parliament and the European Council of 9 August 2002.[12] Agreement on a new proposal with some changes was obtained in the European Council on 5 November 2002. Further negotiations resulted in Common Position No 25/2003, adopted by the European Council on 24 March 2003.[13] In a second reading, the European Parliament voted on twenty-one new amendments on 2 July 2003, all of which were accepted by the European Commission. This allowed the final text of the Prospectus Directive to be adopted smoothly.

3 Legal framework and modifications

3. The Prospectus Directive amends Directive 2001/34 of 28 May 2001 on the admission of securities to official stock exchange listings and on information to be published on those securities[14] to the extent the latter also regulated the information to be made available upon admission to trading on a regulated market. Moreover, the provisions of Directive 2001/34 on the publication of listing particulars for admission to trading have been deleted (Art. 27 Dir.); however, this directive continues to regulate the conditions for admission to trading on a regulated market and the publication of information and other obligations following admission to trading.

The Prospectus Directive furthermore repeals Directive 89/298 of 17 April 1989 coordinating the requirements for the drawing up, scrutiny and distribution of the prospectus to be published when transferable securities are offered to the public.[15] Any references to the Directive of 17 April 1989 in other legislative documents should henceforth be construed to refer to the Prospectus Directive (Art. 28 Dir.).

The Prospectus Directive and Directive 2001/34 of 28 May 2001 on the admission of securities to official stock exchange listing and on information to be published on those securities, should be read together as creating a single system. The Prospectus Directive deals with the information that must be published when securities are admitted to trading on a regulated market and when a public offering is made, while Directive 2001/34 of 28 May 2001 regulates the information that must be made available when securities are listed on an official stock exchange. The provisions relating to publication of information in the latter directive have been replaced by Directive 2004/109 of 15 December 2004 on the harmonisation of transparency requirements in relation to information about issuers whose securities are

[12] *Ibid.*, C 20 of 28 January 2003. [13] *Ibid.*, C 125 of 27 May 2003.

[14] *Ibid.*, L 184 of 6 July 2001.

[15] *Ibid.*, L 124 of 5 May 1989. This directive created an incomplete and complex mechanism of mutual recognition which did not achieve the objective of a single European passport (first recital to the Prospectus Directive).

admitted to trading on a regulated market.[16] The deadline for transposition of Directive 2004/109 by the Member States was 20 January 2007.

4. The Prospectus Directive is complemented by Commission Regulation 809/2004 of 29 April 2004 (the 'Prospectus Regulation') implementing the Prospectus Directive as regards information contained in prospectuses as well as the format, incorporation by reference and publication of such prospectuses and dissemination of advertisements (the 'Prospectus Regulation' or 'Reg.').[17] The Prospectus Regulation defines the minimum information that must be included in the prospectus and related documents. Guidance in applying the Prospectus Regulation can be found in the CESR's recommendations for consistent implementation of the Prospectus Regulation and in the answers contained in the document 'Frequently asked questions regarding Prospectuses: Common positions agreed by CESR Members',[18] and the summary records of the Informal Meetings of the delegates of the competent authorities of the Member States which met with the Commission. Two summary records are available on the Internet: (1) the Summary record of the 3rd Informal Meeting of 26 January 2005 on Prospectus Transposition (hereafter, 'Summary record of the 3rd Informal Meeting of 26 January 2005'); and, (2) the Summary record of the 4th Informal Meeting of 8 March 2005 on Prospectus Transposition (hereafter, 'Summary record of the 4th Informal Meeting of 8 March 2005').[19]

This legislative technique is in accordance with the Committee of Wise Men's Final Report on the Regulation of European Securities Markets of 15 February 2001 (the 'Lamfalussy-approach'), which proposes legislation on four levels: framework principles, implementing measures, cooperation and enforcement.[20] Level 1 should be limited to defining broad framework principles to be set forth in a directive. Level 2 focuses on the technical implementing measures to be adopted by the Commission, assisted by a committee of experts, in the form of a regulation. The Commission should be able to change these measures easily in order to ensure that they reflect supervisory and market developments.[21] Level 3 is focused on ensuring better cooperation amongst the competent authorities (see no. 80 of this

[16] *Ibid.*, L 390 of 31 December 2004. This directive repeals Title IV of Directive 2001/34 ('Ongoing obligations relating to securities admitted to official listing').

[17] Published for the first time in *Official Journal* L 149 of 30 April 2004, with an amended version in *Official Journal* L 215 of 16 June 2004; *see* Annex II to this book. The Prospectus Regulation has been amended twice, by Regulation 1787/2006 of 4 December 2006 (*Official Journal* L 337 of 5 December 2006) and Regulation 211/2007 of 27 February 2007 (*Official Journal* L 61 of 28 February 2007).

[18] Dated 18 July 2006, *available at* www.cesr.eu.

[19] These summary records can be consulted on internet (www.europa.eu.int/comm/internal_market).

[20] Sixth recital to the Prospectus Directive.

[21] Ninth recital to the Prospectus Directive.

report). At level 4, enforcement is realised by ensuring that the competent authorities wield minimal identical broad powers (see no. 76 of this report). More generally, the forty-seventh recital to the Prospectus Directive announces the establishment of a European Securities Unit to ensure the uniform approval of prospectuses, thus further enhancing the harmonised application of Community law.

In general, the Commission is empowered under the Prospectus Directive to adopt implementing measures concerning the definitions used in the Prospectus Directive in order to take into account technical developments on the financial markets and to ensure uniform application of the Prospectus Directive (Art. 2(4) Dir.).

These implementing measures must be prepared in accordance with Council Decision 1999/468 of 28 June 1999 laying down the procedures for the exercise of implementing powers conferred on the Commission (Art. 24(2) Dir.).[22] In doing so, the Commission must take into account Community legislation and recommendations, economic developments, and disclosure measures relating to the registration of qualified individual investors (Art. 2(4) Dir.). It may not modify the essential provisions of the Prospectus Directive (Art. 24(2) Dir.).

In preparing these implementing measures, the Commission will be assisted by the European Securities Committee (ESC), established by a Commission decision of 6 June 2001.[23]

The forty-first recital to the Prospectus Directive sets forth the principles which the Commission must observe in preparing a regulation containing technical provisions implementing the framework set forth in the Prospectus Directive. These principles are the following:

- the need to ensure confidence in financial markets amongst small investors and small and medium-sized enterprises (SMEs) by promoting high standards of transparency in the financial markets;
- the need to provide investors with a wide range of competing investment opportunities and a level of disclosure and protection tailored to their circumstances;
- the need to ensure that independent regulatory authorities enforce the rules consistently, especially as regards the fight against white-collar crime;
- the need for a high level of transparency and consultation with all market participants and with the European Parliament and the Council;
- the need to encourage innovation in the financial markets if they are to be dynamic and efficient;

[22] *Official Journal* L 184 of 17 July 1999.

[23] *Ibid.*, L 191 of 13 July 2001. This is in accordance with the comitology procedure explained above (see no. 1).

- the need to ensure systemic stability of the financial system by close and reactive monitoring of financial innovation;
- the importance of reducing the cost of, and increasing access to, capital;
- the need to balance, on a long-term basis, the costs and benefits to market participants (including SMEs and small investors) of any implementing measures;
- the need to foster the international competitiveness of the Community's financial markets without prejudice to a much-needed extension of international cooperation;
- the need to achieve a level playing field for all market participants by establishing Community legislation every time it is appropriate;
- the need to respect differences in national financial markets where these do not unduly impinge on the coherence of the single market;
- the need to ensure coherence with other Community legislation in this area, as imbalances in information and a lack of transparency may jeopardise the operation of the markets and above all harm consumers and small investors.

These principles are reflected in the Prospectus Regulation. If the wording of the Prospectus Regulation is not clear, it should be interpreted in accordance with the above principles.

II Application

5. The deadline for transposition of the Prospectus Directive into national law by the Member States was 1 July 2005 (Art. 29 Dir.). Prospectuses approved before such date do not require a new approval under the Prospectus Directive. In the event of public offers, under an ongoing offering programme approved before such date, constituting separate offers, the prospectus will require approval in accordance with the Prospectus Directive.[24]

Most Member States were late in enacting implementing legislation, but all, meanwhile, implemented the Prospectus Directive. On 1 January 2007, Romania and Bulgaria acceded to the EU. Consequently, the Prospectus Directive and the Prospectus Regulation also apply in those countries with immediate effect.

The Prospectus Regulation applies as from 1 July 2005. As it has direct effect, the Prospectus Regulation applies without further action on the part of the Member States.

The Prospectus Directive and the Prospectus Regulation are also applicable in the member states of the European Economic Area (EEA), i.e. Norway, Iceland and Liechtenstein.[25] Therefore, any references in

[24] Summary record of the 4th Informal Meeting of 8 March 2005, p. 5.

[25] Further to the Decision of 8 June 2004 of the EEA Joint Committee, amending Annex IX to the EEA Agreement (*Official Journal*, 25 November 2004).

this report to the European Union or its Member States should be construed to include these three countries as well, unless specified otherwise.

III Scope

1 General remarks

6. The Prospectus Directive applies to prospectuses for the public offering of securities or for the admission of securities to trading on a regulated market in the European Economic Area. Takeover bids with a price paid partly or entirely in securities (as defined below) must also comply with the provisions of the Prospectus Directive unless they are governed by the rules implementing the Directive of 21 April 2004 on takeover bids[26] and such rules are considered equivalent by the competent authority to those set forth in the Prospectus Directive (see no. 13 of this report). In any event, the Prospectus Directive does not apply to a takeover bid if the price is paid in cash regardless of whether the bid complies with the Directive of 21 April 2004, since no securities are offered to the public.

The prospectus obligation and the other obligations contained in the Prospectus Directive apply only to transferable securities. Non-transferable securities are not covered by the Prospectus Directive.[27] Transferable securities are defined as those which are negotiable on the capital markets, with the exception of payment instruments.[28] The following securities are considered negotiable on the capital markets: shares in companies and other securities equivalent to company shares; interests in partnerships or other entities; depositary receipts in respect of shares, bonds or other forms of securitised debt (including depositary receipts in respect of such securities); and any other securities giving the right to acquire or sell any transferable security or giving rise to a cash settlement determined with reference to transferable securities, currencies, interest rates or yields, commodities or other indices or measures,[29] including

[26] *Official Journal* L 142 of 30 April 2004.

[27] Such as non-transferable options granted to employees (see the answer to Question 3 of 'Frequently asked questions regarding Prospectuses: Common positions agreed by CESR Members', 18 July 2006, *available at* www.cesr.eu.

[28] Art. 4(1)(18) of Directive 2004/39 of 21 April 2004 on markets in financial instruments (*Official Journal* L 145 of 30 April 2004). Article 1(a) of the Prospectus Directive refers to Article 1(4) of the Council Directive of 10 May 1993 on investment services in the securities field (*Official Journal* L 141 of 11 June 1993) as last amended by Directive 2000/64 of 7 November 2000 (*Official Journal* L 290 of 17 November 2000). However, this directive has since been repealed by Article 69 of Directive 2004/39 of 21 April 2004, effective 1 May 2006. Any references to the repealed directive should thus be construed to refer to the equivalent terms as defined in the Directive of 21 April 2004. The deadline for transposition of the Directive into national law was 1 May 2006 (Art. 70 of the Directive of 21 April 2004).

[29] *Ibid.*

warrants, covered warrants and certificates, convertible notes and other securities convertible at the investor's option.[30] However, money market instruments – i.e. instruments normally traded on the money market that mature in less than one year – are excluded, although the Member States can decide to extend the scope of their prospectus rules to cover these instruments (Art. 2(1)(a) Dir.).

A prospectus must be prepared and made public in accordance with the Prospectus Directive in two cases: upon (i) an offering of securities to the public (see nos. 10 and 11 of this report); or (ii) an admission of securities to trading on a regulated market situated or operating within an EU Member State (see no. 14 of this report).

A regulated market is defined as '*a multilateral system operated and/or managed by a market operator, which brings together or facilitates the bringing together of multiple third-parties buying and selling interests in financial instruments*[31] *– in the system and in accordance with its non-discretionary rules – in a way that results in a contract, in respect of the financial instruments admitted to trading under its rules and/or systems, and which is authorised and functions regularly and in accordance with the provisions of Title III*' of the Directive 2004/39 of 21 April 2004 on markets in financial instruments.[32] Each Member State must keep a list of the regulated markets for which it is considered the home Member State within the meaning of the Directive of 21 April 2004, and forward this list to the other Member States and the European Commission, which shall publish it in the *Official Journal of the European Communities*.[33]

7. The Prospectus Directive covers all types of securities, regardless of whether they represent equity,[34] and consequently also applies to bonds, including eurobonds.

The Prospectus Directive nevertheless excludes from coverage a long list of securities and offerings (see no. 8 of this report). The public offering and admission to trading of such securities are not subject to the prospectus obligation or to any other provisions of the Prospectus Directive, such as

[30] Twelfth recital to the Prospectus Directive.

[31] The term 'financial instruments' is defined in Section C of Annex I to the Directive of 21 April 2004 on markets in financial instruments.

[32] Article 2(1)(j) of the Prospectus Directive refers to Article 1(13) of the Directive of 10 May 1993 on investment services in the securities field. As mentioned, this directive has been repealed by Article 69 of the Directive of 21 April 2004 on markets in financial instruments, effective 1 May 2006. Any references to the repealed directive should thus be construed to refer to the equivalent terms as defined in the Directive of 21 April 2004 (Art. 69). The current definition of a 'regulated market' is contained in Article 4(1)(14) of the Directive of 21 April 2004.

[33] Art. 47 of the Directive of 21 April 2004.

[34] Twelfth recital to the Prospectus Directive, noting that the broad definition of 'securities' is only valid for the Prospectus Directive and may not be used to interpret other legislative documents.

those regarding advertisements. Thus, if a prospectus is prepared and approved under national law for the public offering or admission to trading of excluded securities, it will not be eligible for the European passport created by the Prospectus Directive, unless in the limited cases defined in no. 9 of this report.

2 Excluded securities

8. The Prospectus Directive does not apply to the following securities and offerings:

(a) units issued by collective investment undertakings other than the closed-end type; units of a collective investment undertaking are defined as securities issued by a collective investment undertaking as representing rights of the participants in this undertaking over its assets; collective investment undertakings other than the closed-end type means trusts and investment companies whose object is the collective investment of capital provided by the public and which operate on the principle of risk-spreading, the units of which are, at the holders' request, repurchased or redeemed, directly or indirectly, out of the undertaking's assets (Art. 2(1)(o) and (p) Dir.);

(b) non-equity securities issued by a Member State or by a Member State's regional or local authorities, a public international body of which one or more Member States are members, the European Central Bank[35] or the central bank of a Member State; non-equity securities are all securities which are not equity securities; equity securities are defined as '*shares and other transferable securities equivalent to shares in companies, as well as any other type of transferable securities giving the right to acquire any of the aforementioned securities as a consequence of their being converted or the rights conferred by them being exercised, provided that securities of the latter type are issued by the issuer of the underlying shares or by an entity belonging to the group of the said issuer*' (Art. 2(1)(b) and (c) Dir.); this derogation shall not apply to securities offered by countries which are not members of the European Economic Area;

(c) shares in the capital of central banks of the Member States;

(d) securities unconditionally and irrevocably guaranteed by a Member State or by a regional or local authority of a Member State;[36]

[35] For a justification of this exemption as regards securities issued by the European Central Bank, *see* the ECB's opinion of 16 November 2001, point 10 (*Official Journal* C 344 of 6 December 2001).

[36] *See* the eleventh recital to the Prospectus Directive and the Common Position adopted by the European Council on 24 March 2003 (*Official Journal* C 125 E of 27 May 2003, 49).

(e) securities issued by associations with legal status or non-profit organisations recognised by a Member State, with a view to obtaining the means necessary to achieve their not-for-profit goals;
(f) non-equity securities issued in a continuous or repeated manner by credit institutions provided these securities (i) are not subordinated, convertible or exchangeable; (ii) do not give rise to a right to subscribe to or acquire other types of securities and are not linked to derivatives; (iii) materialise receipt of repayable deposits; and (iv) are covered by a deposit guarantee scheme under Directive 94/19/EC of 30 May 1994 on deposit-guarantee schemes;[37]
(g) non-fungible capital shares whose main purpose is to provide their holder with a right to occupy an apartment or other form of immovable property or any part thereof and which cannot be sold without relinquishing this right; this exemption is specifically designed to exclude shares in a housing association which each occupant of an apartment or other form of real property is bound to hold and which give rise to special rights that render the shares non-fungible;[38]
(h) securities included in an offering for total consideration of less than €2,500,000, calculated over a period of 12 months;
(i) *bostadsobligationer* issued repeatedly by credit institutions in Sweden whose main purpose is to grant mortgage loans, provided (i) the *bostadsobligationer* issued are of the same series and (ii) are on tap during a specified issuance period; (iii) the terms and conditions of the *bostadsobligationer* are not changed during the issuance period; and (iv) any sums deriving from issuance of the *bostadsobligationer*, in accordance with the issuer's articles of association, are invested in assets that provide sufficient coverage for any liabilities deriving from the securities;[39] and
(j) non-equity securities issued in a continuous or repeated manner by credit institutions where the total consideration for the offer is less than €50,000,000, calculated over a period of 12 months, provided these securities (i) are not subordinated, convertible or exchangeable, and (ii) do not give rise to a right to subscribe to or acquire other types of securities and are not linked to derivatives[40] (Art. 1(2) Dir.); issues

[37] *Official Journal* L135 of 31 May 1994.

[38] Common Position adopted by the European Council on 24 March 2003, *Official Journal* C 125 E of 27 May 2003, 48.

[39] *Bostadsobligationers* are a special type of mortgage-backed bond governed by Swedish law which are exempt from the prospectus obligation owing to their special nature (Common Position adopted by the European Council on 24 March 2003, *Official Journal* C 125 E of 27 May 2003, 48).

[40] These are excluded since the domestic nature of such offerings renders it appropriate to regulate them at the national level (Common Position adopted by the European Council on 24 March 2003, *Official Journal* C 125 E of 27 May 2003, 49).

shall be considered continuous or repeated if they are on tap or concern at least two separate issues of securities of a similar type and/or class[41] over a period of 12 months (Art. 2(1)(l) Dir.).

With respect to the last exemption above, Article 30(2) of the Prospectus Directive provides a transitional provision for Member States that allowed a complete or partial exemption from the obligation to publish a prospectus under (repealed) Directive 89/298 of 17 April 1989 coordinating the requirements for the drawing up, scrutiny and distribution of the prospectus to be published when transferable securities are offered to the public,[42] for the offer to the public (including the admission to trading on a regulated market) of debt securities or other transferable securities equivalent to debt securities issued in a continuous or repeated manner by credit institutions or other financial institutions equivalent to credit institutions that regularly publish their annual accounts and which are, within the European Economic Area, set up or governed by a special law or pursuant to such a law, or are subject to public supervision intended to protect savings. Pursuant to this transitional provision, offerings of such securities by credit and/or financial institutions shall continue to fall outside the scope of the Prospectus Directive regardless of the total consideration and the conditions for the securities, provided, of course, they are issued in a continuous or repeated manner. This transition period applies for five years following the entry into force of the Prospectus Directive, i.e. from 31 December 2003 (Art. 32 Dir.). Member States who provided for such an exemption must bring their legislation into line with Article 1(2)(j) of the Prospectus Directive no later than 31 December 2008.

From (h) above, it follows that public offerings of securities are only subject to the provisions of the Prospectus Directive if the total consideration of the offering is equal to or exceeds €2,500,000 (calculated over a twelve-month period). The value of the offering throughout all countries of the European Economic Area is taken into account in determining whether this threshold has been met.[43] If the offering falls under this threshold, the Member States need not apply the rules of the Prospectus Directive and the Prospectus Regulation, meaning such offerings will be governed for the most part by national law and there is no obligation to harmonise the applicable rules.[44] However, the offeror or issuer can always

[41] This includes not only identical securities but also securities that belong in general terms to a single category, possibly including different products such as debt securities, certificates and warrants or the same product under the same programme, or different features notably in terms of seniority, types of underlying assets or the basis used to determine the redemption amount or coupon payment (*see* the thirteenth recital to the Prospectus Directive). [42] *Official Journal* L 124 of 5 May 1989.

[43] Answer to Question 15 of 'Frequently asked questions regarding Prospectuses: Common positions agreed by CESR Members', 18 July 2006, *available at* www.cesr.eu.

[44] Common Position adopted by the European Council on 24 March 2003, *Official Journal* C 125 E of 27 May 2003, 48.

decide to make an offering below €2,500,000 subject to the provisions of the Prospectus Directive (see no. 9 of this report). In this latter case, a prospectus must be prepared unless the total consideration is less than €100,000, in which event the offering will qualify as a private placement (see no. 11 of this report).[45] Offerings of securities without consideration fall into the latter category.[46]

The threshold of €2,500,000 does not apply to requests for admission to a regulated market, which are governed by the Prospectus Directive regardless of the total value of the securities for which admission to trading is sought.

A public offering or admission to trading of the securities listed above will be subject to the national law of the Member States where the offering is made or where admission to trading is sought. Thus, a prospectus or other publications may be required but need not comply with the provisions of the Prospectus Directive.

9. With respect to the public offering or listing on a regulated market of any of the types of securities mentioned under points (b), (d), (h), (i) and (j) above, the offeror or issuer can always decide voluntarily to prepare a prospectus in accordance with the provisions of the Prospectus Directive (Art. 1(3) Dir.).

In the event of an opt-in, the provisions of the Prospectus Directive, including those regarding the European passport, shall apply. The Member States must allow this possibility and may not provide otherwise in their national laws.

This possibility to opt-in and to benefit from the European passport in accordance with the Prospectus Directive does not apply to the other securities and offerings listed above in no. 8 of this report.[47]

3 Definition of an offer to the public

10. As mentioned above, the offer of transferable securities to the public entails the preparation of a prospectus in accordance with the Prospectus Directive and Prospectus Regulation.

[45] The characterisation of an offering to the public for total consideration of less than €100,000 as a private placement means that the Member States cannot apply to such small offerings their national rules on prospectuses, which shall consequently benefit from the exemption contained in Article 3(2) of the Prospectus Directive. Small offerings of this type are governed by the applicable provisions of the Prospectus Directive (see no. 64 of this report), while offerings for total consideration of €100,000 to €2,500,000 (calculated over 12 months) are excluded as such from the scope of the Prospectus Directive (see the Common Position adopted by the European Council on 24 March 2003, *Official Journal* C 125 E of 27 May 2003, 50), unless the offeror chooses to opt in (see no. 9 of this report).

[46] Answer to Question 4 of 'Frequently asked questions regarding Prospectuses: Common positions agreed by CESR Members', 18 July 2006, *available at* www.cesr.eu.

[47] Summary record of the 3rd Informal Meeting of 26 January 2005, p. 2.

An offer to the public is defined as a communication to persons, regardless of the form, '*presenting sufficient information on the terms of the offer and the securities to be offered, so as to enable an investor to decide to purchase or subscribe to these securities*'. This definition includes the placement of securities through financial intermediaries (Art. 2(1)(d) Dir.).

It follows from this definition that if the communication does not contain '*sufficient information on the terms of the offer and the offered securities*' to '*enable an investor to decide to purchase or subscribe to*' the transferable securities, no public offering is made for purposes of the Prospectus Directive. This implies that a communication which contains insufficient information shall not be considered an offering entailing the preparation of a prospectus under the Prospectus Directive. Of course, this definition is intended to exclude the communication of general information about securities clearly not intended to form part of an offering. Moreover, national legislation can prohibit communications containing insufficient information.[48]

In general, a communication that does not refer to an offer price shall not be considered a public offer, as there is insufficient information about the terms of the offering. However, if the price can be deduced indirectly from the information provided, the communication may qualify as an offer under the above definition. In practice, any communication that mentions the possibility of an offer must be reviewed carefully in light of the above definition of a public offering. If in doubt, it is advisable to contact the competent authority and submit the communication for review.

Based on the above definition, an offering made in accordance with the Prospectus Directive must also enable '*an investor to purchase or subscribe*' to the offered securities. It follows from this wording that allocations of securities where there is no possibility of choice on the part of the recipient, including no right of refusal, do not qualify as public offerings of securities.[49]

IV Obligation to prepare and publish a prospectus and exemptions

1 Offer of securities to the public

A Prospectus obligation and private placements

11. The offering of transferable securities to the public is subject to prior publication of a prospectus (Art. 3(1) Dir.).

The obligation to publish a prospectus does not apply in the following cases: (a) an offering of securities addressed solely to qualified investors; (b) an offering of securities addressed to fewer than 100 persons in a given

[48] National legislation will define what is sufficient information (Summary record of the 3rd Informal Meeting of 26 January 2005, pp. 2–3).

[49] Answer to Question 4 of 'Frequently asked questions regarding Prospectuses: Common positions agreed by CESR Members', 18 July 2006, *available at* www.cesr.eu.

Member State,[50] other than qualified investors; (c) an offering of securities addressed to investors who acquire the securities for total consideration of at least €50,000 per investor for each separate offering; (d) an offering of securities whose denomination per unit amounts to at least €50,000; and/or (e) an offering of securities having total consideration of less than €100,000, calculated over a period of twelve months (Art. 3(2) Dir.).[51] Such offerings do not qualify as public offerings of securities within the meaning of Article 3 of the Prospectus Directive[52] and can be organised without a prospectus. Moreover, any publication of information about the offering, so long as it remains within the above limits, is not subject to prior approval by the competent authority. However, the distribution of such information should comply with the rules discussed under no. 64 of this report.

Gratuitous offerings of securities are treated as small offerings for consideration of less than €100,000.[53] This will not be the case if there are hidden considerations that result in the above threshold being exceeded, for example if the securities are offered in lieu of quantifiable financial benefits in another form.[54]

Any subsequent resale of the securities shall be considered a separate offering subject to the prospectus obligation if it does not fall within one of the above exemptions These exemptions cannot be applied if the securities

[50] The offering can, as a result, be made to 100 persons or more, provided it is made in different Member States and the threshold of less than 100 persons in each Member State is not exceeded.

[51] Generally, offerings for total consideration of less than €2.5 million (calculated over a period of twelve months) fall outside the scope of the Prospectus Directive (see no. 8 of this report), unless the offeror or issuer chooses to have the offering governed by the Prospectus Directive (see no. 9 of this report). In that case, a prospectus must be drafted unless the total consideration is less than €100,000, in which case the exemption for private placements shall apply (see the Common Position adopted by the European Council on 24 March 2003, *Official Journal* C 125 E of 27 May 2003, 50).

[52] In the proposals for the Prospectus Directive, this was clearly stated in the definition of a public offering of securities (*see* Art. 2(2) of the amended proposal, *Official Journal* C 020 E, 28 January 2003). Moving these derogations to Article 3 (*Obligation to publish a prospectus*) could create some confusion as to the difference with the exemptions in Article 4. However, it follows from the Common position adopted by the Council of 4 March 2003 (*Official Journal* C 125 E of 27 May 2003, 50) that it was not the legislature's intent to change the scope of these derogations (*see also* Communication of the Commission of 26 March 2003, COD/2001/0117), which should thus not be considered an offering of securities to the public within the meaning of the Prospectus Directive.

[53] The allocation of securities for free which the recipient cannot refuse does not qualify as an offering of securities to the public for purposes of the Prospectus Directive (*see* no. 10 of this report).

[54] Answer to Question 4 of 'Frequently asked questions regarding Prospectuses: Common positions agreed by CESR Members', 18 July 2006, *available at* www.cesr.eu. However, this is not the case for shares offered for free to employees under an employee share scheme. Such shares shall not be deemed offered in lieu of remuneration, unless expressly provided.

are placed through financial intermediaries and the above conditions are not met for the final placement (Art. 3(2) Dir.).

Qualified investors are deemed not to require the protection of a prospectus as they are thought to have sufficient expertise and knowledge to define the risks represented by the securities offered. The following entities are considered qualified investors: (i) legal entities regulated or authorised to operate in the financial markets, including credit institutions,[55] investment firms, other authorised or regulated financial institutions, insurance companies, collective investment vehicles and their management companies, pension funds and their management companies, commodities dealers, and entities not authorised or regulated for this purpose whose sole object is to invest in securities; (ii) national and regional governments, central banks, international and transnational institutions such as the International Monetary Fund, the European Central Bank, the European Investment Bank and similar international organisations; and (iii) other legal entities that do not qualify as small and medium-sized enterprises (SMEs) (Art. 2(1)(e) Dir.). Small and medium-sized enterprises are companies which, according to their last annual or consolidated accounts, meet at least two of the following three criteria: (i) an average during the financial year of less than 250 employees; (ii) a balance sheet total not exceeding €43 million; and (iii) net annual turnover not exceeding €50 million (Art. 2(1)(f) Dir.). The Commission can adjust these figures to take into account technical developments in the financial markets and to ensure uniform application of the Prospectus Directive (see no. 4 *in fine* of this report).

The above definition of a qualified investor excludes natural persons, even if they operate an enterprise that is not considered an SME by the above standards.

A Member State can characterise as a qualified investor natural persons who reside in that state and who expressly request to be so characterised if they meet at least two of the following criteria: (1) the person has carried out at an average of at least ten transactions of significant size on the securities markets per quarter over the past four quarters; (2) the value of that person's securities portfolio exceeds €500,000; and (3) the person works or has worked for at least one year in the financial sector in a position that requires knowledge of securities investments (Arts 2(1)(e)(iv) and 2(2) Dir.). The Prospectus Directive does not allow the Member States to add additional requirements to the definition of a qualified investor. If a natural person satisfies the above criteria (and national law permits natural persons to be considered qualified investors) the competent authority cannot refuse

[55] A credit institution is an undertaking as defined in Article 1(1)(a) of Directive 2000/12 of 20 March 2000 on the taking up and pursuit of the business of credit institutions (*Official Journal* L 126, 26 May 2000), as amended by Directive 2000/28/EC (*Official Journal* L 275, 27 October 2000)(Art. 2(1)g) Dir.).

to register the natural person as a qualified investor on other grounds. It follows from the above that with respect to cross-border transactions, the qualification of qualified investor will depend on the national law of the Member State where the investor resides.[56]

Moreover, a Member State can choose to authorise as a qualified investor certain SMEs registered in that state who expressly ask to be considered as such (Art. 2(1)(e)(v) Dir.).

If a Member State decides to authorise natural persons or SMEs as qualified investors it must ensure that the competent authority in that state keeps a register of such persons and SMEs. This register must be kept in such manner that an adequate level of data protection is ensured. Any person or SME listed in this register is entitled to request de-characterisation at any time and thus to no longer be considered a qualified investor (Art. 2(3) Dir.). This register must at least be available to all issuers, but Member States may grant wider access subject to the law on data protection.[57]

12. In the event of a private placement, the offeror can decide to prepare a private placement memorandum which can be made available to qualified investors, investors who are prepared to acquire securities for a total consideration of at least €50,000, or persons who are not qualified investors if there are fewer than 100 per Member State. In this case, the content and publication requirements of the Prospectus Directive will not apply. Of course, the national law of the Member State where the private placement is organised may impose specific requirements. In general, the offeror must ensure that the private placement memorandum contains sufficient information so as not to confuse subscribers. The same applies to small offerings.

The private placement memorandum should be distributed in an equal manner to all investors concerned (see no. 64 of this report).

B Exemptions

13. The following offerings are exempt from the prospectus requirement (Art. 4(1) Dir.):

(a) the offering of shares issued in substitution for shares of the same class already issued, if the issuance of such new shares does not involve any increase in the issued capital;
(b) the offering of securities in connection with a takeover by means of an exchange offer, provided a document is available containing information regarded by the competent authority as equivalent to that set forth in the prospectus required by the Prospectus Directive, taking into account the requirements of Community law, in particular the

56 Summary record of the 3rd Informal Meeting of 26 January 2005, p. 3.
57 Summary record of the 4th Informal Meeting of 8 March 2005, p. 2.

Directive of 21 April 2004 on takeover bids;[58] the Prospectus Directive does not refer to the competent authority of the home Member State for purposes of approval of the prospectus; the bidder will ask the supervisory authority in the Member State where the takeover bid is launched or organised, whether its offer document contains equivalent information in comparison with the information required by the Prospectus Directive and the Prospectus Regulation;[59] the equivalence opinion of the above supervisory authority does not imply a passport in this respect; it implies that the competent authorities in other Member States must not accept this equivalence opinion, and will verify each independently whether the information contained in the offer document is equivalent;[60]

(c) the offering or allotment of securities in connection with a merger, provided a document is available containing information regarded by the competent authority as equivalent[61] to that set forth in the prospectus required under the Prospectus Directive, taking into account the requirements of Community law, in particular the Third Directive of 9 October 1978 on mergers of public limited-liability companies[62] and the Directive of 26 October 2005 on cross-border mergers of limited-liability companies;[63] the national authorities will decide whether this exemption can also be invoked for demergers; they may grant this exemption if a document with equivalent information is made available under applicable legislation; [64]

(d) the offering or allotment of shares free of charge to existing shareholders, and dividends paid in the form of shares of the same class as those in respect of which such dividends are paid, provided a document is made available containing information on the number and nature of the shares and the reasons for and details of the offering; this exemption applies to the offering of an option to reinvest dividends in the form of shares instead of receiving cash;[65] and

[58] *Official Journal* L 142 of 30 April 2004.

[59] This is also the opinion of the informal taskforce of representatives of the supervisory authorities organised by the Commission (Summary record of the 3rd Informal Meeting of 26 January 2005, p. 6). During this meeting the Commission stated that it has no immediate plans to adopt implementing measures in respect of the meaning of 'equivalence' in this provision of the Prospectus Directive. See for more details, D. Van Gerven, 'Rules of Community Law applicable to takeover bids', in *Common Legal Framework for Takeover Bids in Europe*, Cambridge University Press, *to be published*.

[60] This is also confirmed by the informal taskforce of representatives of the supervisory authorities organised by the Commission (see the reference in the preceding footnote).

[61] For the notion of equivalence, see (b) above.

[62] *Official Journal*, L 295 of 20 October 1978. [63] *Official Journal*., L 310 of 25 November 2005. [64] Summary record of the 4th Informal Meeting of 8 March 2005, p. 3.

[65] Summary record of the 4th Informal Meeting of 8 March 2005, p. 3.

(e) the offering or allotment of securities to existing or former directors or employees by their employer whose securities are admitted to trading on a regulated market or by an affiliated undertaking,[66] provided a document is made available containing information on the number and nature of the securities and the reasons for and details of the offering; the regulated market must be a market in the European Union that satisfies the criteria set forth under no. 6 of this report; it is apparently not required that the securities offered to the directors and employees also be admitted to trading.

Whether one of the above exemptions is available will be decided on a case by case basis by the competent authorities of the Member State on which territory the securities are offered to the public. An exemption granted in one Member State does not imply a passport to benefit from such exemption in other Member States.[67]

However, if a prospectus is prepared for publication in the cases listed above, it will be subject to the provisions of the Prospectus Directive and must be approved by the competent authority of the home Member State in accordance with the procedure set forth under no. 17 *et seq.* of this report. This follows from Article 13(1) of the Prospectus Directive, which prohibits the publication of a prospectus which has not been approved by the competent authority of the home Member State (see no. 17 of this report).

2 Admission to trading on a regulated market

A Prospectus obligation

14. A request for admission of securities to trading on a regulated market situated or operated within the European Economic Area is in general subject to prior publication of a prospectus (Art. 3(3) Dir.). The exemptions set forth above (no. 11 of this report) do not apply.

B Exemptions

15. There is no obligation to publish a prospectus in the event of admission to trading of the following types of securities:

[66] Directors and employees are considered to have sufficient knowledge of their employer to justify an exemption from the obligation to publish a prospectus (Common Position adopted by the European Council on 24 March 2003, *Official Journal* C 125 E of 27 May 2003, 51). Contrary to Art. 4(2)(f) Dir. (see no. 15(f) of this report), there is no requirement that the offered securities are of the same class as the securities already admitted to trading on a regulated market. The informal taskforce of competent authorities organised by the Commission is of the opinion that this a drafting mistake and that Member States are entitled to require that this condition should also apply with respect to the offering of securities to directors and employees (Summary record of the 4th Informal Meeting of 8 March 2005, pp. 3–4).

[67] Summary record of the 4th Informal Meeting of 8 March 2005, p. 3.

(a) shares representing, over a period of 12 months, less than 10 per cent of the number of shares of the same class already admitted to trading on the same regulated market;
(b) shares issued in substitution for shares of the same class already admitted to trading on the same regulated market, if the issuance of such shares does not involve an increase in the issued capital;
(c) securities offered in connection with a takeover by means of an exchange offer, provided a document is available containing information regarded by the competent authority as equivalent to that set forth in the prospectus required by the Prospectus Directive, taking into account the requirements of Community law, in particular the Directive of 21 April 2004 on takeover bids (see no. 13(b) of this report);[68]
(d) securities offered, allotted or to be allotted in connection with a merger, provided a document is available containing information regarded by the competent authority as equivalent to that set forth in the prospectus required by the Prospectus Directive, taking into account the requirements of Community law, in particular the Third Directive of 9 October 1978 on mergers of public limited-liability companies[69] and the Directive of 26 October 2005 on cross-border mergers of limited-liability companies;[70]
(e) shares offered, allotted or to be allotted free of charge to existing shareholders, and dividends paid in the form of shares of the same class as those in respect of which they are paid, provided the shares are of the same class as those already admitted to trading on the same regulated market and a document is made available containing information on the number and nature of the shares and the reasons for and details of the offering (see also no. 13(d) of this report);
(f) securities offered, allotted or to be allotted to existing or former directors or employees by their employer or an affiliated undertaking, provided the securities in question are of the same class as those already admitted to trading on the same regulated market and a document is made available containing information on the number and nature of the securities and the reasons for and details of the offering; it is not required that the securities offered to directors and employees also be admitted to trading;
(g) shares resulting from the conversion or exchange of other securities or from the exercise of rights conferred by other securities, provided the shares are of the same class as those already admitted to trading on the same regulated market;[71]

[68] *Official Journal* L 142 of 30 April 2004. [69] *Ibid.*, L 295 of 20 October 1978.

[70] *Ibid.*, L 310 of 25 November 2005.

[71] For a discussion of possible abuse, *see* the answer to Question 16 of 'Frequently asked questions regarding Prospectuses: Common positions agreed by CESR Members', 18 July 2006, *available at* www.cesr.eu.

(h) securities already admitted to trading on another regulated market, subject to the following conditions: (i) the securities, or securities of the same class, have been admitted to trading on that other regulated market for more than eighteen months; (ii) for securities first admitted to trading on a regulated market after the date of entry into force of the Prospectus Directive (i.e. 31 December 2003 (Art. 32 Dir.)), the admission to trading on that other regulated market was associated with an approved prospectus made available to the public in accordance with Article 14 of the Prospectus Directive (see no. 57 of this report); (iii) except where (ii) applies, for securities first admitted to trading after 30 June 1983, listing particulars were approved in accordance with the requirements of Directive 80/390 of 17 March 1980 coordinating the requirements for the drawing up, scrutiny and distribution of the listing particulars to be published for the admission of securities to official stock-exchange listings[72] or Directive 2001/34 of 28 May 2001 on the admission of securities to official stock-exchange listings and on information to be published on those securities;[73] (iv) the ongoing obligations for trading on that other regulated market have been complied with; (v) the party seeking the admission of securities to trading on a regulated market under this exemption makes a summary document available to the public in a language accepted by the competent authority of the Member State where the regulated market is located; (vi) the summary document referred to in point (v) is made available to the public in the Member State of the regulated market where admission to trading is sought in the manner set out in Article 14(2) of the Prospectus Directive (see no. 57 of this report); and (vii) the content of the summary document complies with Article 5(2) of the Prospectus Directive (see no. 36 of this report).[74] Furthermore, the summary document shall state where the most recent prospectus can be obtained and where the financial information published by the issuer pursuant to its ongoing disclosure obligations is available (Art. 4(2) Dir.). This last exemption is intended to facilitate the raising of capital on new markets.[75]

As discussed in no. 13 of this report, the granting of an exemption in one Member State does not imply that the same exemption

[72] *Official Journal* L 100 of 17 April 1980.

[73] *Ibid.*, L 184 of 6 July 2001. The Directive 2001/34 has been replaced by Directive 2004/109 of 15 December 2004 on the harmonisation of transparency requirements in relation to information about issuers whose securities are admitted to trading on a regulated market (*Official Journal* L 390 of 31 December 2004).

[74] See also Summary record of the 3rd Informal Meeting of 26 January 2005, pp. 7–8 for more details on this condition.

[75] Common Position adopted by the European Council on 24 March 2003, *Official Journal* C 125 E of 27 May 2003, 51.

automatically applies in other Member States where admission to trading is requested.

As is the case for the exemptions applicable to public offerings (see no. 13 of this report), if the issuer decides, notwithstanding the exemption, to publish a prospectus, the prospectus will be subject to the provisions of the Prospectus Directive and must be approved by the competent authority of the home Member State in accordance with the procedure set forth under no. 17 *et seq*. of this report. This follows from Article 13(1) of the Prospectus Directive, which prohibits the publication of a prospectus that has not been approved by the competent authority of the home Member State (see no. 17 of this report).

The disclosure requirements set forth in the Prospectus Directive do not prevent the Member States from providing additional requirements for the admission to trading of securities to a regulated market. For example, national law typically contains special corporate governance rules. Of course, these requirements may not directly or indirectly restrict the preparation, content or dissemination of a prospectus approved by the competent authority in accordance with the Prospectus Directive.[76]

3 Consequences of exemption

16. When an offeror or issuer qualifies for an exemption from the prospectus requirement under the rules discussed under nos. 13 and 15 above, the competent authorities cannot require the publication of a prospectus. The Member States may not provide in their national laws that a prospectus must be prepared in this case.

However, if the offeror or issuer wishes to publish a prospectus, it must obtain the approval of the competent authority of the home Member State before doing so.

V Prior approval of the competent authority

1 No publication without prior approval

17. A prospectus cannot be published unless it has first been approved by the competent authority of the home Member State (Art. 13(1) Dir.). This applies to all forms of publication to third parties in general (see no. 10 of this report).

As discussed under no. 11 of this report, private placements are not subject to the prospectus requirement and do not qualify as public offerings of securities under the Prospectus Directive. The offeror is entitled to publish an offering memorandum or any other information without the

[76] Fifteenth recital to the Prospectus Directive.

approval of the competent authority, to the extent that this memorandum and/or information concerns a private placement addressed solely to a limited circle of persons (see no. 12 of this report).

2 Competent authority

A Definition

18. Approval entails at least scrutiny of the completeness of the prospectus, including the consistency of the information contained therein and its comprehensiveness (Art. 2(1)(q) Dir.).

Each Member State shall designate a competent authority for the approval of prospectuses, but may entrust specific tasks under the Prospectus Directive to other authorities. However, a prospectus for a cross-border public offering or an admission to trading should be approved by the central competent authority. The competent authority for purposes of the Prospectus Directive should be completely independent from all market participants (Art. 21(1) Dir.[77] See also no. 75 of this report for further discussion of the organisation of the competent authorities).

The competent authority must be an administrative authority independent of the economic players, and organised in such a way as to avoid conflicts of interest.[78]

B Designation of a competent authority

19. The home Member State is defined in function of the issuer's nationality, i.e. the legal entity that issues or proposes to issue securities or the person requesting admission to trading (Art. 2(1)(h) Dir.). This also applies to public offerings. In such a case, the nationality of the issuer of the securities to be offered to the public is the deciding factor. Generally, the issuer and the offeror will be the same entity, or at least members of the same group.

However, if the securities are not equity securities and have a denomination of €1,000 or more (i.e. large-denomination debt securities), the offeror or issuer has a limited choice (see below).

20. If the issuer is based in the European Economic Area, the competent authority is the authority of the Member State where the issuer's registered office is located. This Member State is the home Member State for the purposes of designating a competent authority under the Prospectus Directive.

21. If the issuer is incorporated in a country outside the European Economic Area, the home Member State will be the one where the securities are

[77] Due to its federal structure, Germany has been granted an extension to comply with these rules until 31 December 2008 (Art. 30(3) Dir.; Common Position adopted by the European Council on 24 March 2003, *Official Journal* C 125 E of 27 May 2003, 55).

[78] Thirty-seventh recital to the Prospectus Directive.

intended to be offered to the public for the first time after the date of entry into force of the Prospectus Directive, i.e. after 31 December 2003, or where the first application for admission to trading on a regulated market is made, at the choosing of the issuer, the offeror or the person requesting admission, as the case may be. If the securities are intended to be offered simultaneously to the public in different Member States, the competent authority for purposes of the Prospectus Directive can be the authority in any of these states. The same holds true in the event of a simultaneous request for admission to trading on regulated markets in different Member States.

The Prospectus Directive does not state from which date (following publication of the Prospectus Directive) admission to trading on a regulated market should be taken into account in determining the home Member State. This is important as the home Member State designated in accordance with the above rule is final for equity securities and low-denomination debt securities (i.e. debt securities having a denomination of less than €1,000). Based on a non-binding statement of the European Commission, it appears that the date of transposition of the Prospectus Directive, i.e. 1 July 2005, should be considered the cut-off date (see no. 23 of this report). Any admission to trading *before* that date, provided the securities are still traded on a regulated market on 1 July 2005, will thus determine the home Member State in accordance with the transitional provision contained in Article 30(1) of the Prospectus Directive (see no. 23 of this report). This interpretation accords with the purpose of the Prospectus Directive.

If the offeror or person requesting admission to trading on a regulated market is not the (foreign) issuer, the offeror or person requesting admission will be entitled to select the home Member State in accordance with the above rules. In this case, the issuer can nevertheless choose another home Member State (regardless of its prior choice) on the occasion of a subsequent offering or request for admission to trading on a regulated market in the European Economic Area.[79] In other words, the foreign issuer is not bound by the first choice made by the offeror or person requesting admission to trading. This right of subsequent election is only available in the event that the securities were offered to the public or admitted to trading on a regulated market and the home Member State of the issuer therefore determined by a person other than the issuer itself.[80]

22. The issuer's nationality is not exclusively decisive for issues of large-denomination debt securities, i.e. non-equity securities having a denomination per unit of at least €1,000 or, for non-equity securities denominated in a currency other than euros, nearly equivalent to €1,000, and for issues of non-equity securities giving the right to acquire transferable securities or to

[79] Art. 2(1)(m)(iii) Dir.; Common Position adopted by the European Council on 24 March 2003, *Official Journal* C 125 E of 27 May 2003, p. 50.

[80] Summary record of the 3rd Informal Meeting of 26 January 2005, p. 4.

receive consideration in cash, as a result of their conversion or exercise of the rights conferred by them, provided the issuer of the non-equity securities is not the issuer of the underlying securities or an entity belonging to the same group. The denomination of non-equity securities in a foreign currency should be determined upon submission of the draft prospectus for approval.[81]

For such offerings or admissions to trading on a regulated market, the issuer, offeror or person requesting admission to trading is entitled to choose the home Member State from amongst (i) the Member State where the issuer has its registered office, and (ii) the Member State where the securities were or are to be admitted to trading on a regulated market or where the securities are offered to the public (Art. 2(1)(m) Dir.). They must then submit a prospectus for approval to the competent authority of the selected Member State.

These special rules have been introduced to allow issuers and offerors of large-denomination bonds, i.e. bonds having a denomination of at least €1,000 per unit, and certain derivatives, a certain degree of flexibility in choosing the competent authority, permitting them to choose the competent authority of the Member State where the securities are generally listed and where that authority has the necessary expertise and experience in complex securities.[82] Particularly for eurobonds, the Luxembourg stock exchange is the preferred market.

Under these rules, the offeror or person requesting admission to trading is entitled to select the competent authority from the aforementioned Member States on a transaction-by-transaction basis and is not bound by a prior choice, even if it relates to the same type of securities. It should be noted, however, that the competent authority is entitled to assign its power to approve the prospectus to another competent authority, subject to the latter's agreement (Art. 13(5) Dir.; see also no. 24 of this report). For example, if a person requesting admission to trading of large-denomination debt securities or derivatives, approved in the past by the competent authority of the Member State where the regulated market is located, addresses its request for approval to the competent authority of the Member State of the issuer's registered office, the latter may prefer to assign its power to the competent authority of the Member State where the securities are listed.

The above rules also apply to non-EEA issuers. Of course, in this case there will be no registered office in the European Economic Area, meaning there will be no choice in actuality, as only the competent authority of the Member State where the offering is intended to be made or where the regu-

[81] Question 9 of 'Frequently asked questions regarding Prospectuses: Common positions agreed by CESR Members', 18 July 2006, *available at* www.cesr.eu.

[82] Common Position adopted by the European Council on 24 March 2003, *Official Journal* C 125 E of 27 May 2003, p. 50.

lated market is situated can be selected. This would be different, however, if the offering is made or admission to trading sought in several Member States simultaneously.

23. Article 30(1) of the Prospectus Directive provides for a transitional provision for non-EEA issuers whose '*securities have already been admitted to trading on a regulated market*' in the European Economic Area. These foreign issuers can choose their competent authority '*in accordance with Article 2(1)(m)(iii)*'.

Foreign issuers must have informed the competent authority of their choice by 31 December 2005 (see no. 73 of this report). The competent authority of that Member State will be authorised to approve the prospectus for any future transactions. If the issuer failed to respect this deadline, the rules applicable to other foreign issuers shall apply (see no. 21 of this report).

This transitional provision raises several interpretative issues. First, it does not state before which date the securities should have been admitted to trading on a regulated market in the European Economic Area. Thus, it could be argued that the cut-off date is the date of entry into force of the Prospectus Directive, i.e. 31 December 2003 (Art. 32 Dir.) and, therefore, any time period should refer to, or start running from, such date. Furthermore, its scope is unclear as a result of a general cross-reference to Article 2(1)(m)(iii).

In a non-binding statement, the Internal Market DG indicated that Article 30(1) applies to foreign issuers which '*already ha[ve] equity securities or low denomination debt admitted to trading on a regulated market in at least one EU Member State*' to the extent such foreign issuers have securities that are traded on a regulated market in the European Union on 1 July 2005, i.e. the deadline for transposition of the Prospectus Directive.[83] This statement also indicates that a foreign issuer, whose securities are listed on a regulated market in the European Economic Area on 1 July 2005, must choose the competent authority of the Member State in which its securities are admitted to trading or, if its securities are listed on regulated markets in several Member States, the competent authority of one of these states. If the foreign issuer moreover has made a public offering of equity securities or low-denomination debt securities between 31 December 2003 and 31 December 2005, it may choose the competent authority of the Member State in which it made the offering. In any event, the choice should have been notified by 31 December 2005.[84]

Given the unclear wording of Article 30(1) of the Prospectus Directive, the competent authorities and courts will most likely examine what the

[83] Report of the International Capital Markets Association of November 2005, *available at* www.icma-group.org.

[84] This has been confirmed in the answer to Question 8 of 'Frequently asked questions regarding Prospectuses: Common positions agreed by CESR Members', 18 July 2006, *available at* www.cesr.eu.

foreign issuer actually did. If it notified its choice of Member State by 31 December 2005, as indicated above, and this choice falls within the limits of Article 2(1)(m), the competent authority in this state will prevail (unless it indicates that it is not competent under the above rules).

If the foreign issuer did not notify its choice by 31 December 2005, the provisions of Article 2(1)(m) shall apply, as explained above (see no. 21). In this case, the choice should be based on the first public offering or admission to trading after 31 December 2005. This will also be the case if the securities were offered to the public or if a request for admission to trading on a regulated market was made by an entity other than the issuer during the transition period, and the issuer did not select the home Member State.[85]

C Assignment of authority to approve the prospectus

24. The competent authority of the home Member State where the draft prospectus is filed may transfer its authority to approve the prospectus to the competent authority of another Member State, subject to the latter's consent. This transfer shall be notified to the issuer, the offeror or the person requesting admission to trading within three working days from the date of the decision of the competent authority of the home Member State. If the prospectus comprises several documents (see no. 26, no. 43 and no. 45 of this report), the approval of all those parts of the prospectus must be assigned.[86]

The approval period of ten working days referred to in no. 25 of this report starts on that date (Art. 13(5) Dir.).

3 Approval procedure

25. The competent authority must notify the issuer, the offeror or the person requesting admission to trading (Art. 13(2) Dir.) of its decision on the prospectus within ten working days following submission of the draft. This period is extended to twenty working days if the public offering relates to an issuer without any securities admitted to trading on a regulated market and which has not previously offered securities to the public (Art. 13(3) Dir.). Failure to issue a decision within the aforementioned time period does not indicate approval, however (Art. 13(2) Dir.). The consequences of failure to observe these time limits shall be governed by national law.[87]

[85] Art. 2(1)(m)(iii) Dir.; Common Position adopted by the European Council on 24 March 2003, *Official Journal* C 125 E of 27 May 2003, 50.

[86] Summary record of the 3rd Informal Meeting of 26 January 2005, p. 9. At this Informal Meeting, the Commission mentioned that it is advisable that the competent authority to which approval has been assigned, should also approve any supplements to the prospectus.

[87] Common Position adopted by the European Council on 24 March 2003, *Official Journal* C 125 E of 27 May 2003, p. 53.

If the competent authority finds, on reasonable grounds, that the documents submitted to it are incomplete or that additional information is needed, the time period for approval shall only start to run on the date on which the additional information is provided. Notification that information is missing must occur within the above time periods (Art. 13(4) Dir.).[88]

Approval is valid for twelve months, provided supplements are filed, when required, to update relevant information (see no. 55 of this report).

4 Prospectus consisting of separate documents

26. The Prospectus Directive permits issuers and offerors to split their prospectus into three documents: a registration document containing information about the offeror or issuer, a securities note with information on the securities offered or issued in a specific transaction, and a summary note (see no. 36 of this report). Only information on the securities issued or offered must be prepared for each individual transaction.

Once approved, the registration document may be used for new transactions without re-approval regardless of the Member State in which the offering or issue takes place. The offeror or issuer need only submit the securities note with the summary, if any,[89] containing the information mentioned under no. 43 of this report, for approval to the competent authority (Art. 12(1) Dir.). This rule does not apply, of course, if the registration document is not approved at the time the request for approval of the securities note is made (Art. 12(3) Dir.). In this case, both documents must be approved by the competent authority. The summary note and the securities note are approved separately (Art. 12(2) *in fine* Dir.).

In the event a material change in the registration document (or in any approved supplement, see no. 66 of this report) or a recent development occurs which is liable to affect investors' assessment and should thus be mentioned in the registration document (or supplement), it must be indicated in the securities note (Art. 12(2) Dir.). This applies to all changes and developments since the latest updated registration document or supplement approved and issued in the meantime, as well as to any previous changes or developments omitted without authorisation.

[88] This provision only refers to the time period of ten working days, but it seems reasonable to infer that it would also apply to cases where the time period is extended to twenty working days.

[89] A summary is not required if the prospectus relates to the admission to trading on a regulated market of non-equity securities with a denomination of at least €50,000, provided the applicable national rules of the Member State where admission is requested do not require a summary (Art. 5(2) Dir.; *see also* no. 36 of this report).

5 Liability of the competent authority

27. The liability of the competent authority is governed by national law.

Each Member State shall ensure that the competent authorities of other Member States cannot be held liable under its national law (Art. 13(6) Dir.). The liability of the competent authority of another Member State shall be determined by the laws of that state.

VI Content, format and language of the prospectus and related documents

1 Content and incorporation by reference; permissible omission of information

A Inclusion of all necessary information

28. In general, the prospectus should contain information about the issuer and the securities to be offered or admitted to trading (Art. 5(2) Dir.). An indication of the information which should be included is listed in Annex I to the Prospectus Directive.[90] Annexes II through IV give a general overview of the information to be included in the registration document, the securities note and the summary note in the event the prospectus is divided into three documents (see no. 43 of this report). The Prospectus Regulation defines more precisely the information that must be provided in the prospectus (see no. 29 of this report).[91] The information in the summary note (Annex IV) is identical to that which must be included in the summary portion of a single-document prospectus (Part I of Annex I). The four annexes to the Prospectus Directive are appended to this book as Annex I.

Article 5(1) of the Prospectus Directive contains two main rules regarding the information to be made available in the prospectus.

First, the prospectus should contain all information necessary to enable investors to make an informed assessment of the assets and liabilities, financial position, profit and losses and prospects of the issuer and of any guarantor, and of the rights attached to the securities offered. This information must be presented in an objective manner.[92] This rule stresses that all information necessary to sufficiently inform investors must be made available. Whether the information is sufficient is determined based on the particular nature of the issuer and of the securities being offered or admitted to trading. The general rule is that the information made available should permit investors to make an informed assessment of the risks represented by the securities in order to take a decision with full knowledge

[90] The Annexes to the Prospectus Directive are indicative (Art. 7(3) Dir.).

[91] In the event of a difference between the Annexes to the Prospectus Directive, and the information defined in the Prospectus Regulation, the latter will prevail.

[92] Twentieth recital to the Prospectus Directive.

of the facts.[93] The competent authority may, under certain conditions, permit certain information to be omitted (see no. 38 of this report). The information included must comply with the Community data protection rules.[94]

Second, the information must be presented in an easily analysable and comprehensible form. Since the offering is made to the public, any type of investor should be able to assess the information. This also means that the form in which the information is made available be suitable for any type of public, regardless of its expertise. In this respect, the Prospectus Directive intends to harmonise the presentation and form of information throughout the EEA in order to ensure an equivalent level of investor protection in all Member States.[95]

Ensuring the completeness and suitable presentation of information contained in the prospectus is part of the approval procedure undertaken by the competent authority (see no. 25 of this report).

29. The information to be included in the prospectus is defined in the Prospectus Regulation which implements the Prospectus Directive as regards information contained in prospectuses as well as the format, incorporation by reference and publication of such prospectuses and the dissemination of advertisements.[96] The Prospectus Regulation defines the information that must be included in the applicable prospectus and the information which can be incorporated by reference, as well as the format, publication aspects and the dissemination of advertisements. The Prospectus Regulation is based on applicable standards in the field of financial and non-financial information set out by international securities commissions, in particular the International Organisation of Securities Commissions (IOSCO) (Art. 7(3) Dir.). IOSCO has developed international disclosure standards for cross-border offerings and initial listings by foreign issuers.

The Prospectus Regulation defines information based on the type of issuer and securities offered. The rules contained in the Prospectus Regulation pay particular attention to the following (Art. 7(2) Dir.):

(a) the various types of information needed by investors relating to equity securities as compared to non-equity securities: a consistent approach shall be taken with regard to information required in a prospectus for securities having a similar economic rationale, notably derivatives;
(b) the various types and characteristics of offerings and admissions to trading on a regulated market of non-equity securities; the information

[93] Nineteenth recital to the Prospectus Directive.

[94] Thirty-second recital to the Prospectus Directive.

[95] *See* the twentieth recital to the Prospectus Directive.

[96] Published for the first time in the *Official Journal* L 149 of 30 April 2004, with a corrected version in the *Official Journal* L 215 of 16 June 2004 and appended hereto as Annex II.

required in a prospectus shall be appropriate from the point of view of investors in non-equity securities having a denomination per unit of at least €50,000;

(c) the format used and the information required in prospectuses relating to non-equity securities, including warrants in any form,[97] issued under an offering programme;

(d) the format used and the information required in prospectuses relating to non-equity securities, insofar as these securities are not subordinated, convertible, exchangeable, subject to subscription or acquisition rights or linked to derivatives, issued in a continuous or repeated manner by entities regulated or authorised to operate in the financial markets within the European Economic Area;

(e) the various activities and size of the issuer, in particular small and mid-sized companies; for such companies the information shall be adapted to their size and, where appropriate, to their shorter track record; and

(f) if applicable, the public nature of the issuer.

The Prospectus Regulation must at least provide for inclusion of the information listed in Annex I to the Prospectus Directive (see Annex I to this book).

The Prospectus Regulation is applicable as from 1 July 2005 (Art. 36 Reg.) and contains transitional provisions for specific cases (Art. 35 Reg.).

30. In implementing the Prospectus Regulation, issuers, offerors and their advisers can refer to the CESR's Recommendations for the consistent implementation of the European Commission's Regulation on Prospectuses 809/2004.[98] The purpose of the CESR's Recommendations is twofold. First, they are intended to offer guidelines to issuers, offerors and their advisers when deciding to what extent specific information should be included in a prospectus. Second, they should permit the competent authorities to ensure consistent application of the regulations implementing the Prospectus Directive. The competent authorities will recommend that issuers and offerors prepare their prospectus in accordance with the Recommendations.[99] The Recommendations and their application will be reviewed regularly by the CESR and updated when necessary.

[97] It includes warrants linked to instruments other than securities, which are traded on a regulated market (Summary record of the 3rd Informal Meeting of 26 January 2005, p. 4).

[98] *Available at* the CESR's website, www.cesr-eu.org.

[99] The CESR's members are the chairs of the national authorities entrusted with supervision of application of the securities laws in the Member States. In most countries, these authorities will be designated the competent authority for purposes of the Prospectus Directive.

B Schedules and building blocks: information to be included in the prospectus

31. The Regulation's approach to preparing a prospectus is set forth in a combination of schedules and building blocks (hence the appellation 'building block approach'), listing the items of information which must be included in the prospectus (the 'information items'). A building block is a list of additional information, not included in the applicable schedule, which must be added to the relevant schedule depending on the type of instrument and/or transaction for which the prospectus or base prospectus is prepared (Art. 2(2) Reg.). The schedules list the minimum disclosure requirements, to which building blocks are added, if required.

The Prospectus Regulation provides schedules for the Share Registration Document (Annex I), the Share Securities Notes (Annex III), the Debt and Derivative Securities Registration Document (Annex IV), the Securities Note related to Debt Securities with a denomination per unit of less than €50,000 (Annex V), the Asset-Backed Securities Registration Document (Annex VII),[100] the Debt and Derivative Securities Registration Document (Annex IX), the Depository Receipts issued over shares (Annex X), the Banks Registration Document (Annex XI), the Securities Note for Derivative Securities (Annex XII), the Securities Note for Debt Securities with denomination per unit of at least €50,000 (Annex XIII), the Registration Document for securities issued by collective investment undertakings of the closed-end type (Annex XV), the Registration Document for securities issued by Member States, third countries and their regional and local authorities (Annex XVI), and the Registration Document for securities issued by Public International Bodies[101] and for debt securities guaranteed by an OECD member state (Annex XVII). These schedules stipulate the minimum information that must be included in the prospectus for such securities. The Prospectus Regulation defines which schedule or schedules must be used, depending on the type of securities offered and the nature of the issuer or offeror (Arts. 4–20 Reg.). Information items in the schedules may be omitted if the information or equivalent information is not pertinent (Art. 23(4) Reg.; see also no. 38 of this report, and, with respect to equivalent information, no. 39).

Building blocks are provided for *pro forma* financial information (Annex II), guarantees (Annex VI), additional information on asset-backed

[100] Asset-backed securities are defined as 'securities which (a) represent an interest in assets, including any rights intended to assure servicing, or the receipt or timeliness of receipts by holders of assets of amounts payable there under; or (b) are secured by assets and the terms of which provide for payments which relate to payments or reasonable projections of payments calculated by reference to identified or identifiable assets' (Art. 2(5) Reg.).

[101] These are defined to include public legal entities, established by an international treaty between sovereign states, to which one or more Member States belong (Art. 2(8) Reg.).

securities (Annex VIII), and additional information on underlying shares for some equity securities (Annex XIV).

For guidelines and interpretation of the information items included in the schedules and the building blocks reference is made to the CESR's Recommendations for the consistent implementation of the European Commission's Regulation on Prospectuses 809/2004 (see no. 30 of this report).

Annex XVIII of the Prospectus Regulation contains a table with combinations of schedules and building blocks (the 'Table of Combinations'). This annex indicates which schedules and building blocks must be combined for specific types of securities. Other combinations may be used for securities not mentioned in Annex XVIII (Arts. 21 and 22(3) Reg.). This is also relevant when a base prospectus is prepared (see no. 44 of this report), which must contain the information items required in Annexes I to XVII, depending on the type of issuer and the securities offered.

The competent authority cannot request the inclusion in a prospectus of information items not listed in the annexes. However, it may require, in a specific case, the inclusion of additional information relating to the items mentioned in the annexes if the draft prospectus does not satisfy the Prospectus Directive's disclosure requirements (Arts. 3 and 22(1) Reg.).

If the issuer is a property, mineral, investment, scientific-based or shipping company or a start-up founded less than three years ago, the competent authority is entitled to request adapted information, in addition to the information items listed in the annexes, taking into account the nature of the issuer's activities. In particular, a valuation or expert's report on the issuer's assets may be requested. The competent authority will inform the European Commission of any such request (Art. 23(1) Reg.). The CESR's Recommendations contain guidelines on the additional information about such companies which should be included and on the content of the expert's report.[102]

32. In the event of an offering or admission to trading of securities which are not the same but comparable to the types mentioned in the Table of Combinations (Annex XVIII), relevant information items must be added from other schedules for securities notes provided in the annexes, in the schedule of securities note which is used for the preparation of the prospectus. These items will be added based on the main characteristics of the securities offered (Art. 23(2) Reg.).

In the event the offering or request for admission to trading concerns a new type of securities, the competent authority will decide, in consultation with the issuer, offeror or person requesting admission, what information should be included in the prospectus (Art. 23(3) Reg.). There is no obligation

[102] Chapter III of the CESR's Recommendations for the consistent implementation of the European Commission's Regulation on Prospectuses No 809/2004 (see no. 30 of this report).

to adhere to one of the schedules to the Regulation. This derogation is only available for new types of securities with features completely different from the types mentioned in the Table of Combinations and if the characteristics of this new security are such that a combination of the various information items referred to in the schedules and building blocks is not relevant (Art. 23(3) *in fine* Reg.). In this case, the competent authority shall inform the European Commission of the information included in the prospectus.

33. If the final offer price and the volume of securities to be offered to the public cannot be included in the prospectus, the prospectus must indicate (i) the criteria and/or conditions in accordance with which the offer price and volume of offered securities will be determined or, in the case of price, the maximum price; or, alternatively if the final offer price and the amount of the securities nor the information defined in (i) are included in the prospectus, (ii) that acceptance of the purchase or subscription of securities may be withdrawn no later than two working days following the filing date of the final offer price and volume of offered securities with the competent authority of the home Member State (Art. 8(1) Dir. and no. 19 *et seq*. of this report).

If the prospectus does not include the above information on the price and volume of the offered securities, this information must be filed with the competent authority of the home Member State and published in the manner in which the prospectus is made available to the public (see no. 57 of this report).

C Financial information presented in accordance with IFRS

34. Where, in accordance with the schedules to the Prospectus Regulation, historical financial information must be included in a prospectus, such information must be presented in accordance with the International Financial Reporting Standards (IFRS)[103] prepared by the International Accounting Standards Board (IASB). IFRS were rendered the applicable international accounting standards in the EEA by Regulation 1606/2002 of 19 July 2002 on the application of international accounting standards.[104]

Issuers established in the EEA must publish financial information in accordance with IFRS or such information must be restated to correspond to IFRS. However, restatement is not required for periods predating 1 January 2004 or if an issuer had securities admitted to trading on a regulated market on 1 July 2005, until the issuer publishes its first consolidated annual accounts in accordance with IFRS (Art. 35(1) Reg.).

[103] *See* 20.1 of Annex I, 13.1 of Annex IV, 8.2 of Annex VII, 11.1 of Annex IX, and 20.1 of Annex X to the Prospectus Regulation.

[104] *Official Journal* L 243 of 11 September 2002. IFRS and their amendments were formally adopted by the Commission in Regulation 1725/2003 of 29 September 2003 adopting certain international accounting standards (*Official Journal* L 261 of 13 October 2003) and its subsequent changes.

For issuers that benefit from a (national) transitional provision in accordance with Article 9 of Regulation 1606/2002 of 19 July 2002 (Art. 35(2) Reg.), the relevant date is 1 January 2006. In accordance with this provision, national law may provide that publicly traded companies governed by such law need only prepare their consolidated accounts in accordance with IFRS for financial years starting on or after 1 January 2007, if only their debt securities are admitted to trading on a regulated market in a Member State, or if their securities are admitted to trading in a country outside the EEA and, in the latter case, they have been using internationally accepted standards since a financial year that started before 11 September 2002.

35. Issuers from countries outside the EEA benefit from a transition period, ending on 1 January 2007. The obligation to restate their financial information in accordance with IFRS does not apply to such issuers who have securities admitted to trading on a regulated market on 1 January 2007 and who have presented and prepared historical financial information in accordance with the national accounting standards of a country outside the EEA. In this case, the historical financial information must be accompanied by more detailed and/or additional information if the financial statements included in the prospectus do not give a true and fair view of the issuer's assets and liabilities, financial position and profit and loss (Art. 35(3) Reg.).

After 1 January 2007, foreign issuers must present their financial information in accordance with IFRS or the national accounting standards of a non-EU country, provided such standards are equivalent to IFRS. If this is not the case, the foreign issuer must include in the prospectus restated financial statements (Art. 35(5) Reg.).[105]

However, restatement is not required for a prospectus filed before 1 January 2009 when one of the following conditions is met:

(a) the notes to the financial statements that form part of the historical financial information contain an express and unqualified statement that they comply with IFRS in accordance with IAS 1 (Presentation of Financial Statements);
(b) the historical financial information is prepared in accordance with the generally accepted accounting principles (GAAP) of either Canada, Japan or the United States;
(c) the historical financial information is prepared in accordance with the generally accepted accounting principles of a third country other than Canada, Japan or the United States and the following cumulative conditions are met:

[105] Article 35(5) of the Regulation has been replaced by Regulation 1787/2006 of 4 December 2006 (*Official Journal* L 337 of 5 December 2006).

(i) the authority responsible for national accounting standards in the third country in question has made a public commitment, before the start of the financial year in which the prospectus is filed, to bring this country's standards into line with IFRS;

(ii) that authority has established a work programme demonstrating its intention to work towards convergence by 31 December 2008; and

(iii) the issuer provides the competent authority with satisfactory proof that conditions (i) and (ii) have been met (Art. 35(5A) Reg.).

The European Commission shall encourage convergence between IFRS and Canadian, Japanese and US GAAP.

D Summary

36. As a general rule, the prospectus should contain a summary.

A summary is not required if the prospectus relates to the admission to trading on a regulated market of non-equity securities[106] having a denomination of at least €50,000 (high-denomination non-equity securities), provided the applicable national legislation of the Member State where admission is requested does not require the inclusion of a summary, drafted in the official language of that state (Art. 5(2)(2) Dir.). In this case, investors shall be presumed to have sufficient financial resources to pay for advice on the offer or issue.

37. The summary must briefly convey the essential characteristics and risks associated with the issuer, any guarantor and the securities. It must be drafted in non-technical language, accessible to all, and should normally not exceed 2,500 words.[107] This limit is a guideline, however, not a cap as the number of words will largely depend on the language used.[108] Part I of Annex I to the Prospectus Directive (see Annex I to this book) defines the information which should preferably be included in the summary.[109] The Prospectus Regulation does not provide a schedule or building block for the summary. The issuer, offeror or person requesting admission to trading will thus determine its content (Art. 24 Reg.).

The summary must be drafted in the language in which the prospectus was originally prepared.

The summary must furthermore contain a warning that (1) it should be read as an introduction to the prospectus; (2) any decision to invest in the securities should be based on the prospectus as a whole; (3) if a claim with respect to the information contained in the prospectus is brought before the

[106] For a definition of non-equity securities, *see* no. 8 of this report.

[107] Twenty-first recital to the Prospectus Directive.

[108] Common Position adopted by the European Council on 24 March 2003, *Official Journal* C 125 E of 27 May 2003, 51.

[109] The Annexes to the Directive are indicative (Art. 7(3) Dir.).

courts, the investor may, under applicable national law, have to bear the cost of translating the prospectus before the commencement of legal proceedings; and (4) those persons who have tabled the summary, including any translation thereof, and applied for its notification, shall be held civilly liable but only if the summary is misleading, inaccurate or inconsistent when read together with the rest of the prospectus (Art. 5(2) Dir.). Thus, investors should take care not to read only the summary.

The foregoing emphasises the legal value of the summary. Investors should familiarise themselves with the prospectus in its entirety and should not rely solely on the summary in taking their investment decision. The summary is at best a guideline to better understand the prospectus. Consequently, if the summary is unclear or misleading as regards the nature of the securities offered or other elements fundamental to the investment decision, it will only result in liability if such ambiguity or misinformation cannot be cleared up upon reading the entire prospectus (Art. 6(2) Dir.; see also no. 85 of this report).

E Permitted omissions

38. The competent authority of the home Member State may allow certain information required by the Prospectus Directive or the Prospectus Regulation to be omitted from the prospectus if it is of the opinion that (i) the disclosure of such information would be contrary to the public interest; (ii) the disclosure of such information would be seriously detrimental to the issuer, provided, however, that the omission of such information would not be likely to mislead the public with regard to facts and circumstances essential to an informed assessment of the issuer, offeror or guarantor and of the rights attached to the securities to which the prospectus relates; or (iii) such information is of minor importance to a specific offering or admission to trading on a regulated market and will not influence the assessment of the financial position and prospects of the issuer, offeror or guarantor (Art. 8(2) Dir.). Omission is especially appropriate for sensitive information.[110]

In general, information items included in the schedules and building blocks can be omitted if they are not pertinent and no equivalent information is available (Art. 23(4) Reg.; see also no. 39 of this report for a discussion of equivalent information). The risks can never be eliminated altogether, however.[111]

With respect to the base prospectus, the issuer, offeror or person requesting admission to trading is entitled to omit information items which are unknown at the time the prospectus is approved and which can only be determined at the time of the individual issue (Art. 22(2) Reg.).

110 Twenty-fifth recital to the Prospectus Directive.

111 Answer to Question 7 of 'Frequently asked questions regarding Prospectuses: Common positions agreed by CESR Members', 18 July 2006, *available at* www.cesr.eu.

F Inclusion of equivalent information

39. If certain information required by the Prospectus Regulation is inappropriate as regards the sphere of activity or corporate form of the issuer or the securities to which the prospectus relates, equivalent information must be included. This obligation only applies to the extent such information is available (Art. 8(3) Dir.).

The offeror or issuer shall determine whether information is equivalent.

The offeror or issuer must, in any event, ensure that investors receive adequate information (Art. 8(3) Dir.). This rule will guide the offeror and issuer in determining the manner in which the equivalent information is presented and may furthermore justify the omission of certain equivalent information if such information is liable to confuse investors.

G Incorporation by reference

40. The Prospectus Directive permits the incorporation of information available to the public by reference, without including it in the prospectus. However, information may not be incorporated by reference in the summary (Art. 11(1) *in fine* Dir.).

A prospectus may only incorporate information by reference to one or more previously or simultaneously published documents approved by the competent authority of the home Member State or filed with that authority in accordance with the Prospectus Directive (e.g. information filed in accordance with no. 57 of this report) or the Directive of 28 May 2001 on the admission of securities to official stock-exchange listings and on information to be published on those securities[112] (Art. 11(1) Dir.).[113] The purpose of this rule is to reduce the cost of preparing the prospectus.[114] However, information filed with non-EU authorities may not be incorporated by reference, which may hinder foreign issuers and offerors.

The following documents can be incorporated by reference: (1) annual and interim financial information; (2) documents prepared on the occasion of a specific transaction such as a merger or demerger; (3) audit reports and financial statements; (4) memoranda and articles of association; (5) earlier approved and published prospectuses and/or base prospectuses; (6) regulated information; and (7) circulars to security holders (Art. 28(1) Reg.).

The information to which reference is made should be the latest information available to the offeror or the issuer (Art. 11(1) Reg.). If this is not the case, more recent information must be included in the prospectus, and any reference to the old information shall be deemed invalid. If the information in a document incorporated by reference has been changed, the prospectus shall clearly state this and provide updated information (Art. 28(3) Reg.).

[112] *Official Journal* L 184 of 6 July 2001.

[113] The Prospectus Regulation contains specific rules on the incorporation of information by reference (*see* Art. 28).

[114] Twenty-ninth recital to the Prospectus Directive.

The rules set forth under no. 49 *et seq.* of this report with respect to the use of languages shall apply to any document incorporated by reference (Art. 28(2) Reg.), meaning that issuers and offerors must first verify whether the information to which reference is made is available in the language of the prospectus. If necessary, the document may first need to be translated into an acceptable language and filed in accordance with the above rules.[115]

If the prospectus incorporates information by reference, it must contain a list of cross-references to enable investors to easily identify specific items of information (Art. 11(2) Dir.). This cross-reference list must present in one place of the prospectus a list of the information which has been incorporated by reference. This should be prepared in such manner that it informs the investor in a clear and easily accessible manner, whether the prospectus is complete or whether he will need to consult other documents.[116]

2 Form

A Possibilities

41. The Prospectus Directive allows the publication of a single prospectus or the division of a prospectus into three separate documents (i.e. a registration document, a securities note and a summary note). This possibility exists for both public offerings of securities and the admission of securities to trading.

For certain offerings and admissions to trading, a base prospectus can be approved and used for future transactions. In this case, only a supplement will be required for future transactions.

B Single document

42. In general, the prospectus must be a single document including all information set forth under no. 28 of this report. The information items that must be included in the prospectus are further defined in Annex I to the Prospectus Directive (see Annex I to this book)[117] and the Prospectus Regulation (Annex II to this book).

C Separate documents

43. The use of separate documents is helpful if the offeror or issuer intends to regularly offer or issue transferable securities (outside an offering programme of non-equity securities).[118] In this case, it may be cost-efficient to

[115] Answer to Question 5 of 'Frequently asked questions regarding Prospectuses: Common positions agreed by CESR Members', 18 July 2006, *available at* www.cesr.eu.

[116] Summary record of the 3rd Informal Meeting of 26 January 2005, p. 9.

[117] This Annex is indicative not binding (Art. 7(3) Dir.)

[118] An offering programme is a plan that permits the issue of non-equity securities, including warrants in any form, of a similar type and/or class in a continuous or repeated manner over a specified issuance period (Art. 2(1)(k) Dir.).

prepare a document containing information on the offeror or issuer which can be used for each new transaction. Only information on the securities issued or offered need then be prepared for each new transaction.

In this case, the prospectus will consist of a registration document, a securities note and a summary note (Art. 5(3) Dir.).

The registration document contains information on the issuer. It may be prepared and approved prior to, and outside of, a public offer or request for admission to trading on a regulated market.[119]

The securities note contains information on the securities offered to the public or to be admitted to trading on a regulated market as well as any information which should normally be provided in the registration document if there has been a material change or recent development liable to affect investors' decision since the time of the last approved updated registration document or approval of the last supplement thereto (Art. 12(2) Dir.).

The summary note should contain the information normally included in the summary of a prospectus, i.e. a brief description of the essential characteristics and risks associated with the issuer, any guarantor and the securities (no. 28 of this report). The summary will also include information contained in the registration document and securities note. No summary note is required if the prospectus relates to the admission to trading on a regulated market of non-equity securities[120] having a denomination of at least €50,000 and the national legislation of the Member State where admission is requested does not require that a summary be filed, in the official language of that state, for such an offering (Art. 5(2) Dir.).

The minimum information that must be included in the registration document, securities note and summary note is set forth in Annexes II through IV to the Prospectus Directive (see Annex I to this book)[121] and the Prospectus Regulation (Annex II to this book). Information should not be duplicated unnecessarily in the various documents.[122]

44. Once the registration document has been approved, only the securities note and summary note need be approved and published for subsequent issues, if required (see above). These are approved separately (see no. 26 of this report) and must be published prior to the offering or admission to trading of the securities. The registration document may need to be updated if there is new significant information which should be included in the prospectus (see no. 65 of this report).

The registration document shall remain valid for twelve months following its approval (Art. 9(4) Dir.; see also no. 55 of this report). Thus, during

[119] Summary record of the 3rd Informal Meeting of 26 January 2005, p. 9.

[120] For the definition of non-equity securities, *see* no. 8 of this report.

[121] This Annex is however indicative (Art. 7(3) Dir.)

[122] Fourth recital to the Prospectus Regulation.

this twelve-month period, the issuer or offeror need only provide a securities note and summary for new offerings or requests for admission to trading. The securities note shall reflect any updates to the registration document, when required (see above). If the information in the registration document requires updating during this twelve-month period and no securities note has been prepared, supplements must be prepared and submitted for approval (see no. 66 of this report for the rules applicable to supplements).

If the approved registration document was already published, it suffices to publish the securities note and the summary note, provided that they indicate where the other documents can be obtained (Art. 14(5) Dir.; see no. 60 of this report). Publication of all those documents is required before initiation of the transaction.

D Base prospectus

45. For certain types of securities, it is also possible to include information about the issuer and the securities offered in a base prospectus and to issue a supplement updating the information contained therein for subsequent issues or offerings (Art. 5(4) Dir.). The base prospectus need not necessarily include the final terms of the offering (Art. 2(1)(r) Dir.). This technique is intended to create a fast-track procedure since only the supplement requires approval.[123] The information which must be included in the base prospectus is set forth in Annex I to the Prospectus Directive (see Annex I to this book)[124] and the Prospectus Regulation (Annex II to this book). The base prospectus, like a regular prospectus, must include a summary.

A supplement is only required if, following approval of the base prospectus but before either the final close of the offering for each issue of securities under the base prospectus (for a public offering) or the commencement of trading on the regulated market (for an admission to trading) a significant new factor arises or a material mistake or inaccuracy is discovered relating to the information contained in the base prospectus which is capable of affecting investors' assessment of the securities (Art. 22(7) Reg.). Preparation and approval of the supplement is discussed under no. 65 of this report.

If the final terms of the offer are not included in either the base prospectus or a supplement, they must be provided to investors and filed with the competent authority as soon as practicable when the public offering is made, if possible before the start of the offering. These terms must include the criteria and/or conditions in accordance with which the price and volume of the offered securities are determined or, in the case of price, the maximum price (Art. 5(4) third para Dir.).

[123] Twenty-third recital to the Prospectus Directive.

[124] This Annex is only indicative (Art. 7(3) Dir.)

46. The use of a base prospectus is only permitted for the offering or admission to trading of the following types of securities:

(a) non-equity securities, including warrants in any form,[125] issued under an offering programme (a plan which permits the issuance of non-equity securities, including warrants in any form,[126] of a similar type and/or class[127] in a continuous or repeated manner over a specified period (Art. 2(1)(k) Dir.));
(b) non-equity securities issued in a continuous or repeated manner by credit institutions, (i) where the sums deriving from the issuance of the securities, under national law, are invested in assets that provide sufficient coverage for any liability deriving from the securities until their maturity date; and (ii) where, in the event of insolvency of the credit institution concerned, the amounts are used first to repay capital and interest (without prejudice to the provisions of Directive 2001/24/EC of 4 April 2001 on the reorganisation and winding-up of credit institutions)[128] (Art. 5(4) Dir.);
(c) asset-backed securities; and
(d) warrants (i) which can be converted or exchanged into shares or other transferable securities equivalent to shares, at the issuer's or the investor's discretion, or on the basis of conditions established at the time of the issue or which give, in any other way, the possibility to acquire shares or other transferable securities equivalent to shares; (ii) provided, however, that these shares or other transferable securities equivalent to shares are or will be issued by the issuer of the securities or by an entity belonging to the same group as the issuer and are not yet traded on a regulated market or an equivalent market outside the European Union at the time of approval of the prospectus covering the securities and that the underlying shares or other transferable securities equivalent to shares can be physically delivered (Art. 22(6) Reg.).

Issues shall be considered continuous or repeated if they are on tap or concern at least two separate issues of securities of a similar type and/or class over a period of twelve months (Art. 2(1)(l) Dir.). Securities of a

[125] It includes warrants linked to instruments other than securities, which are traded on a regulated market (Summary record of the 3rd Informal Meeting of 26 January 2005, p. 4).

[126] This wording is intended to cover all warrants, including equity warrants (Common Position adopted by the European Council on 24 March 2003, *Official Journal* C 125 E of 27 May 2003, 52).

[127] This includes not only identical securities but also securities belonging in general terms to one category, possibly including different products, such as debt securities, certificates and warrants, or the same product under the same programme, or different features notably in terms of seniority, type of underlying assets or the basis used to determine the redemption amount or coupon payment (thirteenth recital to the Prospectus Directive).

[128] *Official Journal* L 125 of 5 May 2001.

similar type and/or class include not only identical securities but also securities that belong in general terms to one category, which may include different products, such as debt securities, certificates and warrants, or the same product under the same programme, or different features, notably in terms of seniority, type of underlying assets or the basis used to determine the redemption amount or coupon payment.[129]

47. The base prospectus must contain the information items listed in the appropriate schedules and building blocks set forth in the annexes to the Prospectus Regulation (no. 31 of this report). Information which is not known at the time the base prospectus is approved and which can only be determined at the time of the individual issue may be omitted (Art. 22(2) Reg.) and subsequently included in a supplement at the time of issue.

In addition to the information items listed in the schedules and the building blocks, the base prospectus must include the following information: (1) an indication of the information to be included in the final terms; (2) the method for publication of the final terms, or, if this cannot be determined at the time of approval of the base prospectus, an indication of how the public will be informed about the publication method used; and (3), for non-equity securities issued under an offering programme (see point (a) above), a general description of the offering programme (Art. 22(5) Reg.).

The final terms of the offering, attached to the base prospectus, need only contain the information items from the various securities note schedules used to prepare the base prospectus (Art. 22(4) Reg.).

3 Format

48. The format of the prospectus is defined by the Prospectus Regulation and depends on the manner in which the prospectus has been prepared, i.e. a single document, separate documents or a base prospectus.

If the prospectus is a single document (see no. 42 of this report), it shall consist of the following four parts: (1) a clear and detailed table of contents; (2) a summary; (3) the risks associated with the issuer and the type(s) of security covered; and (4) the other information items listed in the applicable schedules and building blocks (see no. 31 of this report) (Art. 25(1) Reg.).

If the prospectus is split into several documents (see no. 43 of this report), the registration document and securities note shall each consist of the following: (1) a clear and detailed table of contents; (2) as the case may be, the risks associated with the issuer and the type(s) of security covered; and (3) the other information items listed in the applicable schedules and building blocks (Art. 25(2) Reg.). The summary is presented as a separate document distributed at the time of the issuance or offering of the securities.

[129] Thirteenth recital to the Prospectus Directive.

49. A base prospectus consists of the same four parts as an ordinary prospectus (see above) (Art. 26(1) Reg.). The base prospectus must include a summary, even if it covers several types of securities (Art. 26(6) Reg.). Information on each type of security covered must be set forth clearly in the base prospectus (Art. 26(2) Reg.). The same applies to the summary (Art. 26(6) *in fine* Reg.).

The final terms can be included in the base prospectus or presented in the form of a separate document. In the latter case, some information which has been included in the approved base prospectus may be added in accordance with the relevant securities note schedule used to prepare the base prospectus. In this case, the final terms must be presented in such a way that they can be easily identified by investors. Furthermore, the final terms should state clearly and prominently that for complete information on the issuer and offering, the final terms should be read in conjunction with the base prospectus and where the base prospectus is available (Art. 26(5) Reg.).

Several base prospectuses may be included in a single document (Art. 26(8) Reg.). In this case, if the approval of the competent authority of several home Member States is required under the rules of the Prospectus Directive, these authorities shall seek to cooperate and, if possible, assign approval power to one among them (see no. 24 of this report).[130]

If the issuer, offeror or person requesting admission to trading has filed a registration document for a particular type of security in the past and thereafter decides to draw up a base prospectus, the latter document must contain (1) the information contained in the previously or simultaneously approved registration document, which shall be deemed incorporated by reference (in accordance with Art. 28 Reg.), and (2) the information which would otherwise be contained in the relevant securities note, except for the final terms if these are not included in the base prospectus (Art. 26(4) Reg.).

50. The order in which the various parts of the prospectus and base prospectus are presented is mandatory and cannot be changed. However, it is possible to include a cover note containing general information about the issuer.[131]

The issuer, offeror or person requesting admission to trading may freely determine the order in which the information items which must be included in the schedules and building blocks are presented (Art. 25(3) and Art. 26(2) Reg.). Of course, this order should not be misleading or adversely affect investors' possibility to make an informed assessment since this would run contrary to the spirit of Article 5 of the Prospectus Directive. Furthermore, in a base prospectus, information on the various securities offered must be presented separately (Art. 26(2) Reg.).

If the order of information items differs from that presented in the

[130] Twenty-seventh recital to the Prospectus Regulation.

[131] Answer to Question 6 of 'Frequently asked questions regarding Prospectuses: Common positions agreed by CESR Members', 18 July 2006, *available at* www.cesr.eu.

annexes to the Prospectus Regulation, the competent authority of the home Member State may require that a list of cross-references be filed in order to allow it to verify that all required information has been included in the draft prospectus. This list shall identify the page number where each item can be found in the prospectus (Arts. 25(4) and 26(3) Reg.).

4 Language

51. In general, the prospectus is prepared in the language of the home Member State (see no. 19 of this report) (Art. 19(1) Dir.), especially if the public offering or admission to trading is limited to that state. In this case, the law of the home Member State will determine in which language the prospectus (and summary) must be drawn up and published. However, as explained under no. 53 of this report, this will also be the case if the offering is made or the admission to trading is sought in other Member States.

The special rules on the use of languages do not apply if the offering is not considered public within the meaning of Article 3(2) of the Prospectus Directive (see no. 11 of this report). In this case, the documentation sent to investors, such as a private placement memorandum, need not comply with these rules (see no. 12 of this report).

52. When a public offering is made or admission to trading sought outside the home Member State, in one or more other Member States (host Member States), the prospectus must be drafted either in the language accepted by the competent authority of each state or in a language deemed customary in international financial circles. The choice lies with the issuer, the offeror or the person requesting admission to trading (Art. 19(2) Dir.). A language customary in international financial circles would be English, for example. Other languages may qualify, provided that such other language is generally used in international finance in the Member States where the offering is made or the admission to trading sought.[132]

Regardless of the language of the prospectus, the competent authority of each Member State where the public offering is made or the admission to trading sought can require that the summary be translated into the official language of that state (Art. 19(1) Dir.). However, this authority cannot require that the entire prospectus be translated.

Finally, in order to obtain the approval of the competent authority of the home Member State (if the public offering is not made or the admission to trading is not sought in that state), the draft prospectus must be submitted in a language customary in international financial circles or in a language accepted by this authority, at the choosing of the offeror, issuer or person requesting admission to trading (Art. 19(2) Dir.). The summary will be filed in the same language in which the prospectus was prepared for filing (Art. 5(2) Dir.).

[132] Summary record of the 3rd Informal Meeting of 26 January 2005, p. 10.

The foregoing is best illustrated by an example. If a public offering is made in both France and Italy by a Dutch offeror (but not in the Netherlands), the offeror is entitled to prepare the prospectus in either the official languages of both countries or in English. If it chooses the former option, the prospectus must be drafted in both Italian and French. If it decides to draw up the prospectus in English, however, the competent authorities of Italy and France can always request a summary in Italian or French, respectively.

For scrutiny by the competent authority of the home Member State (i.e. the Netherlands) with a view to approval, the Dutch offeror must submit the draft prospectus in either English or Dutch. If the offeror were Belgian, it would probably submit the draft prospectus to the competent Belgian authority in either English or French, so that only an Italian translation would be required. As mentioned, in such event, if the prospectus is in English, the French and Italian authorities can request a translation of the summary into French or Italian, respectively.

53. If a public offering is made or admission to trading on a regulated market sought in more than one Member State, including the home Member State, the prospectus must be prepared and submitted in a language accepted by the competent authority of the home Member State (Art. 19(3) Dir.). The competent authority of that state will decide on the language applicable under national law and may require publication in additional languages if it has more than one official language.

Once approved, the prospectus must be made available in the other states where the offering is made or the admission to trading requested, i.e. the host Member States, either in a language accepted by the competent authority of each host Member State or in a language customary in international financial circles. The offeror, issuer or person requesting admission to trading shall take a decision in this regard (Art. 19(3) Dir.).

Finally, the competent authority of each host Member State may require that the summary be translated into its official language(s) (Art. 19(3) Dir.). If the host Member State has more than one official language, it may require translation of the summary into all of its official languages.

54. Special rules on the use of languages apply in the event admission to trading on a regulated market of non-equity securities with a denomination per unit of at least €50,000 is requested in one or more Member States. In this case the offeror, issuer or person requesting admission may choose to prepare the prospectus either in a language accepted by the competent authorities of the home and host Member States or in a language customary in international financial circles (Art. 19(4) Dir.).

The Member States can provide in their national legislation that, in this case, a summary must be prepared in the official language(s) of that state (Art. 19(4) Dir.). However, there must be an express statutory provision to this end, and a summary must be prepared only if required by national law (see no. 36 of this report).

These special rules do not apply to the public offering of such securities since, in this case, there is no obligation to publish a prospectus (see no. 11 of this report).

5 Term of validity

55. Once approved, the prospectus remains valid for twelve months from its publication date (Art. 9(1) Dir.). This relatively short period of validity is intended to ensure that prospectuses are kept up to date.[133] In order to remain valid, any new significant fact relating to information contained in the prospectus which is capable of affecting investors' assessment of the securities must be made public via a supplement (see no. 66 of this report).

In the event of an offering programme of non-equity securities, a duly filed base prospectus shall remain valid for up to twelve months (Art. 9(2) Dir.). An offering programme is a plan that permits the issue of non-equity securities, including warrants in any form,[134] of a similar type and/or class, in a continuous or repeated manner over a specified issuance period (Art. 2(1)(k) Dir.). Issues are considered to be continuous or repeated if they are on tap or concern at least two separate issues of securities of a similar type and/or class over a twelve-month period (Art. 2(1)(l) Dir.). Securities of a similar type and/or class include not only identical securities but also securities that belong in general terms to one category and may include different products, such as debt securities, certificates and warrants, or the same product under the same programme, as well as different features, notably in terms of seniority, types of underlying assets and the basis for determining the redemption amount or coupon payment.[135]

No time limit applies to base prospectuses for the continuous or repeated issue of non-equity securities by credit institutions where (i) the sums deriving from the issue, under national law, are invested in assets that provide sufficient coverage for any liabilities deriving from the securities until their maturity date, and (ii) in the event of insolvency of the credit institution, the sums are used first to repay capital and interest due (without prejudice to the provisions of Directive 2001/24/EC of 4 April 2001 on the reorganisation and winding-up of credit institutions).[136] In this case, the prospectus shall remain valid until the securities concerned are no longer issued in a continuous or repeated manner or the programme is terminated (Art. 9(3) Dir.).

133 Twenty-sixth recital to the Prospectus Directive.

134 It includes warrants linked to instruments other than securities, which are traded on a regulated market (Summary record of the 3rd Informal Meeting of 26 January 2005, p. 4).

135 Thirteenth recital to the Prospectus Directive.

136 *Official Journal* L 125 of 5 May 2001.

Finally, once approved, a registration document remains valid for twelve consecutive months, provided it is updated with supplements where appropriate (as discussed in no. 66 *et seq.* of this report)(Art. 9(4) Dir.).[137]

VII Publication and advertisements

1 Publication

56. After approval of the prospectus, the issuer, offeror or person requesting admission to trading must file the approved prospectus, in its final form, with the competent authority of the home Member State (see no. 19 of this report) and make it available to the public as soon as practicable and, in any case, reasonably in advance of the offering or admission to trading and no later than the commencement of the offer (Art. 14(1) Dir.). Publication should always be in accordance with the legislation on data protection.[138]

In the event of an initial public offering (IPO) of a class of shares not already admitted to trading on a regulated market in the European Union (as further defined under no. 6 of this report), the prospectus must be made available no later than six working days before the end of the offering (Art. 14(1) Dir.). This time period is to ensure that in the case where the IPO is open for less than six working days, the prospectus is made available sufficient time before admission of the securities to trading.[139]

The text and format of the prospectus (and any supplements) as published or otherwise made available to the public must at all times conform to the original approved version (Art. 14(6) Dir.), meaning it is prohibited to render public any new information useful to investors through other channels, i.e. a supplement or otherwise.[140] However, a significant new fact, material error or inaccuracy capable of affecting investors' assessment of the securities must be made public by a supplement (see no. 66 of this report).

57. Information can be made available to the public through any of the following means:

(a) publication in one or more newspapers circulated throughout, or widely circulated in, the Member States in which the public offering is made or the admission to trading sought; the newspaper must be a

[137] Art. 9(4) Dir. refers erroneously to Art. 10(1); it should refer to Art. 16(1) of the Prospectus Directive (Summary record of the 3rd Informal Meeting of 26 January 2006, p. 8).

[138] Thirty-second recital to the Prospectus Directive; Common Position adopted by the European Council on 24 March 2003, *Official Journal* C 125 E of 27 May 2003, 54.

[139] Summary record of the 3rd Informal Meeting of 26 January 2005, pp. 9–10.

[140] Answer to Question 14 of 'Frequently asked questions regarding Prospectuses: Common positions agreed by CESR Members', 18 July 2006, *available at* www.cesr.eu.

general or financial publication having a national or supra-regional scope; if the competent authority is of the opinion that the selected newspaper does not satisfy the above conditions, it can designate a newspaper whose circulation it deems appropriate taking into account, in particular, the geographic area, population and reading habits in each Member State (Art. 30 Reg.); or

(b) a printed form made available, free of charge, to the public at the market on which the securities are being admitted to trading or at the issuer's registered office and the offices of the financial intermediaries placing or selling the securities, including paying agents; or

(c) in electronic form on the issuer's website and, if applicable, on the website of the financial intermediaries placing or selling the securities, including paying agents; or

(d) in electronic form on the website of the regulated market where the admission to trading is sought; or

(e) in electronic form on the website of the competent authority of the home Member State if the latter has decided to offer this service.

The offeror, issuer or person requesting admission to trading shall determine the means of publication and inform the competent authority of the home Member State accordingly. It is recommended that the publication method take into account the function of the document to be made public and permit investors to access it quickly and in a cost-efficient manner.[141]

The publication method used for the final terms related to a base prospectus must not be the same as that used for the base prospectus itself (Art. 33 Reg.). This refers to the means defined above by which the prospectus is made available to the public. National law may require that a notice be published stating how the final terms are published (Art. 14(3) Dir.; see no. 58 of this report).[142]

The home Member State may require an issuer or offeror publishing a prospectus in accordance with method (a) or (b) above to also post its prospectus on the website of the issuer (or offeror) and, if applicable, that of the financial intermediaries handling the placement or sale of the securities (Art. 14(2) Dir.).

No other publication requirements may be imposed by the Member States.

58. The home Member State may require that a notice be published stating how the prospectus is made available and where it can be obtained by members of the public (Art. 14(3) Dir.). An additional notice may be required when the final terms of a base prospectus are published separately.[143] The

[141] Twenty-ninth recital to the Prospectus Regulation.

[142] Summary record of the 4th Informal Meeting of 8 March 2005, p. 5.

[143] Thirty-third recital to the Prospectus Regulation.

competent authority of the host Member State is not entitled to require that a notice be published if the law of the home Member State does not so require.[144]

The notice must be published in a newspaper with a national or supra-regional circulation, as defined above. However, if the prospectus is published solely for the admission of securities to trading on a regulated market and securities of the same class have already been admitted to that market, the notice can merely be included in the bulletin of that regulated market, regardless of whether it is in paper or electronic form (Art. 31(1) Reg.). The notice must be published the next working day following the publication date of the prospectus (Art. 31(2) Reg.).

The notice must contain the following information:

(a) the issuer's identification details;
(b) the type, class and volume of securities offered and/or in respect of which admission to trading is sought, provided this information is known at the time of publication of the notice;
(c) the proposed timetable for the offering or admission to trading;
(d) a statement that a prospectus has been published and an indication of where it can be obtained;
(e) if the prospectus has been published in paper form, the address where and the period of time for which it is available to the public;
(f) if the prospectus has been published in electronic form, the address where investors can obtain a hard copy; and
(g) the date of the notice (Art. 31(3) Reg.).

59. If the prospectus is made available in electronic form, it must comply with the following rules:

(a) the prospectus must be easily accessible from the website;
(b) the format should be such that the prospectus cannot be modified;
(c) the prospectus must not contain hyperlinks, except where information is incorporated by reference, provided such information is easily and immediately available; and
(d) investors must be able to download and print the prospectus (Art. 29(1) Reg.).

Furthermore, a paper copy must be made available by the issuer, offeror or person requesting admission to trading or by the financial intermediaries placing or selling the securities (Art. 14(7) Dir.) and sent to investors at their first request free of charge. It is not sufficient to allow the investor to inspect a physical copy at a designated place.[145]

[144] Answer to Question 2 of 'Frequently asked questions regarding Prospectuses: Common positions agreed by CESR Members', 18 July 2006, *available at* www.cesr.eu.

[145] Summary record of the 3rd Informal Meeting of 26 January 2005, p. 10.

When a prospectus for a public offering is posted on a website, it is, of course, also available to investors residing outside those countries in which the offering is made. Issuers, financial intermediaries and regulated markets must take measures to avoid targeting residents of Member States and third countries not covered by a public offering of securities (Art. 29(2) Reg.). The Prospectus Regulation mentions one such measure, namely the inclusion of a disclaimer with respect to the intended addressees of the offering. However, if this is not sufficient, other measures will be required.

60. If the prospectus comprises several documents (i.e. a base prospectus and supplements; a registration document, securities note and, if any, a summary note) and/or incorporates information by reference, the documents which make up the prospectus and the information to which reference is made may be published and circulated separately. However, these documents must be made available, free of charge, to the public in accordance with one of the methods set forth under no. 57 of this report.

Each of the aforementioned documents must mention where the other documents that make up the prospectus, or to which it refers, can be obtained (Art. 14(5) Dir.).

61. Prospectuses approved over the last twelve months or a list of these prospectuses with, if available, a hyperlink to the text of the prospectus on the website of the issuer or the regulated market, shall be posted on the website of the competent authority of the home Member State (Art. 14(4) Dir.).

Automatic posting of prospectuses on the competent authority's website is a major step forward, although the latter can decide to publish only a list of prospectuses, along with hyperlinks to the relevant texts (if available), meaning that, in most cases, investors will be able to consult a given prospectus online. If a prospectus is not posted on the website of the issuer or offeror (because there is no obligation to do so; see no. 57 of this report), it can always be viewed on the website of the competent authority. Most investors have access to the Internet, and those who do not can request a paper copy, as explained at no. 57 of this report.

2 Advertisements

62. Any advertisement relating to a public offering of transferable securities, as defined under no. 10 of this report, or to an admission to trading on a regulated market, must comply with the provisions laid down in Article 15 of the Prospectus Directive. Advertisements are announcements (a) relating to a specific offer to the public of securities or to an admission to trading on a regulated market which (b) aim to specifically promote the potential subscription or acquisition of such securities (Art. 2(9) Reg.).

For those securities listed under no. 8 of this report, the rules on advertising shall not apply, except where the offering or admission to trading may be made voluntarily subject to the Prospectus Directive and if the offeror or issuer decides to do so at the time of the offering or admission to trading (see no. 9 of this report).

63. When the advertisement relates to a public offering or an admission to trading on a regulated market for which the Prospectus Directive requires the publication of a prospectus,[146] it must satisfy the following rules:

(a) the advertisement must state that a prospectus has been or will be published and indicate where investors are or will be able to obtain it;
(b) the advertisement must be clearly recognisable as such for a public offering or admission to trading of securities on a regulated market; and
(c) the information in the advertisement must not be inaccurate or misleading and must be consistent with that contained in the prospectus, if already published, or with the information required to be included in the prospectus, if the prospectus has yet to be published (Art. 15(2) and (3) Dir.).

Furthermore, any information concerning the public offering or admission to trading, disclosed in written or oral form, must be consistent with that contained in the prospectus. This rule also applies if the information is made public for purposes other than advertising (Art. 15(4) Dir.).

Article 34 of the Prospectus Regulation lists the manners in which advertisements can be made public (see Annex II to this book). It is not clear whether this list is exhaustive.

64. In the event that no prospectus is required under the Prospectus Directive, any material information provided by the offeror or issuer which is addressed to qualified investors or special categories of investors must be disclosed to all qualified investors or special categories of investors to whom the offer is exclusively addressed. This is also true for the private placement memorandum (see no. 12 of this report) and for information disclosed in the context of meetings relating to the offering of securities, such as road shows or other presentational events (Art. 15(5) Dir.).[147]

When a prospectus is required, the above information must be included in the prospectus or in a supplement (see no. 66 of this report).

65. The competent authority of the home Member State shall ensure that advertisements comply with the above rules (Art. 15(6) Dir.). In this regard, the competent authorities of the host Member State(s) must rely on the competent authority of the home Member State (see no. 79 of this report).

[146] Private placements, within the meaning of Article 3(2) of the Prospectus Directive (defined at no. 11 of this report), are excluded (Common Position adopted by the European Council on 24 March 2003, *Official Journal* C 125 E of 27 May 2003, 54).

[147] Summary record of the 3rd Informal Meeting of 26 January 2005, p. 10.

VIII Supplements – new information

66. In the event of a prospectus being made public, supplements will need to be published for any significant new fact, material error or inaccuracy relating to the information contained in the prospectus, provided the fact, mistake or inaccuracy is such that it is capable of affecting investors' assessment of the securities. This obligation only applies until the close of the offering or the start of trading on the regulated market.

Interim financial statements will not necessarily constitute a significant new fact. This determination will depend on the relevance of the information contained therein, such as the extent to which it differs from financial information previously made public, and the type of securities. If in doubt, it is advisable to publish a supplement.[148]

Information that does not constitute a significant new fact, material error or inaccuracy capable of affecting investors' assessment of the securities cannot be made public through a supplement, since the prospectus cannot be modified following approval (Art. 14(6) Dir.). This holds true even if the information would be useful to investors but is not important enough to affect their assessment of the securities.[149] Of course, this assessment is subjective, to a certain extent.

67. The supplement must be approved in the same manner as the prospectus, and thus by the same authority (Art. 16(1) Dir.). The language of the supplement is determined in accordance with the rules applicable to the prospectus (see no. 49 *et seq*. of this report).

In the event of a cross-border public offering or admission to trading or a public offering or admission to trading in another Member State, the competent authority of that other state (the host Member State) can inform the competent authority of the home Member State of the need to prepare a prospectus due to a significant new fact, material error or inaccuracy. In this case, the competent authority of the home Member State shall examine the information provided (see no. 79 of this report).

The competent authority must decide whether to approve the supplement within seven working days. The supplement shall be published in at least the same way as the prospectus as soon as practicable (Art. 16(1) Dir.).

If required, the summary and any translations thereof shall also be updated by a supplement if this is necessary to take into account new information contained in the supplement to the prospectus (Art. 16(1) Dir.). If the summary must be updated, the issuer, offeror or person requesting admission to trading shall decide whether to issue a new summary (incorporating the new information) or a supplement to the original summary

[148] Answer to Question 9 of 'Frequently asked questions regarding Prospectuses: Common positions agreed by CESR Members', 18 July 2006, *available at* www.cesr.eu.

[149] *Ibid.*, Answer to Question 14.

(containing the new information). If the changes are incorporated into the original summary, this must be done in such a way that investors can easily identify them, in particular by way of footnotes (Arts. 25(5) and 26(7) Reg.).

In the event a supplement is required, investors who have already agreed to purchase or subscribe to the securities (prior to publication of the supplement) shall be entitled to withdraw their acceptance within a given period of time defined in the supplement or prospectus. This period must be at least two working days following publication of the supplement (Art. 16(2) Dir.). If investors fail to exercise their right within this period, they shall not be allowed to withdraw at a later date regardless of the importance of the information contained in the supplement. The supplement or prospectus will define the manner in which this right can be exercised and to whom the withdrawal should be addressed. If no provision is made to this effect, the right can be exercised in any manner (subject to applicable national law) but should be directed to the issuer or offeror.

IX Annual information

68. Issuers whose securities are admitted to trading on a regulated market must prepare, at least annually, a document containing or referring to all information published over the preceding twelve months, both in and outside the European Union (Art. 10(1) Dir.).

This information need not be included in an annual document if it has been published or otherwise made available to the public, in which case it shall suffice to refer to the publication in question, which need not be based in the European Union. However, the information must have been published or made available to the public in accordance with Community and/or national laws or rules on the regulation of securities, issuers of securities and securities markets.[150] If the publication is based outside the European Union, the information must have been published in accordance with that country's national laws or rules on the regulation of securities, issuers of securities and securities markets.

The annual document must refer, at the very least, to the information required under the Company Law Directives, the Directive of 28 May 2001 on the admission of securities to official stock-exchange listings and on information to be published on those securities,[151] and the Regulation of 19 July 2002 on the application of international accounting standards (Art. 10(1) Dir.).[152] The latter Regulation has rendered IFRS applicable (see no. 34 of this report).

[150] *See* the Common Position adopted by the European Council on 24 March 2003, *Official Journal* C 125 E of 27 May 2003, 52.

[151] *Official Journal* L 184 of 6 July 2001.

[152] *Ibid.*, L 243 of 11 September 2002.

If any information contained in the annual document is out of date, a mention should be made to this effect (Art. 27(3) Reg.).

Any reference to information must also state where it can be obtained (Art. 10(2) Dir.).

This information obligation does not apply to issuers of non-equity securities with a denomination per unit of at least €50,000 (Art. 10(3) Dir.), in which case investors are presumed to have sufficient funds to pay for the information.

69. The annual document must be filed with the competent authority of the home Member State after publication of the issuer's financial statements but, in any event, no later than twenty working days following publication of the annual financial statements in the home Member State (Art. 10(2) Dir.; Art. 27(2) Reg.). If the issuer has more than one home Member State, he will file it with the competent authorities of all those states.[153] Filing of the annual document after publication of the issuer's financial statements allows the competent authority to monitor the information made available and ensure that it complies with the issuer's obligations.[154]

Within the above time period, the annual document must also be published in the same way as the prospectus (Art. 27 Reg.; see also no. 57 of this report).

In order to take into account technical developments on the financial markets and to ensure uniform application of the above rules, the Commission may adopt a regulation containing implementing measures in this respect. However, these implementing measures may only relate to the publication method of the abovementioned disclosure requirements and may not entail the imposition of new disclosure requirements (Art. 10(4) Dir.).

X Cross-border offerings and admissions to trading

70. One of the major achievements of the Prospectus Directive is the introduction of the single European passport for prospectuses approved by the competent authority of a given Member State, meaning that, once approved, a prospectus can be used throughout the European Union.

To this effect, Article 17 of the Prospectus Directive states that a prospectus (and supplements) approved by the competent authority of the home Member State (see no. 19 of this report) can be used for a public offering or admission to trading of the same securities in any other Member State, termed host Member States. The competent authorities of host Member States cannot require that a prospectus or its supplements be subject to their approval and cannot impose administrative

[153] Summary record of the 3rd Informal Meeting of 26 January 2005.

[154] Twenty-eighth recital to the Prospectus Directive.

requirements with respect to such a prospectus (and supplements), such as the filing of certain documents or the provision of additional information (Art. 17(1) Dir.). These authorities can only require that the summary be translated into the official language of that state (Art. 19(2) and (3) Dir.; see no. 52 of this report).

If the prospectus is not made available in a language deemed customary in international financial circles, it will also have to be made available in the language accepted by the competent authority of the host Member States (see nos. 52 and 53 of this report).

71. The competent authority of the home Member State which approved the prospectus shall remain competent to approve any supplements, even if they relate to the host Member State where the public offering is made or the admission to trading sought (see no. 79 of this report). The competent authority of the host Member State can, of course, inform the competent authority of the home Member State of any new significant facts, material errors or inaccuracies (Art. 17(2) Dir.). The competent authority of the home state will then bring up the matter with the issuer or offeror and request the preparation of a supplement. If the competent authority of the home Member State refuses to act or the issuer or offeror refuses to prepare a supplement, the competent authority of the host state can take appropriate measures to protect investors (see no. 79 of this report).

The above applies to cross-border public offerings or admissions to trading, i.e. public offerings made in different Member States or admissions to regulated markets situated in different Member States, even if no public offering is made or admission to trading sought in the home Member State.

72. In order for the European passport to be effective, the issuer or person responsible for preparing the prospectus must request that the competent authority of the home Member State inform the competent authority of the host Member State of the approval of the prospectus.

The competent authority of the home Member State must, if the prospectus is approved, send a certificate of approval attesting that the prospectus has been drawn up in accordance with the Prospectus Directive. A copy of the approved prospectus and, if applicable, a translation of the summary made under the responsibility of the issuer or person responsible for drafting the prospectus shall be attached to the certificate (Art. 18(1) Dir.).

In the event the competent authority of the home Member State has authorised that certain information be omitted from the prospectus or if equivalent information has been included, in accordance with Article 8 of the Prospectus Directive, it shall indicate in the certificate of approval that this provision of the Prospectus Directive applies and justify the omission or inclusion of the equivalent information (Art. 18(2) Dir.).

The certificate must be sent within three working days from the request. However, if the request has been made when submitting the draft prospectus for approval, the certificate must be sent within one working day from approval of the prospectus (Art. 18(1) Dir.).

The same procedure must be followed for each supplement approved (Art. 18(1) Dir.).

XI Issuers incorporated outside the European Economic Area

73. Issuers or offerors with their registered office in a country outside the European Economic Area may launch a public offering or request admission to trading of their securities on a regulated market in the European Economic Area. Such foreign issuers need not have their head office or registered office in the European Economic Area in order to make a public offering or request admission to trading on a regulated market. However, if their head office is outside the European Economic Area and their registered office in an EEA Member State, they shall be deemed issuers incorporated in the EEA and therefore subject to the rules applicable to EEA-based issuers. For purposes of determining the competent authority, the home Member State shall be the state in which the issuer's registered office is located (see no. 20 of this report).

Foreign issuers must comply with the following rules in order to make a public offering or request admission to trading on a regulated market in the European Economic Area (Art. 20(1) Dir.).

The prospectus for such a public offering or admission to trading must be prepared in accordance with international standards set by international securities organisations, including the IOSCO disclosure standards.

Furthermore, the information requirements, including with respect to financial information, must be equivalent to those contained in the Prospectus Directive. This is important for foreign issuers governed by legislation that does not require the disclosure of financial statements in the manner required under Community law.

The competent authority of the home Member State (responsible for approving the prospectus; see no. 19 of this report) shall decide whether the prospectus meets the above requirements.

74. In the event of a public offering or request for admission to trading in several Member States, the competent authority of the host Member State, i.e., the state in which the securities are first offered or the admission to trading requested, is solely competent to approve the prospectus (no. 19 of this report). The competent authority of the other host state(s) where the public offering is made or the admission to trading sought must accept the approved prospectus and shall refer to the competent authority of the home Member State in the event of any irregularities (see no. 78 of this report).

The provisions of Articles 17, 18 and 19 of the Prospectus Directive shall apply to such cross-border offerings and admissions to trading (Art. 20(2) Dir.; see nos. 68 *et seq.* and 49 *et seq.* of this report).

Foreign issuers whose securities are traded on a regulated market in the European Economic Area on 1 July 2005 qualify for transitional rules, as explained under no. 23 of this report.

XII Special powers of the competent authorities and sanctions

1 Powers and precautionary measures

A Designation of a competent authority

75. Each Member State must designate a competent authority to scrutinise prospectuses and other documents under the Prospectus Directive. If required by national law, the Member States may designate other administrative authorities to oversee the approval and publication of prospectuses and supplements and supervise advertisements (Art. 21(1) Dir.).

The competent authorities so designated must be completely independent from all market participants (Art. 21(1) third para Dir.).

Until 2011, the Member States may allow the competent authorities to delegate certain specific tasks to other entities. Any such delegation of authority (except for posting on the Internet and the filing of prospectuses) must come to an end no later than 31 December 2011.[155] The delegation must define the tasks as well as the conditions under which they are to be performed. These conditions must stipulate that the entity entrusted with the tasks '*act and be organised in such a manner as to avoid conflict[s] of interest and so that information obtained from carrying out the delegated tasks is not used unfairly or to prevent competition*'. Furthermore, final responsibility for supervising compliance with the Prospectus Directive and its implementing measures and for approving the prospectus must remain with the competent authorities (Art. 21(2) Dir.).

B Powers conferred on the competent authorities

76. The Member States must ensure that their competent authorities have all necessary powers to perform their functions.

A competent authority which has received an application to approve a prospectus, i.e., the competent authority of the home Member State, shall be empowered *at least* to:

[155] Art. 21(2) Dir. The European Commission will review the delegation by 31 December 2008 (Art. 21(2) first para Dir.). The Member States must inform the Commission of any arrangements with respect to the delegation of authority (including the applicable conditions) (Art. 21(2) Dir.).

(a) require issuers, offerors or persons requesting admission to trading to include in the prospectus supplementary information, if necessary for investor protection;
(b) require issuers, offerors or persons requesting admission to trading, and the persons that control them or are controlled by them, to provide information and documents;
(c) require auditors and managers of the issuer, offeror or person requesting admission to trading, as well as financial intermediaries commissioned to carry out the public offering or request admission to trading, to provide information;[156]
(d) suspend a public offering or admission to trading for a maximum of ten consecutive working days on any single occasion, if it has reasonable grounds to suspect that the provisions of the Prospectus Directive have been violated;
(e) prohibit or suspend advertisements for a maximum of ten consecutive working days on any single occasion, if it has reasonable grounds to believe that the provisions of the Prospectus Directive have been violated;
(f) prohibit a public offering if it finds that the provisions of the Prospectus Directive have been violated or if it has reasonable grounds to suspect that they will be;
(g) suspend or ask the relevant markets to suspend trading for a maximum of ten consecutive working days on any single occasion, if it has reasonable grounds to believe that the provisions of the Prospectus Directive have been violated;
(h) prohibit trading on a regulated market if it finds that the provisions of the Prospectus Directive have been violated; and
(i) make public the fact that an issuer is failing to comply with its obligations (Art. 21(3) Dir.).

The words 'at least' indicate that national law may grant the competent authorities additional powers. However, these additional powers must accord with the underlying principles of the Prospectus Directive, as set out in no. 1 of this report, and with the division of authority amongst the competent authority of the home Member State and that of the host Member State and not hinder cooperation between them (see no. 79 of this report).

Where necessary under national law, the competent authority may request that the relevant judicial authority decide on use of the powers referred to in points (d) to (h) above (Art. 21(2) Dir.).

[156] The auditors concerned may not invoke professional secrecy to refuse to communicate the requested information. Of course, the competent authority itself should treat this information as confidential (see no. 81 of this report)(Summary record of the 3rd Informal Meeting of 26 January 2005, p. 11).

77. With respect to securities which have been admitted to trading on a regulated market in the European Economic Area, the competent authority is furthermore empowered to:

(a) require the issuer to disclose all material information liable to affect investors' assessment of the securities in order to protect investors or ensure smooth operation of the market;
(b) suspend, or ask the relevant regulated market to suspend, the securities from trading if, in its opinion, the issuer's situation is such that trading would be detrimental to investors' interests;
(c) ensure that issuers whose securities are traded on regulated markets comply with the publication and information obligations (annual accounts, annual report, semi-annual reports and other relevant documentation) after listing of the securities on a regulated market, as set forth in Articles 102 and 103 of the Directive of 28 May 2001 on the admission of securities to official stock exchange listings and on information to be published on those securities, and that equivalent information is provided to investors and equivalent treatment granted by the issuer to all similarly situated securities holders in all Member States where the public offering is made or the securities are admitted to trading; and
(d) carry out on-site inspections in its territory in accordance with national law in order to verify compliance with the provisions of the Prospectus Directive and its implementing measures. Where necessary under national law, the competent authority or authorities can exercise this power by applying to the relevant judicial authority and/or in cooperation with other authorities (Art. 21(4) Dir.). National law may require that such inspections only be carried out with a court order and/or in collaboration with other authorities.[157]

78. The Member States shall remain entitled to make separate legal and administrative arrangements for overseas European territories for whose external relations they are responsible (Art. 21(5) Dir.).

C Division of powers between the competent authority of the home Member State and that of the host Member State(s)

79. The powers defined under no. 76 of this report can be exercised solely by the competent authority of the home Member State. In the event of a cross-border public offering or an admission to trading on regulated markets in different Member States, the competent authority of the host Member States is not authorised to exercise these powers and must defer to the competent authority of the home Member State.

[157] Common Position adopted by the European Council on 24 March 2003, *Official Journal* C 125 E of 27 May 2003, 56.

Consequently, a decision to suspend or prohibit a public offering or admission to trading on a regulated market because the offeror or issuer has violated the provisions of the Prospectus Directive or if there are reasonable suspicions that it will do so can only be taken by the competent authority of the home Member State.

The competent authority of a host Member State in which securities are offered to the public or admission to trading on a regulated market requested based on a prospectus approved in the home Member State has very little authority over the offering or admission to trading. This is consistent with the concept of the single European passport. The competent authority of the host Member State must accept the prospectus as approved by the competent authority of the home Member State, and any supplements and advertisements are submitted to the latter authority for approval, even if they relate to the host Member State where the public offering is made or admission to trading sought (see nos. 63 and 64 of this report).

If the competent authority of the host Member State discovers that the issuer or the financial institutions in charge of the public offering have committed irregularities or breached the issuer's obligations with respect to admission to trading on a regulated market, it shall inform the competent authority of the home Member State accordingly (Art. 23(1) Dir.). The same rule applies if the competent authority of the host Member State finds significant new facts or material errors or inaccuracies relating to information included in the prospectus which are capable of affecting investors' assessment of the securities (Art. 17(2) Dir.).

The competent authority of the host Member State can intervene only if the breach is not remedied. If the offeror, issuer or financial institution in charge of the public offering persists in violating the relevant statutory or regulatory provisions, notwithstanding the measures taken by the competent authority of the home Member State, the competent authority of the host Member State is entitled to intervene and can take appropriate measures in order to protect investors, after having first informed the competent authority of the home Member State. The same holds true if the measures taken by the competent authority of the home Member State appear inadequate, and the offeror, issuer or financial institution in charge of the public offering persists in breaching the relevant statutory or regulatory provisions (Art. 23(2) Dir.).

The competent authority of the host Member State should also be entitled to act if the competent authority of the home Member State fails to take measures. Communication and coordination between the competent authorities of the home Member State and the host Member State(s) is clearly essential for smooth supervision of cross-border offerings and admissions to trading on regulated markets in different Member States and for the imposition of adequate sanctions.

2 Cooperation between the competent authorities

80. The Prospectus Directive imposes a duty on the competent authorities to cooperate whenever necessary for the purposes of carrying out their duties and making use of their powers in application of the rules laid down in the Prospectus Directive and implementing national laws. This duty includes providing assistance when required (Art. 22(2) Dir.).

The competent authorities shall exchange information and cooperate when an issuer has more than one competent authority in its home Member State because it has various classes of securities. The same applies when approval of the prospectus has been transferred to the competent authority of another Member State (see no. 24 of this report). Cooperation will also be required in the event of a suspension of or ban on trading securities listed on regulated markets in several Member States in order to ensure a level playing field between trading venues and guarantee investor protection (Art. 22(2) Dir.).

Furthermore, the competent authority of the host Member State should be able to request assistance from the competent authority of the home Member State from the time approval of a prospectus or supplement is requested or securities for other reasons scrutinised. This is especially important in the event of a new type or rare form of securities. In return, the competent authority of the home Member State should be entitled to request information from the competent authority of the host Member State on any items specific to the latter's market (Art. 22(2) Dir.). The objective is to exchange know-how and experience in such matters in order to enhance scrutiny and supervision.

The competent authorities should also be entitled to consult with the operators of regulated markets when necessary. This is especially relevant when a decision to suspend trading must be taken. They should also be entitled to ask a regulated market to suspend or prohibit trading (Art. 22(2) Dir.).

3 Duty of confidentiality

81. The competent authorities and their personnel are subject to a duty of confidentiality. This duty also extends to entities to which the competent authorities delegate certain tasks. The information covered by this duty may not be disclosed to any other person or authority, except in accordance with the relevant statutory provisions (Art. 22(1) Dir.).

This duty may not prevent the competent authorities from exchanging confidential information in the framework of their cooperation in application of the Prospectus Directive and continues to apply to any information thus transferred (Art. 22(3) Dir.).

4 Sanctions

82. National law must provide for appropriate sanctions to ensure that the provisions of the Prospectus Directive, the Prospectus Regulation and their implementing legislation are observed. In addition to criminal sanctions, administrative measures and sanctions are also available. The sanctions should be effective, proportional and dissuasive (Art. 25(1) Dir.). The power to impose sanctions or take appropriate measures can be entrusted to the competent authority or another independent authority, in accordance with applicable law.

In general, administrative proceedings are conducted more rapidly than criminal proceedings. For this reason, the Community legislature encourages the Member States to permit the supervisory authorities to impose administrative sanctions, generally including a penalty or publication of the sanction. Administrative sanctions are sanctions within the meaning of Article 6 of the European Convention on Human Rights.[158] Authorities imposing such sanctions must comply with the provisions of this article, which provides for the right to a fair trial within a reasonable period of time before an independent and impartial court, as well as the right to be assisted by counsel, to prepare a defence and to be heard. Article 6 does not stipulate that administrative sanctions cannot be imposed by an administrative court, provided appeal to an independent and impartial court is available (see no. 83 of this report).

Administrative measures include the suspension of a public offering or admission to trading and of trading in listed securities.

The competent authority must have power to render public any measures or sanctions imposed, unless disclosure is liable to seriously jeopardise the financial markets or cause disproportionate damage to the parties involved (Art. 25(2) Dir.).

83. National law must provide for a right to appeal all decisions taken pursuant to the laws, regulations and administrative provisions adopted in accordance with the Prospectus Directive (Art. 26 Dir.). The appeal must be heard by a court, i.e. an independent and impartial judicial body. This is especially important for the administrative sanctions and measures discussed above.

XIII Prospectus liability

84. In several Member States, the persons responsible for the information contained in the prospectus are identified under national law. This is important, as a public offering or issue of securities is, in general, a complicated and lengthy process involving numerous persons and entities. In order to

[158] ECHR, *Oztürk* v. *Germany*, 21 February 1984, Series A, no. 75; *Bendenoun* v. *France*, 24 February 1994, Series A, no 284.

avoid a situation in which investors claiming damages for wrongful representation in a prospectus cannot identify the responsible parties, the law requires that these persons be identified in the prospectus.

Article 6 of the Prospectus Directive instructs the Member States to ensure that the issuer or its corporate bodies, whether they be administrative, managerial or supervisory, the offeror and the person requesting admission to trading on a regulated market or the guarantor can be held liable for the information presented in the prospectus. These persons must be clearly identified in the prospectus. To this end, their name and function or, in the case of legal entities, their name and the address of their registered office must be mentioned. Furthermore, the prospectus must contain a statement by such persons that, to the best of their knowledge, the information contained in the prospectus is in accordance with the facts and that the prospectus contains no omissions likely to affect its import (Art. 6(1) Dir.). Their responsibility may not be limited to certain parts of the prospectus.[159] However, if in addition a guarantor undertakes responsibility, it is admitted that his responsibility is limited to the information required under the Annex VI of the Prospectus Regulation, i.e. the building block on guarantees, provided that this is clearly stated in the prospectus.[160] The same applies to other persons whose responsibility is limited to certain parts of the prospectus, as long as at least one of the above persons is responsible for the entire prospectus.

85. The Member States may go beyond what is required by the Prospectus Directive and indicate other persons who can be held liable for the information contained in the prospectus. Furthermore, the above rules do not prevent investors suing other persons under the rules of tort or other rules in effect under applicable national law.

National law must provide that the statutory provisions on civil liability shall apply to the persons identified as responsible for a prospectus. However, it should not provide that a party can be held civilly liable solely on the basis of a summary or translation. Investors should always read the summary in conjunction with the prospectus. Moreover, a translation should be viewed by investors as nothing more, and they should rely on the original prospectus insofar as possible (see no. 37 of this report). Civil liability may arise, however, if the summary or translation is misleading, inaccurate or inconsistent when read together with the rest of the prospectus (Art. 6(2) Dir.).

XIV Conclusion

86. The European passport and harmonisation of the rules governing the content of prospectuses, as well as the uniform rules on languages, will

159 Summary record of the 4th Informal Meeting of 8 March 2005, p. 4.
160 Summary record of the 3rd Informal Meeting of 26 January 2005, p. 8.

undoubtedly reduce the costs of offerings and admissions to trading on regulated markets and, in general, facilitate the public offering of securities and their admission to trading and thus access to the capital markets for all types of securities.

The Prospectus Directive is the cornerstone of a uniform programme of Community legislation on offering documents for securities offered to the public or for which admission to trading on a regulated market is requested. It creates an EU-wide framework, similar to the securities laws in the United States.[161]

Furthermore, the authorities entrusted with approving prospectuses and supervising public offerings and admissions to trading are forced to adhere to a statutory framework in which their powers are precisely prescribed. In general, issuers and offerors will have to deal with a single competent authority in order to get a prospectus approved, launch a public offering or request admission to trading. Furthermore, the authorities have a duty to cooperate so as to permit smooth cross-border transactions.

The foregoing is especially important for cross-border offerings when the securities are listed on several regulated markets and will furthermore make life much easier for offerors who wish to offer their securities in several Member States simultaneously.

The Commission will assess application of the Prospectus Directive five years after its entry in force, i.e. in 2009,[162] and prepare a report of its findings to be submitted to the European Parliament and the European Council for further consideration. This report will contain, where appropriate, proposals to amend the Prospectus Directive (Art. 31 Dir.). In this respect, the Commission will be assisted by the European Securities Committee.

[161] For a comparative discussion, *see* D. Fischer-Appelt and T. Werlen, 'The EU Prospectus Directive – Content of the Unified European Prospectus Regime and Comparison with U.S. Securities Laws', *Euridia*, 2004, p. 379.

[162] In accordance with Article 32, the Prospectus Directive entered into force on the day of its publication in the *Official Journal of the European Union*, i.e. on 31 December 2003.

PART II

Application in each Member State

National reports for EU Member States

2 Belgium

DIRK VAN GERVEN AND ELKE JANSSENS
NautaDutilh

I Introduction

1. In Belgium, the Prospectus Directive has been implemented by the Act of 16 June 2006 on the public offering of securities and the admission of securities to trading on regulated markets (the 'Prospectus Act'). The rules governing the publication of a prospectus in the event of a public offering of securities or a

request for admission to trading on a regulated market are laid down in the Prospectus Act and the Prospectus Regulation.[1] No other legislation or circulars have been issued by the national supervisory authority, the *Commissie voor het Bank-, Financie- en Assurantiewezen/Commission bancaire, financière et des assurances* (Banking, Finance and Insurance Commission) ('CBFA'). The Prospectus Act entered into force on 1 July 2006.[2]

2. Prior to implementation of the Prospectus Directive, the offering of securities was regulated by the Act of 22 April 2003 on the public offering of securities,[3] the Royal Decree of 31 October 1991 on the prospectus to be published when securities are offered to the public, and the Royal Decree of 18 September 1990 on the prospectus to be published when securities are admitted to trading. This legislation has been, with respect to the public offering of securities and listing on a regulated market, abolished by the Prospectus Act.

3. The Prospectus Act goes beyond implementation of the Prospectus Directive. More specifically, the Prospectus Act distinguishes between harmonised transactions and non-harmonised transactions. Harmonised transactions are those regulated by the Prospectus Directive[4] and are therefore eligible for the European passport. Non-harmonised transactions are (1) the public offering of investment instruments other than securities; (2) the public offering of securities with a total consideration of less than €2.5 million carried out, in whole or in part, in Belgium; and (3) the admission of investment instruments other than securities to trading on a Belgian regulated market, provided a prospectus is published for such a transaction in accordance with the Prospectus Act.[5] Non-harmonised transactions cannot benefit from the European passport. However, the offeror or issuer can make a non-harmonised transaction subject to the rules applicable to harmonised transactions in order to benefit from the European passport to the extent permitted by the Prospectus Directive (see no. 8 of Chapter I of this book).[6] This extension is not available for the admission of securities to trading on an unregulated market, such as Alternext or the *Marché Libre*.

[1] The Banking, Finance and Insurance Commission (CBFA) has issued a short note on the notions of 'qualified investor' and 'professional and institutional investor', dated 10 October 2006.

[2] The Prospectus Regulation and all sufficiently precise, unconditional and clear provisions of the Prospectus Directive granting rights to individuals have applied since 1 July 2005 (CBFA circular of 16 June 2005).

[3] The Act of 22 April 2003 abolished three acts regulating the public offering of securities and the admission of securities to trading on a regulated market (Royal Decree No 185 of 9 July 1935 on the control of banks and the issuance of securities, the Act of 10 June 1964 on the public solicitation of savings, and the Act of 10 July 1969 on the solicitation of public savings).

[4] *See* no. 6 *et seq*. of the general report in volume 1 of this book.

[5] Art. 42 Prospectus Act.

[6] *Ibid.*, Art. 22(2).

The precise scope of the Prospectus Act and the distinction between harmonised, non-harmonised and other transactions is not always clear.[7]

II Competent authority

4. The competent authority for the approval of prospectuses in Belgium is the Banking, Finance and Insurance Commission, abbreviated 'CBFA' in French and Dutch.

With respect to the public offering of securities, the CBFA is competent for:

- the public offering of securities on Belgian territory;
- admissions to trading on Belgian regulated (and unregulated) markets;
- the public offering of securities with a total value of €2.5 million or more, which takes place on the territory of another Member State of the European Economic Area in the event Belgium is the 'home Member State';
- admissions to trading on a regulated market of another Member State of the European Economic Area in the event Belgium is the 'home Member State'.[8]

As was the case prior to enactment of the Prospectus Act, the first criterion to determine whether the CBFA is competent is territorial in scope and is not based on the addressee's nationality. The Prospectus Act added a second (new) extra-territorial criterion based on the issuer's nationality.[9] This is considered an important change in the CBFA's powers.

5. If Belgium is not the home Member State, the CBFA can transfer its authority to approve the prospectus to the Member State where the offering or admission to trading takes place.[10] Such a transfer of authority will only occur when the link with Belgium is remote and the CBFA considers another regulatory authority to be better qualified to examine the prospectus. Likewise, the CBFA can, in similar circumstances, also accept a transfer of powers from the national regulatory authority of another Member State, provided that this authority agrees with the transfer to the CBFA.[11]

[7] For example, it is not clear how the €2.5 million threshold for non-harmonised transactions should be calculated or what the relationship is between the *de minimis* safe harbour and such a non-harmonised transaction. Another example is the exemption for court-ordered public auctions of securities provided for in the Prospectus Act but not in the Prospectus Directive (Art. 16(1)(2) Prospectus Act).

[8] As defined in Article 2(1)(m) Directive and Article 7(1) Prospectus Act; see Chapter I, nos. 20–22.

[9] *See* Section V.2.B of Chapter I of this book.

[10] Art. 40 Prospectus Act.

[11] *Ibid.*, Art. 41.

III Prior approval and appeal procedures

1 Offering of securities to the public

A Procedure

6. It is prohibited to offer securities to the public in Belgium, or to have securities admitted to trading on a regulated market, unless a prospectus has been approved by the CBFA or the competent regulatory authority of another Member State, in accordance with the Prospectus Directive.[12] The procedure set forth in the Prospectus Directive, as discussed in the general report, has been implemented by the Prospectus Act. In addition to the draft prospectus, the applicant should file the following documents: information on the banking syndicate and the analysts' reports including material made available to the analysts; any transfer restrictions on the securities; reports on the issue, if applicable; expert reports to which the draft prospectus refers; and any other document relevant to examining the prospectus.[13]

The CBFA will announce within ten working days of receipt of a request for approval of a prospectus whether it needs more information or if the prospectus is approved. This period is extended to twenty working days if, during the last ten years the CBFA has not reviewed a (base) prospectus for the offeror or issuer relating to a public offering or admission to trading on a regulated market.[14]

If the applicant does not receive a reply from the CBFA within the aforementioned ten-working-day period after having submitted a completed file,[15] it is entitled to send a notice of default to the CBFA. Upon receipt of such a notice, the CBFA has 10 working days within which to either approve the prospectus or request more information. If the CBFA does not react within this time period, the prospectus shall be deemed rejected.[16]

If the prospectus is rejected (or not approved within the statutory time limit), the applicant can file an appeal with the Brussels Court of Appeal. Appeal is not possible if the prospectus is approved.[17] The applicant should first request that the CBFA reconsider its decision within fifteen days of notification thereof.[18] If the CBFA does not change its mind, an appeal should be filed within twenty-one days from the date on which the CBFA was requested to reconsider (but no earlier than fifteen days from the date of this request).

[12] *Ibid.*, Art. 17. [13] *Ibid.*, Art. 32.

[14] Article 32(5) Prospectus Act differs from Article 13(3) of the Directive, which only extends the time limit if the public offering involves securities issued by an issuer that does not have any securities admitted to trading on a regulated market and has not previously offered securities to the public. [15] Art. 32(1) Prospectus Act. [16] *Ibid.*, Art. 32(4).

[17] *Ibid.*, Art. 32(6).

[18] Art. 121(2) of the law of 2 August 2002 on financial markets and financial services.

It is expressly provided that approval of a prospectus does not imply that the CBFA has approved the transaction or assessed its appropriateness or quality or the status of those responsible for it.

B Exemptions

7. Article 18(1) of the Prospectus Act provides exemptions from the obligation to publish a prospectus for certain categories of securities. In addition to the exemptions set forth in Article 4(1) of the Prospectus Directive,[19] specific Belgian exemptions exist.

These exemptions include the following:

(a) the public offering of shares having a total value of less than €2 million of cooperative companies, recognised in accordance with Article 5 of the Act of 20 July 1995, on the National Council for Cooperation, provided that title to or holding of such shares is a condition to performance of services by the cooperative company;
(b) the public offering of securities with a total value of less than €2.5 million to employees within the scope of employee participation plans, as defined in the Act of 22 May 2001 on employee participation in the capital and profits of companies;
(c) the offering of securities to existing or former directors or employees by an undertaking affiliated with the employer, provided these securities are of the same class as the securities already admitted to trading on a regulated market, subject to a document being made available containing information on the number and nature of the securities and the reasons for and details of the offering;[20] and
(d) the offering of securities to existing or former directors or employees by their employer or a company affiliated with the latter, provided the total value of the securities offered is less than €2.5 million, the securities are of the same class as those already admitted to trading on a regularly functioning and publicly accessible market outside the European Economic Area that applies similar information obligations to issuers of securities as applicable in EU regulated markets, and a document is made available containing information on the number and nature of the securities and the reasons for and conditions of the offering.

2 Admission to trading on a regulated market

A Procedure

8. As mentioned above, securities may not be admitted to trading on a regulated market unless a prospectus has been approved by the CBFA or the

[19] *See* nos. 13 and 15 of Chapter I.

[20] This is an extension of exemption (e), defined in no. 13 of Chapter I.

competent regulator of another Member State. In this case, the procedure to request approval of the prospectus is the same as the procedure applicable to a public offering (see no. 6 of this report).

B Exemptions

9. Article 18(2) of the Prospectus Act sets forth exemptions to the obligation to publish a prospectus for the admission to trading on a regulated market of certain categories of securities. The exemptions fully mirror those set forth in Article 4(2) of the Prospectus Directive (see no. 15 of Chapter I).

IV Content and format, language and supplements of the prospectus

1 Content

10. In general, a prospectus should contain all information necessary, taking into account the nature of the issuer and of the securities offered to the public or admitted to trading on a regulated market, to enable investors to make an informed assessment of the assets and liabilities, financial position, financial results and prospects of the offeror, issuer and any guarantor and of the rights attached to such securities.[21] The content of the prospectus should be in accordance with the Prospectus Regulation.[22]

The CBFA may (but is not obliged to) authorise the omission of certain information required by the Prospectus Act or the Prospectus Regulation in the event that[23] (i) the disclosure of such information would be contrary to the public interest; (ii) the disclosure of such information would be seriously detrimental to the issuer, provided the omission is not likely to mislead the public with regard to facts and circumstances essential to an informed assessment of the issuer, offeror or guarantor, if any, and of the rights attached to the securities to which the prospectus relates; or (iii) such information is of minor importance and relates to a specific offer or admission to trading on a regulated market and is not such as to influence the assessment of the financial position and prospects of the issuer, offeror or guarantor, if any.

In addition, the CBFA can grant permission to replace certain information with equivalent adequate information when the requirements of the Prospectus Regulation are inappropriate to the offeror's or issuer's scope of activity or corporate form or to the securities to which the prospectus relates.[24]

[21] Article 24(1) of the Prospectus Act is almost exactly the same as Article 5(1) of the Directive. [22] Art. 26(1) Prospectus Act.

[23] Art. 27(2) Prospectus Act and Art. 8(2) Dir.

[24] Art. 27(3) Prospectus Act and Art. 8(3) Dir.

11. Exceptionally, a prospectus can be drawn up in accordance with the national law of an issuer not having its registered office in the European Economic Area if[25] (i) the information incorporated in the prospectus is equivalent to the requirements of the Prospectus Act and Prospectus Regulation; and (ii) the prospectus is drawn up in accordance with international standards set by international securities commission organisations, including the IOSCO disclosure standards.

12. Due to the uncertainty of market conditions, the offer price and number of securities to be offered are often not mentioned in the prospectus. To the extent the final offer price and number of securities to be offered cannot be mentioned in the prospectus, mention should be made of the maximum offer price and the criteria and/or conditions in accordance with which the offer price and number of offered securities will be determined.

Investors can withdraw their acceptance of the offer or subscription within a period of two working days following the announcement of the final offer price. This announcement shall be made public in the same way as the prospectus.[26]

As provided for in Article 11 of the Prospectus Directive, the CBFA can also permit the incorporation of information by reference in the prospectus (see no. 40 of Chapter I).

2 Format

13. The prospectus can, at the offeror's or issuer's discretion, be drawn up as a single document or as three separate documents. A prospectus consisting of three separate documents should include a registration document (with information relating to the offeror or the issuer), a securities note (with information relating to the securities to be offered or admitted to trading), and a summary note. Listed companies subject to the obligation to draw up an annual report, which intend to make multiple offerings within a single year, will often request that their annual report be approved as a registration document. In this case, when a public offering is envisaged, only the securities note and summary need be prepared. If necessary (due to material changes or recent developments), the securities note can serve to update the registration document.[27]

For the public offering or admission to trading of certain types of securities (such as non-equity securities, including warrants in any form issued under an offering programme, or non-equity securities issued in a continuous or repeated manner by credit institutions), the prospectus can, at the choosing of the issuer, offeror or person requesting admission to

[25] Art. 26(2) Prospectus Act and Art. 20(1) Dir.

[26] Art. 27(1) Prospectus Act and Art. 8(1) Dir.

[27] Art. 28(3) Prospectus Act.

trading on a regulated market, consist of a base prospectus containing all relevant information about the issuer and the securities offered or to be admitted.[28]

3 Supplements

14. In the event a significant factor arises or a material mistake or inaccuracy occurs in the period between approval of the prospectus and the close of the offer or the admission to trading, the issuer (or offeror) should prepare a supplement to the prospectus. This supplement must be approved by the CBFA (or the competent regulator of another Member State, if the prospectus was approved in that state) within a maximum period of seven working days. The summary and any translations should also be amended to take into account the new information included in the supplement.[29]

A supplement (or amendment to the prospectus) can also be required if a prospectus was prepared in accordance with the local law of another Member State of the European Economic Area and additional material information was subsequently provided to qualified or special categories of investors. In this case, the additional material information should be incorporated in the prospectus or in a supplement to the prospectus.[30]

Investors who have already agreed to purchase or subscribe to the securities have a right to withdraw their acceptance within a period of two working days following publication of the supplement.

4 Language

15. The prospectus should be prepared in Dutch, French or a language customary in international financial circles. English is accepted by the CBFA as a language customary in the sphere of international finance. The summary must be prepared both in Dutch and French, unless the advertisements and other documents in relation to the offer or admission have been prepared in only one official language, in which case the summary need only be prepared in that language.[31]

If the prospectus is drafted in English, a Belgian issuer or offeror will also have to draw up a Dutch or French version thereof, depending on the location of its registered office, in accordance with the legislation on the use of languages in Belgium.

If the prospectus is only circulated in Flanders or Wallonia, the CBFA will allow it to be made available in only one language, i.e. Dutch or French.

[28] Art. 29(1) Prospectus Act and Art. 5(4) Dir.
[29] Art. 34 Prospectus Act and Art. 16 Dir.
[30] Art. 59 Prospectus Act and Art. 15(3) Dir.
[31] Art. 31 Prospectus Act.

V Publication and advertisements

1 Method of publication

16. The prospectus should be made available to the public at least three working days before the end of the public offering and no later than the opening of the offering. In the event of an admission to trading on a regulated market without a public offering, the prospectus should be made available to the public at least one working day before the date of admission to trading. If it is the first admission to trading for the securities, the prospectus should be made available at least six working days before the end of the offering.[32]

Publication shall be accomplished in accordance with Article 14(2) of the Prospectus Directive. A prospectus shall be considered to have been made public when it is made available in any of the following ways:

- publication in one or more daily newspapers with nationwide or extensive circulation;
- in a printed document made available free of charge to the public at the authenticity/or of the market on which the securities are being admitted to trading, the issuer's registered office and the offices of the financial intermediaries placing or selling the securities;
- on the website of the offeror or issuer, the CBFA (www.cbfa.be)[33] and/or Euronext (www.euronext.be) and, if any, the financial intermediary.[34]

Before the entry into force of the Prospectus Act, a notice had to be published in one or more newspapers stating how the prospectus had been made generally available. Although the Prospectus Directive still allows the Member States to require such an obligation, the Belgian legislature did not.[35] However, whenever advertisements relating to the transaction are circulated, they should mention that a prospectus has been or will be published and the place where it is or will be possible to obtain a copy thereof.

The (base) prospectus and registration document are valid for a period of twelve months following their publication, provided they are updated when required. The registration document can, of course, only be distributed if it is accompanied by a securities note and summary.[36]

[32] *Ibid.*, Art. 21(1).

[33] All prospectuses approved by the CBFA are published on the CBFA's website in chronological order (a search engine is also available). Only the prospectus drafted in the language approved by the CBFA is published, not all translations or advertisements relating to the transaction.

[34] Art. 21(2) Prospectus Act.

[35] Art. 14(3) Dir.

[36] Art. 54 Prospectus Act and Art. 9 Dir.

2 Advertisements

17. Any type of advertisement relating to an offering of securities to the public or to an admission to trading is subject to specific provisions of the Prospectus Act, in the event that:

- securities are offered on the Belgian territory or securities are admitted to trading on a Belgian regulated market;
- public offerings are made that are not subject to the obligation to draw up a prospectus;[37]
- securities are offered or admitted to trading outside Belgium in a Member State of the European Economic Area, and a prospectus has been drawn up and approved by the CBFA in accordance with the Prospectus Act.

It should be noted that Belgium considers the European passport not to cover advertisements relating to the transaction mentioned in the prospectus. The CBFA shall review advertisements even if the prospectus has been approved in another Member State of the European Economic Area (and this state qualifies as the home Member State in accordance with the Prospectus Directive). This position was firmly criticised during discussions on the Prospectus Act in Parliament.[38] The finance minister, however, was of the opinion that a lack of control of advertising would hurt competition.[39]

Any advertisement made public by the issuer (or offeror) should comply with the following conditions: (i) the document should state that a prospectus has been or will be published and where it can be obtained; (ii) the information contained in the advertisement should be accurate and not misleading; (iii) the information should be consistent with that contained in the prospectus; and (iv) the advertisement must be clearly recognisable as such.

Specific requirements can be imposed by royal decree for the public offering or listing of certain types of securities.[40]

18. The various methods of circulating advertisements are set forth in the Prospectus Regulation (see Annex II to this book). All advertisements should be approved by the CBFA before being circulated. The CBFA will inform the issuer (or offeror) of its decision within a period of five days following receipt of the draft document. If necessary, due to the international character of a transaction, a shorter period can be agreed with the CBFA.

[37] In this case, the advertisements will not be controlled by the CBFA but should meet the requirements of the Prospectus Act (Art. 57(2) Prospectus Act).

[38] Memorie van Toelichting (explanatory memorandum), *Parl. Doc.*, House 2005–2006, no. 51-2344/1, p. 217 and Kamerverslag (Report of the Commission), *Parl. Doc.*, House 2005–2006 no. 51-2344/3, p. 7.

[39] Kamerverslag (Report of the Commission), *Parl. Doc.*, House 2005–2006 no. 51-2344/3, pp. 8–9.

[40] Art. 58(4) Prospectus Act.

19. Depending on the language used for the prospectus and whether the company wishes to circulate advertisements in Wallonia or Flanders, a translation of the advertisement into Dutch, French or a language customary in international financial circles should be submitted for approval to the CBFA.

In the event the prospectus is prepared in only one national language (because the offer is limited to the Brussels-Capital Region, where either French or Dutch can be used, and to one other monolingual region) and the issuer (or offeror) wishes to make publicity in the other region, i.e. the Walloon or Flemish Region, the CBFA will require a translation of the summary of the prospectus into the official language of that region.

20. If advertisements with material information are made available to qualified investors or special categories of investors, such information must (i) be incorporated in the prospectus or a supplement thereto, if there is an obligation to publish a prospectus and (ii) be disclosed to all qualified investors or special categories of investors, if the offer is exclusively addressed to this type of investor. Material information is often given to certain investors during pilot-fishing meetings or road shows. Presentations given or brochures or other documents distributed during such meetings are reviewed by the CBFA. In the event the CBFA is of the opinion that such documents contain material information not included in the prospectus or not made available to other investors, they will oblige the issuer (or offeror) to publish the information in question. Road-show presentations are often published on the company's website.

21. Under no circumstances can reference be made to approval of advertisements by the CBFA in any document, only the fact that the prospectus has been approved.

VI Use of a prospectus approved in other (non-EU and non-EEA) countries

22. If a prospectus is drawn up and approved by the competent authority in accordance with the national law of an issuer whose home Member State is not a Member State of the European Economic Area, the CBFA will accept the prospectus provided[41] (i) the information incorporated in the prospectus (including financial information) is equivalent to the requirements of the Prospectus Act and the Prospectus Regulation, and (ii) the prospectus is drawn up in accordance with the international standards set by international securities commission organisations, including the IOSCO disclosure standards.

As far as the possibility to use a prospectus approved by the regulator of another Member State of the European Economic Area is

[41] Art. 26(2) Prospectus Act and Art. 20(1) Dir.

concerned, Belgium has implemented the provisions of the Prospectus Directive.[42] More specifically, no approval of such a prospectus is required provided:

- the prospectus was approved by the competent authority of another Member State of the European Economic Area in accordance with the Directive's implementing legislation;
- the prospectus is still valid;
- the prospectus is drawn up in Dutch, French or a language customary in international financial circles; if the securities are partly or entirely offered on the Belgian territory, the summary should be in both Dutch and French, but if the documents are only circulated in the Walloon or Flemish Region, a translation into the official language of that region shall suffice;
- the CBFA is notified that the prospectus has been approved by the competent authority of the home Member State and a copy of the prospectus and a translation of the summary are provided.

As mentioned above, the CBFA will review advertisements and all information distributed regarding the prospectus notwithstanding the fact that the advertisements have already been reviewed by the regulatory authority that approved the prospectus.

VII Sanctions

23. The Prospectus Act contains a list of sanctions that can be imposed by the CBFA under specific circumstances.[43] This list does not fully correspond to that set forth in Article 21(3) and (4) of the Prospectus Directive. The CBFA, for example, has the right to order the issuer, offeror or persons requesting admission to trading to take specific measures if it is of the opinion that the public offering or admission to trading could take place under circumstances liable to mislead the public about the assets and liabilities, financial position, financial results and prospects of the issuer (or offeror) and of the rights attached to such securities. The types of orders the CBFA can give are not defined. If the issuer (or offeror or person requesting admission to trading) does not comply with an order issued by the CBFA, a fine of up to €50,000 per day of delay, or €2.5 million per infringement, can be imposed.[44]

24. In the event of a violation of any provision of the Prospectus Act, the CBFA can impose an administrative fine ranging from €2,500 to €2 million.[45]

In addition to administrative fines, violators can also be punished by a prison term ranging from one month to one year and/or a criminal fine of

[42] Art. 36-Art. 38 Prospectus Act. [43] *Ibid.*, Art. 67(2). [44] *Ibid.*, Art. 67(4).
[45] *Ibid.*, Art. 71.

€75 to €15,000 in specific circumstances enumerated in the Prospectus Act. The following acts, for example, are subject to criminal sanctions:

- obstruction of an inspection/audit by the CBFA or the refusal or failure to provide the CBFA with information or documents referred to in the Prospectus Act or providing the CBFA with incomplete or inaccurate information;
- the intentional publication of advertisements containing inaccurate information or information that could mislead the public about the assets and liabilities, financial position, financial results and prospects of the issuer (or offeror) and of the rights attached to the securities;
- the intentional publication of a prospectus, supplement or advertisement that differs from the prospectus, supplement or advertisement approved by the CBFA (or by the competent authority of another Member State).[46]

VIII Prospectus liability

25. The prospectus should clearly indicate and identify the persons responsible for it and any supplements,[47] namely the issuer or the offeror or directors of the latter. These persons must declare in the prospectus that the information contained therein is true and accurate and that no information had been omitted that could alter the meaning of the prospectus. In addition to the directors, other persons may be named responsible for specific parts of the prospectus (and its supplements).

The issuer, offeror and directors named as responsible parties in the prospectus are, notwithstanding any provision to the contrary, jointly liable for any damage caused by any misleading or incorrect information in the prospectus and its supplements, or the omission of information required by the Prospectus Act, the Prospectus Directive or the implementing legislation. The investor's damage shall be presumed to have been caused by the misleading or incorrect information or the omission, if it is such as to create a positive investment climate or positively influence the purchase price of the securities. This presumption can be rebutted, but the burden of proof lies with the issuer, offeror or directors named in the prospectus.

Liability cannot be incurred solely on the basis of a summary of the prospectus or a translation thereof, unless the summary contains misleading, inaccurate or inconsistent information in relation to the prospectus.

26. The above joint liability also extends to the issuer, offeror and any intermediaries appointed by the latter for any damage caused by inaccurate,

[46] *Ibid.*, Art. 69. [47] *Ibid.*, Art. 61.

misleading or inconsistent information included in the advertisements or other documents relating to the offering or the admission to trading or by violation of the rules of the Prospectus Act applicable to advertisements and related documents.[48]

IX Rules applicable to transactions and securities not subject to the Directive and Regulation

27. The Prospectus Act goes beyond the mere transposition of the Prospectus Directive. More specifically, the Belgian legislature chose to apply the rules set forth in the Prospectus Directive to the following transactions:[49]

- public offerings of investment instruments other than securities;
- public offerings of securities with a total consideration of less than €2.5 million partly or entirely carried out on the Belgian territory; and
- the admission of investment instruments other than securities to trading on a Belgian regulated market provided a prospectus is published for such a transaction in accordance with the Prospectus Act.

Save when other specific legislation applies, other public offerings do not require the publication of a prospectus.

X Conclusion

28. The Belgian legislature has faithfully transposed the provisions of the Prospectus Directive into national law.

However, some provisions of the Prospectus Act are surprising. First, the Prospectus Act adds several exemptions to the list of exemptions for approval and publication of a prospectus in the event of a public offering of securities (see no. 7 of this report). Second, the obligation to submit advertisements to the CBFA for approval, even those relating to a cross-border offering in which Belgium acts only as a host Member State, and which have already been approved by the competent authority of the home Member State, may be challenged as going beyond what is permitted by the Prospectus Directive (see no. 17 of this report).

[48] *Ibid.*, Art. 61(4).

[49] *Ibid.*, Art. 42.

3

Czech Republic

PETR KASÍK AND VLASTIMIL PIHERA
Kocián Šolc Balaštík

I Introduction

1. In the Czech legal system, public offering of securities, public security markets and acceptance of securities to these markets are subject to Act No. 256/2004 Coll., the Capital Market Trading Act (hereinafter the 'CMTA'). The CMTA was adopted in 2004 and took effect upon the Czech Republic's accession to the European Union (1 May 2004). Prior to the

adoption of the CMTA, capital market and securities trading issues were subject to Act No. 591/1992 Coll., the Securities Act. In addition to primarily public-law regulation of the capital market, the Securities Act contained general private-law provisions applicable to securities and certain contractual types relating to securities. However, the CMTA was drafted mainly as a public-law regulation replacing the provisions of the Securities Act applicable to these issues up to that time. The only provisions of the Securities Act remaining valid were the ones of a private-law character while the CMTA became the regulation aspiring to take the position of a codex regulating the capital market.

The CMTA has a position of special professional law in the Czech legal system. Any general issues not regulated by the CMTA are, depending on the nature thereof, subject to general private law (in particular the Commercial Code and the Civil Code) or general public law (in particular the Code of Administrative Procedure).

2. Public offering of, public trading with and acceptance of securities for trading on public markets had not been regulated in Czech jurisdiction before the Securities Act was adopted in 1992, introducing the first regulation ever. The Securities Act subjected acceptance of securities for trading on the public market and issue of securities upon public offer to approval by the Ministry of Finance. One of the conditions imposed by the Ministry was the requirement of a prospectus. These initially very limited provisions were soon amended several times, the most significant amendment being the one effective since 1 January 2001.[1] Among other things, the amendment distinguished between a standard prospectus applicable to acceptance on a regulated market (this basically involved listing particulars) and the so-called narrower prospectus applicable to public offers outside the regulated market. These provisions were subsequently replaced by the provisions of the CMTA with the same contents. The most recent major change was introduced by the amendment to the CMTA in 2006 (effective since 7 March 2006),[2] which transcribed the Prospectus Directive.

The public offering of securities and security prospectuses (subject to the Prospectus Directive on the level of European law) is currently set forth in Part 4, Sections 34 through 36*l* of the CMTA. As far as the contents of the prospectus are concerned, the CMTA refers to the directly applicable Prospectus Regulation.

II Competent authority

3. The public offers of securities and the admission of securities to stock exchanges were supervised by the Ministry of Finance between 1992 and

[1] Act no. 362/2000 Coll. [2] Act no. 56/2006 Coll.

1998, and subsequently by the Securities Commission between 1998 and 2006. The Securities Commission was abolished on April 1, 2006 and its powers passed over to the Czech National Bank, which had been in charge of supervising banks before (the so-called integration of the financial market supervision).

The Czech National Bank is a special public institution provided with a position independent from the state executive power (the government) by the Constitution of the Czech Republic. One of the Bank's main tasks is to manage the Czech Republic's currency policies. The Bank's current role as the financial market supervisor is specific in this light. (The only EU countries with a similar model are Ireland and Slovakia.)

III Procedure of prior approval and appeal

1 Obligation to prepare and publish a prospectus

4. The only party authorised to offer investment securities is a party which has published a prospectus approved by the Czech National Bank or a foreign supervisory authority (Section 35 of the CMTA) at the beginning of the public offer at the latest. This formulation indicates that the duty to publish the prospectus is imposed on any party that decides to offer securities. The offeror therefore cannot refer to any other, already published, prospectus in this connection, not even if it applied to the same securities.

The Czech National Bank approves the prospectus upon proposal by the party who drafted it. General rules of administrative procedure apply to the approval proceedings.[3] An appeal may be filed against the Czech National Bank's decision; the appeal is tried and decided by the supreme body of the Czech National Bank – the Bank Council. To demand court review of the decision by the Czech National Bank one must file an administrative lawsuit. Appeals against the decision by first-instance courts, if any, are to be decided by the Supreme Administrative Court.

The Czech National Bank must decide whether or not to approve the prospectus within ten or, if the applicant has no history, twenty, business days of delivery of the application. However, these deadlines do not apply to the appeal proceedings (i.e. the appeal proceedings are not limited in terms of time) and, in addition, any failure to adhere to the deadline in the first-instance proceedings has no impact on the applicant's position, save for the applicant's potential right to claim damages. The Czech National Bank may further demand (Section 36c, subsection 7 of the CMTA) that the prospectus be completed if the presented documents are incomplete or if further information is required. The deadline for the decision commences again after the Czech National Bank has received the additional required information.

[3] Act no. 500/2004 Coll.

2 Public offer

5. A cornerstone for the law applicable to public offers of securities is the definition of the '*public offer of investment securities*' (Section 34 of the CMTA) which is as follows: '*any notification to a wider group of parties containing information on any securities being offered and the terms and conditions for the acquisition thereof which is sufficient for the investor to decide to buy or subscribe for such investment securities*'. This definition, although somewhat complicated, basically follows the definition of the '*offer of securities to the public*' as per the Prospectus Directive (Art. 2(1)(d) Dir.).

The public offer is devised to disclose information which will provide a standard investor with a picture of the main parameters of the transaction and give them the opportunity to evaluate benefits thereof and make the investment decision rather than to disclose all information of the transaction which may be objectively required or which represents essential particulars of the draft agreement. By the newly formulated definition of the public offer in Section 34 of the CMTA the legislator intended to remove the previous doubt whether and under what circumstances may any absence of certain information in a particular notification result in the fact that such notification cannot qualify as a public offer.

However, Czech law contains no explicit provisions that stipulate what to deem as sufficient information for the '*investor to make a decision to buy or subscribe for investment securities*'. This issue has been left up to interpretation by the Czech National Bank and, in particular, the courts. However, taking into account the priority of euro-conform interpretation of Czech law, the conclusion should not differ from the general understanding of public offers as per European legislation (see Chapter 1, no. 10).

The previous case-law of the court and the Securities Commission is applicable even after the 2006 amendment to the CMTA, which formulated primarily the following principles: even information not explicitly contained in the offer but which is available to offer addressees on the basis of the information contained in the offer (such as information available through a telephone line), must be deemed to constitute a part of the offer, as well as any information which can be inferred from the offer in any other manner. Further, any notification published in media distributed or available in the Czech Republic, or any notification posted on the Internet, which is aimed (in terms of its contents) at investors in the Czech Republic, must be deemed to constitute a public offer of securities. (Presentation on Internet sites is considered to be aimed at investors in the Czech Republic, especially if the language of the notification is Czech).

3 Securities, excluded securities

6. The duty to publish the prospectus under Czech law applies to the public offers of investment securities defined in Section 3, subsection 2 of the

CMTA. The definition is identical to the one in Article 1(4) of Directive 93/22/EEC. The Czech legal provisions thus only apply to securities defined by the Prospectus Directive, not to other investment instruments. The duty to publish the prospectus does not apply to public offers of money market instruments or various types of derivatives. Public offering of securities by collective investment funds is subject to special regulations under the Collective Investment Act.[4]

Section 34, subsection 3 of the CMTA lists securities to which the provisions of the CMTA (applicable to public offers and the duty to publish the prospectus) do not apply. The list basically copies Article 1(2) of the Prospectus Directive. The exception is Section 34, subsection 3(g) of the CMTA, whereunder the regulation does not apply to public offers of securities for which the total offered sale price in a period of twelve months does not exceed the amount of €200,000. Imposing such a threshold is a regulatory decision by Czech legislators at their discretion, since the Prospectus Directive makes it possible to provide for such exception up to the limit of €2.5 million (Art. 2(2)(h) Dir.) but not less than €100,000 (Art. 3(2)(e) Dir.) (see Chapter 3, No. 2).

What is somewhat unclear is the issue of whether or not an offeror may opt to draft a prospectus voluntarily under circumstances where the provisions applicable to public offers and prospectuses do not apply. The law fails to resolve this issue explicitly. We believe there is nothing to the contrary in the law and therefore it is appropriate to conclude, using the euro-conform interpretation, that the offeror may take advantage of such option.

4 Exemptions from the duty to publish a prospectus upon public offer

7. The exemptions from the duty to publish a prospectus are imposed in Section 35(2) and Section 35(3) of the CMTA in a substantially similar manner as Article 3 and 4(1) of the Prospectus Directive (see Chapter IV, No. 11).

We consider it appropriate to point out in this connection that the CMTA includes under the definition of qualified investors, in addition to financial institutions and '*small and medium-sized enterprises*' listed in Article 2(1)(e) of the Prospectus Directive, individuals who qualify under at least two of the three predetermined criteria and have been registered in a list of qualified investors by the Czech National Bank or a supervisory authority in a member state of the European Union upon their own request. The criteria are as follows: (i) consummation of transactions of a substantial volume on regulated security markets throughout the four most recent calendar quarters with an average occurrence of at least ten transactions per quarter; (ii) the volume of the managed assets in investment

[4] Act no. 189/2004 Coll.

instruments is higher than the amount equal to €500,000; and (iii) experience in the financial sector on a professional position requiring knowledge of investment in investment instruments for at least one full month (Section 34, subsection 2(d) of the CMTA).

8. It holds, pursuant to the Prospectus Directive, that if securities are offered as consideration in takeover bids there is no need to draft the prospectus if another document is drafted for the takeover bid containing information that the supervisory authority believes to correspond to the information required for the prospectus. Section 35, subsection 3(a) of the CMTA follows the text of the Directive literally and requires that such documents be submitted to the Czech National Bank and available at the issuer's registered office. It also states that whether the '*document*' is sufficient or not is to be resolved by the Czech National Bank and sets forth that if the Czech National Bank '*does not send the decision to the issuer within 15 business days following the delivery of the document, it holds that the Czech National Bank considers the information in the document as equal to the information in the prospectus; if the prospectus proceedings are suspended, the 15-day period shall not continue to run*'. This construction may give rise to a notion that these are independent proceedings regarding approval of some sort of a special document. However, we believe the legislators probably had in mind proceedings on approval of takeover bid publishing under the Commercial Code but the provisions on the approval of takeover bids do not respect the provisions of the CMTA (in particular the fifteen-day period for the decision). Since these provisions have not yet been applied it is not clear how the Czech National Bank would proceed in such a case.

The CMTA applies a similar construction to the exemption regarding offering of securities in connection with the transformation of companies. This is also a situation in which it is not clear what document the Czech National Bank should approve of and experience will verify this. Furthermore, there are no provisions dealing with when such document should be published. The interpretation at hand is that this must basically occur simultaneously with the publication of the draft merger agreement, division project or takeover agreement.

For exemptions applicable to securities offered free-of-charge or as a dividend to shareholders, or securities offered to the management or employees, the CMTA imposes (in accordance with the Prospectus Directive) a requirement that if the exemption is to apply, a document must be delivered to the Czech National Bank and simultaneously be available at the issuer's registered office, containing information on the number and type of securities and information on the offer. Such a document does not have to be comparable to the prospectus in its contents, and is not subject to approval by the Czech National Bank under these circumstances.

5 Admission to trading on a regulated market, exclusions

9. Pursuant to Section 44, subsection 2(a) of the CMTA, shares or bonds may be admitted for trading on a regulated market, *inter alia*, only when the prospectus for such shares or bonds is published and at least one day has passed since publication. The CMTA further imposes certain conditions for admission of securities substituting shares (Section 44, subsection 5 of the CMTA), but there is no requirement for the prospectus to be published among these conditions. The market organiser may impose further conditions for admission of other securities for trading on a regulated market. The market organiser may also impose further requirements beyond the framework of requirements imposed by the CMTA. We believe that this alternative can be assessed as insufficient with respect to the provisions of Article 3(3) of the Prospectus Directive.

The CMTA further lists circumstances under which there is no duty to publish the prospectus upon admission of shares or bonds on the regulated market (Section 44, subsection 4 the CMTA), which basically copies Article 1(2) and Article 4(2) of the Prospectus Directive (see Chapter 4, No. 15).

IV Content and format, language and supplements of the prospectus

1 Content

10. The CMTA imposes only general requirements for the content of the prospectus while the details are contained in the directly applicable Prospectus Regulation. Even in this respect, however, the CMTA mostly quotes the Prospectus Directive. This is why full reference can be made to Chapter 4 in particular. The next section of this document therefore provides a mere general summary of the major principles of the regulation applicable to the prospectus.

The prospectus shall contain information on the issuer, the security involved and a summary of the prospectus. The summary shall contain 'comprehensibly formulated brief characteristics and risks of the issuer of the security and the guarantor, if any' (Section 36, subsection 4 of the CMTA). The summary of the prospectus constitutes a specific part thereof which shall provide a brief (no more than 2,500 words) and comprehensible summary of the contents of the prospectus to give a less knowledgeable investor an essential overview of the substance of the offered security and the risks involved. The CMTA's requirement for the 'comprehensible' formulation must be primarily understood as a requirement for the summary to refrain from using any professional language, which should only be used in the other sections of the prospectus to provide a 'knowledgeable' review. The summary constitutes a part of the entire prospectus and must be assessed in connection with the prospectus.

11. The information in the prospectus can be provided by virtue of a reference to one or several documents previously or simultaneously published and approved by the Czech National Bank or to a document summarising all information that the issuer has published during the most recent year as a part of the performance of its statutory duties. The prospectus shall refer to the most up-to-date documents that must be available to the public throughout the entire duration the prospectus is published and shall contain a list of references.

12. The Czech National Bank may consent to have information that is not substantial to investors, in conflict with public interest or substantially damaging the issuer to be omitted from the prospectus (Section 36e of the CMTA) or approve the so-called preliminary prospectus, i.e. a prospectus without the final price and the number of securities (Section 36d CMTA). It is not required to simultaneously publish the final price and the number of securities with the prospectus but anytime later on, provided the investors are provided with it at least two days after information on the final price and the volume of the issue has been disclosed to the public so that they can recall their acceptance of the public offer.

2 Form and format

13. Identically with the Prospectus Directive, the CMTA stipulates that the prospectus can be drafted as a single prospectus or as a set of three independent documents, each serving as a unified prospectus in regulatory terms. The contents of the prospectus can therefore be divided into (i) a 'registration document' containing information on the issuer of the particular security; (ii) 'securities note' dealing with the security to which the prospectus applies; and (iii) the 'summary'. The summary can be either part of a single prospectus or an independent document that, together with the registration document and the securities note, comprise a combined prospectus. The issuer may, for instance, use an approved registration document for two prospectuses by attaching a different securities note and the summary. If the prospectus comprises several documents it can be published and distributed independently under the terms and conditions imposed for the publication of the prospectus. However, each document must contain information about where to obtain the other documents comprising the prospectus (see Chapter 4, No. 41).

Article 5(4) of the Prospectus Directive and Section 36a of the CMTA set forth that warrants issued under an '*offering programme*' and non-equity securities issued in a continuous or repeated manner can be offered under a single prospectus, the so-called base prospectus. The CMTA defines the offering programme in Section 34, subsection 2(c) as a plan for continuous issue of securities within the issue period but provides no details thereon. Act No. 190/2004 Coll., the Bond Act, indicates that in particular the bond programme, as defined in Section 13 of the Bond Act, constitutes the offering programme. The bond programme is to be approved simultaneously with the base prospectus and both may comprise a single document. The question of whether or not other issue programmes may exist is open but we can conclude that the existence thereof would have to be provided for by generally binding law.

The Prospectus Regulation defines the format of the prospectus and we refer therefore to Chapter VI, No. 48.

3 Supplements

14. The issue of supplements to prospectuses is dealt with in Section 36j of the CMTA, which is a translation of Article 16 of the Prospectus Directive. We may therefore refer to Chapter 8, No. 66.

4 Language

15. The basic rule is that the prospectus must be in Czech if the Czech National Bank is to approve the prospectus for public offering or admission to trading on a regulated market only in the Czech Republic.

Pursuant to Article 19 of the Prospectus Directive, the CMTA requires that where the prospectus is to be approved for a public offer or admission to trading on a regulated market in the Czech Republic and another Member State, the prospectus shall be drawn up in Czech, or in a language accepted by the competent authorities of that Member State, or English, at the discretion of the issuer of the prospectus. In this instance, the prospectus shall be drawn up in two languages. If the prospectus to be approved applies to securities to be admitted for trading on a regulated market in any other Member State excluding the Czech Republic, the prospectus must be presented to the Czech National Bank in the language of the particular Member State and in Czech. The Czech version of the prospectus is for the information of the Czech National Bank and is not approved as such. In this instance the prospectus is to be approved in a single language version only.

If the Czech National Bank is to approve a prospectus for warrants whose nominal value per unit amounts to at least €50,000 to be traded on a regulated market in one or more Member States of the European Union, the prospectus shall be drawn up in either a language accepted by the supervisory authorities of the other Member States (and in Czech in this instance) or in English, at the discretion of the issuer of the prospectus. The Czech National Bank is further authorised to permit a prospectus for securities offered in the Czech Republic to be drafted only in English even in other circumstances if it is for the benefit of the investors (Section 36(g) of the CMTA).

If a prospectus approved by the supervisory authority of another Member State is to be published in the Czech Republic, the only languages shall be Czech or English. If the prospectus is published in English a Czech translation of the summary of the prospectus must be provided.

V Publication and advertisements

1 Method of publication

16. The prospectus shall be published without undue delay after the Czech National Bank has approved it, or after a certificate of approval by another supervisory authority has been delivered to the Czech National Bank. The prospectus shall be published in full by one or several of the following means:

(i) on the issuer's website or on the website of a securities broker if it places or sells the securities;
(ii) in at least one nation-wide daily newspaper and, at the same time, in the manner set forth in (i) above;
(iii) by brochure which shall be available to the public free of charge at the registered office of the organiser of the regulated market on which the securities are to be admitted to trading, or in the issuer's registered office and registered offices of securities brokers if they place or sell the securities and, at the same time, in the manner set forth in (i);
(iv) on the website of the organiser of the regulated market in respect of which the admission to trading has been applied for; or
(v) on the offeror's website if the securities are offered by a party other than the issuer.

If the prospectus comprises several documents or includes references, the documents and the information comprising the prospectus can be published and distributed independently, provided that each document comprising the prospectus or the document to which reference is made are published in accordance with the requirements for prospectus publication referred to above. Each document must contain information on where to obtain the other documents that together form the complete prospectus.

If the prospectus is published only on the Internet, the party who published it (which can be either the issuer, the party who submits the offer, the applicant for admission to trading on an official market or the securities broker who places or sells the securities) must deliver a hard copy of the prospectus to the investor, free of charge, upon request.

Certain problems may arise from the text of Section 36(h) of the CMTA, under which the prospectus shall be published without undue delay after it has been approved. This is a stricter requirement than that imposed by Article 14 of the Prospectus Directive.

2 Advertisements

17. The CMTA regulates the content of advertisements identically to Article 15 of the Prospectus Directive. Therefore, we can conclude that all marketing material must contain the information about the prospectus,

where and when it was published and where it can be obtained. It must be consistent with the prospectus and clearly recognisable (Section 36(k) of the CMTA). Further we refer to Chapter 7, No. 63.

Czech law does not contain any requirement for the regulator to sign off on the marketing materials or any requirement to register the marketing materials with any authority. However, marketing activity is under the supervision of the Czech National Bank.

VI Use of a prospectus approved in other (non EU) countries

18. If the supervisory authority of a country that is not a member of the European Union approves the prospectus of a security, the Czech National Bank cannot accept the prospectus *ipso jure*. Securities can be offered or admitted to trading on a public market only if the Czech National Bank approves the foreign prospectus for such securities. The prospectus must comply with the requirements imposed by Czech and European laws applicable to the contents thereof.

Pursuant to Article 20 of the Prospectus Directive, however, the CMTA makes it possible for the Czech National Bank to approve a prospectus for securities issued by an issuer with its registered office in a country that is not a Member State of the European Union, if the prospectus complies with the law of that country, provided that

(i) the requirements of that country for prospectuses are equal to the requirements imposed by law; and
(ii) the prospectus has been drawn up in compliance with international standards imposed by international organisations of the relevant supervisory authorities.

Under such circumstances, the prospectus for such securities do not have to comply with the formal requirements of the Czech and European laws applicable thereto.

VII Sanctions

19. Issuers of listed securities and parties publicly offering securities are subject to supervision by the Czech National Bank. Section 136 of the CMTA applies to the general powers of the Czech National Bank to order a party subject to supervision who has breached the CMTA or any decision issued in line with the CMTA to remedy the insufficiency corresponding to the nature and seriousness of the breach. The Czech National Bank may, among other measures, suspend public offering of securities, or the admission of securities to trading on a regulated market, for ten business days or to prohibit or suspend the promotion or any notices regarding the public offer or the admission of the securities to trading on a regulated market.

Pursuant to Section 36(c), subsection 7 of the CMTA, the Czech National Bank may demand that the prospectus be supplemented if the presented documents are incomplete or if further information is required. It can be inferred from these provisions (even taking into account Art. 21(3) Dir.) that such requirements can go beyond the explicit requirements listed by law or the Prospectus Regulation, and that the Czech National Bank may do so every time it is required for investor protection.

Pursuant to the Capital Market Supervision Act,[5] the Czech National Bank, when deciding the application for approval of the prospectus, is authorised to request any information and background material from senior managers or auditors of the securities issuer, the party that drafted the prospectus or the securities broker who places the securities. The Capital Market Supervision Act further stipulates a general power for the Czech National Bank to request any information or background material from any party that is subject to the Bank's supervision (including issuers of listed securities, parties publicly offering securities or securities brokers). The Czech National Bank may request any information from other parties if it is necessary for the investigation of any fact indicating a breach of duties regarding protection of insider information or manipulation of the market. The Czech National Bank is further authorised to carry out on-site control of any party subject to the supervision at any time.

The CMTA further grants the Czech National Bank the right to impose cash penalties. The CMTA lists individual offences. Any party which (a) publicly offers securities without having published the prospectus; (b) fails to follow the rules for promotion and other notices regarding public offers or admission of securities to trading on an official market; (c) fails to comply with the terms and conditions for publishing the prospectus and any supplement thereto; (d) fails to carry out remedy by a deadline; or (e) drafts the prospectus in conflict with the rules for drafting prospectuses is subject to a penalty up to CZK 10 million by the Czech National Bank.

VIII Prospectus liability

20. Pursuant to Section 36(b) of the CMTA, the party/parties that drafted the prospectus shall be liable for the accuracy and completeness of the information in the prospectus. Pursuant to Section 36, subsection 5 of the CMTA, the issuer or other party/parties offering the securities or applying for the listing thereof shall draft the prospectus. The legislator apparently declined to impose liability for drafting the prospectus on the particular party that physically drafts the prospectus and instead restricted liability to the party that submits the prospectus to the public. This conclusion cannot be changed by the requirement that the prospectus include information of

[5] Act no. 15/1998 Coll.

parties liable for accurate drafting of the prospectus, including their declaration that to the best of their knowledge the information in the prospectus is true and no facts that could change the meaning of the prospectus have been omitted. The issuer is usually this liable party.

The CMTA also regulates the position of the so-called guarantor of the prospectus. The guarantor is a party who explicitly declares that he assumes liability for the accuracy of the information in the prospectus. Such a party is then liable as the party that drafted the prospectus. However, the guarantee is not obligatory and it is solely at the discretion of the party that drafts the prospectus whether to opt for the guarantee or not.

It may be added that the CMTA fails to deal with the issue of the damage for which such parties are to be liable and how to determine the amount thereof. These issues remain to be resolved empirically. With respect to the absence of any applicable judicature, it can hardly be anticipated how the courts are to approach this issue.

IX Rules applicable to transactions and securities not subject to the Directive and Regulation

21. Transferable securities are the only investment instruments the public offering of which is regulated by Czech law. This is why parties offering, for example, financial-futures contracts could not be subject to the requirements for publishing the prospectus or any other duties relating to public offering under the CMTA. Similarly, advertising material that offers such investment instruments could not be subject to the contents-related requirements of Section 36(k).

A similar conclusion can be reached in respect of public offering of securities excluded from the application of the CMTA, the group of which is basically identical to the exemptions provided for by the Prospectus Directive.

X Conclusion

22. The Czech legislation applicable to public offering of securities is essentially a transposition of the Prospectus Directive. Most of the provisions copy the provisions of the Directive; any potential discrepancies in terms of contents can be attributed to the translation rather than the intention of the legislators. Areas to which the Directive applies only generally and to which national laws are expected to apply (such as the liability for the prospectus and compensation for damage) are dealt with fairly vaguely by the Czech legislation which, combined with minimal experience of the applying of such provisions, results in considerable uncertainty.

The provisions of the CMTA are only limited to the public offering of transferable securities; the public offering of any other investment instruments is not subject to any special regulation. It can be added that no such event has ever occurred in the Czech Republic. The Czech law subjects admission to a regulated market by publishing of a prospectus only for shares and bonds. These insufficiencies are to be removed by a major amendment to the CMTA being prepared which should in particular transpose the Directive on markets in financial instruments (2004/39/EC) and take effect on 1 January 2008. However, no text of the amendment has yet been presented.

The currently applicable Czech law provides for acknowledgement of prospectuses approved by supervisory authorities of other member countries in accordance with the requirements of the Prospectus Directive and imposes no obstacles to international offering of securities, save for the requirement that a Czech summary of the prospectus be published together with the English text thereof.

4 Denmark

VAGN THORUP AND DAVID MOALEM
Kromann Reumert

I Introduction

1. Taking as its point of departure the implementation of the Prospectus Directive, the Danish prospectus regime was substantially revised with effect from 1 July 2005.

Today, the Danish prospectus regime consists of three tiers, of which only Tier 1 is a direct consequence of the implementation of the Prospectus Directive. Figure 1 below illustrates the three current tiers of the Danish prospectus regime.

The Tier 2 legislation encompasses the 'smaller unlisted offerings' and is based on the Danish legislator's desire to ensure investors in these offerings a minimum standard of protection. The legislation is to a large extent similar to that of Tier 1. However, since it is not based on the Prospectus Directive there are certain differences, i.e. the passporting regime is inapplicable to Tier 2-offerings and the Danish Financial Services Authority (*Finanstilsynet*, the 'Danish FSA') is not bound by the EU interpretation of the Prospectus Directive.

Tier 3 deals with offerings which the Prospectus Directive specifically prohibits from being comprised by the obligation to publish a prospectus. Such offerings with an aggregate value below €100,000 are only comprised by the general regulation in the Danish Marketing Practices Act and other general pieces of legislation.

	TYPE OF OFFERING	APPLICABLE LEGISLATION
Tier 1	Offers of securities with an aggregate value above €2.5 million and of securities which are listed or admitted to trading on a regulated market	Prospectus Directive Prospectus Regulation CESR's recommendations The Danish Securities Trading Act, Chapter 6 Executive Order No. 1232/2007 Guidelines No. 9318/2005
Tier 2	Offers of unlisted securities with an aggregate value between €100,000 and €2.5 million	The Danish Securities Trading Act, Chapter 12 Executive Order No. 1231/2007 Guidelines No. 9320/2005
Tier 3	Offers of unlisted securities with an aggregate value below €100,000	Not encompassed by the Prospectus Regulation. The Danish Marketing Act and other acts may be applicable

Figure 1. Overview of the Danish prospectus regime

II Competent authority

2. The Danish Securities Trading Act designates the Danish FSA as the competent authority. Consequently, the Danish FSA is responsible for approving Tier 1 and Tier 2 prospectuses submitted to it. Further, the Danish FSA is responsible for the procedure under the EU prospectus passporting regime.

The Danish FSA charges a fee of DKK 25,000 for the approval of Tier 1 prospectuses. Approval of Tier 2 prospectuses is free of charge.

III Procedure of prior approval and appeal

1 The obligation to publish a prospectus

3. Under the Danish Prospectus regime, the main rule is that any offer of transferable securities to the public in Denmark with an aggregate value above €100,000 entails an obligation to publish a prospectus. In accordance with Section 2b of the Danish Securities Trading Act, an offer of securities to the public is: '*a communication to natural or legal persons in any form and by any means, presenting sufficient information on the terms of the offer and the securities to be offered, so as to enable an investor to decide to purchase or subscribe to these securities*'.

4. It follows from the definition that an offer of transferable securities of an aggregate value above €100,000 will, as a main rule, be an offer of securities to the public and result in an obligation to publish a prospectus. The closer understanding of 'transferable securities' remains to be clarified by the Danish FSA, as no formal position has yet been taken in this respect. It can be expected that the interpretation hereof will be coordinated by CESR.

Based on the comments on the definition of an offer of securities to the Danish public in the preparatory works of the Danish Securities Trading Act, the offeror/issuer must actively take steps to make available to the Danish public sufficient information on the terms of the offer, so as to enable an investor to decide to purchase or subscribe to the securities, including i.e. information on the characteristics, terms and price of the securities, how and when to subscribe to the securities etc., cf. *Folketingstidende* A 2004–05 (1. *samling*), p. 355. Thus, the publication of information and statements and publicity efforts made in advance of a proposed financing which have the effect of conditioning the public mind or arousing the public interest in an issuer or in its securities will normally constitute an offer to the public. Excluded from the definition is presumably communication of general information about securities clearly not intended to form part of an offering, e.g. a communication regarding the securities which does not refer to an offer price (unless the price may easily be deduced indirectly from the information provided). Further, to constitute an 'offer' the (final) investor must be able to make an investment decision, cf. also CESR's interpretation hereof (CESR/07-110 (February 2007), p. 6):

> *in the case of allocations of securities [. . .] where there is no element of choice on the part of the recipient, including no right to repudiate the allocation, there is no 'offer of securities to the public' within the meaning of Article 2.1 d) PD. This is because the definition refers to a communication containing sufficient information 'to enable an investor to decide to' purchase or subscribe for the securities. Where no decision is made by the recipient of the securities, there is no offer for the purposes of the Directive. Such allocations will therefore fall outside the scope of the PD.*

2 Admission to listing or trading on a regulated Danish market

5. The Danish Securities Trading Act distinguishes between (i) a stock exchange and (ii) an authorised marketplace. Both of these types of marketplace constitute a 'regulated market', as defined in MiFID, and offerings which are listed or admitted to trading hereon are therefore encompassed by the Prospectus Directive. In practice, the relevant Danish regulated markets are as follows:

- The Copenhagen Stock Exchange (OMX)
- XtraMarked (OMX)
- The Danish Authorised Market Place

As mentioned under No. II above the Danish FSA is responsible for the approval of prospectuses submitted to the Danish FSA and for the procedure under the EU prospectus passporting regime. This also applies to offers of securities to be listed or admitted to trading on a regulated market in Denmark. However, the marketplaces will also perform a review of the prospectuses and it is customary that they request further information and/or amendments to the prospectus before the securities officially are listed or admitted to trading.

Further to the above, an alternative marketplace, First North – which is basically a multilateral trading facility (MTF), comprised of additional Danish securities regulation – is operated in Copenhagen by the OMX group. Being a non-regulated market in the context of the Prospectus Directive, admission of securities on First North is considered an admission of unlisted securities encompassed by the Tier 2 regulation.

3 Exemptions

6. The exemptions contained in the Danish prospectus legislation are divided into two main categories, namely:

(i) Unlisted securities: securities which are not listed or admitted to trading on a regulated market operating from within the EU/EEA; and
(ii) Listed securities: securities which are listed or admitted to trading on a regulated market (i.e. stock exchanges and similar) operating from within the EU/EEA.

Notably, securities, which are listed or admitted to trading outside (but not inside) the EU/EEA, e.g. on NYSE or NASDAQ belong in the category of unlisted securities for the purposes of the rules. Further, as mentioned under (ii) above, securities to be admitted to trading on First North are considered as unlisted securities.

7. Although the exemptions 1232/2007 follow from two different sets of rules – Executive Order No. 306/2005 for Tier 1 offerings and Executive Order No. 1231/2007 for Tier 2 offerings – the exemptions apply equally to Tier 1 and Tier 2 offerings. Figure 2 below illustrates the applicable exemptions under Danish law.

UNLISTED SECURITIES

- an offer of securities addressed solely to qualified investors
- an offer of securities addressed to fewer than 100 natural or legal persons per Member State or EEA State, other than qualified investors
- an offer of securities addressed to investors who acquire securities for a total consideration of at least € 50,000
- an offer of securities whose denomination per unit amounts to at least € 50,000
- an offer of securities with a total consideration of less than € 100,000, which limit shall be calculated over a period of twelve months
- shares issued in substitution for shares of the same class already issued, if the issuing of such new shares does not involve any increase in the issued capital

LISTED SECURITIES

- shares representing, over a period of twelve months, less than 10 % of the number of shares of the same class already admitted to trading on the same regulated market
- shares issued in substitution for shares of the same class already admitted to trading on the same regulated market, if the issuing of such shares does not involve any increase in the issued capital
- securities offered in connection with a takeover, provided that a document is available containing information which is regarded as being equivalent to that of the prospectus
- securities offered, allotted or to be allotted in connection with a merger, provided that a document is available containing information which is regarded as being equivalent to that of the prospectus

Figure 2. Exemptions under Danish law

UNLISTED SECURITIES

- securities offered in connection with a takeover, provided that a document is available containing information which is regarded as being equivalent to that of the prospectus
- securities offered, allotted or to be allotted in connection with a merger, provided that a document is available containing information which is regarded as being equivalent to that of the prospectus
- shares offered, allotted or to be allotted free of charge to existing shareholders, and dividends paid out in the form of shares of the same class as the shares in respect of which such dividends are paid, provided that a document is made available containing information on the number and nature of the shares and the reasons for and details of the offer
- securities offered, allotted or to be allotted to existing or former directors or employees by their employer which has securities already admitted to trading on a regulated market or by an affiliated undertaking, cf. Section 5(1)(9) of the Danish Financial Business Act, provided that a document is made available containing information on the number and nature of the securities and the reasons for and details of the offer

LISTED SECURITIES

- shares offered, allotted or to be allotted free of charge to existing shareholders, and dividends paid out in the form of shares of the same class as the shares in respect of which such dividends are paid, provided that the said shares are of the same class as the shares already admitted to trading on the same regulated market and that a document is made available containing information on the number and nature of the shares and the reasons for and details of the offer
- securities offered, allotted or to be allotted to existing or former directors or employees by their employer or an affiliated undertaking, cf. Section 5(1)(9) of the Danish Financial Business Act, provided that the said securities are of the same class as the securities already admitted to trading on the same regulated market and that a document is made available containing information on the number and nature of the securities and the reasons for and details of the offer
- shares resulting from the conversion or exchange of other securities or from the exercise of the rights conferred by other securities, provided that the said shares are of the same class as the shares already admitted to trading on the same regulated market
- securities already admitted to trading on another regulated market, provided certain conditions are met

Figure 2. (cont.)

4 The EU Prospectus Passport under Danish law

A Introduction

8. In the context of the Danish legislation regarding the EU Prospectus Passport, the distinction between the three tiers (outlined under no. 1 above) is essential. This is due to the fact that the regulation hereof in the Prospectus Directive only encompasses offers of (a) securities with an aggregate value above €2.5 million and of (b) securities which are listed or admitted to trading on a regulated market within the EU/EEA (i.e. Tier 1 offerings).

For Tier 1 offerings the EU Prospectus Passport requires the EU/EEA Member States to mutually recognise prospectuses approved by the competent authority in any other Member State and thus enabling the cross-border passporting of prospectuses within the EU/EEA.

The Danish regulation of relevance to the EU Prospectus Passport is primarily encompassed by chapters 5, 8 and 9 of the Danish Executive Order No. 1232/2007. Furthermore, the Prospectus Regulation (2004/809/EC) comprises certain provisions regarding the content of the prospectus to be passported.

B Tax Description

9. To comply with the Prospectus Directive, the prospectus must meet the minimum requirements in accordance with the Prospectus Regulation. These requirements include, among other things, a description of the rules on withholding tax in the home member state as well as that of *the member state in which the securities are being offered* (in this case Denmark), cf. Article 6 and Schedule III, Item 4.11 of the Prospectus Regulation, which stipulates that the prospectus must contain (a) information on taxes on the income from the securities withheld at source, and (b) indication as to whether the issuer assumes responsibility for the withholding of taxes at the source.

C Danish Summary

10. The prospectus may be in English or Danish. If the prospectus is in English, the summary must be translated into Danish, cf. Section 29(5) of the Danish Executive Order No. 1232/2007.

The summary may normally not exceed 2,500 words and must be easy to read. The summary must convey the essential characteristics and risks associated with the issuer, any guarantor and the securities. In addition, the summary must convey the following information; cf. Section 15(3) of the Danish Executive Order No. 306/2005:

- The summary should be read as an introduction to the prospectus;
- Any decision to invest in the securities should be based on consideration of the prospectus as a whole by the investor;

- Where a claim relating to the information contained in the prospectus is brought before a court, the plaintiff investor may have to bear the costs of translating the prospectus before the legal proceedings are initiated; and
- Civil liability attaches to those persons who have drafted the summary including any translation thereof, and applied for its notification, but only if the summary is misleading, inaccurate or inconsistent when read together with the other parts of the prospectus in question.

D The filing procedure and commencement of the public offer

11. The filing procedure to be performed in connection with the passporting of the prospectus into Denmark and the commencement of the public offering may in general be outlined as follows:

(i) The prospectus and supplement, if any, must be filed with the competent authority of the relevant EU/EEA Member State.
(ii) The competent authority of the relevant EU/EEA Member State must approve the prospectus and supplement, if any.
(iii) The issuer must request that the competent authority in the relevant EU/EEA Member State issue a Certificate of Approval. The Certificate of Approval must state that the prospectus (and supplement) comply with the Prospectus Directive.
(iv) The issuer must request that the competent authority in the relevant EU/EEA Member State send the Certificate of Approval to the Danish FSA along with a copy of the prospectus (and supplement) and a summary in Danish. The prospectus must be valid at the time of filing, i.e. twelve months from the time of publication in the relevant EU/EEA Member State, cf. Sections 21–23 of the Prospectus Order.
(v) The Danish FSA will confirm its receipt of the Certificate of Approval and the Danish summary (if required) to the competent authority of the relevant EU/EEA Member State.
(vi) The Danish FSA issues a Prospectus Certificate. This Prospectus Certificate will only state that the Danish FSA has received the necessary material under the EU Prospectus Passport regime. The Danish FSA does not charge any filing fees with respect to the issuance of the Prospectus Certificate. The Danish FSA publishes a list of Prospectus Certificates issued within the last twelve months on its web-address: www.ftnet.dk.
(vii) The public offering may commence when the Prospectus Certificate is received from the Danish FSA and the prospectus (and supplement) is considered published.

IV Content and format, language and supplements of the prospectus

1 Content

12. The minimum requirements as to the content of a prospectus are laid down in the Prospectus Regulation and in particular schedules I to XVII, which comprise a rather elaborate outline of the information to be included in the prospectus.

Notwithstanding the detailed schedules of the Prospectus Regulation, Section 23(3) of the Danish Securities Trading Act stipulates the general clause that the prospectus should contain all information necessary to enable investors and their advisors to make an informed assessment of the assets and liabilities, financial position, profit and losses and prospects of the issuer and of any guarantor, and of the rights attached to the securities offered, cf. Article 5(1) of the Prospectus Directive.

The general clause stresses that all information necessary to sufficiently inform investors must be made available. Thus, the prospectus should permit investors to make an informed assessment of the risks represented by the securities in order to make an investment decision with full knowledge of all relevant facts.

2 Format

13. As mentioned under No. I above, the Danish prospectus regime was substantially revised with effect from 1 July 2005 due to the implementation of the Prospectus Directive. Before this implementation a Danish prospectus could only be approved and published as one single coherent document.

As of 1 July 2005 this state of law was changed and the prospectus may today alternatively be prepared as three separate documents in accordance with the Prospectus Directive and the schedules of the Prospectus Regulation; (i) a registration document, (ii) a securities note and (iii) a summary.

In practice, separate documents are used if the offeror/issuer intends to regularly offer or issue transferable securities (outside an offering programme of non-equity securities). In such cases only information on the securities issued or offered will then need to be prepared for each new transaction.

14. For certain types of securities, it is also possible to use base prospectuses. A base prospectus is defined as a document containing (a) all relevant information about the issuer and the securities to be offered to the public or admitted to listing or trading on a stock exchange, an authorised marketplace or a similar regulated market for securities and (b) at the choice of the issuer, the final terms of the offering, cf. Section 10 of Executive Order No. 306/2005.

By using the base prospectus, it is possible to leave out certain information about the securities, which would normally have to be included in the prospectus, i.e. the offer price and number of securities. Base prospectuses may be used in connection with (a) offering programmes or (b) securities issued in a continuous or repeated manner as defined in Sections 6 and 7 of Executive Order No. 306/2005.

Debt issuance programmes commonly use base prospectuses as the legal basis for future offerings under the specific debt issuance programme. Section 22 of the Prospectus Regulation encompasses the minimum information to be included in a base prospectus and its final terms. Section 22(6) of the Prospectus Regulation and Section 17(1) of Executive Order No. 306/2005 outline the categories of non-equity securities for which base prospectuses may be used, e.g. asset backed securities, notes and warrants.

15. If the final terms of the offer cannot be included in either the base prospectus or a supplement, the final terms must be (a) provided to investors and (b) filed with the competent authority in the country in which the prospectus has been approved when each public offering is made, as soon as practicable and, if possible, prior to the beginning of the offering, cf. Section 17(3) of Executive Order No. 306/2005. There is no obligation to file the final terms with the Danish FSA, unless the Danish FSA is the competent authority. However, even though it is not an obligation, the Danish FSA appreciates receiving the final terms.

3 Supplements

16. Any significant new fact, material error or inaccuracy relating to the information contained in the prospectus which occurs until the closing of the offering or the start of trading on a regulated market in Denmark and may affect an investor's assessment of the securities will result in an obligation to publish a supplement to the prospectus, cf. Section 26(1) of Executive Order No. 1232/2007. The supplement must be approved by the Danish FSA within seven business days.

The summary (and any translations thereof) must be updated in accordance with the new information in the supplement, cf. Section 26(2) of Executive Order No. 1232/2007.

In the event a supplement is required, investors who have already agreed to purchase or subscribe to the securities prior to publication of the supplement shall be entitled to withdraw their acceptance within two business days following the publication of the supplement, cf. Section 26(3) of Executive Order No. 1232/2007.

4 Language

17. Section 29 of Executive Order No. 1232/2007 comprises the Danish regulation of the language requirements in connection with the publication of prospectuses.

The prospectus must be prepared in Danish if the offer is restricted to Denmark and Denmark is the home member state, cf. Section 29(1) of Executive Order No. 1232/2007.

If the offer is directed at Denmark and other EU/EEA countries and Denmark is the home member state, the prospectus must be in Danish. Further, the prospectus must be published in a language accepted by the competent authorities in the host member states or in English, cf. Section 29(4) of Executive Order No. 1232/2007.

If the offer is directed at Denmark but the home member state is another EU/EEA Member State, the prospectus may be in either Danish or English. If the prospectus is only prepared in an English version, the issuer/offeror must prepare a Danish translation of the summary, cf. Section 29(5) of Executive Order No. 1232/2007.

The Danish FSA may choose to dispense with the requirement to publish the prospectus in a Danish version, if the specific characteristics of the offer of securities do not entail a consideration for such an investor protection, cf. Section 29(7) of Executive Order No. 1232/2007.

V Publication and advertisements

1 Method of publication

18. The public offering may commence when the prospectus (and supplement) is considered published. The prospectus (and supplement) has to be published as soon as possible following the confirmation from the Danish FSA. The term 'as soon as possible' is yet to be determined in common practice. However, the prospectus (and supplement) must be published no later than at the time of the offer of the securities in Denmark, cf. Section 24 of Executive Order No. 1232/2007.

The following acts are considered Acts of Publication in accordance with Section 25 of Executive Order No. 1232/2007:

- Publication in one or more nationwide Danish newspapers provided the public offering is made via a stock exchange or authorised marketplace in Denmark;
- In written form, placed free of charge at the disposal of the public at the place of business of the market where the securities are listed or admitted to trading, as well as the place of business of the issuer and the financial companies placing or transacting the sale of the securities;
- In electronic form on the website of the issuer and, where applicable,

on the websites of the financial companies placing or transacting the sale of the securities;
- In electronic form, via the information system of the stock exchange, the authorised market or the regulated market where the application for listing or admission for trading is made.

In the event of electronic publication, the prospectus (and supplement) must be available upon the investor's request in physical form, free of charge, from the issuer or the financial companies placing or transacting the sale of the securities, until the prospectus (and supplement) ceases to be valid, cf. Section 25(4) of Executive Order No. 1232/2007.

19. Also, material changes in the information given in the prospectus (and supplement) which take place between the approval of the prospectus and the end of the offer, must be made public in accordance with the above within seven business days, cf. Section 26 of Executive Order No. 1232/2007.

20. If the final terms of the offer cannot be included in either the base prospectus or a supplement, the final terms must be (a) provided to investors and (b) filed with the competent authority in the country in which the prospectus has been approved when each public offering is made as soon as practicable and, if possible, in advance of the beginning of the offer, cf. Section 17(3) of Executive Order No. 1232/2007. There is no obligation to file the final terms with the Danish FSA.

2 Advertisements

21. Advertisement of the offer must satisfy the rules relating to advertisements in Sections 27 and 28 of the Danish Executive Order No. 1232/2007. Accordingly, advertisements regarding the offer shall state the following:

- that the prospectus has been or will be published; and
- indicate where investors are or will be able to obtain it.

Advertisements shall furthermore be clearly recognisable as such, and the information contained in an advertisement must not be inaccurate or misleading. This information shall also be consistent with the information contained in the prospectus, if already published, or with the information required to be in the prospectus, if the prospectus is published afterwards.

All information concerning the offer disclosed in an oral or written form, even if not for advertising purposes, shall be consistent with that contained in the prospectus.

22. Marketing, promotion, etc., of the offer to investors resident/located in Denmark may take place provided that it is carried out fairly and in conformity with the rules of good securities trading practice and good practice for financial businesses laid down in the Danish Securities Trading Act and the Danish Financial Business Act. Said rules contain standards for good mar-

keting and trading practice. Furthermore, please be advised that the Danish Act on Certain Consumer Agreements (implementing the EU Directives 1987/577, 1997/7, 2002/65) encompasses a prohibition against 'cold calls' to consumers and the Danish Fair Marketing Practices Act prohibits unsolicited inquiries through email, an automatic calling system or fax, including to professional investors.

The issuer of the securities is entitled to perform any marketing, promotion, etc., without obtaining licence, cf. Section 9(4) of the Danish Financial Business Act. Any other entities than the issuer itself (intermediaries) must be licensed to carry out investment service in Denmark, e.g. by offering, marketing, promoting, transferring, selling or delivering of the securities, cf. Sections 9, 30, 31 and 33 of the Danish Financial Business Act. A licence to carry out investment service in Denmark may be obtained by virtue of one of the following regulatory authorities:

- through the establishment of a Danish licensed securities dealer;
- through cross-border activity based on an EU investment service licence;
- through a branch in Denmark based on an EU investment service licence; or
- through a licence required for non-EU securities dealers.

Irrespective of whether the marketing, promoting etc. is performed by the issuer or an intermediary, the Danish FSA does not require reviewing/approving of advertisements or other marketing documents in connection with these activities.

VI Use of prospectus approved in other (non EU) countries

23. Section 32 of Executive Order No. 1232/2007 stipulates that if Denmark is the home member state of an issuer having its registered office in a country outside the European Union or EEA, the Danish FSA may approve a prospectus for a Tier 1 offer to the public or for admission to listing or trading in Denmark, drawn up in accordance with the legislation of a country outside the European Union or EEA, provided that:

(i) The prospectus has been drawn up in accordance with international standards set by international securities commission organisations, including the IOSCO disclosure standards;
(ii) The information requirements under the law of the country in question, including information of a financial nature, are equivalent to the requirements under the Prospectus Directive.

The prospectus and approval procedure is comprised by the same language requirements and approval procedures as apply to the EU/EEA prospectuses; cf. Section 33 of Executive Order No. 1232/2007.

VII Sanctions

24. Wilfully or grossly negligent violations of the Danish securities regulation are in general punishable by fine. Companies, etc., (legal entities) may incur criminal liability pursuant to the rules laid down in Chapter 5 of the Danish Penal Code. In case of material violations, the Danish FSA may also issue a public warning against the undertaking in question.

However, in practice, the possible sanctions under Danish law differ depending on the actual scope and character of the particular breach and there are normally no sanctions the first time an offence is committed. Such an offence will in general be met by contact from the Danish FSA and an order to correct the activity, behaviour, etc.

VIII Prospectus liability

25. Article 6 of the Prospectus Directive prescribes that the persons responsible for the prospectus must be clearly identified in the prospectus. To this end, their name and function or, in the case of legal entities, their name and the address of their registered office, must be mentioned. Furthermore, the prospectus must contain a statement by such persons that, to the best of their knowledge, the information contained in the prospectus is in accordance with the facts and that the prospectus contains no omissions likely to affect its import.

Notwithstanding the above, a potential civil liability in connection with a prospectus and offer of securities must be assessed under Danish law, i.e. as civil liability for damages. The Danish prospectus liability derives from the general Danish law of torts. As such, in principle, liability could be attached to anyone who negligently disperses, or aids in the preparation of, the prospectus to the effect that one or more investors suffer a loss, which can be proven to have been caused by the negligent act of the alleged tortfeasor. However, negligence in this respect would most likely require that the alleged tortfeasor had actual or constructive knowledge of material misinformation or omissions in the prospectus at the time when it caused an investor to purchase securities in reliance of the prospectus.

The (quite sparse) Danish case law on prospectus liability has set the liability threshold rather high, which means that even fairly major mistakes in the prospectus do not entail liability, if the prospectus, when read as a whole, cannot be said to be misleading, cf. also the ruling by the Danish Supreme Court in the 'Hafnia-case' (UfR 2002.2067H) regarding an emission in a financial institution (Hafnia), followed by the bankruptcy thereof.

The Danish Supreme Court's ruling in the 'Hafnia-case' showed that liability to pay damages with respect to the offer of securities follows the general Danish principles in this area. Consequently, the ordinary criteria with respect to negligence, adequacy, recoverable losses, own and acceptance of risk apply. It also follows from the ruling that not only must the professional parties on the issuer's side (issuing company, merchant bank, management, auditors, etc.) show proper attention (*caveat venditor*) when offering securities; proper attention (*caveat emptor*) is also required on the part of the investors, professional as well as private.

In its ruling in the Hafnia case, the Danish Supreme Court established the so-called 'materiality criterion' which is thought to be the decisive factor in the future when determining whether prospectus liability arises under Danish law. According to said criterion it will normally be a precondition for the parties responsible for the prospectus (including the company itself) to incur liability towards investors for a 'defect' prospectus (i.e. a prospectus with false, misleading or omitted information) as with respect to the fact that the matters in question take into account other information contained therein of significant relevance with regard to the assessment of the issuing company.

IX Rules applicable to transactions and securities not subject to the Directive and Regulation

26. As mentioned under no. 1 above, the Danish prospectus regime consists of 'three tiers', of which only Tier 1 is a direct implementation of the Prospectus Directive. The Danish prospectus legislation under Tier 2 encompasses the 'smaller unlisted offerings' and is based on the desire of the Danish legislator to ensure investors in these offerings a minimum standard of protection. The legislation is to a large extent similar to that of Tier 1. However, since it is not based on the Prospectus Directive there are certain differences, e.g. that the passporting regime is inapplicable to Tier 2 offerings.

X Conclusion

27. If we take a look back at the period since the Danish implementation of the Prospectus Directive on 1 July 2005, the picture of the harmonisation of the Prospectus Rules – seen from a practical point of view – must be said to have eased the work involved in, for example, cross-border offerings, as well as the communication between the relevant players across EU country borders. To a considerable degree, this is due to the fact that a new European groundwork has now been established in the form of the Prospectus Directive relating to such offerings.

At the same time it must be realised that, as a practitioner, one continuously comes across different interpretations of the EU rules in the specific EU/EEA Member States. In some situations, such differences increasingly constitute practical trade barriers to the players on the securities market. In the same breath it should be noted that several of the unsuitable interpretations/differences arisen since the implementation, have been solved by way of a joint interpretation in the CESR cooperation between the FSAs in Europe. In practice, the said CESR cooperation has contributed significantly to ensuring a consistent interpretation of the Prospectus Directive and thus to ensuring the dismantling of trade barriers between the EU/EEA Member States.

5

Estonia

RAINO PARON AND MONIKA KOOLMEISTER
Raidla & Partners

I Introduction

1. In Estonia, the Estonian Securities Market Act (hereinafter 'SMA') is the main legal act providing, *inter alia*, the general rules on public offers (including prospectuses), takeovers, market abuse, provision of investment services, activities of investment firms, regulated markets and exchanges, as well as supervision of the market participants. The previous European rules on prospectuses specified in the directives 2001/34/EC[1] and 89/298/EEC[2]

[1] Directive 2001/34/EC of the European Parliament and of the Council of 28 May 2001 on the admission of securities to official stock exchange listing and on information to be published on those securities.

[2] Council Directive 89/298/EEC of 17 April 1989 coordinating the requirements for the drawing-up, scrutiny and distribution of the prospectus to be published when transferable securities are offered to the public.

(see Chapter 1, No. 3) were also implemented into Estonian law by incorporation of the relevant rules to the SMA.

In view of the previous legislative tradition, no separate act implementing the Prospectus Directive (hereinafter also 'Dir.', 'the Directive', please see Annex I) was adopted in Estonia. The Prospectus Directive was implemented into Estonian law (i) by amending the SMA and (ii) by the Minister of Finance adopting two regulations specifying the rules on prospectuses provided for in the SMA. There was a short delay in implementing the Directive. The respective amendments to the SMA came into force on 15 November 2005 instead of 1 July 2005, as provided for in the Directive. The Minister of Finance adopted its Regulation No. 90 on 'Procedure and Conditions with Regard to Exceptions on the Information and Data Published in a Prospectus' (hereinafter the 'Omissions Regulation') on 27 December 2005 and Regulation No. 4 on 'The Requirements for the Prospectuses Pertaining to Public Offer, Trading and Listing of Securities' (hereinafter the 'Regulation on the Prospectus Requirements') on 9 January 2006. Also, due to the implementation of the Prospectus Directive, the Tallinn Stock Exchange amended its rules to some extent.

In addition to the SMA and the regulations adopted hereunder, the Estonian Financial Supervision Authority (hereinafter the 'EFSA') has adopted advisory guidelines on 'Rules of Conduct During Public Offer of Securities', applicable as of 1 October 2003. The guidelines apply to public offers of securities admitted to trading on a regulated market or with regard to which such an application has been submitted. As regards content, the guidelines include principles for distribution of the securities, management of information (including inside information) during an offer, as well as requirements on information to be included in a prospectus. Pursuant to the guidelines, the guidelines have to be applied in conformity with the SMA and other laws and regulations. As to implementation of the Prospectus Directive, some of the provisions of the advisory guidelines may not be applied due to the amendments in law. As the guidelines have advisory character only, this chapter will not further analyse the advice set forth therein. However, if an offer is made in Estonia, it is always advisable to adhere to the advice provided in the guidelines.

II Competent authority

2. The SMA has been amended in the light of Article 21(1) of the Prospectus Directive requiring each Member State to designate an independent central competent administrative authority responsible for carrying out the obligations provided for in the Prospectus Directive (see Chapter 1, No. 18). The EFSA has been designated as the Estonian independent central competent administrative authority in the meaning of Article 21(1)

of the Prospectus Directive. Pursuant to Articles 15(1), 132(1)[1] and 157 of the SMA, both the prospectus to be published upon public offers and upon admission to trading have to be registered with the EFSA.

Pursuant to Article 4 of the Estonian Financial Supervision Authority Act, the EFSA is a public legal entity with autonomous competence and independent budget operating alongside the Bank of Estonia (the Estonian central bank). The EFSA conducts financial supervision in the name of the state and is independent in the conduct of financial supervision.

3. In respect of the authorities of the EFSA, the following applies. In cases where Estonia is the home Member State of the issuer, the EFSA, pursuant to Article 36(1) of the SMA, is entitled to request, by its precept (an administrative act), that the public offer of securities be terminated or suspended if:

(i) the requirements of the SMA and laws established on the basis thereof or other laws regulating public offers are violated, or there is reason to believe that the specified requirements will be violated;
(ii) the terms and conditions of the offer as described in the prospectus have not been complied with;
(iii) the information submitted upon registration of the prospectus is inaccurate to a significant extent.

In its precept suspending the offer, the EFSA will oblige the offeror to eliminate the circumstances causing the suspension of the offer. While eliminating such circumstances, the offeror may resume the offer with the permission of the EFSA.

With regard to admission to trading, the EFSA, in order to (i) protect the interests of investors; (ii) avoid danger to the regular and lawful operation of the market; or (iii) protect any other significant interest or avoid any other threat, is also entitled to issue a precept to an operator of a regulated securities market for suspension of trading of certain securities on the market for at most ten consecutive working days on any single occasion if the requirements provided for in the SMA (including the prospectus requirements) have been infringed or there are reasonable grounds for believing that the requirements provided for in the SMA will be infringed (Art. 136(1)(1) of the SMA). Further, the EFSA is entitled to issue a precept to an operator of the market for cessation of trading of securities (Art. 137(1) of the SMA).[3]

Also, in order to verify the information submitted along with the application to register the prospectus, the EFSA may request that more specific information and documents be submitted, perform on-site inspections, order an assessment or special audit, consult state databases and obtain

[3] See Chapter 1, No. 74.

oral explanations (from the issuer, the offeror, all members of the management board of the issuer or of the body substituting it, their representatives and, in the event of justified need, third parties) in respect of the content of documents and facts relevant in deciding to register a prospectus (Art. 18(4), 132[1] (1), 157 of the SMA).

4. It should be noted that although prior to implementation of the Prospectus Directive, pursuant to the SMA, scrutiny of prospectuses with regard to admission to a market did not fall within the authority of the EFSA, but within the authority of the respective market, the SMA has not made use of the possibility to temporarily delegate the powers of the EFSA to the respective markets (cf. Art. 21(2) Dir., see Chapter 1, No. 75).

5. As required by the Prospectus Directive, the SMA includes rules on designation of the competent authority (see Chapter 1, Nos. 19–23). In the case of an issuer registered in Estonia, the home Member State is Estonia (Art. 13[1](1) of the SMA). Also, rules with regard to large denomination non-equity issuers or offerors and issuers of a third country provided for in the Prospectus Directive have been implemented into Estonian law. Pursuant to Article 13(2)[1] of the SMA, the home Member State of an issuer of a third state is Estonia or another Member State where securities are offered to the public or where securities are applied for to be admitted to trading for the first time. However, it is not clear from the wording of the SMA, as to which point in time has to be taken into account upon deciding where the securities are offered or admitted to trading for the first time (pursuant to Art. 2(1)(m)(iii) of the Prospectus Directive, the date of entry into force of the Directive is of importance).

As an exception, no transitional provision, as provided for in Article 30(1) of the Prospectus Directive, has been implemented into Estonian law (see Chapter 1, No. 21) as, at the time of implementation of the Prospectus Directive, there were no issuers incorporated in a third country whose securities would have already been admitted to trading on a regulated market in Estonia.

III Procedure of prior approval and appeal

6. If the home Member State of the issuer or offeror is Estonia, a prospectus (or, a securities note or a summary) shall be registered with the EFSA prior to being made public and the offer or admission being announced (Art. 16 (1), 132[1] (1), 157 of the SMA).

Pursuant to the Prospectus Directive, a prospectus has to be drawn up when (i) securities are offered to the public, or (ii) admitted to trading on a regulated market. According to the SMA, however, a prospectus has to be drawn up when (i) securities are offered to the public ('a public offering prospectus'), (ii) the securities are admitted to trading on a regulated market ('a trading prospectus')[4] and (iii) the securities are admitted to trading on an exchange ('a listing prospectus')[5]. Nevertheless, despite the division into three by the SMA, there is no conflict with the Prospectus Directive because the rules of the SMA on (ii) and (iii) are identical. Thus, the division into three in the context of prospectuses has terminological difference only. Therefore, throughout this chapter, the term of 'admission to trading' is used to denote both admission of securities for trading on exchanges as well as on other regulated markets.

7. Contrary to the Prospectus Directive, the SMA does not include a definition of a 'public offer', but only a definition of an 'offer of securities'. Pursuant to Article 11 of the SMA, an offer of securities means a communication to a person 'in any form and by any means, which is sufficiently exact as to the terms of the offer and the securities to be offered enabling an investor to decide to purchase or subscribe to these securities'. However, each offer of securities (as defined above) is considered to be public pursuant to Article 12(1) of the SMA with the exception of (see also Chapter 1, No. 11):

(i) an offer of securities addressed solely to qualified investors, or
(ii) an offer of securities addressed to fewer than ninety-nine persons per Member State, other than qualified investors, or
(iii) an offer of securities addressed to investors who acquire securities for a total consideration of at least €50,000 per investor, for each separate offer, or
(iv) an offer of securities whose denomination per unit amounts to at least €50,000, or
(v) an issue or offer of securities with a total consideration of less than €100,000 in a period of twelve months.

The SMA does not specify whether the exemption of an offer of €100,000 for a period of twelve months applies if the offer made has a total consideration less than €100,000 in Estonia or in all Member States altogether. However, as the exception of an offer to fewer than ninety-nine persons is expressly stipulated to apply with regard to ninety-nine persons per Member State and such a wording is not used with regard to the €100,000 exception, it can be argued that the total consideration has to be calculated EEA-wide.

In practice, the private offering exception (as provided in the first paragraph of this chapter, no. 7) often is made use of by addressing the offer to qualified investors only. Therefore, the 'qualified investor' exception is of

4 The official translation uses the term 'particulars' instead of a 'prospectus', however, for the sake of clarity, the term 'prospectus' is used in this chapter.

5 Pursuant to Art. 150 of the SMA, an exchange is a market, where listed securities are traded.

great importance in practice. The Prospectus Directive provides only an indicative list of qualified investors (Art. 2(1)(e), see also Chapter 1, No. 11), leaving the exact list of 'qualified investors' to each Member State. Pursuant to Article 6(2) of the SMA, professional investors are:

(i) an Estonian or foreign credit institution, investment firm, management company, investment fund, insurance undertaking or another person subject to financial supervision;
(ii) the Republic of Estonia or a foreign state, or a local or regional government or the central bank of Estonia or of a foreign state;
(iii) an international organisation, including the International Monetary Fund, the European Central Bank, the European Investment Bank;
(iv) an Estonian or foreign financial institution whose only business activity is investment in securities;
(v) a small or medium-sized enterprise (hereinafter SME) which pursuant to Article 237 of the SMA has been entered into a list kept by the EFSA;[6]
(vi) an Estonian or foreign company that is not a SME;
(vii) a natural person who pursuant to Article 237 of the SMA has been entered into a list kept by the EFSA and who meets at least two of the following requirements: (i) the investor has carried out transactions of a significant size on securities markets at an average frequency of, at least, ten per quarter over the previous four quarters; (ii) the volume of the securities portfolio of the investor exceeds €500,000; (iii) the investor works or has worked for at least one year in the financial sector in a professional position which requires knowledge of securities investment;
(viii) a SME of another Member State or a natural person who is registered as a qualified investor in the other Member State.

8. The exemptions from the obligation to draw up a prospectus as provided for in Article 4 of the Prospectus Directive have been implemented into Estonian law without any special variations from the wording of the Prospectus Directive. Similarly to Article 4 (1)(e) of the Prospectus Directive, the SMA does not stipulate whether trading on the same regulated market is a precondition for application of the exception.

Also, the cases exempted from the applicability of the Prospectus Directive (Art. 1(2) Dir.) have been implemented into Estonian law (as circumstances where a prospectus does not have to be published). However,

[6] Pursuant to Art. 6(3) of the SMA, a SME is a company which according to its last annual report or consolidated accounts meets at least two of the following criteria: (i) the average number of employees of the SME during the financial year is less than 250; (ii) the annual balance sheet total of the SME does not exceed €43 million; (iii) the annual turnover of the SME does not exceed €50 million.

the exception provided for in Article 1(2)(h) of the Prospectus Directive has been broadly interpreted by Estonian law. Pursuant to the SMA, if an (i) offer or (ii) admission to trading concerns securities of an offer with a total consideration of less than €2.5 million, which limit shall be calculated over a period of twelve months, the issuer, offeror or person seeking admission to trading may prepare and make public a prospectus pursuant to the requirements established either (a) in chapters 2 and 3 of the Prospectus Regulation or (b) in the 'Regulation on the Prospectus Requirements' (Art. 132^3(4), 17(4) of the SMA). Thus, Estonian law has made use of the possibility provided for in the Prospectus Directive stipulating special prospectus rules with regard to offers with a total consideration between €2.5 million and €100,000. In doing so, the SMA has extended the possibility to opt out of the Prospectus Directive to admissions to trading of securities being part of an offer with a total consideration of less than €2.5 million. It may be argued that the wording of Article 1 (2)(h) of the Prospectus Directive does not entitle a Member State to extend the exception to admission to trading, and pursuant to the strict reading of the Prospectus Directive, upon admission of securities to a regulated market, a prospectus would have to be drawn up every time, unless securities stipulated in Article 4 (2) of the Prospectus Directive are concerned.

The content of the prospectus drawn up pursuant to the 'Regulation on the Prospectus Requirements' is described in no. 25 of this chapter.

9. After drawing up the prospectus, if the home Member State of the issuer is Estonia, the prospectus shall be registered with the EFSA prior to being made public and the offer or admission being announced. For registration, an application shall be filed. If the home Member State of the issuer of the securities offered is not Estonia, an application for the registration of a prospectus may be submitted to the EFSA by the securities market supervisory authority of another Member State. The prospectus and, if the issuer and the offeror have articles of association, copies thereof, shall be appended to the application. If the documents submitted upon filing the application do not meet the requirements prescribed by law, and/or the prospectus, in the opinion of the EFSA, does not include all the necessary information taking into account the interests of investors, the EFSA shall request, within ten working days of the filing of the application, that the documents be brought into compliance with the law or be amended (Articles 18, 132^1, 157 of the SMA). Otherwise, the decision to register or not to register a prospectus has to be made in ten working days (see also Chapter I, No. 25).

The EFSA is entitled to extend the term for deciding to register the prospectus to twenty working days if the public offer involves securities issued by an issuer who does not have any securities admitted to trading on a market and who has not previously offered securities to the public. The wording of the SMA is not clear as to whether offers and admissions in Estonia only are included, or whether offers and admissions in other Member States or third countries also are of importance in deciding the extension of the scrutiny period.

If the EFSA refuses registration of the prospectus, it shall give reasons for its decision. The EFSA, pursuant to Articles 21, 132[1], 157 of the SMA, is entitled to refuse registration of a prospectus if:

(i) the conditions of the offer are contrary to legislation in force or the articles of association of the issuer;
(ii) the prospectus does not meet the requirements established by law and the deficiencies are significant;
(iii) the offeror does not submit all the documents prescribed by law, or the documents are inconsistent, or the prospectus, in the opinion of the EFSA, does not include all the necessary information taking account of the interests of investors.

Thus the scope of the EFSA's scrutiny is broader than stipulated in the Prospectus Directive. Pursuant to the Prospectus Directive, scrutiny shall include scrutiny of the completeness of the prospectus, including the consistency of the information contained therein and its comprehensiveness (Art. 2(1)(q) Dir.). The EFSA, however, may also conduct an analysis of whether the articles of association of the issuer entitle the offer to be made or securities to be admitted to trading. However, the Prospectus Directive does not prohibit national law from providing additional scrutiny when compared to the Prospectus Directive. In that regard, the Estonian regulation may be considered as conforming to the Prospectus Directive.

The EFSA shall deliver the decision concerning registration or refusal to register a prospectus to the applicant immediately. Failure to make a decision within the given time frame is not considered to constitute a registration (Article 20(5), 132[1], 157 of the SMA).

10. In the case of failure to register the prospectus in the time frame given by law, the issuer, offeror or the person seeking admission may file with an administrative court a claim for issuing of an unissued administrative act (the unissued administrative act being the decision on registration or refusal to register). In principle, the Estonian State Liability Act entitles the issuer to claim compensation for damages caused upon the exercise of powers of a public authority if the issuer, offeror or the person asking admission to trading can prove that it sustained damages. Thus, the issuer, offeror or the person seeking admission to trading may also claim damages from the state in case of failure of the EFSA to make a decision within the given time frame. Loss of income is not compensated for if the EFSA proves that it is not at fault in causing the damage.

Also, upon refusal by the EFSA to register the prospectus, an appeal may be filed with an administrative court by the issuer, offeror or the person seeking admission. However, in the case of a refusal to register a prospectus, it has to be considered that the EFSA has certain discretion upon deciding whether to register the prospectus or not (above all, whether the prospectus is comprehensive and consistent). Thus, if the claim of the issuer, offeror or person seeking admission to trading to register the prospectus and invalidate the decision of refusal to register the prospectus is satisfied by the administrative court, the court is likely to order the EFSA to reconsider the application for registration and shall not render a decision itself on whether the prospectus should be registered or not. However, if pursuant to the circumstances of the case, the EFSA has no grounds to refuse to register the prospectus, the court may order the EFSA to reconsider the matter without further consideration of the circumstances (see also Art. 6 of the Estonian State Liability Act).

11. Due to the new principle of the European Passport, implemented on the basis of the Prospectus Directive, further registration and scrutiny of a prospectus already registered and scrutinised by another Member State (i.e. in cases where Estonia is a host Member State) is not required (see chapter 1, No. 70). However, in such cases, prior to the prospectus being made public and the offer being announced in Estonia, the EFSA shall be informed thereof through the securities market supervisory agency of the home Member State of the issuer or offeror or the person asking admission, and the following documents shall be appended to the notification pursuant to Articles 16(3), 132[1], 157 of the SMA:

- (i) the registration certificate of the prospectus issued by the securities market supervisory agency of the home Member State of the issuer, offeror or person seeking admission, which must contain confirmation that the prospectus has been drawn up pursuant to the requirements for prospectuses provided for in EU legislation and information concerning the omissions made with regard to the information contained in the prospectus in accordance with the provisions of EU legislation and the reasons for the specified exceptions;
- (ii) a transcript of the prospectus (or, a transcript of the securities note and summary, if applicable) in Estonian or English or, with the consent of the EFSA, in another language;
- (iii) at the request of the EFSA, a translation of the summary of the prospectus into Estonian.

12. However, although the principle of the European Passport has been implemented into the SMA, the Listing Rules of the Tallinn Stock Exchange, nevertheless, contrary to the SMA and the Prospectus Directive, may require submission of additional information for the

review of the Tallinn Stock Exchange. If the Tallinn Stock Exchange, as the stock exchange operator, does not admit the securities to trading, although the prospectus has been registered pursuant to the requirements of the SMA, pursuant to Articles 133(1) and 157 of the SMA, a person seeking admission to trading has the right to file an action with a court or, subject to agreement between the parties, the arbitral tribunal for recognition of the right of a security to be admitted for trading and for obliging the operator to admit the security for trading.

13. The issuer registered in Estonia is required to notify the EFSA of any offer of securities issued and offered thereby in a foreign state (Art. 39(1) of the SMA).

IV Content and format, language and supplements of the prospectus

1 Content

14. Pursuant to the SMA, the prospectus has to correspond to the content and format requirements provided in Chapters II and III of the Prospectus Regulation (see Chapter 1, No. 31).

As a general guideline, Article 14^1(1) of the SMA stipulates that a prospectus shall contain all information necessary to enable investors to make an informed assessment of the assets and liabilities, financial position, profit and losses, and prospects of the issuer and of any guarantor, and of the rights attached to such securities, presented in an easily analysable and comprehensible form and, according to the particular nature of the issuer and of the securities offered to the public.

Further, as stipulated in Article 8(2) of the Prospectus Directive, not all of the information provided for in the Prospectus Regulation has to be included in the prospectus where grounds for the omission of certain information exist (see Chapter 1, No. 38). In Estonia, the Omissions Regulation provides for the procedure for applying for an exception. The Omissions Regulation requires the applicant, depending on the grounds for omission, respectively, to submit information on the exact public interest which is contravened by disclosure or sufficient evidence that disclosure of certain information would be seriously detrimental to the issuer or is only of minor importance or also information. The application for omission shall be reviewed in ten working days.

Also, based on the Prospectus Directive, there are reduced publicity standards with regard to admission to trading of non-equity securities having a denomination of at least €50,000.

Further, there are special prospectus requirements in case an issuer, offeror or person requesting admission to trading may draw up a prospectus pursuant to the 'Regulation on Prospectus Requirements' (Nos. 8 and 25 of this chapter).

2 Format

15. As mentioned above, the SMA refers to the format requirements of Chapters II and III of the Prospectus Regulation. For the sake of clarity, the SMA specifically stipulates that a prospectus may consist of one document or several separate documents. If the prospectus consists of separate documents, it will have the following parts: (i) a registration document containing information on the issuer, (ii) a securities note containing information concerning the securities to be offered to the public and (iii) a summary (see also Chapter 1, Nos. 41–50).

Pursuant to Article $14^1(2)$ of the SMA, both a prospectus consisting of one as well as of several separate documents shall contain a summary (see Chapter 1, No. 36) which, in a brief manner and in non-technical language, conveys the essential characteristics of and risks associated with the issuer, any guarantor and the securities. The summary shall also contain a warning that:

(i) the summary should be read as an introduction to the prospectus and any decision to invest in the securities should be based on consideration of the prospectus as a whole by the investor;
(ii) where a claim relating to the information contained in a prospectus is brought before a court, the plaintiff investor might, under the national legislation of the home Member State or host Member State, have to bear the costs of translating the prospectus before legal proceedings are initiated;
(iii) no civil liability shall attach to any person solely on the basis of the summary, including any translation thereof, unless the summary is misleading, inaccurate or inconsistent when read together with the other parts of the prospectus.

Due to implementation of the Prospectus Directive, incorporation by reference is possible (Art. $14^1(4)$ of the SMA). In addition, a base prospectus can be drawn up pursuant to the requirements stipulated in Chapters II and III of the Prospectus Regulation (see Chapter 1, No. 45).

3 Supplements

16. Pursuant to Article 23 and Article 132^4 of the SMA, any new significant circumstances, mistakes or inaccuracies relating to the information included in the prospectus, which are capable of affecting the assessment of the securities and which become known between the time when the prospectus is registered and the final closing of the offer to the public, or the time when trading on a market begins, shall be immediately stated by the offeror, issuer or person asking admission to trading in a supplement to the prospectus. A supplement to a prospectus is an integral part of the prospectus (see Chapter 1, No. 66).

A supplement to a prospectus shall be registered with the EFSA (see no. 9 and the following of this chapter) or the securities market supervisory agency of the home Member State of the issuer and shall be made public in the same way and in accordance with at least the same arrangements as were applied when the prospectus to which the corresponding supplement is appended was made public. The EFSA shall decide to register the supplement or refuse registration in seven working days (Art. 23(3) of the SMA).

In cases where Estonia is the home Member State, the EFSA is entitled to request, by its precept, that the offeror, issuer or person seeking admission to trading make a supplement public.

4 Language

17. In the case of a prospectus registered with the EFSA, pursuant to Article 32, 132[1], 157 of the SMA, a notice of an offer (see this chapter, No. 19), the prospectus, supplements to the prospectus (see this chapter, No. 16) and other documents and notices pertaining to the issuer and the securities offered shall be prepared and published (i) in Estonian, (ii) in English or, (iii) provided that the interests of investors are not damaged, in another language, with the permission of the EFSA. If the prospectus is not published in Estonian, the EFSA may demand that the summary of the prospectus be translated into Estonian and be published (cf. Chapter 1, Nos. 51–53). Thus, even if the offer to the public is made or admission to trading is sought only in Estonia, the prospectus still does not have to be drawn up in Estonian, but may be drawn up in English or any other language accepted by the EFSA.

The SMA specifies that if the documents and notices are compiled in Estonian and in another language as well and if their wording differs or if it is possible to interpret them differently, the wording of the relevant document in Estonian or its translation into Estonian takes precedence.

Further, in the case of a prospectus which is registered with the securities market supervisory authority of another Member State, a notice of an offer, the prospectus, supplements to the prospectus and other documents and notices pertaining to the issuer and the securities offered shall be published in English or, by agreement of the EFSA, the home Member State of the issuer and the securities market supervisory agencies of other host Member States, in another language. If the prospectus is not published in Estonian, the EFSA may demand that the summary of the prospectus be translated into Estonian and published.

In respect of language rules, the style of the language is relevant. The SMA, based on the Prospectus Directive, provides the following guidance. The prospectus itself has to be easily analysable and comprehensible – this rule may also be regarded as a criterion applicable to the language. The summary of the prospectus, however, has to be formulated in non-technical language, conveying the essential characteristics and risks associated with the issuer, any guarantor and the securities (Art. $14^1(1)$ of the SMA). Thus, it may be argued that different language standards apply to the summary and other parts of the prospectus, demanding that the summary of the prospectus would be easily understood by non-qualified investors, whereas other parts of the prospectus, if so required by the SMA, may include technical language (i.e. language understandable mainly to qualified investors).

V Publication and advertisements

1 Method of publication

18. Pursuant to Estonian law (Art. 15(3), $132^2(2)$, 157 of the SMA), a prospectus shall be published (taking into account the requirements provided for in Articles 29 and 30 of the Prospectus Regulation) by one of the methods described below:

(i) in at least one national daily newspaper;
(ii) in a printed form to be made available, free of charge, to the public at the registered office of the issuer and at the offices of the financial intermediaries placing or selling the securities, including intermediaries of payments made on the securities of the issuer or, in the case of admission to trading, at the registered office of the operator of the market;
(iii) on the website of the persons specified in clause (ii) above;
(iv) on the website of the securities market supervisory authority of the home Member State of the issuer (or, in the case of a public offer, on the website of another person or agency responsible for the registration of the prospectus).

Thus, the SMA has not made use of the option to publish a prospectus on the website of the EFSA. However, the SMA does recognise making the prospectus public on the website of the securities market supervisory agency of the home Member State in the case of public offers (see Chapter 1, No. 57).

In the case of public offers, the prospectus has to be made public no later than on the day on which the public offer of securities is announced (Art. 15(2) of the SMA). In the case of admission to trading, the prospectus shall be made public not later than on the date on which securities are admitted to trading on a market, with the exception of an initial public offer of a class of shares not already admitted to trading on a market. In the latter case, the trading prospectus shall be accessible to the public within at least six working days preceding the end of the offer (Art. $132^2(2)$ and (3) of the SMA). The SMA does not specify whether the latter applies in cases where the shares have not previously been admitted to trading on a market in

Estonia, the EU or elsewhere. Please also note that the SMA does not include a requirement to make a prospectus public as soon as practicable (cf. Art. 14(1) Dir.).

19. Estonia has made use of the option, referred to in Article 14(3) of the Prospectus Directive, to require the publication of a notice of an offer stating how the prospectus has been made available and where it can be obtained. Pursuant to Article 29(3) of the SMA, if the offeror is obliged to draw up a prospectus, the offeror shall announce the offer before the public offer begins by publishing a relevant notice (hereinafter 'notice of offer') in at least one national daily newspaper pursuant to the procedure provided for in Article 31 of the Prospectus Regulation. A notice of offer shall contain the information required in Article 31 (3) of the Prospectus Regulation.

2 Advertisements

20. Pursuant to Article 31(1) of the SMA, a notice of an offer and any other advertising pertaining to the offer disclosed orally or in writing, including information not disclosed for advertising purposes, may not be inexact, misleading or in contradiction with information to be found in the prospectus (see Chapter 1, No. 62). A notice of an offer and any advertising materials pertaining to the offer shall be submitted to the EFSA prior to the offer being made public. The EFSA, however, does not have to approve of the advertising materials nor register such materials beforehand. An offer may be advertised only after the announcement of the offer as described in No. 19 of this chapter.

Advertising of an offer or admission to trading shall comply with the requirements provided for in Article 34 of the Prospectus Regulation as well as Chapter II and Article 15 of the Advertising Act (provided below) and should include information about places where the prospectus is made public and can be obtained. Pursuant to Article 15 of the Estonian Advertising Act, *inter alia*, advertising of financial services shall be understandable, unambiguous and shall ensure clear and easy understanding of all conditions of the services being offered, in particular the actual interest rate, all other service-related costs and the terms of payment. Advertising of financial services shall also not contain direct or indirect comparisons to competing services that contain information that is not directly and easily comparable.

If Estonia is the home Member State of the issuer, the EFSA is entitled, by its precept, to prohibit or suspend advertisements concerning a public offer for a maximum of ten consecutive working days on any single occasion, if it has reasonable grounds for believing that the rules on advertising have been infringed. Upon suspension of the broadcast of advertising, the EFSA shall require, by its precept, the issuer, offeror or person seeking admission of securities to a market to eliminate the circumstances that were the bases for suspending the broadcasting of advertising. Upon permission of the EFSA, the issuer, offeror or person seeking admission of securities to a market may continue to broadcast advertising while eliminating those circumstances regarded as bases for suspending the advertising.

21. Further, the SMA has also implemented into Estonian law the equal treatment rule stipulated in Article 15(5) of the Prospectus Directive. Accordingly, even if the drawing up of a prospectus is not required, material information, including information disclosed in the context of meetings relating to offers of securities, provided by an issuer, offeror, or a person asking admission to trading and addressed to qualified investors or a special category of investors, shall be disclosed to all qualified investors or special categories of investors to whom the offer is exclusively addressed.

VI Use of prospectus approved in other (non EU) countries

22. In order for a prospectus of an issuer in a third country to be registered with the EFSA, the following documents shall be submitted to the EFSA pursuant to Article 37(1) of the SMA (cf. Chapter 1, No. 73):

(i) an application for registration;
(ii) the prospectus, and if the issuer, offeror or person seeking admission to trading have articles of association, copies thereof;
(iii) a certificate of registration of the prospectus issued by a competent securities market supervisory agency of the home country of the issuer or another document permitting the prospectus to be made public or permitting trading on a regulated securities market or certifying the listing on the stock exchange, if the issue of such document is required;
(iv) a copy of the audited annual report of the issuer for the previous economic year which, upon request of the EFSA, shall be submitted together with translation of the report into Estonian;
(v) upon submission of a prospectus in a foreign language, a translation thereof into Estonian if requested by the EFSA;
(vi) an agreement with a professional securities market participant located in Estonia to 'carry out' the issue;
(vii) a description of the terms and conditions of the offer of securities.

Thus, pursuant to Article 37 of the SMA, for 'carrying out the issue' (a term not defined, but considered to include placing, advertising, and introducing, as well as selling, securities) of securities of an issuer in a third country, an Estonian professional securities market participant has to be involved each time.

Further, the EFSA is entitled to request additional information about the legislation in force in the home country of the issuer, offeror or person seeking admission to trading.

As an exception from the general rule that a prospectus shall not be registered unless it complies with the requirements on prospectuses provided for in the SMA, the EFSA may register a prospectus of an issuer in a third country if in the opinion of the EFSA, the following conditions are met:

(i) the prospectus has been drawn up in accordance with international standards set by international organisations of securities supervision authorities, including the IOSCO disclosure standards;
(ii) the information requirements are equivalent to the requirements established in the SMA, legislation established on the basis thereof and the Prospectus Regulation.

There is no explicit rule in the SMA, however, stipulating that the EFSA may register a prospectus of a third country. The issuer, offeror or person seeking admission to trading only in the case where Estonia is the home state of such a person, the SMA should be interpreted in line with Article 20 of the Prospectus Directive.

VII Sanctions

23. Pursuant to the forty-third recital to the Prospectus Directive, Member States should lay down a system of sanctions for breaches of the national provisions adopted pursuant to the Prospectus Directive and should take all the measures necessary to ensure that these sanctions are applied. The sanctions thus provided for should be effective, proportional and dissuasive. Article 25 of the Prospectus Directive specifies that a Member State shall ensure that the appropriate administrative measures can be taken or administrative sanctions be imposed against the persons responsible, where the provisions adopted in the implementation of the Prospectus Directive have not been complied with (Chapter 1, No. 82).

In connection with offering of securities and publication of a prospectus, pursuant to the SMA, administrative sanctions for the following violations exist:

- Failure to register a public offer prospectus, a trading or listing prospectus beforehand with the EFSA or another competent securities market supervisory agency or conducting an offer of securities without a prospectus (Art. 237[1] of the SMA);
- Violation of requirements to make public a public offer prospectus or, a trading or listing prospectus (Art. 237[2] of the SMA, see this chapter, Nos. 18–19);
- Violation of the procedure for the announcement or suspension of an offer of securities (Art. 237[3] of the SMA);
- Provision of incorrect or inaccurate information to possible investors in a prospectus or in any other manner by an offeror and violation of

the requirement to inform all potential investors on equal terms during an offer of securities (Art. 237^4 of the SMA). However, there is no explicit provision stating that the sanction is also applicable with regard to issuers or persons seeking admission to trading, or other persons liable under the prospectus liability regulation;

- Advertising by an offeror of an offer of securities before announcing the offer, publishing misleading advertising about the offer, presenting in an advertisement information which has not been presented in the prospectus, or failure to submit advertising materials concerning an offer to the EFSA prior to the publication of such materials (Art. 237^5 of the SMA). In this case there is also no explicit provision stating that the sanction is applicable also with regard to issuers or persons seeking admission to trading;
- Violation of the obligation to repurchase securities if a supplement to a prospectus has been published or the registered and published prospectus included neither the final offer price and amount of securities, nor the maximum price, or the criteria in accordance with which the final price and the amount of the securities will be determined (Art. 237^6 of the SMA);
- Failure by the offeror to present in a supplement to the prospectus information concerning changes in the information provided in the prospectus affecting or being able to affect the price of the securities, or any other relevant information (Art. 237^7 of the SMA). In this case there is also no explicit provision stating that the sanction is applicable also with regard to issuers or persons seeking admission to trading.

As punishment for all of the administrative offences (väärtegu) described above, a fine of up to 200–300 fine units[7] is imposed. The same acts, if committed by a legal entity, are punishable by a fine of up to 50,000 Estonian kroons (approximately €3,205).

Considering (i) the small amount of fees and that (ii) with regard to several administrative offences, the law applies only to public offers (but not to admission to trading), it is arguable whether effective sanctions for breaches have been introduced by the SMA.

Furthermore, in other cases, if (i) as a result of supervision, the EFSA has discovered violations of the SMA and legislation issued on the basis thereof, or the rules and regulations of a regulated market or of the articles of association of a securities market participant; or (ii) in order to prevent violations of law or if other circumstances emerge which endanger or may endanger the interests of the investors or the interests of the securities market as a whole; or (iii) it is necessary to protect the interests of investors or to ensure the transparency of the market, the EFSA is entitled to issue a

[7] A fine unit is the base amount of a fine and is equal to sixty Estonian kroons (approximately € 4).

percept (an administrative act). With its percept, the EFSA, *inter alia*, is entitled to (Art. 235 of the SMA):

(i) prohibit certain transactions or activities from being conducted, or to establish restrictions on their volume;
(ii) demand that an issuer whose securities are offered publicly disclose information promptly, if the obligation to disclose such information arises from the SMA;
(iii) demand that an operator of a regulated market suspends or terminates trading;
(iv) demand that an issuer terminates violation of requirements of legislation of a foreign state;
(v) request other acts to ensure compliance with the SMA.

Pursuant to Article 25(2) of the Prospectus Directive, Member States shall provide that the competent authority may disclose to the public every measure or sanction that has been imposed for infringement of the provisions adopted pursuant to the Prospectus Directive, unless the disclosure would seriously jeopardise the financial markets or cause disproportionate damage to the parties involved. Pursuant to Article 53(2) of the Financial Supervisory Authority Act, resolutions of the management board of the EFSA are not public, unless mentioned in a special law. The SMA does not have a provision concerning disclosure, thus, disclosure per strict reading of the law would not be possible. However, in the case of breaches of the SMA it is settled practice of the EFSA to make violations public.

VIII Prospectus liability

24. As noted in Chapter 1, No. 84, pursuant to Article 6 of the Prospectus Directive, the Member States have to ensure that the issuer or its corporate bodies, whether they be administrative, managerial or supervisory, the offeror and the person requesting admission to trading on a regulated market or the guarantor can be held liable for the information presented in the prospectus. Except for the restriction of liability rule with regard to the summary (see No. 15 of this chapter), the Prospectus Directive does stipulate (i) the preconditions, (ii) manner of liability (joint and several, partial liability, etc.), (iii) the scope of liability (liability for the prospectus as a whole or parts thereof). Thus, each of the Member States is entitled to provide for its own rules. In Estonia, the following rules apply.

Pursuant to Article 24 of the SMA, the correctness and completeness of information included in a prospectus shall be confirmed in the prospectus by the issuer and, if existent, by the offeror. Whether the issuer and offeror are liable jointly and severally or partly, is not specifically stipulated, but it may be assumed that joint and several liability applies. An auditor shall confirm the accuracy of the information presented in the annual or semi-annual reports contained in the prospectus by his or her signature.

If the prospectus contains information which is significant for the purpose of assessing the value of the securities and such information proves to be different from the actual circumstances, the issuer or the offeror shall compensate the owner of the security for damage sustained thereby due to the difference between the actual circumstances and the information presented in the prospectus, provided that the issuer or offeror was, or should have been, aware of such difference. This also applies if the prospectus is incomplete due to the omission of relevant facts, provided that the incompleteness of the prospectus results from the issuer or the offeror hiding the facts. Based on the restriction of liability rule with regard to the summary provided in Article 6(2) of the Prospectus Directive, the above rules apply to the summary of a prospectus, including any translation thereof, only if the summary is misleading, inaccurate or inconsistent when read together with other parts of the prospectus. The obligation to compensate for damage rests with the issuer or offeror also if a third party is the source of the information presented in the prospectus.

A person liable under prospectus liability rules is entitled to compensate for the damage by acquiring the security from the person that sustained the damage for the price that the latter paid to acquire the offered security. By acquiring securities in this manner from the person that sustained the damage, the person causing the damage is released from the obligation to compensate for any other damage to the person that sustained the damage. In case of securities traded on a market, the person who causes the damage has the right to compensate for the damage by acquiring a security traded on a market from the person who sustained the damage for the price that the latter paid for the security, or for the sales price of the security immediately after admission of the security to trading on the market (Art. $132^1(3)$ and 158 of the SMA). Thus, in fact, the persons liable for the prospectus can limit their liability to the price paid by the investor and are not liable for further compensation.

Further, the liability is restricted with regard to qualified investors who should, *a priori*, be able to detect that certain information in the prospectus is not correct. Hence, pursuant to Article 26(2) of the SMA, an issuer or offeror shall not be obliged to compensate for damage if the person who sustained the damage was aware, at the moment of acquiring the security, that the prospectus which was the basis for the offer was incomplete or contained inaccurate information. The same applies if a qualified investor who sustains damage should have realised, at the moment of acquiring the security, and by exercising due care in its activities, that the information contained in the prospectus was inaccurate or incomplete, unless liability for the damage caused derives from deliberate acts of the person causing the damage.

The limitation period for a claim under prospectus liability is five years as of the beginning of the offer of the relevant security on the basis of a prospectus that contains inaccurate information or is incomplete. Any agreements that exclude, limit or reduce compensation under the prospectus liability or the limitation period shall be null and void.

As the Prospectus Directive does not provide for an obligation to include a special clause on civil liability in cases where no prospectus is published at all, the SMA also does not provide for such a clause. However, as noted in No. 23 of this chapter, failure to publish a prospectus constitutes an administrative offence (*väärtegu*). It may also be argued that tort rules apply but there is no respective court practice in that regard.

Further, Estonian law also does not include a special rule on 'soft data' (profit forecasts or estimates, trend information) contained in prospectuses. Thus, it is advisable for issuers and offerors to consider the absence of a milder liability rule upon publication of estimates in the prospectus.

Also, no special rule on conflict of laws is provided in the SMA with regard to the prospectus liability rule. It may be argued that tort rules apply in determining the applicable law, but, there is no respective court practice in that regard. A European conflict of laws rule, however, would be necessary for the sake of clarity.

IX Rules applicable to transactions and securities not subject to the Directive and Regulation

25. As described above in No. 8 of this chapter, if (i) an offer, or (ii) admission to trading concerns securities of an offer with a total consideration of less than €2.5 million, which limit shall be calculated over a period of twelve months, the issuer, offeror or person asking admission to trading may prepare and make public a prospectus pursuant to the requirements established (a) in Chapters 2 and 3 of the Prospectus Regulation, or (b) in the 'Regulation on the Prospectus Requirements'. However, certain securities are excluded from the application of the 'Regulation on the Prospectus Requirements' (subscription rights, investment fund units and derivative instruments and money market instruments issued by an Estonian credit institution or foreign person). With regard to excluded securities, no special domestic rules apply.

In cases where the issuer, offeror or person seeking admission to trading is entitled to draw up a prospectus pursuant to the 'Regulation on the Prospectus Requirements', the following applies. The 'Regulation on the Prospectus Requirements' includes special chapters on prospectuses for (i) equity, (ii) bond, (iii) depositary receipt issuers. Further, additional rules on prospectuses of shares with pre-emptive rights to subscribe new shares, convertible securities, bonds guaranteed by legal persons and bonds traded on a market are provided.

When compared to the requirements of the Prospectus Regulation, the 'Regulation on the Prospectus Requirements' requires publication of less information. Also, the prospectus has to be comprised of one document and no summary has to be included.[8] The 'Regulation on the Prospectus Requirements' does also not explicitly provide for the possibility of incorporating information in the prospectus by means of reference. Further, there is no special section for risk factors. Only the annual report of the last financial year has to be presented (instead of the last three years as provided for in the Prospectus Regulation). In addition, the 'Regulation on the Prospectus Requirements' does not include any special methods on presentation of pro forma data[9] and the issuer does not have to refer to whether it complies with the corporate governance regime of Estonia. Further, many additional minor differences with regard to the information to be made public exist when compared to the Prospectus Regulation.

The 'Regulation on the Prospectus Requirements' does not include any language rules; thus, the rules described above in No. 17 of this chapter should apply.

Adoption of the requirement to publish a prospectus even in cases where it is not required by European law, demonstrates the intent to secure a high level of investor protection. However, prospectuses drawn up pursuant to the 'Regulation on the Prospectus Requirements' do not benefit from the advantages of the European Passport.

X Conclusion

26. The Prospectus Directive has been implemented in Estonian law by amending the SMA, as well as adopting the 'Omissions Regulation' and the 'Regulation on the Prospectus Requirements' hereunder. The implementation can mostly be regarded as complying with the Prospectus Directive and the principles therein; however, a few inconsistencies with the Prospectus Directive may be regarded as still existing.

As one of the main changes resulting from the implementation of the Prospectus Directive into Estonian law, the SMA, with the purpose of enhancing investor protection and facilitating information symmetry, made use of the option to stipulate that a prospectus has to be drawn up and scrutinised even in the case of an offer with a total consideration in between €2.5 million and €100,000 during a period of twelve months.

[8] However, this question should be discussed with the EFSA, as it may not be excluded that the EFSA is of the understanding that the summary requirement applies also with regard to the prospectuses drawn up pursuant to the 'Regulation on the Prospectus Requirements'.

[9] However, the 'Regulation on the Prospectus Requirements' stipulates that pro forma reports have to be presented in the case of securities issued in the course of mergers, divisions, partial or total transfer of assets and obligations, takeovers or transfer of assets other than cash.

The implementation of the language rules of the Prospectus Directive into Estonian law enables the conduct of an entirely domestic offer or admission to trading by publishing a prospectus drawn up in English only. Even the summary must be prepared in Estonian only if requested by the EFSA. Such implementation refers to the aim of enhancing and facilitating the making of offers and admissions to trading.

As requested in the Prospectus Directive, the SMA includes a prospectus liability regulation and sanctions for breach of the prospectus rules. Whether the sanctions as provided at present are effective in reaching the aims of the Prospectus Directive is disputable.

To sum up, the implementation of the Prospectus Directive provides the legal framework in Estonia necessary for establishment of a common European capital market. Many provisions of the SMA require unified European interpretation in order for the idea of a common European capital market to have full effect. In our opinion, the 'Lamfalussy-approach' (Chapter 1, No. 4) seems an efficient vehicle to achieve that end, and to reduce different interpretations existent at present of the national laws.

6

Greece

VASSILIKI LAZARAKOU AND GEORGE GEORGIOU
Zepos & Yannopoulos

I Introduction

1 General

1. Directive 2003/71 of the European Parliament and of the Council (the 'Prospectus Directive' or 'Dir.') has been implemented in Greece by way of Law 3401/2005 (the 'Law') on the 'Prospectus for securities offered to the public and admitted for trading' which entered into force on 17 October 2005. The new law repealed the pre-existing legal framework, consisting mainly of two Presidential Decrees, namely, Decree 348/1985 implementing Directive 80/390 and Decree 52/1992 implementing Directive 89/298.

In the explanatory report of the law (the 'Ex. Rep.') it is specifically provided that the objective of the legislator is to reinforce investor protection and to ensure market efficiency.[1] The Prospectus Directive is characterised as an important tool for the integration of the internal market since it facilitates enterprises' access to investment capital throughout the Community. The consummation of the European capital market is further advanced through the granting to the issuers of a 'European passport' by way of which they will be in a position to offer their securities and to have them admitted to European Union regulated markets.[2]

Apart from the Law, which implements the Prospectus Directive, Regulation 809/2004 (the 'Prospectus Regulation' or 'Reg.') is also directly applicable. The Prospectus Regulation provides for the specificities of the prospectus publication. For reasons of clarity specific reference is made to the Prospectus Regulation in Article 7 of the Law.

In summary, the general Greek legal framework for the publication of a prospectus when securities are offered to the public, or admitted to trading on an organised market that is established or operates in Greece, consists of the Law which implemented the Prospectus Directive and the Prospectus Regulation directly applicable in Greece.

2 Scope

2. The Law sets out the requirements for the drawing up, approval and distribution of the prospectus to be published when securities are offered to the public or admitted to trading on a regulated market situated or operating in Greece.[3]

The Prospectus obligation applies only to securities and not to funds or non transferable products. Specifically, the definition of securities includes transferable securities (shares in companies and other transferable securities equivalent to shares in companies, bonds and other debt securities equivalent to bonds, which are negotiable on the capital markets, as well as any other title that is tradeable and gives the right to acquire any other

[1] Ex. Rep. p. 1. [2] Ex. Rep. p. 1. [3] Art. 1(2) of the Law.

transferable security by subscription or exchange, or gives rise to a cash settlement) as well as the titles of the money market, i.e. financial instruments usually traded in the money market, which have a duration of above twelve months.

3. The Law does not apply to:[4]

(i) units issued by collective investment undertakings other than the closed-end type; collective investment undertakings other than the closed-end type means mutual funds and investment companies whose object is the collective investment of capital provided by the public and which operate on the principle of risk-spreading, the units of which are, at the holders' request, repurchased or redeemed, directly or indirectly, out of the undertaking's assets;[5]

(ii) non-equity securities issued by a Member State or by a Member State's regional or local authorities including municipalities, a public international body of which one or more Member States are members, the European Central Bank or the central bank of a Member State; non-equity securities are all securities which are not equity securities; equity securities means shares and other transferable securities equivalent to shares in companies, as well as any other type of transferable securities giving the right to acquire any of the aforementioned securities as a consequence of their being converted or the rights conferred by them being exercised, provided that securities of the latter type are issued by the issuer of the underlying shares or by an entity belonging to the group of the said issuer;[6]

(iii) shares in the capital of central banks of the Member States;

(iv) securities unconditionally and irrevocably guaranteed by a Member State or by a regional or local authority of a Member State, including the municipalities;

(v) securities issued by associations which benefit from a special legal status or non-profit organisations recognised by a Member State, with a view to obtaining the means necessary to achieve their not-for-profit goals;

(vi) non-equity securities issued in a continuous or repeated manner by credit institutions provided the following requirements are met cumulatively: the securities (a) are not subordinated, convertible or exchangeable; (b) do not give rise to a right to subscribe to or acquire other types of securities and are not linked to derivatives; (c) materialise receipt of repayable deposits; and (d) are covered by a deposit guarantee scheme according to the Law 2832/2000;

(vii) non-exchangeable shares or capital units whose main purpose is to provide their holder with a right to occupy an apartment or other

[4] Art. 1(3) of the Law. [5] Art. 2(1)(p) of the Law. [6] Art. 2(1)(b) and (c) of the Law.

form of immovable property or any part thereof and which cannot be sold without relinquishing this right;

(viii) securities included in a public offer for total consideration of less than €2.5 million, calculated over a period of twelve months;

(ix) non-equity securities issued in a continuous or repeated manner by credit institutions where the total consideration for the offer is less than €50 million, calculated over a period of twelve months, provided the following requirements are met cumulatively: the securities (a) are not subordinated, convertible or exchangeable; (b) do not give rise to a right to subscribe to or acquire other types of securities; and (c) are not linked to derivatives; issues shall be considered continuous or repeated if they are on tap or concern at least two separate issues of securities of a similar type or class over a period of twelve months.[7]

In cases (ii), (iv), (viii) and (ix) the issuer, offeror or person asking for admission to trading on a regulated market may choose to draw up a prospectus according to the Law.[8]

In cases (ii) and (iv) through (ix), by virtue of a decision of the Minister of Economy and Finance, which is issued further to a proposal by the CMC, the minimum information in connection with the offered securities may be determined, the dissemination means for this information, limitations in connection with the on-sale or the admission of those securities to a regulated market, as well as any other issue or detail in connection with the above.[9]

Furthermore, the Law provides for specific exemptions where the prospectus is not required to be outlined below.

II Competent authority

4. The Law designated the Capital Market Commission (the 'CMC') as the administrative authority responsible for ensuring the application of the Law and for monitoring the observance of the obligations arising out of the provisions of the Law and the Prospectus Regulation.[10]

When the CMC receives an application for approving a prospectus it is empowered to:

(i) require issuers, offerors or persons asking for admission to trading on a regulated market and their underwriters or advisers to include in the prospectus supplementary information, if necessary for investor protection;

(ii) require issuers, offerors or persons asking for admission to trading on a regulated market, and the persons that control them or are controlled by them, to provide information and documents;

[7] Art. 2(1)(m) of the Law. [8] Art. 1(4) of the Law. [9] Art. 1(5) of the Law.
[10] Art. 21(1) of the Law.

(iii) require auditors and managers of the issuer, offeror or person asking for admission to trading on a regulated market, as well as their underwriters or advisers commissioned to carry out the offer to the public or ask for admission to trading, to provide information;
(iv) suspend a public offer or admission to trading for a maximum of ten consecutive working days on any single occasion if it has reasonable grounds for suspecting that the provisions of the Law have been infringed;
(v) prohibit a public offer if it finds that the provisions of the Law have been infringed or if it has reasonable grounds for suspecting that they would be infringed;
(vi) suspend or ask the relevant regulated markets to suspend trading on a regulated market for a maximum of ten consecutive working days on any single occasion if it has reasonable grounds for believing that the provisions of the Law have been infringed;
(vii) prohibit trading on a regulated market if it finds that the provisions of the Law have been infringed;
(viii) prohibit or suspend advertisements for a maximum of ten consecutive working days on any single occasion if it has reasonable grounds for believing that the provisions of the Law have been infringed;
(ix) make public the fact that a person mentioned above in subparagraphs (ii) and (iii) is failing to comply with its obligations arising out of the Law.[11]

In cases of emergency, the Execution Committee of the CMC may proceed to the actions referred to in points (iv) to (viii) above. In such cases the relevant decision is ratified in the next meeting of the CMC Board of Directors.[12]

III Procedure of prior approval and appeal

1 General

A General rule

5. Article 3 of the Law sets out the general rule, i.e. the obligation to publish a prospectus in case of public offer of securities or where admission to a regulated market is sought. Unlike previous legislation, the Law includes a definition of what constitutes an 'offer of securities to the public'. The term 'public offer of securities' is thus defined as a public communication in any form and by any means, which is addressed to the public and contains sufficient information on the terms of the offer or subscription and the securities to be offered, so as to enable an investor to decide to purchase or subscribe to these securities. This definition also applies to the placing of

[11] Art. 21(2) of the Law. [12] Art. 21(3) of the Law.

securities through underwriters or advisers.[13] The Law has adopted the terminology of the European Union legislative texts and uses the term 'public offer' as a general notion comprising both the public subscription by way of issuing new securities and the public disposal of already existing securities. The law applies irrespective of the legal reason for which new securities are issued, e.g. due to capital increase by way of cash injection or by way of capitalisation of reserves, due to a merger etc.[14]

This obligation to publish a prospectus applies, provided that the offering does not fall in one of the exemptions. Failure to publish a prospectus entails the administrative sanctions set out in Article 24 of the Law; however, the validity of an offer effected in violation of the said obligation is not questioned.[15]

B Exemption re: types of offer (private placement exemptions)

6. Specifically, it is stated in Article 3 of the Law that neither the publication of a prospectus nor the prior approval by the CMC on the basis of the Law and of Article 10 of Law 876/79 (see below) are required in case of the following types of offer (private placements):[16]

(i) an offer of securities addressed solely to qualified investors; and/or
(ii) an offer of securities addressed to fewer than 100 natural or legal persons per Member State, other than qualified investors; and/or
(iii) an offer of securities addressed to investors who acquire securities for a total consideration of at least €50,000 per investor, for each separate offer; and/or
(iv) an offer of securities whose denomination per unit amounts to at least €50,000; and/or
(v) an offer of securities with a total consideration of less than €100,000, which limit shall be calculated over a period of twelve months.

Not all above private placement exceptions have been used in practice. Furthermore, the term *'qualified investors'* is now defined in the new Law and includes a number of persons not covered under the previous regime. Specifically, it includes:

(i) legal entities which are authorised or regulated to operate in the financial markets, including: credit institutions, investment firms, other authorised or regulated financial institutions, insurance companies, collective investment schemes and their management companies, pension funds and their management companies, commodity dealers, as well as entities not so authorised or regulated whose corporate purpose is solely to invest in securities;

[13] Art. 2(1)(d) of the Law. [14] Ex. Rep. p. 1. [15] Ex. Rep. p. 2.
[16] Art. 3(2) of the Law.

(ii) national and regional governments, central banks, international and supranational institutions such as the International Monetary Fund, the European Central Bank, the European Investment Bank and other similar international organisations;
(iii) legal entities which are not 'small and medium-sized enterprises' (as such term is defined below);
(iv) natural persons and 'small and medium-sized enterprises', included in the 'register of qualified investors' (as such term is described below) subject to mutual recognition, if the issuer, the offeror or the person asking for the listing of the securities has its seat in another Member State. The term *'small and medium-sized enterprises'* is specifically defined in the law.

The '*register of qualified investors*' is a register kept by the CMC in which, after an application is filed, small and medium-sized enterprises which have their seat in Greece as well as natural persons who reside in Greece may be registered. For the natural persons specifically, the Law states special criteria that should be met in order to be registered therein.

In addition, in general an approval must be granted by the CMC in all cases where persons aim to induce the public to invest in any kind of instruments, and which was used as a catch-all provision. Specifically, under Article 10 of Law 876/1979, it is prohibited for natural or legal persons 'to perform in any way whatsoever advertisements, notifications, declarations or announcements to the public aiming to attracting the public for investing money in all kinds of monetary instruments as well as the collection of the savings of the public for participating in any kind of investments unless a special permission has been granted by the CMC'.

The Law lifted the necessity of prior CMC approval based on Article 10 of Law 876/1979 if one of the above-mentioned exemptions for the issuance of prospectus applies. Thus, in cases where, for example, the financial instruments to be offered are not considered by the CMC as falling under the definition of securities for the purposes of the Law, Article 10 of Law 876/1979 will not be applicable, if the sale falls under one of the aforementioned exemptions. This is not the case however if such financial instrument is the unit or share of a mutual fund or collective investment, for which other specific rules apply.

According to the Law any subsequent resale of securities which were previously the subject of one or more of the types of offer mentioned above shall be regarded as a separate offer.[17] This provision was very important because in the previous framework there was no reference to on-sale of securities and the CMC accepted that both the offeror and the issuer are liable. By this new provision the critical issue would be to determine which person is the offeror.

[17] Art. 3(4) of the Law.

C Exemptions re: types of securities offered

7. The obligation to publish a prospectus shall not apply and a licence by the CMC shall not be required in the event that the following types of securities are offered to the public:

(i) shares issued in substitution for shares of the same class already issued, if the issuing of such new shares does not involve any increase in the issued capital;
(ii) securities offered in connection with a takeover by means of an exchange offer, provided that a document containing information equivalent to that of the prospectus, is made available to the public and notified to the CMC;
(iii) securities offered, allotted or to be allotted in connection with a merger, provided that a document containing information equivalent to that of the prospectus, is made available to the public and notified to the CMC;
(iv) shares offered, allotted or to be allotted free of charge to existing shareholders, and dividends paid out in the form of shares of the same class as the shares in respect of which such dividends are paid, provided that a document containing information on the number and nature of the shares and the reasons for and details of the offer, is made available to the public and notified to the CMC;
(v) securities offered, allotted or to be allotted to existing or former members of the board of directors or employees by their employer or by an affiliated undertaking (as defined in the Greek law on corporations), provided that a document containing information on the number and nature of the shares and the reasons for and details of the offer, is made available to the public and notified to the CMC.

8. The obligation to publish a prospectus shall not apply to the admission to trading on a regulated market of the following types of securities:

(i) shares representing, over a period of twelve months, less than 10 per cent of the number of shares of the same class already admitted to trading on the same regulated market;
(ii) shares issued in substitution for shares of the same class already admitted to trading on the same regulated market, if the issuing of such shares does not involve any increase in the issued capital;
(iii) securities offered in connection with a takeover bid by means of an exchange offer, provided that a document containing information equivalent to that of the prospectus, is made available to the public and notified to the CMC;

(iv) securities offered, allotted or to be allotted in connection with a merger, provided that a document containing information equivalent to that of the prospectus, is made available to the public and notified to the CMC;

(v) shares offered, allotted or to be allotted free of charge to existing shareholders, and dividends paid out in the form of shares of the same class as the shares in respect of which such dividends are paid, provided that the said shares are of the same class as the shares already admitted to trading on the same regulated market and that a document, containing information on the number and nature of the shares and the reasons for and details of the offer, is made available to the public and notified to the CMC;

(vi) securities offered, allotted or to be allotted to existing or former directors or employees by their employer or an affiliated undertaking (as defined in the Greek law on corporations), provided that the said securities are of the same class as the securities already admitted to trading on the same regulated market and that a document, containing information on the number and nature of the securities and the reasons for and detail of the offer, is made available to the public and notified to the CMC;

(vii) shares resulting from the conversion or exchange of other securities or from the exercise of the rights conferred by other securities, provided that the said shares are of the same class as the shares already admitted to trading on the same regulated market;

(viii) securities already admitted to trading on another regulated market, provided that the following conditions are met cumulatively:

  (a) that these securities, or securities of the same class, have been admitted to trading on that other regulated market for more than eighteen months;

  (b) that when the securities were admitted to trading on a regulated market for the first time, listing particulars were approved in accordance with Presidential Decree 348/1985[18] or the respective applicable national legislation implementing into national law Directives 80/390/EEC and 2001/34/EC;

  (c) that the ongoing obligations for trading on that other regulated market have been fulfilled;

  (d) that the person seeking the admission of a security to trading on a regulated market makes a summary document available to the public in a language accepted by the CMC, which shall state where the most recent prospectus can be obtained and where the financial information published by the issuer pursuant to its ongoing disclosure obligations is available.

[18] See above under I1.

The last exemption is particularly important for the purposes of facilitating the parallel admission to trading in more than one organised market of the European Union.

2 Approval

A Approval of a domestic prospectus

9. No prospectus can be published until it has been approved by the CMC.[19]

The CMC notifies the issuer, the offeror or the person asking for admission to trading on a regulated market, as the case may be, of its decision regarding the approval of the prospectus within ten working days of the submission of the draft prospectus.[20]

10. The time limit referred to in Article 13(2) of the Law is extended to twenty working days if the public offer involves securities issued by an issuer which does not have any securities admitted to trading on a regulated market and who has not previously offered securities to the public.[21] This is because there is hitherto no information in connection with this issuer.

11. If the CMC finds that the documents submitted are incomplete or that supplementary information is needed, it notifies the issuer, the offeror or the person asking for admission to trading on a regulated market within ten working days of the submission of the application. In such case the time limits referred to in Article 13(2) and (3) apply only from the date on which such information is provided by the issuer, the offeror or the person asking for admission to trading on a regulated market.[22]

12. The CMC may transfer the approval of a prospectus to the competent authority of another Member State, subject to the agreement of that authority. This transfer is notified to the issuer, the offeror or the person asking for admission to trading on a regulated market within three working days from the date of the decision taken by the CMC. The time limits for the competent authority of the other Member State, referred to in Article 13(2) and (3) apply from the date of that notification.[23]

If the approval of a prospectus has been transferred to the CMC by the competent authority of another Member State the time limits for the CMC referred to in Article 13(2) and (3) apply from the date of the notification from that other competent authority.[24]

B Approval of a prospectus approved in an EU country

13. If Greece is the host Member State and an offer to the public or admission to trading on a regulated market is about to be carried out in Greece or in another Member State, the prospectus approved by the home Member

[19] Art. 13(1) of the Law. [20] Art. 13(2) of the Law. [21] Art. 13(3) of the Law.
[22] Art. 13(4) of the Law. [23] Art. 13(5) of the Law. [24] Art. 13(6) of the Law.

State, and any supplements thereto, is valid for the public offer or the admission to trading in Greece, provided that the CMC is notified in accordance with Article 18 of the Law. In such case no approval of the prospectus by the CMC is required.[25] This procedure, outlined in the Prospectus Directive and, accordingly, in the Law, was an important introduction to the legal framework since it facilitates and simplifies offerings made in the EU.

If there are significant new factors, material mistakes or inaccuracies, as referred to in Article 16, arising since the approval of the prospectus, the CMC may draw the attention of the competent authority of the home Member State to the need for issuance of a supplement, so that the latter may request its publication.[26]

C Notification to another EU country of the prospectus approved in Greece

14. If Greece is the home Member State the CMC provides, at the request of the issuer or the person responsible for drawing up the prospectus, the competent authority of the host Member State with a certificate of approval and a copy of the prospectus. If applicable, this notification is accompanied by a translation of the summary produced under the responsibility of the issuer or person responsible for drawing up the prospectus. The same procedure is followed for any supplement to the prospectus.[27]

The certification of approval certifies that the prospectus was drawn up in accordance with the provisions of the Law when Greece is the home Member State or in accordance with the legislation implementing Directive 2003/71 in the home Member State, when Greece is the host Member State.[28]

Cases under 2.2 and 2.3, above, introduce into Greek law the notion of 'European passport' of a prospectus that has been duly approved by a competent authority. The European passport allows issuers, already in possession of an approved prospectus, to offer their securities to the public of other Member States or to admit them to trading in organised markets of other Member States, the only procedural requirement being the transmission of the certificate of approval from the home Member State to the host Member State.

In this way offers of securities may transcend European borders and parallel admissions in more than one European organised market may be effected. As a result of this more relaxed and flexible system, retail or institutional investors enjoy more investment options, while administration costs incurred by the issuer are significantly reduced.[29]

[25] Art. 17(1) of the Law. Additionally the authorisation required by Art. 10 of Law 876/1979 is not applicable in this case. [26] Art. 17(2) of the Law. [27] Art. 18(1) of the Law.
[28] Art. 18(2) of the Law. [29] See Ex. Rep. p. 5.

IV Content and format, language and supplements of the prospectus

1 Content

15. The prospectus contains all information which, according to the particular nature of the issuer and of the securities offered to the public or admitted to trading on a regulated market, is necessary to enable investors to make an informed assessment of the assets and liabilities, financial position, profit and losses, and prospects of the issuer and of any guarantor, and of the rights attaching to such securities. This information is presented in an easily analysable and comprehensible form.[30]

The prospectus contains information concerning the issuer and the securities to be offered to the public or to be admitted to trading on a regulated market. The particular information that must be included in the prospectus is contained in the Prospectus Regulation to which the Law refers directly in Article 7.

16. The prospectus also includes a summary conveying the most important information contained in the prospectus. By way of indication the summary must contain the following items:

(i) identity of directors, senior management, advisers and auditors;
(ii) offer statistics and expected timetable;
(iii) key information concerning the degree of indebtedness and other selected financial data for the issuer, the capitalisation, the reasons for the offer and the use of proceeds and the risk factors;
(iv) information concerning history and development of the issuer and overview of its business activities;
(v) operating and financial review of the issuer in a consolidated way and its prospects;
(vi) major shareholders and related-party transactions;
(vii) details of the offer or admission to trading concerning, for example, the number and percentage of the securities offered or admitted, the plan for the distribution of the securities, the selling shareholders, the dilution of existing shareholders' percentage, the organised market in which the securities will be admitted and the expenses of the issue;
(viii) information on the issuer's share capital and its articles of association;
(ix) documents on display for the public and way to access them.[31]

The summary must be drafted in the language in which the prospectus is originally drafted. Additionally, it should contain a warning that:

(i) it should be read as an introduction to the prospectus;
(ii) any decision to invest in the securities should be based on consideration of the prospectus as a whole by the investor;

[30] Art. 5(1) of the Law. [31] Art. 5(2) of the Law.

(iii) where a claim relating to the information contained in a prospectus is brought before a court, the plaintiff investor might have to bear the costs of translating the prospectus in whole or in part before the legal proceedings are initiated; and
(iv) civil liability lies with those persons who have submitted the summary including any translation thereof, and applied for its notification, but only if the summary is misleading, inaccurate or inconsistent when read together with the other parts of the prospectus.

Where the prospectus relates to the admission to trading on a regulated market of non-equity securities having a denomination of at least €50,000, there shall be no requirement to provide a summary.[32]

17. The final offer price and amount of securities which will be offered to the public are notified to the CMC and published by the issuer or the offeror in accordance with the requirements of the Law.[33]

The Law includes an authorisation to the CMC, according to which the CMC may provide, by virtue of a decision to this effect, the way securities are to be distributed to the investors, the methods of determination of the final offer price (including the book-building method), the possible maximum percentage by which the maximum price of the price range may exceed the minimum, the categories of investors that may participate in the procedure of determining the offer price and any other relevant issue or detail.[34]

The relevant CMC decision issued in this respect is decision 1/364/5.12.2005, which set out the specifics for the distribution of the securities to the investors as well as the rules for determining the securities' final offer price. Certain of the important provisions of this decision are the following:

- If the book-building method is selected, the securities are divided in two categories, one for qualified investors and one for non-qualified investors;
- The percentage allocated to each category may not be less than a minimum percentage of the total number of securities offered;
- The maximum percentage of securities that a non-qualified investor may acquire may not exceed 2 per cent of the total number of securities offered, while the maximum percentage for qualified investors is 4 per cent of the total number of securities offered;
- If the demand does not cover the supply in one of the two categories, securities are transferred to the category where demand has not been satisfied fully;
- The book-building process lasts three working days;

[32] Art. 5(3) of the Law. [33] Art. 8(1) of the Law. [34] Art. 8(2) of the Law.

- The underwriter or, if not existent, the issuer or selling shareholder determines the price range, which may not exceed the minimum price by more than 20 per cent.

Additionally, by virtue of CMC decision 4/379/18.4.2006, the parallel offer of securities to a limited circle of persons together with the public offer, has been provided. In particular a parallel offer has been defined as the offer to the personnel or to the BoD members of the issuer and affiliated entities or to less than 100 persons cooperating with the issuer. The price for the securities offered to the personnel or the BoD members may be lower than the offer price of the shares publicly offered by up to 10 per cent, while the price in case of offer to the issuer's partners may not be lower than the offer price of the shares publicly offered. The securities offered to this limited circle of persons may not exceed 5 per cent of the total number of securities offered. A relevant section on this parallel must be included in the prospectus.

If the final offer price and the amount of securities offered to the public cannot be included in the prospectus, the criteria, and the conditions in accordance with which the above elements will be determined or, in the case of price, the maximum price, are disclosed in the prospectus. If the above information may not be included in the prospectus, the acceptances of the purchase or subscription of securities may be withdrawn within two working days of the final offer price and amount of securities which will be offered to the public have been determined. This option must be clearly stated in the prospectus and it must be included in the announcement to the public.[35]

18. The CMC may authorise the omission from the prospectus of certain information provided for in the Law if it considers that:

(i) disclosure of such information would be contrary to the public interest; or
(ii) disclosure of such information would be seriously detrimental to the issuer, provided that the omission would not be likely to mislead the public with regard to facts and circumstances essential for an informed assessment of the issuer, offeror or guarantor, if any, and of the rights attached to the securities to which the prospectus relates; or
(iii) such information is of minor importance only for a specific offer or admission to trading on a regulated market and is not such as will influence the assessment of the financial position and prospects of the issuer, offeror or guarantor, if any.[36]

Without prejudice to the adequate information of investors, where, exceptionally, certain information required to be included in a prospectus is inappropriate to the issuer's sphere of activity or to the legal form of the issuer or to the securities to which the prospectus relates, the prospectus shall

[35] Art. 8(3) of the Law. [36] Art. 8(4) of the Law.

contain information equivalent to the required information. If there is no such information, this requirement shall not apply.[37]

19. A prospectus is valid for twelve months after its publication for offers to the public or admissions to trading on a regulated market, provided that the prospectus is completed by supplements if required pursuant to Article 16.[38]

In the case of an offering programme, the base prospectus, previously filed, is valid for a period of up to twelve months.[39]

In the case of non-equity securities referred to in Article 5(5)(b) of the Law (for which see below under the section 'Format'), the prospectus is valid until no more of the securities concerned are issued in a continuous or repeated manner.[40]

A registration document, as referred to in Article 5(4) of the Law (for which see below under the section 'Format'), previously filed with the CMC, is valid for a period of up to twelve months provided that it has been updated in accordance with Article 10(1) of the Law (for which see below under the section 'Supplements'). The registration document accompanied by the securities note, updated if applicable in accordance with Article 12(2) of the Law (for which see below under the section 'Supplements'), and the summary note is considered to constitute a valid prospectus.[41]

20. The particular procedure and the specific documentation that has to be submitted together with the prospectus are outlined in CMC decision 3/398/22.9.2006.

2 Format

21. The issuer, offeror or person asking for the admission to trading on a regulated market may draw up the prospectus as a single document or separate documents. A prospectus composed of separate documents shall divide the required information into a registration document, a securities note and a summary note. The registration document shall contain the information relating to the issuer. The securities note shall contain the information concerning the securities offered to the public or to be admitted to trading on a regulated market.[42]

22. For the following types of securities, the prospectus can, at the choice of the issuer, offeror or person asking for the admission to trading on a regulated market consist of a base prospectus:

(i) non-equity securities, including warrants in any form, issued under an offering programme;
(ii) non-equity securities issued in a continuous or repeated manner by credit institutions provided, (a) the sums deriving from the issue of

[37] Art. 8(5) of the Law. [38] Art. 9(1) of the Law. [39] Art. 9(2) of the Law.
[40] Art. 9(3) of the Law. [41] Art. 9(4) of the Law. [42] Art. 5(4) of the Law.

the said securities are placed in assets which provide sufficient coverage for the liability deriving from securities until their maturity date; (b) in the event of the insolvency of the related credit institution, the said sums are intended, as a priority, to repay the capital and interest falling due.[43]

The base prospectus contains all the information pertaining to the issuer and the securities which will be subject to a public offer or admission to trading in a regulated market, as well as the final terms of the offer. If the final terms of the offer are not included in either the base prospectus or a supplement, the final terms shall be provided to investors and filed with the CMC when each public offer is made as soon as practicable and if possible in advance of the beginning of each offer.[44]

The information given in the base prospectus shall be supplemented, if necessary, in accordance with Article 16, with updated information on the issuer and on the securities to be offered to the public or to be admitted to trading on a regulated market.[45]

3 Supplements

A Yearly updates

23. Issuers whose securities are admitted to trading on a regulated market in Greece at least annually publish a document that contains or refers to all information that they have published or made available to the public over the preceding twelve months in compliance with their obligations under Community and national legislation and concern the securities, issuers of securities and securities markets.[46]

The document is filed with the CMC after the publication of the financial statement and it states where the information referred to can be obtained.[47]

The above obligation does not apply to issuers of non-equity securities whose denomination per unit amounts to at least €50,000.[48] This exception aims to relieve some issuers of securities that do not target retail investors from excessive workload.

B Incorporation by reference

24. Information may be incorporated in the prospectus by reference to one or more previously or simultaneously published documents that have been approved by the CMC or filed with it in accordance with the Law. This information must be the latest available to the issuer. The summary must not incorporate information by reference.[49]

[43] Art. 5(5) of the Law. [44] Art. 5(6) of the Law. [45] Art. 5(7) of the Law.
[46] Art. 10(1) of the Law. [47] Art. 10(2) of the Law. [48] Art. 10(3) of the Law.
[49] Art. 11(1) of the Law.

When information is incorporated by reference, a cross-reference list must be provided in order to enable investors to identify easily specific items of information.[50]

This option facilitates the procedure of drawing up the prospectus and reduces the cost incurred by the issuers without at the same time jeopardising investors' protection.[51]

C Prospectuses consisting of separate documents

25. An issuer which already has a registration document approved by the CMC may draw up only the securities note and the summary note when securities are offered to the public or admitted to trading on a regulated market. The securities and summary notes are submitted separately for approval.[52]

In this case, the securities note provides information if there has been a material change or recent development which could affect investors' assessments of the issuer and the securities since the latest updated registration document or any supplement, as provided for in Article 16 of the Law, was approved.[53]

Where an issuer has only filed a registration document without approval, the entire documentation, including updated information, is subject to approval.[54]

This new way of prospectus-drafting introduced by the Law, aims to facilitate matters for the issuers and the procedure itself.

D Supplements to the prospectus

26. Every significant new factor, material mistake or inaccuracy relating to the information included in the prospectus which is capable of affecting the assessment of the securities and which arises or is noted between the time when the prospectus is approved and the final closing of the offer to the public or, as the case may be, the time when trading on a regulated market begins, is mentioned in a supplement to the prospectus.[55]

Such a supplement is approved in the same way at the latest within seven working days of its submission for approval and published in accordance with the same arrangements as were applied when the original prospectus was published. The summary, and any translations thereof, shall also be supplemented, if necessary to take into account the new information included in the supplement.[56]

Investors who have already agreed to purchase or subscribe for the securities before the supplement is published have the right, exercisable within a time limit of three working days after publication of the supplement, to withdraw their acceptances or subscriptions.[57]

[50] Art. 11(2) of the Law. [51] Ex. Rep. p. 4. [52] Art. 12(1) of the Law.
[53] Art. 12(2) of the Law. [54] Art. 12(3) of the Law. [55] Art. 16(1) of the Law.
[56] Art. 16(2) of the Law. [57] Art. 16(3) of the Law.

4 Language

27. The new provisions about language will further enhance the public offerings in more than one EU Member States. Especially if Greece is the host Member State, the offeror's cost is significantly reduced since the translation will only concern the summary and not the whole prospectus.

If Greece is the home Member State and an offer to the public is made or admission to trading on a regulated market is sought only in Greece, the prospectus is drawn up in Greek.[58]

If Greece is the home Member State and an offer to the public is made or admission to trading on a regulated market is sought in one or more Member States excluding Greece, the prospectus is drawn up either in Greek or in a language widely used in the international finance sector, at the choice of the issuer, offeror or person asking for admission, as the case may be.[59]

If Greece is the home Member State and an offer to the public is made or admission to trading on a regulated market is sought in more than one Member State including Greece, the prospectus must be drawn up in Greek and must also be made available either in a language accepted by the competent authorities of each host Member State or in a language widely used in the international finance sector, at the choice of the issuer, offeror, or person asking for admission to trading, as the case may be.[60]

As mentioned above, the CMC may request only for the summary to be translated into Greek, if Greece is the host Member State.[61]

If Greece is the home Member State and admission to trading on a regulated market of non-equity securities whose denomination per unit amounts to at least €50,000 is sought on an organised market, the prospectus can be drawn up in a language widely used in the international finance sector, at the choice of the issuer, offeror or person asking for admission to trading, as the case may be.[62]

V Publication and advertisements

1 Methods of publication

28. Once approved, the prospectus is filed with the CMC and is made available to the public by the issuer, offeror or person asking for admission to trading on a regulated market as soon as practicable. The exact timing is laid down in the Law.

The prospectus shall be deemed available to the public when published in the ways provided for in the Law.

The issuer, offeror or person asking for the admission to trading on a regulated market publishes a notice in one or more financial or political

[58] Art. 19(1) of the Law. [59] Art. 19(2) of the Law. [60] Art. 19(3) of the Law.
[61] Art. 19(4) of the Law. [62] Art. 19(5) of the Law.

daily newspapers circulated throughout, or widely circulated in Greece, as well as in the Daily Price Index of the organised market, stating how the prospectus has been made available and where it can be obtained by the public.[63] It is apparent that the attempt of the legislator is to ensure access to all persons.

The CMC publishes on its website over a period of twelve months the list of prospectuses, including, if applicable, a hyperlink to the prospectus published on the website of the issuer, or on the website of the regulated market.[64]

In the case of a prospectus comprising several documents and/or incorporating information by reference, the documents and information comprising the prospectus may be published and circulated separately provided that the said documents are made available, free of charge, to the public, in accordance with the arrangements established in Article 14(2) of the Law. Each document indicates where the other constituent documents of the full prospectus may be obtained.[65]

The text and the format of the prospectus, and/or the supplements to the prospectus, published or made available to the public, must at all times be identical to the original version approved by the CMC.[66]

Where the prospectus is made available by publication in electronic form, a paper copy must nevertheless be delivered to the investor, upon his request and free of charge, by the issuer, the offeror, the person asking for admission to trading or the underwriters or advisers placing or selling the securities.[67]

2 Advertisements

29. Any type of advertisement relating either to an offer to the public of securities or to an admission to trading on a regulated market must observe the principles contained in Article 15(2)–(5) of the Law. Article 15(2)–(4) of the Law applies only to cases where the issuer, the offeror or the person applying for admission to trading is covered by the obligation to draw up a prospectus.[68]

Advertisements must state that a prospectus has been or will be published and indicate where investors are or will be able to obtain it.[69]

Advertisements shall be clearly recognisable as such. The information contained in an advertisement shall not be inaccurate, or misleading. This information shall also be consistent with the information contained in the prospectus, if already published, or with the information required to be in the prospectus, if the prospectus is published afterwards.[70] In any case, all information concerning the offer to the public or the admission to trading on a

[63] Art. 14(3) of the Law. [64] Art. 14(4) of the Law. [65] Art. 14(5) of the Law.
[66] Art. 14(6) of the Law. [67] Art. 14(7) of the Law. [68] Art. 15(1) of the Law.
[69] Art. 15(2) of the Law. [70] Art. 15(3) of the Law.

regulated market disclosed in an oral or written form, even if not for advertising purposes, must be consistent with that contained in the prospectus.[71]

When according to the Law no prospectus is required, material information provided by an issuer or an offeror and addressed to qualified investors or special categories of investors, including information disclosed in the context of meetings relating to offers of securities, must be disclosed to all qualified investors or special categories of investors to whom the offer is exclusively addressed. Where a prospectus is required to be published, such information must be included in the prospectus or in a supplement to the prospectus.[72]

Advertisements published in view of a public offer of securities or admission to trading in an organised market must be submitted to the CMC at least two working days prior to their publication.[73]

Note that in Greece, under the general consumer law as well, advertisements should observe specific rules, such as accuracy, etc.

VI Use of prospectus approved in other (non-EU) countries

30. If Greece is the home Member State of issuers having their registered office in a third country, the CMC may approve a prospectus for an offer to the public or for admission to trading on a regulated market, drawn up in accordance with the legislation of a third country, provided that:

(i) the prospectus has been drawn up in accordance with international standards set by the International Organisation of Securities Commissions (IOSCO); and
(ii) the information requirements, including information of a financial nature, are equivalent to the requirements under the Law[74] and the Regulation.

If Greece is the home Member State and securities issued by an issuer incorporated in a third country are offered to the public or admitted to trading on a regulated market of another Member State, the requirements set out in Articles 17– 19 of the Law apply.[75]

VII Sanctions

31. In the case of violation of the provisions of the Law, the decisions that are issued in accordance with the Law or Regulation 809/2004, the CMC may reprimand or impose a fine, within the limits set by the Law. In determining the precise amount of the fine the CMC takes into account especially the violation's likelihood of inflicting damage to the investors and the

[71] Art. 15(4) of the Law. [72] Art. 15(5) of the Law. [73] Art. 15(6) of the Law.
[74] Art. 20(1) of the Law. [75] Art. 20(2) of the Law.

smooth operation of the market, possible profit-making by the offender and possible recidivism on its part.[76]

Apart from the administrative sanctions outlined above, the CMC may also take precautionary measures when Greece is the host Member State and it finds that irregularities have been committed by the issuer, or by the underwriters or advisers in charge of the public offer, or that breaches have been committed of the obligations attaching to the issuer of securities admitted to a regulated market. In that case, the CMC refers these findings to the competent authority of the home Member State.[77]

If, despite the measures taken by the competent authority of the home Member State, the issuer, underwriter or adviser in charge of the public offer persists in breaching the relevant legal or regulatory provisions, the CMC takes all the appropriate measures in order to protect investors, informs the Commission at the earliest opportunity and informs the competent authority of the home Member State thereon.[78]

VIII Prospectus liability

32. Responsibility for the information given in a prospectus lies with:

(i) the issuer, the offeror, the person asking for the admission to trading on a regulated market, as the case may be;
(ii) the members of the Board of Directors of the aforementioned persons; and
(iii) underwriters or advisers.[79]

Persons other than those mentioned above are responsible for the information contained in separate distinct parts of the prospectus provided that it is clearly specified in it for which particular parts these persons are responsible.[80]

The persons responsible must be clearly identified in the prospectus by their names and functions or, in the case of legal persons, their names and registered offices, as well as declarations by them that, to the best of their knowledge, the information contained in the prospectus is in accordance with the facts and that the prospectus makes no omission likely to affect its import.[81]

The responsible persons referred to above are liable against investors who have acquired securities within the first twelve months of publication of the prospectus, for any damage that they have suffered due to the fault of the responsible persons as to the accuracy or the completeness of the prospectus. The aggrieved party must prove the damage that he suffered as well as the causal link between the fault of the responsible persons and the

[76] Art. 24(1) of the Law. [77] Art. 23(1) of the Law. [78] Art. 23(2) of the Law.
[79] Art. 6(1) of the Law. [80] Art. 6(2) of the Law. [81] Art. 6(3) of the Law.

damage. The responsible persons must prove that they are not at fault. There exists a limitation period for any civil action against the responsible persons starting from the publication of the prospectus.[82] The special civil liability provisions of the Law do not exclude the application of the general civil law liability provisions. Any limitation of liability clause is null and void against the investors. No civil liability attaches to any person solely on the basis of the summary, including any translation thereof, unless it is misleading, inaccurate or inconsistent when read together with the other parts of the prospectus.[83]

The investors entitled to compensation are not only those that have acquired the securities directly from the issuer further to the public offer or the request for admission to trading, but also those who have acquired the securities in the market, i.e. in a derivative way, within twelve months of the publication of the prospectus.[84]

IX Conclusion

33. The law has introduced a number of issues and notions which were either non-existent or modified in comparison with the previous regime.

An issue which must be noted is the differentiation in the private placement exemptions and the introduction of the notion of qualified investors. In the past regime there was, instead, reference to a limited number of investors but without specifying a number. Furthermore, there was no definition of qualified investors or a register thereof. Thus the Law provides further clarity on this issue.

Another innovation is the explicit reference in the Law to the approval required under the catch-all provision of Article 10 of Law 876/79. The new regime provides for more legal safety since its operation is now clarified.

Finally, a major issue is the introduction of the European passport and other rules (e.g. language of the prospectus). The European passport and the uniform rules across the EU relating to the prospectus and the procedure will significantly facilitate the public offering of securities on more than one EU organised market.

Furthermore, the competent authorities will attempt to adopt common interpretation of the relevant procedures and thus provide legal safety for the issuers wishing to offer securities in more than one EU Member State.

Specifically, in Greece the CMC tends to adopt the same position with other competent authorities of the Member States when the EU passport procedure is followed. In addition, the timing for the approval of public offers seems to be significantly reduced. At present, there is no well

[82] Previously one year. [83] See Art. 25 of the Law.

[84] Ex. Rep. p. 5. According to the pre-existing regime compensation could be claimed only by those acquiring securities directly from the issuer, offeror, etc.

established precedent in Greece on all issues covered by the Law, since its enactment is rather recent.

Today, there still exist different interpretations among competent regulatory authorities on specific issues which could be eliminated following the deliberations that take place in several EU committees and the practical implementation of the Law. In general, it must be mentioned that the new regime of Prospectuses tries to harmonise different past practices. In our opinion, the provision of sufficient information to the public will still be the focus of any interpretation followed by the regulatory authorities.

7 Hungary

JACQUES DE SERVIGNY
Gide Loyrette Nouel

I Introduction

1. The European Union has always believed that easier access to capital would increase productivity, job creation and growth in Europe. Although the importance of access to capital was recognised, the existing prospectus regime did not provide a coherent system and, rather, created obstacles to raising capital across the European Union. The biggest obstacle was the lack of harmonised procedures and regulations across Member States.

Therefore, the Directive 2003/71/EC of the European Parliament and of the Council of 4 November 2003 on the prospectus to be published when securities are offered to the public or admitted to trading and amending Directive 2001/34/EC (further the 'Prospectus Directive') was introduced. The Prospectus Directive improved market efficiency through the possibility of issuing a single approved prospectus that enables issuers to raise capital across the European Union without further approval or administrative arrangements.

Furthermore, the Prospectus Directive requires harmonised standards of publication for issues of securities that are offered to the public or admitted to trading on a regulated market in the European Union. The aim is to ensure better investor protection.

The Prospectus Directive is complemented by Commission Regulation No. 809/2004 of 29 April 2004, implementing the Prospectus Directive as regards information contained in the prospectus as well as the format, incorporation by reference and publication of such prospectuses and dissemination of advertisements (further the 'Prospectus Regulation').

2. The Prospectus Directive introduces a regime whereby prospectuses for securities need to be approved by only one competent authority of a single Member State (the home Member State). This feature of the system is called the 'passport-effect'. Once accepted and approved by the competent authority of a Member State, issuers may use the same prospectus with relation to an offer to the public in any Member State or application for admission of securities to trading on any regulated market situated in any Member State.

3. In Hungary the Prospectus Directive was implemented by Act LXII of 2005 on the modification of Act CXX of 2001 on the Capital Market.[1] The modification entered into force on 1 July 2005. All modifications were incorporated into the Act on the Capital Market (further the 'Act').

II Competent Authority

4. The designated authority in Hungary for the approval of the prospectus is the State Financial Institutions Commission (further the 'SFIC'), which is an administrative agency of the government. The status of the SFIC is ruled by a so-called 'status act', Act CXXIV of 1999 on Government Control of Financial Institutions. The SFIC is a budgetary agency vested with powers and authorisations to oversee the sector. It reports directly to the Minister of Finance.[2] The SFIC's jurisdiction includes the supervision of the activities of organisations and individuals falling under the scope of (among others) the Act on the Capital Market. The activity of the SFIC is not ruled by the above act but by other acts. For example, pursuant to the Act on the Capital Market the supervision of private and public offering of securities belongs to the competence of the SFIC.

[1] Please note that the amendment law does not only contain the rules of the Prospectus Directive, but other rules as well that amended the Act on the Capital Market.

[2] Art. 1 of the Act on the Government Control of Financial Institutions.

5. The SFIC complies with the requirements of the Prospectus Directive regarding the status of the approving authority,[3] namely (i) to be designated as the only competent authority to approve prospectuses in order to avoid unnecessary costs and different responsibilities due to a variety of competent authorities in Member States, and (ii) to be responsible for supervising compliance with the Prospectus Directive. Moreover, the SFIC is an administrative authority independent of the economic players and organised in such a way in order to avoid conflicts of interests, as it is also required in the Prospectus Directive.

6. According to Article 36 (1) of the Act on the Capital Market the SFIC shall authorise the publication of the prospectus. The SFIC's authorisation is not required for the publication of a prospectus or public announcement if it has been authorised by the competent supervisory authority of another Member State of the European Union, and if they provide proof to the SFIC that the prospectus or abridged prospectus is in compliance with the regulations of the European Union.

III Procedure of prior approval

1 General remarks

A Condition of publicly offering securities

7. In order to publicly offer securities the issuer or the offeror shall – in general – (i) contract with an investment service provider; (ii) prepare a prospectus; and (iii) make a public offer. Pursuant to the Act on the Capital Market the issuer, the offeror or the person requesting admission to trading on a regulated market shall publish an issue prospectus (hereinafter referred to as 'prospectus') in connection with the public offering of securities or their admission to trading on a regulated market and a public offer (hereinafter referred to as 'public announcement') – with the exception of the admission of securities to trading in a regulated market.

B Definition of public offering and regulated market

8. In this respect public offering of securities shall mean when securities are offered to any investors by means other than private offering.[4]

9. Pursuant to the regulation the regulated market shall mean the exchange market or another regulated market of a Member State of the European Union for the sale and purchase of securities under fixed rules and controlled by supply and demand, and which satisfies the following criteria:[5]

[3] Thirty-seventh recital to the Prospectus Directive.
[4] Art. 5 (1) point 80 of the Act on the Capital Market.
[5] Art. 5 (1) point 29 of the Act on the Capital Market.

(i) membership of or access to, such market is subject to regulations and market standards approved by the competent supervisory authority;
(ii) it operates regularly at specific hours;
(iii) the activities and transactions of all traders are subject to certain minimum requirements (capital requirement, deposit requirements, etc.);
(iv) the publication of prices and quantities is mandatory (at the start, during and at the end of each day's trading the prices and the volume dealt of each instrument must be published);
(v) the minimum requirements for the admission of financial instruments are defined;
(vi) issuers of financial instruments trading on the market shall publish all information which may affect the buying and selling price or any form of price variations of the financial instruments (transparency);
(vii) all traders are required to disclose the particulars of their transactions to the competent supervisory authority;
(viii) it must be included in the lists prepared by Member States on their regulated markets and sent to the other Member States and the European Commission for information purposes.

C Investment service provider

10. Pursuant to Article 23 (1) of the Act on the Capital Market the issuer or the offeror shall contract an investment service provider for the organisation and conduct of the public offering of securities, unless:

(i) the public offering takes place by admission to trading on a regulated market;
(ii) government securities are offered by the issuer himself;
(iii) a credit institution or investment firm offers to issue its own securities; or
(iv) a foreign-registered credit institution or a foreign-registered investment firm offers its own securities in issue by way of its branch office.

11. An investment service provider shall mean an investment firm or a credit institution that is engaged in investment services and in activities auxiliary to investment services, but not including clearing houses and central depositories.[6]

D Exceptions – when issuing a prospectus is not compulsory

(i) Prospectus is not compulsory at all

12. A prospectus or a public announcement is not required:

(a) in connection with the offering of money-market instruments with an original maturity of less than twelve months;

[6] Art. 5 (1) point 17 of the Act on the Capital Market.

(b) in connection with the offering of investment certificates of an open-ended investment fund;
(c) in connection with securities that were already offered publicly.[7]

In the above cases the issuer shall inform the SFIC concerning the placement of securities within fifteen days following the conclusion of the procedure and the SFIC shall have the right to check the procedure to determine as to whether it was conducted in compliance with the conditions above.[8]

(ii) In relation to securities already offered publicly

13. It is not required to have another prospectus or public announcement in connection with securities that were already offered publicly, where:

(a) an issuer issues substitute securities of the same class and type as the securities it has issued previously, and these new substituted securities will not result, as a consequence, in the increase of the issued equity capital;
(b) when equity securities are offered in payment for acquiring any participating interests in a corporation within the framework of a public purchase offer, provided that a document containing information relating to the offered securities or the issuer of such securities that is deemed equivalent by the SFIC to those contained in the prospectus, is already available to the investors concerned;
(c) when equity securities are offered for payment underlying the merger of companies, provided that a document containing information relating to the offered securities or the issuer of such securities that is deemed equivalent by the SFIC to those contained in the prospectus, is already available to the investors concerned;
(d) when a company provides shares to its shareholders free of charge from its assets other than from the share capital, or provides securities in payment of dividend of the same class and type as the ones upon which the dividend is paid;
(e) when the issuer or its affiliated company sells or provides securities to their employees, executive officers, supervisory board members, or to their former employees, executive officers, or supervisory board members, provided that a) the issuer already has other securities admitted for trading on a regulated market, and b) information concerning the number and type of securities and the reasons and circumstances in which such securities have been sold or provided are available.[9]

(iii) Admission of securities to trading on a regulated market

[7] Art. 21 (2) of the Act on the Capital Market.
[8] Art. 21 (3) of the Act on the Capital Market.
[9] Art. 22 (1) of the Act on the Capital Market.

14. Special rules are set out with regard to trading on a regulated market. In the course of an admission of securities to trading on a regulated market a prospectus is not required to be issued in the following cases:

(a) if securities of the same class and type have already been admitted to trading in the same regulated market, and within twelve months the quantity of securities to be admitted shall not exceed 10 per cent of the quantity of securities previously admitted to the regulated market;
(b) if the securities issued to substitute securities of the same class and type have already been admitted to trading in the same regulated market, and if these substituted securities will not result, as a consequence, in the increase of the issued equity capital;
(c) when equity securities are offered in payment for acquiring any participating interests in a corporation within the framework of a public purchase offer, provided that a document containing information relating to the offered securities or the issuer of such securities that is deemed equivalent by the SFIC to those contained in the prospectus, is already available to the investors concerned;
(d) when equity securities are offered for payment underlying the merger of companies, provided that a document containing information relating to the offered securities or the issuer of such securities that is deemed equivalent by the SFIC to those contained in the prospectus, is already available to the investors concerned;
(e) when a company provides shares to its shareholders, free of charge from its assets other than from the share capital, or provides securities in payment of dividend of the same class and type as the ones upon which the dividend is paid, provided that these securities have already been admitted to trading in the same regulated market;
(f) when the issuer or its affiliated company sells or provides securities to the issuer's employees, executive officers, supervisory board members, or to its former employees, executive officers, supervisory board members, provided that securities of the same class have already been admitted to trading in the same regulated market;
(g) in connection with the admission of shares derived from the conversion of certain securities, or from the exercise of rights afforded by such securities, provided that securities of the same type or class have already been admitted to trading in the same regulated market;
(h) if these securities have already been admitted to trading in another regulated market, provided:
    (i) that these securities or securities of the same series have been admitted to trading in another regulated market at least eighteen months previously;
    (ii) that a prospectus has already been published in accordance with the laws of another Member State;

(iii) that the requirements for keeping the securities in circulation are properly satisfied;
(iv) that the person applying for admission to trading on a regulated market publishes an executive summary in Hungarian. The executive summary shall contain an indication of the venue where the last issued prospectus and the most recent financial information published under the obligation of regular disclosure is made available to the investors for review.[10]

In the cases of points (e)–(h) the issuer or the person applying for admission to trading on a regulated market shall disclose to the SFIC and make available to the investors affected information concerning the type and quantity of the securities to be issued, and the reasons and circumstances in which such securities are to be offered.[11]

E Issue program

15. Debt securities may also be offered to the public within the framework of an issue program. An issue program may be devised to offer various types of debt securities using various types of placement methods.[12]

16. An issue program shall mean an operation in which an issuer publicly issues a series of debt securities or investment certificates of a close-ended investment fund at certain intervals, the basic conditions of which are announced by the issuer or the fund manager when the program is initiated, and where the issuer or the fund manager specifies the individual characteristics of each issue.

F Secondary securities

17. An investment service provider or a central depository that is authorised to undertake subscription guarantees and to provide custodial services for securities, or to provide securities account management services may issue secondary securities – under an agreement with the issuer – on the securities in their possession, and when so instructed by the owners of the securities that were issued as part of a series.[13]

18. Secondary securities shall contain: a) the name of the issuer; b) all components of the underlying principal securities; c) the securities code of the secondary securities; d) the place and date of issue of the secondary securities; e) the aggregate face value of the entire series in placement; f) the quantity of securities in placement; and g) the signature of the issuer of printed securities.[14]

[10] Art. 22 (4) of the Act on the Capital Market.
[11] Art. 22 (6) of the Act on the Capital Market.
[12] Art. 23 (2) of the Act on the Capital Market.
[13] Art. 24 (1) of the Act on the Capital Market.
[14] Art. 24 (2) of the Act on the Capital Market.

During the life of secondary securities no rights may be exercised through the underlying principal securities.[15]

G Nullity

19. The subscription of securities, including the purchase contract, shall be null and void in the absence of a prospectus approved by the SFIC and without having published a public announcement, also without the involvement of an investment service provider.[16]

20. Furthermore, the subscription of securities, including the purchase contract, shall also be null and void where the shares of a privately held limited liability company are offered publicly or presented for admission to trading on a regulated market in the absence of a decision by the general meeting for the company's transformation.[17]

21. In the above cases the issuer or the person requesting admission of the securities to trading on a regulated market shall be subject to joint and several liability for any and all damages sustained by the investors.[18]

2 The approval of the SFIC

A General remarks

22. The publication of the prospectus and the public offer shall be authorised by the SFIC.

B Application

23. The procedure of the authorisation by the SFIC can be initiated by application.

24. The application shall contain the following:[19]

(i) a draft version of the prospectus;
(ii) a draft of the transcript of the public announcement;
(iii) a draft of the subscription sheet, if placement takes place by subscription;
(iv) a draft of the auction sheet, if placement takes place by auction;
(v) a draft of the transcript of the securities, or a draft of the written instrument on dematerialised securities;
(vi) proof of payment of administration fees and service charges;
(vii) if the issuer is a business association or a cooperative, the instruments of incorporation;

[15] Art. 24 (3) of the Act on the Capital Market.
[16] Art. 25 (1) of the Act on the Capital Market.
[17] Art. 25 (1) of the Act on the Capital Market.
[18] Art. 25 (2) of the Act on the Capital Market.
[19] Art. 38 (1) of the Act on the Capital Market.

(viii) the issuer's resolution on the public offer;
(ix) in connection with the public offering of the shares of a privately held limited liability company, or their admission to trading on a regulated market, the resolution of the general meeting concerning the amendment of the instruments of incorporation;
(x) the contract between the investment service provider hired to organise and execute the marketing procedure and the issuer, or a draft agreement, or the contracts between the various investment service providers participating in the marketing procedure.

25. Upon the request of an issuer that has its head office in a third country the SFIC may authorise publication of a prospectus if it pertains to securities planned to be offered to the public in Hungary, or requesting admission to trading on a regulated market in Hungary, and if the prospectus:

(i) is in compliance with the regulations of the European Union; or
(ii) is in compliance with standards set by international organisations, including the IOSCO disclosure standards, and
(iii) the requirements concerning the information contained in the prospectus, including information of a financial nature, are equivalent to the requirements under the Act on the Capital Market.[20]

C Supporting documents

26. When requested by the SFIC the issuer, the offeror, the person requesting admission of the securities to trading on a regulated market and the broker/dealer, furthermore, the auditors and executive officers of these persons, their owners holding a controlling interest, or the legal person in which the issuer, the offeror, the person requesting admission of the securities to trading on a regulated market, and the broker/dealer holds a controlling interest, must provide proof in the form of data and documents to verify the information contained in the prospectus.[21]

D Higher-than-average risk

27. Where investment in any particular security carries higher-than-average risks from the investor's point of view, in particular (i) if the issuer of debt securities operates for less than one year; (ii) if following the issue of debt securities the amount of credit liabilities of the issuer is in excess of the issuer's equity capital; or (iii) if the liability of the issuer, the offeror, the person requesting admission of the securities to trading on a regulated market and the broker/dealer is not joint and several, the SFIC shall instruct the issuer, the offeror or the person requesting admission of the securities to trading on a regulated market to expressly indicate such

[20] Art. 37 (1) of the Act on the Capital Market.
[21] Art. 38 (2) of the Act on the Capital Market.

exposure in the beginning of the prospectus and in all announcements and advertisements.[22]

E Corrections

28. The issuer, the offeror, the person requesting admission of the securities to trading on a regulated market and the broker/dealer must immediately notify the SFIC in the event of becoming aware of any fact or circumstance during the authorisation procedure that facilitates corrections (revision, amendment) to be made in the draft prospectus submitted.[23]

F Procedural deadline for the SFIC

29. In general the SFIC shall give the authorisation in ten business days. In case of the first public offer of the issuer the deadline is twenty business days. During this time the SFIC examines whether the legal conditions are complied with in order to authorise the publication of the prospectus and public offer.[24]

30. The SFIC may request additional documents in a further ten business days. The deadline starts when the application arrives at the SFIC. The procedure deadline cannot be extended.

G Refusal of the application

31. The SFIC shall refuse to grant authorisation if the prospectus does not conform to the provisions of this Act and other legal regulations, or if the intended purpose of the placement is to misuse some right, or if the broker/dealer or the issuer fails to comply with the measures required by the SFIC in the course of the procedure.[25]

H Validity of the prospectus

32. The prospectus shall remain valid for twelve months. The securities may be offered to the public or admitted to trading on a regulated market within twelve months of the date of publication of the prospectus, within the validity period of the prospectus.[26]

33. An abridged prospectus published within the framework of an issue programme shall also remain valid for twelve months. In connection with the placement of mortgage bonds by way of a progressive issue, or if they are offered at least twice within a twelve-month period, the abridged prospectus

[22] Art. 38 (4) of the Act on the Capital Market.
[23] Art. 38 (5) of the Act on the Capital Market.
[24] Art. 38 (3) of the Act on the Capital Market.
[25] Art. 38 (5) of the Act on the Capital Market.
[26] Art. 31 (1) of the Act on the Capital Market.

shall be valid until the conclusion of the entire offering procedure, with the exception that the last procedure for placement must commence within twelve months.[27]

34. The registration document shall also remain valid for twelve months if the issuer is in compliance with the obligation of disclosure specified in the rules concerning summary report.[28]

35. Consequently, if the issuer has a registration document that has been approved within the previous twelve months, it is sufficient to publish the securities list and the executive summary for the public offering of securities. In this case the securities list shall indicate all changes of importance that took place pertaining to the issuer since the approval of the registration document, and which may have any bearing on the assessment of the issuer. The registration document accompanied by the securities list and the executive summary authorised in a separate procedure shall be considered to constitute a valid prospectus.[29]

IV Content and format, language and supplements of the prospectus

1 Content

36. The Prospectus Directive and the Act on the Capital Market establish requirements in relation to the content of the prospectus. The requirements aim to support the unified and common standards for prospectuses.

A General requirements

37. All prospectuses must include the information necessary for investors to be able to make an informed assessment of the issuer, or the person who has provided guarantees for the commitments embodied in securities, in terms of market position, financial standing, business and legal aspects, any foreseeable future developments and the prospects of the issuer and of the rights attaching to such securities.[30]

38. All data, information, statements and analysis contained in a prospectus for public offering, or in an announcement published in relation to such a prospectus or the securities to which it pertains, must be true and correct, and shall be sufficient to achieve the objective defined above.[31]

39. The prospectus or the public announcement must not contain any misleading information, nor any statement and/or analysis likely to draw a

27 Art. 31 (2) of the Act on the Capital Market.
28 Art. 31 (3) of the Act on the Capital Market.
29 Art. 31 (4) of the Act on the Capital Market.
30 Art. 26 (1) of the Act on the Capital Market.
31 Art. 26 (2) of the Act on the Capital Market.

misconclusion, and must not conceal any fact that might jeopardise the objective described above.[32]

B Parts of the prospectus

40. Each prospectus shall consist of a registration document, a securities list and the executive summary. The prospectus may also be prepared in a single consolidated document (consolidated prospectus).[33]

41. It is not necessary to include an executive summary in a prospectus that is made in connection with the admission of debt securities to trading on a regulated market where the nominal value of these securities is at least €50,000, or its equivalent in any other currency translated by the official Hungarian National Bank exchange rate in effect on the day of placement, not including when the securities are planned for admission to trading on a regulated market in Hungary as well and the prospectus is prepared in a language other than Hungarian.[34]

(i) The content of the executive summary

42. The executive summary shall contain concise information in a clear and understandable fashion, in the original language of the prospectus, concerning the issuer or the person who has provided guarantees for the commitments embodied in securities, and concerning the key characteristics and main risks of the securities.

43. Moreover the executive summary shall also contain an indication:

(a) that the executive summary is the introductory part of the prospectus;
(b) that investment decisions should be made in full knowledge of the prospectus;
(c) if any action is filed in connection with the information contained in the prospectus, national laws of the Member State may require that the plaintiff bears the costs of the translation of the prospectus before the judicial proceedings; and
(d) the person undertaking responsibility for the contents of the executive summary, or the person translating the executive summary shall be subject to liability for damages sustained by the investor, if the executive summary is misleading or inaccurate, or if it is not in harmony with other segments of the prospectus.[35]

C The manner of indicating the information in the prospectus

44. If the quantity or final offer price of the securities offered cannot be disclosed in the prospectus, then:

[32] Art. 26 (3) of the Act on the Capital Market.
[33] Art. 26 (4) of the Act on the Capital Market.
[34] Art. 26 (5) of the Act on the Capital Market.
[35] Art. 27 (1) of the Act on the Capital Market.

(a) the maximum price of the securities must be indicated along with the criteria or conditions, based upon which the quantity or final offer price of the securities offered is determined; or
(b) the investor shall be given the opportunity to withdraw his offer for the purchase of securities within two business days following disclosure of the final offer price or the quantity of securities offered.[36]

45. The final offer price of the securities or the quantity of securities offered must be made available to the public. The SFIC shall be informed without delay.[37]

D Authorisation for leaving out some information

46. The SFIC may authorise leaving out certain information from the prospectus, if:

(a) publishing the information in question is against public interest;
(b) publishing the information in question is likely to cause serious harm to the issuer and leaving it out is not misleading in terms of the assessment of the issuer, the offeror or the person who has provided guarantees for the commitments embodied in securities, or for the assessment of the rights afforded by such securities;
(c) the information is insignificant for the purposes of offering and it has no bearing concerning the assessment of the financial position of the issuer or the person who has provided guarantees for the commitments embodied in securities.[38]

47. Where information that is prescribed mandatory by law cannot be construed with respect to the issuer's scope of activities or the securities, the prospectus shall contain information that is similar and is able to reflect special characteristics of the issuer or the securities.[39]

E Reference

48. The prospectus may contain the necessary information by way of reference. Reference may only be made to documents that have been approved by or notified to the SFIC, and that have been published previously or simultaneously with the prospectus. Where any part of the information is incorporated in the prospectus by reference, a cross-reference list must be provided in order to enable investors to identify easily specific items of information.[40]

49. The executive summary shall not incorporate information by reference.[41]

[36] Art. 27 (2) of the Act on the Capital Market.
[37] Art. 27 (3) of the Act on the Capital Market.
[38] Art. 27 (7) of the Act on the Capital Market.
[39] Art. 27 (8) of the Act on the Capital Market.
[40] Art. 28 (1) of the Act on the Capital Market.
[41] Art. 28 (2) of the Act on the Capital Market.

2 Format

50. Detailed measures regarding the format and contents of prospectuses are not contained in the Prospectus Directive. Instead, the Commission Regulation (EC) No. 809/2004 (further: the 'Prospectus Regulation') approved by Member States in accordance with the terms of the Directive, prescribes in detail the information that will need to be contained in a prospectus. This includes the format of the documents.[42]

The Prospectus Regulation sets out different minimum disclosure requirements for different products being offered or admitted to trading, depending on the type of information needed by investors in each case.

3 Supplements

A Procedure rules

(i) Procedure initiated by the SFIC

51. If the SFIC learns about any material fact or circumstance between the time of authorisation for publication and the closing of the marketing procedure or the trading of securities in a regulated market that warrants any supplement to the prospectus or the abridged prospectus, the SFIC shall order them to be supplemented upon a hearing with the issuer and the broker/dealer.[43]

(ii) Supplement further to application by the issuer

52. The issuer, the offeror, the person requesting admission of the securities to trading on a regulated market and the broker/dealer must take immediate measures for supplementing the prospectus or abridged prospectus upon learning of any material fact or circumstance between the time of authorisation and the closing of the marketing procedure, or the commencement of trading of the securities in a regulated market that warrants any supplement to the prospectus or to the abridged prospectus.[44]

(iii) Assessment of the supplements

53. The publication of any supplement to the prospectus or the abridged prospectus shall be subject to authorisation by the SFIC. Authorisation of the publication of these supplements shall be subject to the provisions for the authorisation of publication of the prospectus, with the exception that the SFIC makes a decision concerning the application within seven business days.[45]

[42] Art. 25 and 26 of the Prospectus Regulation.
[43] Art. 32 (1) of the Act on the Capital Market.
[44] Art. 32 (2) of the Act on the Capital Market.
[45] Art. 32 (3) of the Act on the Capital Market.

54. The issuer and the broker/dealer shall promptly notify the public concerning the supplement of the prospectus as authorised by the SFIC under the provisions governing the publication of prospectuses.[46]

(iv) Possible suspension of the marketing procedure

55. In the above cases the SFIC may order the suspension of the marketing procedure until the supplement is published.[47]

B Liability in connection with suspension

(i) Right of withdrawal

56. If any supplement is added to the prospectus during the marketing procedure or prior to the commencement of trading in a regulated market, any investor who has entered into an agreement to subscribe or purchase securities before the supplement was made available to the public shall be entitled to withdraw his declaration of acceptance or to avoid the agreement.

57. The investor may exercise the right of avoidance within fifteen days from the date when the supplement was published. In the event of cancellation the issuer, the offeror, the person requesting admission of the securities to trading on a regulated market, and the broker/dealer shall be under joint and several liabilities to compensate the investor for all costs and damages sustained in connection with the subscription or purchase.

58. An allocation procedure may not be initiated for a period of fifteen days following the publication of the supplement.[48]

4 Language

A Securities offered only in Hungary

59. Where an applicant that has its registered office in Hungary or in a third country intends to offer securities to the public or to request admission to trading on a regulated market only in Hungary, the prospectus shall be prepared in a language approved by the SFIC.[49]

B Securities offered in Member States excluding Hungary

60. Where an offer to the public is made or admission to trading on a regulated market is sought in one or more Member States excluding Hungary, the prospectus shall be drawn up either in a language accepted by the competent supervisory authorities of those Member States or in a language customary in the sphere of international finance, at the choice of the applicant.[50]

[46] Art. 32 (4) of the Act on the Capital Market.
[47] Art. 32 (5) of the Act on the Capital Market.
[48] Art. 33 (1) of the Act on the Capital Market.
[49] Art. 43 (1) of the Act on the Capital Market.
[50] Art. 43 (2) of the Act on the Capital Market.

61. If, in the application of the above case, the applicant chooses a language that is considered customary in the sphere of international finance, an executive summary must be submitted to the SFIC translated into the language of the Member State concerned, if it is required according to the regulations in effect in that Member State.[51]

62. In connection with its proceedings referred to in points 59 and 60, above, the SFIC may prescribe that the prospectus shall also have to be drawn up in a language accepted by the SFIC or in a language customary in the sphere of international finance, at the choice of the applicant.[52]

C Securities offered in Hungary as well as in other Member States

63. Where an offer to the public is made or admission to trading on a regulated market is sought in Hungary and in any other Member States, the prospectus shall also have to be drawn up in a language accepted by the SFIC and either in a language accepted by the competent supervisory authority of that Member State or in a language customary in the sphere of international finance, at the choice of the applicant.[53]

D Other cases

64. Where an offer to the public is made in Hungary and the issuer draws up the prospectus in a language other than Hungarian, the executive summary must be prepared in Hungarian as well. If the issuer, the offeror, or the person requesting admission of the securities to trading on a regulated market publishes the prospectus in Hungary by authorisation of the competent supervisory authority of another Member State, the executive summary must be prepared in Hungarian as well.[54]

65. Where admission to trading on a regulated market is sought with respect to debt securities whose nominal value is at least €50,000, or its equivalent in any other currency translated by the official MNB exchange rate in effect on the day of placement, the prospectus shall be drawn up in a language accepted by all competent supervisory authorities concerned or in a language customary in the sphere of international finance. Where admission to trading on a regulated market is sought in Hungary and the prospectus is drawn up in a language other than Hungarian, the executive summary must be prepared and published in Hungarian as well.[55]

[51] Art. 43 (3) of the Act on the Capital Market.
[52] Art. 43 (4) of the Act on the Capital Market.
[53] Art. 43 (5) of the Act on the Capital Market.
[54] Art. 43 (6) of the Act on the Capital Market.
[55] Art. 43 (7) of the Act on the Capital Market.

V Publication and advertisements

1 Method of publication

A Rules of publication

66. With the consent of the SFIC, the prospectus shall be published before the opening of the placement procedure, or before the commencement of trading on a regulated market:

(a) in one or more of the following media:
  - in a daily newspaper of nationwide circulation; or
  - on the website of the issuer, and of the broker/dealer, if applicable; or
  - on the website of the regulated market where the securities in question are traded; or
  - on the SFIC's website, if the SFIC provides such service in compliance with the obligation of publication prescribed in the Act on the Capital Market.

or

(b) it shall be distributed free of charge at all sales locations, at the issuer's registered office or in the designated areas of a regulated market.[56]

67. If the issuer publishes the prospectus at all sales locations, or in a daily newspaper of nationwide circulation, the SFIC may order the issuer to display the prospectus also on its website.

68. With respect to the publication in a daily newspaper, the prospectus shall be published in all Member States where the securities are offered publicly, or presented for admission to trading on a regulated market, in at least one daily newspaper of broad circulation.[57]

69. Where a prospectus is published through electronic channels, the issuer, the offeror, the person requesting admission of the securities to trading on a regulated market, or the broker/dealer shall supply a printed version as well, free of charge, upon the investor's request. When published through electronic channels easy access to the prospectus must be ensured until the securities to which it pertains are in circulation.[58]

70. If the prospectus is comprised of separate documents, or it contains any reference, these documents and the information may be published separately. In this case each document shall contain an indication as to the place where the other documents or the entire prospectus is available for review.[59]

[56] Art. 34 (3) of the Act on the Capital Market.

[57] Art. 34 (6) of the Act on the Capital Market.

[58] Art. 34 (7) and (8) of the Act on the Capital Market.

[59] Art. 34 (9) of the Act on the Capital Market.

71. The prospectus and the amendments of the prospectus must be published as authorised by the SFIC in terms of content and form, inside the validity period of the prospectus.[60]

72. The SFIC shall display on its website the information it has received from the persons subject to the obligation of publication concerning their means of compliance with the obligation of publication.[61]

B Date of publication

73. Where a securities series is offered to the public at the time of issue and the duration of the marketing procedure is less than six business days, the prospectus shall be published at least six business days before the conclusion of the marketing procedure.[62]

2 Advertisement

74. Any type of document – other than a prospectus, abridged prospectus or a public announcement – relating to an offer to the public of securities published by the issuer, the offeror, an investment service provider functioning as broker/dealer or underwriting subscription guarantees, or by the person requesting admission of the securities to trading on a regulated market for the information of investors, shall be considered an advertisement.[63]

All documents specified above shall be clearly recognisable as advertisements.

75. The information contained in an advertisement shall not be inaccurate, or misleading. This information shall also be consistent with the information contained in the prospectus.[64]

76. Advertisements shall state that a prospectus relating to an offer to the public of securities has been or will be published and indicate where investors are or will be able to obtain it.[65]

77. The draft of all advertisements shall be submitted to the SFIC at least five business days before the conclusion of the marketing procedure or before the commencement of trading on a regulated market. The SFIC may ban the publication of the advertisement if it contains any information that is in conflict with the draft version submitted and approved for publication as well as any information that is misleading.[66]

[60] Art. 34 (10) of the Act on the Capital Market.
[61] Art. 34 (11) of the Act on the Capital Market.
[62] Art. 34 (2) of the Act on the Capital Market.
[63] Art. 35 (1) of the Act on the Capital Market.
[64] Art. 35 (3) of the Act on the Capital Market.
[65] Art. 35 (4) of the Act on the Capital Market.
[66] Art. 35 (5) of the Act on the Capital Market.

78. The SFIC's failure to respond within five business days following submission of the advertisement shall be construed as approval for publication under the legal provisions governing the powers and jurisdiction of the SFIC.[67]

VI Use of the prospectus approved in other (non-EU) countries

1 A prospectus already authorised in other Member States

79. An issuer that has a registered office in Hungary may submit the prospectus or abridged prospectus for authorisation to the competent supervisory authority of another Member State of the European Union, if:

(i) it pertains to debt securities with a nominal value of at least €1,000 or its equivalent in any other currency translated by the official (National Bank of Hungary) exchange rate in effect on the day of placement; or

(ii) it pertains to debt securities giving the right to acquire any securities or money as a consequence of their being converted or the rights conferred by them being exercised, provided that the issuer of these securities and the issuer of the securities to be obtained is not the same, or that the issuers do not belong to the same group of companies.[68]

80. Within the meaning of the above rule, the issuer, the offeror or the person requesting admission of the securities to trading on a regulated market may file for authorisation for the publication of a prospectus or abridged prospectus in the Member State in which the securities are planned to be offered to the public, or in which their admission to trading on a regulated market is requested.[69]

2 Referring the application to the competent authority of another Member State

81. The SFIC may forward an application for authorisation to the competent supervisory authority of another Member State subject to approval by the competent supervisory authority of that other Member State. The SFIC shall inform the applicant concerning the transfer of his application for authorisation within three business days following the date of its decision.[70]

82. The SFIC may authorise publication of a prospectus or abridged prospectus upon an application submitted to the competent supervisory authority of another Member State when requested by the competent supervisory authority of that other Member State. The time limit for adopting a

[67] Art. 35 (6) of the Act on the Capital Market.
[68] Art. 36 (3) of the Act on the Capital Market.
[69] Art. 36 (4) of the Act on the Capital Market.
[70] Art. 39 (1) of the Act on the Capital Market.

decision for the granting or refusal of the authorisation shall commence on the day when the competent supervisory authority of the other Member State notifies the applicant concerning the transfer of his application.[71]

3 Official certificate by the SFIC

83. The SFIC shall provide an official certificate at the request of the applicant to the competent supervisory authority of another Member State to verify that the prospectus or abridged prospectus has been authorised under this Act for publication within the preceding twelve months and is in compliance with the regulations of the European Union. Together with the official certificate the SFIC shall also send to the competent supervisory authority of the other Member State the prospectus and – if required by the regulations of that Member State – the executive summary the applicant has submitted translated into another language.[72]

84. If the SFIC has authorised leaving out any information from the prospectus, this shall be indicated – including the reasons – in the official certificate.[73]

85. The SFIC shall send the official certificate to the competent supervisory authority of another Member State within three business days from the date of receipt of the request, or if the request was submitted together with the application for authorisation of the prospectus for publication, on the business day that follows the date of authorisation of the prospectus for publication.[74]

VII Sanctions

1 Authority measures

86. If the SFIC finds that an issuer or broker/dealer that is established in another Member State is in violation of the regulations on public offering, or that the issuer of securities that has been admitted to trading on a regulated market in Hungary has breached the obligations relating to keeping the securities in circulation, it shall notify the competent supervisory authority of the Member State where the issuer is established.[75]

87. If the issuer or broker/dealer fails to terminate its unlawful conduct in spite of or in the absence of, any measures taken by the competent supervisory authority of the Member State where the issuer is established upon the notice above, the SFIC shall take the measures necessary for the protection

[71] Art. 39 (2) of the Act on the Capital Market.
[72] Art. 40 (1) of the Act on the Capital Market.
[73] Art. 40 (2) of the Act on the Capital Market.
[74] Art. 40 (3) of the Act on the Capital Market.
[75] Art. 399 (3) of the Act on the Capital Market.

of investors. The SFIC shall notify the competent supervisory authority of the other Member State prior to taking the measures. The SFIC shall notify the European Commission concerning the measures taken.[76]

88. The SFIC shall assess and weigh the data and information available and shall take measures and/or impose sanctions consistent with the gravity of the violation, breach or negligence in relation

(i) to the operation of the institution in question;
(ii) to the clients of the institution; or
(iii) to the operation of the capital markets.[77]

89. The SFIC shall have powers to take the following measures and/or to impose the following sanctions in connection with the obligation of prospectus publication: (i) impose fines in the cases and in the measure prescribed by law;[78] (ii) suspend the offering and subscription of securities and the trading of investment instruments;[79] (iii) initiate procedures with other competent authorities;[80] (iv) if before the closing of the marketing procedure the SFIC learns about any material fact or circumstance, based on which authorisation for the publication of the prospectus should have been rejected or that is of significant injury to the investors' interests, the SFIC shall withdraw its authorisation granted for the publication of the prospectus and shall compel the issuer and the broker/dealer to terminate the marketing procedure within the prescribed deadline;[81] (v) in the event of any failure to comply with the obligation of public disclosure as prescribed in the Act on the Capital Market, the SFIC shall publish the information to which the failure pertains in accordance with Section 40 at the expense of the defaulting party.[82]

If there is a lawsuit filed for the review of the SFIC's decision defined in point (v) above, the court shall rule on the case in an expedited proceeding. The hearing shall be scheduled on or before the eight days following the date on which charges are filed at the court, if no other action is required.[83]

90. If the offering of the securities contained therein took place in violation of law, and there is reasonable cause to retain such securities on the account in order to prevent any injury to third parties a further sanction may be that the SFIC restrict access to the account.[84]

[76] Art. 399 (4) of the Act on the Capital Market.
[77] Art. 399 (5) of the Act on the Capital Market.
[78] Art. 400 (1) *point m)* of the Act on the Capital Market.
[79] Art. 400 (1) *point n)* of the Act on the Capital Market.
[80] Art. 400 (1) *point p)* of the Act on the Capital Market.
[81] Art. 400 (1) *point v)* of the Act on the Capital Market.
[82] Art. 400 (1) *point w)* of the Act on the Capital Market.
[83] Art. 400 (2) of the Act on the Capital Market.
[84] Art. 400 (5) *point a)* of the Act on the Capital Market.

2 Supervision fines

91. Among other issuers, investment service providers shall be subject to a fine imposed by the SFIC for any violation, circumvention, evasion, non-fulfilment or late fulfilment of the obligations set out in the Act on the Capital Market and in legal regulations enacted under its authorisation.[85]

92. The amount of a fine shall be determined according to the gravity of non-compliance with the requirements laid down in the Act on the Capital Market, in specific other legislation and/or in the SFIC resolutions, or to the weight of negligence and the financial advantage received.[86]

93. The amount of the fine shall be between HUF 200,000 and 10 million (approx. €780–38,500) for any breach of, negligence or partial compliance with the obligations relating to public offerings and prospectuses.[87]

VIII Prospectus liability

94. The issuer and the broker/dealer (or the broker/dealer acting as the syndicate leader where applicable), the person who has provided guarantees for the commitments embodied in securities, the offeror or the person requesting admission of the securities for trading on a regulated market, shall be subject to joint and several liability for any and all damage caused to an investor by supplying misleading information or by concealing material information in connection with the offering of securities. The prospectus shall contain precise information concerning the person who/that is held liable for the contents of the prospectus or any part of it, including the name and address of this person and his role in the offering procedure. The liability of any person shall cover all information contained in the prospectus, as well as the lack of any necessary information.[88]

95. A signed declaration of liability shall be annexed to the prospectus by all persons held liable above. The declaration shall stipulate that all data and information in the prospectus are true and correct, and that it contains all information necessary for investors to make an informed assessment of the issuer or the person who has provided guarantees for the commitments embodied in securities and the securities to which it pertains.[89]

96. No civil liability shall attach to any person solely on the basis of the executive summary, including the translation thereof into any language,

[85] Art. 405 (1) of the Act on the Capital Market.
[86] Art. 406 (1) of the Act on the Capital Market.
[87] Art. 406 (2) of the Act on the Capital Market.
[88] Art. 29 (1) of the Act on the Capital Market.
[89] Art. 29 (2) of the Act on the Capital Market.

unless it is misleading, inaccurate or inconsistent when read together with the other parts of the prospectus.

97. The person referred to above shall be subject to the liability defined under Section 29 of the Act on the Capital Market for five years from the publication of the public announcement to which it pertains. This liability cannot be validly excluded or limited.[90]

IX Rules applicable to transactions and securities not subject to the Directive and the Regulation

98. Article 1(2) of the Prospectus Directive lists the securities which are not subject to it. However, the Act on the Capital Market sets out special rules in connection with some securities that are not covered by the Prospectus Directive. These are the (i) securities of international financial institutions; (ii) securities of credit institutions; (iii) securities of local governments.

99. In connection with the offering of debt securities to the public or their admission to trading on a regulated market by the international financial institutions referred to in Schedule No. 1 to the Act on the Capital Market, or by any public international bodies of which one or more Member States are members, if they are offered or admitted to trading on a regulated market only in Hungary, instead of the prospectus a public offer prospectus approved by the SFIC may be published.[91]

100. In connection with the offering of debt securities issued by credit institutions to the public or their admission to trading on a regulated market, if they are offered or admitted to trading on a regulated market only in Hungary, the same rule may be used as above, i.e. instead of a prospectus a public offer prospectus may be published:

(a) in the case of similar securities offered within the framework of an issue programme, if these securities:
  - are not subordinated, convertible or exchangeable;
  - do not give a right to subscribe to or acquire other types of securities and are not linked to a derivative instrument;
  - constitute reception of repayable deposits; and
  - are covered by a deposit guarantee scheme of the National Deposit Insurance Fund.

(b) in the case of similar securities offered within the framework of an issue programme, if the issue price of all securities offered remains below €50 million within a twelve-month period following the initial offering, or its equivalent in another currency as translated by the

[90] Art. 29 (3) of the Act on the Capital Market.
[91] Art. 45 (1) of the Act on the Capital Market.

official National Bank exchange rate in effect on the day when the decision for offering has been adopted, and these securities:

- are not subordinated, convertible or exchangeable;
- do not give a right to subscribe to or acquire other types of securities and that they are not linked to a derivative instrument.[92]

The public offer prospectus shall remain in effect for twelve months from the date of the SFIC's approval.[93]

101. In connection with the offering of debt securities issued by a local government or by the regional or local authorities of any Member State of the European Union or securities guaranteed by a local government or by the regional or local authorities of any Member State of the European Union to the public or their admission to trading on a regulated market, if they are offered or admitted to trading on a regulated market only in Hungary, instead of the prospectus the issuer may draw up a special prospectus; a template thereof is annexed to the Act on the Capital Market.[94]

X Conclusion

102. The Prospectus Directive creates a new and flexible system for the authorisation of prospectuses in the European Union. Hungary has modified its capital market regulations in order to fulfil the requirements of the European Union. The new 'passport system' was available from 1 July 2005. The benefit to Hungarian issuers wishing to raise capital using this 'passporting' facility is significant.

[92] Art. 45 (2) of the Act on the Capital Market.
[93] Art. 45 (3) of the Act on the Capital Market.
[94] Art. 46 of the Act on the Capital Market.

8

Latvia

DACE SILAVA-TOMSONE, TOMS SULMANIS AND AIGARS GOZITIS
Lejinś, Torgāns & Partners

I Introduction

1. The financial law of the Republic of Latvia (hereinafter 'Latvia') consists of a number of laws, regulations and instructions, most of which are

adopted by the Financial and Capital Market Commission, the Latvian Central Depository and the market makers.

All laws applicable to the securities market in Latvia may be divided into the following categories:

(i) laws (adopted by the Parliament) and regulations (adopted by the Cabinet of Ministers);
(ii) regulations adopted by the Financial and Capital Market Commission ('Commission');
(iii) rules, instructions adopted by the Riga Stock Exchange (hereinafter 'RSE') and Latvian Central Depository (hereinafter 'LCD').

The main body of legislation governing the securities market is the Financial Instruments Market Law, adopted on 20 November 2003, effective as of 1 January 2004 (hereinafter 'Financial Instruments Law'). It is a comparatively new law, which replaces and supplements the old Law on Securities; however, since its adoption it has been amended five times. The Financial Instruments Law complies to a large extent with the requirements of the European Union financial services legislation, of which the most important are requirements for the financial instruments to be listed in the Main List and information to be disclosed thereto; requirements for the prospectuses regarding the public offer of transferable securities; requirements for the use of inside information and prohibition of market manipulations.

Participants in the financial instruments market in Latvia are credit institutions providing investment services or ancillary (non-core) investment services, investment brokerage firms, issuers, investors, companies that pursuant to law are entitled to manage collective investment undertakings, market makers, the Latvian Central Depository and other persons who engage in the activities governed by the Financial Instruments Law.[1]

The Financial Instruments Law governs the procedure by which financial instruments are publicly offered and circulated, investment services and ancillary (non-core) investment services provided, and participants in the financial instruments market licensed and supervised, and establishes the rights and obligations of participants in the financial instrument market.

The Financial Instruments Law regulates the public circulation of only those financial instruments included in the regulated market.

The Law on Investment Management Companies, adopted 18 December 1997, effective as of 1 July 1998, provides that the main activity of investment management companies is investment fund management; in addition this Law sets forth requirements under which the investment man-

[1] Financial Instruments Market Law, adopted on 20 November 2003, effective as of 1 January 2004, Art. 1

agement companies may perform individual management of investors' financial instruments in accordance with the investor's authorisation; and may provide consultation on investments in financial instruments.

The Investor Protection Law, adopted 8 November 2001, effective as of 1 January 2002, established a mandatory investor protection scheme concerning compensation of investors who have invested in financial instruments.

The Law on the Prevention of Laundering of Proceeds Derived from Criminal Activities, adopted 18 December 1997, effective as of 1 June 1998, determines the duties and rights of the persons referred to in this Law, and their supervisory and control authorities, regarding the prevention of laundering proceeds from crime.

Apart from specific provisions established in the Financial Instruments Law, in relation to corporate and shareholder matters, brokerage companies and credit institutions are governed by the Commercial Law, adopted 13 April 2000, effective as of 1 January 2002, and the Group of Companies Law, adopted 23 March 2000, effective as of 27 April 2000.

A separate law regulates the issuance of mortgage bonds, the Law on Mortgage Bonds, adopted 10 September 1998, effective as of 13 October 1998. The issue and circulation of mortgage bonds is regulated by this law and the Financial Instruments Law.

Brokerage companies and credit institutions that provide investment services in respect of the financial instruments admitted to trading on the regulated market shall comply with the regulations of the respective person organising the market; and brokerage companies and credit institutions that provide investment services in respect of the financial instruments registered with the LCD shall comply with the regulations of the LCD.

RSE, the only market maker in Latvia, adopts rules on requirements set forth for the issuers and financial instruments being listed at the RSE, as well as rules of trading. The rules and instructions of the LCD provide provisions on keeping, registering, clearing and settlement of financial instruments in Latvia.

One of the most relevant regulatory enactments as regards the preparation and issuing of prospectuses is RSE Rules on Listing and Trading of Financial Instruments on the Markets Regulated by the Exchange, approved by the RSE Management Board meeting on 18 May 2007 (hereinafter 'RSE Rules').

II Competent authority

1 Financial and Capital Market Commission

2. The Financial and Capital Market Commission was established and operates according to the Law on Financial and Capital Market Commission, adopted 1 June 2000, effective as of 1 July 2001.

The target of the Commission's activities is to protect the interests of investors, depositors and the insured, and to promote the development and stability of the financial and capital market, i.e. the Commission is the supervisor of the financial market. The Commission has authority:

(i) to issue regulations and directives, governing activities of financial and capital market participants;
(ii) to request and receive information necessary for the execution of its functions from financial and capital market participants;
(iii) to, in cases stipulated under the regulations, set forth restrictions on the activities of financial and capital market participants;
(iv) to examine compliance of the activities of financial and capital market participants with the legislation, and regulations and directives of the Commission;
(v) to apply sanctions set forth by the regulatory requirement to financial and capital market participants and their officials, if the said requirements are violated;
(vi) to participate in the general meeting of financial and capital market participants, to initiate meetings of financial and capital market participants' management bodies, specify items for their agenda, and participate therein;
(vii) to request and receive, from the Commercial Register and other public institutions, any information required for execution of its functions free of charge;
(viii) to cooperate with foreign financial and capital market supervision authorities and, by mutual consent, exchange information necessary to execute its functions set forth by law.[2]

2 Riga Stock Exchange (RSE)

3. The RSE is the sole market maker in Latvia. According to the Financial Instruments Law, one of the market maker's functions is to supervise the issuers of financial instruments admitted to trading on the market maker's regulated markets. Thus the RSE is also a supervisor.

3 Latvian Central Depository (LCD)

4. The LCD is a company that makes book entries of and accounts for the financial instruments that are in public circulation in the Republic of Latvia, and ensures the settlement of financial instruments and cash in transactions in financial instruments on the regulated market, as well as

[2] Law on the Financial and Capital Market Commission, adopted on June 1 2000, in effect as of July 1 2001, Art. 7.

the settlement of financial instruments among custodians.[3] According to the Financial Instruments Law, one of the LCD's functions is to control the activities of the market participants in relation to rules and regulations adopted by the LCD.

III Procedures of prior approval and appeal

1 Public offer

5. According to the Financial Instruments Law a public offer may be made only after the Commission's permission to make a public offer has been received and a prospectus has been published in compliance with the requirements of the said law.[4]

An initial public offer (hereinafter 'public offer') means the provision of information by the means of any intermediary regarding the conditions of an offer and the offered transferable securities that allows investors to make a decision on either purchasing or underwriting the securities.[5]

6. To receive permission to make a public offer, an issuer or a person making the public offer shall submit an application to the Commission together with two originals of the issue prospectus (prepared in accordance with the Financial Instruments Law and the Prospectus Regulation) and the text of the issue prospectus in an electronic form; and the decision of the issuer on the issue of transferable securities and the public offer if the person that makes a public offer is a legal entity.[6]

The following information shall be provided by an issuer in the application:

(i) issuer's registration number, place and institution, name, legal address, phone number, as well as fax number and email address (if such exists);
(ii) the type of transferable securities, category, total number and the par value of a single transferable security;
(iii) anticipated trade or distribution date;
(iv) countries in which an issuer or a person making a public offer intends to offer transferable securities to the public.

[3] Financial Instruments Market Law, adopted on 20 November 2003, effective as of 1 January 2004, Art. 1.
[4] Financial Instruments Market Law, adopted on 20 November 2003, effective as of 1 January 2004, Art. 14 (1).
[5] Financial Instruments Market Law, adopted on 20 November 2003, effective as of 1 January 2004, Art. 139.
[6] Financial Instruments Market Law, adopted on 20 November 2003, effective as of 1 January 2004, Art. 14(2).

7. The Commission shall review the application and the accompanying documents and take a decision on granting or refusing permission to make a public offer within ten working days of the receipt of the documents required by regulatory provisions, and prepared and formatted in compliance with the requirements of regulatory provisions.[7]

If the Commission finds, on reasonable grounds, that the documents submitted to it are incomplete or that supplementary information is needed, it shall notify the issuer within ten working days of the submission of the application. The time limits referred to above shall apply only from the date on which such information is provided by the issuer or person asking to make a public offer.

The time limits referred to above can be extended to twenty working days by the Commission if the public offer involves securities issued by an issuer who does not have any securities admitted to trading on a regulated market and who has not previously offered securities to the public.

If the Commission fails to give a decision on the prospectus within the limits laid down in the Financial Instruments Law, this shall not constitute the right to make a public offer for an issuer or a person asking to make a public offer. In this case the Commission shall send to an issuer or a person asking to make a public offer an explanation about the suspension of the application, indicating when the decision to allow a public offer or refusal thereof will be taken.

The Commission shall decide to refuse permission where the submitted documents contain information that fails to comply with the requirements set out in the law and other regulatory provisions; and provide reasons regarding the failure to comply with the requirements set out in regulatory provisions.

Upon deciding to grant permission to make a public offer, the prospectus is considered to be registered with the Commission. The Commission posts the text of the decision and of the issue prospectus on its website.[8]

2 Admission to trading

8. The Financial Instruments Law provides that the requirements for the admission of financial instruments to trading on regulated markets shall be established by the respective market maker. The decision on admitting financial instruments to trading on regulated markets is taken by the management board of a market maker on the basis of an issuer's application.[9]

[7] Financial Instruments Market Law, adopted on 20 November 2003, effective as of 1 January 2004, Art. 14(4), (5).

[8] Financial Instruments Market Law, adopted on 20 November 2003, effective as of 1 January 2004, Art. 14.

[9] Financial Instruments Market Law, adopted on 20 November 2003, effective as of 1 January 2004, Art. 41(5), (6).

The issuer submits the application for the admission of financial instruments to trading on the regulated market to a market maker not later than three months from the registration of the prospectus with the Commission. Within ten days from the date of receipt of the issuer's application the market maker makes a decision on admitting financial instruments to trading on the regulated market.[10]

RSE, the only market maker in Latvia, adopts rules on requirements set forth for the issuers and financial instruments being listed at the RSE, as well as rules of trading. RSE Rules set additional requirements that a potential issuer or person making a public offer shall comply with.

Financial instruments may be listed and traded on the following RSE lists:

(i) Main list;
(ii) Second list;
(iii) Debt securities list;
(iv) Investment fund list.

Listing is the inclusion of financial instruments on the RSE list and trading with them. The listing procedure starts as of the moment when the issuer has submitted to the RSE an application for the listing and trading of the financial instruments issued by it (hereinafter 'listing application').[11]

9. The RSE Management Board is also entitled to take conditional listing decisions. Namely, if on the moment of submitting the listing application, the issuer applying for listing, or the financial instruments issued by it, do not conform to the provisions of the RSE Rules but the RSE Management Board considers that the issuer and the financial instruments issued by it will conform to the requirements for the issuers and financial instruments set forth in the RSE Rules after the primary placement, public offering or other activities that will be carried out after passing the listing decision, before the term set in RSE Rules. In this resolution the RSE shall determine the conditions to be met by the issuer, as well as the term for the fulfilment of these conditions.[12]

In addition to the above requirements, the issuer has to enter into the listing agreement with RSE within five trading days as from the adoption of the listing decision, but no later than three trading days prior to the listing

[10] Financial Instruments Market Law, adopted on 20 November 2003, effective as of 1 January 2004, Art. 50(2).

[11] RSE Rules on Listing and Trading of Financial Instruments on the Markets Regulated by the Exchange, approved by the RSE Supervisory Board meeting on 18 May 2007, Art. 9.1.2.

[12] RSE Rules on Listing and Trading of Financial Instruments on the Markets Regulated by the Exchange, approved by the RSE Supervisory Board meeting on 18 May 2007, Art. 10.2.

date. The agreement shall determine the obligation of the issuer to comply with the RSE Rules. The RSE shall not commence trading with the financial instruments of the issuer until the listing agreement is entered into.

10. The RSE Rules set forth different requirements as to the amount and type of information to be submitted, depending upon the type of financial instruments the issuer intends to trade and, subsequently, on which trading list. As an insight, the following information is required to be submitted to the RSE if the issuer intends to trade shares on the RSE main list:

(i) a copy of the issuer's registration certificate or similar document which certifies the legal status of the issuer (the fact of registration), certified by a public notary and information about the resolutions of the managing institutions of the issuer that have been adopted before submitting the listing application, but not yet registered with the Commercial Register;
(ii) a copy of the Articles of Association/Charter of the issuer, certified by a public notary;
(iii) the issuer's management;
(iv) a copy of the issuer's shareholders' meeting resolution on amendments to the Articles of Association/Charter and increasing of share capital (not yet registered with the Commercial Registry), as well as a copy of the proposal for the amendments to the Articles of Association/Charter approved by the management board of the issuer;
(v) copies of annual reports certified by a certified auditor (also in electronic form) for the last three years;
(vi) issue prospectus or an equivalent document, also in electronic form, that has been drawn up and registered in compliance with the provisions of the Financial Instruments Law;
(vii) if an agreement with an RSE member on market making for the financial instruments of the issuer has been concluded, the information about the conclusion of the agreement and description of the main provisions of the agreement;
(viii) the resolution of the managing institution authorised by the issuer on submitting the listing application;
(ix) statement about conformity of the issuer and its financial instruments to the requirements set forth in the RSE rules for listing.[13]

[13] RSE Rules on Listing and Trading of Financial Instruments on the Markets Regulated by the Exchange, approved by the RSE Management Board meeting on 18 May 2007, Art. 9.3.1.

On individual occasions the RSE management board shall have the right to resolve that some of the documents referred to above and to be appended to the listing application shall not be required to pass the listing decision.

There are also other general requirements set forth in relation to the issuer. Thus, the issuer which wants to have the financial instruments issued by it listed on an RSE list has to be registered and acting in compliance with the regulatory enactments of the country of registration:

(i) the issuers economic activity, including legal and economic standing, has to be such that does not threaten the interests of the investors;
(ii) the issuer's Articles of Association (Charter) shall conform to the regulatory enactments regulating the activities of the issuer. The issuer shall ensure that the Articles of Association (Charter) are publicly accessible at the issuer's Office and on the website of the issuer, if applicable.[14]

The RSE has the right not to include in the list financial instruments of an issuer against which insolvency or bankruptcy procedures have been initiated during the two years before submitting the listing application, or which has had regular insolvency problems during the said period.

There are specific requirements for financial instruments determined in the RSE Rules:

(i) only freely transferable financial instruments may be listed on the RSE lists and the transfer right of the financial instruments may not be restricted by the Articles of Association/Charter of the issuer;
(ii) the financial instruments registered for listing shall be book-entered with the LCD or another foreign central depository with which the RSE and/or the LCD has entered into agreement on cooperation in provision of settlement;
(iii) only dematerialised financial instruments may be registered for listing;
(iv) the financial instruments registered for listing have to conform to the provisions of the regulatory enactments applied to them and they have to be issued in compliance with the provisions of the said regulatory enactments, Articles of Association/Charter of the issuer or other documents regulating the activity of the issuer.

[14] RSE Rules on Listing and Trading of Financial Instruments on the Markets Regulated by the Exchange, approved by the RSE Management Board meeting on 18 May 2007, Art. 4.1.

11. The RSE Management Board shall pass a listing decision or refusal of listing within ten days of the issuer submitting the listing application and the documents set forth in RSE Rules. If the RSE Management Board requires additional information from the issuer, the examination term of the listing application shall be counted from the moment of disclosing the required information to the RSE.

The RSE, after the RSE Management Board has passed the listing decision, shall send, without delay, written notification of the adopted decision to the issuer, the Commission and the LCD. In addition, the RSE will publish the decision, without delay, on the RSE website.

3 Exemptions

12. There are also exemptions to the obligation to draw up a prospectus set forth in the Financial Instruments Law, i.e. it is not required to draw up prospectus if the following transferable securities are issued:

(i) shares issued in substitution for shares of the same class already issued, if the issuing of such new shares does not involve any increase in the issued capital;
(ii) securities offered in connection with a takeover of the company by means of an exchange offer, provided that a document is available containing information which is regarded by the Commission as being equivalent to that of the prospectus, taking into account the requirements of Community legislation;
(iii) securities offered, allotted or to be allotted in connection with a merger, provided that a document is available containing information which is regarded by the Commission as being equivalent to that of the prospectus, taking into account the requirements of Community legislation;
(iv) shares offered, allotted or to be allotted free of charge to existing shareholders, and dividends paid out in the form of shares of the same class as the shares in respect of which such dividends are paid, provided that a document is made available containing information on the number and nature of the shares and the reasons for and details of the offer;
(v) securities offered, allotted or to be allotted to existing or former directors or employees by their employer which has securities already admitted to trading on a regulated market or by an affiliated undertaking, provided that a document is made available containing information on the number and nature of the securities and the reasons for and details of the offer.

In addition, the offer is not considered to be public and the requirement to draw up a prospectus is not applicable in cases of:

(i) an offer addressed solely to qualified investors; and/or
(ii) an offer addressed to fewer than 100 natural or legal persons per Member State, other than qualified investors; and/or
(iii) an offer of transferable securities addressed to investors who acquire securities for a total consideration of at least €50,000 per investor, for each separate offer; and/or
(iv) an offer of transferable securities whose denomination per unit amounts to at least €50,000; and/or
(v) an offer of transferable securities with a total consideration of less than €100,000, which limit shall be calculated over a period of twelve months.[15]

4 Appeal of the listing decision

13. If the Commission has taken the decision not to grant permission for an issuer to make a public offer, its decision can be challenged in line with the regulatory enactments in force in Latvia. The Financial Instruments Law states that an administrative act issued by the Commission, or an actual action of the Commission may be disputed in accordance with general legal provisions regulating the administrative process, unless otherwise provided for by law.

Where the Commission examines documents repeatedly, it is not entitled to point out deficiencies or inaccuracies in the information already examined if these deficiencies or inaccuracies were not pointed out in previous examinations, except in cases where the Commission learns new information.

Appeal in court of an administrative act issued by the Commission shall not suspend the execution of the act, where the administrative act issued by the Commission is a decision on one of the following issues:

(i) restriction of the right of an investment brokerage company or a credit institution to provide investment services or to hold financial instruments;
(ii) cancelling licences issued to an investment brokerage company for the provision of investment services and non-core investment services;
(iii) cancelling a licence for organising a regulated market;
(iv) suspension of trade in financial instruments;
(v) request that any influence of persons having acquired a qualifying holding in a regulated market maker, the Latvian Central Depository or an investment brokerage company is immediately terminated;

[15] Financial Instruments Market Law, adopted on 20 November 2003, effective as of 1 January 2004, Art. 16.

(vi) request for the recall of a member of a board of directors or council of the regulated market maker, the Latvian Central Depository or investment brokerage company; and
(vii) prohibition of the exercising of voting rights.[16]

14. According to the Administrative Procedure Law (Article 79 (1)), the decision of the Commission can be disputed within a one-month period from the day it comes into effect, but if the administrative act does not indicate where and within what time period it may be disputed, within a one-year period from the day it comes into effect.

The RSE Rules provide the procedure on how its decisions can be appealed. There are two possible dispute resolution patterns. One relates to matters that also fall within the competence of the Commission; the other is purely subject to the legal relationships of the RSE and its participants.

In the former case, the decision of the RSE can be further challenged in the Commission, whereas in the latter case the appeal of the respective decision can be made in accordance with the dispute resolution procedure established in the RSE Rules.

If the RSE Management Board has passed the decision to refuse the listing, the issuer shall have the right to appeal the decision of the RSE Management Board to the Commission within thirty days of the issuer receiving the respective resolution.

If the RSE Management Board has rejected the delisting application, or has decided on delisting upon its own initiative, the issuer or the asset management company may appeal such decision to the Commission within thirty days of receiving the decision.[17]

15. All other disputes arising between the RSE and the issuers, and between the issuers and investors, which may not be solved by settlement between the parties, shall be examined by the Arbitration Court of the Latvian Chamber of Commerce and Industry in compliance with the rules of the Arbitration Court, or by the Commission in compliance with the provisions of the Law.

The issuers shall have the right to dispute the resolutions adopted by the RSE Management Board within thirty days of the adoption of the resolution.[18]

[16] Financial Instruments Market Law, adopted on 20 November 2003, effective as of 1 January 2004, Art. 4(4).

[17] RSE Rules on Listing and Trading of Financial Instruments on the Markets Regulated by the Exchange, approved by the RSE Supervisory Board meeting on 18 May 2007, Art. 10.6, Art. 12.5.

[18] RSE Rules on Listing and Trading of Financial Instruments on the Markets Regulated by the Exchange, approved by the RSE Management Board meeting on 18 May 2007, Art. 33.

IV Content and format, language and supplements of the prospectus

1 Content

16. The requirements for the preparation of prospectuses are provided in the Financial Instruments Law, RSE Rules and other applicable regulatory enactments.

The Financial Instruments Law requires that the prospectus shall contain in an easily analysable and comprehensible form all information which, according to the particular nature of the issuer and of the transferable securities that will be subject to the public offer on a regulated market, is necessary to enable investors to make an informed assessment of the assets and liabilities, financial position, profits and losses, and prospects of the issuer and of any guarantor, and of the rights attaching to securities.

17. The prospectus can, at the choice of the issuer or person asking for the admission to a regulated market, be prepared as a single document or several separate documents. If the prospectus is drawn up as several separate documents, each of the separate documents shall be registered with the Commission and accompanied by the summary.

A prospectus composed of several separate documents shall divide the required information into:

(i) The registration document where the information relating to the issuer is contained;
(ii) The securities note where the information concerning the securities offered to the public is contained;
(iii) The summary that, in a brief manner and in non-technical language, conveys the essential characteristics and risks associated with the issuer, any guarantor (if one exists) and the securities, in the language in which the prospectus was originally drawn up. The summary shall also contain a warning that:
  - it should be read as an introduction to the prospectus;
  - any decision to invest in the securities should be based on consideration of the prospectus as a whole by the investor;
  - where a claim relating to the information contained in a prospectus is brought before a court, the plaintiff investor might, under the national legislation of the Member States, have to bear the costs of translating the prospectus before the legal proceedings are initiated; and
  - civil liability attaches to those persons who have provided the summary, including any translation thereof, and applied for its notification, but only if the summary is misleading, inaccurate

or inconsistent when read together with the other parts of the prospectus.

The detailed information as to the information to be included in the prospectus and the contents of the prospectus shall be determined in line with the Prospectus Regulation.

If the information to be included in the prospectus in accordance with the Prospectus Regulation does not correspond to the issuer's type of activity, legal form or transferable securities that will be offered to the public, then the information of equivalent nature should be included in the prospectus. If there is no such information of equivalent nature, then no information at all should be included in the prospectus.[19]

2 Format

18. There are two institutions where an issuer has to submit required documentation, i.e. the Commission and the RSE. Both institutions ask to submit needed documentation in both paper and electronic form. The Commission requires submission of an application to the Commission, together with two originals of the issue prospectus, drawn up in accordance with the Prospectus Regulation and the text of the issue prospectus in an electronic form.[20] The RSE sets forth the obligation to disclose to the RSE the electronic version in compliance with the procedure determined by the RSE.[21]

3 Supplements

19. The Financial Instruments Law states that each significant new factor, material mistake or inaccuracy relating to the information included in the prospectus, which is capable of affecting the assessment of the securities and which arises or is noted between the time when the prospectus is approved and the final closing of the offer of transferable securities to the public, shall be supplemented with updates prepared by the issuer or the person who asked to include transferable securities in a regulated market.

An issuer or a person asking to include transferable securities in a regulated market shall submit to the Commission the supplements of the prospectus, which in turn shall register them within seven days following

[19] Financial Instruments Market Law, adopted on 20 November 2003, effective as of 1 January 2004, Art. 17.

[20] Financial Instruments Market Law, adopted on 20 November 2003, effective as of 1 January 2004, Art. 14.

[21] RSE Rules on Listing and Trading of Financial Instruments on the Markets Regulated by the Exchange, approved by the RSE Management Board meeting on 18 May 2007, Art. 9.1.

the receipt of all required documents. An issuer or a person asking to include transferable securities in a regulated market shall also supplement the summary and its translation if it is required to take into account new information that is included in the supplements.

Such a supplement shall be approved in the same way in a maximum of seven working days and published in accordance with at least the same arrangements as were applied when the original prospectus was published.

Investors who have already agreed to purchase or subscribe for the securities before the supplement is published have the right, exercisable within two working days from the publication of the supplement, to withdraw their acceptances.[22]

4 Language

20. If the admission of transferable securities is requested in a regulated market of Latvia, the prospectus shall be drawn up in the official (Latvian) language.

If the inclusion of transferable securities will be asked in a regulated market of one or more EU Member States excluding Latvia, an issuer or a person asking the admission of transferable securities in a regulated market shall draw up the prospectus either in a language accepted by the Commission and competent authorities of those Member States, or in a language customary in the sphere of international finance.

If an issuer or a person making a public offer from another Member State asks to admit transferable securities on a regulated market of Latvia, the summary of the prospectus shall be drawn up in the official (Latvian) language.

If the admission of transferable securities is requested in a regulated market of one or more EU Member States, including Latvia, the prospectus shall be drawn up in the official (Latvian) language and made available either in a language accepted by the competent authorities of each host Member State, or in a language customary in the sphere of international finance.

If the admission of transferable securities is requested in a regulated market of one or more EU Member States in respect to transferable securities that are non-equity securities and whose denomination per unit amounts to at least €50,000, the prospectus shall be drawn up either in a language accepted by the Commission and host Member States or in a language customary in the sphere of international finance.[23]

21. There are also requirements as to the use of language determined by the RSE. It is provided that when drawing up notifications and other

[22] Financial Instruments Market Law, adopted on 20 November 2003, effective as of 1 January 2004, Art. 45.

[23] Financial Instruments Market Law, adopted on 20 November 2003, effective as of 1 January 2004, Art. 49^1.

information to be provided and disclosed to the RSE, the issuer shall conform to the following requirements:

(i) issuers with a registered address in Latvia shall prepare and submit to the RSE all notifications and financial reports in Latvian and also in English;
(ii) issuers with a registered address abroad may submit to the RSE all notifications and reports in English only.[24]

V Publication and advertisements

1 Method of publication

22. When the Commission has passed the decision on the registration of a prospectus it must be made available to the public. It can be done by one of the following publishing methods:

(i) inclusion in one or more newspapers circulated throughout, or widely circulated in, the Member States in which the offer to the public is made or the admission to trading is sought;
(ii) in a printed form to be made available, free of charge, to the public at the offices of the market maker on which the transferable securities are being admitted to trading, or at the registered office of the issuer and at the offices of the financial intermediaries placing or selling the securities, including payment agents;
(iii) in an electronic form on the issuer's website and on the website of the financial intermediaries placing or selling the securities, including payment agents;
(iv) in electronic form on the website of the Commission.

The Commission has a right to request issuers which publish their prospectus either in newspapers or in a printed form to also publish the prospectus in an electronic form. In addition, the Commission is entitled also to request the issuer to publish an announcement in which information as to how the prospectus will be made available to the public, and where it can be obtained by the public, is indicated.

In the case of a prospectus comprising several documents and incorporating information by reference, the documents and information making up the prospectus may be published and circulated separately provided that the said documents are made available, free of charge, to the public by means of publishing them on the issuer's website. Each document shall

[24] RSE Rules on Listing and Trading of Financial Instruments on the Markets Regulated by the Exchange, approved by the RSE Management Board meeting on 18 May 2007, Art. 13.4.

indicate where the other constituent documents of the full prospectus may be obtained.

The text and the format of the prospectus and any supplements, published or made available to the public, must at all times be identical to the original version approved by the Commission.

Where the prospectus is made available by publication in electronic form, a paper copy must nevertheless be delivered to the investor, upon his request and free of charge, by the issuer or a person asking the admission of transferable securities to a regulated market.[25]

2 Advertisements

23. The Financial Instruments Law defines rules on the advertisement of a public offer. The advertising of transferable securities to be included in the regulated market may be commenced only from the day when the prospectus becomes available to the public, i.e. after it has been registered with the Commission.

It is prohibited to include in the advertisement of transferable securities that will be included in a regulated market inaccurate or misleading information, or information that contradicts information already provided in the prospectus. The information must also be consistent with the information contained in the prospectus, if already published, or with the information required to be in the prospectus, if the prospectus is published afterwards.

The advertising may not include any misleading information or information which is contrary to the information specified in the prospectus, and must specify where and when it will be possible to obtain the prospectus. The advertisement must be clearly recognisable as such.

All information concerning the inclusion of transferable securities in a regulated market disclosed in an oral or written form, even if not for advertising purposes, must be consistent with that contained in the prospectus.[26]

VI Use of prospectus approved in other (non EU) countries

24. The Commission is entitled to approve the prospectus of issuers having their registered office in a third country and drawn up in accordance with the legislation of a third country, provided that:

(i) the prospectus has been drawn up in accordance with international standards set by international securities commission organisations, including the IOSCO disclosure standards;

[25] Financial Instruments Market Law, adopted on 20 November 2003, effective as of 1 January 2004, Art. 51.

[26] Financial Instruments Market Law, adopted on 20 November 2003, effective as of 1 January 2004, Art. 24.

(ii) the information requirements, including information of a financial nature, are equivalent to the requirements under the Financial Instruments Law.

If transferable securities, issued by an issuer incorporated in a third country, are admitted on a regulated market of an EU Member State other than the home Member State, the requirements applicable to the approval of prospectus for use among Member States apply.

VII Sanctions

1 Sanctions applied by the Commission

25. There are several types of sanctions that could be applied in case of violations of the Financial Instruments Law and other regulatory enactments. The Commission is entitled to:

(i) suspend a public offer or admission to trading for a maximum of ten consecutive working days on any single occasion if it has reasonable grounds for suspecting that the provisions of the Financial Instruments Law have been infringed;
(ii) prohibit or suspend advertisements for a maximum of ten consecutive working days on any single occasion if it has reasonable grounds for believing that the provisions of the Financial Instruments Law have been infringed;
(iii) prohibit a public offer if it finds that the provisions of the Financial Instruments Law have been infringed or if it has reasonable grounds for suspecting that they would be infringed;
(iv) suspend or ask the relevant regulated markets to suspend trading on a regulated market for a maximum of ten consecutive working days on any single occasion if it has reasonable grounds for believing that the provisions of the Financial Instruments Law have been infringed;
(v) prohibit trading on a regulated market if it finds that the provisions of the Financial Instruments Law have been infringed;
(vi) make public the fact that an issuer is failing to comply with its obligations.[27]

The Commission is also empowered at the stage when the securities have been admitted to trading on a regulated market to:

(i) suspend or ask the relevant regulated market maker to suspend the securities from trading if, in its opinion, the issuer's situation is such that trading would be detrimental to investors' interests;

[27] Financial Instruments Market Law, adopted on 20 November 2003, effective as of 1 January 2004, Art. 55[1].

(ii) ensure that issuers whose securities are traded on regulated markets comply with the obligations provided for in regulatory enactments and that equivalent information is provided to investors and equivalent treatment is granted by the issuer to all securities holders who are in the same position, in all Member States where the offer to the public is made or the securities are admitted to trading;

(iii) carry out on-site inspections in order to verify compliance with the provisions of the Financial Instruments Law.

26. The Financial Instruments Law contains rules that are applicable where violations of the Law have taken place. Thus, the Commission has a right to impose a fine up to the amount of LVL 10,000 (approximately €14,300) for making a public offer disregarding the requirements defined in the Financial Instruments Law.

For other violations of the Financial Instruments Law or administrative acts issued pursuant to it, the Commission has a right to issue a warning or impose a fine up to the amount of LVL 10,000.

For the violation of requirements for making a public offer, the inclusion of financial instruments in a regulated market and the Prospectus Regulation, the Commission has a right to issue a warning or impose a fine up to the amount of LVL 10,000.[28]

2 Sanctions applied by the RSE

27. In addition to those sanctions which the Commission is entitled to apply, there are also sanctions determined in the RSE Rules that the market maker – the RSE – is empowered to apply.

If the issuer, its employees or members of its management board and supervisory board have violated provisions of RSE Rules or if the investment activities of the issuer, its authorised person, auditor, a member of the management board and supervisory board have violated provisions of these RSE Rules, or if the issuer or the said persons have not complied with the resolutions or instructions of the RSE, the RSE may apply the following sanctions on the issuer:

(i) issue a warning;
(ii) impose a fine;
(iii) suspend trading with the financial instruments of the issuer;
(iv) delist the financial instruments of the issuer from the RSE lists.[29]

[28] Financial Instruments Market Law, adopted on 20 November 2003, effective as of 1 January 2004, Art. 148.

[29] RSE Rules on Listing and Trading of Financial Instruments on the Markets Regulated by the Exchange, approved by the RSE Management Board meeting on 18 May 2007, Art. 32.1.

The RSE Management Board shall have the right to adopt a resolution on issuing a warning to the issuer, if the issuer has violated provisions of RSE Rules advising the issuer, without delay, in writing about the warning and the circumstances on the basis of which the resolution was adopted.

The RSE Management Board shall have the right to adopt a resolution on imposing a fine if the issuer, its employee or a member of its management board or supervisory board has materially violated the provisions of the RSE Rules, if the issuer has not eliminated the violation upon warning issued by the RSE or if in the result of the violation the interests of the investors have been violated. In the resolution the RSE Management Board shall determine the date before which the fine has to be paid.

28. The RSE shall have the right to impose on the issuer a fine from LVL 50 to LVL 20,000 (approximately €72 to €29,000). When determining the amount of the fine, the RSE Management Board shall assess the severity of the violation and its influence on the provision of the functioning of a regular and transparent market.[30]

29. In extraordinary circumstances, in order to protect the interest of the investors, the RSE may suspend trading with the financial instruments of the issuer.

The RSE Management Board shall adopt the resolution on resuming of trading with the securities, if the circumstances on the basis of which the resolution on suspension of trading was adopted have been eliminated.

The RSE Management Board has the right to pass a delisting decision in the following cases:

(i) if the issuer or the financial instruments issued by it do not conform to the requirements specified in the RSE Rules;
(ii) the issuer or the members of its management board or supervisory board or employees have repeatedly or materially violated provisions of the RSE Rules or the Law;
(iii) if the interruption of the trade with financial instruments has been longer than six months and if the issuer has not taken measures to eliminate the circumstances on the basis of which trading was suspended;
(iv) other circumstances, as a result of which it is not possible to continue trading with the financial instruments of the issuer in compliance with the procedure determined in the RSE Rules, have occurred;

[30] RSE Rules on Listing and Trading of Financial Instruments on the Markets Regulated by the Exchange, approved by the RSE Management Board meeting on 18 May 2007, Art. 32.2., Art. 32.3.

(v) the issuer has not paid the specified listing fee to the RSE upon repeated notice.[31]

VIII Prospectus liability

30. The prospectus shall be approved by the shareholders' meeting or its authorised management body or official of the issuer.

The management body of the issuer or person asking to include transferable securities in a regulated market and guarantor (if one exists) are responsible for the contents of the prospectus.

A prospectus shall specify the given name, surname, personal identification number (if any) and position of the responsible members of the management bodies of the issuer. The prospectus shall also include a notification by such person stating that, according to the information available to this person, the information included in the prospectus conforms to actual circumstances, as well as that no facts have been concealed which may affect the meaning of the information included in the prospectus. If a person is not responsible for all of the information included in a prospectus, the prospectus shall specify the part for which the relevant person is responsible.

By bringing an action to a court according to general procedures, the investor may claim for damages from persons specified in a prospectus who are responsible for the correctness of the information included therein, provided that the investor has incurred losses due to false or incomplete information having been included in the prospectus.

Investors may not claim for damages from persons specified in a prospectus if it has made the choice only on the basis of a summary or its translation, except cases when the summary is misleading or contradicts the other parts of the prospectus.[32]

IX Rules applicable to transactions and securities not subject to the Directive and Regulation

31. The Financial Instruments Law provides that it is permitted to admit on a regulated market financial instruments the alienation of which is not restricted. And as a general rule it is stated that in order to include transferable securities in a regulated market it is required to publish a prospectus, which has been drawn up pursuant to the aforementioned law. However, there is an exemption that foresees certain cases when it is not mandatory to

[31] RSE Rules on Listing and Trading of Financial Instruments on the Markets Regulated by the Exchange, approved by the RSE Management Board meeting on 18 May 2007, Art. 32.6.

[32] Financial Instruments Market Law, adopted on 20 November 2003, effective as of 1 January 2004, Art. 46.

draw up a prospectus. In cases where an issuer or a person is asking to admit to a regulated market the following transferable securities, there is no statutory requirement to draw up a prospectus:

(i) non-equity securities issued by a Member State or by one of a Member State's regional or local authorities, by public international bodies of which one or more Member States are members, by the European Central Bank or by the central banks of the Member States;

(ii) securities unconditionally and irrevocably guaranteed by a Member State or by one of the Member State's regional or local authorities;

(iii) *'bostadsobligationer'* issued repeatedly by credit institutions in Sweden whose main purpose is to grant mortgage loans, provided that:
- the *'bostadsobligationer'* issued are of the same series;
- the *'bostadsobligationer'* are issued on an ongoing basis during a specified issuing period;
- the terms and conditions of the *'bostadsobligationer'* are not changed during the issuing period;
- the sums deriving from the issue of the said *'bostadsobligationer'*, in accordance with the articles of association of the issuer, are placed in assets which provide sufficient coverage for the liability deriving from securities;

(iv) non-equity securities issued in a continuous or repeated manner by credit institutions where the total consideration of the offer is less than €50 million, which limit shall be calculated over a period of twelve months, provided that these securities:
- are not subordinated, convertible or exchangeable;
- do not give a right to subscribe to or acquire other types of securities and that they are not linked to a derivative instrument.[33]

X Conclusion

32. It can be concluded that the requirements of the Prospectus Directive are fully transposed into the laws and regulations of Latvia. The vast majority of the requirements of the Prospectus Directive are incorporated in the Financial Instruments Law; however, the Financial Instruments Law also contains references to the Prospectus Regulation in the relevant cases. There are no deviations identified in the laws and regulations that would witness that part or any requirement of the Prospectus Directive would have been neglected. Therefore, it can be concluded that the main aim of the

[33] Financial Instruments Market Law, adopted on 20 November 2003, effective as of 1 January 2004, Art. 3.

Prospectus Directive, i.e. to harmonise requirements for the drawing up, approval and distribution of the prospectus to be published when securities are offered to the public or admitted to trading on a regulated market situated or operating within a Member State,[34] is achieved.

[34] 'Dir.' Art.1.

9

Lithuania

IRMANTAS NORKUS AND EVA SUDUIKO
Norcous & Partners

I Introduction

1 Implementing laws and legal framework

1. Directive 2003/71/EC of the European Parliament and of the Council of 4 November 2003 on the prospectus to be published when securities are offered to the public or admitted to trading (the 'Prospectus Directive' or 'Dir.'), amending Directive 2001/34/EC, was fully implemented in Lithuania in July 2005.

In particular, the Prospectus Directive was implemented by: (i) amending and supplementing the Law on Securities Market of the Republic of Lithuania (No. I-1169 of 16 January 1996) (the 'Law on Securities Market'); and (ii) adopting the Resolution of the Securities Commission of the Republic of Lithuania Concerning the Approval of the Rules on the Drawing up and Approval of the Prospectus of Securities and the Rules on the Disclosure of Information (No. 1k-21 of 15 July 2005) (the 'Rules'). It should be noted that in February 2007 the Law on Securities Market was replaced by the Law on Securities of the Republic of Lithuania (No. X-102 of January 2007) (the Law).

2. The Law and the Rules together with directly applicable Commission Regulation 809/2004 of 29 April 2004, implementing the Prospectus Directive as regards information contained in prospectuses, as well as the format, incorporation by reference and publication of such prospectuses and dissemination of advertisements (the 'Prospectus Regulation' or 'Reg.') provide the legal framework for offers of securities to the public in Lithuania and admission of securities to trading on a regulated market in Lithuania.

3. The requirements of the Prospectus Directive to a large extent were nearly literally transposed into the Law and the Rules. This applies, for example, to the definitions used in the Prospectus Directive, exemptions from the obligation to publish the prospectus, content and form of the prospectus, method of publishing of the prospectus, and rules relating to advertisements.

4. It is noteworthy that there is no relevant case law on the provisions of the Law and the Rules implementing the requirements of the Prospectus Directive as yet. Moreover, clarifications of the Law and the Rules by the competent authority in Lithuania, the Securities Commission of the Republic of Lithuania, are rather rare.

5. Before implementing the Prospectus Directive, requirements of Lithuanian law relating to the public offer of securities and admission of securities to official stock exchange listing complied with the provisions of Council Directive 89/298/EEC of 17 April 1989, coordinating the requirements for the drawing-up, scrutiny and distribution of the prospectus to be

published when transferable securities are offered to the public, and Directive 2001/34/EC of the European Parliament and of the Council of 28 May 2001 on the admission of securities to official stock exchange listing and on information to be published on those securities.

2 Scope of the Law

6. The provisions of the Law concerning the prospectus requirement and other obligations related thereto apply to the following transferable equity securities:

(i) shares of public companies, and depository receipts in respect of such shares;
(ii) corporate bonds and other securities, certifying indebtedness of the issuer and conferring on the holder thereof the right to receive from the issuer, within the established time limits and in the established order, the cash amount equivalent to the nominal value, interest and other equivalent remuneration, also depository receipts in respect of such securities; and
(iii) securities conferring the right to acquire or transfer securities referred to in items (i) and (ii) above, or giving rise to the cash settlements determined with reference to securities or exchange rates, interest rates, yield of non-equity securities, stock exchange indexes or other similar measures.

7. In accordance with the Law, the requirements relating to the drawing up, approval and publication of the prospectus do not apply to the following securities:

(i) securities issued (to be issued) by open-type collective investment undertakings;
(ii) non-equity securities issued (or to be issued) by a Member State or by its regional or local authorities, by the European Central Bank or central banks of the Member States, by public international organisations of which at least one Member State is a member;
(iii) shares in the capital of central banks of the Member States;
(iv) securities unconditionally and irrevocably guaranteed by a Member State or by one of a Member State's regional or local authorities;
(v) non-equity securities issued in a continuous or repeated manner by credit institutions, provided that such securities are not subordinated, converted or exchangeable, do not give a right to subscribe to or acquire other types of securities, are not linked to a financial derivative, materialise the reception of repayable deposits, and are covered by a deposit guarantee scheme;
(vi) publicly offered securities issued by an issuer incorporated in a

Member State, where the total consideration for the offer is less than €2.5 million, calculated over a period of twelve months;

(vii) non-equity securities issued in a continuous and repeated manner by credit institutions, where the total consideration for the offer is less than €50 million, calculated over a period of twelve months, provided that such securities are not subordinated, converted or exchangeable, do not give a right to subscribe to or acquire other types of securities, and are not linked to a financial derivative.

The securities and offerings listed above are exempted from the application of the Prospectus Directive too (see Article 1(2) of the Prospectus Directive and Chapter 1, Nos. 8 and 9). It should be noted, however, that the Law does not implement all the exemptions specified in Article 1(2) of the Prospectus Directive. In particular, exemptions specified in Articles 1(2)(e), 1(2)(g) and 1(2)(i) of the Prospectus Directive were not transposed into the Law.

II Competent authority

8. The Securities Commission of the Republic of Lithuania (the 'Lithuanian Securities Commission' or 'LSC') (*Vertybinių popierių komisija*) is an independent body performing the overall supervision of the securities market in Lithuania. The LSC is also the competent authority for the purposes of the Prospectus Directive in Lithuania.

III Procedure of prior approval and appeal

1 Offer of securities to the public

A Prospectus obligation

9. The offer of securities to the public may be exercised in Lithuania only after the drawing up, approval and publication of the prospectus in accordance with the requirements established in the Law, the Rules, and the Prospectus Regulation.

10. The definition of the offer of securities to the public established in the Law follows the wording of the definition set forth in Article 2(1)(d) of the Prospectus Directive (see also Chapter 1, No. 10). The Law only additionally clarifies that communication to persons on the basis of trading on a regulated market in Lithuania is not deemed to be the offer of securities to the public within the meaning of the Law.

B Exemptions

11. The obligation to publish the prospectus does not apply in a number of instances – all transposed into the Law from Article 3 of the Prospectus Directive (see also Chapter 1, Nos. 11 and 12).

12. The Law provides that natural persons or small and medium-sized enterprises can be considered as qualified investors if they meet criteria identical to those set out in Article 2 of the Prospectus Directive (see also Chapter 1, No. 11).

13. In accordance with the Law, the LSC is entitled to establish general exemptions from the prospectus requirement in case of the offer of securities to the public. Such general exemptions from the prospectus obligation are specified in the Rules, which implement all exemptions from the obligation to publish the prospectus specified in Article 4(1) of the Prospectus Directive (see also Chapter 1, No. 13).

14. In certain cases, namely those established in Articles 4(1)(b) and 4(1)(c) of the Prospectus Directive, in order to qualify for an exemption, a document containing certain information regarding the offer and securities has to be approved by the LSC as appropriate. For the purposes of the recognition of the document as appropriate, a written application with the said document enclosed has to be delivered to the LSC. To be appropriate the document should contain sufficient information about the offer and securities. Having concluded that the submitted document is appropriate, the LSC notifies the applicant within five working days of the possibility that preparing a prospectus will not be necessary. In all other cases, exemptions from the prospectus requirement in case of the offer of securities to the public are automatically available by operation of the Law and the Rules and require no application or filing.

2 Admission to trading on a regulated market

A Prospectus obligation

15. Securities may be admitted to trading on a regulated market situated or operating within the territory of Lithuania only after the drawing up, approval and publication of the prospectus in accordance with the requirements established in the Law, the Rules, and the Prospectus Regulation.

16. According to the Resolution of the Lithuanian Securities Commission Regarding the List of the Regulated Markets (No. 18–28 of 6 September 2007), the regulated markets in Lithuania include the following trading lists of the Vilnius Stock Exchange: (i) Main List; (ii) Secondary List; and (iii) Debt Securities List.

B Exemptions

17. In accordance with the Law, the LSC establishes general exemptions from the prospectus obligation applicable in certain cases of securities' admission to trading on a regulated market in Lithuania. These general exemptions are listed in the Rules and are the same as those specified in Article 4(2) of the Prospectus Directive (see also Chapter 1, No.15).

18. In order to qualify for an exemption from the prospectus obligation specified in Articles from 4(2)(c) and 4(2)(d) of the Prospectus Directive, a document containing certain information relating to the securities to be admitted to trading on a regulated market in Lithuania has to be approved by the LSC as appropriate. The document is recognised as appropriate in accordance with the procedure specified above in no.14 of this report. In all other cases, the exemptions from the prospectus requirement in case of admission of securities to trading on a regulated market in Lithuania apply automatically.

3 Approval of the prospectus

19. In accordance with the Law, no prospectus may be published until it has been approved by the LSC or the competent authority of another Member State.

20. The decision of the LSC on approval of the prospectus has to be adopted within the terms specified in the Law, fully complying in this respect with the requirements of Article 13 of the Prospectus Directive (see also Chapter 1, No. 25).

21. Pursuant to the Law, in the event the LSC does not pass any decision regarding the approval of the prospectus within the prescribed time period, the prospectus cannot be deemed to be approved and, consequently, may not be published.

It should be noted that a failure to act by the LSC may be appealed in accordance with the procedure defined in no. 24 of this report.

22. The LSC passes a decision on approval of the prospectus only after reviewing the prospectus for its completeness, including its compatibility and comprehensiveness. The LSC may refuse to approve the prospectus in the following instances:

(i) in case of the failure to provide information in the prospectus in compliance with the requirements of Lithuanian law;
(ii) in case of the failure to provide the documents or explanations stipulated in the regulations of the LSC;
(iii) in case of submission of false documents or information to the LSC; or
(iv) in case the securities have been issued in violation of Lithuanian law.

23. The approval of the prospectus by the LSC means that information contained in the prospectus complies with the requirements of Lithuanian law and the prospectus may be made available for the public. Such approval by the LSC, however, does not confirm the correctness of information provided in the prospectus and may not be regarded as recommendation by the LSC to investors.

4 Right of appeal

24. The acts of or failure to act by the LSC may be appealed to the administrative court in accordance with the procedure laid down in the Law on Administrative Procedure of the Republic of Lithuania (No. VIII-1029 of 14 January 1999).

This law provides that if the LSC delays adoption of the decision, a complaint regarding such delay may be lodged within two months from the day of expiry of a time limit set for the adoption of the decision. A question about the acceptance of the received complaint has to be resolved within seven days. If the complaint is accepted, the preparatory stage of administrative proceedings has to be finalised within one month, by adopting a court ruling to examine the case, and a decision on the subject-matter of the complaint has to be passed within two months of adoption of the said ruling.

IV Content and format, language and supplements of the prospectus

1 Content

25. The prospectus content requirements set forth in the Prospectus Directive (see Chapter 1, Nos. 28 through 40) were implemented into the Law and the Rules without any substantial modifications.

26. In addition to the requirements of the Prospectus Directive and the Prospectus Regulation relating to the content of the prospectus, the Rules provide that (i) information provided in the prospectus has to be objective and easily comparable, and (ii) the statements of the prospectus must be supported by specific projects, concluded transactions, plans, or other specific estimations.

27. The Lithuanian legislator has included in the Law a requirement to produce a summary if the prospectus relates to the admission to trading on a regulated market of non-equity securities with a denomination of at least €50,000 (Article 5(2) of the Prospectus Directive gives the Member States an option to choose whether to require such summary, see also Chapter 1, No. 36). The summary has to be drafted in the Lithuanian language (see no. 36 of this report).

28. The Prospectus Directive allows certain information to be omitted from the prospectus (see Article 8(2) of the Prospectus Directive and Chapter 1, No. 38). The Rules specify that in case of the omission of information in the prospectus, the explanatory note has to be attached to the prospectus specifying the information omitted as well as the reasons for such omission. If the LSC holds that certain information was omitted from the prospectus

without sufficient grounds, it may instruct provision of such information in the prospectus.

2 Form and format

29. The main provisions of the Prospectus Directive in combination with the Prospectus Regulation concerning the form and the format of the prospectus (see Chapter 1, Nos. 41 through 50) were closely reiterated in the Law and the Rules.

30. In accordance with the Rules, if the items, which must be included in the schedules and building blocks of the prospectus, are presented in the order determined at the discretion of the issuer, offeror or person requesting admission to trading (Art. 25(3) and Art. 26(2) Reg., see also Chapter 1, No. 50), i.e. differently from the order presented in the annexes to the Prospectus Regulation, a list of cross-references indicating the page numbers where each item can be found in the prospectus has to be filed with the LSC. It should be noted, however, that when approving the prospectus, the LSC is entitled to require that information items are arranged in the sequence specified in the annexes to the Prospectus Regulation.

3 Supplements

31. The requirements of the Prospectus Directive relating to the supplements of the prospectus (see Article 16 of the Prospectus Directive and Chapter 1, Nos. 66 and 67) were implemented into the Law and the Rules without any substantial differences in the wording.

32. The Prospectus Directive provides that investors who committed themselves to purchasing or subscribing for securities prior to the publication of the supplement, are entitled to withdraw their acceptance at least two working days following the publication of the supplement (Art. 16(2) Dir.). It is noteworthy that the Law has extended the time limit for such withdrawal to five working days. Moreover, the Law requires that in such cases the issuer, offeror or person seeking admission to trading repays contributions to the investors within ten working days without any deductions.

33. In addition to the requirements relating to the supplements set forth in the Prospectus Directive, the Law provides that a supplement to the prospectus has also to be drawn up if during the primary public offering the issuer having consent of the LSC decides to modify the procedure or time limits for the distribution of or payment for securities. In such events, the investors are also entitled to withdraw their commitments to purchase or subscribe for the securities. This right may be exercised within a period specified above in no. 32 of this report.

4 Language

34. The prospectus language requirements set out in the Law fully implement the provisions of the Prospectus Directive (see Article 19 of the Prospectus Directive and Chapter 1, Nos. 51 through 54).

35. In Lithuania, a language referred to in the Prospectus Directive as the 'language to be accepted by the competent authority of the home Member State' should be Lithuanian.

36. According to the Law, where the prospectus is drawn up in a language other than Lithuanian and the offering of securities to the public is being made or admission of securities is sought on a regulated market in Lithuania, the LSC has to be provided with a summary translated into Lithuanian.

In addition, the Lithuanian legislator has decided to require a summary drawn up in Lithuanian in case of admission of non-equity securities of the nominal value not less than €50,000 to trading on a regulated market in Lithuania (Article 5(2) of the Prospectus Directive permitted the Member States to choose whether to require such summary, see also Chapter 1, No. 36).

V Publication and advertisements

1 Method of publication

37. In accordance with the Law, the prospectus has to be published as soon as practicable and, in any case (including the initial public offering mentioned in Article 14(1) of the Prospectus Directive), in advance of the offering or admission to trading of securities involved.

38. The prospectus has to be published by the means specified in the Law, which nearly verbatim repeats the provisions of Article 14(2) of the Prospectus Directive (see also Chapter 1, Nos. 56 through 61).

In particular, the Law provides that the prospectus is deemed to have been made available if published through one of the following means:

(i) in at least one newspaper circulated throughout Lithuania in case of the offering of securities to the public or admission thereof to trading on a regulated market of Lithuania;
(ii) in the form of a brochure handed out free of charge to all persons wishing to receive it in the registered office of the issuer, or the registered office of the operator of the market on which securities will be traded, or the offices of intermediaries of public trading in securities (including paying agents), placing or selling securities;
(iii) in electronic form on the website of the issuer and websites of intermediaries (including paying agents) placing or selling securities; or

(iv) in electronic form on the website of the operator of a regulated market, in which admission to trading is sought.

In case of publication of the prospectus in accordance with the methods identified in items (i) and (ii) above, the prospectus has to be also published in electronic form provided in item (iii) above.

39. The Lithuanian legislator has not implemented the method of publication established in Article 14(1)(e) of the Prospectus Directive, pursuant to which publication can be made by posting the prospectus on the competent authority's website (see also chapter 1, No. 57).

40. The Law does not require publication of a notice stating how the prospectus has been made available and where it can be obtained by the public, which the Member States may require pursuant to Article 14(3) of the Prospectus Directive (see also chapter 1, No. 58).

41. The Law, implementing the requirement set forth in Article 14(4) of the Prospectus Directive, requires the LSC to publish on its website the prospectuses approved during a period of twelve months. All such prospectuses can be found at the following address: www.lsc.lt (the official website of the LSC).

2 Advertisements

42. The wording of the requirements of the Prospectus Directive relating to advertisements (see Article 15 of the Prospectus Directive and Chapter 1, Nos. 62 through 65) is thoroughly transposed into the Law.

43. The Law provides that in case of infringement of the requirements relating to advertisements, the LSC may prohibit the advertising or suspend it for a period not exceeding ten days.

VI Use of prospectuses approved in other (non-EU) countries

44. Prospectuses approved in other (non-EU) countries may not be used for the purposes of the offering of securities to the public or admission thereof to trading on a regulated market in Lithuania. According to the Law, securities may be offered to the public or admitted to trading on a regulated market only after publication of the prospectus approved by the LSC or the competent authority of another Member State. The Law provides that the LSC may approve the prospectus of a foreign issuer if the said prospectus is drawn up in accordance with the requirements set forth in the Prospectus Directive (see Article 20(1) of the Prospectus Directive and Chapter 1, Nos. 73 and 74).

VII Sanctions

1 Illegal acts

45. The Law does not provide for a detailed list of unlawful acts. In fact, any infringement of the Law may entail negative consequences for the persons violating requirements of the Law.

46. Any person who infringes the Law is obliged to (i) act in compliance with the instructions of the LSC and restore the situation to its original condition, (ii) compensate for the loss incurred, and (iii) fulfil sanctions imposed by the LSC.

47. In case of violation of the requirements of the Law and the Rules relating to the prospectus requirements, the LSC may impose appropriate sanctions specified in the Law (e.g. suspend or prohibit offering to the public or trading, suspend advertising, impose pecuniary penalties).

It is noteworthy that pecuniary penalties may be imposed only for the infringements clearly specified in the Law. In particular, the LSC may impose pecuniary sanctions on issuers, intermediaries, or other legal entities organising or conducting public offering of securities or trading on a regulated market, if the prospectus has not been published in advance or where the public offering or trading on a regulated market has been prohibited or suspended. The fines for such breaches may amount (i) up to LTL 100,000 (*c.* €28,962) in cases where the total nominal value of securities offered to the public or admitted to trading on a regulated market is lower than LTL 100,000, and (ii) up to the total nominal value of securities offered to the public or admitted to trading on a regulated market, in cases where the total nominal value of such securities exceeds LTL 100,000. Moreover, the legal entities, which fail to ensure that each investor is provided with a possibility to familiarise with the prospectus, may be fined up to LTL 100,000 (*c.* €28,962).

The application of pecuniary penalties to legal entities as specified above does not exempt their managers from statutory civil liability, administrative, or criminal liability. It should be noted, however, that violation of the requirements relating to the prospectuses set forth in the Law does not entail criminal liability. Such liability may arise only in cases of insider trading, or market manipulation. As regards administrative liability, infringements of the laws governing the securities market may be subject to fines ranging from LTL 1,000 (*c.* €290) to LTL 5,000 (*c.* €1,450).

2 Procedure of imposing pecuniary penalties

48. Pecuniary penalties are imposed by the LSC in accordance with the procedure established in the Law on Markets in Financial Instruments (No. X1014) of 18 January 2007.

49. The procedure of imposing pecuniary penalties may be divided into two stages (i) the preparatory stage; and (ii) the main stage.

During the preparatory stage, the LSC must inform a person whose actions are subject to investigation of his right to submit explanations in relation to the actions being investigated. The term for submission of the said explanations is established by the LSC and, in any case, may not be shorter than five days. Afterwards the LSC has to inform the said person about the date and the venue of the LSC's meeting, in which the question of imposition of a pecuniary penalty will be discussed.

In the main stage, the LSC analyses the material relating to the suspected violation. During this stage, a person whose actions are subject to investigation is entitled, *inter alia*, to familiarise himself with the investigation material, comment on his actions, provide evidence and submit explanations. Having investigated all the material, the LSC adopts one of the following decisions: (i) to impose a pecuniary penalty specified under the Law; (ii) to terminate the investigation due to the absence of violation or statutory basis to impose a penalty; or (iii) to continue the investigation.

When imposing pecuniary penalties, the LSC must take into account the following: (i) amount of the loss incurred due to the violation; (ii) duration of the violation; (iii) amount of illegal proceeds the person gained from the violation; and (iv) aggravating (e.g. interference into the investigation carried out by the LSC, concealment or continuance of violation) and attenuating (e.g. prevention of detrimental effects of the violation, assistance to the LSC, reimbursement of losses) circumstances.

Decisions of the LSC to impose a pecuniary penalty may be appealed to the administrative court within one month in accordance with the procedure established in the Law on Administrative Procedure of the Republic of Lithuania (No. VIII-1029 of 14 January 1999).

50. It is noteworthy that the LSC may impose pecuniary penalties only if not more than two years have passed since the date of infringement or the date such infringement was revealed (in case of continuous violation).

51. Pecuniary penalties have to be paid within one month after receipt of the decision of the LSC concerning the imposition of the pecuniary penalty. In case of a failure to pay the fine within the prescribed time limit, the due sum is enforced in accordance with the procedure established in the Civil Code of Procedure of the Republic of Lithuania (No. IX-743 of 28 February 2002).

VIII Prospectus liability

52. The Lithuanian rules relating to the prospectus liability follow the requirements set out in the Prospectus Directive (see Article 6 of the Prospectus Directive and Chapter 1, Nos. 84 and 85).

53. Pursuant to the Law, a list of persons who are required to accept responsibility for the accuracy and completeness of information provided in the prospectus, includes the issuer or its administrative, management, or supervisory bodies, the offeror, the person asking for admission to trading on a regulated market, or the guarantor. The list is not exhaustive, however. The Law provides that liability for information in the prospectus may be placed on other persons as well.

54. In addition to the requirement for the statement of responsible persons relating to information contained in the prospectus (see Article 6(1) of the Prospectus Directive and Chapter 1, No. 85), the Rules require that all persons liable sign the prospectus.

55. In accordance with the Law, in case of a false statement or omission of information in the prospectus, the investor has a right to claim indemnity from persons responsible in accordance with the provisions of the Civil Code of the Republic of Lithuania (No. VIII-1864 of 18 July 2000).

It should be noted that the Lithuanian law does not provide for any specific regime with regard to civil liability attaching to the prospectus and, therefore, the general rules of civil liability would apply in case of a defective prospectus. Pursuant to the said rules, an investor may claim indemnification for all losses (direct and indirect) if the following three elements exist: (i) information contained in the prospectus was inaccurate or incomplete; (ii) the investor suffered damages due to the defective prospectus; and (iii) such damage was caused by the misleading information provided in the prospectus.

IX Rules applicable to transactions and securities not subject to the Prospectus Directive and the Prospectus Regulation

56. The provisions of the Law concerning the drawing up, approval and publication of the prospectus do not apply to a number of securities, the list of which is provided in no. 7 of this report.

It should be noted that some of the said securities (e.g. securities issued by collective investment undertakings) fall within the scope of other laws establishing the requirements relating to such securities and their offer, while other securities and offerings thereof are unregulated by Lithuanian law.

Notwithstanding the above, provisions of the Law on prohibition of insider dealing and manipulation of the market would apply to securities which are exempted from the prospectus obligation and other related requirements of the Law. Moreover, as any other contract, transactions relating to such securities would be subject to the general principles of Lithuanian contract law. These principles are based on the Principles of International Commercial Contracts prepared by UNIDROIT (1994), while special provisions governing different types of contracts are based on the Principles of European Contract Law prepared by the Commission of the European

Contract Law (2000) and, *inter alia*, include the freedom of contract, binding character of a contract, prevalence of the mandatory rules, equality of contracting parties, good faith, fair dealing and cooperation.

X Conclusion

57. The Lithuanian laws have comprehensively implemented the Prospectus Directive as of July 2005. As mentioned in No. 3 of this report, the Law and the Rules to a large extent follow very closely the wording of the Prospectus Directive. Neither the Law nor the Rules establish any material national variations from the Prospectus Directive, which could result in barriers to cross-border securities offerings. Therefore, the issuers of other Member States should access the Lithuanian securities market effectively and easily.

10

Luxembourg

JOSÉE WEYDERT AND FRANCK-OLIVIER CERA
NautaDutilh

I Introduction

1. The Prospectus Directive was implemented in the Grand Duchy of Luxembourg by an act of 10 July 2005 on prospectuses for securities (the '**Prospectus Act**' or '**Act**').[1] The Prospectus Act applies together with the Prospectus Regulation which contains the detailed provisions to be included in prospectuses prepared for an offer of securities to the public or an admission to trading on a regulated market.

2. The Prospectus Act goes beyond the implementation of the Prospectus Directive. It is divided into four Parts. Part I includes the definitions used throughout the Prospectus Act. Part II has the same scope as the Prospectus Directive and applies to all those issuers that fall within the scope of the Prospectus Directive. Part III sets out the legal framework which applies to issuers and transactions that fall outside of the scope of the Prospectus Directive. Part IV sets out the rules which apply in relation to the Euro MTF, the alternative market and for which the rules and regulations of the Luxembourg Stock Exchange apply and the former authority is the competent authority.

The law grants authority to the *Commission de Surveillance du Secteur Financier* (the 'CSSF') to approve prospectuses in relation to transactions falling within the scope of Part II and to offer securities to the public in the framework of Part III of the Prospectus Act. The mission of the CSSF also extends to the supervision of compliance with the rules set out by the Prospectus Act. In particular, the CSSF is granted with power of investigation and power to issue administrative sanctions.

3. The Prospectus Act is supplemented by various circulars issued by the CSSF:

(i) CSSF Circular 05/224 of 15 December 2005 on the choice of the home Member State for third-country issuers whose securities were admitted to trading as at 1 July 2005;
(ii) CSSF Circular 05/225 of 16 December 2005 on the notion of offer to the public of securities and the obligation to publish a prospectus;
(iii) CSSF Circular 05/226 of 16 December 2005 giving a general overview of the Prospectus Act and technical specifications regarding communications to the CSSF;
(iv) CSSF Circular 05/210 of 10 October 2005 on the information to be given in the simplified prospectus for securities that are not covered by the Prospectus Directive; and
(v) CSSF Circular 06/272 of 21 December 2006 on technical specifications regarding communications to the CSSF, in the framework of offer of

[1] Mémorial A 98 of 12 July 2005.

securities to the public by *sociétés d'investissement en capital à risque* (SICARs) and admission to trading on a regulated market of securities issued by SICARs.

In addition, the CSSF has issued a whole set of guidelines as to interpretation of the Prospectus Act, to which reference is made throughout this report.

II Competent authority

4. The CSSF is the sole competent authority for approving a prospectus for the purposes of offering securities to the public or for admitting securities to trading on a regulated market, when Luxembourg is the home Member State (Art. 7(1) Act). This includes the approval of a prospectus in relation to securities admitted to trading on a regulated market issued by a SICAR[2] or the offer to the public of securities issued by a SICAR.[3]

For the purpose of approving a prospectus subject to Part II of the Prospectus Act, Luxembourg transferred the delegation of functions from the CSSF to the Luxembourg Stock Exchange in order to increase transparency and efficiency of the procedure.[4]

5. Luxembourg will be the home Member State for issuers of equity or low-denomination non-equity securities (i.e. in denominations of less than €1,000), having their registered office in Luxembourg (Art. 2(h)(i) and (ii) Act).

EEA and non-EEA issuers of all other types of securities such as non-equity securities with denominations of at least €1,000 continue to have free choice of their home Member State. Those issuers may choose the home state, i.e. the state of their registered office (not applicable for non-EEA issuers[5]), the state where the securities are offered to the public or admitted to a regulated market (Art. 2 (h)(ii) Act). This provision allows for example the issuer or the offeror complying with one of the above mentioned criteria to submit a eurobond prospectus to the CSSF for approval and benefit from the CSSF's expertise for such type of securities.[6]

The home Member State for non-EEA issuers of equity or non-equity denominations of less than €1,000 having their registered office in a non-EEA country is, either the Member State where the securities are first offered to the public after the Prospectus Directive came into force,[7] or where admission to trading is first sought, at the choosing of the issuer, the offeror or the person requesting admission, as the case may be (Art. 2 (h)(iii) Act).

[2] An act of 15 June 2004 has created the *société d'investissement en capital à risque*, the Luxembourg investment company in risk capital.

[3] CSSF Circular 06/272 of 21 December 2006, no. 1, p. 2.

[4] CSSF Guideline 'Le nouveau "régime prospectus" en 40 Questions/Réponses', no. 4, p. 4.

[5] CSSF Circular 05/224 of 15 December 2005, p. 2.

[6] See Chapter 1, no. 22.

[7] 31 December 2003.

6. Article 62 of the Prospectus Act contains transitional provisions for determining the home Member State in the case of a non-EEA issuer already having equity securities or low denomination debt admitted to trading on a regulated market located in Luxembourg. In such a case, the issuer could choose Luxembourg as the home Member State if it had notified its decision to the CSSF by 31 January 2005 at the latest.

7. In relation to Article 2 (h)(iii) of the Prospectus Act, no provision mentions from which date admission to trading on a regulated market should be taken into account for determining the home Member State purposes. A non-binding statement of the European Commission,[8] confirmed by a CSSF Circular[9] stated that the date of transposition of the Prospectus Directive, i.e. 1 July 2005, should be considered as the cut-off date. Pursuant to that non-binding statement, when an issuer had securities admitted to trading on several regulated markets as at 1 July 2005 (without having regard to the date on which such securities were admitted to such regulated market), the issuer could choose one of the Member States where securities were admitted to a regulated market without taking into consideration where first admission on a regulated market was sought.

For non-EEA issuers that are concerned by Article 62 of the Prospectus Act but that did not notify their decision to choose Luxembourg as home Member State by 31 December 2005, the provisions of Article 2(h)(iii) shall apply.[10]

8. The filing of prospectus approval application may be submitted either in paper format, which could also include a computer based documentation such as CDs or DVDs, by way of electronic filing on the CSSF electronic platform (www.e-file.lu) if the applicant is connected to such platform or through email (prospectus.approval@cssf.lu).[11]

The application shall include the following documents:[12]

(i) a list including the accurate designation of all documents provided in the application;
(ii) the purpose of the application (reference to the chapter of the Prospectus Act under which admission to trading or public offering is required and designation of the Member State in which public offering or admission to trading is contemplated);
(iii) details of the entity in charge of the filing and name of a person in charge of the matter (name, address, email address, telephone number);

[8] Internal Market DG statement dated 3 October 2005; see also Chapter 1, no. 21.
[9] CSSF Circular 05/224 of 15 December 2005, p. 3.
[10] CSSF Circular 05/224 of 15 December 2005, p. 3.
[11] CSSF Circular 05/226 of 16 December 2005, no. II 2, p. 7.
[12] CSSF Circular 05/226 of 16 December 2005, no. II 2, p. 8.

(iv) details of the issuer (or the offeror or the person applying for admission on a regulated market) in the name of which the application is made (name, address, email address, telephone number);
(v) details of the agent of the issuer (or of the offeror or the person applying for admission on a regulated market) in charge of receiving all notifications (name, address, email address, telephone number);
(vi) details of the agent in charge of receiving the invoice (from the CSSF) and the tax (name, address, email address, telephone number);
(vii) details of the person in charge of confirming that the filed draft prospectus is the final version for the purpose of approval and publication of the prospectus (name, address, email address, telephone number);
(viii) the contemplated timetable of the transaction and intended date of approval of the prospectus.

9. The CSSF shall notify its decision relating to the prospectus approval within ten working days as from the submission of the draft prospectus if:

(i) admission to a regulated market is requested; or
(ii) the public offering relates to an issuer all or part of whose securities have been previously offered to the public or have already been admitted to a regulated market (Art. 7(2) Act), by email with confirmation by a separate mail.[13]

If none of the conditions of (ii) above is met, the approval period is extended to 20 working days (Art. 7(3) Act).

If the CSSF finds, on reasonable grounds, that the documents submitted are incomplete or that additional information is needed, the time period for approval shall only start to run on the date on which the additional information is provided. Notification that information is missing must occur within the above time periods[14] (Art. 7(5) Act).

The time period starts running as from the working day following the day of submission of the draft prospectus.[15]

10. In the case of a passporting of the prospectus, the CSSF may deliver an approval certificate to the relevant competent EU authorities together with a translation of the summary drafted under the responsibility of the issuer or of the person in charge of drafting the prospectus, if need be (Art. 19 Act).

Failure by the CCSF to issue a decision within the abovementioned time period is deemed to be a refusal.[16] The issuer may agree with the CSSF that the approval of the prospectus will be notified at a later date than the

[13] CSSF Circular 05/226 of 16 December 2005, no. 4, p. 9.

[14] Even though the Prospectus Act only refers to the ten-day period, we believe that this would also apply to cases where the twenty working days period is applicable (see Chapter 1, no. 25).

[15] CSSF Circular 05/226 of 16 December 2005, no. 3, p. 9.

[16] This rule complies with the Luxembourg rules of public law.

time period of notification of the decision provided by the Prospectus Act.[17]

11. A claim against any decision of the CSSF shall be lodged before the Luxembourg administrative court[18] within three months of notification of the decision. The judgment of the administrative court may be appealed before the Luxembourg administrative appeal court within forty days from the judgment notification. The time periods during which a recourse may be lodged cannot be extended (Art. 27(1) Act).

No recourse has any suspension effect with regard to the CSSF decision unless suspended execution is granted by the president of the Luxembourg administrative court. Suspended execution is granted if (i) execution of the CSSF decision may entail serious and definitive damage; and (ii) the legal arguments against the CSSF decision appear serious (Art. 27(2) Act).

In addition, the president of the Luxembourg administrative court may grant interim measures to safeguard interests of the parties (Art. 27(2) Act).

12. The submission to the CSSF for prospectus approval entails payment of a tax ranging from €1,500 to €2,500 depending on the nature of the prospectus.[19] This tax is not due in relation to passporting procedures where the prospectus was approved by another Member State.[20]

13. As set out expressly in the Prospectus Act, the approval of a prospectus by the CSSF does not imply that the prudential authority takes any position as to the economic or financial opportunity of the transaction or the status or good standing of the issuer (Art. 7(7) Act).

14. Along with the Prospectus Directive, the Prospectus Act provides that the CSSF may transfer the approval of a prospectus to the competent authority of another Member State. This decision must be notified to the issuer, the offeror or the person requesting admission to trading on a regulated market within three working days from the date of the CSSF' s decision which decision shall be made within the time period provided by the Prospectus Act for any prospectus approval (Art. 7(6) Act).

15. In addition, in the framework of complex transactions, it is common practice to provide the CSSF with a first draft prospectus for preliminary advice and comments of the prudential authority.[21]

[17] CSSF Circular 05/226 of 16 December 2005, no. 3, p. 9.

[18] *Tribunal Administratif.*

[19] Grand Ducal Regulation of 10 November 2003 on taxes to be received by the CSSF, as amended by Grand Ducal Regulation of 3 August 2005 (Mémorial A – no. 143 of 2 September 2005).

[20] CSSF Guideline 'Le nouveau "régime prospectus" en 40 Questions/Réponses', no. 39, p. 24.

[21] Position confirmed by the CSSF Circular 05/226 of 16 December 2005, no. 2, p. 8.

16. Provided that supplements are filed, when required, to update relevant information (see also no. 33. of this report), the approval by the CSSF is valid for twelve months as from publication of the prospectus (Art. 11(1) Act).

17. The area of competition of the CSSF is governed by the Luxembourg act of 23 December 1998 relating to the creation of the CSSF (the '**Law on CSSF**') as amended.[22] The CSSF is a public body that shall remain under the supervision of the Luxembourg minister in charge of the financial sector (Art. 20(1) Law on CSSF). The CSSF supervision does not aim at guaranteeing individual interests of companies or supervised professionals, but at protecting the public interest (Art. 20(1) Law on CSSF). Pursuant to the Law on CSSF, the civil liability of the CSSF may be held only in the case of gross negligence in the choice and the implementation of the means used by it in furtherance of its mission of public service (Art. 20(2) Law on CSSF). In addition, damages and a link between the gross negligence and the damages shall be proved by the claimant in order to successfully file a claim against the CSSF.

III Procedure of prior approval and appeal

As a preliminary remark, one may note that Part II of the Prospectus Act (which derives from the Prospectus Directive implementation) excludes units issued by collective investment undertakings other than of closed-end type from its scope of application. The CSSF has confirmed, however, that securities issued by a securitisation fund subject to the Luxembourg law of 22 March 2004 on securitisation shall fall within the scope of Part II of the Prospectus Act.[23] For the purpose of drafting the prospectus and choosing the schedules of the Prospectus Regulation, the securities of such securitisation funds shall be viewed as securities other than those equity type securities.[24]

1 Offer of securities to the public

A Prospectus obligation

18. The offering of securities to the public in Luxembourg is subject to the prior publication of a prospectus (Art. 5 Act).

Prior to the Prospectus Act, no definition of offer of securities to the public was spelled out. An offer of securities to sophisticated or institutional investors, or to a limited number of identified existing clients of a credit insti-

[22] Comments on Article 7 of the draft Prospectus Act, p. 45.

[23] CSSF Guideline ' Questions/Réponses: Le nouveau "régime prospectus" – Partie II ', no. 58, p. 8.

[24] Schedule XV of the Prospectus Regulation relating to closed-end type collective investment undertakings shall be used.

tution or an investment firm that was not subject to extensive advertising, fell outside the scope of public offer, and used to be viewed by the CSSF as a private placement for which no prospectus or approval was required.

19. The Prospectus Act has implemented word for word the definition provided by the Prospectus Directive. Under the Act, an offer of securities to the public means '*a communication to persons in any form and by any means, presenting sufficient information on the terms of the offer and the securities to be offered, so as to enable an investor to decide to purchase or subscribe to these securities. The definition includes the placing of securities through financial intermediaries*' (Art. 2(1)(l) Act).

The definition of offer of securities to the public provided by the Prospectus Act is not applicable to securities outside the scope of the Prospectus Act, such as units issued by open-ended investment funds.[25]

To trigger the requirement to publish a prospectus, the information dispatched to potential investors must contain information on the terms of the offer and the securities concerned. This means that the nature of the security and its main characteristics should be communicated to the investors, that the selling price of the securities should be determined or determinable and that the investors should receive information on the procedure for acceptance and the acceptance period. To that extent, the medium used to make the offer is irrelevant and the mere communication of information or investment advice on securities or an issuer, without securities being offered for subscription or purchase, is not considered an offer to the public as long as it does not provide sufficient information on the terms of the offer and the securities to be offered.

The concept of 'persons' (Art. 2(1)(l) Act) does not either imply a distinction between institutional investors and non-professional clients.

CSSF Circular 05/225[26] sets out that the elements that constitute an offer to the public shall be analysed from a territorial point of view. This means that the location of the offer, i.e. the place of characteristic execution (place of the offer) and the place of residence of the public canvassed by the offer shall be taken into consideration to determine whether the Prospectus Act shall be complied with. As a consequence, (i) an offer of securities made from Luxembourg even to non-residents shall comply with the Prospectus Act and (ii) an offer of securities by a Luxembourg issuer in a foreign country is subject to that foreign country's legislation. However, the Prospectus Act will not apply to offers made abroad to persons residing in Luxembourg or offers made in foreign media available in Luxembourg if the Luxembourg market is not canvassed.

20. In relation to the resale on the secondary market, the Prospectus Act provides that any subsequent resale of securities which were previously the

[25] CSSF Circular 05/225 of 16 December 2005, p. 2.

[26] CSSF Circular 05/225 of 16 December 2005, no. 3.

subject of a public offer shall be regarded as a separate offer (Art. 5(2) Act). This means that, unless the secondary offer exemption is met, the prospectus requirement provided by the Prospectus Act shall be complied with. For example, a qualified investor, who initially subscribed for the securities and intends to resell them, needs to verify whether this resale falls under the scope of the Prospectus Act.

CSSF Circular 05/225 also addresses the issue of resale on the secondary market and confirms that if an investment manager advises the purchase of a particular security to a client without holding it, this activity shall fall outside the scope of the Prospectus Act.[27]

B Exemptions

21. The Prospectus Act provides for exemptions of publication of a prospectus in the following circumstances:

(i) offer of securities to qualified investors. The Prospectus Act (Art. 2(1)(j) Act) implements the definition of qualified investors provided by the Directive (Art. 2(1)(e) Dir.) and confirms that small and medium-sized enterprises (Art. 2(1)(r) Act) and natural persons to be entered into a special register may opt in for being considered as qualified investors;[28] and/or
(ii) offer of securities to less than 100 persons (other than qualified investors) in Luxembourg; and/or
(iii) denomination of at least €50,000; and/or
(iv) total consideration per investor amounts to at least €50,000; and/or
(v) total consideration of the offer is less than €100,000 which limit is calculated over a period of twelve months (Art. 5(2) Act).

In addition, the Prospectus Act provides for prospectus exemption in case of offer of the same types of securities which are spelled out in the Prospectus Directive (Art. 5(3) Act). In particular, granting options to current or former employees or directors of the issuer which allow them to subscribe for securities does not fall within the scope of the obligation to publish a prospectus provided that the options are not negotiable on the capital markets and are exclusively in relation to the employment contract or directorship.[29]

[27] CSSF Circular 05/225 of 16 December 2005, no. 2(b), p. 4.

[28] Entities not authorised or regulated pursuant to the Luxembourg law of 5 April 1993 on the financial sector (the '**Banking Law**') may also be considered as qualified entities provided that their corporate purpose is restricted to investment in securities. In particular, the CSSF has confirmed that Soparfis and special purpose vehicles may be eligible as 'qualified investors' (Guideline delivered by the CSSF named 'Le nouveau "regime prospectus" en 40 Questions/Réponses', no. 24, p. 14).

[29] CSSF Circular 05/225 of 16 December 2005, no. 1 p. 3.

2 Admission to trading on a regulated market

A Prospectus obligation

22. Any admission of securities to trading on a regulated market, as defined in the Directive 2004/39 of 21 April 2004 on markets in financial instruments is subject to prior publication of a prospectus (Art. 6 Act).

B Exemptions

The Act (Art. 6 Act) provided for the same exemptions of publication of a prospectus in the case of admission of securities to trading on a regulated market (Art. 4(2) Dir.).

IV Content and format, language and supplements of the prospectus

1 Content

A Inclusion of all necessary information

23. The Prospectus shall contain all information necessary to enable investors to make an informed assessment of the assets and liabilities, financial position, profit and losses prospects of the issuer and of any guarantor, and of the rights attached to the securities offered (Art. 8(1) Act). In addition, the information must be presented in an easily analysable and understandable form (Art. 8(1) Act; see also Chapter 1, no. 29 for a description of the content of the prospectus as provided by the Prospectus Regulation).

In Luxembourg issuers are often special purpose vehicles issuing asset backed securities. Those entities, like any other, must include audited accounts in the prospectus.[30] However if the special purpose vehicle has not carried out any activity between the date of its incorporation and the submission of the registration document and has not drafted financial accounts, a declaration shall be made by the issuer on that fact in the registration document and the issuer shall be exempt from preparing such accounting document.[31] The CSSF has confirmed that 'carrying out an activity' relates to the principal activity of the issuer that shall be analysed in the context of its corporate purpose.[32] If the special purpose vehicle does not issue asset backed securities, no exemption is provided by the Prospectus Regulation or the Prospectus Act and the special purpose vehicle shall then request the CSSF to grant an exemption on the ground that the required information is of minor importance (Art. 10(2) Act).

[30] Schedule VII of the Prospectus Regulation.

[31] Item 8.1 of Schedule VII of the Prospectus Regulation.

[32] CSSF Guideline 'Questions/Réponses: Le nouveau "régime prospectus" – Partie II', no. 52, p. 4.

The CSSF has confirmed that Article 26 of the Prospectus Regulation may be interpreted in such a way that the order in which the prospectus is tabled may be different from the order which the Prospectus Regulation provides for.[33] In particular, it is not compulsory to table the section on risk factors immediately after the summary, as suggested by Article 26 of the Prospectus Regulation. In addition, information not required by any schedule or building block may be included anywhere in the prospectus.

In Luxembourg, it is also common practice to list or offer fiduciary certificates or notes issued on a fiduciary basis by a fiduciary bank. In this context, the CSSF confirmed that the following schedules shall be used for drawing up the prospectus: Schedule XIII ('securities note'), Schedule XIII, section 4 (for describing the terms and conditions of the underlying issuer), Schedule IX ('registration document' for the description of the underlying issuer) and Schedule X, section 2 (for describing the fiduciary notes issuer).[34] In addition, the CSSF confirmed that the information to be provided on the fiduciary bank shall be identical to the information to be provided on the issuer, as mentioned in the schedule relating to the underlying issuer.[35]

The CSSF also confirmed that for 'tier 1' issuances, the securities shall be considered as debt securities if no convertible right and no voting right is granted to the holder of those securities.[36]

B Financial information presented in accordance with IFRS

24. According to Article 9 of Regulation 1606/2002 of 19 July 2002 on the application of international accounting standards, publicly traded companies shall prepare their consolidated accounts in accordance with IFRS for financial years starting on or after 1 January 2007 (see Chapter 1, no. 34).

It is anticipated that the Directive 2004/109 of 15 December 2004 on the harmonisation of transparency requirements in relation to information about issuers whose securities are admitted to trading on a regulated market[37] (see Chapter 1, no. 3), will be implemented in Luxembourg by the end of 2007. However the CSSF currently recognises US GAAP as equivalent to IFRS for approving prospectuses.

With respect to a guarantor of an issue of securities, there is no obligation for the guarantor to provide its financial accounts under IFRS, unless its home state obliges it to do so.[38]

[33] CSSF Guideline 'Le nouveau "régime prospectus" en 40 Questions/Réponses', no. 30, p. 18.

[34] CSSF Guideline 'Questions/Réponses: Le nouveau "régime prospectus" – Partie II ', no. 51, p. 4.

[35] CSSF Guideline 'Le nouveau "régime prospectus" en 40 Questions/Réponses', no. 31, p. 18.

[36] CSSF Guideline 'Le nouveau "régime prospectus" en 40 Questions/Réponses', no. 32, p. 19. [37] *Official Journal* L 390 of 31 December 2004.

[38] CSSF Guideline 'Le nouveau "régime prospectus" en 40 Questions/Réponses', no. 36, p. 22.

In relation to the presentation of the accounts, the CSSF confirmed that in relation to historical financial information for two accounting years, annual accounts may be included in the same document.[39]

When mentioning the identity of Luxembourg auditors of the accounts of the issuer or guarantor, one shall refer to the *Institut des réviseurs d'entreprises* which is the supervisory authority of auditors in Luxembourg.[40]

C Summary

25. The Prospectus Act requires that the prospectus contains a summary conveying the main characteristics and risks associated with the issuer, any guarantor and the securities (Art. 8(2) Act).

The summary shall be drafted in non-technical language, accessible to all and shall include the information listed in Schedule I of the Prospectus Act.

No summary is required for above €50,000 denomination issues of non-equity securities admitted to trading on a regulated market.

The Prospectus Act provides that the summary shall be read as an introduction to the prospectus and its content may trigger liability of the persons having tabled the summary only if the summary is unclear or misleading and cannot be clarified by reading the entire prospectus (Art. 8(2)(d) and 9(2)Act and see Chapter 1, no. 37).

D Permitted omissions

26. The Prospectus Act has transposed the Prospectus Directive without any amendment.

Therefore, the CSSF accepts that certain information required by the Prospectus Act or the Prospectus Regulation may be omitted from the prospectus if it believes that:

(i) the disclosure of such information would be contrary to the public interest; or
(ii) the disclosure of such information would be seriously detrimental to the issuer, provided, however, that the omission of such information would not be likely to mislead the public with regard to facts and circumstances essential to an informed assessment of the issuer, offeror or guarantor and of the rights attached to the securities to which the prospectus relates; or
(iii) such information is of minor importance to a specific offering or admission to trading on a regulated market and will not influence the assessment of the financial position and prospects of the issuer, offeror or guarantor (Art. 10(2) Act).

[39] CSSF Guideline 'Questions/Réponses: Le nouveau "régime prospectus" – Partie II ', no. 49, p. 3.

[40] CSSF Guideline 'Le nouveau "régime prospectus" en 40 Questions/Réponses', no. 38, p. 23.

In general, information items included in the schedules and building blocks can be omitted if they are not pertinent and no equivalent information is available (Art. 23(4) Reg. and see Chap. 1, no. 39). The Prospectus Act provides that, in exceptional cases, where the information required by the Prospectus Act is not adapted to the activity or the legal form of the issuer or the securities, the prospectus shall contain equivalent information to the required information (Art. 10(3) Act). The CSSF has so far not issued any interpretative circular regarding the concept of 'equivalent information'.

With respect to the base prospectus, the issuer, offeror or person requesting admission to trading on a regulated market is entitled to omit information items which are unknown at the time the prospectus is approved and which can only be determined at the time of the individual issue (Art. 22(2) Reg. and see Chap. 1, no. 39).

The Prospectus Act also allows that the final price of the securities or the volume of the securities to be offered may not be contained in the prospectus. This information shall then be published once available and any investors that have already agreed to purchase or subscribe the securities are granted a two-working days withdrawal period (Art. 10(1)(b) Act).

E Incorporation by reference

In principle, only previously or simultaneously published documents approved by or filed with the CSSF may be incorporated by reference (Art. 15(1) Act). The Prospectus Regulation mentions the types of documents that can be incorporated by reference (Art. 28(1) Reg.). No document may be incorporated by reference in the summary (Art. 15(1) Act).

A document incorporated by reference may be in another language than the prospectus as long as it is in one of the four languages accepted by the CSSF (see no. 31 of this report).

2 Format

27. The document provided to the CSSF for approval is generally named 'prospectus'. However, some jurisdictions such as the United States call it 'offering memorandum'. The CSSF then requires that the cover page of that offering memorandum includes the following: '*This offering memorandum comprises a prospectus for the purposes of Article 5.4 of the Prospectus Directive*'.[41] However, the CSSF takes a more prudent approach in relation to the use of '*pricing supplement*' instead of '*final terms*' since a supplement is in principle subject to a prior approval by the CSSF, but not the final terms.[42]

[41] CSSF Guideline 'Questions/Réponses: Le nouveau "régime prospectus" – Partie II ', no. 46, p. 2.

[42] CSSF Guideline 'Le nouveau "régime prospectus" en 40 Questions/Réponses', no. 15, p. 11.

28. The Prospectus Act suggests various formats for a prospectus, the traditional single-document format, a collection of three separate documents or a base prospectus.

A Single document format

Under this format, the prospectus shall contain information relating to the issuer, the programme and the securities as required by the Prospectus Act and the Prospectus Regulation, in addition to a summary which conveys the essential characteristics and risks associated with the issuer, any guarantor and the securities in a brief manner and non technical language and contain a risk warning to the reader (Art. 8(2) Act).

No summary is required for debt securities whose denomination amounts at least to €50,000 (Art. 8(2) Act).

B Collection of three separate documents

Under this second format, the following documents have to be prepared:

- a registration document including information on the issuer;
- a securities note including information about the securities to be offered to the public or admitted to a regulated market;
- a summary note, including summary of the registration document and securities note (Art. 8(3) Act).

In such a case, a single registration document may be used, within the period validity of the prospectus, in connection with several offers to the public or admission to trading on a regulated market. Only a securities note and a summary note need to be submitted to the CSSF for approval.

C Base prospectus

Under this format, debt securities or warrants either issued under a programme or issued in a continuous or repeated manner by credit institutions (subject to additional requirements) may be issued under a base prospectus including all information required by the Prospectus Act on the issuer, the programme and the securities. The final terms of each issue, including the final pricing terms and the terms that specifically apply to the issue shall be separately filed with the CSSF if not already included in the base prospectus (Art. 8(4) Act) and investors that have already agreed to purchase or subscribe the securities are granted a two-working-days withdrawal period (Art. 10(1)(b) Act).

The CSSF confirmed that final terms may not amend the general terms and conditions of the programme on a general basis and for future tranches. They may only affect tranches issued under those final terms and for a particular trade.[43]

[43] CSSF Guideline 'Questions/Réponses: Le nouveau "régime prospectus" – Partie II ', no. 47, p. 3.

29. Issuers sometimes intend to use the same prospectus for several purposes. This practice is, to some extent accepted by the CSSF. For example, the CSSF accepts that a single base prospectus be used for the admission of securities on a regulated market and the admission of securities on the Euro MTF market (the Luxembourg alternative market), as long as this way to proceed does not impair the clarity of the prospectus.[44]

The same holds true in the case of a multiple-issuers programme. Such a programme may be subject to the drafting of a single prospectus provided that the CSSF considers this presentation justified. In particular, the CSSF will scrutinise the relationship between issuers, i.e. whether they are part of the same group of companies. The issuers shall bring evidence of the relationship amongst them that justifies the drafting of a single prospectus.[45]

In order to improve efficiency, the CSSF accepts the submission of a standardised prospectus such as a 'Unitary Prospectus' or 'Draw-Down Prospectus' in the case of structured products such as credit-linked notes. Such a document which is aimed at describing the underlying securities and which generally incorporates the base prospectus by reference is generally approved by the CSSF within a shorter time frame[46] than the normal approval period.

3 Supplements

30. If, prior to the closing of the offer or the start of trading on the regulated market, either a significant new fact, material error or inaccuracy relating to the information included in the prospectus, which is capable of affecting the investors' assessment of the securities occurs, a supplement shall be submitted for CSSF approval in the same manner as the prospectus (Art. 13 Act). In such a case, the summary and any translations must also be supplemented to take into account the additional information (Art. 13(1) Act).

A 'red herring' prospectus may be approved without inclusion of the number of securities to be issued (or offered to the public or admitted to trading on a regulated market) or the exact price of the securities (as long as the prospectus contains the method of calculation of the price).[47]

In relation to annual accounts or interim annual accounts, the issuer shall draft a supplement to be submitted for CSSF approval each time it considers the information contained in the annual accounts constitutes a significant new fact.[48]

[44] CSSF Guideline 'Le nouveau "régime prospectus" en 40 Questions/Réponses', no. 16, p. 11.

[45] CSSF Guideline 'Questions/Réponses: Le nouveau "régime prospectus" – Partie II ', no. 45, p. 2.

[46] CSSF Guideline 'Le nouveau "régime prospectus" en 40 Questions/Réponses', no. 13, p. 9.

[47] CSSF Guideline 'Le nouveau "régime prospectus" en 40 Questions/Réponses', no. 6, p. 5.

[48] CSSF Guideline 'Questions/Réponses: Le nouveau "régime prospectus" – Partie II ', no. 54, p. 5.

In addition, the CSSF has confirmed that the supplement shall only amend or update general information included in the prospectus and shall not be used to describe or issue a specific tranche; latter information shall only be included in the final terms.[49]

4 Language

31. When Luxembourg is home or host Member State, the CSSF accepts a prospectus and a summary drafted in any of the following languages: English, French, German or Luxemburgish (Art. 20 Act).

For documents incorporated by reference, the CSSF accepts that the language of a document incorporated by reference be different from the language used in the prospectus provided that that language be one of the four languages accepted by the CSSF and that it is accepted by any potential other prudential authority of another Member State.[50]

V Publication and advertisements

1 Method of publication

32. In Luxembourg no notice stating how the prospectus has been made available to, and where it can be obtained by, the public needs to be published. Indeed, this option is provided by the Prospectus Directive but has not been retained by Luxembourg.

The Prospectus Act provides for all the means of publication contemplated by the Prospectus Directive.[51] The prospectus may be published:

(i) by insertion in one or more newspapers widely circulated in Luxembourg such as *D'Wort*; or
(ii) in printed form made available, free of charge, at the office of the Luxembourg Stock Exchange or at the registered office of the issuer and at the office of the financial intermediaries placing or selling the securities, including the Luxembourg paying agents; or
(iii) in electronic form on the issuer's website or, as applicable, on the website of the financial intermediaries; or
(iv) in electronic form on the website of the regulated market where admission to trading is sought (Art. 16(2) Act).

The prospectus needs to be published by the CSSF on the website of the Luxembourg Stock Exchange (www.bourse.lu) for a period of at least twelve months.[52] Investors will thereby be able to have effective, in principle free-of-charge and real-time access to information.

[49] CSSF Guideline 'Le nouveau "régime prospectus" en 40 Questions/Réponses', no. 11, p. 8.
[50] CSSF Guideline 'Le nouveau "régime prospectus" en 40 Questions/Réponses', no. 27, p. 16.
[51] CSSF Circular 05/226 of 16 December 2005, p. 5.
[52] CSSF Guideline 'Le nouveau "régime prospectus" en 40 Questions/Réponses', no.7, p. 5.

Notwithstanding the above, this does not prevent the issuer from using additional means of publication.

Moreover, each investor may receive a printed form of the prospectus upon request to the issuer, offeror, person who asked for the admission of securities to trading on a regulated market or to the financial intermediaries placing or selling the securities concerned (Art. 16(7) Act).

2 Advertisements

33. Advertisements are announcements (a) relating to a specific offer to the public of securities or to an admission to trading on a regulated market which (b) aim to specifically promote the potential subscription or acquisition of such securities (Art. 2(9) Reg.).

Any advertisement relating to an offering of securities to the public or an admission of securities to trading on a regulated market, shall comply with the provisions laid down in Article 17 of the Prospectus Act.

Therefore the advertisement must comply with the following rules:

(i) investors must be able to identify the advertisement as such and the publicity must make reference to the prospectus and indicate the place where the prospectus is made available (Art. 17(2) Act);
(ii) the advertisement must be clearly recognisable as such for a public offering or admission to trading of securities on a regulated market (Art. 17(3) Act);
(iii) the information in the advertisement must not be inaccurate or misleading and must be consistent with that contained in the prospectus, if the prospectus has yet to be published (Art. 17(3) Act).

In addition, any information concerning the public offering or admission to trading, disclosed in written or oral form, must be consistent with that contained in the prospectus. This rule also applies if the information is made public for purposes other than advertising (Art. 17(4) Act).

In the event no prospectus is required under the Prospectus Act, any material information provided by the offeror or issuer which is addressed to qualified investors or special categories of investors, must be disclosed to all qualified investors or special categories of investors to whom the offer is exclusively addressed. When a prospectus is required, the above information must be included in the prospectus or in a supplement (Art. 17(5) Act).

The CSSF is empowered to check whether the advertising activity complies with the Prospectus Act. There is, however, no obligation to submit advertisements to the CSSF for prior approval (Art. 17(6) Act).

VI Use of prospectus approved in other (non EU) countries

34. Along with the Prospectus Directive, the Prospectus Act provides that when Luxembourg is the home Member State with respect to issuers having

their registered office in a third country, the CSSF may approve a prospectus for an offer to the public or for admission to trading on a regulated market drawn up in accordance with the legislation of a third country, provided that:

(i) the prospectus has been drawn up in accordance with international standards set by international securities commission organisations, including the International Organization of Securities Commissions (IOSCO) disclosure standards;
(ii) the information requirements, including information of a financial nature, are equivalent to the requirements under the Prospectus Act;
(iii) the prospectus shall be drawn up in a language accepted by the CSSF (Art. 21(1) Act).

It is necessary to specify in this context that the IOSCO has so far only set up disclosure standards in respect to equity securities (not for non-equity securities).

VII Sanctions

35. In order to ensure that the provisions of the Prospectus Act are complied with, both criminal sanctions (Art. 26 Act) and administrative measures and sanctions (Art. 25 Act) are available, in addition to civil liability actions.

(i) civil liability: Luxembourg general civil liability rules apply for the drafting of the prospectus. Civil liability is excluded on the sole basis of the summary (including its translation) unless its content is misleading, inaccurate or inconsistent when read together with the other parts of the prospectus;
(ii) criminal liability: in the case of a public offer of securities, any failure to have a prospectus approved by the CSSF is punished by a fine ranging from €250 to €125,000 (Art. 26 Act);
(iii) administrative sanctions : any infringement of the Prospectus Act and any failure to cooperate with the CSSF may be punished by an administrative fine ranging from €125 to €125,000 (Art. 25(1) Act).

The CSSF may disclose to the public every measure or sanction that has been imposed for infringement of the provisions adopted pursuant to the Prospectus Act, unless the disclosure would seriously jeopardise the financial markets or cause disproportionate damage to the parties involved (Art. 25(3) Act).

VIII Prospectus liability

36. According to Article 9(1) of the Prospectus Act the responsibility for the information provided in the prospectus is attached to the issuer, the offeror or the person who requests the admission to trading on a regulated market.

The persons responsible for the information included in the prospectus must be clearly identified in the prospectus by their names and functions or, in the case of legal persons, their names and registered offices (Art. 9(1) Act). Those persons shall make a statement in the prospectus pursuant to which, to the best of their knowledge, the information contained in the prospectus is in accordance with the facts and that the prospectus makes no omission likely to affect its import (Art. 9(2) Act).

Pursuant to the Prospectus Act, neither the directors nor the managers are responsible for the information contained in the prospectus unless they ask for the admission of securities to trading on a regulated market (Art. 9(1) Act).[53] However, pursuant to the Prospectus Act, the directors, the managers of the issuer, the offeror or the persons who request admission to trading on a regulated market are liable for the content of the prospectus if they apply for admission to trading on a regulated market.

The provisions of common right as regards civil liability in Luxembourg (laws, regulation and administrative provisions) apply to those persons responsible for the information given in a prospectus.

Unless the summary or translation is misleading or inconsistent when read together with the rest of the prospectus, no civil liability is attached to the summary or its translation (Art. 9 (2) Act).

IX Rules applicable to transactions and securities not subject to the Directive and Regulation

37. The Prospectus Act goes beyond the mere transposition of the Prospectus Directive.

38. In relation to securities excluded from the passported regime and for which the opt-in option has not been exercised (see Chap. 1, no. 9), Part III of the Prospectus Act sets out the rules of approval of a prospectus in relation to the offering of securities to the public or the admission of securities to trading on a regulated market (Art. 28 through 60 Act).

The main differences with the regime set out in Part II of the Prospectus Act are the following:

(i) the securities do not benefit from the European passport, i.e. cannot be freely offered to the public in the Member States or traded on another regulated market without additional approval by the competent authority of the other relevant Member State;
(ii) the prospectus shall not be as detailed as the prospectus drafted pursuant to Part I of the Prospectus Act and, in particular, no summary is needed;
(iii) no annual information is required;

[53] Comments on Article 9 of the draft Prospectus Act, p. 46.

(iv) incorporation by reference of future documents such as annual accounts is possible;
(v) the Luxembourg Stock Exchange is competent for approving a prospectus in case of application to trading on a regulated market;
(vi) no reference is made to civil or criminal liability so that for such matters the general rules of Luxembourg law shall be applicable.

39. Luxembourg has also created the Euro MTF market, an alternative market under which the securities may be traded. The trading is conditional upon the drafting of a prospectus in accordance with the rules and regulations of the Luxembourg Stock Exchange which is competent for approving such prospectus.

However, the Euro MTF market is not a regulated market in the meaning of the Directive 2004/39 of 21 April 2004 on markets in financial instruments and therefore is not included in the list of regulated markets published by the European Commission. However, the Euro MTF market is considered as a regulated market in Luxembourg; it is under the supervision of the CSSF and open to the public.[54]

The CSSF confirmed that a sole prospectus may be drafted for two programmes, one relating to the trading on a regulated market and one relating to the trading on the Euro MTF market, provided that the prospectus remains clear.[55] Along those lines, the CSSF confirmed that the same securities may be admitted to trading on a regulated market and the Euro MTF market.[56]

Securities listed on a regulated market may be transferred without formalities to the Euro MTF market. The issuer shall address a letter to the Luxembourg Stock Exchange requesting such transfer.

X Conclusion

40. The CSSF has developed a true practice and expertise in the handling of the regulatory aspects of a prospectus for a public offer of securities and admission to trading on a regulated market. This is partly due to the willingness of Luxembourg to remain one of the world's prominent sites for debt securities and to cope with the flexibility and innovation required by the international financial market and its players.

[54] Release of the CSSF dated 29 August 2005.

[55] CSSF Guideline 'Le nouveau "régime prospectus" en 40 Questions/Réponses', no. 16, p. 11.

[56] CSSF Guideline 'Le nouveau "régime prospectus" en 40 Questions/Réponses', no. 17, p. 8.

11

The Netherlands

JAN PAUL FRANX
NautaDutilh

I Introduction

1 Legal framework and legislative history

1. In the Netherlands, the offering of securities was traditionally regulated by the Act on the Supervision of Securities Trade 1995 (ASST 1995). The ASST 1995 contained general standards, which were further elaborated in the Decree on the Supervision of Securities Trade 1995 (the 'ASST Decree'). Exemptions from the obligation to publish a prospectus in particular types of situations were provided for by the Exemption Regulation ASST 1995.

2. As per 1 July 2005, the Prospectus Directive was implemented in the Netherlands by the entry into force of an Act amending the ASST 1995 to that effect,[1] a Decree amending the ASST Decree[2] and a regulation amending the Exemption Regulation ASST 1995.[3] Already at the time of implementation, it was known that the aforementioned implementing legal framework would be of a temporary nature. In 2005, the Dutch legislator was already preparing a major legislative operation for the purpose of renewing the entire legal framework for financial markets. A new Act on Financial Supervision was being prepared, in which a major part of the existing securities laws would be integrated, including the ASST. This Act on the Financial Supervision, which entered into force on 1 January 2007, will hereafter be referred to as the AFS 2007.[4] Virtually all of the provisions of the former ASST 1995 and the ASST Decree 1995 have been transmitted to the AFS 2007, generally without the intention of making any changes to the substance of those provisions. Also, certain exemptions from the obligation to publish a prospectus, which were previously contained in the Exemption Regulation ASST 1995, have been 'upgraded' to the level of a formal act by transmitting them as well to the AFS 2007 in the form of exceptions to its scope of application. As a result, the regulatory framework of the AFS 2007 now consists of the Act itself, providing for the obligation to publish a prospectus when securities are offered to the public or admitted to trading on a regulated market in the Netherlands and implementing Article 3(2), 4(1) and 4(2) Dir. in the form of exceptions to the scope of application of the Act. Additionally, a new Exemption Regulation AFS 2007[5] has come into force, implementing Article 1(2) Dir.[6]

[1] Act of 23 June 2005, *Staatsblad* 2005, p. 328.

[2] Decree of 23 June 2005, *Staatsblad* 2005, p. 329.

[3] Regulation of 29 June 2005, *Staatscourant* 1 July 2005, no. 125.

[4] Act of 28 September 2006, *Staatsblad* 2006, 475.

[5] Regulation of 15 November 2006, *Staatscourant* 23 November 2006, no. 229.

[6] It being understood that the exemptions of Art. 1(2)(a) Dir. with respect to securities issued by open-end investment institutions and Art. 1(2)(g) Dir. with respect to rights to occupy an apartment have been taken care of by excluding these from the definition of 'security' contained in Article 1:1 AFS 2007.

2 Definitions

3. In this paragraph some remarks will be made with respect to the way in which certain key concepts have been defined in the AFS 2007: securities (to be divided into equity and non-equity securities) and offer of securities to the public.

A Securities

4. The definition of 'securities' is set out in Article 1:1 AFS 2007 and is narrowly related to the definition of the same concept in Article 2(1)(a) Dir. A key element of the definition is that securities should be negotiable instruments. Securities as defined in Article 1:1 AFS 2007 are deemed to include, among others, negotiable shares, negotiable depositary receipts for shares, negotiable rights of joint ownership in a closed-end collective investment institution and negotiable rights in a limited partnership. The definition also covers negotiable bonds, convertible bonds and warrants. According to the explanatory memoranda to the bill of the AFS 2007,[7] options and futures will not qualify as securities. It is explained that this can be inferred, *inter alia*, from the definition of 'securities' in the Prospectus Directive in combination with the definition of 'financial instruments' in the MiFID[8]. It is further explained that under the Prospectus Directive, the term 'securities' only refers to documents of value that have been issued by an issuer and that do not qualify as financial instruments in the form of agreements.

From the foregoing, it follows that the 'negotiable' element is an important part of the definition of securities. A condition for negotiability is the potential transferability of the instrument to third parties. In addition, an instrument is negotiable if it is usually traded on the capital markets. A feature of an instrument indicating that the instrument is negotiable is its degree of standardisation. As this degree increases, the degree of negotiability will normally increase. As shares in a private limited liability company, even if they are subject to transfer restrictions, are transferable and have a certain degree of standardisation, it is fair to assume that such shares are also negotiable.

Units issued by open-end investment institutions, rights to occupy an apartment and money market instruments having a maturity of less than twelve months have been excluded from the definition of securities in the AFS 2007.

The definition of 'equity securities' in Article 5(1)(d) AFS 2007 closely follows the definition of Article 2(1)(b) Dir. However, the definition of 'non-equity securities' in Article 5(1)(e) is more elaborate than the residual class of instruments covered by Article 2(1)(c) Dir. In the AFS 2007, three subclasses of non-equity securities are explicitly distinguished: (i) securities

[7] Kamerstukken II, 2005–2006, 29 708, no. 19, p. 367. [8] Dir. 2004/39/EC.

which, upon conversion or exchange entitle their owner to acquire securities of which the issuer is not the issuer of the exchangeable securities or an entity belonging to the group of that issuer; (ii) securities which, upon the exercise of the rights attached thereto, provide for settlement in money; and (iii) any other security not being an equity security. The distinction between equity and non-equity securities as well as the distinction between the aforementioned different subclasses of non-equity securities is to a considerable extent decisive for the question which national regulator is competent to approve the prospectus.

B Offer of securities to the public

5. The definition of 'offer of securities to the public' contained in Article 5(1)(a) AFS 2007 is partly based on the definition of Article 2(1)(d) Dir. It should concern a sufficiently specified offer addressed to more than one person to purchase or otherwise acquire securities or an invitation to a third party to make such an offer. The term 'offer' refers to an offer under Netherlands contract law within the meaning of Article 6:217(1) of the Dutch Civil Code.

The part of the definition covering invitations to make an offer is relevant for situations in which no formal offer to purchase or sell in the meaning of Article 6:217(1) Dutch Civil Code is made, but parties are in a more preliminary stage of negotiations with respect to a potential securities transaction. For instance, opening the order book for subscriptions by investors in the framework of a book building procedure prior to an IPO is under Dutch contract law generally considered to constitute an invitation to make an offer in the sense of Article 6:217(1) Dutch Civil Code, but at the same time constitutes an 'offer of securities to the public' under the AFS 2007. In other words, the concept of 'offer' under Dutch securities law is broader than the same concept under Dutch contract law.

II Competent authority

6. The competent authority for approving prospectuses in the Netherlands is the *Stichting Autoriteit Financiële Markten* (Authority for the Financial Markets, or AFM). The competence of the AFM is based on the definition of 'home Member State' contained in Article 2(1)(m) Dir. Therefore, whether the AFM is competent to approve a prospectus will depend on a number of circumstances: first, the issuer's place of business in accordance with applicable law or its articles of association (i.e. situated in the Netherlands, in another Member State, or outside the European Union); second, the type of securities which are offered (i.e. equity or non-equity securities); third, the place where the offer of securities is made may be relevant. In practice, the most important category of situations in which the AFM will be competent to approve the prospectus

includes the offering of equity securities or non-equity securities with a nominal value per security of less than €1,000 by an issuer with registered office in the Netherlands.

Pursuant to Article 5:7 AFS 2007, the AFM is authorised to accept a transfer of competence to approve a prospectus by the national regulator of another Member State. Vice versa, Article 5:8 AFS 2007 provides that the AFM may transfer its competence to approve a prospectus to the national regulator of another Member State, provided that such regulator accepts this transfer. The explanatory documentation to the bill of the AFS 2007 states that a transfer of competence by the AFM to another regulator should only occur on the basis of important reasons, for example if an offer of securities to the public is made by an issuer which has its registered office in the Netherlands, but does not perform any economic activity in the Netherlands and carries out all its activities in another Member State, and intends to make an offer of securities to the public addressed only to persons resident in that other Member State.[9]

III Procedure of prior approval and appeal

1 Offer of securities to the public

7. Article 5:2 AFS 2007 provides that it is prohibited to offer securities to the public in the Netherlands or to have securities admitted to trading on a regulated market in the Netherlands, unless a prospectus has been approved by the AFM or by a competent regulator of another Member State and subsequently has been published. The explanatory documents to the bill of the AFS 2007 state that in the approval process the prospectus should be tested on completeness, consistency and accessibility. In this context, 'completeness' should be interpreted as the prospectus containing the information necessary for the investor to make an informed assessment with respect to the assets, the financial position, the results and the prospects of the issuer and the information required to be included pursuant to the Prospectus Regulation.

It is important to note that the prohibition to offer non-negotiable securities (i.e. not covered by the Prospectus Directive) without making a prospectus generally available, which prohibition was still contained in the ASST 1995, has not been transmitted to the AFS 2007. Non-negotiable instruments do not qualify as 'securities' within the meaning of the Prospectus Directive and the AFS 2007.

Exceptions from the prohibition to offer securities to the public based on Article 3(2) and Article 4(1) Dir. have been implemented by Article 5:3 AFS 2007. Reference is made to the chapter on general provisions of community law in this book.

[9] Kamerstukken II, 2005–2006, 29 708, no. 19, p. 568.

2 Admission to trading on a regulated market

8. As set out above under III.1, Article 5:2 AFS 2007 also prohibits the admission of securities to trading on a regulated market in the Netherlands without making an approved prospectus generally available. The exceptions to this prohibition, which are based on Article 4(2) Dir., are implemented by Article 5:4 AFS 2007. Reference is made to the chapter on general provisions of community law in this book.

3 Exemption Regulation AFS 2007

9. The exemptions contained in Article 1(2) Dir. have been implemented in a new Exemption Regulation AFS 2007.[10]

4 No individual exemptions

10. Previously, the ASST 1995 provided for the authority of the AFM to grant individual exemptions from the prohibition to offer securities or admit securities to trading on a regulated market without making an approved prospectus available. The AFS 2007 no longer provides for this possibility, arguing that it is not in conformity with the Prospectus Directive, which only includes generally applicable exceptions and exemptions from the obligation to publish a prospectus.

5 Procedure

11. Based on Article 13(2), (3) and (4) Dir., the AFS 2007 provides in Article 5:9a that the AFM shall announce its decision regarding the approval of the prospectus to the applicant within a time limit of ten working days of receipt of the application for approval. This time limit is extended to twenty working days in the case of an IPO. If the documents submitted by the applicant are incomplete, the AFM shall give the applicant the opportunity to supplement the application within a time limit to be determined by the AFM. If the applicant fails to supplement the application within this time limit, the AFM may decide not to consider the application any further.

6 Appeal

12. Against decisions of the AFM on the application to approve a prospectus appeal can be instituted by any directly interested party with the Central Administrative Business Court (*College van Beroep voor het Bedrijfsleven*) within six weeks after the date on which the decision is published.

[10] Regulation of 15 November 2006, *Staatscourant* 23 November 2006, no. 229.

IV Content and format, language and supplements of the prospectus

1 Content

13. Article 5:13 AFS 2007 provides that a prospectus shall contain all information which, taking into account the nature of the issuer and of the securities offered to the public or admitted to trading on a regulated market, is necessary to enable investors to make an informed assessment of the assets and liabilities, financial position, financial results and prospects of the issuer and of any guarantor and of the rights attaching to such securities, including without limitation the information referred to in Articles 3 through 23 Prospectus Regulation and the annexes thereto. Thus, the main rule for contents of the prospectus contained in Article 5 Dir. is almost literally implemented into national law. Additionally, Article 5:13(2) AFS 2007 provides that the information to be included in the prospectus should not conflict with any other information with respect to the issuer, which may be known to the AFM. The information should be presented in a form that is comprehensible to a reasonably informed and prudent investor.

Article 5:14 FSA 2007 provides that the summary of the prospectus should be brief and should be drawn up in language which is comprehensible to a reasonably informed and prudently operating person and should convey the essential characteristics and risks. In the explanatory memorandum to the bill of the AFS 2007, reference is made to Recital 21 Dir., in which it is provided that a summary should not normally exceed 2,500 words. The summary should contain a warning to the effect that it should be read as an introduction to the prospectus and any decision to invest in the issuer should be based on consideration of the prospectus as a whole. The warning should contain a statement to the effect that, briefly put, the summary can only result in civil liability in combination with other parts of the prospectus.

Article 5:17 AFS 2007 provides for the possibility of incorporating information in the prospectus by reference. Reference can only be made to documents published previously or simultaneously with the prospectus, which have been filed with, or approved by, the competent regulator of a Member State. Consequently, in accordance with the system of Article 11 Dir., future information cannot be incorporated by reference. The possibility of incorporating future information could increase the flexibility of making securities offerings under offering programs.[11] It is not allowed to incorporate information by reference in the summary.

Article 5:18 AFS 2007 provides for the possibility of omitting the final amount of securities to be offered, or the final offer price or exchange ratio,

[11] In the USA the shelf registration system permits incorporating information contained in future filings with the SEC in advance by reference in the prospectus.

from the prospectus if this information is not yet known. The explanatory memorandum to the bill of the AFS 2007 states that the term 'offer price' should be widely interpreted. This includes, amongst other things, the coupon premium and conversion premium, and the conversion price in the case of convertible shares. Instead of stating the offer price or the amount of securities offered to the public, it will be sufficient to insert the criteria or conditions which are applied in determining these. As soon as the offer price and the amount of securities have been fixed, this information should be published and filed with the AFM.

2 Format

14. Article 5:15 AFS 2007 provides that a prospectus can be drawn up, at the discretion of the issuer, as a single document or as three separate documents. A prospectus consisting of one single document should at least contain the information referred to in Article 5:13 AFS 2007 (see paragraph IV.1 above) and a summary complying with article 5:14 AFS 2007 (see also IV.1 above). Additionally, Article 25(1) Reg. contains a number of supplemental requirements concerning the format of the single-document prospectus.

A prospectus consisting of three separate documents should include a registration document with information relating to the issuer, a securities note with information relating to the securities to be offered or admitted to trading and a summary note. Using a tripartite prospectus may be useful if the issuer intends to make multiple offerings of different types of securities within one year (being the term within which the approval by the competent authority of a registration document remains valid). All three parts of a tripartite prospectus need to be approved by the AFM. If the information relating to the issuer has changed at the time of making the offering, the securities note may update the registration document.

Article 5:16 AFS 2007 provides for the possibility to use a base prospectus, mainly in the event that the issuer will offer non-equity securities in the framework of a debt issuance program. The final terms of the offering can be omitted from the base prospectus and can be published and deposited with the AFM at the time of each individual offering of debt securities. These final terms do not need to be approved by the AFM. It is important to note that the AFM will see to it that final terms are only used to communicate information to the market which has already been provided for as an option in the base prospectus. In other words, final terms may complete the information of the offering, but not supplement the information in comparison with the base prospectus itself. In the latter case, a supplemental prospectus requiring approval by the AFM should be drawn up and published. Article 26(1) through (4) and (8) Reg. contains provisions for the format of a base prospectus.

3 Supplements

15. Article 5:23 AFS 2007 provides that, in the event of a significant new factor, material mistake or inaccuracy occurring in the period between approval of the prospectus and closing of the offer of securities, the issuer or offeror should draw up a document supplementing the prospectus. This supplemental prospectus requires approval by the AFM or the competent regulator of another member state. If the AFM has previously approved the prospectus, it will also be competent to approve any supplemental prospectus. The AFM should take the decision whether or not to approve the supplemental prospectus within seven working days of receipt of the document. Subsequently, the supplemental prospectus has to be published.

Article 5:23(6) and (7) provides that any party which has made an offer aimed at the conclusion of an agreement on the purchase or acquisition of the securities offered or to be admitted to trading on the regulated market, will have the right to withdraw the offer or rescind the agreement within two working days after the publication of a supplemental prospectus. In view of this, it will be preferable in the context of a book-building process not to have a supplemental prospectus published during the last two working days before allocation of the shares and commencement of trading.

4 Language

16. Article 5:19 AFS 2007 contains provisions with respect to the language in which the prospectus should be drawn up. Generally, it closely follows the structure of article 19 Dir. The explanatory memorandum to the bill of the AFS 2007 expressly confirms that English is, in the opinion of the legislator, a language which is customary in the sphere of international finance. It further mentions the possibility for the AFM to formulate a policy as to whether the summary of a prospectus drawn up in a language other than Dutch, should be translated into Dutch. In practice, the AFM will not require a Dutch translation of the summary of a prospectus drawn up in English.

V Publication and advertisements

1 Method of publication

17. Article 14 Dir., providing for the different methods of publication of a prospectus, is implemented in Article 5:21 AFS 2007. The prospectus should be made generally available to the public after it has been approved. In the explanatory memorandum it is stated that a prospectus is generally available if it has been published and is accessible to potential investors. The term 'accessible' refers to the possibility of taking note of the content of the prospectus. In this context a prospectus consisting of various parts has only been made generally available when all its parts have been published.

The prospectus can be made generally available at the latest at the time of offering the securities to the public or admitting the securities to trading on a regulated market. The explanatory memorandum states that, as the duration of an offer of securities may fluctuate greatly, depending on the type of transaction, by not stipulating a minimum term it is left to the offeror to determine when it wants to make the prospectus generally available.[12] In the event of an IPO, a prospectus should be published at least six working days before the end of the offer or admission, in order to give the investor sufficient reading time to make an informed assessment.

Article 5:21(3) AFS 2007 provides for the different means of publication set out by Article 14(2) Dir.: (a) publication in a daily newspaper; (b) in a separate printed document; (c) on the website of the issuer, possibly in combination with the website of the underwriter; (d) on the website of the respective regulated market; or (e) on the website of the AFM. As to (d), it should be noted that Euronext Amsterdam facilitates publication of prospectuses on its website, which is only accessible for investors identifying themselves as residents in the Netherlands. As to (e), it should be noted that for the time being, the AFM does not facilitate publication of the full text of prospectuses on its website. Rather, the website of the AFM contains a list of approved prospectuses, often with a hyperlink to the website of the issuer.

Article 14(3) Dir. offers member states a choice between requiring and not requiring that a notice be published stating how the prospectus has been made generally available. This possibility has not been taken up by the Dutch legislator. The explanatory memorandum states that imposing the obligation to publish this notice entails an administrative burden, while its added value is questionable. It is up to the issuer to determine for itself how the offer of the securities for the admission to trading will be announced, taking into account the requirements of Article 5:20 AFS 2007 (which provision implements Article 15 Dir.).[13]

Article 5:22 AFS 2007, implementing Article 9 Dir., provides that a prospectus will be valid for further offers of securities or admissions of securities to trading on a regulated market during a period of twelve months after it has been made generally available, provided that it is updated by a supplemental prospectus in accordance with article 5:23 AFS 2007 (see paragraph IV.3 above) if necessary. A base prospectus of a debt issuance program is also valid for a period of twelve months after publication.

2 Advertisements

18. Article 5:20 AFS 2007, implementing Article 15 Dir., provides for certain rules with respect to advertisements relating to an offer of securities

[12] Kamerstukken II, 2005–2006, 29 708, no. 19, p. 577.

[13] Kamerstukken II, 2005–2006, 29 708, no. 19, p. 578.

to the public or admission of securities to trading on a regulated market. An advertisement should be recognisable as such and the information contained in the advertisement should be consistent with the information included in the prospectus. The methods of dissemination of advertisements are enumerated in Article 34 Reg.

Article 5:20(3) AFS 2007 provides that certain information furnished to investors during special meetings (including road shows) should also be in the prospectus or in a prospectus supplement. The provision refers to 'essential information . . . which is relevant for the assessment of the assets and liabilities, financial position, financial results and the prospects of the issuer and the rights attaching to the securities'. Although the terms 'essential' and 'relevant' indicate different levels of importance, it is generally acknowledged in practice that breakdowns and further elaborations of financial information included in the prospectus, which are usually provided to professional investors during road shows, do not shed a different light on the financial information included in the prospectus as a whole and are generally deemed too technical and therefore not 'essential' for other (retail) investors.

Although during the preparatory stage of an offering, advertisements and press releases are usually sent in draft to the AFM, the AFM is not prepared to review and comment upon these drafts. Consequently, if the contents of a press release incurs the risk of having a promotional nature, it may be prudent to treat the press release as an advertisement for the purpose of article 5:20 AFS 2007/Article 15 Dir. by making it recognisable as such and including a reference to the prospectus. Thus, the provision for advertisements may serve as a safe harbour for any communication of a promotional nature relating to an offering or admission.

VI Use of prospectus approved in other (non EU) countries

19. Article 5:11 AFS 2007, implementing Article 17 and 18 Dir., provides for the possibility of using a prospectus approved by the regulator of another Member State for offerings to the public or admissions of securities to trading on the regulated market in the Netherlands. In that case, the AFM's approval of the prospectus will not be required. Instead, the regulator of the other Member State will provide the AFM with a certificate of approval attesting that the prospectus was drawn up in accordance with the Prospectus Directive and a copy of the approved prospectus.

VII Sanctions

20. Article 5:25 AFS 2007 authorises the AFM to give an order to take certain specific action to an issuer or offeror in the event that the provisions of the AFS 2007 relating to the offering of securities or the provisions of

the Prospectus Regulation have not been complied with. For instance, if securities have been offered to the public without drawing up a prospectus at all, the AFM may order the issuer to draw up a prospectus within a specific period of time. Paragraph 2 of Article 5:25 AFS 2007 provides that an order issued by the AFM may not negatively affect any agreements entered into by the issuer or offeror and any third party. It is considered that the authority to nullify specific agreements would enable the AFM to serve the interests of specific market parties, which is deemed to be inconsistent with the general duty of the AFM to serve the public interest.

VIII Prospectus liability

21. Under Dutch civil law, a claim of an investor based on prospectus liability will generally be qualified as a claim based on tort. The Netherlands courts will assume jurisdiction if the defendant has its registered office in the Netherlands or damage has been inflicted in the Netherlands.

Under the Dutch Act providing conflict of laws rules with respect to actions based on tort (*Wet Conflictenrecht Onrechtmatige Daad 2001*), the main rule provides for applicability of the national law of the state in the territory of which the tort has taken place. Consequently, the Dutch courts will apply Netherlands law with respect to claims based on prospectus liability relating to securities offerings in the Netherlands.

The legal framework for prospectus liability is contained in Article 6:194–196 of the Dutch Civil Code. These provisions relate to liability for misleading (promotional) statements in general and form a specific class of provisions dealing with tort liability. Publishing or co-publishing a misleading prospectus will constitute a tort committed by the issuer and the lead manager. In practice, investors will first try to recover their damages by addressing the lead manager. In its still leading decision in Re Coop[14], the Dutch Supreme Court has ruled that claims against the lead manager based on prospectus liability should be rejected, if the lead manager is able to demonstrate that it has carried out an adequate due diligence investigation with respect to the issuer and its business in connection with drawing up the prospectus. If an adequate due diligence investigation has been carried out, the misleading character of the prospectus cannot be imputed to the lead manager. As a result, imputation, being one of the constitutive elements of tort under Dutch civil law, will be lacking.

In the Netherlands, there is no longer any regulatory obligation to carry out due diligence in preparation of a securities offering or listing.[15] However, in order to avoid unnecessary exposure of the lead manager and

[14] Hoge Raad 2 December 1994, NJ 1996, 246 (re Coop).

[15] The regulations of Euronext Amsterdam used to provide for a due diligence obligation until 1 July 2005, the date of implementation of the Prospectus Directive.

maintain his due diligence defence under the terms of the Coop decision of the Dutch Supreme Court, in practice, an adequate due diligence investigation will have to be carried out.

In view of the limited scope of Article 6(2) Dir., implementation of the Prospectus Directive in the Netherlands as per 1 July 2005 has not resulted in any changes of the prospectus liability regime under Dutch civil law.

IX Rules applicable to transactions and securities not subject to the Directive and Regulation

22. Securities which are not negotiable are not covered by the Directive and the Regulation and are therefore beyond the scope of the Dutch implementing legislation. As a result, an offer to the public of non-negotiable securities is not subject to the obligation of drawing up a prospectus. Examples of this type of securities are non-negotiable options and futures. To determine whether a security is negotiable, refer to paragraph I.2.A above. Depending on the type of non-negotiable financial instrument, an investor in such an instrument may be protected in a different manner under Dutch law, for instance by reason of the offeror or intermediary of the instrument being subject to a regulatory regime providing for a duty of care towards the investor, or the issuer of the instruments qualifying as an investment institution and thus being subject to the obligation to draw up a (more concise) prospectus under the regulatory regime for investment institutions.

X Conclusion

23. Implementation of the Prospectus Directive into the legislation of the Netherlands has been timely and quite precise. Recent changes to the structure of the legal framework have not so much been caused by implementation of the Prospectus Directive, but rather by the major legislative operation of integrating the most substantial part of the regulatory framework for the financial markets in one act, the Act on the Financial Supervision 2007.

International securities offerings are facilitated in the Netherlands by the AFM not requiring a Dutch translation of the summary of an English-language prospectus, thereby avoiding market parties having to spend additional time and costs.

12
Poland

DANUTA PAJEWSKA AND JAKUB PIETRUSZKA
Wardyński & Partners

I Introduction

1. The recent history of the Polish capital market begins in the 1990s, when new regulations on financial institutions and instruments were adopted. That meant that in 1991 the Polish stock exchange was reopened, after an absence of over fifty years.

2. In 2005, a year after Poland's accession to the European Union, new regulations on the capital market were introduced by three pieces of legislation:

(i) The Act on Public Offering, Conditions Governing the Introduction of Financial Instruments to Organised Trading, and Public Companies;
(ii) The Act on Trading in Financial Instruments;
(iii) The Act on Capital Market Supervision.

3. In 2006, the above Acts were amended by the Act on Financial Market Supervision. All of those Acts fully adapt Polish legislation to the European Union law on capital markets, and in many instances by direct implementation, or reference, to the European Union directives and regulations.

4. In the Polish legal system, the Prospectus Directive and Prospectus Regulation were implemented into the Act on Public Offering, Conditions Governing the Introduction of Financial Instruments to Organised Trading, and Public Companies, and the following information is based mainly on those provisions.

II Competent authority

5. On 19 September 2006, with the entry into force of the Act of 21 July 2006 on supervision of the financial market, the new administrative authority, the **Financial Supervision Commission** ('Commission'), commenced its activities. It took over the responsibilities of the Polish Securities and Exchange Commission and of the Insurance and Pension Funds Supervisory Commission.

The Commission's activities are supervised by the President of the Polish Council of Ministers.

6. The Commission is composed of a Chairperson, two Vice-Chairpersons and four members.

7. The members of the Commission are:

(i) the minister responsible for financial institutions or such minister's representative;
(ii) the minister responsible for social security or such minister's representative;
(iii) the Governor of the National Bank of Poland or Deputy Governor of the National Bank of Poland, delegated by the Governor;
(iv) a representative of the President of the Republic of Poland.

8. The Commission's responsibilities comprise the following:

(i) exercising supervision, as defined in No. 9 below, over the financial market;

(ii) fostering the proper operation of the financial market;
(iii) promoting the development and competitiveness of the financial market;
(iv) taking educational and informative actions related to the operation of the financial market;
(v) participating in the preparation of drafts of legal acts related to financial market supervision;
(vi) creating opportunities for amicable and conciliatory resolution of disputes between financial market participants, including, in particular, disputes arising from contractual relationships between the entities subject to the Commission's supervision and the customers buying their services.

9. Supervision of the financial market shall comprise the following:

(i) capital market supervision,[1]
(ii) banking supervision,[2]
(iii) pensions supervision,[3]
(iv) insurance supervision,[4]
(v) supervision over electronic money institutions.[5]

10. In civil law cases arising from the relationships entered into in connection with participation in trading on the banking, pension, insurance or capital market, or relating to entities operating on those markets, the Commission's Chairperson shall have the powers of a prosecutor ensuing from the provisions of the Code of Civil Procedure.

11. In instances of offences committed within the scope of rules granting Commission supervision, indicated in No. 9 above, or pertaining to any acts aimed against the interests of the market participants, committed in connection with the activities of the entities operating on that market, the

[1] Governed by the provisions of the Act on Trading in Financial Instruments of 29 July 2005, the Act on Public Offering, Conditions Governing the Introduction of Financial Instruments to Organised Trading and Public Companies dated 29 July 2005, the Act on Investment Funds of 27 May 2004, the Act on Commodity Exchanges of 26 October 2000 and the Act on Capital Market Supervision of 29 July 2005.

[2] Governed by the provisions of the Banking Law of 29 August 1997, the Act on the National Bank of Poland of 29 August 1997 and the Act on the Operation of Cooperative Banks, Their Associations and Associating Banks dated 7 December 2000.

[3] Governed by the provisions of the Act on the Organisation and Operation of Pension Funds of 28 August 1997, the Act on Occupational Pension Programs of 20 April 2004, the Act on Personal Pension Accounts of 20 April 2004 and the Act on Insurance and Pension Fund Supervision and the Insurance Ombudsman dated 22 May 2003.

[4] Governed by the provisions of the Act on Insurance Activity of 22 May 2003, the Act on Insurance Intermediation of 22 May 2003, the Act on Insurance and Pension Funds Supervision and the Insurance Ombudsman dated 22 May 2003 and the Act on Premium Subsidies for Farm Crops and Livestock Insurance dated 7 July 2005.

[5] Governed by the provisions of the Electronic Payment Instruments Act of 12 September 2002.

Commission Chairperson, upon being petitioned, is vested with those rights that an aggrieved party has in criminal proceedings.

III Procedure of prior approval and appeal

1 Approval procedure

12. In the case of securities issued by an issuer for which the Republic of Poland is the home state, in order to obtain approval of the issue prospectus drawn up as a single document, the issuer or selling shareholder shall – acting through an investment firm – lodge with the Commission an application containing:

(i) business name and registered office of the issuer;
(ii) basic information on the securities covered by the issue prospectus, in particular details as to the number, type, and par value of the securities;
(iii) designation of the investment firm which will offer the securities covered by the application.

13. The following shall be attached to the application:

(i) The issue prospectus shall be drawn up in the Polish language, subject to No. 14 below;
(ii) The articles of association, the deed of incorporation or such other documents connected with incorporation, activities, and organisation of the issuer as might be required under pertinent laws;
(iii) A resolution concerning issuance of securities by way of a public offering or seeking admission of securities to trading on a regulated market and dematerialisation of the securities, as adopted by the appropriate decision-making body of the issuer or, in the case of an issue prospectus referring to shares, the pertinent resolution of the General Shareholders Meeting of a joint-stock company;
(iv) Specification of the information which is covered by the issuer's or the selling shareholder's request for authorisation of omission of certain information from the issue prospectus, along with a statement of reason for such request;
(v) Specification of the information whose inclusion in the issue prospectus is not possible, along with a description of the specific features of the information or circumstances which justify such omission from the prospectus, subject to No. 14 below.

14. If the public offering or admission to trading on a regulated market is to occur exclusively in a Member State other than the Republic of Poland, the issue prospectus attached to the application referred to in No. 13 above may be drawn up in the Polish or the English language, at the issuer's or the selling shareholder's discretion.

15. The Commission shall hand down its decision on approval of the issue prospectus within ten business days of submission of the application, subject to No. 16 below.

16. In the case of an issuer whose existing securities issued and subscribed for have not been offered in a public offering and have not been admitted to trading on a regulated market, the Commission shall hand down its decision on approval of an issue prospectus relating to securities of such an issuer within twenty business days following submission of the application.

17. Where the submitted documentation is incomplete, or where additional information is required, the Commission may – within the scope necessary for verification of the facts set out in the issue prospectus – demand the provision of other documents and information concerning the financial or legal situation of the issuer by:

(i) The issuer;
(ii) The selling shareholder;
(iii) The qualified auditor of financial statements who has audited the financial statements of the issuer contained in the issue prospectus;
(iv) The investment firm which will offer the securities;
(v) A parent entity or a subsidiary of the issuer or of the selling shareholder.

18. Where the submitted documentation is incomplete, the Commission shall, within a period not exceeding ten business days following the submission of such documentation, notify the applicant of the need to supplement that documentation.

19. The Commission may demand inclusion of additional information in the issue prospectus within the scope, and subject to the conditions defined in Article 23 of the Prospectus Regulation.

20. If the situation described in No 17 or 19 arises, the time limits defined in No. 15 shall be counted from the day on which the documentation has been supplemented or the information called for has been submitted.

21. The Commission may decline to approve an issue prospectus if it does not comply, in its form or substance, with the requirements laid down in pertinent laws.

22. In its decision on approval of the issue prospectus, the Commission may, at the issuer's request, authorise the omission from the prospectus of information whose disclosure:

(i) would be contrary to the public interest;
(ii) would be seriously detrimental to the issuer – provided that the omission would not mislead investors in general as to the facts and

circumstances material for assessment of the securities or of the situation of the issuer;

(iii) is of minor importance to the specific offering or admission to trading on a regulated market, provided that the omission would not mislead investors in general as to the facts and circumstances material for assessment of the securities or of the situation of the issuer.

23. Securities of an issuer having its registered office in a Member State for which the Republic of Poland is a host state may be offered in a public offering or admitted to trading on a regulated market in the Republic of Poland provided that the Commission receives from the competent authority in the issuer's home state:

(i) A notification document confirming approval of the issue prospectus relating to such securities and defining the scope of information:
  (a) whose omission from the issue prospectus has been authorised by the competent authority, or
  (b) not included in the issue prospectus on account of the nature of the issuer's activities, its legal form, the securities in question, or of other reasonable considerations which justify omission of such information from the prospectus, along with a statement of reason for such authorisation or non-inclusion;

(ii) A copy of the approved issue prospectus, drawn up and updated in compliance with the law of such Member State, along with a translation into Polish of the part of the issue prospectus setting out a summary of the information contained therein.

24. Upon receipt of the documents referred to in No. 23 above, the Commission shall promptly notify the issuer or the selling shareholder, as appropriate.

25. The issuer or the selling shareholder shall be obligated to make available to the public the issue prospectus referred to in No. 23(ii) above, drawn up in Polish or English, as chosen by the issuer or by the selling shareholder. In the case of an issue prospectus drawn up in English, the issuer or the selling shareholder shall be obligated to make available to the public, along with the issue prospectus, the summary note or the summary which is a part of a prospectus drawn up as a single document in Polish.

26. The issue prospectus shall not be made available in the Republic of Poland prior to receipt from the Commission of the notification referred to in No. 24 above.

27. Provisions of No. 23–26 above shall apply accordingly to the supplements referred to in No. 45 below approved by the competent authority in the issuer's home state. If the Commission does not receive notification confirming approval by the competent authority in the issuer's home state

of the supplement referring to an event known to the Commission which might materially affect assessment of the security, the Commission should request such competent authority to take appropriate measures to clarify the situation.

28. Provisions of Nos. 23–27 above shall apply accordingly to an issuer having its registered office in a state other than a Member State which has designated a Member State other than the Republic of Poland as its home state.

2 Exemptions

29. The public offering or the admission of securities to trading on a regulated market shall require the drawing up of an issue prospectus, its approval by the Commission, and its being made available to the public, subject to Nos. 30–33 below.

30. Drawing up of the issue prospectus, its approval, and making it available to the public subject, shall not be required **in the case of a public offering or admission to trading on a regulated market** of:

(i) Non-equity securities issued by the State Treasury or by the National Bank of Poland;
(ii) Non-equity securities issued by a Member State other than the Republic of Poland, by a Member State's regional or local authorities, including local government bodies, by a Member State's central bank, by the European Central Bank, or by public international bodies of which one or more Member States are members;
(iii) Securities unconditionally and irrevocably guaranteed by the State Treasury, by a Member State, or by a Member State's regional or local authorities, including local government bodies;
(iv) Shares in the capital of the central bank of a Member State;
(v) Securities issued by the entities referred to in the Law on Public-Benefit and Voluntary Activities of 24 April 2003, or entities of a similar nature which have registered offices in a Member State other than the Republic of Poland, where the issue proceeds are to be devoted exclusively towards implementation of goals defined in the articles of association of such entities;
(vi) Non-equity securities issued in a continuous or repeated manner in cycles comprising at least two offerings executed within an interval of not more than twelve months by a credit institution with its registered office in a Member State, where such non-equity securities are not subordinated, convertible, or exchangeable, do not incorporate the right to subscribe for or acquire other types of securities, and do not comprise an underlying instrument for securities defined in the Act on Trading in Financial Instruments, and the total value of these securities' offering over a period of twelve consecutive months, calculated

on the basis of the issue price, is less than €50 million or the zloty equivalent thereof, calculated at the mid exchange rate for the euro quoted by the National Bank of Poland for the day on which the issue price of these securities is defined;

(vii) Non-fungible shares of capital whose main purpose is to provide the holder with a right to occupy a flat or other form of real estate or part thereof, where such shares may not be disposed of without forfeiting such right.

31. Drawing up of the issue prospectus, its approval, and making it available to the public, shall not be required **in the case of a public offering**:

(i) Addressed exclusively to qualified investors;

(ii) Addressed exclusively to investors each of whom acquires securities of a value, calculated on the basis of the issue price or selling price, of at least €50,000 or the zloty equivalent thereof, calculated at the mid exchange rate for the euro quoted by the National Bank of Poland for the day on which that price is defined;

(iii) Concerning securities whose par value per unit amounts to not less than €50,000 or the zloty equivalent thereof, calculated at the mid exchange rate for the euro quoted by the National Bank of Poland for the day on which the par value of those securities is defined;

(iv) Concerning securities whose total value, calculated on the basis of the issue price or selling price, does not exceed – over a period of twelve consecutive months – €100,000 or the zloty equivalent thereof, calculated in the manner defined in point (ii);

(v) Comprising exclusively:

  (a) Delivery of securities to shareholders in the target company in connection with the acquisition of another company by the issuer,

  (b) Delivery of securities to the shareholders in a company merging with the issuer in connection with the issuer's merger with another company,

  (c) Offering or delivery of shares:

    - To shareholders, on a free-of-charge basis (from the company's resources), or
    - As payment of dividend in respect of shares, where the shares being delivered are of the same type as those in respect of which the dividend is being paid out,

  (d) Offering or delivery of securities of an issuer whose securities are admitted to trading on a regulated market, by the issuer or a related undertaking within the meaning of the Accountancy Act of September 29 September 1994, to current or former directors or employees of such issuer or affiliate,

   (e) Delivery of shares to shareholders in substitution of existing shares of the same type, where such delivery does not entail an increase in the share capital of the issuer;
(vi) Securities, where the total value of their issue over the period of twelve consecutive months, calculated on the basis of the issue price, is less than €2.5 million or the zloty equivalent thereof, calculated at the mid exchange rate quoted by the National Bank of Poland for the day on which the issue price of those securities is defined.

32. Drawing up of the issue prospectus, its approval, and making it available to the public, shall not be required where **admission to trading on a regulated market** is sought for:

(i) Shares representing, over a period of twelve consecutive months, less than 10 per cent of all an issuer's shares of the same type admitted to trading on the same regulated market;
(ii) Shares delivered in substitution of existing shares, which are of the same type as the substituted shares admitted to trading on the same regulated market, where such delivery does not entail an increase in the share capital of the issuer;
(iii) Shares in a company whose other shares of the same type are admitted to trading on the same regulated market, where the purpose of the offering or delivery of shares was to enable holders of other securities of that company to exercise their rights;
(iv) Securities delivered to shareholders in the target company in connection with the acquisition of another company by the issuer;
(v) Securities delivered to shareholders in a company merging with the issuer in connection with the issuer's merger with another company;
(vi) Shares in a company whose other shares of the same type are admitted to trading on the same regulated market, where such shares were offered or delivered:
   (a) To shareholders, on a free-of-charge basis (from the company's resources), or
   (b) As payment of dividend in respect of shares, where the shares being delivered are of the same type as those in respect of which the dividend is being paid out;
(vii) Securities of the same type as other securities of that issuer admitted to trading on the same regulated market, which were offered or delivered by the issuer or its affiliate to current or former directors or employees of such issuer or affiliate;
(viii) Securities admitted to trading on another regulated market where:
   (a) These securities or other securities of the same type of the same issuer have been admitted to trading on such other regulated market for at least eighteen months, and

(b) First-time admission of these securities, or other securities of the same type, to trading on such other regulated market occurred after 31 December 2003 and was preceded by approval of the issue prospectus and making it available to the public, and
(c) Listing particulars made available to the public in connection with such admission occurring after 1 July 1983 and before 31 December 2003 had been drawn up and approved in compliance with the European Union laws in force at that time, and
(d) The issuer fulfils the ongoing obligations related to admission to trading on such other regulated market.

33. If a public offering or seeking admission to trading on a regulated market concerns the securities referred to in No. 30(i)–(iii), No. 30(vi) and No. 31(vi) above, this Chapter III shall apply *mutatis mutandis* if the issuer or the selling shareholder decides accordingly.

3 Information memorandum

34. In the cases described in Nos. 31(v)(a)(b), and 32(iv)(v) above, the issuer or the selling shareholder shall submit to the Commission a notification meeting the requirements referred to in No. 12 and No. 13(ii)–(v) above, enclosing with it the information memorandum of a scope complying with that required for an issue prospectus under Articles 2 through 26, Article 28 and Article 35 of the Prospectus Regulation, and making this information memorandum available to interested investors.

35. Not later than twenty business days following submission of the notification, the Commission may raise an objection in respect of execution of the public offering or to seeking admission of the securities to trading on a regulated market on the basis of the information memorandum to which such notification refers if the information memorandum does not comply, in terms of its form or substance, with the requirements laid down in pertinent laws. In raising the objection, the Commission proscribes execution of the public offering or seeking admission of securities to trading on a regulated market on the basis of that information memorandum.

36. The information memorandum may omit information, the disclosure of which:

(i) would be contrary to the public interest;
(ii) would be seriously detrimental to the issuer – provided that the omission would not mislead investors in general as to the facts and circumstances material for assessment of the securities or of the situation of the issuer;
(iii) is of minor importance to the specific offering or admission to trading on a regulated market, provided that the omission would not mislead

investors in general as to the facts and circumstances material for assessment of the securities or of the situation of the issuer.

– where the Commission has authorised such omission before the information memorandum is made available.

37. Provisions of Nos. 34–36 above shall not apply to the public offering referred to in No. 31(i)–(iv) and in No. 31(v)(e) above.

38. The information memorandum may not be made available to the public prior to the lapse of the deadline laid down in No. 35 above.

IV Content and format, language and supplements of the prospectus

1 Content

39. The issue prospectus should contain true, accurate, and complete information material for assessment of the economic and financial standing, assets and development prospects of the issuer and the guarantor of liabilities under the securities (the guarantor), taking into account the type of issuer and the type of securities which are to be offered in the public offering or admitted to trading on a regulated market, as well as information concerning the rights and obligations associated with such securities. Information set out in the issue prospectus should be formulated in language comprehensible to investors and in a manner enabling assessment of those entities' situation.

40. Information may be incorporated in the issue prospectus by way of reference to one or more documents made available to the public concurrently, or at an earlier date, which have been provided to, or approved by, the Commission. This information should be the most up-to-date information available to the issuer. Where information is incorporated by reference, the issue prospectus shall be accompanied by a list of such references comprising the information, which must be included in the issue prospectus under applicable laws, as well as the documents in question. Neither the summary note nor the summary which is a part of a prospectus drawn up as a single document may include information incorporated by reference. Detailed rules governing incorporation of information by reference are laid down in Article 28 of the Prospectus Regulation.

41. If a requirement to include certain information in the issue prospectus does not apply directly on account of the nature of the issuer's activities, its legal form, the securities in question, or of other reasonable considerations, the issue prospectus shall include information of a nature corresponding to the information mandated by such requirement, provided that this shall not mislead investors generally as to the facts and circumstances material for assessment of the securities in question or the situation of the issuer.

42. The summary note and the summary which is a part of a prospectus drawn up as a single document shall set out, subject to Article 24 of the Prospectus Regulation, in a concise manner and in non-technical language, the most important information and risk factors pertaining to the issuer, the guarantor, the securities, and their offering or their admission to trading on a regulated market, as well as an express statement to the effect that:

(i) it should be read as an introduction to the prospectus;
(ii) any decision to invest in the securities should be based on consideration of the prospectus as a whole by the investor;
(iii) any investor bringing a claim with respect to the contents of the issue prospectus shall bear the cost of any translation of such issue prospectus required before the commencement of court proceedings;
(iv) the persons drawing up the summary note or the summary which is a part of a prospectus drawn up as a single document, along with any translation thereof, shall be liable only for damage occurring where the summary note is misleading, inaccurate, or inconsistent when read together with other parts of the issue prospectus.

43. In the event that the base issue prospectus updated in accordance with rules provided in Nos. 50–57 below does not include information concerning detailed terms and conditions of individual offerings, the issuer or the selling shareholder shall provide to the Commission information on detailed terms and conditions of each offering and will make it available to the public in the same manner as stipulated for issue prospectuses subject to Article 22, Article 26 and Article 33 of the Prospectus Regulation. The requirements arising from Nos. 50–57 below shall not apply to information concerning detailed terms and conditions of an offering which is provided in such a manner; in such an event, the base issue prospectus should meet at least the condition laid down in No. 45 (i) below.

44. The detailed conditions to be met by the issue prospectus, the means of drawing up the issue prospectus, and the terms on which the Commission may demand inclusion of additional information in the issue prospectus are laid down in Article 2 through Article 26, Article 28 and Article 35 of the Prospectus Regulation, subject to the provisions of No. 74 and Polish accountancy rules.

45. The issue prospectus need not specify the issue price or selling price of the securities, or the final number of securities offered, provided that:

(i) The issue prospectus specifies at least the maximum price or the criteria and rules governing definition of the final issue price or selling price for the securities or the final number of securities offered, or
(ii) The issue prospectus indicates that a person who has placed a subscription order prior to the release to the public of information on the

price or the number of securities offered to the public shall have the right to rescind his subscription order by lodging a written statement to that effect with the investment firm acting as the offeror with respect to the securities within two business days following the date on which the information was released.

46. The issuer or the selling shareholder shall change the date of allotment of the securities as appropriate in order to enable the investor to effect such rescission in accordance with No. 45 (ii) above.

47. The issuer or the selling shareholder shall promptly notify the Commission of the final issue price or selling price and of the number of securities offered and make this information available to the public by the same means in which the issue prospectus was made available and in accordance with the procedure laid down in the Act on Public Offering, Conditions Governing the Introduction of Financial Instruments to Organised Trading and Public Companies.

2 Format

48. The issue prospectus shall be drawn up in the form of:

(i) A single document, or
(ii) Separate documents comprising the registration document, the securities note, and the summary note.

49. In the case of public offering or admission to trading on a regulated market of:

(i) Non-equity securities or subscription warrants equivalent as regards the nature of the rights incorporated therein which are issued at a specific time, in a continuous or repeated manner in cycles comprising at least two offerings executed within an interval not exceeding twelve months (offering programme), or
(ii) Non-equity securities issued by a credit institution in a continuous or repeated manner in cycles comprising at least two offerings executed within an interval not exceeding twelve months, where proceeds from such offerings are invested in assets of a value corresponding to at least the value of liabilities arising from such securities until their maturity, and provided also that, in the event of insolvency of the issuer, disputed amounts shall enjoy priority in repayment of the principal and interest due.

The issuer or the selling shareholder shall draw up an issue prospectus constituting a base issue prospectus.

3 Supplements

50. The issuer or the selling shareholder shall promptly – and no later than within twenty-four hours – provide to the Commission, in the form of a

supplement to the issue prospectus along with an application for its approval, information about any and all events or circumstances which might materially affect assessment of the securities, and of which the issuer or the selling shareholder became aware after approval of the issue prospectus and by the day of:

(i) Allotment of the securities, announcement that the subscription for or sale of securities is not successful, or announcement of abandonment of the subscription for or sale of the securities by the issuer or of cancellation of the subscription or sale – where the securities offered in the public offering are not subject to the procedure of admission to trading on a regulated market, or;
(ii) Listing of the securities on the regulated market.

51. The supplement shall be subject to approval by the Commission in accordance with provisions of Nos. 15, 17–20 and 22 above, with the applicable deadline not exceeding seven business days following submission of the application for approval of the supplement.

52. The Commission may refuse to approve the supplement if the supplement does not comply, in its form or substance, with pertinent laws. In refusing the approval, the Commission shall order that the commencement of the public offering be withheld, that the public offering already underway be discontinued, or that the admission of the securities to trading on a regulated market on the basis of the issue prospectus covering these securities be withheld.

53. The issuer or the selling shareholder should make available to the public the supplement to a published issue prospectus promptly upon approval of such supplement by the Commission. The supplement shall be made available by the same means as the issue prospectus or one of the documents referred to in No. 48 (ii), not later than 24 hours following receipt of the decision on approval of the supplement.

54. In the event that, following commencement of the subscription or sale, a supplement concerning events or circumstances arising prior to the allotment of the securities of which the issuer or the selling shareholder became aware prior to such allotment is made available to the public, a person who subscribed for those securities before the supplement is made available may rescind their subscription by lodging a written statement to that effect with the investment firm acting as the offeror in respect of those securities within two business days following the date on which the supplement was made available. The issuer or the selling shareholder shall change the date of allotment of the securities as appropriate in order to enable the investor to effect such rescission.

55. Subject to an agreement with a competent authority in another Member State, the Commission shall transfer to such authority approval of the

supplement submitted to the Commission by an issuer for which the Republic of Poland is the home state if the Commission had previously transferred to that body approval of the issue prospectus or documents referred to in No. 48 (ii) above in accordance with Polish rules on transfer of the approval of an issue prospectus or the documents referred to in No. 48 (ii) to the competent authority of another Member State.

56. Provisions of Nos. 50 and 51 shall apply accordingly to consideration by the Commission of an application for approval of a supplement transferred to the Commission by a competent authority in another Member State subject to the agreement referred to in No. 55 above.

57. The obligation to provide information in the form of a supplement to the issue prospectus shall remain without prejudice to the obligation laid down in the Act on Public Offering, Conditions Governing the Introduction of Financial Instruments to Organised Trading and Public Companies.

4 Language

58. Securities of an issuer having its registered office in a Member State for which the Republic of Poland is a host state may be offered in a public offering or admitted to trading on a regulated market in the Republic of Poland, provided that the Commission receives from the competent authority in the issuer's home state *inter alia* a copy of the approved issue prospectus, drawn up and updated in compliance with the law of such Member State, along with a translation into Polish of the part of the issue prospectus setting out a summary of the information contained therein.

59. The issuer or the selling shareholder shall be obligated to make available to the public the issue prospectus referred to in No. 23 (ii) above, drawn up in the Polish or the English language, as chosen by the issuer or by the selling shareholder. In the case of an issue prospectus drawn up in the English language, the issuer or the selling shareholder shall be obligated to make available to the public, along with the issue prospectus, the summary note or the summary which is a part of a prospectus drawn up as a single document in the Polish language.

V Publication and advertisements

1 Methods of publication

60. Following approval of the issue prospectus, the issuer or the selling shareholder shall submit its final version to the Commission and make the issue prospectus available to the public.

61. The issuer or the selling shareholder shall, subject to No. 62 below, make the issue prospectus available to the public at such time as to enable

the investors to peruse information set out therein, but not later than on the day of commencement of subscription for or sale of the securities covered by the issue prospectus – if the securities are offered in a public offering, or on the day on which the securities are admitted to trading on the regulated market – if the securities have not been offered in a public offering before.

62. In the case of the initial public offering of shares which are to be subsequently admitted to trading on a regulated market, where shares of the same type of that issuer have not yet been admitted to trading on a regulated market, the issue prospectus should be made available to the public not later than six business days prior to the closing of subscription for or sale of the shares.

63. The issuer or the selling shareholder shall make available to the public an issue prospectus drawn up in the Polish language, subject to Nos. 64 and 25 above.

64. In the case of non-equity securities for which admission to trading on a regulated market is sought and the par value per unit amounts to at least €50,000 or the zloty equivalent thereof, calculated at the mid exchange rate for the euro quoted by the National Bank of Poland for the day on which the resolution on the offering of these securities is adopted, the issue prospectus made available to the public should be drawn up in a language agreed upon by the Commission with competent authorities of the Member States in which such admission will be sought or in the English language, as chosen by the issuer or the selling shareholder. In such an event, the issuer or the selling shareholder shall be obligated to make available to the public, along with the issue prospectus, a summary note or a summary which is a part of a prospectus drawn up as a single document in the Polish language.

65. The issuer or the selling shareholder shall make the issue prospectus available to the public by at least one of the following means:

(i) Publication in at least one Polish newspaper of a nationwide circulation;
(ii) In the printed form, made available free of charge at the registered office of the company operating the regulated market on which the securities are to be admitted to trading or at the registered office of the issuer and the registered office of the investment firm acting as the offeror, on the basis of an agreement concluded with the issuer, and at customer service points of entities participating in the subscription for sale of the securities, in a print run sufficient to ensure availability of the issue prospectus to interested persons and efficient execution of the public offering or admission to trading on a regulated market;

(iii) In electronic form on the Internet – on the issuer's website and on websites of the entities participating in the subscription for or sale of the securities, as appropriate;
(iv) In electronic form on the Internet – on the website of the company operating the regulated market on which the securities are to be admitted to trading.

66. The issuer or the selling shareholder shall publish information concerning the form and time frame of making the issue prospectus available to the public in accordance with Article 31 of the Prospectus Regulation, and will forward this information to the Commission.

67. The Commission shall publish on its website information on the issue prospectus approved and made available to the public, along with links to websites of the issuer or of the company operating the regulated market on which the electronic version of such issue prospectus has been posted. The issuer or the selling shareholder shall notify the Commission two days before the day of making available of the issue prospectus to the public or the date on which the issue prospectus will be made available on the Internet, specifying the relevant website.

68. Where the issue prospectus is made available in its electronic form only, the entity making the issue prospectus available shall, at the request of an interested party submitted within the validity period of the issue prospectus, make available a free of-charge printed copy of that issue prospectus at the place at which such request was accepted.

69. Detailed rules governing making available of the issue prospectus to the public are laid down in Articles 29 and 30 of the Prospectus Regulation.

2 Advertisements

70. The issuer or the selling shareholder may conduct promotional activities within the meaning of Article 29 and Article 34 of the Prospectus Regulation and in the form specified therein.

71. Where promotional activities are conducted, all promotional materials should expressly state:

(i) that such materials are of a purely promotional or advertising nature;
(ii) that the issue prospectus has been, or will be, published;
(iii) the places at which the issue prospectus is, or will be, available.

72. Information presented as part of the promotional activities may not contradict the information contained in the issue prospectus and may not mislead investors as to the situation of the issuer and the assessment of its securities.

73. Where drawing up, approval, and making available of the issue prospectus to the public is not statutorily required, any and all information presented to investors as part of promotional activities should be made available in the same scope to all the entities to which the public offering is addressed or which will participate in trading in these securities on the regulated market.

VI Use of prospectus approved in other (non EU) countries

74. In the case of an issuer having its registered office in a state other than a Member State, the issue prospectus may be drawn up on the basis of the laws of the state in which such issuer has its registered office, provided that it is drawn up in compliance with appropriate standards of the International Organisation of Securities Commissions (IOSCO) and that the information contained in such issue prospectus meets the requirements laid down in Nos. 39–43 and in Nos. 45–49 as well as in Article 2 through Articles 26, 28 and 35 of the Prospectus Regulation.

VII Sanctions

1 Administrative sanctions

75. If the issuer, the selling shareholder, or any other entity participating in a public offering on behalf of, or on instructions from, the issuer or the selling shareholder, violates the law in connection with a public offering in the Republic of Poland, or there is a reasonable suspicion that such violation has occurred or may occur, the Commission may, subject to Nos. 77–78 below:

(i) Order that the commencement of such public offering be withheld or that such public offering already underway be discontinued, in each case for a period of not more than ten business days, or
(ii) Proscribe the commencement or continuation of the public offering, or
(iii) Publish, at the expense of the issuer or the selling shareholder, information concerning the illegal activities with respect to the public offering.

76. If the issuer, the selling shareholder, or any other entity participating in a public offering on behalf of, or on instructions from, the issuer or the selling shareholder, violates the law in connection with the seeking of admission of securities to trading on a regulated market in the Republic of Poland, or there is a reasonable suspicion that such violation has occurred or may occur, the Commission may, subject to Nos. 77–78 below:

(i) Order that the admission of the securities to trading on a regulated market be withheld for a period of not more than ten business days;
(ii) Proscribe admission of the securities to trading on a regulated market;

(iii) Publish, at the expense of the issuer or the selling shareholder, information concerning the illegal activities with respect to seeking of admission of securities to trading on a regulated market.

77. The Commission may apply the measures provided for in Nos. 75 or 76 above also if the contents of the issue prospectus, the information memorandum, or other listing particulars submitted to the Commission or made available to the public indicate that:

(i) The public offering or admission of the securities to trading on a regulated market would materially compromise investors' interests;
(ii) Establishment or incorporation of the issuer was effected in gross violation of applicable laws and the consequences of such violation continue;
(iii) Activities of the issuer were, or are, conducted in gross violation of applicable laws and the consequences of such violation continue; or
(iv) The legal status of the securities does not comply with applicable laws.

78. If the circumstances which served as the basis for the decision referred to in No. 75(i) or 75(ii), in Article 76.1 or 76.2, or in No. 77 above cease to apply, the Commission, acting at the issuer's or the selling shareholder's request or on an *ex officio* basis, may repeal such decision.

79. If the issuer for whom the Republic of Poland is a host state violates, or is reasonably suspected to have violated the law, the Commission shall notify of the same the competent authority in such issuer's home state.

80. If, despite notification by the Commission, the competent authority of the issuer's home state does not take measures to prevent further violation of the statutory provisions, or if such measures prove ineffective, the Commission may, with a view to protecting the interests of investors and having first notified such authority, apply vis-à-vis the issuer the measures provided for in Nos. 77 or 78 above. The Commission shall promptly notify the minister responsible for financial institutions that it has taken such measures; the minister, in turn, shall notify the European Commission.

81. The Code of Administrative Procedure provides that the Commission's decisions are not subject to appeal; however, a dissatisfied party can apply to the Commission with a request for reconsideration.

82. If an issuer or selling shareholder fails to perform or unduly performs any of its statutory obligations, arising from the Act on Public Offering, Conditions Governing the Introduction of Financial Instruments to Organised Trading and Public Companies or fails to perform or unduly performs the order referred to in Article 16.1, infringes upon the proscription referred to in Article 16.2, or fails to perform or unduly performs the

obligations referred to in Article 22.4 and 22.7, Article 26.5 and 26.7, Article 27, Article 29 through Article 31 and Article 33 of the Prospectus Regulation, the Commission may:

(i) issue a decision excluding given securities from trading on a regulated market for a definite or indefinite period, or
(ii) impose, taking into account in particular the financial standing of the entity on which the penalty is to be imposed, a pecuniary penalty of up to PLN 1 million or
(iii) apply both these sanctions jointly.

2 Criminal sanctions

83. Whosoever publicly proposes the acquisition of securities without the statutorily required approval of an issue prospectus, submission of a notification including an information memorandum or making such a document available to the public or to interested investors, shall be liable to a fine of up to PLN 1 million or a penalty of imprisonment for up to two years, or to both these penalties jointly.

84. Whosoever offers to the public acquisition of securities covered by an information memorandum concerning a public offering prior to the lapse of the deadline for the Commission's raising objections concerning the notification referred to in No. 83 or in defiance of such an objection, shall be liable to the same penalty.

85. In the event of a lesser crime, the perpetrator of the act specified in Nos. 83 or 84 shall be liable to a fine of up to PLN 250,000.

86. If a person responsible for the information contained in an issue prospectus or other information documents, or other information connected with a public offering, or admission or seeking admission of securities or other financial instruments to trading on a regulated market, or information referred to in No. 50, delivers untrue data or suppresses true data thus materially affecting such information, such person shall be liable to a fine of up to PLN 5 million or a penalty of imprisonment for from six months to five years, or to both these penalties jointly.

87. Whosoever commits the act specified in No. 86, acting on behalf or in the interest of a legal person or an organisational unit without legal personality shall be liable to the same penalty.

VIII Prospectus liability

88. The validity period of an issue prospectus drawn up as a single document shall be twelve months from the date when it is first made available to the public.

89. The validity period of a registration document shall be twelve months from the date of its approval. The validity of the registration document shall also expire if the registration document is not updated in keeping with the deadline set out in No. 50 above.

90. Under the circumstances described in No. 49 above, the validity period of an issue prospectus shall expire on the day on which the offering of securities issued under the issue prospectus is closed.

91. No information made available to the public by the issuer, the selling shareholder, or by other entities participating in the offering on behalf of, or on instructions from, the issuer or the selling shareholder may contradict information contained in the issue prospectus.

92. The liability for damage caused by public disclosure of untrue information or omission of the information which should have been included in the documents prepared and made available in connection with a public offering of securities, admission of securities or financial instruments other than securities to trading on a regulated market or seeking such admission shall rest with the issuer, the firm commitment underwriter, the guarantor, the selling shareholder or entity which seeks admission of financial instruments other than securities to trading on a regulated market, as well as the persons which prepared such information or participated in the preparation thereof, unless neither these entities nor the persons they are responsible for, are not guilty, subject to No. 93 below.

93. Persons preparing a summary or translation thereof shall be liable exclusively for damage caused in the event that such a summary or translation is misleading, inaccurate or inconsistent when read with other parts of the issue prospectus.

IX Rules applicable to transactions and securities not subject to the Directive and Regulation

1 Excluded transactions

94. See Chapter III, No. 37.

2 Excluded securities

95. Under Polish law, the following securities are excluded from the scope of application of the Directive and Regulation:

(i) promissory notes and cheques as defined in the Promissory Note and Cheque Act;
(ii) bank securities as defined in the Banking Law, and other non-equity securities serving to confirm receipt of a repayable deposit and

covered by a deposit guarantee scheme, which are issued in a continuous or repeated manner by a credit institution with a registered office in a Member State, are not subordinated, convertible or exchangeable, do not give a right to subscribe for or acquire other types of securities, and do not comprise an underlying instrument for securities defined in the Act on Trading in Financial Instruments;

(iii) securities comprising money market instruments as defined in the Act on Trading in Financial Instruments, maturing within a year from the date of their acquisition in primary trading.

X Conclusion

96. All the above regulations aim to express the idea of a single market where a prospectus for securities offered to the public, or admitted to trading, approved by a single authority, proves to be sufficient in other Member States of the European Union. The harmonisation and unification of Polish law on prospectuses to EU standards improves access to the Polish market, by reduction of costs, and by less time-consuming effort for public offerings of securities and the admission of them to trading on a regulated market. The framework of a European passport means that the uniform rules are especially useful for those cross-border operations of offerors that seek to offer securities in several Member states, simultaneously.

13

Portugal

JOSÉ ALVES DO CARMO, AND JOSÉ MIGUEL OLIVEIRA AND ARIFO AMADA
Barrocas Sarmento Neves

I Introduction

1. The 'Prospectus Directive' was transposed into Portuguese law through Decree-Law 52/2006 of 15 March 2006 (the Decree-Law).

With the transposition of the 'Prospectus Directive', the Decree-Law has introduced some substantial changes in the following Portuguese Legislation:

(i) Securities Code (the 'SC'), approved by Decree-Law 486/99 of 13 November 1999;
(ii) Companies Code, approved by Decree-Law 262/86 of 3 November 1986;
(iii) Commercial Registry Code, approved by Decree-Law 403/86 of 3 December 1986;

(iv) Legal Regime on Mortgage Backed Securities, approved by Decree-Law 125/90 of 16 April 1990;
(v) Legal Regime on Cashiers Securities, approved by Decree-Law 408/91 of 17 October 1991;
(vi) Legal Regime on Collective Investment Institutions, approved by Decree-Law 252/2003 of 17 October 2003;
(vii) Legal Regime on Securitisation, approved by Decree-Law 453/99 of 5 November 1999;
(viii) Legal Regime on Commercial Notes, approved by Decree-Law 69/2004 of 25 March 2004.

The aforementioned statutes, and subsequent amendments, represent, together with the Decree-Law, the basic legal framework for all matters relating to prospectuses on public offers and the rules relating to the admission to trading of listed securities.

Please note, however, that the Decree-Law does not only cover prospectuses for public offers and the trading of listed securities. Additionally, it transposed into the Portuguese legal system Directive no. 2003/6/CE of the European Parliament and Council of 28 January 2003 regarding the abuse of privileged information and market manipulation, which are, however, beyond the scope of this report.

The legislator's introduction to the Decree-Law indicates that even though the 'Prospectus Directive' is addressed to all public offers, in practice it is intended to address distribution public offers. Therefore, our analysis will focus only on distribution public offers.

II Competent Authority

2. In accordance with article 145 of the SC, as amended by the Decree-Law, the competent Portuguese authority is the *Comissão do Mercado de Valores Mobiliários* ('Securities Market Commission', or the 'CMVM'). It should be noted that while article 145 is included in the public offers section of the SC, according to Article 238 of the SC, it also applies to the admission to trading of listed securities.

Under the provisions of Article 145.1 of the SC, the CMVM is the authority with powers to approve any prospectuses relating to:

(i) the public distribution offers where the issuers have their registered seat in Portugal;
(ii) the acquisition of the shares and securities was permitted because the issuer of these securities is also the issuer of securities or securities belonging to a legal entity in a group relationship with the issuer and other securities with a nominal value which is less than €1,000.

Furthermore, Article 145.2 of the SC provides that the Member State where the issuer has its registered seat, or where the securities were or will be accepted to trade on a regulated market or offered to the public (depending upon the choice of the issuer or offeror), is competent to approve the prospectus in the following two situations: (a) securities which do not represent share capital with a nominal unit value of, at least, €1,000; (b) securities not representing share capital which, as a result of their conversion or of the exercise of rights attributed by them, grant the right to acquire other securities or to receive a certain amount in money, provided that the same issuer of these securities is not the issuer of the underlying securities or an entity belonging to the latter.

In addition, it should be noted that in relation to securities which are not covered by Article 145.2, Article 145.3 of the SC provides in connection with any prospectus where the issuer is incorporated in a non European country that the competent authority to approve the prospectus may, depending upon the choice of the issuer or offeror, be the authority of the country where the securities are to be offered or admitted to trade on a regulated market for the first time. Nevertheless, this is also dependent on any subsequent choice made by the issuers or offerors of a third party country if the Member State of origin has not been elected by them.

Under Article 145.5.6 of the SC, the CMVM may decide to delegate its power to approve the prospectus to the competent authority of another Member State if the latter authority agrees to this delegation. In addition, this delegation must be notified to the issuer or offeror within three days of the CMVM's decision.

In relation to takeovers, Article 145 A of the SC provides that the CMVM has power to supervise takeovers which target securities issued by companies subject to the Portuguese substantive law, as long as the securities have been admitted to trading on a regulated market situated or operating in Portugal or are not admitted to trading on a regulated market. The CMVM also has power to supervise the takeovers of (a) companies incorporated in another jurisdiction, provided that those securities are exclusively admitted to trade on a regulated market situated or operating in Portugal or, (b) if they are not admitted to trade in a Member State where the registered seat of the issuer is located they have been admitted to trade in a regulated market seated or operating in Portugal.

Finally, the SC also contemplates the concept of the 'European Passport Prospectus'. According to Article 146 of the SC, which also applies to admissions to trading under Article 238 of the SC, a prospectus approved in another Member State for a public offer distribution to be conducted in Portugal or in another Member State, is valid and effective in Portugal as long as the CMVM receives from the foreign competent authority: (a) a certificate of approval declaring that the prospectus was prepared in accordance with Directive No. 2003/71/CE, of 4 November 2003, and which justifies, if applicable, why it is unnecessary to include such information in the prospectus; (b) as well as a copy of the prospectus and, where applicable, a summary translation of its contents.

III Procedure of prior approval and appeal

3. According to Article 114 of the SC, a public offer distribution prospectus must be approved by the CMVM, while the takeovers themselves are subject to prior registration with the CMVM. On the other hand, Articles 140.1 and 236.1 of the SC, provide that the prospectus may only be published after it is approved by the CMVM in accordance with the provisions of the 'Prospectus Directive', with it being clear that the prior approval procedure is an indispensable requirement.

The amendments introduced by the Decree-Law resulted in substantial changes to the public offers procedure. Before these amendments the focus of the public offer procedure was on the registration approved and granted by the CMVM. The recent changes in the supervision of public offers has shifted the focus to the approval of the prospectus in much the same way as what was already in place for admissions to trading on regulated markets.

Indeed, the preamble of the Decree-Law provides that this move is justified on the grounds that it is necessary in order to avoid a competitive disadvantage of national issuers when facing their foreign competitors and also to speed up the prospectus approval procedure. Nonetheless, this does not mean that the supervisory powers of the CMVM have been diminished given the fact that it can always decide to suspend or withdraw the offer.

In relation to the approval procedure itself, which is the same for both the public offers and admissions to trading, Article 115 of the SC requires the prospectus approval request to be submitted to the CMVM with the following documents:

- (i) A copy of the shareholder resolution passed approving the issue of the offer, as well as the necessary management decisions;
- (ii) A copy of the articles of association of the securities issuer;
- (iii) A copy of the offeror's articles of association;
- (iv) An up-to-date companies' registration certificate for the issuer;
- (v) An up-to-date companies' registration certificate for the offeror;
- (vi) copies of the management and financial reports, the opinions of the statutory audit committee and certified accounts for the issuer for the periods required by EU Regulation 809/2004, 29 April 2004;
- (vii) A report or statement from an auditor, prepared in accordance with Articles 8 and 9 of the SC which requires that the auditor be registered with the CMVM;
- (viii) The identification code of the securities which are the object of the offer;

(ix) A copy of the contract entered into with the financial intermediary assisting in the operation;
(x) A copy of the placement contract and of the consortium placement contract, if any;
(xi) A copy of the market incentive contract, the stabilisation contract and the supplementary lot distribution option contract, if any;
(xii) A draft of the prospectus;
(xiii) Pro forma financial information, when required;
(xiv) A draft of the offer announcement, when required;
(xv) Expert reports, when required.

4. Most of the documents referred to above were already necessary under the legislation previous to the 'Prospectus Directive'. However, the documents at vi), xiii), xiv) and xv) are new requirements introduced by the Decree-Law. Furthermore, issuers or offerors with their legal registered seat in Portugal must also present a statement from the Social Security and Tax Services declaring that their obligations to these entities have been fulfilled.

Nevertheless, it should be noted that, according to Article 115.2 of the SC, these documents need not be submitted if it is indicated in the application that they have already been lodged with the CMVM and are up to date. Furthermore, under Article 115.3 which is also a new provision introduced by the Decree Law, the CMVM may request the issuer or offeror to provide any additional information deemed necessary to analyse the offer. This need for additional information must be justified, according to Article 118.3 of the SC, and communicated to the offeror within ten business days of the date when the request was presented.

Another innovation introduced by the Decree Law is Article 118 of the SC which provides that, after the aforementioned request is presented, the CMVM must approve the prospectus within ten business days, unless it considers that the issuers did not present a public offer for distribution or have requested an admission to trading on a regulated market, in which case the time period is twenty business days. Moreover, these deadlines run from the date the request is filed or additional information has been requested and if a decision is not given within the referred deadlines, Article 118.4 provides that the request is to be considered as having been refused.

Furthermore, Article 119 of the SC provides that the CMVM may only refuse to approve the prospectus if any of the documents referred to above are false or not in accordance with legal requirements. However, before such a refusal, the CMVM must request that the offeror correct any irregularities in his request. In so far as any appeal against the refusal of the CMVM is concerned, there are no specific provisions, which means that the decisions can be challenged through the courts.

Before analysing the exemptions, it seems convenient to briefly outline certain aspects of the preliminary prospectus provided for at Articles 164 and 165 of the SC. According to those provisions, it is possible to gather information on the intentions of investors to assess the viability of a distribution public offer after the disclosure of a preliminary prospectus which must be approved by the CMVM. The request for this prospectus must be submitted to the CMVM accompanied by some of the documents referred to under Article 115 above and the draft preliminary prospectus which must comply with the Prospectus Regulation.

To conclude the prior approval procedure, a brief reference needs to be made to the circumstances where there is no need to obtain prior approval of the prospectus: i.e. the exemptions.

First, according to Article 111 and 236.2(a) of the SC, the public offer or admissions to trade regime outlined above does not apply to the following situations and accordingly there is no need to follow the prospectus approval procedure:

(i) Public offers for the distribution of securities, which are not representative of share capital, issued by a Member State or by one of its regional or local authorities and public offers for the distribution of securities which benefit from an unconditional and irrevocable guarantee by one of those Members States or regional or local authorities;
(ii) Public offers of securities issued by the European Central Bank or by the central bank of one of the Member States;
(iii) Public offers of securities issued by an open collective investment institution which are conducted by the issuer on its behalf;
(iv) Offers made in a CMVM-registered market which are presented exclusively through that market's communication methods and which are not preceded or accompanied by any sort of prospecting or promotion to undetermined recipients;
(v) Public offers for the distribution of securities with a nominal value per unit equal or superior to €50,000 or with a subscription or sale price by the recipient equal or superior to that amount;
(vi) Public offers for the distribution of securities, which are not representative of share capital, issued by international public institutions to which one or several Member States belong;
(vii) Public offers for the distribution of securities issued by associations or non profit entities, recognised by a Member State, aimed at obtaining the necessary funds to achieve their non-profit goals;
(viii) Public offers for the distribution of securities, which are not representative of share capital, issued continuously or repeatedly by credit institutions, provided that those securities:
    - are not subordinated, convertible or likely to be traded;
    - do not grant the right to acquire other types of securities and are not associated to a derivative instrument;
    - certify the reception of reimbursable deposits;

- are covered by the Deposit Guarantee Fund foreseen in the General Regime for Credit Institutions and Financial Companies or by another deposit guarantee fund under the terms of Directive no. 94/19/CE, European Parliament and Council, of 30 May, regarding the deposit guarantee system;

(ix) Public offers for the distribution of securities with a total value which is less than €2.5 million and this limit is to be calculated taking into account all offers taking place during a period of twelve months;

(x) Public offers for the distribution of securities, which are not representative of share capital, issued continuously or repeatedly by credit institutions when the offer's total value is less than €50 million and this limit is to be calculated taking into account all offers taking place during a period of twelve months, provided that such securities:
  - are not subordinated, convertible or likely to be traded;
  - do not grant the right to acquire other types of securities and are not associated to a derivative instrument;

(xi) Public offers for the subscription of shares issued in substitution of shares of the same category already issued, as long as the issuing of the new shares does not result in an increase of the share capital already issued;

(xii) Takeover of securities issued by collective investment institutions incorporated as companies.

In the situations referred to in (i), (ii), (ix) and (x) above it should also be noted that although there is no need to have a prospectus approved, if the issuer decides to prepare a prospectus then this will be governed by these rules.

Article 143 of the SC, in its turn, commences by stating that every public offer must be preceded by the publication of a prospectus. As referred to above, there certain types of public offers, under Article 111 of the SC, to which these rules of the SC do not apply. However, there also other types of public offers to which those rules do apply with the exception of the requirement for a prior prospectus which still applies; these are as follows:

(i) Offers of securities to be attributed, due to a merger, to at least 100 shareholders who are not qualified investors, as long as a document with information deemed by the CMVM as equivalent to the one in a prospectus is available at least fifteen days before the general meeting;

(ii) Payment of profits in the form of shares of the same category as the shares in respect of which the payment is being made, as long as a document with information on the number and nature of the shares, as well as the offer's reasons and characteristics, is available;

(iii) Offers for the distribution of securities to members of the board or employees, existing or former, by the employer when the latter has securities admitted to trading on a regulated market or through a company controlled by it, as long as a document with information on the number and nature of the shares, as well as the offer's reasons and characteristics, is available.

In the above cases, even though there is no obligation to present a prospectus, the offeror may do so, in which case these rules apply in their entirety.

On the other hand, Article 236 of the SC, which deals with the admission to trading, states, at paragraph 2(a), that the prospectus is not required for the admission of securities referred to in (i) to (iv) and (vi) to (xi) of article 111 of the SC, as described above, as well as those set out at article 143.2 of the SC. Furthermore, Article 236.2 of the SC also establishes that there is no need to obtain a prospectus for the admission to trading of:

(i) Shares offered, attributed or to be attributed for no consideration to existing shareholders and profits paid in the form of shares of the same category of shares in respect of which the payment is being made, provided that these shares are of the same category as those already admitted to trading on a regulated market and a document with information on the number and nature of the shares, as well as the offer's reasons and characteristics, is available;

(ii) Securities offered, attributed or to be attributed to members of the board, existing and former, by the employer or a company controlled by the latter, provided that these securities are of the same category as those already admitted to trading on the same regulated market and a document with information on the number and nature of the shares, as well as the offer's reasons and characteristics, is available;

(iii) Shares which represent, during a twelve-month period, less than 10 per cent of the number of shares of the same category already admitted to trading on the same regulated market;

(iv) Shares resulting from the conversion or exchange of other securities or of the exercise of rights granted by other securities, provided that those are of the same category as the shares already admitted to trading on the same regulated market;

(v) Securities already admitted to trading on another regulated market in the following circumstances:
   - Those securities, or securities of the same category, must have been admitted to trading on this other regulated market for over eighteen months;
   - For securities admitted to trading for the first time on a regulated market, the admission to trading in this other market must have been accompanied by the publication of a prospectus pursuant to Article 140 of the SC;
   - Except where the previous paragraph is applicable, for securities admitted to trading for the first time after 30 June 1983, the prospectus must have been approved in accordance with the

requirements of Directive no. 80/390/CE, of the Council, of 27 March or of Directive 2001/34/CE, of the Council, of 28 May;

- All the requirements for trading in this other regulated market must have been observed;
- The entity requesting admission under this exception must have prepared a summary which is made available to the public in a language approved by the CMVM;
- The content of the summary must fulfil the provisions of Article 135 A of the SC, as well as indicate where the most recent prospectus can be obtained and where the financial information, published by the issuer according to his legal obligations, is available.

IV Content and format, language and supplements of the prospectus

1 Content

5. In relation to the content of the prospectus, Article 135 of the SC begins by stating, following the Prospectus Directive, that the prospectus must contain complete, accurate, up-to-date, clear, objective and legally permitted information allowing the recipients to properly analyse the operation.

Under Article 135-A of the SC, one of the new additions to the SC resulting from the transposition of the Prospectus Directive, regardless of the chosen format, any public offer for the distribution of securities must include a summary which presents the main characteristics and the risks associated with the issuer, the guarantor and the securities. It is also worth mentioning that, under the terms of Article 238 of the SC, these rules on the summary of the prospectus also apply to the admission to trading. The referred summary must state that:

(i) Liability for the prospectus is excluded if the damages deriving from the prospectus are only due to its summary, or any of its translations, unless the latter contains deceitful, inaccurate and incoherent information when analysed together with the remaining documents of the prospectus;
(ii) It is a mere introduction to the prospectus;
(iii) Any decision in relation to investing in the securities must be based on the information included in the prospectus as a whole.

However, Article 238 of the SC, relating to the prospectus for the admission to trading, stipulates that the presentation of a summary is not compulsory in admissions to trading on a regulated market where the securities are not representative of share capital and have a nominal value of, at least, €50,000.

On the other hand, according to Article 136 of the SC, which establishes the common content of the prospectus, the latter must include the following information:

(i) The identity of those liable for its content;
(ii) The offer's objectives;
(iii) The issuer and the activity it carries out;
(iv) The offeror and the activity it carries out;
(v) The administration and auditing structure of the issuer;
(vi) The composition of the issuer's and offeror's corporate bodies;
(vii) The financial intermediaries included in the placement consortium, if any.

Although most of the rules on the prospectus for public offers apply to the admission to trading, in this case, according to Article 238 of the SC, only the matters referred to in (i), (iii) and (v) to (vii) must be considered for the admissions to trading prospectuses.

6. Having described the common content of the prospectus, the SC goes on and describes, respectively, in Articles 137 and 138 the content for the prospectus of a distribution public offer and takeover. For the distribution public offer, Article 137 of the SC determines that the content of the prospectus must comply with the Prospectus Regulation and that it should include statements by the people liable for its content certifying that, to the best of their knowledge, the information in the prospectus is accurate and there are no relevant omissions. Furthermore, and still under Article 137, if the offer is over securities admitted or likely to be admitted to trading on a regulated market located or operating in Portugal or in another Member State, a single prospectus may be approved and used, provided that it satisfies the requirements for both operations. These provisions are also applicable to admissions to trading under Article 238 of the SC.

In relation to takeovers, Article 138 of the SC states that the prospectus must contain information on the following:

(i) All matters referred to in Article 183-A of the SC, which was introduced by the Decree-Law and deals with the announcement of the offer, as follows:
  - identification and corporate seat of the offeror, issuer and financial intermediaries responsible for the assistance and placement of the offer;
  - amount and characteristics of the securities which the offer is aimed at;
  - type of offer;
  - position in which the financial intermediaries take part in the operation;
  - offer price and global amount, as well as nature and terms of payment;
  - offer deadline;
  - criteria for the proportional division;
  - offer conditions;

- percentage of voting rights in the target company held by the offeror and others who are related to him under the terms of Article 20 of the SC;
- places for the advertisement of the prospectus;
- entity in charge of analysing and publishing the offer results.

(ii) The consideration offered and its justification, and, if it is in securities, issued or to be issued, the prospectus must also include all the information that would be required if the securities were the object of a public offer;
(iii) The minimum and maximum amounts of securities that the offeror intends to acquire;
(iv) The percentage of voting rights that, according to Article 20 of the SC, may be exercised by the offeror in the target company;
(v) The percentage of voting rights that, according to Article 20 of the SC, may be exercised by the target company in the offeror company;
(vi) The entities related to the offeror in the ways set out at Article 20;
(vii) Details of securities of the same class as those that are the object of the offer, and have been acquired in the previous six months by the issuer or anyone in a relationship with it as set out at Article 20 of the SC, indicating the acquisition dates, amount and consideration;
(viii) The purposes of the acquisition, particularly in respect of the maintenance of listings on a regulated market of the securities which are the object of the offer, the maintenance of the status of public company, the continuity or amendment of the business activity developed by the target company and by companies that have a control or group relationship with it, its human resources policy and financial strategy;
(ix) The possible implications of the success of the offer on the offeror's financial situation;
(x) The shareholders' agreements, entered into by the offeror or any entity described at Article 20 of the SC, with significant influence on the target company;
(xi) The agreements entered into between the offeror or any entity described at Article 20 of the SC and the members of the governing bodies of the target company, including any special advantages that may have been stipulated in their favour;
(xii) The method of payment of the consideration when the securities that are the object of the offer are also listed on a regulated market located or functioning abroad;
(xiii) The proposed settlement in case of suppression of voting rights under Article 182-A of the SC, as well as the methods of payment and of calculating the amount;
(xiv) The national legislation applicable to the contracts between the offeror and the holders of securities of the target company, following

the acceptance of the offer, as well as the competent courts to solve any conflicts arising from the operation;

(xv) Any expenses or burdens for the recipients.

One of the new prospectus rules introduced by the Decree-Law relates to incorporation by reference. As established by Article 136-A, which also applies to admissions to trading in view of Article 238 of the SC, the incorporation of information in the prospectus by reference to other documents previously or simultaneously published and which have been approved by or notified to the CMVM, is allowed. Nevertheless, the summary of the prospectus cannot have information incorporated by reference.

In relation to the content of the prospectus, we should like to conclude this report by referring briefly to the fact that it is possible to withhold certain information from the prospectus. Article 141 of the SC, which also applies to admissions to trading in view of Article 238 of the SC, states that, upon request of the issuer or offeror, the CMVM may not require the inclusion of certain information in the prospectus, provided that:

(i) The publication of such information is against the public interest;

(ii) The publication of such information is particularly harmful to the issuer, as long as the omission is not likely to mislead the public regarding facts and circumstances which are essential to properly evaluate the issuer, offeror or guarantor, as well as the rights inherent to the securities at stake;

(iii) This information is of minor importance to the offer and is not likely to influence the evaluation of the financial position and perspectives of the issuer, offeror or guarantor.

2 Format

7. The format of the prospectus is regulated by Article 135-B of the SC on public offers for the distribution of securities, which also applies to admissions to trading due to Article 238 of the SC. According to Article 135-B of the SC, the prospectus for the distribution of public offers may be prepared in the form of a single document or separate documents. A prospectus with separate documents includes a registration document, a note on the securities and a summary. The registration document should contain information regarding the issuer and must have been previously submitted to the CMVM for approval or mere presentation, while the note on the securities must contain information regarding the target securities.

Article 135-C of the SC, also introduced into Portuguese legislation by the Prospectus Directive and which applies to admissions to trading under Article 238 of the SC, describes the base prospectus. Article 135-C provides that a single base prospectus, with information regarding the issuer and the securities, may be used in public offers for the distribution of:

(i) Securities which are not representative of share capital, including warrants, issued within an offer program;

(ii) Securities which are not representative of share capital issued continuously or repeatedly by a credit institution as long as:
- The amounts resulting from the issuance of those securities are invested in assets which ensure a sufficient cover for the liabilities arising from the securities until its respective maturity date;
- In case of bankruptcy of the credit institution, the referred amounts are destined, as first priority, to reimburse the invested capital and pay the respective interest.

3 Supplements

8. Supplements which may be required after the approval of the prospectus are dealt with by Article 142 of the SC, which states that if, between the date of approval of the prospectus and the end of the deadline for the offer, any irregularities are detected in the prospectus, any new event occurs or a new fact which was not considered before is now known that might be relevant to the decision of the recipients, the approval of an addendum or amendment must be requested from the CMVM.

This request must be approved within seven days and published according to the provisions of Article 140 of the SC, described below. The summary and its translations should also be completed or amended, if necessary, to include the information contained in the addendum or amendment.

Finally, Article 135-C of the SC, on the base prospectus considered above, also foresees the use of supplements. Article 135-C (3), provides that the base prospectus must be complemented, if necessary, with updated information on the issuer and the securities by an addendum.

4 Language

9. In relation to public offers Article 163-A of the SC indicates that the prospectus may be, in whole or in part, prepared in a language usually used in international financial markets where its presentation does not derive from a legal obligation, it has been prepared within a public offer addressed to several States or if the issuer's personal law is foreign. Nevertheless, in what is a new amendment introduced by the Decree-Law, in the latter two situations, the CMVM may require that the prospectus also be presented in the Portuguese language.

In respect of the language of the prospectus for admissions to trading on a regulated market, the relevant article is 237-A of the SC, which includes a provision similar to Article 163-A of the SC but goes somewhat further. According to this, the prospectus may be written in a language usually used in international financial markets if:

(i) The securities to be admitted have a nominal value equal or superior to €50,000, or, if securities without a nominal value are at stake, the initial foreseen value for the admission is equal or superior to that amount;
(ii) It has been prepared within an admission request to markets of several States;
(iii) The issuer's personal law is foreign;
(iv) It is destined to markets or market segment which, due to their characteristics, are only accessible to qualified investors.

This last circumstance was not contemplated in the SC prior to the transposition of the Prospectus Directive and was introduced by the Decree-Law.

Finally, as determined by Article 163-A of the SC for public offers, Article 237-A of the SC establishes that in the situations referred to in ii) and iii) the CMVM may require that the prospectus is also presented in the Portuguese language.

V Publication and advertisements

1 Method of publication

10. The publication of the prospectus is provided for by Article 140 of the SC, which also applies to the admission to trading in view of Article 238 of the SC. According to this provision, which was substantially changed by the Decree-Law, after its approval, the final version of the prospectus must be sent to the CMVM and made available to the public. The prospectus may be published in the following ways:

(i) Publication in one or more national newspapers or, if not national, of high circulation;
(ii) Printed and placed, free of charge, and available to the public at the premises of the market to which the admission to trading of the securities was requested, or at the headquarters of the issuer and in the agencies of the financial intermediaries responsible for the securities' placement, including the issuer's financial services;
(iii) Posted on the issuer's website and, if applicable, on the financial intermediaries' website on the Internet, including the issuer's financial services;
(iv) Posted on the website of the regulated market in respect of which the admission to trading was requested;
(v) Posted on the CMVM's website.

If the prospectus has several documents and/or contains information incorporated by reference to other documents, such documents and information may be published separately, as long as they are made available to the public, free of charge, through the means referred to above. Moreover, the publication of the prospectus, according to Article 140.10 of the SC, must always be in compliance with the Prospectus Regulation.

In respect of the publication of the base prospectus, Article 135-C(4) of the SC specifically provides that, where the offer's final conditions are not included in the base prospectus or in an addendum, these should be disclosed to the investors and communicated to the CMVM as soon as it is viable and, if possible, before the beginning of the offer. This disclosure must also be made in compliance with the Prospectus Regulation.

2 Advertisements

11. Articles 121 and 122 of the SC govern the prospectus advertisements. According to article 121, the publicity regarding public offers must:

(i) Be in accordance with Article 7 of the SC, i.e. it has to be complete, accurate, updated, clear, objective and legally permissible;
(ii) Make a reference to the future existence or availability of the prospectus and indicate how to obtain it;
(iii) Be reconcilable with the content of the prospectus.

It should also be stated that all of the advertising material pertaining to the offer must be approved by the CMVM.

Under the terms of Article 122 of the SC, if the CMVM considers that, after the preliminary review of the request, the approval of the prospectus or the registration of the offer is viable, it may authorise advertisements before the approval of the prospectus or the granting of the registration, as long as this does not cause any difficulties to the recipients or market.

On the other hand, Article 140-A, which was introduced by the Decree-Law, determines that if the prospectus for public offers is only published through the websites on the Internet, as referred to in iii), iv) and v), above, an announcement on the availability of the prospectus must be made. The content and publication of the referred announcement must be in compliance with the 'Prospectus Regulation'.

VI Use of prospectus approved in other non European Union countries

12. The use of a prospectus approved in other non European Union countries is regulated by Article 147 of the SC, which was substantially amended by the Decree-Law and also applies to admissions to trading by virtue of Article 238 of the SC. These provisions determine that the CMVM may approve a prospectus of a public offer for the distribution of securities of an issuer with its corporate seat in a non European Union State prepared according to the legislation of a non-European Union State as long as it has been prepared in compliance with international standards established by international organisations of securities supervisors, including the IOSCO

standards, and it contains information, namely of a financial nature, equivalent to that provided for in the SC and the Prospectus Regulation.

Furthermore, Article 147.2 of the SC also provides that the prospectus approved under it must observe the rules under article 146 of the SC, analysed above at II.

VII Sanctions

13. Under Article 131 of the SC, the CMVM may order the withdrawal of an offer or prevent its launch if it considers that the offer is invalid or breaches any rule which cannot be remedied. Article 133 establishes that the CMVM may suspend the offer on the same grounds.

Moreover, according to Article 393.1(a) and Article 394.1 of the SC, the situations listed below constitute serious offences which, under Article 388 of the SC, may result in the payment of a fine of between €25,000 to €2.5 million:

(i) The undertaking of a public offering without prior approval of the prospectus or prior registration with the CMVM;
(ii) The disclosure of a public offer of distribution, decided or planned, and the acceptance of orders of subscription or acquisition, before the publication of the prospectus or, if a takeover is at stake, before the publication of the announcement;
(iii) The disclosure of a prospectus, respective addenda and rectification of the base prospectus, without the prior approval of the competent authority;
(iv) The breach of the duty of disclosure of the prospectus, the base prospectus, respective addendums and rectifications or the offer's final conditions;
(v) The breach of the duty of disclosure, including, in the prospectus, the base prospectus, respective addendums and rectifications or the offer's final conditions, information which is complete, accurate, updated, clear, objective and legally permissible according to the Prospectus Regulation;
(vi) The admission to trading of securities in breach of the rules;
(vii) The lack of disclosure of the admission prospectus, of the respective addendums and rectifications, or of necessary information for its update, or its disclosure without prior approval by the competent authority.

In addition, according to Article 393.2 of the SC, the following circumstances constitute a serious offence which, according to Article 388 of the SC, may result in the payment of a fine of between €12,500 to €1.25 million:

(i) The gathering of investment intentions without a prior approval of a preliminary prospectus by the CMVM or prior to the disclosure of the same;
(ii) The breach of the duty to include the references list in the prospectus when this contains information incorporated by reference.

However, Article 404 of the SC stipulates that other accessory penalties, such the loss of all the profits obtained with the violation at stake, among others, may be applied instead of the fine.

VIII Prospectus liability

14. Liability for the prospectus is provided for by Articles 149 to 154 of the SC for public offers, which, however, also apply to admissions to trading due to Article 243 of the SC.

According to Article 149 of the SC, the offeror or members of its board, the issuer or members of its board, the promoters where they exist, the members of the statutory audit committee, the auditing companies, the auditors, persons who certified or analysed the accounting documents upon which the prospectus is based and other persons accepting responsibility for any information, prediction or study included in the prospectus, may be liable for damages arising from irregularities in the prospectus' content under Article 135 of the SC, unless they prove that it was not their fault.

On the other hand, according to Article 150 of the SC, the offeror is always liable, regardless of fault, whenever the members of its board, the financial intermediaries, or other people accepting responsibility for any information, prediction or study included in the prospectus are liable. Likewise, the issuer is always liable, regardless of fault, whenever members of its board, promoters, members of the statutory audit committee, auditing companies, auditors and other people who certified or analysed the accounting documents on which the prospectus is based are liable. Additionally, the chief of the placement intermediaries' consortium is always liable, regardless of fault, whenever one of the members of the consortium is liable. Furthermore, if several people are liable, according to Article 151 of the SC, their responsibility is joint and several.

Finally, the compensation due must be sufficient to place the injured party in the same situation it would have been in if, at the moment of the acquisition of the securities, the content of the prospectus had been in accordance with Article 135 of the SC. Nevertheless, the right to compensation must be exercised within six months of acquiring knowledge on the irregularity of the content of the prospectus and it cannot be exercised, in any event, two years after the disclosure of the offer's result.

IX Rules applicable to transactions and securities not subject to the Directive and Regulation

15. The rules to be applied to transactions and securities not subject to the 'Prospectus Directive' and 'Prospectus Regulation' are those resulting from the basic principles and rules of Portuguese International Law.

X Conclusion

16. In conclusion, we should like to say that in our view the legislator of the Decree-Law was reasonable in ensuring that all the innovations of the 'Prospectus Directive' and the 'Prospectus Regulation' were provided for in our national legislation, thereby contributing to the harmonising of the European Union Member States legislation.

14 Slovakia

MICHAELA JURKOVÁ
Čechová & Partners

I Introduction

1. Public offers of securities which fall under the scope of Directive 2003/71/EC of the European Parliament and of the Council of 4 November 2003 on the prospectus to be published when securities are offered to the public or admitted to trading and amending Directive 2001/34/EC (the 'Prospectus Directive' or 'Dir.') are regulated in Slovakia by Act No.

566/2001 Coll. of 9 November 2001 on securities and investment services and amending and supplementing certain other acts, as amended (the 'Securities Act'). As far as the admission of securities to trading on a regulated market is concerned, it is covered by Act No. 429/2002 Coll. on the stock exchange, as amended ('Stock Exchange Act'), with the exception of rules regulating the preparation and approval of the prospectus used for the purpose of admission of securities to trading on a regulated market.

2. Already since its entering into force on 1 January 2002, the Securities Act also regulated, *inter alia*, public offers of securities, including approval and publication of the prospectus; however, it was only Act No. 336/2005 Coll. of 23 June 2005, amending and supplementing Act No. 566/2001 Coll. on securities and investment services and amending and supplementing certain other acts, as amended (the Securities Act), and amending and supplementing certain other acts ('the Amendment') that transposed the Prospectus Directive into Slovak legislation. The Amendment became effective on 1 August 2005, which means that Slovakia transposed the Prospectus Directive with a one-month delay.

As mentioned in the explanatory report to the draft Amendment published by the Government of Slovakia, 'the legal regulation of public offers of securities and of prospectuses before Act No. 336/2005 Coll. was covered by the Securities Act and by the Stock Exchange Act, which two acts implemented the original framework of the European Union for public offers and prospectuses of securities. That meant that the issuers of securities had to comply with two legal acts when preparing the prospectuses of securities, which two acts stipulated different prerequisites of prospectuses and different procedures for their approval depending on the fact whether the offer was made on a regulated market (stock exchange) or on non-regulated market. Two different authorities had the competence to approve the prospectuses: (a) Financial Market Authority (*Úrad pre finančný trh*), a former authority for supervision of financial markets, which approved the prospectuses prepared under the Securities Act, and in certain cases also the prospectus for listing of securities on a stock exchange; and (b) Bratislava Stock Exchange (*Burza cenných papierov v Bratislave, a.s.*), which approved the prospectus for listing securities under the Stock Exchange Act, when the issuer had not yet its prospectus approved by the Financial Market Authority. These doubled procedures might have been discouraging issuers from acquiring the capital through financial markets.'[1]

The new legal regulation introduced by the Amendment simplified the administrative procedures for approval of prospectuses by determining only one competent authority, the Financial Market Authority, replaced by the National Bank of Slovakia as of 1 January 2006. Under the previously

[1] Explanatory Report to draft Act No. 336/2005 published at www.government.gov.sk

valid legislation, three different prospectuses existed: prospectus of securities for public offer, prospectus of securities in the scope of prospectus for listed securities and prospectus for listed securities; the latter two were used for admission to trading on a regulated market. The Amendment deleted the provisions concerning approval of the prospectus from the Stock Exchange Act, and thus the three types of prospectus have been replaced with one prospectus approved by the National Bank of Slovakia under the Securities Act and used for both public offers of securities, as well as admission of securities to trading on a regulated market (which otherwise remains regulated by the Stock Exchange Act). The new legislation also brought shorter time periods for approval of a prospectus.

3. As far as the contents of the prospectus are concerned, they are specified in the Securities Act only by references to Commission Regulation (EC) No. 809/2004 of 29 April 2004 implementing Directive 2003/71/EC of the European Parliament and of the Council as regards information contained in prospectuses as well as the format, incorporation by reference and publication of such prospectuses and dissemination of advertisements (the 'Prospectus Regulation' or 'Reg.').

The former Financial Market Authority together with the Ministry of Finance of the Slovak Republic and professionals active on the financial markets prepared a document entitled 'Essentials of the contents of the securities prospectus for offer to the public and for admission to trading on a regulated market' (*Obsahové náležitosti prospektu cenného papiera pre realizáciu verejnej ponuky a pre prijatie cenných papierov k obchodovaniu na regulovanom trhu*, the 'Prospectus Essentials'). The document is currently available on the web site of the National Bank of Slovakia[2] and it mostly repeats the provisions of the Prospectus Directive and the Prospectus Regulation concerning the contents of the prospectus.

II Competent authority

4. Starting from 1 January 2006, the National Bank of Slovakia, which is also a central bank of Slovakia, became the supervising authority over the financial markets based on Act No. 747/2004 Coll. on financial market supervision and amending and supplementing certain other acts, as amended (the 'Financial Market Supervision Act'), and replaced the previously existing Financial Market Authority, which was dissolved by this act.

According to the Securities Act, the National Bank of Slovakia is the central competent administrative authority in accordance with Article 21 of the Prospectus Directive for carrying out the obligations provided for in the Prospectus Directive, including approval of prospectuses of securities.

[2] www.nbs.sk/DFT/KAPTRH/VP/OBSNAL.PDF

The Slovakian legislator does not give the National Bank of Slovakia the possibility to delegate its tasks, as allowed by Article 21 (2) of the Prospectus Directive.

III Procedure of prior approval and appeal

1 Public offer of securities

5. Public offering of securities is regulated in Sections 120 through 125(h) of the Securities Act. It is defined, for the purposes of the Securities Act, as any communication to a wider scope of persons in any form and by any means, presenting sufficient information on the terms of the offer of securities and on the securities offered, so as to enable an investor to decide to purchase or subscribe to these securities. This definition shall also be applicable to the placing of securities through securities brokers[3] or foreign securities brokers, if executed in the manner described in the previous sentence.

Public offer of securities without a prior publication of an approved prospectus is forbidden, if not stipulated otherwise by the Securities Act, i.e. unless the exemptions mentioned below apply.

6. The application for approval of the prospectus is to be submitted by the issuer, offeror or person asking for admission to trading on a regulated market to the National Bank of Slovakia, if Slovakia is the home Member State of the issuer.

The definition of the home Member State of the issuer corresponds to the one included in the Prospectus Directive. The home Member State means:

- (i) for issuers with their registered seat in a Member State, that are not mentioned under (ii) below, the Member State where the respective issuer has its registered seat;
- (ii) the Member State where the issuer has its registered seat or where the securities were or are to be admitted to trading on a regulated market or where the securities are offered to the public, for issues of non-equity securities: (a) whose denomination per unit amounts to at least €1,000, and (b) which give the right to acquire any transferable securities or to receive a cash amount as a consequence of their being converted or the rights conferred by them being exercised, provided that the issuer of the non-equity securities is not the issuer of the underlying securities or an entity belonging to the group of the latter issuer;
- (iii) for the issuers incorporated in a third country that are not mentioned under (ii) above, the Member State where the securities are intended to be offered to the public for the first time after 31 December 2003 or

[3] The term 'securities broker' is used by the Securities Act for entities having the licence for performance of investment/financial services.

where the first application for admission to trading on a regulated market is made; however the right of the issuer to choose the home Member State shall remain unaffected.

7. The National Bank of Slovakia must decide on approval of the prospectus and notify the applicant of the decision within ten working days after the submission of the draft proposal. This time period is extended up to twenty working days if the public offer of securities concerns the securities of an issuer whose securities have not yet been admitted to trading on a regulated market and who until the date of the application has not offered securities to the public.

If the National Bank of Slovakia finds out that the draft prospectus is not complete or that certain additional data need to be supplemented in accordance with the Prospectus Regulation, it must inform the applicant thereof within the period of ten working days following the submission of the application. If it is necessary for the protection of investors, the National Bank of Slovakia may ask that the prospectus be supplemented with additional data. In such case, the time periods for the decision of the National Bank of Slovakia start on the date when the applicant provides the requested additional data.

The failure of the National Bank of Slovakia to decide within the above-mentioned periods shall not be considered as approval of the prospectus; the National Bank of Slovakia must inform the applicant without undue delay about its failure to meet the term for decisions and the reasons thereof.

8. When examining the prospectus, the National Bank of Slovakia examines mainly its completeness, mutual compliance of the submitted information and their comprehensibility. The approved prospectuses are kept by the National Bank of Slovakia.

9. Even in cases when the National Bank of Slovakia is a competent authority for approval of the prospectus, it may transfer the approval to a competent authority of another Member State after having agreed with that other authority. Similarly, the National Bank of Slovakia may approve a prospectus for the approval of which the authority of another Member State is competent upon the agreement with this other competent authority. The applicant must be informed within three working days of a decision to transfer the approval and the time periods for the issue of an approval start on the date the applicant is informed.

10. The application of general rules of administrative proceedings being excluded, the proceedings before the National Bank of Slovakia are governed by the Financial Market Supervision Act, stipulating, e.g. the prerequisites of the application, rules of procedure, definition of the participant in the proceedings, methods of delivery of documents, etc.

The decision of the National Bank of Slovakia may be subject to an appeal which shall be submitted to the department of the National Bank of Slovakia that has issued the relevant decision within fifteen calendar days following the delivery of the decision to the applicant. It is the Council of the National Bank of Slovakia that will decide on the appeal.

The valid and effective decision of the National Bank of Slovakia can be opposed by submitting an action to the Supreme Court of Slovakia.

2 Admission to trading

11. Procedure of admission of securities to trading on a regulated market is regulated by the Stock Exchange Act. The Stock Exchange Act differentiates between a market of listed securities and a regulated free market. The application for admission to trading on any of them requires submission, together with the application, of a securities prospectus approved by the National Bank of Slovakia in accordance with the Securities Act.

According to the Stock Exchange Act, securities can be traded on a regulated market as of the day following the publication of their prospectus.

12. The application for admission to trading on a market of listed securities may be submitted either by the issuer of securities or by a member of the stock exchange. The application for admission to trading on a regulated free market may be submitted either by the issuer or by a member of the stock exchange, unless the law provides otherwise. 'Unless the law provides otherwise' refers mainly to the competence of the stock exchange to decide on admission of securities to trading on a regulated free market upon its own discretion, without an application being submitted by the issuer of the relevant securities.

If the stock exchange decides to admit to trading securities without an application by their issuers, it must notify the issuers thereof at least thirty days in advance. The issuer has the right to forbid the trading with the securities within a period of thirty days after the decision on admission to trading was adopted, by a written notification delivered to the stock exchange. If the issuer does not forbid the trading according to the previous sentence, the securities can be traded on a regulated free market, even without the issuer's approval.

13. If the securities and the issuer meet the conditions stipulated by law and by the rules of the stock exchange, the stock exchange will decide on admission to trading within sixty days of receipt of the application. On the one hand, the Stock Exchange Act states that this period can be extended up to six months in case of simultaneous application in one or more other Member States.

On the other hand, the Stock Exchange Act states that if an application for listing of the same securities on the Slovakian stock exchange and simultaneously on a stock exchange with a seat in another Member State is made, or if on such stock exchanges the decision-making process is going on simultaneously, the Slovakian stock exchange shall coordinate its activity with the competent body in the other Member State and shall take the measures necessary for making the procedure faster and simpler. This should apply especially with respect to fulfilment, or discharge from fulfilment, of additional requirements for admission to trading stipulated by the Slovakian stock exchange or the competent body of the other Member State above the minimum scope prescribed by the legal regulation of the European Union on admission to trading of securities on a market of listed securities. The same applies to evaluation of a request for admission to trading on a market of listed securities of securities which are already listed on a stock exchange of another Member State. The Slovakian stock exchange may refuse such request if the issuer does not meet its obligations resulting from listing of its securities in the other Member State.

14. The stock exchange must issue a written decision on the application for admission to trading and notify the applicant about the decision without undue delay. If the stock exchange does not issue a decision within the aforementioned sixty-day time period, the issuance of the decision can be claimed at the court.

15. The stock exchange must publish a notice on admission to trading of securities on a market of listed securities in newspapers circulated throughout Slovakia containing stock exchange news. At least the following information must be published: name of securities, business name of the issuer, the date of admission to trading on a market of listed securities and the date of the beginning of trading.

3 Exemptions

A Exemptions applicable to offer of securities to the public

16. Duty to publish an approved prospectus does not apply to an offer of securities to the public, if the offer is:

- (i) addressed solely to qualified investors;
- (ii) addressed to fewer than 100 natural or legal persons per Member State, other than qualified investors;
- (iii) addressed to investors who on the basis of this offer acquire securities in a total value of at least €50,000 per one investor;
- (iv) an offer where the nominal value or the price per unit amounts to at least €50,000; or
- (v) with a total value of less than €100,000, which limit shall be calculated over a period of twelve months.

17. For the purposes of the exemption mentioned under (i) above, the qualified investor is defined by the Securities Act as:

(i) securities broker, financial institution or legal entity, the principal scope of business of which is investing in the investment instruments;
(ii) state authority, municipality or upper regional unit,[4] state authority and self-government unit of another state, the National Bank of Slovakia, central bank of another state, the International Monetary Fund, the European Central Bank, the European Investment Bank, and other similar international organisations;
(iii) commercial company or cooperative which is not a small or medium sized enterprise (i.e. which fulfils at least two of the following conditions according to its latest annual individual or consolidated financial statements: (a) average number of employees over the accounting period is lower than 250; (b) total value of its assets does not exceed €43 million; (c) annual net turnover does not exceed €50 million);
(iv) natural person residing in the territory of Slovakia recognised as a qualified investor by the National Bank of Slovakia upon the request made by the natural person; a natural person residing in another Member State will be recognised as a qualified investor upon fulfilment of requirements of that other Member State;
(v) small or medium-sized enterprise with its seat in Slovakia recognised as a qualified investor upon its request by the National Bank of Slovakia, if it meets at least two of the three conditions mentioned above under (iii); a small or medium sized enterprise having its seat in another Member State is considered as a qualified investor if it meets the conditions of that other Member State.

The natural person resident in Slovakia can be recognised as a qualified investor by the National Bank of Slovakia, if he/she meets at least two of the following conditions:

(i) the investor has carried out transactions of a significant size on securities markets at an average frequency of, at least, ten per quarter over the previous four quarters, while a significant transaction is a transaction with the value exceeding €6,000;
(ii) the size of the investor's securities portfolio exceeds €500,000;
(iii) the investor works or has worked for at least one year in the financial sector in a professional position which requires knowledge of securities investment.

The National Bank of Slovakia administers the register of natural persons residing in Slovakia and of small and medium-sized companies with their

[4] Self-governmental unit in Slovakia at the level of regions.

seat in Slovakia that were recognised as qualified investors; the National Bank of Slovakia must make the data from the register available to the issuers of securities upon their written request.

The National Bank of Slovakia deletes a natural person or a small or medium-sized enterprise from the list of qualified investors upon their own request or if they cease to meet any of the aforementioned conditions.

18. The Securities Act further excludes application of the obligation to publish a prospectus to the public offers of certain types of securities, which correspond to the exemptions provided for in Article 4(1) of the Prospectus Directive. These exemptions also include securities offered, allotted or to be allotted to existing or former directors or employees by their employer which has securities already admitted to trading on a regulated market or by an affiliated undertaking, provided that a document is made available containing information on the number and nature of the securities and the reasons for and details of the offer. According to a recent unofficial statement of the National Bank of Slovakia (given in a particular case), the information on the number of the securities, if not available, can be replaced in that document by the information on the manner of calculation of the total number of securities which are subject to the offer.

19. The provisions of the Securities Act on approval and publication of securities prospectuses further do not apply to the securities as listed in Article 1(2) of the Prospectus Directive. However, a prospectus may be prepared for the securities listed below if the issuer, offeror or person asking for admission to trading so decides:

(i) non-equity securities issued by a Member State or by one of a Member State's regional or local authorities, by public international bodies of which one or more Member States are members, by the European Central Bank or by the central banks of the Member States;
(ii) securities unconditionally and irrevocably guaranteed by a Member State or by one of a Member State's regional or local authorities;
(iii) non-equity securities issued in a continuous or repeated manner by banks or foreign banks where the total consideration of the offer is less than €50 million, which limit shall be calculated over a period of twelve months, provided that these securities (a) are not subordinated, convertible or exchangeable; (b) do not give a right to subscribe to or acquire other types of securities and that they are not linked to a derivative instrument; and
(iv) securities that are subject of a public offer where the total consideration of the offer is less than €2.5 million, calculated over a period of twelve months.

In the case of securities under (iv) above where the total consideration of the offer is more than €100,000 and at the same time less than €2.5 million, calculated over a period of 12 months, the provisions of the Securities Act regulating the prospectus, its approval and publication apply; however, excluding the provisions concerning cooperation of Member States.

B Exemptions applicable to admission of securities to trading

20. Pursuant to the Stock Exchange Act, the duty to submit the approved prospectus together with application for admission of securities to trading on a regulated market and to publish a prospectus does not apply in the following cases:

(i) shares representing, over a period of twelve months, less than 10 per cent of the number of shares of the same class already admitted to trading on the same stock exchange;
(ii) shares issued in substitution for shares of the same class already admitted to trading on the same stock exchange, if the issuing of such shares does not involve any increase in the registered capital of the issuer;
(iii) securities offered in connection with a takeover by means of an exchange offer, provided that a document is available containing information which is regarded by the National Bank of Slovakia as being equivalent to that of the prospectus;
(iv) securities offered in connection with a merger or amalgamation, provided that a document is available containing information which is regarded by the National Bank of Slovakia as being equivalent to that of the prospectus;
(v) shares offered free of charge to existing shareholders, and dividends paid out in the form of shares of the same class as the shares in respect of which such dividends are paid, provided that the said shares are of the same class as the shares already admitted to trading on the same stock exchange and that a documents is made available containing information on the number and nature of the shares and the reasons for and details of the offer;
(vi) securities offered to existing or former members of statutory, supervisory or managing bodies or employees by their employer or an affiliated undertaking, provided that the said securities are of the same class as the securities already admitted to trading on the same stock exchange and that a document is made available containing information on the number and nature of the shares and the reasons for and details of the offer;
(vii) shares acquired by exchange of other securities or from the exercise of the rights conferred by other securities, provided that the said shares are of the same class as the shares already admitted to trading on the same stock exchange;
(viii) securities already admitted to trading on another regulated market, on the following conditions:

(a) that these securities, or securities of the same class, have been admitted to trading on that other regulated market for more than eighteen months;
(b) that, for securities first admitted to trading on a regulated market after 31 December 2003, the admission to trading on that other regulated market was associated with an approved prospectus made available to the public in conformity with the Securities Act;
(c) that, except where (b) applies, for securities first admitted to listing after 30 June 1983, the prospectuses were approved in compliance with the Stock Exchange Act or the Securities Act, or with the laws of the Member State regulating prospectuses and admission to trading on a regulated market;
(d) that these securities continue meeting the requirements for trading on that other regulated market;
(e) that the person seeking the admission of a security to trading on a regulated market makes a summary document available to the public in a Slovakian language in the manner specified under the Securities Act in the Member State of the regulated market where the admission to trading is sought; the contents of the summary document shall comply with the Securities Act and the document shall state where the most recent prospectus can be obtained and where the information published by the issuer pursuant to his ongoing disclosure obligations is available;

(ix) securities to which the provisions on public offer of securities of the Securities Act do not apply, excluding the securities where the right to voluntary elaboration of a prospectus has been used in accordance with the Securities Act.

IV Content and format, language and supplements of the prospectus

1 Content

21. According to Section 121 of the Securities Act, the prospectus shall contain all the information which is due to the nature of the issuer and the nature of the securities (publicly offered or admitted for trading) necessary for the investors to be able to make a correct evaluation of the issuer, its assets and liabilities, financial situation, profit and loss and perspectives, and of persons that took over the guarantees for repayment of the securities, or proceeds and rights related to the securities.

The information in the prospectus must be provided in a comprehensive and transparent manner.

The prospectus must contain the data on the issuer, data on the securities, and the summary stating in a brief and comprehensive manner the basic characteristics of the issuer, of the securities, and persons providing the guarantee.

22. The summary must contain a notice that:

(i) it represents only an introduction to the prospectus;
(ii) any investor's decision must result from the evaluation of the prospectus as a whole;
(iii) in case of an action brought to a court by the investor with respect to the information contained in the prospectus, the petitioner may be obliged to bear the costs of translation of the prospectus into the language of the Member State where the action was brought;
(iv) in case of damage resulting from the summary containing misleading or inaccurate information or information which contradicts the data contained in the other parts of the prospectus, the persons responsible for data contained in the prospectus and persons responsible for the summary or its translation are liable for damages.

The summary is not required in case of a request for admission to trading on a regulated market of non-equity securities with a nominal value or price of at least €50,000 per one individual security. This does not apply when non-equity securities are requested to be admitted for trading on a regulated market in one or more Member States, in which case the prospectus shall be prepared in the Slovak language and in a language accepted by the authorities of the host Member State or only in a language commonly used in international finance chosen by the issuer, offeror or person asking for the admission to trading; in such a case the summary must be translated into Slovak.

2 Format

23. The prospectus may be prepared as one document, or as a document consisting of three individual/separate documents, being:

(i) a registration document containing the data on the issuer;
(ii) a description of securities containing data on the securities which are the subject of the public offer or of admission to trading; and
(iii) a summary document containing the data which are otherwise contained in the summary.

As a general rule, the prospectus must be prepared in compliance with the Prospectus Regulation.

24. The data can be included in the prospectus also in the form of references to one or more documents published previously or at the same time as the prospectus, and approved by the National Bank of Slovakia, or submitted to the National Bank of Slovakia in compliance with the Securities Act or

Stock Exchange Act, or to the competent authority of another Member State. Such data must be the most recent data available to the issuer. The list of cross-references must be included in the prospectus.

The above does not apply to the summary where the data must not be included in the form of references.

25. The prospectus can be prepared as a base prospectus in the case of the following securities:

(i) non-equity securities and option certificates (warrants) issued under an offering programme;
(ii) non-equity securities issued in a continuous or repeated manner by banks or foreign banks, if:
   (a) the proceeds deriving from their issue are placed in assets which provide sufficient coverage for the liability deriving from securities;
   (b) proceeds deriving from their issue are intended, as a priority, to repay the capital and interest falling due in case of insolvency of the related bank or a foreign bank.

The base prospectus is a prospectus containing all important information concerning the issuer and the securities, which is prepared in compliance with the Prospectus Regulation.

26. If the base prospectus does not contain the final terms of the public offer of securities, these shall be notified to the investors and submitted to the National Bank of Slovakia for each individual public offer of securities at the moment of the beginning of the offer, at the latest. In such a case, either (a) the prospectus must contain at least the criteria and conditions according to which the final price and number of the securities will be determined, or in case of price also maximum price, or (b) the investors must be provided with a possibility to withdraw their acceptance of the public offer at least two working days after the final price and number of securities is made public.

3 Supplements

27. If during an offering programme or in the course of continuous or repeated issue of securities, important changes occur to the data mentioned in the base prospectus, these data must be supplemented or amended in the form of a supplement (in compliance with Section 125c of the Securities Act).

Every significant new factor, material mistake or inaccuracy relating to the information included in the prospectus which is capable of affecting the assessment of the securities and which arises or is noted between the time when the prospectus is approved and the final closing of the offer to the public, or the time when trading on a regulated market begins, must be mentioned in a supplement to the prospectus.

The rules applicable to approval of the prospectus apply also to the approval of a supplement by the National Bank of Slovakia, however, the National Bank of Slovakia has seven working days for approval of the supplement (while in the case of the prospectus itself, the time period is ten working days). The supplement shall be published in the same way as the original prospectus. If necessary, the summary and any translation thereof must also be supplemented.

Investors who have already agreed to purchase or subscribe for the securities before the supplement is published have the right to withdraw their acceptance within the period which is stipulated by the Securities Act to be two working days (the minimum period provided in the Prospectus Directive).

4 Language

28. Where an offer to the public is made or admission to trading on a regulated market is sought only in the territory of Slovakia, the prospectus shall be drawn up in Slovak (the official language of Slovakia).

29. When an offer is made or an admission is sought exclusively in another Member State (i.e. not in Slovakia, which, however, is the home Member State), the prospectus must be drawn up in the language accepted by the competent authority of the other host Member State or in a language customary in the sphere of international finance, at the choice of the issuer, offeror or person asking for admission to trading. If requested by the competent authority of the host Member State, this person must provide a translation of the summary into one or more official languages of the host Member State.

For the purposes of approval of the prospectus according to the previous paragraph, the prospectus must be submitted to the National Bank of Slovakia in Slovak or in a language customary in the sphere of international finance.

30. When an offer is made or an admission to trading is sought in Slovakia and, at the same time, in another Member State, the prospectus must be drawn up in Slovak and also in a language accepted by the competent authority of each host Member State or a language customary in the sphere of international finance. The summary must be translated into the official language or official languages of the host Member State if the competent authority of the host Member State requested so. The National Bank of Slovakia may require from the issuer of another Member State, the offeror or a person asking for admission to trading translation of the summary into Slovak if the offer is made or admission to trading is sought in Slovakia and another Member State.

31. When admission to trading on a regulated market of non-equity securities whose denomination per unit amounts to at least €50,000 is sought in one or more Member States, the prospectus must be drawn up in Slovak and a language accepted by the competent authority of the host Member

State, or only in the language customary in the sphere of international finance, at the choice of the issuer, offeror or persons asking for admission to trading. The summary must be translated into Slovak.

V Publication and advertisements

1 Method of publication of prospectus

32. The prospectus must be made available to the public at a reasonable time in advance of the offer to the public or the admission to trading of the securities – at the latest on the day when the offer of securities to the public or the trading on the regulated market with the securities begins. The obligation is imposed on the issuer, offeror or person asking for admission to trading on a regulated market.

In the case of an initial public offer of a class of shares not already admitted to trading on a regulated market that is to be admitted to trading for the first time, the prospectus must be made available to the public at least six working days before the end of the offer; however, the general ban on publicly offering securities without previous publication of a prospectus shall remain unaffected.

33. The methods of publication stipulated by the Securities Act correspond to those provided in Article 14(2) of the Prospectus Directive. The National Bank of Slovakia does not, for the time being, offer the service of publication of the prospectus in electronic form on its website. The Securities Act gives the National Bank of Slovakia an obligation to publish on its website over a period of twelve months only a list of prospectuses approved including, if applicable, a hyperlink to the prospectus published on the website of the issuer or on the website of the regulated market.

The Securities Act requires the issuers having published their prospectus in newspapers or in printed form (Article 14(2) (a) and (b) Dir.) to make it available also in electronic form on their website or on the website of financial institutions placing or selling the securities, including paying agents (Article 14(2) (c) Dir.), if securities of a total value exceeding €20 million are offered to the public.

34. In addition, in the case of publication of the prospectus in accordance with (b) through (e) of Article 14(2) of the Prospectus Directive, the Securities Act imposes an obligation to publish a notice stating how the prospectus was made public and where it can be obtained. Such notice must be published in daily newspapers circulated throughout, or widely circulated in, the Member States in which the offer to the public is made or the admission to trading is sought.

35. The Slovak Securities Act, in accordance with the Prospectus Directive allows, in the case of a prospectus comprising several documents and/or

incorporating information by reference, the documents and information making up the prospectus to be published and circulated separately provided that the said documents are made available to the public in accordance with Article 14(2) of the Prospectus Directive. Each document must indicate where the other constituent documents of the full prospectus may be obtained.

The text and format of the prospectus, and/or the supplements to the prospectus published or made available to the public, must be identical to the version of the prospectus approved by the National Bank of Slovakia.

The investors have the right to receive, upon their request and free of charge, a paper copy of the prospectus that has been made available by publication in electronic form.

2 Advertisements

36. Any notice, advertisement, poster or other document ('advertisements') relating to a public offer of securities or to admission to trading on a regulated market must contain the information that a prospectus has been or will be published and where it can be obtained, save for the cases when the prospectus is not required.

The purpose of the advertisement must be clearly evident. The information contained therein must not be inaccurate or misleading, and must be consistent with the information published, or to be published in the prospectus, if the prospectus is required. Also any information concerning the offer to the public of securities or admission to trading on a regulated market disclosed in an oral or written form, even if not for advertising purposes, must be consistent with those contained in the prospectus.

37. When, according to the Securities Act, a prospectus is not required, material information addressed to qualified investors or special categories of investors, including information disclosed in the context of meetings relating to offers of securities, must be disclosed to all qualified investors or special categories of investors to whom the offer is exclusively addressed. When a prospectus is required, such information shall be included in the prospectus or in a supplement to the prospectus.

38. There is no obligation for the advertisements to be approved by, or even filed with the National Bank of Slovakia. However, the National Bank of Slovakia has the right to forbid or suspend for a period of ten working days, the publication of an advertisement if it finds out that its publication or further circulation would breach the provisions of the Securities Act or of the Regulation.

None of the aforementioned provisions of the Securities Act shall affect the provisions of the Regulation.

VI Use of prospectus approved in other (non EU) countries

39. The National Bank of Slovakia may approve a prospectus for an offer to the public or for admission to trading on a regulated market for an issuer having its registered office in a third country (i.e. a non-EU country), drawn up in accordance with the legislation of such third country, provided that:

(i) the prospectus has been drawn up in accordance with international standards set by international securities commission organisations, including the rules concerning disclosure of information to the public; and provided that
(ii) the information requirements including information of a financial nature, are equivalent to the requirements under the Securities Act.

In the case of an offer to the public or admission to trading on a regulated market of securities, issued by an issuer incorporated in a third country, executed in a Member State other than the home Member State, the rules governing the cooperation between the Member States when an offer or an admission to trading within the European Union is concerned, apply.

VII Sanctions

40. If the National Bank of Slovakia finds deficiencies in the activities of the securities issuer, offeror, or person asking for admission to trading consisting in breaching of duties imposed by the Securities Act or in circumventing other provisions of the Securities Act or other applicable laws, the National Bank of Slovakia may:

(i) impose on the issuer, offeror or person asking for admission to trading the following sanctions: (a) levy remedy measures for removing deficiencies, (b) impose a fine of SKK 10,000 to SKK 20 million (approx. €285 to €571,428), (c) impose a duty to publish a correction of incomplete, incorrect or untrue information published by the issuer, offeror or person asking for admission to trading under their legal obligation;
(ii) suspend issuing securities for a maximum of ten working days;
(iii) forbid the issuer or offeror issuing the securities.

VIII Prospectus liability

41. According to the Securities Act, the issuer, its statutory body, managing body or supervisory body, natural person or legal entity being the offeror is responsible for the data contained in the prospectus, as well as the person requesting the admission of securities to trading on a regulated market or a

person that provided a guarantee for payment of the securities or their proceeds, or the person that prepared the prospectus.

The responsible persons are liable for the damage resulting from the incorrectness of the data included in the prospectus. The persons responsible for the summary or its translation are liable for the damage resulting from the fact that the summary contained misleading or inaccurate information, or that the information provided in the summary was not in compliance with the remaining parts of the prospectus.

42. The responsible persons must be clearly indicated in the prospectus. In the case of natural persons, their name, surname and position, and in the case of legal entities their business name and registered seat, must be indicated.

The prospectus must contain a declaration by the responsible persons that according to their best knowledge the data in the prospectus correspond to the reality, and that nothing which could influence the importance of the prospectus for correct evaluation of the issuer or securities, has been left out of the prospectus.

43. According to Section 159(1) of the Securities Act, the liability for damage resulting under the Securities Act is governed by the relevant provisions of Act No. 513/1991 Coll. the Commercial Code, as amended (the 'Commercial Code'). The liability for damage under the Commercial Code is an objective liability that arises notwithstanding the existence of the fault on the side of the liable person. The liable person may be exempted only if he/she proves the existence of circumstances excluding the liability, which are defined as obstacles that arose independently of the will of the obliged person and that prevent the obliged person to fulfil his/her obligation, provided it cannot be reasonably presumed that the obliged person could reverse or overcome these obstacles or their consequences and that he/she could anticipate such obstacles at the time of creation of his/her obligation.

IX Rules applicable to transactions and securities not subject to the Directive and Regulation

44. Under the Slovakian Securities Act, securities that are the subject of an offer to the public of a total value lower than €2.5 million, but exceeding €100,000, are subject to the obligation to publish a prospectus approved by the National Bank of Slovakia; however, the provisions concerning cooperation between the Member States do not apply in this case.

The units issued by collective investment undertakings other than the closed-end type, which are exempted from the application of the Prospectus Directive, are subject to special legal regulation of Act No. 594/2003 Coll. on collective investment and amending and supplementing certain other acts, as amended.

Other securities excluded from the application of the Prospectus Directive are subject to general provisions of the Securities Act regulating the issue of securities.

X Conclusion

45. The Slovakian legislator transposed into Slovakian law the provisions of the Prospectus Directive by amending the Securities Act, regulating the offer of securities to the public, and the Stock Exchange Act, covering the admission to trading on a regulated market. As a result, only one prospectus is currently required for the public offer of securities and for admission of securities to trading on a regulated market instead of the previous three different prospectuses required.

In principle, the Slovakian laws largely repeat the provisions of the Prospectus Directive, and as regards the contents of the prospectus, the Slovakian legislator limits itself to the references to the provisions of the Prospectus Regulation, which is directly applicable in all Member States.

15

United Kingdom

NIGEL BOARDMAN
Slaughter and May

I Introduction

1. The Financial Services Authority ('FSA') is the United Kingdom's regulatory authority for the financial services industry and wields statutory powers under the Financial Services and Markets Act 2000 ('FSMA') to make rules, policy and codes and to issue guidance to regulated firms. Most of this guidance is contained in the thirty-five-volume FSA Handbook of

Rules and Guidance ('FSA Handbook'), comprised of sourcebooks, manuals and other high-level standards applicable to all firms authorised by the FSA. The FSA exercises its functions in conjunction with HM Treasury, which is responsible in this regard for implementing the necessary legislative changes required to transpose the Prospectus Directive ('Prospectus Directive') into national law.

2. In the UK, transposition of Community legislation on financial services is usually carried out by a combination of amendments proposed by the government to primary or secondary legislation and by the FSA to its Handbook. The Treasury and the FSA have noted that the Prospectus Directive calls for 'maximum harmonisation' for the most part and, as a result, the Member States have relatively little leeway in implementing it.

Implementation of the Prospectus Directive in the UK has been achieved by:

- (i) Amendments to Part VI of FSMA on the powers and responsibilities of the FSA and the requirements for the listing of securities that appear on the Official List;
- (ii) The Prospectus Regulations 2005[1] ('Prospectus Regulations 2005') have amended FSMA by setting out, amongst other things, the basic circumstances under which a prospectus is required;
- (iii) The introduction of new FSA rules and guidance;
- (iv) The new FSA rules will take the form of a new section to the FSA Handbook, which will replace the existing listing rules in their entirety. The new section will be split into three parts:
  - (a) Listing Rules ('Listing Rules'): these shall apply to the issuers of admitted securities and to those seeking admission to the Official List and have been radically overhauled as a result of transposition of the Market Abuse Directive and the Prospectus Directive and by the FSA's review of the listing procedure;
  - (b) Disclosure and Transparency Rules ('Disclosure and Transparency Rules');
  - (c) Prospectus Rules ('Prospectus Rules'): these shall apply (1) whenever there is a (listed or unlisted) public offering in the UK; and (2) where securities are admitted to a regulated market in the UK. These rules focus on the format of a prospectus, the information that must be contained therein and the approval process.
- (v) The direct effect of the Prospectus Regulation, published on 30 April 2004 ('Prospectus Regulation').
- (vi) Adoption by the FSA of the Committee of European Securities Regulators' ('CESR') Recommendations, published in February

[1] Statutory Instrument 2005/1433.

2005.[2] The CESR's Recommendations ('CESR Recommendations') are indirectly incorporated into the new scheme through the Prospectus Rules,[3] which state that the Recommendations shall be taken into account in determining the effect of the Prospectus Directive. In determining whether relevant statutory provisions have been observed, the FSA will take into account compliance with the CESR Recommendations.

3. Pursuant to transposition of the Prospectus Directive, the new prospectus scheme supersedes the old listing rules and the Public Offer of Securities Regulations 1995 ('POS Regulations'), which have been repealed.

II Competent authority

4. The FSA, as the UK's financial services regulator, is authorised to act as the competent authority in the UK with respect to the approval of prospectuses and is referred to in this capacity as the UK Listing Authority.[4] Amendments have been made to Part VI of FSMA to provide a statutory framework within which the FSA operates as the competent authority for purposes of the Prospectus Directive.

III Prior approval procedure and appeal

1 Approval

5. Section 87A(1) of FSMA provides for approval of prospectuses by the FSA. The FSA may not approve a prospectus unless it is satisfied that:

(i) the UK is the home Member State for the issuer of the transferable securities to which the prospectus relates;
(ii) the prospectus contains the information necessary to enable investors to make an informed assessment of:
  (a) the assets and liabilities, financial position, profits and losses, and prospects of the issuer of the transferable securities and of any guarantor; and
  (b) the rights attached to the transferable securities.
(iii) all other requirements imposed by or in accordance with Part VI of the FSMA or the Prospectus Directive have been complied with (insofar as these relate to a prospectus for the transferable securities in question).

6. Issuers who wish to apply for approval of a prospectus will be required to submit to the FSA a draft prospectus, a registration document or a

[2] The Committee of European Securities Regulators' Recommendations for the consistent implementation of the European Commission's Regulation on Prospectuses No 809/2004.
[3] Prospectus Rules 1.1.6 G and 1.1.8G. [4] Sec. 72(1) FSMA; Prospectus Rule 1.1.2G.

securities note and summary (as the case may be) together with all the documents stipulated in Prospectus Rule 3.1.1R.

The FSA must notify the applicant of its decision within ten working days or, in the case of a new issuer, twenty working days from the first working day after the date on which the application is received. However, if the FSA requests specific documents or information from the applicant in writing, this period starts to run the day after the applicant complies with the request.

The FSA must notify the applicant in writing of its decision to approve or reject a prospectus and, in the latter case, explain why the prospectus was refused and inform the applicant of its right to refer the matter to the courts.

2 Clarification of a 'public offering'

7. Transposition of the Prospectus Directive has resulted in a fundamental change to the UK regulatory scheme in relation to what constitutes a public offering.

8. By introducing a pan-European definition of an 'offering of securities to the public', the Prospectus Directive creates a situation whereby all offerings of securities (whether listed or not) shall require a prospectus unless an exemption applies. Under the Prospectus Directive, all prospectuses for public offerings must be approved by the FSA. This is a fundamental change from the previous system, which required that prospectuses relating to unlisted securities be filed with Companies House but did not require that they be approved.

The Treasury initially noted that the definition contained in the Directive is extremely broad and potentially ambiguous, especially in view of the provision that renders any subsequent resale an offering in its own right. The Treasury was also concerned that this broad definition could affect trading on the secondary markets. For instance, there were concerns that normal secondary-market communications, such as the posting of prices by traders on electronic dealing systems, could amount to an 'offering of securities to the public'.

There was therefore a consensus that the Prospectus Directive's broad definition of a public offering needed to be clarified. To implement this definition, the Treasury incorporated it directly into Part VI of FSMA but added a clarification that a public offering does not include a communication in connection with trading on:

- a regulated market; or
- a multilateral trading facility; or
- any market prescribed for the market abuse regulations under Section 118 of FSMA.[5]

[5] Sec. 130A FSMA.

9. The broad wording of the Prospectus Directive means that a secondary offering of listed securities could amount to a public offering for which a prospectus is required. Under the old scheme, once securities had been admitted to trading they could be sold by their holders in a public offering without a prospectus. Now, however, if major shareholders of a company coming to market wish to retain their right to sell their shares, they will either need to negotiate an agreement with the issuer to secure access to all information necessary to publish a prospectus or ensure that the securities are sold in an exempt transaction (for example, to qualified investors or to no more than 100 investors in any Member State).

If an issuer issues a prospectus in relation to a secondary offering, a party offering its shares in connection with that offering will not be jointly liable for the prospectus if (1) the issuer is responsible for the prospectus in accordance with the Prospectus Rules; (2) the prospectus was drawn up primarily by the issuer or by one or more persons acting on the issuer's behalf; and (3) the offeror is making the offer in association with the issuer.

3 Exemptions from the prospectus requirement

10. There are a number of exemptions from the prospectus requirement, which can be divided into the following categories:

(i) Exemptions that apply to offerings of transferable securities to the public.

Exempt 'offerings' are listed in Section 86(1) of FSMA. Exempt 'securities' are listed in Parts 1 and 2 of Schedule 11A to the FSMA and in Prospectus Rule 1.2.2R.

The exempt securities listed in Prospectus Rule 1.2.2R fall into three categories:

(a) securities that are not in fact being 'offered' because existing shareholders receive them by way of an existing right, for example, (1) shares issued in substitution for outstanding shares of the same class; (2) an issuance of new shares that does not involve an increase in the company's share capital; and (3) shares offered free of charge to existing shareholders and dividends paid in the form of shares of the same class as those for which the dividends are paid;

(b) securities offered in connection with certain transactions, such as takeovers or mergers, provided a document is made available containing information the FSA regards as 'equivalent' to that contained in a prospectus; an 'equivalent document' is not a prospectus for the purposes of the Prospectus Directive and is thus not eligible for the European passport; and

(c) securities offered to employees or former employees which are already admitted to trading on a regulated market.

(ii) Exemptions that apply only to the admission of transferable securities to trading on a regulated market.

Exempt 'securities' for this purpose are listed in Part 1 of Schedule 11A to the FSMA and in Prospectus Rule 1.2.3R.

The exempt securities listed in Prospectus Rule 1.2.3R fall into two main categories:

(a) those that mirror the securities which are exempt in a public offering (see (i) above); and
(b) additional exemptions which companies may use in connection with the exemption relating to the admission of transferable securities to trading on a registered market includes:
    - an exemption for the admission of shares representing, over a twelve-month period, less than 10 per cent of shares of the same class already admitted to trading on the same regulated market;
    - an exemption for shares resulting from the conversion of other securities or the exercise of rights (i.e. warrants, options or convertibles, so long as it does not result in a public offering); and
    - an exemption that permits the admission of securities where there is no prospectus to 'passport' into the UK but the company nevertheless meets certain conditions (i.e. the securities have been traded on another regulated market for at least eighteen months).

11. Although most of these exemptions are similar to those available under the old prospectus and listing rules there are some important differences.

(i) 'Fewer than 100 investors' exemption under Section 86(i) of FSMA: With respect to the exemption in cases where an offering is made to fewer than 100 people per EEA member state, the Treasury initially proposed requiring the formal aggregation of the number of offerees over a twelve-month period in order to prevent successive offerings of the same securities being made to groups of ninety-nine persons at a time. The Treasury subsequently abandoned this proposal. It is now up to the FSA to determine, on a case-by-case basis, whether a number of successive offerings constitutes a single offering or a series of different offerings (and thus whether the exemption applies). It is therefore the FSA's job to identify and stop potential abuse. The possibility to make an offering, without a prospectus, to 100 non-sophisticated investors per EEA member state (possibly in addition to qualified investors) or to any number of investors outside the EEA amounts to a considerable relaxation of the former UK rules.

(ii) 'Qualified investor' exemption under Section 86(i) of FSMA: One of the most significant exemptions relates to offerings to 'qualified investors', which is broader than the 'professionals only' exemption available under the old scheme and includes small and medium-sized enterprises and individuals who satisfy certain criteria set out in the Prospectus Directive and who are registered as qualified investors with the FSA. The FSA has decided to allow such investors to 'self-certify' that they satisfy certain criteria. The adoption of qualified investor rules and a qualified investor register permits self-certification by prospective qualified investors in lieu of certification by solicitors or accountants, as originally proposed.

For the purposes of this exemption, it was necessary to clarify the treatment of offerings made to discretionary private-client brokers. The Treasury's implementing regulations have introduced a provision in Section 86 of FSMA to ensure that the existing position is maintained, i.e. offerings to discretionary brokers are understood to be addressed to the brokers themselves (and not their clients) and are thus eligible for the qualified investor exemption. The Treasury wanted to ensure that the fundraising costs incurred by small and medium-sized companies were not unnecessarily increased.

(iii) Professional Securities Market (PSM): In response to concerns that implementation of, *inter alia*, the Prospectus Directive could drive international issuers away from the UK, the London Stock Exchange has created a new market for specialist debt and equity-linked securities (such as Eurobonds, convertible and asset-backed securities and depositary receipts). Securities admitted to this market will often benefit from an exemption from the prospectus obligation, since they are offered in high minimum denominations or marketed only to qualified investors. This 'unregulated' debt market will undoubtedly be especially welcomed by non-EEA issuers of non-equity securities with denominations of less than €50,000 (retail debt), who would otherwise be subject to heightened regulation, including the requirement to prepare IFRS accounts. The minimum disclosure requirements for PSM issuers will be limited to those applicable to wholesale securities, regardless of the denomination.

IV Content, language and supplements

12. The Listing and Prospectus Rules have been revised to implement the Prospectus Directive's more detailed provisions on the approval, form and content of prospectuses.

1 General content requirements

13. The Prospectus Rules introduce a number of changes to the content requirements for prospectuses, although the overall disclosure standard (set

by new Section 87A of FSMA) remains similar. As before, a prospectus must contain all information necessary to enable investors to make an informed assessment of the assets and liabilities, financial position, profit and losses and prospects of the issuer and of any guarantor and of the rights attached to the securities.

The Prospectus Rules reflect the Prospectus Directive's requirement that a prospectus drawn up as a single document include the following parts in the following order:

(i) a clear and detailed table of contents;
(ii) a summary not exceeding 2,500 words, which briefly and in non-technical language conveys the essential characteristics of, and risks associated with, the issuer, any guarantor and the securities;
(iii) the risk factors linked to the issuer and the type of securities covered by the issue; and
(iv) the information items set out in the schedules to, and 'building blocks'[6] in, the Prospectus Regulation appropriate for the type of issue in question.[7]

2 Format

14. The Prospectus Rules set out two main options for the format of a prospectus: either a single document (including a summary) containing all requisite information or a three-part prospectus consisting of a registration document, a securities note and a summary note.[8]

The advantage of the new format is that the registration document is valid for twelve months and can therefore be used in connection with other offerings or the admission to trading of different securities within that period of time.

Although a similar shelf-registration facility was available under the old listing rules for listings with the London Stock Exchange, it was seldom used by issuers. It is, however, widely expected that shelf-registration will become more popular under the Prospectus Directive, for example when issuers decide to launch a rights issue. In effect, the reduced disclosure obligations applicable to rights issues under the previous legislation (allowing a circular or abridged prospectus rather than a full prospectus) are not reflected in the Prospectus Directive. Therefore, any rights issue to the public, at any level, will now require a full prospectus. This change could persuade UK issuers to file an annual registration document as part of the tripartite prospectus structure introduced by the Prospectus Directive so that when an issuer decides to launch a rights issue, it need only submit a securities note (to update the 'shelf'-registration document) and a summary for approval.

[6] The 'building block' approach requires an issuer to construct the content of its prospectus from the separate schedules and building blocks in the Prospectus Regulation.

[7] Prospectus Rule 2.2.10R.

[8] Prospectus Rules 2.2.1-2.2.3R.

3 Detailed requirements

15. The Prospectus Directive imposes few new obligations on companies with securities admitted to trading on a regulated market. The main new obligations relate to the requirement to provide annual information and to include a summary in their prospectus.

The detailed prospectus requirements are mainly contained in the Prospectus Rules, although some aspects are also regulated by new provisions of FSMA. Many of the detailed content requirements are similar to those contained in the old listing rules, but there are significant differences, which are outlined below:

(i) Summary: Sections 87A(5) and (6) of FSMA set out the summary requirement. A prospectus must contain a summary, unless it pertains to the admission to trading of non-equity transferable securities with a denomination of at least €50,000. The summary must mention not only the issuer's and the securities' essential characteristics but also the risks associated with them and contain a warning that it should be read as an introduction to the prospectus and that any decision to invest should be based on the prospectus taken as a whole.[9] Consequently, the FSA has abolished the provisions[10] for mini-prospectuses, offering notices and summary particulars, as their function is now satisfied by the summary.

(ii) Working-capital statement: The Prospectus Directive requires the inclusion of a working-capital statement in all prospectuses for equity issues. This is a significant change for FSA-regulated entities, such as banks, which were previously not usually required to make such a statement, although the FSA cannot change the Prospectus Directive's requirement in this regard, it has set out an alternative for regulated issuers who cannot make a clean statement about their working capital for the coming twelve months; such issuers may be listed as long as the FSA is satisfied they meet applicable solvency and capital-adequacy requirements and are expected to do so for the next twelve months.[11]

(iii) Incorporation by reference: Prior to implementation of the Prospectus Directive, UK law did not allow issuers to incorporate information in a prospectus by reference. In a major change from previous practice, however, incorporation by reference is now permitted.[12] Information may be incorporated in a prospectus not reference not only to documents previously approved by the FSA, but by reference to documents that have been approved by the competent authority of the home Member State. The FSA requires that hard copies of all documents to be incorporated by reference be submitted for vetting and approval, along with the rest of the prospectus.

[9] Prospectus Rule 2.1.2. [10] Rules 8.10, 8.11 and 8.12 of the old Listing Rules.
[11] Listing Rule 6.1.18G. [12] Prospectus Rule 2.4.

(iv) Risk factors: Risk factors specific to the issuer or its industry must be disclosed prominently in a section entitled 'Risk Factors'.

(v) Financial information: One of the most important changes brought about by the Prospectus Directive is that financial information in a prospectus must be prepared in accordance with International Accounting Standards (IAS) or 'equivalent accounting standards'. The old listing rules required applicants to produce three years of accounts prepared in accordance with UK GAAP. Under the new rules, three years of audited accounts are required, thus allowing issuers to benefit from the more liberal Prospectus Rules, which only require that the last two years' accounts have been prepared in accordance with IAS or equivalent standards. The CESR Recommendations state that Canadian, Japanese and US GAAP, taken as a whole, should be deemed equivalent to IFRS, subject to a number of additional disclosure requirements. In addition, where an issuer has a complex financial history or has made a significant financial commitment such that the inclusion of financial information relating to an entity other than the issuer is necessary to enable investors to make an informed assessment of the issuer and the securities, such financial information shall be deemed to relate to the issuer and the competent authority of the home Member State shall have the power to request that such financial information be included in the prospectus. This is to ensure that financial information relating to entities that were legally separate from the issuer at the time when such financial information was drawn up are included in cases where such entities subsequently become part of the issuer's legal group.

(vi) Operating and financial review: An operating and financial review (OFR) must be included in a prospectus for equity securities, indicating the causes of any material changes from year to year in the financial information to the extent necessary to understand the issuer's business as a whole. In certain respects, the OFR contained in a prospectus resembles that found in a company's annual report, but there are significant differences. The prospectus OFR will normally resemble a US 'MD1A' section (management's discussion and analysis of the company's financial position and operating results), which can already be found in most IPO prospectuses but will now become standard for all equity transactions.

(vii) Annual disclosure list: Issuers whose securities are admitted to trading on a regulated market will be required to file an annual update with the competent authority of their home Member State containing or referring to all information published or made available to the public over the previous twelve months pursuant to obligations imposed on the issuer by securities regulators in the EEA and elsewhere. In order to satisfy this requirement, the FSA allows issuers to file a list (the so-called Annual Information Update List) stating where this information can be obtained, indicating the date of its publication and filing, and including a short description. Appropriate disclaimers should be included to ensure that investors do not rely on information that is not directed to them or which may be out of date. This list should be filed through a regulatory information service within twenty days of the date on which the issuer's annual accounts are filed with the FSA.[13]

4 Prospectus supplements

16. As under the old scheme, a supplement to a prospectus must be published if any significant new fact arises or material mistake or inaccuracy in the prospectus comes to light from the time of approval of the prospectus to either the close of the offering or the commencement of trading, as the case may be.[14] This is largely similar to the previous scheme put in place by the old listing rules and the POS Regulations.

5 Language

17. The FSA requires that all prospectuses submitted to it for approval be drafted in English. In general, however, it will require an English translation of the *summary* of a non-FSA approved prospectus if the issuer is making a public offering of securities. For issuers seeking admission to trading on a regulated market, the Prospectus Directive introduces a new option, allowing a Member State to require such an issuer of high-denomination non-equity securities to produce a summary in the official language of that state. For reasons of market efficiency, the UK has not enacted this option, meaning that such issuers are not required to produce a summary in English.

In brief, an offeror must ensure that the summary is translated into English if (1) an offering is made in the UK; (2) a prospectus containing a summary and relating to transferable securities has been approved by the competent authority of another EEA member state; and (3) the prospectus is drawn up in a language other than English that is customary in the sphere of international finance.[15] The FSA will consider a language to be customary in the sphere of international finance if documents in that language are accepted for scrutiny and filing in at least three capital markets in each of Europe, Asia and the Americas.

V Publication and advertisements

1 Publication method

18. Under the new rules, a prospectus is deemed to have been made available to the public when published either:[16]

[13] Prospectus Rule 5.2.8. [14] Sec. 87G FSMA. [15] Prospectus Rule 4.1.6.
[16] Prospectus Rule 3.2.4.

(i) in one or more newspapers circulated throughout, or widely circulated in, the EEA member states in which the offering is made or the admission to trading sought;
(ii) in a printed form made available to the public at the offices of the regulated market or at the issuer's registered office and at the offices of the financial intermediaries;
(iii) in electronic form on the issuer's website; or
(iv) in electronic form on the website of the regulated market.

Website publication: In keeping with the option made available to home Member States by the Prospectus Directive, the Treasury had initially proposed requiring issuers to post an electronic copy of the prospectus on their website, in addition to publication in paper form. This suggestion prompted concern, as some issuers may not have a website and, furthermore, prospectuses would then be internationally accessible, which could result in inadvertent breaches of foreign security laws. The Treasury therefore decided not to require online posting.

The FSA posts a list of all prospectuses approved during the past twelve months on its website.[17]

Publication of notices: The Treasury proposed that issuers be required to publish a notice stating how their prospectus had been made available to the public and where it could be obtained. However, the FSA decided not to adopt this requirement in order to avoid placing an unnecessary burden on debt issuers, which currently need not publish such a newspaper notice. Had the FSA gone along with the Treasury's proposal, it would have had to make both debt and equity transactions subject to this requirement, which would run contrary to its approach of not requiring such a notice for specialist debt transactions.

2 Advertisements

19. The FSA rules, which previously applied only to advertisements for listed securities, have been superseded by the Prospectus Directive.

There are now new requirements for advertisements relating to a public offering or a request for admission to trading.[18] Such advertisements must, amongst other things, state that a prospectus has been or will be published and indicate where it can be obtained. Information in the advertisement must be consistent with that contained in the prospectus. The FSA has clarified that a written advertisement should contain a prominent statement that it is not a prospectus.

VI Use of prospectuses approved in non-EU countries

20. Recognition of third-country prospectuses: The Prospectus Rules allow the FSA to approve a prospectus drawn up by a non-EU issuer in accordance

[17] Prospectus Rule 3.2.7G. [18] Prospectus Rule 3.3.2R.

with its national law if the UK is the home Member State in relation to that issuer and if it is satisfied that the prospectus has been drawn up in accordance with appropriate international standards and that the applicable information requirements are equivalent to the new prospectus scheme.[19] The FSA has not issued any guidelines on when this power may be used and has merely stated that '[w]e anticipate that once a few prospectuses drawn up according to the laws of a third country are determined to be equivalent, sufficient precedent would have been set to provide issuers with a degree of certainty on which third country prospectuses are broadly judged to be equivalent'.[20] The FSA will therefore determine whether a prospectus meets these criteria on a case-by-case basis and will judge each application on its merits.

Under Sections 87H and 87I of FSMA, a prospectus approved by the competent authority of an EEA country other than the UK shall not be deemed approved by the FSA until that other authority has provided the FSA with (1) a certificate of approval; (2) a copy of the prospectus as approved; and (3) if requested by the FSA, a translation of the summary of the prospectus.[21]

VII Sanctions

21. The FSA has the authority to impose the following sanctions for breach of any relevant provision of the FSMA, the Prospectus Rules or any other provision enacted in accordance with the Prospectus Directive (an 'applicable provision'):

(i) Suspension or prohibition of the offering to the public:[22] The FSA can (1) require the offeror to suspend the offering for a period not to exceed ten working days; and/or (2) require a person not to advertise the offering or to take such steps as the FSA may request to suspend any existing advertising for the offering for a period not to exceed ten working days. If the FSA has reasonable grounds to suspect that an applicable provision will be violated or if it finds that such a provision has indeed been violated, it can require the offeror to withdraw the offering.

(ii) Suspension or prohibition of the admission to trading on a regulated market:[23] If the securities have not yet been admitted to trading, the FSA can (1) require a person requesting admission to suspend the request for a period not to exceed ten working days; and/or (2) require that person not to advertise the securities in question or to take such steps as the FSA may specify to suspend any existing advertisement in connection with those securities for a period not to exceed ten working days. If the securities have already been admitted to trading, the FSA can require the market operator to (1) suspend trading in the

[19] Prospectus Rule 4.2. [20] FSA Policy Statement 05/7. [21] Prospectus Rule 5.3.1UK.
[22] Sec. 87K FSMA. [23] *Ibid.*, Sec. 87L.

securities for a period of up to ten working days; and/or (2) require that person not to advertise the securities or to take such steps as the FSA may specify to suspend any existing advertisement in connection with the securities, for a period of up to ten working days.

If the FSA proposes any of the actions outlined above, it must give written notice to the person(s) concerned, stating the reasons for the proposed action and informing them that they are entitled to make representations to the FSA and of the date on which the action will take effect as well as of their right to refer the matter to the Financial Services and Markets Tribunal.

(iii) Public censure of issuer:[24] If the FSA finds that an issuer of transferable securities, a person offering such securities to the public or a person requesting admission of such securities to a regulated market is failing to comply with its obligations under an applicable provision, it may publish a statement to this effect. If the FSA proposes this sanction, it must first send the person concerned a warning letter setting out the terms of the proposed statement. If, after considering any representations made in response to the warning letter, the FSA decides to publish the statement nonetheless, it must notify the person concerned of its decision and of the terms of the statement. That person is then entitled to refer the matter to the Financial Services and Markets Tribunal.

VIII Prospectus liability

22. The Treasury has conferred powers on the FSA to make rules determining liability for prospectuses. The Prospectus Rules contain provisions on statutory liability for prospectuses.[25] The new scheme is broadly similar to the old, although a distinction is made between prospectuses for shares, warrants or options issued by an issuer to subscribe for its equity and other transferable securities, on the one hand, and all other types of transferable securities, on the other. In the latter case, the issuer's directors cannot be held liable for the prospectus. One key change under the new scheme is that the issuer and its directors must accept responsibility for the entire prospectus. The practice under the old takeover rules of allowing issuers to release themselves from liability with respect to information on the target company contained in listing particulars is not reflected in the new scheme.

Prospectus Rule 5.5.3(1)R provides a definition of equity securities for the purposes of determining statutory liability for prospectuses, while Prospectus Rule 5.5.3(2)R lists those persons who can be held liable for a prospectus.

Under the new scheme, issuers and their directors share responsibility for equity (share) prospectuses, while issuers alone are responsible for prospectuses relating to other types of securities.

[24] *Ibid.*, Sec. 87M. [25] Prospectus Rule 5.5.

In addition, Prospectus Rule 2.1.7R transposes the Prospectus Directive provision that civil liability attaches to the persons responsible for the summary, including any translation thereof, but only if the summary is misleading, inaccurate or inconsistent when read together with other parts of the prospectus.

IX Rules applicable to transactions and securities not subject to the Directive and Regulation

23. Under the new scheme, the new Listing Rules will apply to transactions and securities not subject to the Prospectus Directive and Regulation. Listing particulars will only be required under the Listing Rules where:

(i) an issuer applies for admission to the Official List of securities listed in Part 1 of Schedule 11A to FSMA; or
(ii) an issuer applies for admission to the Official List of any other specialist securities for which a prospectus is not required under the Directive.

Specialist securities are defined in the Listing Rules as securities which, owing to their nature, are normally bought and traded by a limited number of investors who are particularly knowledgeable in investment matters. As a matter of policy, the FSA believes that the content of listing particulars should follow, insofar as practicable, the most appropriate building blocks set out in the Prospectus Directive. Listing particulars will therefore effectively contain the same information as a prospectus for that type of security. Issuers of specialist securities (i.e. debt securities and convertible bonds, but not depositary receipts) are required to prepare listing particulars with the same content requirements applicable to wholesale debt (or, if relevant, wholesale asset-backed securities) under the Prospectus Rules, including information on the underlying security where appropriate, irrespective of the denomination. Issuers of depositary receipts are required to prepare listing particulars with the same content requirements as apply to wholesale depositary receipts under the Prospectus Rules.

X Conclusion

1 Additional important points

A Eligibility

24. It is important to note that the Prospectus Directive only harmonises rules in relation to prospectuses. The Listing Rules contain a number of obligations which are 'super-equivalent' to the requirements of the Prospectus Directive. In particular, a company listed on the Official List must comply with super-equivalent eligibility requirements, continuing

obligations and rules in relation to sponsors. This means that a prospectus which is 'passported' into the UK is in itself no guarantee of admission to the Official List, as the issuer must still satisfy the super-equivalent Listing Rules requirements.

B Clarification of a 'regulated market'

25. The Prospectus Directive requires issuers to publish a prospectus in connection with the admission of securities to trading on a regulated market (unless an exemption applies). The definition referred to in the Directive (which is also that used in the Markets in Financial Instruments Directive (2004/39)) is broader than the old listing rules, which were limited to admission to the Official List. The Member States are responsible for maintaining a list of their 'regulated markets'. The Treasury has published a list of regulated markets in the UK:

REGULATED MARKETS OPERATED BY THE LONDON STOCK EXCHANGE	**OTHER REGULATED MARKETS**
Domestic Market	The London International Financial Futures and Options Exchange (LIFFE)
Specialist Fixed Market	Regulated Market segment for SMS Securities and Regulated Market segment for pan-European securities operated by Virt-x
Gilt Edged and Fixed Interest Market	EDX
International Retail Service (Regulated Segment)	The PLUS-listed market operated by PLUS Markets plc.
International Order Book (Regulated Segment)	
Dutch Trading Service (order book only)	
International Bulletin Board (regulated segment order book only)	

The Treasury has also clarified that the Alternative Investment Market (AIM) ceased to be a regulated market on 12 October 2004. Therefore, the Prospectus Directive does not apply to applications for admission to trading on AIM. On 3 May 2005, the LSE confirmed that as from 1 July 2005, the standard of information required for AIM admission, which does not constitute a public offering under the Prospectus Directive, will be based on the requirements of the Directive, with certain carve-outs, and known as AIM-PD. This will effectively establish a standard similar to the POS Regulations, which have been superseded.

PART III

National reports for EEA Member States

16

Norway

SOLVEIG FAGERHEIM BUGGE AND SVERRE TYRHAUG
Thommessen

I Introduction

1. Norway is not a member of the EU, but a party to the EEA Agreement. Directive 2003/71 of the European Parliament and of the Council of 4 November 2003 on the prospectus to be published when securities are offered to the public or admitted to trading (the 'Prospectus Directive' or 'Dir.') was implemented into the EEA Agreement in June 2004[1] and the Norwegian Government approved the implementation in November 2004.[2]

The Prospectus Directive and the complementing Commission Regulation 809/2004 of 29 April 2004 implementing the Prospectus Directive as regards information contained in prospectuses as well as the format, incorporation by reference and publication of such prospectuses and dissemination of advertisements (the 'Prospectus Regulation' or 'Reg.') were then implemented into Norwegian law through the adoption of the Act of 10 June 2005 No. 42 on amendments to the Securities Trading Act, etc. (implementation of the Prospectus Directive) (the 'Act of Amendment'), and the adoption of a number of supplementary regulations on 9 December 2005.[3]

The Act of Amendment inserted a revised Chapter 5, titled 'Prospectus Requirements in Connection with Public Offerings and Admission to Trading', into the Norwegian Act of 19 June 1997 No. 79 on Securities Trading. In June 2007, a new Norwegian Act on securities trading was adopted (the Act of 29 June 2007 No.75 on Securities Trading the 'Securities Trading Act' or the 'STA') replacing the Act of 19 June 1997 No. 79. The prospectus rules of the previous Act are continued in Chapter 7 of the new Act.[4] The Securities Trading Act is one of several acts governing securities trading in Norway.[5] Other than the prospectus rules set out in Chapter 7, the Act contains provisions regarding the licensing and activities of investment firms and clearing houses, general rules for trading on Norwegian regulated market places for securities, disclosure requirements relating to listed companies, insider trading and market abuse, and mandatory and voluntary offer requirements.

[1] Further to the Decision on 8 June 2004 of the EEA Joint Committee, amending Annex IX to the EEA Agreement (*Official Journal*, 25 November 2004).

[2] Cf. St.prp. No. 80 (2003–2004) and Innst. S. No. 19 (2004–2005).

[3] The Regulation on Information in a Prospectus (FOR-2005-12-09-1422), the Regulation on the control of prospectuses (FOR-2005-12-09-1423), the Regulation on exemptions from the prospectus obligation (FOR-2005-12-09-1424), and the Regulation on transitional rules in relation to amendments to the prospectus rules in Chapter 5 of the Securities Trading Act (FOR-2005-12-09-1425).

[4] For the purposes of the preparation of this report, an unofficial translation of the Securities Trading Act used and distributed by *Kredittilsynet* (the Financial Supervisory Authority of Norway) has been used.

[5] Other acts include the Stock Exchange Act of 29 June 2007 No. 74 and the Regulation on regulated markets (the Stock Exchange Regulation), the Public Limited Companies Act of 13 June 1997 No. 45 and the Securities Registration Act of 5 July 2002 No. 64.

The supplementary regulations adopted on 9 December 2005 are titled (1) the Regulation on information in a prospectus,[6] (2) the Regulation on the control of prospectuses,[7] (3) the Regulation on exemptions from the prospectus obligation[8] and (4) the Regulation on transitional rules in relation to amendments to the prospectus rules in Chapter 5 of the Securities Trading Act.[9]

Both the new Chapter 7 of the Securities Trading Act and the prospectus rules of the Regulation to the Securities Trading Act entered into force on 1 November 2007.[10]

The authority to control and approve prospectuses under the new prospectus regime has, as described in Section II below, been delegated to Oslo Børs (the Oslo Stock Exchange). In two circulars published following the adoption of the regime, Oslo Børs provides guidelines on the understanding and application of the new prospectus rules. The two circulars are titled (1) Circular No. 9/2005 New rules for prospectuses in Chapter 5 of the Securities Trading Act and related regulations – implementation of the Prospectus Directive ('Circular No. 9/2005') and (2) Circular No. 3/2006 Control, approval and publication of prospectuses ('Circular No. 3/2006').

2. This report gives an overview of the Norwegian rules applicable to prospectuses to be produced when securities are offered to the public or admitted to trading on a stock exchange or an authorised market place. The main focus is on the rules applicable to transactions and securities subject to the Prospectus Directive and the Prospectus Regulation, i.e. transactions and securities for which a so-called EEA prospectus is to be produced. As a general rule, this is the case for (1) admissions to trading of transferable securities on a regulated market place, and (2) offerings of transferable securities where the aggregate consideration is at least €2.5 million calculated over a twelve-month period. The rules applicable to transactions and securities not subject to the Prospectus Directive and the Prospectus Regulation, e.g. offerings of transferable securities where the consideration is less than €2.5 million and mergers and demergers, will only be briefly described in Section IX below.

II Competent authority

3. Under the Prospectus Directive, each Member State has an obligation to designate a competent authority for the approval of prospectuses (Art. 21(1) Dir., see also Chapter 1, No. 18 *et seq.*).

In Norway, the overall responsibility for the approval of EEA prospectuses has been assigned to *Kredittilsynet* (the Financial Supervisory

[6] FOR-2005-12-09-1422. [7] FOR-2005-12-09-1423. [8] FOR-2005-12-09-1424.
[9] FOR-2005-12-09-1425. [10] FOR-2007-06-29-876.

Authority of Norway) pursuant to Section 5-8 (6) of the Securities Trading Act. The operational responsibility for approval of EEA prospectuses has, however, been delegated to Oslo Børs under the Regulation to the Securities Trading Act.[11] Oslo Børs is therefore, in practice, the relevant Norwegian prospectus authority.

III Procedure of prior approval and appeal

1 Obligation to produce prospectus

A Introduction

4. The obligation to produce a prospectus in accordance with Chapter 5 of the Securities Trading Act may arise in the following two situations; (1) in connection with offers to subscribe for or purchase transferable securities, cf. Section 5-2 of the Securities Trading Act, and (2) upon admission to trading of transferable securities on a regulated market place, cf. Section 7-3 of the Securities Trading Act. The two scenarios will be described in further detail in Sections B and C below.

Under both scenarios, the obligation to produce a prospectus applies to 'transferable securities'. This term, which is defined in Section 2-2 (2) of the Securities Trading Act, includes equity securities such as shares, primary capital certificates, convertible bonds and rights to purchase or subscribe for securities issued by a company for its own securities, and non-equity securities such as bonds and rights to purchase or subscribe for securities issued by a party other than the issuer of the underlying securities.

B Obligation to produce a prospectus in connection with a public offer

5. Section 7-2 of the Securities Trading Act states that a prospectus must be produced where an offer to subscribe for or purchase transferable securities is directed at 100 or more persons in the Norwegian securities market, and involves an amount of at least €100,000, calculated over a twelve-month period.

The Prospectus Directive imposes an obligation to produce a prospectus for 'any offer of securities to be made to the public' (Art. 3(1) Dir.; see also Chapter 1, No. 11). The positive obligation to produce a prospectus is thus described somewhat differently in the Prospectus Directive and the Securities Trading Act. This does, however, not necessarily entail a difference in meaning. Oslo Børs has stated that it assumes that the exemption for an offer directed at fewer than 100 persons represents the definitive statement of whether an offer shall be deemed not to be made to the public.

Offers of securities for a total consideration of less than €2,500,000 calculated over a twelve-month period fall outside the Prospectus Directive

[11] Cf. Section 7-3 of the Regulation to the Securities Trading Act. See also Art. 21 (2) Dir.

unless the offerer or issuer chooses to have the offering governed by the Prospectus Directive, see Chapter 1, Nos. 8 through 9. This regulation of the scope of the Prospectus Directive is reflected in Chapter 7 of the Securities Trading Act. Pursuant to Section 7-7 of the Act, a prospectus prepared in connection with offers of securities where the consideration is at least €2.5 million calculated over a twelve-month period, shall be deemed to be an EEA prospectus and will thus be subject to the provisions of the Act applicable to EEA prospectuses. A prospectus prepared in connection with offers of securities where the consideration is between €100,000 and €2.5 million will in general only be subject to the less stringent rules applicable to the so-called registration prospectuses (national prospectuses), see Section IX below.

The obligation to produce a prospectus in connection with an offer of securities to the public is consequently dependent on (1) the number of persons to whom the offer is directed, and (2) the aggregate consideration for the offer. When determining whether the applicable thresholds in the Securities Trading Act are met, guidance may be sought in the Appendix to Circular No. 9/2005.[12]

6. As regards the number of persons threshold, Oslo Børs takes the view that the deciding factor is the number of persons who receive the offer, and not the number of persons who choose to accept the offer.

In a situation where an investment manager subscribes on behalf of a number of investors on the basis of discretionary investment management mandates, the investment manager will, according to Oslo Børs, generally be seen as a single person for the purposes of calculating the number of persons.[13]

As opposed to the situation for the consideration thresholds, the number of persons threshold is to be calculated on the basis of each individual offer, and not on a twelve-month basis. Oslo Børs has stated that in the event that two or more formally separate offers are made, each of which addressed to fewer than 100 persons, but jointly to more than 100 persons, due consideration must be given to whether the offers in reality should be seen as a single offer. The general concepts of circumvention will play a central role in this regard.[14]

7. As regards the consideration thresholds of €100,000 and €2.5 million Oslo Børs takes the view that the consideration shall be calculated for an offer in its entirety, regardless of how the consideration might be divided between the different Member States. And if an offer relates to different types of securities, the threshold amounts shall be calculated separately for each type of security.

[12] Cf. the Appendix to Circular No. 9/2005 pp. 6–7.

[13] See also the preparatory works of Chapter 5 of the 1997 Securities Trading Act (Ot.prp. No. 69 (2004–2005) p. 22).

[14] Cf. the Appendix to Circular No. 9/2005 p. 7.

The twelve-month period forming the basis for the calculation of the consideration thresholds, shall be calculated from the date the last offer was made.

In the event that an issuer makes two subsequent offers within a twelve-month period which individually trigger the obligation to produce a national registration prospectus, but jointly exceed the €2.5 million threshold, Oslo Børs is of the opinion that the issuer will be required to produce a registration prospectus for the first offer and an EEA prospectus for the second offer.

C Obligation to produce a prospectus upon admission to trading

8. as regards the obligation to produce a prospectus upon admission to trading, section 7-3 of the securities trading act states that a prospectus must be produced where transferable securities are admitted to listing on a regulated market place, and that this includes an increase in share capital by a company with listed shares. the obligation to produce a prospectus applies regardless of whether an application is required for the admission to trading.[15]

All prospectuses regarding admissions to trading on a stock exchange or an authorised market place are deemed to be EEA prospectuses pursuant to Section 5-7 of the Securities Trading Act and are consequently subject to the rules of the Act applicable to such prospectuses.

D Exemptions from the obligation to produce a prospectus

(i) Public offers

9. Section 7-4 of the Securities Trading Act provides certain specific exemptions from the obligation to produce a prospectus in connection with public offers. The exemptions include offers referring to non-equity securities offered by a state, by a central bank or guaranteed by a state, offers referring to non-equity securities issued continuously and repeatedly by financial institutions, offers made in connection with a merger or the exchange of shares in the same company or an acquisition, offers of shares to existing shareholders with no consideration paid and offers to employees or board members.

As regards offers made in connection with mergers and acquisitions, a document containing information being equivalent to that of a prospectus must be submitted to Oslo Børs for control.[16] For offers made free of charge to existing shareholders or current or former employees or board members, a document containing information on the category and number of securities, as well as the background and conditions for the offer, must be prepared, but such a document is not subject to any control or approval by Oslo Børs. Listed companies must publish the aforementioned documents through a stock exchange notification.[17]

[15] Further to the preparatory works of Chapter 5 of the Act of 19 June 1997 No. 79 on Securities Trading (Ot.prp. No. 69 (2004–2005) p. 21).

[16] Cf. Oslo Børs' Circular No. 9/2005 p. 4.

[17] l.c.

Further, some of the exemptions set out in Article 3 (2) of the Prospectus Directive are reflected in Section 7-4 of the Securities Trading Act, namely the exemptions for offers directed at professional investors and offers of securities issued in minimum lots of €50,000.

As regards the exemption for offers directed at professional investors, more specific rules have been laid down in the Regulation to the Securities Trading Act. Section 7-1 of the Regulation determines which investors are deemed to be 'professional'. This includes legal persons approved or regulated for the purposes of activities in the financial markets, central banks and other authorities, and legal persons with investment in securities as their sole business objective. Furthermore, legal entities of a certain size in terms of employees, assets and turnover and certain natural persons with particular experience in the securities market can require to be registered as professional investors.

In accordance with Article 2(1)(e) of the Prospectus Directive, the right to require registration as a professional investor only applies to legal and natural persons which are domiciled or have their registered office in Norway.[18]

The exemptions can be combined. For example, an issuer can offer securities to up to 99 non-professional investors at a minimum subscription and allotment below €50,000, and additional securities to professional investors or investors where the minimum subscription and allocation is above €50,000.

(ii) Admission to trading

10. Section 7-5 of the Securities Trading Act provides certain specific exemptions from the obligation to produce a prospectus upon admission to trading. In the same way as for public offers, exemptions relating to non-equity securities issued by a state or a central bank or guaranteed by a state, non-equity securities issued continuously and repeatedly by financial institutions, securities listed in connection with a merger or the exchange of shares in the same company or an acquisition, offers of shares to existing shareholders with no consideration paid and offers of securities to employees or board members have been given.

In addition, Section 7-5 provides exemptions for increases in capital where the number of shares issued amounts to less than ten per cent of the number of shares already listed in the same class of shares. The 10 per cent threshold is calculated on a rolling twelve-month basis. There are also exemptions related to the exercise of certain rights (typically shares issued as a result of the exercise of convertible bonds) and for certain securities listed on another regulated market. As for the latter exemption, more specific conditions have been laid down in Section 7-2 of the Regulation to the Securities Trading Act.

[18] Cf. the Appendix to Circular No. 9/2005 p. 14.

As regards the 10 per cent threshold applicable to share capital increases, Oslo Børs has stated that it assumes that only increases in share capital not covered by any other exemption from the obligation to produce a prospectus, should be included.

(iii) Discretionary exemptions

11. In addition to the exemptions set out in Sections 7-4 and 7-5 of the Securities Trading Act, the prospectus authority has, under Section 7-6, been given discretionary powers to grant exemptions from the obligation to produce a prospectus in certain specific cases, including offers and admissions to trading of securities issued by ideal organisations, short-term debt instruments, bonds issued by municipalities or county authorities and securities guaranteed by municipalities or county authorities.

2 Approval procedure

12. Pursuant to Section 7-7 (2) of the Securities Trading Act, an EEA prospectus cannot be published until it has been approved. Prior to publication, such a prospectus must consequently be submitted to Oslo Børs for control.

The control of prospectuses regarding securities of the same class as securities already admitted to trading on a regulated market, shall, pursuant to Section 7-8 (3) of the Securities Trading Act, be concluded no later than five working days after Oslo Børs has received a complete prospectus. The same applies to the control of prospectuses regarding securities for which a prospectus previously has been prepared pursuant to the rules regarding public offers. In other cases, the control shall be concluded no later than 10 working days after Oslo Børs has received a complete prospectus.

Section 7-8 (3) of the Securities Trading Act applies to the control of *complete* prospectuses. For such prospectuses, Oslo Børs will notify the issuer of whether the prospectus has been approved, or whether additional information is required, within the said deadlines.[19] If additional information is required, the deadlines will run from the submission of the additional information (Art. 13(4) Dir.).

As an alternative to the submission of a complete prospectus for control, Oslo Børs offers a more informal control procedure, cf. Circular No. 3/2006. An offerer, issuer or other person requesting admission to trading can submit a *draft* prospectus to Oslo Børs for control, and Oslo Børs will provide feedback on the prospectus within the following tentative time limits:

(i) For prospectuses regarding securities which are listed or which have been applied for listing on a stock exchange or a regulated market, Oslo Børs can normally be expected to provide its first feedback

[19] Cf. Circular 3/2006 p. 2.

within five working days from receipt of a draft prospectus.

(ii) For prospectuses regarding offers to purchase or subscribe for securities which are not listed or applied for listing, Oslo Børs can normally be expected to provide its first feedback within ten working days of receiving a draft prospectus. In the event that it is important, for the purpose of the accomplishment of the offer, to have the prospectus approved earlier, Oslo Børs can be requested to carry out the prospectus control within the deadlines applicable to listed securities.

Oslo Børs has made it clear that a longer case-handling time must be expected in the event that draft prospectuses that have not been sufficiently prepared, are submitted for control. And if a previously approved prospectus/registration document is resubmitted for control due to new offers or requests for admission to trading made within the prospectus'/registration document's period of validity; see Section IV.2 below, Oslo Børs has stated that it will try to reduce its outlined case-handling time.

For offer prospectuses and listing prospectuses for shares and primary capital certificates, a complete and approved prospectus must be submitted to Oslo Børs in PDF-format no later than 4.30 pm the day before the offer period commences or the securities are admitted to trading, unless otherwise agreed with the case handlers of Oslo Børs. In the event of an initial public offering (IPO) of a class of shares not already admitted to trading, prospectuses must be submitted to Oslo Børs no later than 2.00 pm the day before admission to trading. For offers and listings of bonds and other types of securities, the approved prospectus must be submitted to the stock exchange no later than 2.00 pm the day before commencement of the offer or the listing.

For prospectuses used cross-border into Norway, a notification that the prospectus has been prepared in accordance with the Prospectus Directive and approved by the home competent authority must be received by Oslo Børs within the above-mentioned deadlines, cf. Section 7-9 (1) of the Securities Trading Act.

3 Appeal

13. Decisions made by Oslo Børs as part of the prospectus control may be appealed to *Børsklagenemnda* (the Stock Exchange Appeals Committee), cf. Section 7-8 of the Regulation to the Securities Trading Act.

IV Content and format, language and supplements to the prospectus

1 Content

14. In line with Article 5 (1) of the Prospectus Directive, Section 7-13 of the Securities Trading Act contains a general provision on the information required to be included in an EEA prospectus. Such a prospectus shall

contain information necessary to enable the investors to make a well-informed assessment of the issuer's and any guarantor's financial position and prospects and of rights attached to the securities in question. The information shall be given in an easily understandable and analysable form.

Another content requirement is set out in Section 7-18 of the Securities Trading Act. A prospectus must contain a statement from the persons responsible for it, see Section VIII below. Although Section 7-18 specifically mentions information which must be included in such a statement, the content of the statement must nonetheless satisfy the requirements of the relevant Annexes to the Prospectus Regulation.

The more specific content requirements for an EEA prospectus follow from the Prospectus Regulation and its Annexes, which are incorporated into Norwegian law through Article 7-13 of the Regulation to the Securities Trading Act. For an overview of the content requirements of the Prospectus Regulation and its Annexes, please see Chapter 1, No. 29 *et seq.*

The prospectus authority may, pursuant to Section 7-16 of the Securities Trading Act, allow certain required information to be omitted from a prospectus. The provision contains a list of such information which corresponds to the information mentioned in Articles 8(2) and 8(3) of the Prospectus Directive, see Chapter 1, Nos. 38 through 39.

2 Format

15. In accordance with the Prospectus Directive, a prospectus prepared under the Securities Trading Act can be produced as one document or as several separate documents, i.e. a registration document, a securities note and a summary note, cf. Section 7-14 of the Securities Trading Act.[20]

A registration document shall, as stated in Article 9(4) of the Prospectus Directive, remain valid for twelve months following its approval, cf. Section 7-12 (3) of the Securities Trading Act. An issuer, offerer or other person requesting admission to trading can consequently use a registration document for new offerings or requests for admission to trading within the twelve-month validity period, and will hence only have to prepare a new securities note and summary note, and potentially a supplement updating the information in the registration document. According to Oslo Børs, this option will be available regardless of whether the first prospectus was produced as a single document or as several separate documents.[21]

Pursuant to Section 7-14 (1) *in fine* of the Securities Trading Act, a prospectus prepared in connection with a loan scheme may be structured as a base prospectus, see Chapter 1, No. 45 *et seq.*, in accordance with further

[20] See Chapter 1, No. 41 *et seq.*

[21] Cf. the Appendix to Circular No. 9/2005 p. 17.

rules to be laid down in a regulation. Such rules have been given in Sections 7-15 through 7-19 of the Regulation to the Securities Trading Act.

Section 7-14 (2) of the Securities Trading Act permits information to be incorporated into the prospectus by reference to other documents, see Chapter 1, No. 40. It follows explicitly from Section 7-14 (2) that only information included in previously approved or registered prospectuses can be incorporated in such a manner. Pursuant to the Prospectus Directive, *any document* that has been approved by or submitted to the competent prospectus authority in accordance with the Prospectus Directive or the Directive of 28 May 2001 on the admission to trading of securities to official stock-exchange listings and on information to be published on those securities, can be incorporated by reference. Different documents from which information can be incorporated by reference have also been specified in Article 28 (1) of the Prospectus Regulation. Despite the wording of Section 7-14 (2) of the Securities Trading Act, Oslo Børs has taken the view that all information which can be incorporated by reference pursuant to the Prospectus Directive and the Prospectus Regulation, can also be incorporated by reference in an EEA prospectus produced under the Norwegian Securities Trading Act.[22]

In the event of incorporation by reference, a reference list showing where the relevant information can be found must be made available, cf. Section 7-14 (2) of the Securities Trading Act and Article 11 (1) of the Prospectus Directive.

Information cannot be incorporated into the summary of a prospectus by reference, cf. Section 7-14 (2) *in fine* of the Securities Trading Act and Article 11 (2) of the Prospectus Directive.

3 Supplements

16. Any new fact, material error or inaccuracy which may be of significance for the assessment of the securities, and which is brought to light between the publication of the prospectus and the expiry of the acceptance period or the admission to trading, shall appear in a supplement to the prospectus, cf. Section 7-15 of the Securities Trading Act. The supplement must be approved by the prospectus authority in accordance with Section 7-7 of the Securities Trading Act and published without undue delay in accordance with Section 7-19, see Section V.1 below.

The Committee of European Securities Regulators (CESR) has considered whether interim financial statements will constitute a significant new fact which must be published as a supplementary prospectus and has concluded that this is not necessarily the case, see Chapter 1, No. 66. Oslo Børs has, contrary to this, taken the view that the contents of interim financial

[22] Appendix to Circular No. 9/2005 p. 19.

statements normally will be of such significance that a supplementary prospectus should be issued if interim financial statements are published during the time period specified in Section 7-15 of the Securities Trading Act.[23]

When a supplement to a prospectus is published, an acceptance of an offer made before the publication of the supplement may be withdrawn within two days, cf. Section 7-21 (2) of the Securities Trading Act.

4 Language

17. Section 7-17 of the Securities Trading Act provides that prospectuses shall be produced in Norwegian, English, Swedish or Danish. If a prospectus is produced in English, Swedish or Danish, the prospectus authority can require that the summary of the prospectus is translated into Norwegian.

Oslo Børs is of the view that all the documents that make up a prospectus, including documents incorporated by reference, must be produced in the same language. Exemptions from this rule may be granted in special circumstances.[24]

V Publication and advertisements

1 Method of publication

18. In conformity with Article 14 (1) of the Prospectus Directive, an EEA prospectus must, pursuant to Section 7-19 of the Securities Trading Act, be made available to the public no later than the day the offer period commences or the securities are admitted to trading, or, in the event of an initial public offering (IPO) of a class of shares not already admitted to trading, no later than six days before the end of the offer period.

A prospectus shall be deemed available to the public when published in any of the following ways:

(i) by insertion in at least one national newspaper;
(ii) by being made available to the public free of charge at the offerer's office or at the office of the marketplace and with the investment firm placing the offer;
(iii) by being made available electronically on the offerer's or the marketplace's website and on the website of any investment firms placing the offer;
(iv) by being made available on the website of Oslo Børs.

If an offerer or issuer wishes to publish a prospectus on the website of Oslo Børs, this must be communicated to Oslo Børs when the first draft of the prospectus is submitted to control, at the latest. In the event that an offerer

[23] Cf. the Appendix to Circular No. 9/2005 p. 20. [24] *Ibid.* p. 23.

or issuer wants to publish a prospectus on the website of Oslo Børs merely as a supplement to publication of the prospectus elsewhere, this can be achieved through the issue of a stock exchange notification containing a link to the prospectus.[25]

Where an offer prospectus is published electronically on the websites of the offerer, the investment firm(s) placing the offer or Oslo Børs, reasonable steps must in accordance with Article 29(2) of the Commission Regulation be taken to avoid targeting residents in Member States or third countries where the offer does not take place.[26]

Where a prospectus is made available to the public in any of the ways described under (ii) through (iv) above, a notice stating where the prospectus is available must be inserted in a national newspaper. In accordance with Article 31(2) of the Commission Regulation, the notice must be published no later than the first working day following publication of the prospectus. The notice must contain the information specified in Article 31(3) of the Prospectus Regulation. For prospectuses regarding admission to trading on Oslo Børs of shares in a class of shares already admitted to trading, the notice may, instead, be sent as a stock exchange notification, cf. Article 31(3) of the Prospectus Regulation.

19. In order to ensure that no public offers are made and that no securities are listed without a prospectus having been made available to the public pursuant to the rules of the Prospectus Directive, the offerer, issuer or person requesting admission to trading must no later than the day before the offer period starts or the securities are admitted to trading send a statement to Oslo Børs containing the following information:

(i) the chosen method of publication;
(ii) where the prospectus has been or will be made available to the public;
(iii) confirmation that the prospectus already has been or will be published within the deadlines described above; and
(iv) confirmation that the prospectus is or will be inserted in a national newspaper or published through Oslo Børs' information system.[27]

The statement must be submitted within the deadlines for submission of a complete and approved prospectus.

20. For prospectuses regarding admission to trading on Oslo Børs of shares in a class of shares already admitted to trading, it can be agreed with Oslo Børs that admission to trading can take place on the same day as (1) the prospectus is approved, (2) the statement mentioned above is submitted and (3) the prospectus is made available to the public.[28]

[25] Cf. Circular No. 3/2006 p. 6.
[26] Cf. the Appendix to Circular No. 9/2005 p. 27.
[27] Cf. Circular No. 3/2006 p. 6.
[28] *Ibid.* p. 7 and Section 11.4(3) of Oslo Børs' Continuing Obligations for Stock Exchange Listed Companies.

Based on the statement from the offerer, issuer or person requesting admission to trading, Oslo Børs will, in the case of prospectuses relating to securities which have been admitted to trading or where an application has been made for the admission to trading, publish a stock exchange notification stating that the prospectus has been approved and made available to the public.[29]

21. The obligation to submit a statement as mentioned above applies equally to prospectuses used cross-border into Norway, cf. Section 7-9 of the Securities Trading Act (but with no obligation to make a public announcement through an advertisement in a national Norwegian newspaper if this has already been done in another EU-country).

2 Advertisements

22. Advertisements in connection with an offer must meet the requirements set out in Section 7-20 of the Securities Trading Act, which implements Article 15 of the Prospectus Directive, see Chapter 1, Nos. 62 through 65. Such advertisements must state that further information is given in the prospectus and indicate where the prospectus can be obtained.

Oslo Børs has given further guidance on the content requirements of advertisements in its Circular No. 4/2004 on publication of announcements etc. in connection with offers of transferable securities that require a prospectus.[30] Pursuant to the Circular, advertisements shall normally not include specific information on the company or the securities offered. If such information nonetheless is included, the content of the advertisement must be fairly balanced and must not present a more positive picture of the offer or the securities in question than the prospectus. Information on the major risk factors associated with the securities in question must also be provided.[31]

VI Use of prospectus approved in other (non EU) countries

23. A prospectus drawn up by an issuer or offerer with a registered head office in a country outside the EEA in accordance with the prospectus rules of

[29] l.c.

[30] Although published in 2004, Oslo Børs has stated that the guidelines given in the Circular are valid also after the entry into force of the new prospectus rules, Cf. the Appendix to Circular No. 9/2005 pp. 4 and 28 and Circular No. 3/2006 p. 7.

[31] Oslo Børs has in a statement from 2006 criticised a company for breach of Section 7-20 of the Act of 19 June 1997 No. 79 on Securities Trading (equivalent to Section 7-20 of the current Securities Trading Act) and Oslo Børs' guidelines in connection with an advertisement published in one of Norway's financial papers regarding with the initial public offering of the company's shares (Oslo Børs' Decisions and Statements 2006, p. 24). The description of the company given in the advertisement was in Oslo Børs' view incomplete and unbalanced. Further, the advertisement did not contain any adverse information and there was no reference to the prospectus in the advertisement.

this country can, pursuant to Section 7-7 (5) of the Securities Trading Act, cf. Article 20(1) of the Prospectus Directive, be approved by the Norwegian prospectus authority, provided that the prospectus has been produced in accordance with international standards and contains the information required for an EEA prospectus pursuant to Chapter 7 of the Securities Trading Act.[32]

Under the Prospectus Directive, it is a condition for the approval of prospectuses produced in accordance with the prospectus rules of a country outside the EEA that the rules of the country in question comply with the IOSCO disclosure standards; see Chapter 1, No. 73. Oslo Børs has accordingly expressed the view that it will be able to approve a prospectus related to an issuer with a registered head office outside the EEA provided that the prospectus rules of the relevant jurisdiction comply with the IOSCO disclosure standards.[33]

When Oslo Børs receives a prospectus produced in accordance with the prospectus rules of a country outside the EEA, it will check that the information provided in the prospectus is sufficiently equivalent to the information required for an EEA prospectus. Once it has gained more experience with such prospectuses, it will consider publishing a list of countries with acceptable prospectus rules as suggested by the European Securities Forum.[34]

VII Sanctions

24. Violation of the obligations laid down in Chapter 7 of the Securities Trading Act may, pursuant to Article 17-1 of the Act, be sanctioned with administrative fines. The Regulation to the Securities Trading Act provides a more detailed regulation of the process for imposition and calculation of such fines. For issuers of listed securities, the maximum administrative fine which can be imposed is ten times the yearly listing fee for each violation which can be sanctioned with an administrative fine. For other issuers or offerers, it follows from the regulation that an administrative fine shall be calculated having regard to the seriousness of the violation and the calculation principles applicable to issuers of listed securities.[35]

The Regulation to the Securities Trading Act also gives Oslo Børs the authority to suspend an offer or prohibit an advertisement for a maximum of ten consecutive working days if it has reasonable grounds for suspecting that the prospectus rules have been violated.[36]

[32] In Section 7-7 (5) of the Securities Trading Act, the wording '*issuers* with a registered head office in a country outside the EEA' (our italics) is used. It must, however, be assumed that the provision applies to prospectuses in relation to every offer or admission to listing of transferable securities. See also the Appendix to Circular No. 9/2005 p. 23.

[33] Cf. the Appendix to Circular No. 9/2005 p. 24. [34] l.c.

[35] Cf. Section 7-7 of the Regulation to the Securities Trading Act.

[36] Cf. Section 7-6(c) and (d) of the Regulation to the Securities Trading Act, Cf. Art. 21(2)(d) and (e) Dir.

VIII Prospectus liability

25. Pursuant to Section 7-18 of the Securities Trading Act, a prospectus must identify the persons responsible for it, and these persons must sign a statement of responsibility as described in Section IV.10 above.

For prospectuses regarding offers to purchase or subscribe for shares made by the issuer of the shares, and for prospectuses regarding admission to trading, the issuer's board of directors must assume responsibility for the prospectus. For other types of securities, the Securities Trading Act does not contain any specific provision on prospectus responsibility. Oslo Børs has, in conformity with Article 6(1) of the Prospectus Directive, taken the view that the issuer's executive management or board of directors can assume responsibility for the prospectus in such cases.[37]

Article 6 (2) of the Prospectus Directive provides that the Member States must ensure that their laws, regulations and administrative provisions on civil liability apply to those persons responsible for the information given in a prospectus, see Chapter 1, No. 85. The Securities Trading Act does not contain any provision to this effect. Pursuant to the preparatory works of the 1997 Securities Trading Act, such a provision was considered unnecessary as the civil liability of persons responsible for the information given in a prospectus will be governed by general statutory and non-statutory national law.[38]

IX Rules applicable to transactions and securities not subject to the Directive and Regulation

1 Registration prospectuses

26. Under Chapter 7 of the Securities Trading Act, a registration prospectus must be produced for offers to subscribe for or purchase transferable securities with a total consideration between €100,000 and €2.5 million directed at 100 or more persons in the Norwegian securities market, cf. Sections 7-2 and 7-7 of the Securities Trading Act. The obligation to produce a registration prospectus applies regardless of whether the securities are listed on a stock exchange.

Compared to the rules applicable to EEA prospectuses, the requirements for the contents of a registration prospectus, which are set out in Section 7-14 of the Regulation to the Securities Trading Act, are less comprehensive. Further, a registration prospectus is not subject to control or approval by Oslo Børs (or any other prospectus authority). Pursuant to Section 7-10 of the Securities Trading Act, a registration prospectus shall instead be registered with the Norwegian Register of Business Enterprises.

As a registration prospectus does not satisfy the requirements of the Prospectus Directive and the Prospectus Regulation, it cannot be used cross-border within the EEA.

[37] Cf. the Appendix to Circular No. 9/2005 p. 21.

[38] Cf. Ot.prp. No. 69 (2004–2005) p. 59.

2 Mergers, demergers etc

27. The former Stock Exchange Regulation[39] at one stage imposed an obligation to produce a prospectus when a listed company participated in a merger or demerger or carried out a reverse takeover. This obligation was revoked in connection with the entry into force of the new prospectus rules.

In Circular No. 9/2005 and its Appendix, Oslo Børs expresses the view that it will be entitled to impose an obligation to (1) produce a limited prospectus or information document in the case of certain transactions falling outside the scope of the Prospectus Directive; and (2) produce a more extensive prospectus or information document in the case of certain other transactions falling outside the scope of the Prospectus Directive.

This has been followed from Oslo Børs in its Continuing Obligations for Stock Exchange Listed Companies (the 'Continuing Obligations'). Pursuant to the Continuing Obligations, a listed company must publish an extended stock exchange notification in the event that it enters into an agreement for acquisition or divestment of a business or an asset resulting in a change of more than five per cent in the company's assets, revenue or profit/loss. The extended stock exchange notification must fulfil various specific content requirements. For example, information about the parties and the transaction, including information about the consideration, the financing and the significance for the company must be given. An extended stock exchange notification must be published before the opening of the stock exchange on the third working day after the agreement has been entered into.[40]

Moreover, Oslo Børs requires that a listed company produce an information document ('mini-prospectus') in the event that it enters into an agreement resulting in a change of more than 25 per cent calculated on the basis of the principles used to determine whether pro forma financial information must be provided in a prospectus, cf. Annex 1 Section 20.2 Reg. and CESR/06–054b Part II Chapter 6. In the same way as for extended stock exchange notifications, the information document must fulfil certain specific content requirements. The content requirements for an information document are more extensive than the content requirements for an extended stock exchange notification. The information document must at the latest be published twenty working days after the agreement has been entered into and it must be submitted to Oslo Børs for control before it is published.[41]

[39] FOR-1994-01-17-30. [40] Cf. Section 3.4 of the Continuing Obligations

[40] Cf. Section 3.5 of the Continuing Obligations.

PART IV

Annexes

Annex I

Council Directive (EC) No 2003/71 of 4 November 2003 on the prospectus to be published when securities are offered to the public or admitted to trading (the Prospectus Directive)

DIRECTIVE 2003/71/EC OF THE EUROPEAN PARLIAMENT AND OF THE COUNCIL

of 4 November 2003

on the prospectus to be published when securities are offered to the public or admitted to trading and amending Directive 2001/34/EC

(Text with EEA relevance)

THE EUROPEAN PARLIAMENT AND THE COUNCIL OF THE EUROPEAN UNION,

Having regard to the Treaty establishing the European Community, and in particular Articles 44 and 95 thereof,

Having regard to the proposal from the Commission (1),

Having regard to the opinion of the European Economic and Social Committee (2),

Having regard to the opinion of the European Central Bank (3),

Acting in accordance with the procedure laid down in Article 251 of the Treaty (4),

Whereas:

(1) Council Directives 80/390/EEC of 17 March 1980 coordinating the requirements for the drawing up, scrutiny and distribution of the listing particulars to be published for the admission of securities to official stock exchange listing (5) and 89/298/EEC of 17 April 1989 coordinating the requirements for the drawing up, scrutiny and distribution of the prospectus to be published when transferable securities are offered to the public (6) were adopted several years ago introducing a partial and complex mutual recognition mechanism which is unable to achieve the objective of the single passport provided for by this Directive. Those directives should be upgraded, updated and grouped together into a single text.

(2) Meanwhile, Directive 80/390/EEC was integrated into Directive 2001/34/EC of the European Parliament and of the Council of 28 May 2001 on the admission of securities to official stock exchange listing and on information to be published on those securities (7), which codifies several directives in the field of listed securities.

(3) For reasons of consistency, however, it is appropriate to regroup the provisions of Directive 2001/34/EC which stem from Directive 80/390/EEC together with Directive 89/298/EEC and to amend Directive 2001/34/EC accordingly.

(4) This Directive constitutes an instrument essential to the achievement of the internal market as set out in timetable form in the Commission communications 'Risk capital action plan' and 'Implementing the framework for financial market: Action Plan' facilitating the widest possible access to investment capital on a Community-wide basis, including for small and medium-sized enterprises (SMEs) and start-ups, by granting a single passport to the issuer.

(5) On 17 July 2000, the Council set up the Committee of Wise Men on the regulation of European securities markets. In its initial report of 9 November 2000 the Committee stresses the lack of an agreed definition of public offer of securities, with the result that the same operation is regarded as a private placement in some Member States and not in others; the current system discourages firms from raising capital on a Community-wide basis and therefore from having real access to a large, liquid and integrated financial market.

(6) In its final report of 15 February 2001 the Committee of Wise Men proposed the introduction of new legislative techniques based on a four-level approach, namely framework principles, implementing measures, cooperation and enforcement. Level 1, the directive, should confine itself to broad, general 'framework' principles, while Level 2 should contain technical implementing measures to be adopted by the Commission with the assistance of a committee.

(7) The Stockholm European Council of 23 and 24 March 2001 endorsed the final report of the Committee of Wise Men and the proposed four-level approach to make the regulatory process for Community securities legislation more efficient and transparent.

(8) The resolution of the European Parliament of 5 February 2002 on the implementation of financial services legislation also endorsed the Committee of Wise Men's final report, on the basis of the solemn declaration made before Parliament the same day by the Commission and the letter of 2 October 2001 addressed by the Internal Market Commissioner to the chairman of Parliament's Committee on Economic and Monetary Affairs with regard to the safeguards for the European Parliament's role in this process.

(1) OJ C 240 E, 28.8.2001, p. 272 and OJ C 20 E, 28.1.2003, p. 122.
(2) OJ C 80, 3.4.2002, p. 52.
(3) OJ C 344, 6.12.2001, p. 4.
(4) Opinion of the European Parliament of 14 March 2002 (OJ C 47 E, 27.2.2003, p. 417), Council Common Position of 24 March 2003 (OJ C 125 E, 27.5.2003, p. 21) and Position of the European Parliament of 2 July 2003 (not yet published in the Official Journal). Decision of the Council of 15 July 2003.
(5) OJ L 100, 17.4.1980, p. 1. Directive as last amended by Directive of the European Parliament and of the Council 94/18/EC (OJ L 135, 31.5.1994, p. 1).
(6) OJ L 124, 5.5.1989, p. 8.
(7) OJ L 184, 6.7.2001, p. 1.

(9) According to the Stockholm European Council, Level 2 implementing measures should be used more frequently to ensure that technical provisions can be kept up to date with market and supervisory developments and deadlines should be set for all stages of Level 2.

(10) The aim of this Directive and its implementing measures is to ensure investor protection and market efficiency, in accordance with high regulatory standards adopted in the relevant international fora.

(11) Non-equity securities issued by a Member State or by one of a Member State's regional or local authorities, by public international bodies of which one or more Member States are members, by the European Central Bank or by the central banks of the Member States are not covered by this Directive and thus remain unaffected by this Directive; the abovementioned issuers of such securities may, however, if they so choose, draw up a prospectus in accordance with this Directive.

(12) Full coverage of equity and non-equity securities offered to the public or admitted to trading on regulated markets as defined by Council Directive 93/22/EEC of 10 May 1993 on investment services in the securities field [1], and not only securities which have been admitted to the official lists of stock exchanges, is also needed to ensure investor protection. The wide definition of securities in this Directive, which includes warrants and covered warrants and certificates, is only valid for this Directive and consequently in no way affects the various definitions of financial instruments used in national legislation for other purposes, such as taxation. Some of the securities defined in this Directive entitle the holder to acquire transferable securities or to receive a cash amount through a cash settlement determined by reference to other instruments, notably transferable securities, currencies, interest rates or yields, commodities or other indices or measures. Depositary receipts and convertible notes, e.g. securities convertible at the option of the investor, fall within the definition of non-equity securities set out in this Directive.

(13) Issuance of securities having a similar type and/or class in the case of non-equity securities issued on the basis of an offering programme, including warrants and certificates in any form, as well as the case of securities issued in a continuous or repeated manner, should be understood as covering not only identical securities but also securities that belong in general terms to one category. These securities may include different products, such as debt securities, certificates and warrants, or the same product under the same programme, and may have different features notably in terms of seniority, types of underlying, or the basis on which to determine the redemption amount or coupon payment.

(14) The grant to the issuer of a single passport, valid throughout the Community, and the application of the country of origin principle require the identification of the home Member State as the one best placed to regulate the issuer for the purposes of this Directive.

(15) The disclosure requirements of the present Directive do not prevent a Member State or a competent authority or an exchange through its rule book to impose other particular requirements in the context of admission to trading of securities on a regulated market (notably regarding corporate governance). Such requirements may not directly or indirectly restrict the drawing up, the content and the dissemination of a prospectus approved by a competent authority.

(16) One of the objectives of this Directive is to protect investors. It is therefore appropriate to take account of the different requirements for protection of the various categories of investors and their level of expertise. Disclosure provided by the prospectus is not required for offers limited to qualified investors. In contrast, any resale to the public or public trading through admission to trading on a regulated market requires the publication of a prospectus.

(17) Issuers, offerors or persons asking for the admission to trading on a regulated market of securities which are exempted from the obligation to publish a prospectus will benefit from the single passport if they comply with this Directive.

(18) The provision of full information concerning securities and issuers of those securities promotes, together with rules on the conduct of business, the protection of investors. Moreover, such information provides an effective means of increasing confidence in securities and thus of contributing to the proper functioning and development of securities markets. The appropriate way to make this information available is to publish a prospectus.

(19) Investment in securities, like any other form of investment, involves risk. Safeguards for the protection of the interests of actual and potential investors are required in all Member States in order to enable them to make an informed assessment of such risks and thus to take investment decisions in full knowledge of the facts.

[1] OJ L 141, 11.6.1993, p. 27. Directive as last amended by Directive 2000/64/EC of the European Parliament and of the Council (OJ L 290, 17.11.2000, p. 27).

(20) Such information, which needs to be sufficient and as objective as possible as regards the financial circumstances of the issuer and the rights attaching to the securities, should be provided in an easily analysable and comprehensible form. Harmonisation of the information contained in the prospectus should provide equivalent investor protection at Community level.

(21) Information is a key factor in investor protection; a summary conveying the essential characteristics of, and risks associated with, the issuer, any guarantor and the securities should be included in the prospectus. To ensure easy access to this information, the summary should be written in non-technical language and normally should not exceed 2 500 words in the language in which the prospectus was originally drawn up.

(22) Best practices have been adopted at international level in order to allow cross-border offers of equities to be made using a single set of disclosure standards established by the International Organisation of Securities Commissions (IOSCO); the IOSCO disclosure standards ([1]) will upgrade information available for the markets and investors and at the same time will simplify the procedure for Community issuers wishing to raise capital in third countries. The Directive also calls for tailored disclosure standards to be adopted for other types of securities and issuers.

(23) Fast-track procedures for issuers admitted to trading on a regulated market and frequently raising capital on these markets require the introduction at Community level of a new format of prospectuses for offering programmes or mortgage bonds and a new registration document system. Issuers may choose not to use those formats and therefore to draft the prospectus as a single document.

(24) The content of a base prospectus should, in particular, take into account the need for flexibility in relation to the information to be provided about the securities.

(25) Omission of sensitive information to be included in a prospectus should be allowed through a derogation granted by the competent authority in certain circumstances in order to avoid detrimental situations for an issuer.

(26) A clear time limit should be set for the validity of a prospectus in order to avoid outdated information.

([1]) International disclosure standards for cross-border offering and initial listings by foreign issuers, Part I, International Organisation of Securities Commissions, September 1998.

(27) Investors should be protected by ensuring publication of reliable information. The issuers whose securities are admitted to trading on a regulated market are subject to an ongoing disclosure obligation but are not required to publish updated information regularly. Further to this obligation, issuers should, at least annually, list all relevant information published or made available to the public over the preceding 12 months, including information provided to the various reporting requirements laid down in other Community legislation. This should make it possible to ensure the publication of consistent and easily understandable information on a regular basis. To avoid excessive burdens for certain issuers, issuers of non-equity securities with high minimum denomination should not be required to meet this obligation.

(28) It is necessary for the annual information to be provided by issuers whose securities are admitted to trading on a regulated market to be appropriately monitored by Member States in accordance with their obligations under the provisions of Community and national law concerning the regulation of securities, issuers of securities and securities markets.

(29) The opportunity of allowing issuers to incorporate by reference documents containing the information to be disclosed in a prospectus — provided that the documents incorporated by reference have been previously filed with or accepted by the competent authority — should facilitate the procedure of drawing up a prospectus and lower the costs for the issuers without endangering investor protection.

(30) Differences regarding the efficiency, methods and timing of the checking of the information given in a prospectus not only make it more difficult for undertakings to raise capital or to obtain admission to trading on a regulated market in more than one Member State but also hinder the acquisition by investors established in one Member State of securities offered by an issuer established in another Member State or admitted to trading in another Member State. These differences should be eliminated by harmonising the rules and regulations in order to achieve an adequate degree of equivalence of the safeguards required in each Member State to ensure the provision of information which is sufficient and as objective as possible for actual or potential securities holders.

(31) To facilitate circulation of the various documents making up the prospectus, the use of electronic communication facilities such as the Internet should be encouraged. The prospectus should always be delivered in paper form, free of charge to investors on request.

(32) The prospectus should be filed with the relevant competent authority and be made available to the public by the issuer, the offeror or the person asking for admission to trading on a regulated market, subject to European Union provisions relating to data protection.

(33) It is also necessary, in order to avoid loopholes in Community legislation which would undermine public confidence and therefore prejudice the proper functioning of financial markets, to harmonise advertisements.

(34) Any new matter liable to influence the assessment of the investment, arising after the publication of the prospectus but before the closing of the offer or the start of trading on a regulated market, should be properly evaluated by investors and therefore requires the approval and dissemination of a supplement to the prospectus.

(35) The obligation for an issuer to translate the full prospectus into all the relevant official languages discourages cross-border offers or multiple trading. To facilitate cross-border offers, where the prospectus is drawn up in a language that is customary in the sphere of international finance, the host or home Member State should only be entitled to require a summary in its official language(s).

(36) The competent authority of the host Member State should be entitled to receive a certificate from the competent authority of the home Member State which states that the prospectus has been drawn up in accordance with this Directive. In order to ensure that the purposes of this Directive will be fully achieved, it is also necessary to include within its scope securities issued by issuers governed by the laws of third countries.

(37) A variety of competent authorities in Member States, having different responsibilities, may create unnecessary costs and overlapping of responsibilities without providing any additional benefit. In each Member State one single competent authority should be designated to approve prospectuses and to assume responsibility for supervising compliance with this Directive. Under strict conditions, a Member State should be allowed to designate more than one competent authority, but only one will assume the duties for international cooperation. Such an authority or authorities should be established as an administrative authority and in such a form that their independence from economic actors is guaranteed and conflicts of interest are avoided. The designation of a competent authority for prospectus approval should not exclude cooperation between that authority and other entities, with a view to guaranteeing efficient scrutiny and approval of prospectuses in the interest of issuers, investors, markets participants and markets alike. Any delegation of tasks relating to the obligations provided for in this Directive and in its implementing measures should be reviewed, in accordance with Article 31, five years after the date of entry into force of this Directive and should, except for publication on the Internet of approved prospectuses, and the filing of prospectuses as mentioned in Article 14, end eight years after the entry into force of this Directive.

(38) A common minimum set of powers for the competent authorities will guarantee the effectiveness of their supervision. The flow of information to the markets required by Directive 2001/34/EC should be ensured and action against breaches should be taken by competent authorities.

(39) For the purposes of carrying out their duties, cooperation between competent authorities of the Member States is required.

(40) Technical guidance and implementing measures for the rules laid down in this Directive may from time to time be necessary to take into account developments on financial markets. The Commission should accordingly be empowered to adopt implementing measures, provided that these do not modify the essential elements of this Directive and provided that the Commission acts in accordance with the principles set out in this Directive, after consulting the European Securities Committee established by Commission Decision 2001/528/EC ([1]).

(41) In exercising its implementing powers in accordance with this Directive, the Commission should respect the following principles:

— the need to ensure confidence in financial markets among small investors and small and medium-sized enterprises (SMEs) by promoting high standards of transparency in financial markets,

— the need to provide investors with a wide range of competing investment opportunities and a level of disclosure and protection tailored to their circumstances,

— the need to ensure that independent regulatory authorities enforce the rules consistently, especially as regards the fight against white-collar crime,

— the need for a high level of transparency and consultation with all market participants and with the European Parliament and the Council,

([1]) OJ L 191, 13.7.2001, p. 45.

— the need to encourage innovation in financial markets if they are to be dynamic and efficient,

— the need to ensure systemic stability of the financial system by close and reactive monitoring of financial innovation,

— the importance of reducing the cost of, and increasing access to, capital,

— the need to balance, on a long-term basis, the costs and benefits to market participants (including SMEs and small investors) of any implementing measures,

— the need to foster the international competitiveness of the Community's financial markets without prejudice to a much-needed extension of international cooperation,

— the need to achieve a level playing field for all market participants by establishing Community legislation every time it is appropriate,

— the need to respect differences in national financial markets where these do not unduly impinge on the coherence of the single market,

— the need to ensure coherence with other Community legislation in this area, as imbalances in information and a lack of transparency may jeopardise the operation of the markets and above all harm consumers and small investors.

(42) The European Parliament should be given a period of three months from the first transmission of draft implementing measures to allow it to examine them and to give its opinion. However, in urgent and duly justified cases, this period may be shortened. If, within that period, a resolution is passed by the European Parliament, the Commission should re-examine the draft measures.

(43) Member States should lay down a system of sanctions for breaches of the national provisions adopted pursuant to this Directive and should take all the measures necessary to ensure that these sanctions are applied. The sanctions thus provided for should be effective, proportional and dissuasive.

(44) Provision should be made for the right of judicial review of decisions taken by Member States' competent authorities in respect of the application of this Directive.

(45) In accordance with the principle of proportionality, it is necessary and appropriate for the achievement of the basic objective of ensuring the completion of a single securities market to lay down rules on a single passport for issuers. This Directive does not go beyond what is necessary in order to achieve the objectives pursued in accordance with the third paragraph of Article 5 of the Treaty.

(46) The assessment made by the Commission of the application of this Directive should focus in particular on the process of approval of prospectuses by the competent authorities of the Member States, and more generally on the application of the home-country principle, and whether or not problems of investor protection and market efficiency might result from this application; the Commission should also examine the functioning of Article 10.

(47) For future developments of this Directive, consideration should be given to the matter of deciding which approval mechanism should be adopted to enhance further the uniform application of Community legislation on prospectuses, including the possible establishment of a European Securities Unit.

(48) This Directive respects the fundamental rights and observes the principles recognised in particular by the Charter of Fundamental Rights of the European Union.

(49) The measures necessary for the implementation of this Directive should be adopted in accordance with Council Decision 1999/468/EC of 28 June 1999 laying down the procedures for the exercise of implementing powers conferred on the Commission [1],

HAVE ADOPTED THIS DIRECTIVE:

CHAPTER I

GENERAL PROVISIONS

Article 1

Purpose and scope

1. The purpose of this Directive is to harmonise requirements for the drawing up, approval and distribution of the prospectus to be published when securities are offered to the public or admitted to trading on a regulated market situated or operating within a Member State.

2. This Directive shall not apply to:

(a) units issued by collective investment undertakings other than the closed-end type;

(b) non-equity securities issued by a Member State or by one of a Member State's regional or local authorities, by public international bodies of which one or more Member States are members, by the European Central Bank or by the central banks of the Member States;

(c) shares in the capital of central banks of the Member States;

[1] OJ L 184, 17.7.1999, p. 23.

(d) securities unconditionally and irrevocably guaranteed by a Member State or by one of a Member State's regional or local authorities;

(e) securities issued by associations with legal status or non-profit-making bodies, recognised by a Member State, with a view to their obtaining the means necessary to achieve their non-profit-making objectives;

(f) non-equity securities issued in a continuous or repeated manner by credit institutions provided that these securities:

(i) are not subordinated, convertible or exchangeable;

(ii) do not give a right to subscribe to or acquire other types of securities and that they are not linked to a derivative instrument;

(iii) materialise reception of repayable deposits;

(iv) are covered by a deposit guarantee scheme under Directive 94/19/EC of the European Parliament and of the Council on deposit-guarantee schemes [1];

(g) non-fungible shares of capital whose main purpose is to provide the holder with a right to occupy an apartment, or other form of immovable property or a part thereof and where the shares cannot be sold on without this right being given up;

(h) securities included in an offer where the total consideration of the offer is less than EUR 2 500 000, which limit shall be calculated over a period of 12 months;

(i) 'bostadsobligationer' issued repeatedly by credit institutions in Sweden whose main purpose is to grant mortgage loans, provided that

(i) the 'bostadsobligationer' issued are of the same series;

(ii) the 'bostadsobligationer' are issued on tap during a specified issuing period;

(iii) the terms and conditions of the 'bostadsobligationer' are not changed during the issuing period;

(iv) the sums deriving from the issue of the said 'bostadsobligationer', in accordance with the articles of association of the issuer, are placed in assets which provide sufficient coverage for the liability deriving from securities;

(j) non-equity securities issued in a continuous or repeated manner by credit institutions where the total consideration of the offer is less than EUR 50 000 000, which limit shall be calculated over a period of 12 months, provided that these securities:

(i) are not subordinated, convertible or exchangeable;

(ii) do not give a right to subscribe to or acquire other types of securities and that they are not linked to a derivative instrument.

[1] OJ L 135, 31.5.1994, p. 5.

3. Notwithstanding paragraph 2(b), (d), (h), (i) and (j), an issuer, an offeror or a person asking for admission to trading on a regulated market shall be entitled to draw up a prospectus in accordance with this Directive when securities are offered to the public or admitted to trading.

Article 2

Definitions

1. For the purposes of this Directive, the following definitions shall apply:

(a) 'securities' means transferable securities as defined by Article 1(4) of Directive 93/22/EEC with the exception of money market instruments as defined by Article 1(5) of Directive 93/22/EEC, having a maturity of less than 12 months. For these instruments national legislation may be applicable;

(b) 'equity securities' means shares and other transferable securities equivalent to shares in companies, as well as any other type of transferable securities giving the right to acquire any of the aforementioned securities as a consequence of their being converted or the rights conferred by them being exercised, provided that securities of the latter type are issued by the issuer of the underlying shares or by an entity belonging to the group of the said issuer;

(c) 'non-equity securities' means all securities that are not equity securities;

(d) 'offer of securities to the public' means a communication to persons in any form and by any means, presenting sufficient information on the terms of the offer and the securities to be offered, so as to enable an investor to decide to purchase or subscribe to these securities. This definition shall also be applicable to the placing of securities through financial intermediaries;

(e) 'qualified investors' means:

(i) legal entities which are authorised or regulated to operate in the financial markets, including: credit institutions, investment firms, other authorised or regulated financial institutions, insurance companies, collective investment schemes and their management companies, pension funds and their management companies, commodity dealers, as well as entities not so authorised or regulated whose corporate purpose is solely to invest in securities;

(ii) national and regional governments, central banks, international and supranational institutions such as the International Monetary Fund, the European Central Bank, the European Investment Bank and other similar international organisations;

(iii) other legal entities which do not meet two of the three criteria set out in paragraph (f);

(iv) certain natural persons: subject to mutual recognition, a Member State may choose to authorise natural persons who are resident in the Member State and who expressly ask to be considered as qualified investors if these persons meet at least two of the criteria set out in paragraph 2;

(v) certain SMEs: subject to mutual recognition, a Member State may choose to authorise SMEs which have their registered office in that Member State and who expressly ask to be considered as qualified investors;

(f) 'small and medium-sized enterprises' means companies, which, according to their last annual or consolidated accounts, meet at least two of the following three criteria: an average number of employees during the financial year of less than 250, a total balance sheet not exceeding EUR 43 000 000 and an annual net turnover not exceeding EUR 50 000 000;

(g) 'credit institution' means an undertaking as defined by Article 1(1)(a) of Directive 2000/12/EC of the European Parliament and of the Council of 20 March 2000 relating to the taking up and pursuit of the business of credit institutions [1];

(h) 'issuer' means a legal entity which issues or proposes to issue securities;

(i) 'person making an offer' (or 'offeror') means a legal entity or individual which offers securities to the public;

(j) 'regulated market' means a market as defined by Article 1(13) of Directive 93/22/EEC;

(k) 'offering programme' means a plan which would permit the issuance of non-equity securities, including warrants in any form, having a similar type and/or class, in a continuous or repeated manner during a specified issuing period;

(l) 'securities issued in a continuous or repeated manner' means issues on tap or at least two separate issues of securities of a similar type and/or class over a period of 12 months;

(m) 'home Member State' means:

(i) for all Community issuers of securities which are not mentioned in (ii), the Member State where the issuer has its registered office;

(ii) for any issues of non-equity securities whose denomination per unit amounts to at least EUR 1 000, and for any issues of non-equity securities giving the right to acquire any transferable securities or to receive a cash amount, as a consequence of their being converted or the rights conferred by them being exercised, provided that the issuer of the non-equity securities is not the issuer of the underlying securities or an entity belonging to the group of the latter issuer, the Member State where the issuer has its registered office, or where the securities were or are to be admitted to trading on a regulated market or where the securities are offered to the public, at the choice of the issuer, the offeror or the person asking for admission, as the case may be. The same regime shall be applicable to non-equity securities in a currency other than euro, provided that the value of such minimum denomination is nearly equivalent to EUR 1 000;

(iii) for all issuers of securities incorporated in a third country, which are not mentioned in (ii), the Member State where the securities are intended to be offered to the public for the first time after the date of entry into force of this Directive or where the first application for admission to trading on a regulated market is made, at the choice of the issuer, the offeror or the person asking for admission, as the case may be, subject to a subsequent election by issuers incorporated in a third country if the home Member State was not determined by their choice;

(n) 'host Member State' means the State where an offer to the public is made or admission to trading is sought, when different from the home Member State;

(o) 'collective investment undertaking other than the closed-end type' means unit trusts and investment companies:

(i) the object of which is the collective investment of capital provided by the public, and which operate on the principle of risk-spreading;

(ii) the units of which are, at the holder's request, repurchased or redeemed, directly or indirectly, out of the assets of these undertakings;

(p) 'units of a collective investment undertaking' mean securities issued by a collective investment undertaking as representing the rights of the participants in such an undertaking over its assets;

(q) 'approval' means the positive act at the outcome of the scrutiny of the completeness of the prospectus by the home Member State's competent authority including the consistency of the information given and its comprehensibility;

(r) 'base prospectus' means a prospectus containing all relevant information as specified in Articles 5, 7 and 16 in case there is a supplement, concerning the issuer and the securities to be offered to the public or admitted to trading, and, at the choice of the issuer, the final terms of the offering.

2. For the purposes of paragraph 1(e)(iv) the criteria are as follows:

(a) the investor has carried out transactions of a significant size on securities markets at an average frequency of, at least, 10 per quarter over the previous four quarters;

(b) the size of the investor's securities portfolio exceeds EUR 0,5 million;

[1] OJ L 126, 26.5.2000, p. 1. Directive as last amended by Directive 2000/28/EC (OJ L 275, 27.10.2000, p. 37).

(c) the investor works or has worked for at least one year in the financial sector in a professional position which requires knowledge of securities investment.

3. For the purposes of paragraphs 1(e)(iv) and (v) the following shall apply:

Each competent authority shall ensure that appropriate mechanisms are in place for a register of natural persons and SMEs considered as qualified investors, taking into account the need to ensure an adequate level of data protection. The register shall be available to all issuers. Each natural person or SME wishing to be considered as a qualified investor shall register and each registered investor may decide to opt out at any moment.

4. In order to take account of technical developments on financial markets and to ensure uniform application of this Directive, the Commission shall, in accordance with the procedure set out in Article 24(2), adopt implementing measures concerning the definitions referred to in paragraph 1, including adjustment of the figures used for the definition of SMEs, taking into account Community legislation and recommendations as well as economic developments and disclosure measures relating to the registration of individual qualified investors.

Article 3

Obligation to publish a prospectus

1. Member States shall not allow any offer of securities to be made to the public within their territories without prior publication of a prospectus.

2. The obligation to publish a prospectus shall not apply to the following types of offer:

(a) an offer of securities addressed solely to qualified investors; and/or

(b) an offer of securities addressed to fewer than 100 natural or legal persons per Member State, other than qualified investors; and/or

(c) an offer of securities addressed to investors who acquire securities for a total consideration of at least EUR 50 000 per investor, for each separate offer; and/or

(d) an offer of securities whose denomination per unit amounts to at least EUR 50 000; and/or

(e) an offer of securities with a total consideration of less than EUR 100 000, which limit shall be calculated over a period of 12 months.

However, any subsequent resale of securities which were previously the subject of one or more of the types of offer mentioned in this paragraph shall be regarded as a separate offer and the definition set out in Article 2(1)(d) shall apply for the purpose of deciding whether that resale is an offer of securities to the public. The placement of securities through financial intermediaries shall be subject to publication of a prospectus if none of the conditions (a) to (e) are met for the final placement.

3. Member States shall ensure that any admission of securities to trading on a regulated market situated or operating within their territories is subject to the publication of a prospectus.

Article 4

Exemptions from the obligation to publish a prospectus

1. The obligation to publish a prospectus shall not apply to offers of securities to the public of the following types of securities:

(a) shares issued in substitution for shares of the same class already issued, if the issuing of such new shares does not involve any increase in the issued capital;

(b) securities offered in connection with a takeover by means of an exchange offer, provided that a document is available containing information which is regarded by the competent authority as being equivalent to that of the prospectus, taking into account the requirements of Community legislation;

(c) securities offered, allotted or to be allotted in connection with a merger, provided that a document is available containing information which is regarded by the competent authority as being equivalent to that of the prospectus, taking into account the requirements of Community legislation;

(d) shares offered, allotted or to be allotted free of charge to existing shareholders, and dividends paid out in the form of shares of the same class as the shares in respect of which such dividends are paid, provided that a document is made available containing information on the number and nature of the shares and the reasons for and details of the offer;

(e) securities offered, allotted or to be allotted to existing or former directors or employees by their employer which has securities already admitted to trading on a regulated market or by an affiliated undertaking, provided that a document is made available containing information on the number and nature of the securities and the reasons for and details of the offer.

2. The obligation to publish a prospectus shall not apply to the admission to trading on a regulated market of the following types of securities:

(a) shares representing, over a period of 12 months, less than 10 per cent of the number of shares of the same class already admitted to trading on the same regulated market;

(b) shares issued in substitution for shares of the same class already admitted to trading on the same regulated market, if the issuing of such shares does not involve any increase in the issued capital;

(c) securities offered in connection with a takeover by means of an exchange offer, provided that a document is available containing information which is regarded by the competent authority as being equivalent to that of the prospectus, taking into account the requirements of Community legislation;

(d) securities offered, allotted or to be allotted in connection with a merger, provided that a document is available containing information which is regarded by the competent authority as being equivalent to that of the prospectus, taking into account the requirements of Community legislation;

(e) shares offered, allotted or to be allotted free of charge to existing shareholders, and dividends paid out in the form of shares of the same class as the shares in respect of which such dividends are paid, provided that the said shares are of the same class as the shares already admitted to trading on the same regulated market and that a document is made available containing information on the number and nature of the shares and the reasons for and details of the offer;

(f) securities offered, allotted or to be allotted to existing or former directors or employees by their employer or an affiliated undertaking, provided that the said securities are of the same class as the securities already admitted to trading on the same regulated market and that a document is made available containing information on the number and nature of the securities and the reasons for and detail of the offer;

(g) shares resulting from the conversion or exchange of other securities or from the exercise of the rights conferred by other securities, provided that the said shares are of the same class as the shares already admitted to trading on the same regulated market;

(h) securities already admitted to trading on another regulated market, on the following conditions:

(i) that these securities, or securities of the same class, have been admitted to trading on that other regulated market for more than 18 months;

(ii) that, for securities first admitted to trading on a regulated market after the date of entry into force of this Directive, the admission to trading on that other regulated market was associated with an approved prospectus made available to the public in conformity with Article 14;

(iii) that, except where (ii) applies, for securities first admitted to listing after 30 June 1983, listing particulars were approved in accordance with the requirements of Directive 80/390/EEC or Directive 2001/34/EC;

(iv) that the ongoing obligations for trading on that other regulated market have been fulfilled;

(v) that the person seeking the admission of a security to trading on a regulated market under this exemption makes a summary document available to the public in a language accepted by the competent authority of the Member State of the regulated market where admission is sought;

(vi) that the summary document referred to in (v) is made available to the public in the Member State of the regulated market where admission to trading is sought in the manner set out in Article 14(2); and

(vii) that the contents of the summary document shall comply with Article 5(2). Furthermore the document shall state where the most recent prospectus can be obtained and where the financial information published by the issuer pursuant to his ongoing disclosure obligations is available.

3. In order to take account of technical developments on financial markets and to ensure uniform application of this Directive, the Commission shall, in accordance with the procedure referred to in Article 24(2), adopt implementing measures concerning paragraphs 1(b), 1(c), 2(c) and 2(d), notably in relation to the meaning of equivalence.

CHAPTER II

DRAWING UP OF THE PROSPECTUS

Article 5

The prospectus

1. Without prejudice to Article 8(2), the prospectus shall contain all information which, according to the particular nature of the issuer and of the securities offered to the public or admitted to trading on a regulated market, is necessary to enable investors to make an informed assessment of the assets and liabilities, financial position, profit and losses, and prospects of the issuer and of any guarantor, and of the rights attaching to such securities. This information shall be presented in an easily analysable and comprehensible form.

2. The prospectus shall contain information concerning the issuer and the securities to be offered to the public or to be admitted to trading on a regulated market. It shall also include a summary. The summary shall, in a brief manner and in non-technical language, convey the essential characteristics and risks associated with the issuer, any guarantor and the securities, in the language in which the prospectus was originally drawn up. The summary shall also contain a warning that:

(a) it should be read as an introduction to the prospectus;

(b) any decision to invest in the securities should be based on consideration of the prospectus as a whole by the investor;

(c) where a claim relating to the information contained in a prospectus is brought before a court, the plaintiff investor might, under the national legislation of the Member States, have to bear the costs of translating the prospectus before the legal proceedings are initiated; and

(d) civil liability attaches to those persons who have tabled the summary including any translation thereof, and applied for its notification, but only if the summary is misleading, inaccurate or inconsistent when read together with the other parts of the prospectus.

Where the prospectus relates to the admission to trading on a regulated market of non-equity securities having a denomination of at least EUR 50 000, there shall be no requirement to provide a summary except when requested by a Member State as provided for in Article 19(4).

3. Subject to paragraph 4, the issuer, offeror or person asking for the admission to trading on a regulated market may draw up the prospectus as a single document or separate documents. A prospectus composed of separate documents shall divide the required information into a registration document, a securities note and a summary note. The registration document shall contain the information relating to the issuer. The securities note shall contain the information concerning the securities offered to the public or to be admitted to trading on a regulated market.

4. For the following types of securities, the prospectus can, at the choice of the issuer, offeror or person asking for the admission to trading on a regulated market consist of a base prospectus containing all relevant information concerning the issuer and the securities offered to the public or to be admitted to trading on a regulated market:

(a) non-equity securities, including warrants in any form, issued under an offering programme;

(b) non-equity securities issued in a continuous or repeated manner by credit institutions,

(i) where the sums deriving from the issue of the said securities, under national legislation, are placed in assets which provide sufficient coverage for the liability deriving from securities until their maturity date;

(ii) where, in the event of the insolvency of the related credit institution, the said sums are intended, as a priority, to repay the capital and interest falling due, without prejudice to the provisions of Directive 2001/24/EC of the European Parliament and of the Council of 4 April 2001 on the reorganisation and winding up of credit institutions [1].

The information given in the base prospectus shall be supplemented, if necessary, in accordance with Article 16, with updated information on the issuer and on the securities to be offered to the public or to be admitted to trading on a regulated market.

If the final terms of the offer are not included in either the base prospectus or a supplement, the final terms shall be provided to investors and filed with the competent authority when each public offer is made as soon as practicable and if possible in advance of the beginning of the offer. The provisions of Article 8(1)(a) shall be applicable in any such case.

[1] OJ L 125, 5.5.2001, p. 15.

5. In order to take account of technical developments on financial markets and to ensure uniform application of this Directive, the Commission shall, in accordance with the procedure referred to in Article 24(2), adopt implementing measures concerning the format of the prospectus or base prospectus and supplements.

Article 6

Responsibility attaching to the prospectus

1. Member States shall ensure that responsibility for the information given in a prospectus attaches at least to the issuer or its administrative, management or supervisory bodies, the offeror, the person asking for the admission to trading on a regulated market or the guarantor, as the case may be. The persons responsible shall be clearly identified in the prospectus by their names and functions or, in the case of legal persons, their names and registered offices, as well as declarations by them that, to the best of their knowledge, the information contained in the prospectus is in accordance with the facts and that the prospectus makes no omission likely to affect its import.

2. Member States shall ensure that their laws, regulation and administrative provisions on civil liability apply to those persons responsible for the information given in a prospectus.

However, Member States shall ensure that no civil liability shall attach to any person solely on the basis of the summary, including any translation thereof, unless it is misleading, inaccurate or inconsistent when read together with the other parts of the prospectus.

Article 7

Minimum information

1. Detailed implementing measures regarding the specific information which must be included in a prospectus, avoiding duplication of information when a prospectus is composed of separate documents, shall be adopted by the Commission in accordance with the procedure referred to in Article 24(2). The first set of implementing measures shall be adopted by 1 July 2004.

2. In particular, for the elaboration of the various models of prospectuses, account shall be taken of the following:

(a) the various types of information needed by investors relating to equity securities as compared with non-equity securities; a consistent approach shall be taken with regard to information required in a prospectus for securities which have a similar economic rationale, notably derivative securities;

(b) the various types and characteristics of offers and admissions to trading on a regulated market of non-equity securities. The information required in a prospectus shall be appropriate from the point of view of the investors concerned for non-equity securities having a denomination per unit of at least EUR 50 000;

(c) the format used and the information required in prospectuses relating to non-equity securities, including warrants in any form, issued under an offering programme;

(d) the format used and the information required in prospectuses relating to non-equity securities, in so far as these securities are not subordinated, convertible, exchangeable, subject to subscription or acquisition rights or linked to derivative instruments, issued in a continuous or repeated manner by entities authorised or regulated to operate in the financial markets within the European Economic Area;

(e) the various activities and size of the issuer, in particular SMEs. For such companies the information shall be adapted to their size and, where appropriate, to their shorter track record;

(f) if applicable, the public nature of the issuer.

3. The implementing measures referred to in paragraph 1 shall be based on the standards in the field of financial and non-financial information set out by international securities commission organisations, and in particular by IOSCO and on the indicative Annexes to this Directive.

Article 8

Omission of information

1. Member States shall ensure that where the final offer price and amount of securities which will be offered to the public cannot be included in the prospectus:

(a) the criteria, and/or the conditions in accordance with which the above elements will be determined or, in the case of price, the maximum price, are disclosed in the prospectus; or

(b) the acceptances of the purchase or subscription of securities may be withdrawn for not less than two working days after the final offer price and amount of securities which will be offered to the public have been filed.

The final offer price and amount of securities shall be filed with the competent authority of the home Member State and published in accordance with the arrangements provided for in Article 14(2).

2. The competent authority of the home Member State may authorise the omission from the prospectus of certain information provided for in this Directive or in the implementing measures referred to in Article 7(1), if it considers that:

(a) disclosure of such information would be contrary to the public interest; or

(b) disclosure of such information would be seriously detrimental to the issuer, provided that the omission would not be likely to mislead the public with regard to facts and circumstances essential for an informed assessment of the issuer, offeror or guarantor, if any, and of the rights attached to the securities to which the prospectus relates; or

(c) such information is of minor importance only for a specific offer or admission to trading on a regulated market and is not such as will influence the assessment of the financial position and prospects of the issuer, offeror or guarantor, if any.

3. Without prejudice to the adequate information of investors, where, exceptionally, certain information required by implementing measures referred to in Article 7(1) to be included in a prospectus is inappropriate to the issuer's sphere of activity or to the legal form of the issuer or to the securities to which the prospectus relates, the prospectus shall contain information equivalent to the required information. If there is no such information, this requirement shall not apply.

4. In order to take account of technical developments on financial markets and to ensure uniform application of this Directive, the Commission shall, in accordance with the procedure referred to in Article 24(2), adopt implementing measures concerning paragraph 2.

Article 9

Validity of a prospectus, base prospectus and registration document

1. A prospectus shall be valid for 12 months after its publication for offers to the public or admissions to trading on a regulated market, provided that the prospectus is completed by any supplements required pursuant to Article 16.

2. In the case of an offering programme, the base prospectus, previously filed, shall be valid for a period of up to 12 months.

3. In the case of non-equity securities referred to in Article 5(4)(b), the prospectus shall be valid until no more of the securities concerned are issued in a continuous or repeated manner.

4. A registration document, as referred to in Article 5(3), previously filed, shall be valid for a period of up to 12 months provided that it has been updated in accordance with Article 10(1). The registration document accompanied by the securities note, updated if applicable in accordance with Article 12, and the summary note shall be considered to constitute a valid prospectus.

Article 10

Information

1. Issuers whose securities are admitted to trading on a regulated market shall at least annually provide a document that contains or refers to all information that they have published or made available to the public over the preceding 12 months in one or more Member States and in third countries in compliance with their obligations under Community and national laws and rules dealing with the regulation of securities, issuers of securities and securities markets. Issuers shall refer at least to the information required pursuant to company law directives, Directive 2001/34/EC and Regulation (EC) No 1606/2002 of the European Parliament and of the Council of 19 July 2002 on the application of international accounting standards ([1]).

2. The document shall be filed with the competent authority of the home Member State after the publication of the financial statement. Where the document refers to information, it shall be stated where the information can be obtained.

3. The obligation set out in paragraph 1 shall not apply to issuers of non-equity securities whose denomination per unit amounts to at least EUR 50 000.

4. In order to take account of technical developments on financial markets and to ensure uniform application of this Directive, the Commission may, in accordance with the procedure referred to in Article 24(2), adopt implementing measures concerning paragraph 1. These measures will relate only to the method of publication of the disclosure requirements mentioned in paragraph 1 and will not entail new disclosure requirements. The first set of implementing measures shall be adopted by 1 July 2004.

([1]) OJ L 243, 11.9.2002, p. 1.

Article 11

Incorporation by reference

1. Member States shall allow information to be incorporated in the prospectus by reference to one or more previously or simultaneously published documents that have been approved by the competent authority of the home Member State or filed with it in accordance with this Directive, in particular pursuant to Article 10, or with Titles IV and V of Directive 2001/34/EC. This information shall be the latest available to the issuer. The summary shall not incorporate information by reference.

2. When information is incorporated by reference, a cross-reference list must be provided in order to enable investors to identify easily specific items of information.

3. In order to take account of technical developments on financial markets and to ensure uniform application of this Directive, the Commission shall, in accordance with the procedure referred to in Article 24(2), adopt implementing measures concerning the information to be incorporated by reference. The first set of implementing measures shall be adopted by 1 July 2004.

Article 12

Prospectuses consisting of separate documents

1. An issuer which already has a registration document approved by the competent authority shall be required to draw up only the securities note and the summary note when securities are offered to the public or admitted to trading on a regulated market.

2. In this case, the securities note shall provide information that would normally be provided in the registration document if there has been a material change or recent development which could affect investors' assessments since the latest updated registration document or any supplement as provided for in Article 16 was approved. The securities and summary notes shall be subject to a separate approval.

3. Where an issuer has only filed a registration document without approval, the entire documentation, including updated information, shall be subject to approval.

CHAPTER III

ARRANGEMENTS FOR APPROVAL AND PUBLICATION OF THE PROSPECTUS

Article 13

Approval of the prospectus

1. No prospectus shall be published until it has been approved by the competent authority of the home Member State.

2. This competent authority shall notify the issuer, the offeror or the person asking for admission to trading on a regulated market, as the case may be, of its decision regarding the approval of the prospectus within 10 working days of the submission of the draft prospectus.

If the competent authority fails to give a decision on the prospectus within the time limits laid down in this paragraph and paragraph 3, this shall not be deemed to constitute approval of the application.

3. The time limit referred to in paragraph 2 shall be extended to 20 working days if the public offer involves securities issued by an issuer which does not have any securities admitted to trading on a regulated market and who has not previously offered securities to the public.

4. If the competent authority finds, on reasonable grounds, that the documents submitted to it are incomplete or that supplementary information is needed, the time limits referred to in paragraphs 2 and 3 shall apply only from the date on which such information is provided by the issuer, the offeror or the person asking for admission to trading on a regulated market.

In the case referred to in paragraph 2 the competent authority should notify the issuer if the documents are incomplete within 10 working days of the submission of the application.

5. The competent authority of the home Member State may transfer the approval of a prospectus to the competent authority of another Member State, subject to the agreement of that authority. Furthermore, this transfer shall be notified to the issuer, the offeror or the person asking for admission to trading on a regulated market within three working days from the date of the decision taken by the competent authority of the home Member State. The time limit referred to in paragraph 2 shall apply from that date.

6. This Directive shall not affect the competent authority's liability, which shall continue to be governed solely by national law.

Member States shall ensure that their national provisions on the liability of competent authorities apply only to approvals of prospectuses by their competent authority or authorities.

7. In order to take account of technical developments on financial markets and to ensure uniform application of this Directive, the Commission may, in accordance with the procedure referred to in Article 24(2), adopt implementing measures concerning the conditions in accordance with which time limits may be adjusted.

Article 14

Publication of the prospectus

1. Once approved, the prospectus shall be filed with the competent authority of the home Member State and shall be made available to the public by the issuer, offeror or person asking for admission to trading on a regulated market as soon as practicable and in any case, at a reasonable time in advance of, and at the latest at the beginning of, the offer to the public or the admission to trading of the securities involved. In addition, in the case of an initial public offer of a class of shares not already admitted to trading on a regulated market that is to be admitted to trading for the first time, the prospectus shall be available at least six working days before the end of the offer.

2. The prospectus shall be deemed available to the public when published either:

(a) by insertion in one or more newspapers circulated throughout, or widely circulated in, the Member States in which the offer to the public is made or the admission to trading is sought; or

(b) in a printed form to be made available, free of charge, to the public at the offices of the market on which the securities are being admitted to trading, or at the registered office of the issuer and at the offices of the financial intermediaries placing or selling the securities, including paying agents; or

(c) in an electronic form on the issuer's website and, if applicable, on the website of the financial intermediaries placing or selling the securities, including paying agents; or

(d) in an electronic form on the website of the regulated market where the admission to trading is sought; or

(e) in electronic form on the website of the competent authority of the home Member State if the said authority has decided to offer this service.

A home Member State may require issuers which publish their prospectus in accordance with (a) or (b) also to publish their prospectus in an electronic form in accordance with (c).

3. In addition, a home Member State may require publication of a notice stating how the prospectus has been made available and where it can be obtained by the public.

4. The competent authority of the home Member State shall publish on its website over a period of 12 months, at its choice, all the prospectuses approved, or at least the list of prospectuses approved in accordance with Article 13, including, if applicable, a hyperlink to the prospectus published on the website of the issuer, or on the website of the regulated market.

5. In the case of a prospectus comprising several documents and/or incorporating information by reference, the documents and information making up the prospectus may be published and circulated separately provided that the said documents are made available, free of charge, to the public, in accordance with the arrangements established in paragraph 2. Each document shall indicate where the other constituent documents of the full prospectus may be obtained.

6. The text and the format of the prospectus, and/or the supplements to the prospectus, published or made available to the public, shall at all times be identical to the original version approved by the competent authority of the home Member State.

7. Where the prospectus is made available by publication in electronic form, a paper copy must nevertheless be delivered to the investor, upon his request and free of charge, by the issuer, the offeror, the person asking for admission to trading or the financial intermediaries placing or selling the securities.

8. In order to take account of technical developments on financial markets and to ensure uniform application of the Directive, the Commission shall, in accordance with the procedure referred to in Article 24(2), adopt implementing measures concerning paragraphs 1, 2, 3 and 4. The first set of implementing measures shall be adopted by 1 July 2004.

Article 15

Advertisements

1. Any type of advertisements relating either to an offer to the public of securities or to an admission to trading on a regulated market shall observe the principles contained in paragraphs 2 to 5. Paragraphs 2 to 4 shall apply only to cases where the issuer, the offeror or the person applying for admission to trading is covered by the obligation to draw up a prospectus.

2. Advertisements shall state that a prospectus has been or will be published and indicate where investors are or will be able to obtain it.

3. Advertisements shall be clearly recognisable as such. The information contained in an advertisement shall not be inaccurate, or misleading. This information shall also be consistent with the information contained in the prospectus, if already published, or with the information required to be in the prospectus, if the prospectus is published afterwards.

4. In any case, all information concerning the offer to the public or the admission to trading on a regulated market disclosed in an oral or written form, even if not for advertising purposes, shall be consistent with that contained in the prospectus.

5. When according to this Directive no prospectus is required, material information provided by an issuer or an offeror and addressed to qualified investors or special categories of investors, including information disclosed in the context of meetings relating to offers of securities, shall be disclosed to all qualified investors or special categories of investors to whom the offer is exclusively addressed. Where a prospectus is required to be published, such information shall be included in the prospectus or in a supplement to the prospectus in accordance with Article 16(1).

6. The competent authority of the home Member State shall have the power to exercise control over the compliance of advertising activity, relating to a public offer of securities or an admission to trading on a regulated market, with the principles referred to in paragraphs 2 to 5.

7. In order to take account of technical developments on financial markets and to ensure uniform application of this Directive, the Commission shall, in accordance with the procedure referred to in Article 24(2), adopt implementing measures concerning the dissemination of advertisements announcing the intention to offer securities to the public or the admission to trading on a regulated market, in particular before the prospectus has been made available to the public or before the opening of the subscription, and concerning paragraph 4. The first set of implementing measures shall be adopted by the Commission by 1 July 2004.

Article 16

Supplements to the prospectus

1. Every significant new factor, material mistake or inaccuracy relating to the information included in the prospectus which is capable of affecting the assessment of the securities and which arises or is noted between the time when the prospectus is approved and the final closing of the offer to the public or, as the case may be, the time when trading on a regulated market begins, shall be mentioned in a supplement to the prospectus. Such a supplement shall be approved in the same way in a maximum of seven working days and published in accordance with at least the same arrangements as were applied when the original prospectus was published. The summary, and any translations thereof, shall also be supplemented, if necessary to take into account the new information included in the supplement.

2. Investors who have already agreed to purchase or subscribe for the securities before the supplement is published shall have the right, exercisable within a time limit which shall not be shorter than two working days after the publication of the supplement, to withdraw their acceptances.

CHAPTER IV

CROSS-BORDER OFFERS AND ADMISSION TO TRADING

Article 17

Community scope of approvals of prospectuses

1. Without prejudice to Article 23, where an offer to the public or admission to trading on a regulated market is provided for in one or more Member States, or in a Member State other than the home Member State, the prospectus approved by the home Member State and any supplements thereto shall be valid for the public offer or the admission to trading in any number of host Member States, provided that the competent authority of each host Member State is notified in accordance with Article 18. Competent authorities of host Member States shall not undertake any approval or administrative procedures relating to prospectuses.

2. If there are significant new factors, material mistakes or inaccuracies, as referred to in Article 16, arising since the approval of the prospectus, the competent authority of the home Member State shall require the publication of a supplement to be approved as provided for in Article 13(1). The competent authority of the host Member State may draw the attention of the competent authority of the home Member State to the need for any new information.

Article 18

Notification

1. The competent authority of the home Member State shall, at the request of the issuer or the person responsible for drawing up the prospectus and within three working days following that request or, if the request is submitted together with the draft prospectus, within one working day after the approval of the prospectus provide the competent authority of the host Member State with a certificate of approval attesting that the prospectus has been drawn up in accordance with this Directive and with a copy of the said prospectus. If applicable, this notification shall be accompanied by a translation of the summary produced under the responsibility of the issuer or person responsible for drawing up the prospectus. The same procedure shall be followed for any supplement to the prospectus.

2. The application of the provisions of Article 8(2) and (3) shall be stated in the certificate, as well as its justification.

CHAPTER V

USE OF LANGUAGES AND ISSUERS INCORPORATED IN THIRD COUNTRIES

Article 19

Use of languages

1. Where an offer to the public is made or admission to trading on a regulated market is sought only in the home Member State, the prospectus shall be drawn up in a language accepted by the competent authority of the home Member State.

2. Where an offer to the public is made or admission to trading on a regulated market is sought in one or more Member States excluding the home Member State, the prospectus shall be drawn up either in a language accepted by the competent authorities of those Member States or in a language customary in the sphere of international finance, at the choice of the issuer, offeror or person asking for admission, as the case may be. The competent authority of each host Member State may only require that the summary be translated into its official language(s).

For the purpose of the scrutiny by the competent authority of the home Member State, the prospectus shall be drawn up either in a language accepted by this authority or in a language customary in the sphere of international finance, at the choice of the issuer, offeror or person asking for admission to trading, as the case may be.

3. Where an offer to the public is made or admission to trading on a regulated market is sought in more than one Member State including the home Member State, the prospectus shall be drawn up in a language accepted by the competent authority of the home Member State and shall also be made available either in a language accepted by the competent authorities of each host Member State or in a language customary in the sphere of international finance, at the choice of the issuer, offeror, or person asking for admission to trading, as the case may be. The competent authority of each host Member State may only require that the summary referred to in Article 5(2) be translated into its official language(s).

4. Where admission to trading on a regulated market of non-equity securities whose denomination per unit amounts to at least EUR 50 000 is sought in one or more Member States, the prospectus shall be drawn up either in a language accepted by the competent authorities of the home and host Member States or in a language customary in the sphere of international finance, at the choice of the issuer, offeror or person asking for admission to trading, as the case may be. Member States may choose to require in their national legislation that a summary be drawn up in their official language(s).

Article 20

Issuers incorporated in third countries

1. The competent authority of the home Member State of issuers having their registered office in a third country may approve a prospectus for an offer to the public or for admission to trading on a regulated market, drawn up in accordance with the legislation of a third country, provided that:

(a) the prospectus has been drawn up in accordance with international standards set by international securities commission organisations, including the IOSCO disclosure standards;

(b) the information requirements, including information of a financial nature, are equivalent to the requirements under this Directive.

2. In the case of an offer to the public or admission to trading on a regulated market of securities, issued by an issuer incorporated in a third country, in a Member State other than the home Member State, the requirements set out in Articles 17, 18 and 19 shall apply.

3. In order to ensure uniform application of this Directive, the Commission may adopt implementing measures in accordance with the procedure referred to in Article 24(2), stating that a third country ensures the equivalence of prospectuses drawn up in that country with this Directive, by reason of its national law or of practices or procedures based on international standards set by international organisations, including the IOSCO disclosure standards.

CHAPTER VI

COMPETENT AUTHORITIES

Article 21

Powers

1. Each Member State shall designate a central competent administrative authority responsible for carrying out the obligations provided for in this Directive and for ensuring that the provisions adopted pursuant to this Directive are applied.

However, a Member State may, if so required by national law, designate other administrative authorities to apply Chapter III.

These competent authorities shall be completely independent from all market participants.

If an offer of securities is made to the public or admission to trading on a regulated market is sought in a Member State other than the home Member State, only the central competent administrative authority designated by each Member State shall be entitled to approve the prospectus.

2. Member States may allow their competent authority or authorities to delegate tasks. Except for delegation of the publication on the Internet of approved prospectuses and the filing of prospectuses as mentioned in Article 14, any delegation of tasks relating to the obligations provided for in this Directive and in its implementing measures shall be reviewed, in accordance with Article 31 by 31 December 2008, and shall end on 31 December 2011. Any delegation of tasks to entities other than the authorities referred to in paragraph 1 shall be made in a specific manner stating the tasks to be undertaken and the conditions under which they are to be carried out.

These conditions shall include a clause obliging the entity in question to act and be organised in such a manner as to avoid conflict of interest and so that information obtained from carrying out the delegated tasks is not used unfairly or to prevent competition. In any case, the final responsibility for supervising compliance with this Directive and with its implementing measures and for approving the prospectus shall lie with the competent authority or authorities designated in accordance with paragraph 1.

Member States shall inform the Commission and the competent authorities of other Member States of any arrangements entered into with regard to delegation of tasks, including the precise conditions regulating such delegation.

3. Each competent authority shall have all the powers necessary for the performance of its functions. A competent authority that has received an application for approving a prospectus shall be empowered at least to:

(a) require issuers, offerors or persons asking for admission to trading on a regulated market to include in the prospectus supplementary information, if necessary for investor protection;

(b) require issuers, offerors or persons asking for admission to trading on a regulated market, and the persons that control them or are controlled by them, to provide information and documents;

(c) require auditors and managers of the issuer, offeror or person asking for admission to trading on a regulated market, as well as financial intermediaries commissioned to carry out the offer to the public or ask for admission to trading, to provide information;

(d) suspend a public offer or admission to trading for a maximum of 10 consecutive working days on any single occasion if it has reasonable grounds for suspecting that the provisions of this Directive have been infringed;

(e) prohibit or suspend advertisements for a maximum of 10 consecutive working days on any single occasion if it has reasonable grounds for believing that the provisions of this Directive have been infringed;

(f) prohibit a public offer if it finds that the provisions of this Directive have been infringed or if it has reasonable grounds for suspecting that they would be infringed;

(g) suspend or ask the relevant regulated markets to suspend trading on a regulated market for a maximum of 10 consecutive working days on any single occasion if it has reasonable grounds for believing that the provisions of this Directive have been infringed;

(h) prohibit trading on a regulated market if it finds that the provisions of this Directive have been infringed;

(i) make public the fact that an issuer is failing to comply with its obligations.

Where necessary under national law, the competent authority may ask the relevant judicial authority to decide on the use of the powers referred to in points (d) to (h) above.

4. Each competent authority shall also, once the securities have been admitted to trading on a regulated market, be empowered to:

(a) require the issuer to disclose all material information which may have an effect on the assessment of the securities admitted to trading on regulated markets in order to ensure investor protection or the smooth operation of the market;

(b) suspend or ask the relevant regulated market to suspend the securities from trading if, in its opinion, the issuer's situation is such that trading would be detrimental to investors' interests;

(c) ensure that issuers whose securities are traded on regulated markets comply with the obligations provided for in Articles 102 and 103 of Directive 2001/34/EC and that equivalent information is provided to investors and equivalent treatment is granted by the issuer to all securities holders who are in the same position, in all Member States where the offer to the public is made or the securities are admitted to trading;

(d) carry out on-site inspections in its territory in accordance with national law, in order to verify compliance with the provisions of this Directive and its implementing measures. Where necessary under national law, the competent authority or authorities may use this power by applying to the relevant judicial authority and/or in cooperation with other authorities.

5. Paragraphs 1 to 4 shall be without prejudice to the possibility for a Member State to make separate legal and administrative arrangements for overseas European territories for whose external relations that Member State is responsible.

Article 22

Professional secrecy and cooperation between authorities

1. The obligation of professional secrecy shall apply to all persons who work or have worked for the competent authority and for entities to which competent authorities may have delegated certain tasks. Information covered by professional secrecy may not be disclosed to any other person or authority except in accordance with provisions laid down by law.

2. Competent authorities of Member States shall cooperate with each other whenever necessary for the purpose of carrying out their duties and making use of their powers. Competent authorities shall render assistance to competent authorities of other Member States. In particular, they shall exchange information and cooperate when an issuer has more than one home competent authority because of its various classes of securities, or where the approval of a prospectus has been transferred to the competent authority of another Member State pursuant to Article 13(5). They shall also closely cooperate when requiring suspension or prohibition of trading for securities traded in various Member States in order to ensure a level playing field between trading venues and protection of investors. Where appropriate, the competent authority of the host Member State may request the assistance of the competent authority of the home Member State from the stage at which the case is scrutinised, in particular as regards a new type or rare forms of securities. The competent authority of the home Member State may ask for information from the competent authority of the host Member State on any items specific to the relevant market.

Without prejudice to Article 21, the competent authorities of Member States may consult with operators of regulated markets as necessary and, in particular, when deciding to suspend, or to ask a regulated market to suspend or prohibit trading.

3. Paragraph 1 shall not prevent the competent authorities from exchanging confidential information. Information thus exchanged shall be covered by the obligation of professional secrecy, to which the persons employed or formerly employed by the competent authorities receiving the information are subject.

Article 23

Precautionary measures

1. Where the competent authority of the host Member State finds that irregularities have been committed by the issuer or by the financial institutions in charge of the public offer or that breaches have been committed of the obligations attaching to the issuer by reason of the fact that the securities are admitted to trading on a regulated market, it shall refer these findings to the competent authority of the home Member State.

2. If, despite the measures taken by the competent authority of the home Member State or because such measures prove inadequate, the issuer or the financial institution in charge of the public offer persists in breaching the relevant legal or regulatory provisions, the competent authority of the host Member State, after informing the competent authority of the home Member State, shall take all the appropriate measures in order to protect investors. The Commission shall be informed of such measures at the earliest opportunity.

CHAPTER VII

IMPLEMENTING MEASURES

Article 24

Committee procedure

1. The Commission shall be assisted by the European Securities Committee, instituted by Decision 2001/528/EC (hereinafter referred to as 'the Committee').

2. Where reference is made to this paragraph, Articles 5 and 7 of Decision 1999/468/EC shall apply, having regard to the provisions of Article 8 thereof and provided that the implementing measures adopted in accordance with this procedure do not modify the essential provisions of this Directive.

The period laid down in Article 5(6) of Decision 1999/468/EC shall be set at three months.

3. The Committee shall adopt its rules of procedure.

4. Without prejudice to the implementing measures already adopted, on the expiry of a four-year period following the entry into force of this Directive the application of its provisions providing for the adoption of technical rules and decisions in accordance with the procedure referred to in paragraph 2 shall be suspended. On a proposal from the Commission, the European Parliament and the Council may renew the provisions concerned in accordance with the procedure laid down in Article 251 of the Treaty and, to that end, shall review them prior to the expiry of the four-year period.

Article 25

Sanctions

1. Without prejudice to the right of Member States to impose criminal sanctions and without prejudice to their civil liability regime, Member States shall ensure, in conformity with their national law, that the appropriate administrative measures can be taken or administrative sanctions be imposed against the persons responsible, where the provisions adopted in the implementation of this Directive have not been complied with. Member States shall ensure that these measures are effective, proportionate and dissuasive.

2. Member States shall provide that the competent authority may disclose to the public every measure or sanction that has been imposed for infringement of the provisions adopted pursuant to this Directive, unless the disclosure would seriously jeopardise the financial markets or cause disproportionate damage to the parties involved.

Article 26

Right of appeal

Member States shall ensure that decisions taken pursuant to laws, regulations and administrative provisions adopted in accordance with this Directive are subject to the right to appeal to the courts.

CHAPTER VIII

TRANSITIONAL AND FINAL PROVISIONS

Article 27

Amendments

With effect from the date set out in Article 29, Directive 2001/34/EC is hereby amended as follows:

1. Articles 3, 20 to 41, 98 to 101, 104 and 108(2)(c)(ii) shall be deleted;
2. in Article 107(3), the first subparagraph shall be deleted;
3. in Article 108(2)(a), the words 'the conditions of establishment, the control and circulation of listing particulars to be published for admission' shall be deleted;
4. Annex I shall be deleted.

Article 28

Repeal

With effect from the date indicated in Article 29, Directive 89/298/EEC shall be repealed. References to the repealed Directive shall be construed as references to this Directive.

Article 29

Transposition

Member States shall bring into force the laws, regulations and administrative provisions necessary to comply with this Directive not later than 1 July 2005. They shall forthwith inform the Commission thereof. When Member States adopt those measures they shall contain a reference to this Directive or shall be accompanied by such a reference on the occasion of their official publication. The methods for making such reference shall be laid down by Member States.

Article 30

Transitional provision

1. Issuers which are incorporated in a third country and whose securities have already been admitted to trading on a regulated market shall choose their competent authority in accordance with Article 2(1)(m)(iii) and notify their decision to the competent authority of their chosen home Member State by 31 December 2005.

2. By way of derogation from Article 3, Member States which have used the exemption in Article 5(a) of Directive 89/298/EEC may continue to allow credit institutions or other financial institutions equivalent to credit institutions which are not covered by Article 1(2)(j) of this Directive to offer debt securities or other transferable securities equivalent to debt securities issued in a continuous or repeated manner within their territory for five years following the date of entry into force of this Directive.

3. By way of derogation from Article 29, the Federal Republic of Germany shall comply with Article 21(1) by 31 December 2008.

Article 31

Review

Five years after the date of entry into force of this Directive, the Commission shall make an assessment of the application of this Directive and present a report to the European Parliament and the Council, accompanied where appropriate by proposals for its review.

Article 32

Entry into force

This Directive shall enter into force on the day of its publication in the *Official Journal of the European Union*.

Article 33

Addressees

This Directive is addressed to the Member States.

Done at Brussels, 4 November 2003.

For the European Parliament	*For the Council*
The President	*The President*
P. COX	G. ALEMANNO

ANNEX I

PROSPECTUS

I. **Summary**

The summary shall provide in a few pages the most important information included in the prospectus, covering at least the following items:

A. identity of directors, senior management, advisers and auditors

B. offer statistics and expected timetable

C. key information concerning selected financial data; capitalisation and indebtedness; reasons for the offer and use of proceeds; risk factors

D. information concerning the issuer
- history and development of the issuer
- business overview

E. operating and financial review and prospects
- research and development, patents and licences, etc.
- trends

F. directors, senior management and employees

G. major shareholders and related-party transactions

H. financial information
- consolidated statement and other financial information
- significant changes

I. details of the offer and admission to trading
- offer and admission to trading
- plan for distribution
- markets
- selling shareholders
- dilution (equity securities only)
- expenses of the issue

J. additional information
- share capital
- memorandum and articles of association
- documents on display

II. **Identity of directors, senior management, advisers and auditors**

The purpose is to identify the company representatives and other individuals involved in the company's offer or admission to trading; these are the persons responsible for drawing up the prospectus as required by Article 5 of the Directive and those responsible for auditing the financial statements.

III. **Offer statistics and expected timetable**

The purpose is to provide key information regarding the conduct of any offer and the identification of important dates relating to that offer.

A. Offer statistics

B. Method and expected timetable

IV. **Key information**

The purpose is to summarise key information about the company's financial condition, capitalisation and risk factors. If the financial statements included in the document are restated to reflect material changes in the company's group structure or accounting policies, the selected financial data must also be restated.

A. Selected financial data

B. Capitalisation and indebtedness

C. Reasons for the offer and use of proceeds

D. Risk factors

V. **Information on the company**

The purpose is to provide information about the company's business operations, the products it makes or the services it provides, and the factors which affect the business. It is also intended to provide information regarding the adequacy and suitability of the company's properties, plant and equipment, as well as its plans for future capacity increases or decreases.

A. History and development of the company

B. Business overview

C. Organisational structure

D. Property, plant and equipment

VI. **Operating and financial review and prospects**

The purpose is to provide the management's explanation of factors that have affected the company's financial condition and results of operations for the historical periods covered by the financial statements, and management's assessment of factors and trends which are expected to have a material effect on the company's financial condition and results of operations in future periods.

A. Operating results

B. Liquidity and capital resources

C. Research and development, patents and licences, etc.

D. Trends

VII. **Directors, senior management and employees**

The purpose is to provide information concerning the company's directors and managers that will allow investors to assess their experience, qualifications and levels of remuneration, as well as their relationship with the company.

A. Directors and senior management

B. Remuneration

C. Board practices

D. Employees

E. Share ownership

VIII. **Major shareholders and related-party transactions**

The purpose is to provide information regarding the major shareholders and others that may control or have an influence on the company. It also provides information regarding transactions the company has entered into with persons affiliated with the company and whether the terms of such transactions are fair to the company.

A. Major shareholders

B. Related-party transactions

C. Interests of experts and advisers

IX. **Financial information**

The purpose is to specify which financial statements must be included in the document, as well as the periods to be covered, the age of the financial statements and other information of a financial nature. The accounting and auditing principles that will be accepted for use in preparation and audit of the financial statements will be determined in accordance with international accounting and auditing standards.

A. Consolidated statements and other financial information

B. Significant changes

X. **Details of the offer and admission to trading details**

The purpose is to provide information regarding the offer and the admission to trading of securities, the plan for distribution of the securities and related matters.

A. Offer and admission to trading

B. Plan for distribution

C. Markets

D. Holders of securities who are selling

E. Dilution (for equity securities only)

F. Expenses of the issue

XI. **Additional information**

The purpose is to provide information, most of which is of a statutory nature, that is not covered elsewhere in the prospectus.

A. Share capital

B. Memorandum and articles of association

C. Material contracts

D. Exchange controls

E. Taxation

F. Dividends and paying agents

G. Statement by experts

H. Documents on display

I. Subsidiary information

ANNEX II

REGISTRATION DOCUMENT

I. **Identity of directors, senior management, advisers and auditors**

The purpose is to identify the company representatives and other individuals involved in the company's offer or admission to trading; these are the persons responsible for drawing up the prospectus and those responsible for auditing the financial statements.

II. **Key information about the issuer**

The purpose is to summarise key information about the company's financial condition, capitalisation and risk factors. If the financial statements included in the document are restated to reflect material changes in the company's group structure or accounting policies, the selected financial data must also be restated.

A. Selected financial data

B. Capitalisation and indebtedness

C. Risk factors

III. **Information on the company**

The purpose is to provide information about the company's business operations, the products it makes or the services it provides and the factors which affect the business. It is also intended to provide information regarding the adequacy and suitability of the company's properties, plants and equipment, as well as its plans for future capacity increases or decreases.

A. History and development of the company

B. Business overview

C. Organisational structure

D. Property, plants and equipment

IV. **Operating and financial review and prospects**

The purpose is to provide the management's explanation of factors that have affected the company's financial condition and results of operations for the historical periods covered by the financial statements, and management's assessment of factors and trends which are expected to have a material effect on the company's financial condition and results of operations in future periods.

A. Operating results

B. Liquidity and capital resources

C. Research and development, patents and licences, etc.

D. Trends

V. **Directors, senior management and employees**

The purpose is to provide information concerning the company's directors and managers that will allow investors to assess their experience, qualifications and levels of remuneration, as well as their relationship with the company.

A. Directors and senior management

B. Remuneration

C. Board practices

D. Employees

E. Share ownership

VI. **Major shareholders and related-party transactions**

The purpose is to provide information regarding the major shareholders and others that may control or have an influence on the company. It also provides information regarding transactions the company has entered into with persons affiliated with the company and whether the terms of such transactions are fair to the company.

A. Major shareholders

B. Related-party transactions

C. Interests of experts and advisers

VII. **Financial information**

The purpose is to specify which financial statements must be included in the document, as well as the periods to be covered, the age of the financial statements and other information of a financial nature. The accounting and auditing principles that will be accepted for use in preparation and audit of the financial statements will be determined in accordance with international accounting and auditing standards.

A. Consolidated statements and other financial information

B. Significant changes

VIII. **Additional information**

The purpose is to provide information, most of which is of a statutory nature, that is not covered elsewhere in the prospectus.

A. Share capital

B. Memorandum and articles of association

C. Material contracts

D. Statement by experts

E. Documents on display

F. Subsidiary information

ANNEX III

SECURITIES NOTE

I. **Identity of directors, senior management, advisers and auditors**

The purpose is to identify the company representatives and other individuals involved in the company's offer or admission to trading; these are the persons responsible for drawing up the prospectus and those responsible for auditing the financial statements.

II. **Offer statistics and expected timetable**

The purpose is to provide key information regarding the conduct of any offer and the identification of important dates relating to that offer.

A. Offer statistics

B. Method and expected timetable

III. **Key information about the issuer**

The purpose is to summarise key information about the company's financial condition, capitalisation and risk factors. If the financial statements included in the document are restated to reflect material changes in the company's group structure or accounting policies, the selected financial data must also be restated.

A. Capitalisation and indebtedness

B. Reasons for the offer and use of proceeds

C. Risk factors

IV. **Interests of experts**

The purpose is to provide information regarding transactions the company has entered into with experts or advisers employed on a contingent basis.

V. **Details of the offer and admission to trading**

The purpose is to provide information regarding the offer and the admission to trading of securities, the plan for distribution of the securities and related matters.

A. Offer and admission to trading

B. Plan for distribution

C. Markets

D. Selling securities holders

E. Dilution (for equity securities only)

F. Expenses of the issue

VI. **Additional information**

The purpose is to provide information, most of which is of a statutory nature, that is not covered elsewhere in the prospectus.

A. Exchange controls

B. Taxation

C. Dividends and paying agents

D. Statement by experts

E. Documents on display

ANNEX IV

SUMMARY NOTE

The summary note shall provide in a few pages the most important information included in the prospectus, covering at least the following items:

- identity of directors, senior management, advisers and auditors
- offer statistics and expected timetable
- key information concerning selected financial data; capitalisation and indebtedness; reasons for the offer and use of proceeds; risk factors
- information concerning the issuer
  - history and development of the issuer
  - business overview
- operating and financial review and prospects
  - research and development, patents and licences, etc.
  - trends
- directors, senior management and employees
- major shareholders and related-party transactions
- financial information
  - consolidated statement and other financial information
  - significant changes
- details on the offer and admission to trading
  - offer and admission to trading
  - plan for distribution
  - markets
  - selling shareholders
  - dilution (for equity securities only)
  - expenses of the issue
- additional information
  - share capital
  - memorandum and articles of incorporation
  - documents available for inspection

Annex II

Commission Regulation (EC) No 809/2004 of 29 April 2004 implementing the Prospectus Directive as regards information contained in prospectuses as well as the format, incorporation by reference and publication of such prospectuses and dissemination of advertisements (the Prospectus Regulation)

►B

COMMISSION REGULATION (EC) No 809/2004

of 29 April 2004

implementing Directive 2003/71/EC of the European Parliament and of the Council as regards information contained in prospectuses as well as the format, incorporation by reference and publication of such prospectuses and dissemination of advertisements

(Text with EEA relevance)

(OJ L 215, 16.6.2004, p. 3)

Amended by:

		Official Journal		
		No	page	date
►M1	Commission Regulation (EC) No 1787/2006 of 4 December 2006	L 337	17	5.12.2006
►M2	Commission Regulation (EC) No 211/2007 of 27 February 2007	L 61	24	28.2.2007

▼B

COMMISSION REGULATION (EC) No 809/2004

of 29 April 2004

implementing Directive 2003/71/EC of the European Parliament and of the Council as regards information contained in prospectuses as well as the format, incorporation by reference and publication of such prospectuses and dissemination of advertisements

(Text with EEA relevance)

THE COMMISSION OF THE EUROPEAN COMMUNITIES,

Having regard to the Treaty establishing the European Community,

Having regard to Directive 2003/71/EC of the European Parliament and the Council of 4 November 2003 on the prospectus to be published when securities are offered to the public or admitted to trading and amending Directive 2001/34/EC [1], and in particular Article 5(5), Article 7, Article 10(4), Article 11(3), Article 14(8) and Article 15(7) thereof,

After consulting the Committee of European Securities Regulators (CESR) [2] for technical advice,

Whereas:

(1) Directive 2003/71/EC lays down principles to be observed when drawing up prospectuses. These principles need to be supplemented as far as the information to be given therein, the format and aspects of publication, the information to be incorporated by reference in a prospectus and dissemination of advertisements are concerned.

(2) Depending on the type of issuer and securities involved, a typology of minimum information requirements should be established corresponding to those schedules that are in practice most frequently applied. The schedules should be based on the information items required in the IOSCO 'Disclosure Standards for cross-border offering and initial listings' (part I) and on the existing schedules of Directive 2001/34/EC of the European Parliament and of the Council of 28 May on the admission of securities to official stock exchange listing and on information to be published on those securities [3].

(3) Information given by the issuer, the offeror or the person asking for admission to trading on a regulated market, according to this Regulation, should be subject to European Union provisions relating to data protection.

(4) Care should be taken that, in those cases where a prospectus is composed of separate documents, duplication of information is avoided; to this end separate detailed schedules for the registration document and for the securities note, adapted to the particular type of issuer and the securities concerned, should be laid down in order to cover each type of security.

(5) The issuer, the offeror or the person asking for admission to trading on a regulated market are entitled to include in a prospectus or base prospectus additional information going beyond the information items provided for in the schedules and building blocks. Any additional information provided should be

(1) 1 OJ L 345, 31.12.2003, p. 64.
(2) 2 CESR was established by Commission Decision 2001/527/EC (OJ L 191, 13.7.2001, p. 43).
(3) OJ L 184, 6.7.2001, p. 1. Directive as last amended by Directive 2003/71/EC.

▼B

appropriate to the type of securities or the nature of the issuer involved.

(6) In most cases, given the variety of issuers, the types of securities, the involvement or not of a third party as a guarantor, whether or not there is a listing etc, one single schedule will not give the appropriate information for an investor to make his investment decision. Therefore the combination of various schedules should be possible. A non exhaustive table of combinations, providing for different possible combinations of schedules and 'building blocks' for most of the different type of securities, should be set up in order to assist issuers when drafting their prospectus.

(7) The share registration document schedule should be applicable to shares and other transferable securities equivalent to shares but also to other securities giving access to the capital of the issuer by way of conversion or exchange. In the latter case this schedule should not be used where the underlying shares to be delivered have already been issued before the issuance of the securities giving access to the capital of the issuer; however this schedule should be used where the underlying shares to be delivered have already been issued but are not yet admitted to trading on a regulated market.

(8) Voluntary disclosure of profit forecasts in a share registration document should be presented in a consistent and comparable manner and accompanied by a statement prepared by independent accountants or auditors. This information should not be confused with the disclosure of known trends or other factual data with material impact on the issuers' prospects. Moreover, they should provide an explanation of any changes in disclosure policy relating to profit forecasts when supplementing a prospectus or drafting a new prospectus.

(9) Pro forma financial information is needed in case of significant gross change, i. e. a variation of more than 25 % relative to one or more indicators of the size of the issuer's business, in the situation of an issuer due to a particular transaction, with the exception of those situations where merger accounting is required.

(10) The schedule for the share securities note should be applicable to any class of share since it considers information regarding a description of the rights attached to the securities and the procedure for the exercise of any rights attached to the securities.

(11) Some debt securities such as structured bonds incorporate certain elements of a derivative security, therefore additional disclosure requirements related to the derivative component in the interest payment should be included in the securities note schedule for debt securities.

(12) The additional 'building block' related to guarantee should apply to any obligation in relation to any kind of security.

(13) The asset backed securities registration document should not apply to mortgage bonds as provided for in Article 5(4)(b) of Directive 2003/71/EC and other covered bonds. The same should apply for the asset backed securities additional 'building block' that has to be combined with the securities note for debt securities.

(14) Wholesale investors should be able to make their investment decision on other elements than those taken into consideration by retail investors. Therefore a differentiated content of prospectus is necessary for debt and derivative securities aimed at those investors who purchase debt or derivative securities with a denomination per unit of at least EUR 50 000 or a denomination in another currency provided that the value of such

▼B

minimum denomination when converted to EURO amounts to at least EURO 50 000.

(15) In the context of depository receipts, emphasis should be put on the issuer of the underlying shares and not on the issuer of the depository receipt. Where there is legal recourse to the depository over and above a breach of its fiduciary or agency duties, the risk factors section in the prospectus should contain full information on this fact and on the circumstances of such recourse. Where a prospectus is drafted as a tripartite document (i.e. registration document, securities note and summary), the registration document should be limited to the information on the depository.

(16) The banks registration document schedule should be applicable to banks from third countries which do not fall under the definition of credit institution provided for in Article 1(1)(a) of Directive 2000/12/EC of the European Parliament and of the Council of 20 March 2000 relating to the taking up and pursuit of the business of credit institutions ([1]) but have their registered office in a state which is a member of the OECD.

(17) If a special purpose vehicle issues debt and derivative securities guaranteed by a bank, it should not use the banks registration document schedule.

(18) The schedule 'securities note for derivative securities' should be applicable to securities which are not covered by the other schedules and building blocks. The scope of this schedule is determined by reference to the other two generic categories of shares and debt securities. In order to provide a clear and comprehensive explanation to help investors understand how the value of their investment is affected by the value of the underlying, issuers should be able to use appropriate examples on a voluntary basis. For instance, for some complex derivatives securities, examples might be the most effective way to explain the nature of those securities.

(19) The additional information 'building block' on the underlying share for certain equity securities should be added to the securities note for debt securities or substitute the item referring to 'information required in respect of the underlying' of the schedule securities note for derivative securities, depending on the characteristics of the securities being issued.

(20) Member States and their regional or local authorities are outside the scope of Directive 2003/71/EC. However, they may choose to produce a prospectus in accordance with this Directive. Third country sovereign issuers and their regional or local authorities are not outside the scope of Directive 2003/71/EC and are obliged to produce a prospectus if they wish to make a public offer of securities in the Community or wish their securities to be admitted to trading on a regulated market. For those cases, particular schedules should be used for the securities issued by States, their regional and local authorities and by public international bodies.

(21) A base prospectus and its final terms should contain the same information as a prospectus. All the general principles applicable to a prospectus are applicable also to the final terms. Nevertheless, where the final terms are not included in the base prospectus they do not have to be approved by the competent authority.

(22) For some categories of issuers the competent authority should be entitled to require adapted information going beyond the information items included in the schedules and building blocks

([1]) OJ L 126, 26.5.2000, p. 1. Directive as last amended by the 2003 Act of Accession.

▼B

because of the particular nature of the activities carried out by those issuers. A precise and restrictive list of issuers for which adapted information may be required is necessary. The adapted information requirements for each category of issuers included in this list should be appropriate and proportionate to the type of business involved. The Committee of European Securities Regulators could actively try to reach convergence on these information requirements within the Community. Inclusion of new categories in the list should be restricted to those cases where this can be duly justified.

(23) In the case of completely new types of securities which cannot be covered by the existing schedules or any of their combinations, the issuer should still have the possibility to apply for approval for a prospectus. In those cases he should be able to discuss the content of the information to be provided with the competent authority. The prospectus approved by the competent authority under those circumstances should benefit from the single passport established in Directive 2003/71/EC. The competent authority should always try to find similarities and make use as much as possible of existing schedules. Any additional information requirements should be proportionate and appropriate to the type of securities involved.

(24) Certain information items required in the schedules and building blocks or equivalent information items are not relevant to a particular security and thus may be inapplicable in some specific cases; in those cases the issuer should have the possibility to omit this information.

(25) The enhanced flexibility in the articulation of the base prospectus with its final terms compared to a single issue prospectus should not hamper the easy access to material information for investors.

(26) With respect to base prospectuses, it should be set out in an easily identifiable manner which kind of information will have to be included as final terms. This requirement should be able to be satisfied in a number of different ways, for example, if the base prospectus contains blanks for any information to be inserted in the final terms or if the base prospectus contains a list of the missing information.

(27) Where a single document includes more than one base prospectus and each base prospectus would require approval by a different home competent authority, the respective competent authorities should act in cooperation and, where appropriate, transfer the approval of the prospectus in accordance with Article 13(5) of Directive 2003/71/EC, so that the approval by only one competent authority is sufficient for the entire document.

(28) Historical financial information as required in the schedules should principally be presented in accordance with Regulation (EC) No 1606/2002 of the European Parliament and of the Council of 19 July 2002 on the application of international accounting standard [1] or Member States' accounting standards. Specific requirements should, however, be laid down for third country issuers.

(29) For the purposes of publication of the document referred to in Article 10 of Directive 2003/71/EC, issuers should be allowed to choose the method of publication they consider adequate among those referred to in Article 14 of that Directive. In selecting the method of publication they should consider the objective of the document and that it should permit investors a fast and cost-efficient access to that information.

(1) OJ L 243, 11.9.2002, p. 1.

▼B

(30) The aim of incorporation by reference, as provided for in Article 11 of Directive 2003/71/EC, is to simplify and reduce the costs of drafting a prospectus; however this aim should not be achieved to the detriment of other interests the prospectus is meant to protect. For instance, the fact that the natural location of the information required is the prospectus, and that the information should be presented in an easily and comprehensible form, should also be considered. Particular attention should be granted to the language used for information incorporated by reference and its consistency with the prospectus itself. Information incorporated by reference may refer to historical data, however if this information is no more relevant due to material change, this should be clearly stated in the prospectus and the updated information should also be provided.

(31) Where a prospectus is published in electronic form, additional safety measures compared to traditional means of publication, using best practices available, are necessary in order to maintain the integrity of the information, to avoid manipulation or modification from unauthorised persons, to avoid altering its comprehensibility and to escape from possible adverse consequences from different approaches on offer of securities to the public in third countries.

(32) The newspaper chosen for the publication of a prospectus should have a wide area of distribution and a high circulation.

(33) A home Member State should be able to require publication of a notice stating how the prospectus has been made available and where it can be obtained by the public. Where a home Member State requires publication of notices in its legislation, the content of such a notice should be kept to the necessary items information to avoid duplication with the summary. These home Member States may also require that an additional notice in relation to the final terms of a base prospectus is to be published.

(34) In order to facilitate centralising useful information for investors a mention should be included in the list of approved prospectuses posted in the web-site of the competent authority of the home Member State, indicating how a prospectus has been published and where it can be obtained.

(35) Member States should ensure effective compliance of advertising rules concerning public offers and admission to trading on a regulated market. Proper co-ordination between competent authorities should be achieved in cross-border offerings or cross-border admission to trading.

(36) In view of the interval between the entry into force of Regulation (EC) No 1606/2002 and the production of certain of its effects, a number of transitional arrangements for historical financial information to be included in a prospectus should be provided for, in order to prevent excessive burden on issuers and enable them to adapt the way they prepare and present historical financial information within a reasonable period of time after the entry into force of Directive 2003/71/EC.

(37) The obligation to restate in a prospectus historical financial information according to Regulation (EC) N° 1606/2002 does not cover securities with a denomination per unit of at least EUR 50 000; consequently such transitional arrangements are not necessary for such securities.

(38) For reasons of coherence it is appropriate that this Regulation applies from the date of transposition of Directive 2003/71/EC.

(39) Whereas the measures provided for in this Regulation are in accordance with the opinion of the European Securities Committee,

▼B

HAS ADOPTED THIS REGULATION:

CHAPTER I

SUBJECT MATTER AND DEFINITIONS

Article 1

Subject matter

This Regulation lays down:

1. the format of prospectus referred to in Article 5 of Directive 2003/71/EC;
2. the minimum information requirements to be included in a prospectus provided for in Article 7 of Directive 2003/71/EC;
3. the method of publication referred to in Article 10 of Directive 2003/71/EC;
4. the modalities according to which information can be incorporated by reference in a prospectus provided for in Article 11 of Directive 2003/71/EC;
5. the publication methods of a prospectus in order to ensure that a prospectus is publicly available according to Article 14 of Directive 2003/71/EC;
6. the methods of dissemination of advertisements referred to in Article 15 of Directive 2003/71/EC.

Article 2

Definitions

For the purposes of this Regulation, the following definitions shall apply in addition to those laid down in Directive 2003/71/EC:

1. 'schedule' means a list of minimum information requirements adapted to the particular nature of the different types of issuers and/or the different securities involved;
2. 'building block' means a list of additional information requirements, not included in one of the schedules, to be added to one or more schedules, as the case may be, depending on the type of instrument and/or transaction for which a prospectus or base prospectus is drawn up;
3. 'risk factors' means a list of risks which are specific to the situation of the issuer and/or the securities and which are material for taking investment decisions;
4. 'special purpose vehicle' means an issuer whose objects and purposes are primarily the issue of securities;
5. 'asset backed securities' means securities which:

   (a) represent an interest in assets, including any rights intended to assure servicing, or the receipt or timeliness of receipts by holders of assets of amounts payable there under;

   or

   (b) are secured by assets and the terms of which provide for payments which relate to payments or reasonable projections of payments calculated by reference to identified or identifiable assets;

▼B

6. 'umbrella collective investment undertaking' means a collective investment undertaking invested in one or more collective investment undertakings, the asset of which is composed of separate class(es) or designation(s) of securities;

7. 'property collective investment undertaking' means a collective investment undertaking whose investment objective is the participation in the holding of property in the long term;

8. 'public international body' means a legal entity of public nature established by an international treaty between sovereign States and of which one or more Member States are members;

9. 'advertisement' means announcements:

   (a) relating to an specific offer to the public of securities or to an admission to trading on a regulated market;

   and

   (b) aiming to specifically promote the potential subscription or acquisition of securities.

10. 'profit forecast' means a form of words which expressly states or by implication indicates a figure or a minimum or maximum figure for the likely level of profits or losses for the current financial period and/or financial periods subsequent to that period, or contains data from which a calculation of such a figure for future profits or losses may be made, even if no particular figure is mentioned and the word 'profit' is not used.

11. 'profit estimate' means a profit forecast for a financial period which has expired and for which results have not yet been published.

12. 'regulated information' means all information which the issuer, or any person who has applied for the admission of securities to trading on a regulated market without the issuer's consent, is required to disclose under Directive 2001/34/EC or under Article 6 of Directive 2003/6/EC of the European Parliament and of the Council [1].

CHAPTER II

MINIMUM INFORMATION

Article 3

Minimum information to be included in a prospectus

A prospectus shall be drawn up by using one or a combination of the following schedules and building blocks set out in Articles 4 to 20, according to the combinations for various types of securities provided for in Article 21.

A prospectus shall contain the information items required in Annexes I to XVII depending on the type of issuer and securities involved, provided for in the schedules and building blocks set out in Articles 4 to 20. ►M2 Subject to Article 4a(1), a competent authority shall not request that a prospectus contain information items which are not included in Annexes I to XVII. ◄

In order to ensure conformity with the obligation referred to in Article 5 (1) of Directive 2003/71/EC, the competent authority of the home Member State, when approving a prospectus in accordance with Article 13 of that Directive, may require that the information provided by the issuer, the offeror or the person asking for admission

(1) OJ L 96, 12.4.2003, p. 16

▼B

to trading on a regulated market be completed, for each of the information items, on a case by case basis.

Article 4

Share registration document schedule

1 For the share registration document information shall be given in accordance with the schedule set out in Annex I.

2 The schedule set out in paragraph 1 shall apply to the following:

1. shares and other transferable securities equivalent to shares;

2. other securities which comply with the following conditions:

   (a) they can be converted or exchanged into shares or other transferable securities equivalent to shares, at the issuer's or at the investor's discretion, or on the basis of the conditions established a the moment of the issue, or give, in any other way, the possibility to acquire shares or other transferable securities equivalent to shares;

   and

   (b) provided that these shares or other transferable securities equivalent to shares are or will be issued by the issuer of the security and are not yet traded on a regulated market or an equivalent market outside the Community at the time of the approval of the prospectus covering the securities, and that the underlying shares or other transferable securities equivalent to shares can be delivered with physical settlement.

▼M2

Article 4a

Share registration document schedule in cases of complex financial history or significant financial commitment

1. Where the issuer of a security covered by Article 4(2) has a complex financial history, or has made a significant financial commitment, and in consequence the inclusion in the registration document of certain items of financial information relating to an entity other than the issuer is necessary in order to satisfy the obligation laid down in Article 5(1) of Directive 2003/71/EC, those items of financial information shall be deemed to relate to the issuer. The competent authority of the home Member State shall in such cases request that the issuer, the offeror or the person asking for admission to trading include those items of information in the registration document.

Those items of financial information may include pro forma information prepared in accordance with Annex II. In this context, where the issuer has made a significant financial commitment any such pro forma information shall illustrate the anticipated effects of the transaction that the issuer has agreed to undertake, and references in Annex II to 'the transaction' shall be read accordingly.

2. The competent authority shall base any request pursuant to paragraph 1 on the requirements set out in item 20.1 of Annex I as regards the content of financial information and the applicable accounting and auditing principles, subject to any modification which is appropriate in view of any of the following factors:

(a) the nature of the securities;

(b) the nature and range of information already included in the prospectus, and the existence of financial information relating to

▼M2

an entity other than the issuer in a form that might be included in a prospectus without modification;

(c) the facts of the case, including the economic substance of the transactions by which the issuer has acquired or disposed of its business undertaking or any part of it, and the specific nature of that undertaking;

(d) the ability of the issuer to obtain financial information relating to another entity with reasonable effort.

Where, in the individual case, the obligation laid down in Article 5(1) of Directive 2003/71/EC may be satisfied in more than one way, preference shall be given to the way that is the least costly or onerous.

3. Paragraph 1 is without prejudice to the responsibility under national law of any other person, including the persons referred to in Article 6(1) of Directive 2003/71/EC, for the information contained in the prospectus. In particular, those persons shall be responsible for the inclusion in the registration document of any items of information requested by the competent authority pursuant to paragraph 1.

4. For the purposes of paragraph 1, an issuer shall be treated as having a complex financial history if all of the following conditions apply:

(a) its entire business undertaking at the time that the prospectus is drawn up is not accurately represented in the historical financial information which it is required to provide under item 20.1 of Annex I;

(b) that inaccuracy will affect the ability of an investor to make an informed assessment as mentioned in Article 5(1) of Directive 2003/71/EC; and

(c) information relating to its business undertaking that is necessary for an investor to make such an assessment is included in financial information relating to another entity.

5. For the purposes of paragraph 1, an issuer shall be treated as having made a significant financial commitment if it has entered into a binding agreement to undertake a transaction which, on completion, is likely to give rise to a significant gross change.

In this context, the fact that an agreement makes completion of the transaction subject to conditions, including approval by a regulatory authority, shall not prevent that agreement from being treated as binding if it is reasonably certain that those conditions will be fulfilled.

In particular, an agreement shall be treated as binding where it makes the completion of the transaction conditional on the outcome of the offer of the securities that are the subject matter of the prospectus or, in the case of a proposed takeover, if the offer of securities that are the subject matter of the prospectus has the objective of funding that takeover.

6. For the purposes of paragraph 5 of this Article, and of item 20.2 of Annex I, a significant gross change means a variation of more than 25 %, relative to one or more indicators of the size of the issuer's business, in the situation of an issuer.

▼B

Article 5

Pro forma financial information building block

For pro forma financial information, information shall be given in accordance with the building block set out in Annex II.

▼B

Pro forma financial information should be preceded by an introductory explanatory paragraph that states in clear terms the purpose of including this information in the prospectus.

Article 6

Share securities note schedule

1 For the share securities note information is necessary to be given in accordance with the schedule set out in Annex III.

2 The schedule shall apply to shares and other transferable securities equivalent to shares.

Article 7

Debt and derivative securities registration document schedule for securities with a denomination per unit of less than EUR 50 000

For the debt and derivative securities registration document concerning securities which are not covered in Article 4 with a denomination per unit of less than EUR 50 000 or, where there is no individual denomination, securities that can only be acquired on issue for less than EUR 50 000 per security, information shall be given in accordance with the schedule set out in Annex IV.

Article 8

Securities note schedule for debt securities with a denomination per unit of less than EUR 50 000

1 For the securities note for debt securities with a denomination per unit of less than EUR 50 000 information shall be given in accordance with the schedule set out in Annex V.

2 The schedule shall apply to debt where the issuer has an obligation arising on issue to pay the investor 100 % of the nominal value in addition to which there may be also an interest payment.

Article 9

Guarantees building block

For guarantees information shall be given in accordance with the building block set out in Annex VI.

Article 10

Asset backed securities registration document schedule

For the asset backed securities registration document information shall be given in accordance with the schedule set out in Annex VII.

Article 11

Asset backed securities building block

For the additional information building block to the securities note for asset backed securities information shall be given in accordance with the building block set out in Annex VIII.

▼B

Article 12

Debt and derivative securities registration document schedule for securities with a denomination per unit of at least EUR 50 000

For the debt and derivative securities registration document concerning securities which are not covered in Article 4 with a denomination per unit of at least EUR 50 000 or, where there is no individual denomination, securities that can only be acquired on issue for at least EUR 50 000 per security, information shall be given in accordance with the schedule set out in Annex IX.

Article 13

Depository receipts schedule

For depository receipts issued over shares information shall be given in accordance with the schedule set out in Annex X.

Article 14

Banks registration document schedule

1 For the banks registration document for debt and derivative securities and those securities which are not covered by Article 4 information shall be given in accordance with the schedule set out in Annex XI.

2 The schedule set out in paragraph 1 shall apply to credit institutions as defined in point (a) of Article 1(1) of Directive 2000/12/EC as well as to third country credit institutions which do not fall under that definition but have their registered office in a state which is a member of the OECD.

These entities may also use alternatively the registration document schedules provided for under in Articles 7 and 12.

Article 15

Securities note schedule for derivative securities

1 For the securities note for derivative securities information shall be given in accordance with the schedule set out in Annex XII.

2 The schedule shall apply to securities which are not in the scope of application of the other securities note schedules referred to in Articles 6, 8 and 16, including certain securities where the payment and/or delivery obligations are linked to an underlying.

Article 16

Securities note schedule for debt securities with a denomination per unit of at least EUR 50 000

1 For the securities note for debt securities with a denomination per unit of at least EUR 50 000 information shall be given in accordance with the schedule set out in Annex XIII.

2 The schedule shall apply to debt where the issuer has an obligation arising on issue to pay the investor 100 % of the nominal value in addition to which there may be also an interest payment.

▼B

Article 17

Additional information building block on the underlying share

1 For the additional information on the underlying share, the description of the underlying share shall be given in accordance with the building block set out in Annex XIV.

In addition, if the issuer of the underlying share is an entity belonging to the same group, the information required by the schedule referred to in Article 4 shall be given in respect of that issuer.

2 The additional information referred to in the first subparagraph of paragraph 1 shall only apply to those securities which comply with both of the following conditions:

1. they can be converted or exchanged into shares or other transferable securities equivalent to shares, at the issuer's or at the investor's discretion, or on the basis of the conditions established a the moment of the issue or give, in any other way, the possibility to acquire shares or other transferable securities equivalent to shares;

   and

2. provided that these shares or other transferable securities equivalent to shares are or will be issued by the issuer of the security or by an entity belonging to the group of that issuer and are not yet traded on a regulated market or an equivalent market outside the Community at the time of the approval of the prospectus covering the securities, and that the underlying shares or other transferable securities equivalent to shares can be delivered with physical settlement.

Article 18

Registration document schedule for collective investment undertakings of the closed-end type

1 In addition to the information required pursuant to items 1, 2, 3, 4, 5.1, 7, 9.1, 9.2.1, 9.2.3, 10.4, 13, 14, 15, 16, 17.2, 18, 19, 20, 21, 22, 23, 24, 25 of Annex I, for the registration document for securities issued by collective investment undertakings of the closed-end type information shall be given in accordance with the schedule set out in Annex XV.

2 The schedule shall apply to collective investment undertakings of the closed-end type holding a portfolio of assets on behalf of investors that:

1. are recognised by national law in the Member State in which it is incorporated as a collective investment undertaking of the closed end type;

   or

2. do not take or seek to take legal or management control of any of the issuers of its underlying investments. In such a case, legal control and/or participation in the administrative, management or supervisory bodies of the underlying issuer(s) may be taken where such action is incidental to the primary investment objective, necessary for the protection of shareholders and only in circumstances where the collective investment undertaking will not exercise significant management control over the operations of that underlying issuer(s).

▼B

Article 19

Registration document schedule for Member States, third countries and their regional and local authorities

1 For the registration document for securities issued by Member States, third countries and their regional and local authorities information shall be given in accordance with the schedule set out in Annex XVI.

2 The schedule shall apply to all types of securities issued by Member States, third countries and their regional and local authorities.

Article 20

Registration document schedule for public international bodies and for issuers of debt securities guaranteed by a member state of the OECD

1 For the registration document for securities issued by public international bodies and for securities unconditionally and irrevocably guaranteed, on the basis of national legislation, by a state which is member of the OECD information shall be given in accordance with the schedule set out in Annex XVII.

2 The schedule shall apply to:

— all types of securities issued by public international bodies,

— to debt securities unconditionally and irrevocably guaranteed, on the basis of national legislation, by a state which is member of the OECD.

Article 21

Combination of schedules and building blocks

1 The use of the combinations provided for in the table set out in Annex XVIII shall be mandatory when drawing up prospectuses for the types of securities to which those combinations correspond according to this table.

However, for securities not covered by those combinations further combinations may be used.

2 The most comprehensive and stringent registration document schedule, i.e. the most demanding schedule in term of number of information items and the extent of the information included in them, may always be used to issue securities for which a less comprehensive and stringent registration document schedule is provided for, according to the following ranking of schedules:

1. share registration document schedule;

2. debt and derivative securities registration document schedule for securities with a denomination per unit of less than EUR 50 000;

3. debt and derivative securities registration document schedule for securities with a denomination per unit at least EUR 50 000.

Article 22

Minimum information to be included in a base prospectus and its related final terms

1 A base prospectus shall be drawn up by using one or a combination of schedules and building blocks provided for in Articles 4 to 20

▼B

according to the combinations for various types of securities set out in Annex XVIII.

A base prospectus shall contain the information items required in Annexes I to XVII depending on the type of issuer and securities involved, provided for in the schedules and building blocks set out in Articles 4 to 20. A competent authority shall not request that a base prospectus contains information items which are not included in Annexes I to XVII.

In order to ensure conformity with the obligation referred to in Article 5 (1) of Directive 2003/71/EC, the competent authority of the home Member State, when approving a base prospectus in accordance with Article 13 of that Directive, may require that the information provided by the issuer, the offeror or the person asking for admission to trading on a regulated market be completed, for each of the information items, on a case by case basis.

2 The issuer, the offeror or the person asking for admission to trading on a regulated market may omit information items which are not known when the base prospectus is approved and which can only be determined at the time of the individual issue.

3 The use of the combinations provided for in the table in Annex XVIII shall be mandatory when drawing up base prospectuses for the types of securities to which those combinations correspond according to this table.

However, for securities not covered by those combinations further combinations may be used.

4 The final terms attached to a base prospectus shall only contain the information items from the various securities note schedules according to which the base prospectus is drawn up.

5 In addition to the information items set out in the schedules and building blocks referred to in Articles 4 to 20 the following information shall be included in a base prospectus:

1. indication on the information that will be included in the final terms;
2. the method of publication of the final terms; if the issuer is not in a position to determine, at the time of the approval of the prospectus, the method of publication of the final terms, an indication of how the public will be informed about which method will be used for the publication of the final terms;
3. in the case of issues of non equity securities according to point (a) of Article 5(4) of Directive 2003/71/EC, a general description of the programme.

6 Only the following categories of securities may be contained in a base prospectus and its related final terms covering issues of various types of securities:

1. asset backed securities;
2. warrants falling under Article 17;
3. non-equity securities provided for under point (b) of Article 5(4) of Directive 2003/71/EC;
4. all other non-equity securities including warrants with the exception of those mentioned in (2).

In drawing up a base prospectus the issuer, the offeror or the person asking for admission to trading on a regulated market shall clearly segregate the specific information on each of the different securities included in these categories.

7 Where an event envisaged under Article 16(1) of Directive 2003/71/EC occurs between the time that the base prospectus has been approved and the final closing of the offer of each issue of secu-

▼B

rities under the base prospectus or, as the case may be, the time that trading on a regulated market of those securities begins, the issuer, the offeror or the person asking for admission to trading on a regulated market shall publish a supplement prior to the final closing of the offer or the admission of those securities to trading.

Article 23

Adaptations to the minimum information given in prospectuses and base prospectuses

1 Notwithstanding Articles 3 second paragraph and 22(1) second subparagraph, where the issuer's activities fall under one of the categories included in Annex XIX, the competent authority of the home Member State, taking into consideration the specific nature of the activities involved, may ask for adapted information, in addition to the information items included in the schedules and building blocks set out in Articles 4 to 20, including, where appropriate, a valuation or other expert's report on the assets of the issuer, in order to comply with the obligation referred to in Article 5(1) of Directive 2003/71/EC. The competent authority shall forthwith inform the Commission thereof.

In order to obtain the inclusion of a new category in Annex XIX a Member State shall notify its request to the Commission. The Commission shall update this list following the Committee procedure provided for in Article 24 of Directive 2003/71/EC.

2 By way of derogation of Articles 3 to 22, where an issuer, an offeror or a person asking for admission to trading on a regulated market applies for approval of a prospectus or a base prospectus for a security which is not the same but comparable to the various types of securities mentioned in the table of combinations set out in Annex XVIII, the issuer, the offeror or the person asking for admission to trading on a regulated market shall add the relevant information items from another securities note schedule provided for in Articles 4 to 20 to the main securities note schedule chosen. This addition shall be done in accordance with the main characteristics of the securities being offered to the public or admitted to trading on a regulated market.

3 By way of derogation of Articles 3 to 22, where an issuer, an offeror or a person asking for admission to trading on a regulated market applies for approval of a prospectus or a base prospectus for a new type of security, the issuer, the offeror or the person asking for admission to trading on a regulated market shall notify a draft prospectus or base prospectus to the competent authority of the home Member State.

The competent authority shall decide, in consultation with the issuer, the offeror or the person asking for admission to trading on a regulated market, what information shall be included in the prospectus or base prospectus in order to comply with the obligation referred to in Article 5 (1) of Directive 2003/71/EC. The competent authority shall forthwith inform the Commission thereof.

The derogation referred to in the first subparagraph shall only apply in case of a new type of security which has features completely different from the various types of securities mentioned in Annex XVIII, if the characteristics of this new security are such that a combination of the different information items referred to in the schedules and building blocks provided for in Articles 4 to 20 is not pertinent.

4 By way of derogation of Articles 3 to 22, in the cases where one of the information items required in one of the schedules or building blocks referred to in 4 to 20 or equivalent information is not pertinent to the issuer, to the offer or to the securities to which the prospectus relates, that information may be omitted.

▼B

Article 24

Content of the summary of prospectus and base prospectus

The issuer, the offeror or the person asking for admission to trading on a regulated market shall determine on its own the detailed content of the summary to the prospectus or base prospectus referred to in Article 5(2) of Directive 2003/71/EC.

CHAPTER III

FORMAT OF THE PROSPECTUS, BASE PROSPECTUS AND SUPPLEMENTS

Article 25

Format of the prospectus

1 Where an issuer, an offeror or a person asking for the admission to trading on a regulated market chooses, according to Article 5(3) of Directive 2003/71/EC to draw up a prospectus as a single document, the prospectus shall be composed of the following parts in the following order:

1. a clear and detailed table of contents;
2. the summary provided for in Article 5 (2) of Directive 2003/71/EC;
3. the risk factors linked to the issuer and the type of security covered by the issue;
4. the other information items included in the schedules and building blocks according to which the prospectus is drawn up.

2 Where an issuer, an offeror or a person asking for the admission to trading on a regulated market chooses, according to in Article 5(3) of Directive 2003/71/EC, to draw up a prospectus composed of separate documents, the securities note and the registration document shall be each composed of the following parts in the following order:

1. a clear and detailed table of content;
2. as the case may be, the risk factors linked to the issuer and the type of security covered by the issue;
3. the other information items included in the schedules and building blocks according to which the prospectus is drawn up.

3 In the cases mentioned in paragraphs 1 and 2, the issuer, the offeror or the person asking for admission to trading on a regulated market shall be free in defining the order in the presentation of the required information items included in the schedules and building blocks according to which the prospectus is drawn up.

4 Where the order of the items does not coincide with the order of the information provided for in the schedules and building blocks according to which the prospectus is drawn up, the competent authority of the home Member State may ask the issuer, the offeror or the person asking for the admission to trading on a regulated market to provide a cross reference list for the purpose of checking the prospectus before its approval. Such list shall identify the pages where each item can be found in the prospectus.

5 Where the summary of a prospectus must be supplemented according to Article 16(1) of Directive 2003/71/EC, the issuer, the offeror or the person asking for admission to trading on a regulated market shall decide on a case-by-case basis whether to integrate the new

▼B

information in the original summary by producing a new summary, or to produce a supplement to the summary.

If the new information is integrated in the original summary, the issuer, the offeror or the person asking for admission to trading on a regulated market shall ensure that investors can easily identify the changes, in particular by way of footnotes.

Article 26

Format of the base prospectus and its related final terms

1 Where an issuer, an offeror or a person asking for the admission to trading on a regulated market chooses, according to Article 5 (4) of Directive 2003/71/EC to draw up a base prospectus, the base prospectus shall be composed of the following parts in the following order:

1. a clear and detailed table of contents;
2. the summary provided for in Article 5 (2) of Directive 2003/71/EC;
3. the risk factors linked to the issuer and the type of security or securities covered by the issue(s);
4. the other information items included in the schedules and building blocks according to which the prospectus is drawn up.

2 Notwithstanding paragraph 1, the issuer, the offeror or the person asking for admission to trading on a regulated market shall be free in defining the order in the presentation of the required information items included in the schedules and building blocks according to which the prospectus is drawn up. The information on the different securities contained in the base prospectus shall be clearly segregated.

3 Where the order of the items does not coincide with the order of the information provided for by the schedules and building blocks according to which the prospectus is drawn up, the home competent authority may ask the issuer, the offeror or the person asking for admission to trading on a regulated market to provide a cross reference list for the purpose of checking the prospectus before its approval. Such list should identify the pages where each item can be found in the prospectus.

4 In case the issuer, the offeror or the person asking for admission to trading on a regulated market has previously filed a registration document for a particular type of security and, at a later stage, chooses to draw up base prospectus in conformity with the conditions provided for in points (a) and (b) of Article 5(4) of Directive 2003/71/EC, the base prospectus shall contain:

1. the information contained in the previously or simultaneously filed and approved registration document which shall be incorporated by reference, following the conditions provided for in Article 28 of this Regulation;
2. the information which would otherwise be contained in the relevant securities note less the final terms where the final terms are not included in the base prospectus.

5 The final terms attached to a base prospectus shall be presented in the form of a separate document containing only the final terms or by inclusion of the final terms into the base prospectus.

In the case that the final terms are included in a separate document containing only the final terms, they may replicate some information which has been included in the approved base prospectus according to the relevant securities note schedule that has been used for drawing up the base prospectus. In this case the final terms have to be presented in such a way that they can be easily identified as such.

▼B

A clear and prominent statement shall be inserted in the final terms indicating that the full information on the issuer and on the offer is only available on the basis of the combination of base prospectus and final terms and where the base prospectus is available.

6 Where a base prospectus relates to different securities, the issuer, the offeror or the person asking for admission to trading on a regulated market shall include a single summary in the base prospectus for all securities. The information on the different securities contained in the summary, however, shall be clearly segregated.

7 Where the summary of a base prospectus must be supplemented according to Article 16(1) of Directive 2003/71/EC, the issuer, the offeror or the person asking for admission to trading on a regulated market shall decide on a case-by-case basis whether to integrate the new information in the original summary by producing a new summary, or by producing a supplement to the summary.

If the new information is integrated in the original summary of the base prospectus by producing a new summary, the issuer, the offeror or the person asking for admission to trading on a regulated market shall ensure that investors can easily identify the changes, in particular by way of footnotes.

8 Issuers, offerors or persons asking for admission to trading on a regulated market may compile in one single document two or more different base prospectuses.

CHAPTER IV

INFORMATION AND INCORPORATION BY REFERENCE

Article 27

Publication of the document referred to in Article 10(1) of Directive 2003/71/EC

1 The document referred to in Article 10(1) of Directive 2003/71/EC shall be made available to the public, at the choice of the issuer, the offeror or the person asking for admission to trading on a regulated market, through one of the means permitted under Article 14 of that Directive in the home Member State of the issuer.

2 The document shall be filed with the competent authority of the home Member State and made available to the public at the latest 20 working days after the publication of the annual financial statements in the home Member State.

3 The document shall include a statement indicating that some information may be out-of-date, if such is the case.

Article 28

Arrangements for incorporation by reference

1 Information may be incorporated by reference in a prospectus or base prospectus, notably if it is contained in one the following documents:

1. annual and interim financial information;
2. documents prepared on the occasion of a specific transaction such as a merger or de-merger;
3. audit reports and financial statements;
4. memorandum and articles of association;

▼B

5. earlier approved and published prospectuses and/or base prospectuses;

6. regulated information;

7. circulars to security holders.

2 The documents containing information that may be incorporated by reference in a prospectus or base prospectus or in the documents composing it shall be drawn up following the provisions of Article 19 of Directive 2003/71/EC.

3 If a document which may be incorporated by reference contains information which has undergone material changes, the prospectus or base prospectus shall clearly state such a circumstance and shall give the updated information.

4 The issuer, the offeror or the person asking for admission to trading on a regulated market may incorporate information in a prospectus or base prospectus by making reference only to certain parts of a document, provided that it states that the non- incorporated parts are either not relevant for the investor or covered elsewhere in the prospectus.

5 When incorporating information by reference, issuers, offerors or persons asking for admission to trading on a regulated market shall endeavour not to endanger investor protection in terms of comprehensibility and accessibility of the information.

CHAPTER V

PUBLICATION AND DISSEMINATION OF ADVERTISEMENTS

Article 29

Publication in electronic form

1 The publication of the prospectus or base prospectus in electronic form, either pursuant to points (c) (d) and (e) of Article 14(2) of Directive 2003/71/EC, or as an additional means of availability, shall be subject to the following requirements:

1. the prospectus or base prospectus shall be easily accessible when entering the web-site;

2. the file format shall be such that the prospectus or base prospectus cannot be modified;

3. the prospectus or base prospectus shall not contain hyper-links, with exception of links to the electronic addresses where information incorporated by reference is available;

4. the investors shall have the possibility of downloading and printing the prospectus or base prospectus.

The exception referred to in point 3 of the first subparagraph shall only be valid for documents incorporated by reference; those documents shall be available with easy and immediate technical arrangements.

2 If a prospectus or base prospectus for offer of securities to the public is made available on the web-sites of issuers and financial intermediaries or of regulated markets, these shall take measures, to avoid targeting residents in Members States or third countries where the offer of securities to the public does not take place, such as the insertion of a disclaimer as to who are the addressees of the offer.

▼B

Article 30

Publication in newspapers

1 In order to comply with point (a) of Article 14(2) of Directive 2003/71/EC the publication of a prospectus or a base prospectus shall be made in a general or financial information newspaper having national or supra-regional scope;

2 If the competent authority is of the opinion that the newspaper chosen for publication does not comply with the requirements set out in paragraph 1, it shall determine a newspaper whose circulation is deemed appropriate for this purpose taking into account, in particular, the geographic area, number of inhabitants and reading habits in each Member State.

Article 31

Publication of the notice

1 If a Member State makes use of the option, referred to in Article 14(3) of Directive 2003/71/EC, to require the publication of a notice stating how the prospectus or base prospectus has been made available and where it can be obtained by the public, that notice shall be published in a newspaper that fulfils the requirements for publication of prospectuses according to Article 30 of this Regulation.

If the notice relates to a prospectus or base prospectus published for the only purpose of admission of securities to trading on a regulated market where securities of the same class are already admitted, it may alternatively be inserted in the gazette of that regulated market, irrespective of whether that gazette is in paper copy or electronic form.

2 The notice shall be published no later than the next working day following the date of publication of the prospectus or base prospectus pursuant to Article 14(1) of Directive 2003/71/EC.

3 The notice shall contain the following information:

1. the identification of the issuer;
2. the type, class and amount of the securities to be offered and/or in respect of which admission to trading is sought, provided that these elements are known at the time of the publication of the notice;
3. the intended time schedule of the offer/admission to trading;
4. a statement that a prospectus or base prospectus has been published and where it can be obtained;
5. if the prospectus or base prospectus has been published in a printed form, the addresses where and the period of time during which such printed forms are available to the public;
6. if the prospectus or base prospectus has been published in electronic form, the addresses to which investors shall refer to ask for a paper copy;
7. the date of the notice.

Article 32

List of approved prospectuses

The list of the approved prospectuses and base prospectuses published on the web-site of the competent authority, in accordance with Article 14(4) of Directive 2003/71/EC, shall mention how such prospectuses have been made available and where they can be obtained.

▼B

Article 33

Publication of the final terms of base prospectuses

The publication method for final terms related to a base prospectus does not have to be the same as the one used for the base prospectus as long as the publication method used is one of the publication methods indicated in Article 14 of the Directive 2003/71/EC.

Article 34

Dissemination of advertisements

Advertisements related to an offer to the public of securities or to an admission to trading on a regulated market may be disseminated to the public by interested parties, such as issuer, offeror or person asking for admission, the financial intermediaries that participate in the placing and/or underwriting of securities, notably by one of the following means of communication:

1. addressed or unaddressed printed matter;
2. electronic message or advertisement received via a mobile telephone or pager;
3. standard letter;
4. Press advertising with or without order form;
5. catalogue;
6. telephone with or without human intervention;
7. seminars and presentations;
8. radio;
9. videophone;
10. videotext;
11. electronic mail;
12. facsimile machine (fax);
13. television;
14. notice;
15. bill;
16. poster;
17. brochure;
18. web posting including internet banners.

CHAPTER VI

TRANSITIONAL AND FINAL PROVISIONS

Article 35

Historical financial information

1 The obligation for Community issuers to restate in a prospectus historical financial information according to Regulation (EC) No 1606/2002, set out in Annex I item 20.1, Annex IV item 13.1, Annex VII items 8.2, Annex X items 20.1 and Annex XI item 11.1 shall not apply to any period earlier than 1 January 2004 or, where an issuer has securities admitted to trading on a regulated market on 1 July

▼B

2005, until the issuer has published its first consolidated annual accounts with accordance with Regulation (EC) No 1606/2002.

2 Where a Community issuer is subject to transitional national provisions adopted pursuant Article 9 of Regulation (EC) No 1606/2002, the obligation to restate in a prospectus historical financial information does not apply to any period earlier than 1 January 2006 or, where an issuer has securities admitted to trading on a regulated market on 1 July 2005, until the issuer has published its first consolidated annual accounts with accordance with Regulation (EC) No 1606/2002.

3 Until 1 January 2007 the obligation to restate in a prospectus historical financial information according to Regulation (EC) No 1606/2002, set out in Annex I item 20.1, Annex IV item 13.1, Annex VII items 8.2, Annex X items 20.1 and Annex XI item 11.1 shall not apply to issuers from third countries:

1. who have their securities admitted to trading on a regulated market on 1 January 2007;

   and

2. who have presented and prepared historical financial information according to the national accounting standards of a third country.

In this case, historical financial information shall be accompanied with more detailed and/or additional information if the financial statements included in the prospectus do not give a true and fair view of the issuer's assets and liabilities, financial position and profit and loss.

4 Third country issuers having prepared historical financial information according to internationally accepted standards as referred to in Article 9 of Regulation (EC) No 1606/2002 may use that information in any prospectus filed before 1 January 2007, without being subject to restatement obligations.

▼M1

5. Subject to paragraph 5A, from 1 January 2007, third country issuers referred to in paragraphs 3 and 4 shall present their historical financial information in accordance with international accounting standards adopted under Regulation (EC) No 1606/2002 or a third country's national accounting standards equivalent to those standards. If such historical financial information is not in accordance with any such standards, it must be presented in the form of restated financial statements.

5A. Third country issuers are not subject to a requirement, under Annex I, item 20.1; Annex IV, item 13.1; Annex VII, item 8.2; Annex X, item 20.1 or Annex XI, item 11.1, to restate historical financial information or to a requirement under Annex VII, item 8.2. bis; Annex IX, item 11.1; or Annex X, item 20.1.bis, to provide a narrative description of the differences between international accounting standards adopted under Regulation (EC) No 1606/2002 and the accounting principles in accordance with which such information is drawn up, included in a prospectus filed with a competent authority before 1 January 2009, where one of the following conditions is met:

(a) the notes to the financial statements that form part of the historical financial information contain an explicit and unreserved statement that they comply with International Financial Reporting Standards in accordance with IAS 1 Presentation of Financial Statements;

(b) the historical financial information is prepared in accordance with the Generally Accepted Accounting Principles of either Canada, Japan or the United States of America;

(c) the historical financial information is prepared in accordance with the Generally Accepted Accounting Principles of a third country other than Canada, Japan or the United States of America, and the following conditions are satisfied:

▼M1

(i) the third country authority responsible for the national accounting standards in question has made a public commitment, before the start of the financial year in which the prospectus is filed, to converge those standards with International Financial Reporting Standards;

(ii) that authority has established a work programme which demonstrates the intention to progress towards convergence before 31 December 2008; and

(iii) the issuer provides evidence that satisfies the competent authority that the conditions in (i) and (ii) are met.

5B. By 1 April 2007, the Commission shall present to the European Securities Committee and the European Parliament a first report on the work timetable of the authorities responsible for national accounting standards in the US, Japan and Canada for the convergence between IFRS and the Generally Accepted Accounting Principles of those countries.

The Commission shall closely monitor, and regularly inform the European Securities Committee and the European Parliament about the amount of progress in the convergence between International Financial Reporting Standards and the Generally Accepted Accounting Principles of Canada, Japan and the United States of America and of progress on the elimination of reconciliation requirements that apply to Community issuers in those countries. In particular, it shall inform the European Securities Committee and the European Parliament immediately if the process is not proceeding satisfactorily.

5C. The Commission shall also regularly inform the European Securities Committee and the European Parliament about the development of regulatory discussions and the amount of progress in the convergence between International Financial Reporting Standards and the Generally Accepted Accounting Principles of third countries mentioned in paragraph 5A(c) and progress towards the elimination of any reconciliation requirements. In particular, the Commission shall inform the European Securities Committee and the European Parliament immediately if the process is not proceeding satisfactorily.

5D. In addition to the obligations under paragraphs 5B and 5C, the Commission shall engage in and maintain a regular dialogue with third country authorities and, before 1 April 2008 at the latest, the Commission shall present a report to the European Securities Committee and to the European Parliament on the progress in convergence and progress towards the elimination of any reconciliation requirements that apply to Community issuers under the rules of a third country covered by paragraph 5A (b) or (c). The Commission may request or require another person to prepare the report.

5E. At least six months before 1 January 2009, the Commission shall ensure a determination of the equivalence of the Generally Accepted Accounting Principles of third countries, pursuant to a definition of equivalence and an equivalence mechanism that it will have established before 1 January 2008 in accordance with the procedure referred to in Article 24 of Directive 2003/71/EC. When complying with this paragraph, the Commission shall first consult the Committee of European Securities Regulators on the appropriateness of the definition of equivalence, the equivalence mechanism and the determination of the equivalence that is made.

▼B

6 The provisions of this Article shall also apply to Annex VI, item 3.

▼B

Article 36

Entry into force

This Regulation shall enter into force in Member States on the twentieth day after its publication in the *Official Journal of the European Union.*

It shall apply from 1 July 2005.

This Regulation shall be binding in its entirety and directly applicable in all Member States.

▼B

ANNEXES

Annexes I to XVII: Schedules and building blocks

Annex XVIII: Table of combinations of schedules and building blocks

Annex XIX: List of specialist issuers

▼B

ANNEX I

Minimum Disclosure Requirements for the Share Registration Document (schedule)

1. **PERSONS RESPONSIBLE**

1.1. All persons responsible for the information given in the Registration Document and, as the case may be, for certain parts of it, with, in the latter case, an indication of such parts. In the case of natural persons including members of the issuer's administrative, management or supervisory bodies indicate the name and function of the person; in case of legal persons indicate the name and registered office.

1.2. A declaration by those responsible for the registration document that, having taken all reasonable care to ensure that such is the case, the information contained in the registration document is, to the best of their knowledge, in accordance with the facts and contains no omission likely to affect its import. As the case may be, a declaration by those responsible for certain parts of the registration document that, having taken all reasonable care to ensure that such is the case, the information contained in the part of the registration document for which they are responsible is, to the best of their knowledge, in accordance with the facts and contains no omission likely to affect its import.

2. **STATUTORY AUDITORS**

2.1. Names and addresses of the issuer's auditors for the period covered by the historical financial information (together with their membership in a professional body).

2.2. If auditors have resigned, been removed or not been re-appointed during the period covered by the historical financial information, indicate details if material.

3. **SELECTED FINANCIAL INFORMATION**

3.1. Selected historical financial information regarding the issuer, presented for each financial year for the period covered by the historical financial information, and any subsequent interim financial period, in the same currency as the financial information.

The selected historical financial information must provide the key figures that summarise the financial condition of the issuer.

3.2. If selected financial information for interim periods is provided, comparative data from the same period in the prior financial year must also be provided, except that the requirement for comparative balance sheet information is satisfied by presenting the year end balance sheet information.

4. **RISK FACTORS**

Prominent disclosure of risk factors that are specific to the issuer or its industry in a section headed 'Risk Factors'.

5. **INFORMATION ABOUT THE ISSUER**

5.1. *History and development of the issuer*

5.1.1. The legal and commercial name of the issuer

5.1.2. The place of registration of the issuer and its registration number

5.1.3. The date of incorporation and the length of life of the issuer, except where indefinite

5.1.4. The domicile and legal form of the issuer, the legislation under which the issuer operates, its country of incorporation, and the address and telephone number of its registered office (or principal place of business if different from its registered office)

5.1.5. The important events in the development of the issuer's business.

5.2. *Investments*

5.2.1. A description, (including the amount) of the issuer's principal investments for each financial year for the period covered by the

▼B

historical financial information up to the date of the registration document

5.2.2. A description of the issuer's principal investments that are in progress, including the geographic distribution of these investments (home and abroad) and the method of financing (internal or external)

5.2.3. Information concerning the issuer's principal future investments on which its management bodies have already made firm commitments.

6. **BUSINESS OVERVIEW**

6.1. *Principal Activities*

6.1.1. A description of, and key factors relating to, the nature of the issuer's operations and its principal activities, stating the main categories of products sold and/or services performed for each financial year for the period covered by the historical financial information;

and

6.1.2. An indication of any significant new products and/or services that have been introduced and, to the extent the development of new products or services has been publicly disclosed, give the status of development.

6.2. *Principal Markets*

A description of the principal markets in which the issuer competes, including a breakdown of total revenues by category of activity and geographic market for each financial year for the period covered by the historical financial information.

6.3. Where the information given pursuant to items 6.1 and 6.2 has been influenced by exceptional factors, mention that fact.

6.4. If material to the issuer's business or profitability, a summary information regarding the extent to which the issuer is dependent, on patents or licences, industrial, commercial or financial contracts or new manufacturing processes.

6.5. The basis for any statements made by the issuer regarding its competitive position.

7. **ORGANISATIONAL STRUCTURE**

7.1. If the issuer is part of a group, a brief description of the group and the issuer's position within the group.

7.2. A list of the issuer's significant subsidiaries, including name, country of incorporation or residence, proportion of ownership interest and, if different, proportion of voting power held.

8. **PROPERTY, PLANTS AND EQUIPMENT**

8.1. Information regarding any existing or planned material tangible fixed assets, including leased properties, and any major encumbrances thereon.

8.2. A description of any environmental issues that may affect the issuer's utilisation of the tangible fixed assets.

9. **OPERATING AND FINANCIAL REVIEW**

9.1. *Financial Condition*

To the extent not covered elsewhere in the registration document, provide a description of the issuer's financial condition, changes in financial condition and results of operations for each year and interim period, for which historical financial information is required, including the causes of material changes from year to year in the financial information to the extent necessary for an understanding of the issuer's business as a whole.

9.2. *Operating Results*

9.2.1. Information regarding significant factors, including unusual or infrequent events or new developments, materially affecting the issuer's income from operations, indicating the extent to which income was so affected.

▼B

9.2.2. Where the financial statements disclose material changes in net sales or revenues, provide a narrative discussion of the reasons for such changes.

9.2.3. Information regarding any governmental, economic, fiscal, monetary or political policies or factors that have materially affected, or could materially affect, directly or indirectly, the issuer's operations.

10. **CAPITAL RESOURCES**

10.1. Information concerning the issuer's capital resources (both short and long term);

10.2. An explanation of the sources and amounts of and a narrative description of the issuer's cash flows;

10.3. Information on the borrowing requirements and funding structure of the issuer;

10.4. Information regarding any restrictions on the use of capital resources that have materially affected, or could materially affect, directly or indirectly, the issuer's operations.

10.5. Information regarding the anticipated sources of funds needed to fulfil commitments referred to in items 5.2.3 and 8.1.

11. **RESEARCH AND DEVELOPMENT, PATENTS AND LICENCES**

Where material, provide a description of the issuer's research and development policies for each financial year for the period covered by the historical financial information, including the amount spent on issuer-sponsored research and development activities.

12. **TREND INFORMATION**

12.1. The most significant recent trends in production, sales and inventory, and costs and selling prices since the end of the last financial year to the date of the registration document.

12.2. Information on any known trends, uncertainties, demands, commitments or events that are reasonably likely to have a material effect on the issuer's prospects for at least the current financial year.

13. **PROFIT FORECASTS OR ESTIMATES**

If an issuer chooses to include a profit forecast or a profit estimate the registration document must contain the information set out in items 13.1 and 13.2:

13.1. A statement setting out the principal assumptions upon which the issuer has based its forecast, or estimate.

There must be a clear distinction between assumptions about factors which the members of the administrative, management or supervisory bodies can influence and assumptions about factors which are exclusively outside the influence of the members of the administrative, management or supervisory bodies; the assumptions must be readily understandable by investors, be specific and precise and not relate to the general accuracy of the estimates underlying the forecast.

13.2. A report prepared by independent accountants or auditors stating that in the opinion of the independent accountants or auditors the forecast or estimate has been properly compiled on the basis stated and that the basis of accounting used for the profit forecast or estimate is consistent with the accounting policies of the issuer.

13.3. The profit forecast or estimate must be prepared on a basis comparable with the historical financial information.

13.4. If a profit forecast in a prospectus has been published which is still outstanding, then provide a statement setting out whether or not that forecast is still correct as at the time of the registration document, and an explanation of why such forecast is no longer valid if that is the case.

▼B

14. **ADMINISTRATIVE, MANAGEMENT, AND SUPERVISORY BODIES AND SENIOR MANAGEMENT**

14.1. Names, business addresses and functions in the issuer of the following persons and an indication of the principal activities performed by them outside that issuer where these are significant with respect to that issuer:

(a) members of the administrative, management or supervisory bodies;

(b) partners with unlimited liability, in the case of a limited partnership with a share capital;

(c) founders, if the issuer has been established for fewer than five years;

and

(d) any senior manager who is relevant to establishing that the issuer has the appropriate expertise and experience for the management of the issuer's business.

The nature of any family relationship between any of those persons.

In the case of each member of the administrative, management or supervisory bodies of the issuer and of each person mentioned in points (b) and (d) of the first subparagraph, details of that person's relevant management expertise and experience and the following information:

(a) the names of all companies and partnerships of which such person has been a member of the administrative, management or supervisory bodies or partner at any time in the previous five years, indicating whether or not the individual is still a member of the administrative, management or supervisory bodies or partner. It is not necessary to list all the subsidiaries of an issuer of which the person is also a member of the administrative, management or supervisory bodies;

(b) any convictions in relation to fraudulent offences for at least the previous five years;

(c) details of any bankruptcies, receiverships or liquidations with which a person described in (a) and (d) of the first subparagraph who was acting in the capacity of any of the positions set out in (a) and (d) of the first subparagraph was associated for at least the previous five years;

(d) details of any official public incrimination and/or sanctions of such person by statutory or regulatory authorities (including designated professional bodies) and whether such person has ever been disqualified by a court from acting as a member of the administrative, management or supervisory bodies of an issuer or from acting in the management or conduct of the affairs of any issuer for at least the previous five years.

If there is no such information to be disclosed, a statement to that effect is to be made.

14.2. Administrative, Management, and Supervisory bodies' and Senior Management conflicts of interests

Potential conflicts of interests between any duties to the issuer, of the persons referred to in item 14.1 and their private interests and or other duties must be clearly stated. In the event that there are no such conflicts, a statement to that effect must be made.

Any arrangement or understanding with major shareholders, customers, suppliers or others, pursuant to which any person referred to in item 14.1 was selected as a member of the administrative, management or supervisory bodies or member of senior management.

Details of any restrictions agreed by the persons referred to in item 14.1 on the disposal within a certain period of time of their holdings in the issuer's securities.

15. **REMUNERATION AND BENEFITS**

In relation to the last full financial year for those persons referred to in points (a) and (d) of the first subparagraph of item 14.1:

▼B

15.1. The amount of remuneration paid (including any contingent or deferred compensation), and benefits in kind granted to such persons by the issuer and its subsidiaries for services in all capacities to the issuer and its subsidiaries by any person.

That information must be provided on an individual basis unless individual disclosure is not required in the issuer's home country and is not otherwise publicly disclosed by the issuer.

15.2. The total amounts set aside or accrued by the issuer or its subsidiaries to provide pension, retirement or similar benefits.

16. **BOARD PRACTICES**

In relation to the issuer's last completed financial year, and unless otherwise specified, with respect to those persons referred to in point (a) of the first subparagraph of 14.1:

16.1. Date of expiration of the current term of office, if applicable, and the period during which the person has served in that office.

16.2. Information about members of the administrative, management or supervisory bodies' service contracts with the issuer or any of its subsidiaries providing for benefits upon termination of employment, or an appropriate negative statement.

16.3. Information about the issuer's audit committee and remuneration committee, including the names of committee members and a summary of the terms of reference under which the committee operates.

16.4. A statement as to whether or not the issuer complies with its country's of incorporation corporate governance regime(s). In the event that the issuer does not comply with such a regime, a statement to that effect must be included together with an explanation regarding why the issuer does not comply with such regime.

17. **EMPLOYEES**

17.1. Either the number of employees at the end of the period or the average for each financial year for the period covered by the historical financial information up to the date of the registration document (and changes in such numbers, if material) and, if possible and material, a breakdown of persons employed by main category of activity and geographic location. If the issuer employs a significant number of temporary employees, include disclosure of the number of temporary employees on average during the most recent financial year.

17.2. Shareholdings and stock options

With respect to each person referred to in points (a) and (d) of the first subparagraph of item 14.1. provide information as to their share ownership and any options over such shares in the issuer as of the most recent practicable date.

17.3. Description of any arrangements for involving the employees in the capital of the issuer.

18. **MAJOR SHAREHOLDERS**

18.1. In so far as is known to the issuer, the name of any person other than a member of the administrative, management or supervisory bodies who, directly or indirectly, has an interest in the issuer's capital or voting rights which is notifiable under the issuer's national law, together with the amount of each such person's interest or, if there are no such persons, an appropriate negative statement.

18.2. Whether the issuer's major shareholders have different voting rights, or an appropriate negative statement.

18.3. To the extent known to the issuer, state whether the issuer is directly or indirectly owned or controlled and by whom and describe the nature of such control and describe the measures in place to ensure that such control is not abused.

18.4. A description of any arrangements, known to the issuer, the operation of which may at a subsequent date result in a change in control of the issuer.

▼B

19. **RELATED PARTY TRANSACTIONS**

Details of related party transactions (which for these purposes are those set out in the Standards adopted according to the Regulation (EC) No 1606/2002), that the issuer has entered into during the period covered by the historical financial information and up to the date of the registration document, must be disclosed in accordance with the respective standard adopted according to Regulation (EC) No 1606/2002 if applicable.

If such standards do not apply to the issuer the following information must be disclosed:

(a) the nature and extent of any transactions which are - as a single transaction or in their entirety - material to the issuer. Where such related party transactions are not concluded at arm's length provide an explanation of why these transactions were not concluded at arms length. In the case of outstanding loans including guarantees of any kind indicate the amount outstanding;

(b) the amount or the percentage to which related party transactions form part of the turnover of the issuer.

20. **FINANCIAL INFORMATION CONCERNING THE ISSUER'S ASSETS AND LIABILITIES, FINANCIAL POSITION AND PROFITS AND LOSSES**

20.1. *Historical Financial Information*

Audited historical financial information covering the latest 3 financial years (or such shorter period that the issuer has been in operation), and the audit report in respect of each year. ►**M2** If the issuer has changed its accounting reference date during the period for which historical financial information is required, the audited historical information shall cover at least 36 months, or the entire period for which the issuer has been in operation, whichever is the shorter. ◄ Such financial information must be prepared according to Regulation (EC) No 1606/2002, or if not applicable to a Member State national accounting standards for issuers from the Community. For third country issuers, such financial information must be prepared according to the international accounting standards adopted pursuant to the procedure of Article 3 of Regulation (EC) No 1606/2002 or to a third country's national accounting standards equivalent to these standards. If such financial information is not equivalent to these standards, it must be presented in the form of restated financial statements.

The last two years audited historical financial information must be presented and prepared in a form consistent with that which will be adopted in the issuer's next published annual financial statements having regard to accounting standards and policies and legislation applicable to such annual financial statements.

If the issuer has been operating in its current sphere of economic activity for less than one year, the audited historical financial information covering that period must be prepared in accordance with the standards applicable to annual financial statements under the Regulation (EC) No 1606/2002, or if not applicable to a Member State national accounting standards where the issuer is an issuer from the Community. For third country issuers, the historical financial information must be prepared according to the international accounting standards adopted pursuant to the procedure of Article 3 of Regulation (EC) No 1606/2002 or to a third country's national accounting standards equivalent to these standards. This historical financial information must be audited.

If the audited financial information is prepared according to national accounting standards, the financial information required under this heading must include at least:

(a) balance sheet;

(b) income statement;

(c) a statement showing either all changes in equity or changes in equity other than those arising from capital transactions with owners and distributions to owners;

▼B

(d) cash flow statement;

(e) accounting policies and explanatory notes.

The historical annual financial information must be independently audited or reported on as to whether or not, for the purposes of the registration document, it gives a true and fair view, in accordance with auditing standards applicable in a Member State or an equivalent standard.

20.2. *Pro forma financial information*

In the case of a significant gross change, a description of how the transaction might have affected the assets and liabilities and earnings of the issuer, had the transaction been undertaken at the commencement of the period being reported on or at the date reported.

This requirement will normally be satisfied by the inclusion of pro forma financial information.

This pro forma financial information is to be presented as set out in Annex II and must include the information indicated therein.

Pro forma financial information must be accompanied by a report prepared by independent accountants or auditors.

20.3. *Financial statements*

If the issuer prepares both own and consolidated annual financial statements, include at least the consolidated annual financial statements in the registration document.

20.4. *Auditing of historical annual financial information*

20.4.1. A statement that the historical financial information has been audited. If audit reports on the historical financial information have been refused by the statutory auditors or if they contain qualifications or disclaimers, such refusal or such qualifications or disclaimers must be reproduced in full and the reasons given.

20.4.2. Indication of other information in the registration document which has been audited by the auditors.

20.4.3. Where financial data in the registration document is not extracted from the issuer's audited financial statements state the source of the data and state that the data is unaudited.

20.5. *Age of latest financial information*

20.5.1. The last year of audited financial information may not be older than one of the following:

(a) 18 months from the date of the registration document if the issuer includes audited interim financial statements in the registration document;

(b) 15 months from the date of the registration document if the issuer includes unaudited interim financial statements in the registration document.

20.6. *Interim and other financial information*

20.6.1. If the issuer has published quarterly or half yearly financial information since the date of its last audited financial statements, these must be included in the registration document. If the quarterly or half yearly financial information has been reviewed or audited, the audit or review report must also be included. If the quarterly or half yearly financial information is unaudited or has not been reviewed state that fact.

20.6.2. If the registration document is dated more than nine months after the end of the last audited financial year, it must contain interim financial information, which may be unaudited (in which case that fact must be stated) covering at least the first six months of the financial year.

The interim financial information must include comparative statements for the same period in the prior financial year, except that the requirement for comparative balance sheet information may be satisfied by presenting the years end balance sheet.

▼B

20.7. *Dividend policy*

A description of the issuer's policy on dividend distributions and any restrictions thereon.

20.7.1. The amount of the dividend per share for each financial year for the period covered by the historical financial information adjusted, where the number of shares in the issuer has changed, to make it comparable.

20.8. *Legal and arbitration proceedings*

Information on any governmental, legal or arbitration proceedings (including any such proceedings which are pending or threatened of which the issuer is aware), during a period covering at least the previous 12 months which may have, or have had in the recent past significant effects on the issuer and/or group's financial position or profitability, or provide an appropriate negative statement.

20.9. *Significant change in the issuer's financial or trading position*

A description of any significant change in the financial or trading position of the group which has occurred since the end of the last financial period for which either audited financial information or interim financial information have been published, or provide an appropriate negative statement.

21. **ADDITIONAL INFORMATION**

21.1. *Share Capital*

The following information as of the date of the most recent balance sheet included in the historical financial information:

21.1.1. The amount of issued capital, and for each class of share capital:

(a) the number of shares authorised;

(b) the number of shares issued and fully paid and issued but not fully paid;

(c) the par value per share, or that the shares have no par value;

and

(d) a reconciliation of the number of shares outstanding at the beginning and end of the year. If more than 10 % of capital has been paid for with assets other than cash within the period covered by the historical financial information, state that fact.

21.1.2. If there are shares not representing capital, state the number and main characteristics of such shares.

21.1.3. The number, book value and face value of shares in the issuer held by or on behalf of the issuer itself or by subsidiaries of the issuer.

21.1.4. The amount of any convertible securities, exchangeable securities or securities with warrants, with an indication of the conditions governing and the procedures for conversion, exchange or subscription.

21.1.5. Information about and terms of any acquisition rights and or obligations over authorised but unissued capital or an undertaking to increase the capital.

21.1.6. Information about any capital of any member of the group which is under option or agreed conditionally or unconditionally to be put under option and details of such options including those persons to whom such options relate.

21.1.7. A history of share capital, highlighting information about any changes, for the period covered by the historical financial information.

21.2. *Memorandum and Articles of Association*

21.2.1. A description of the issuer's objects and purposes and where they can be found in the memorandum and articles of association.

21.2.2. A summary of any provisions of the issuer's articles of association, statutes, charter or bylaws with respect to the members of the administrative, management and supervisory bodies.

21.2.3. A description of the rights, preferences and restrictions attaching to each class of the existing shares.

▼B

21.2.4. A description of what action is necessary to change the rights of holders of the shares, indicating where the conditions are more significant than is required by law.

21.2.5. A description of the conditions governing the manner in which annual general meetings and extraordinary general meetings of shareholders are called including the conditions of admission.

21.2.6. A brief description of any provision of the issuer's articles of association, statutes, charter or bylaws that would have an effect of delaying, deferring or preventing a change in control of the issuer.

21.2.7. An indication of the articles of association, statutes, charter or bylaw provisions, if any, governing the ownership threshold above which shareholder ownership must be disclosed.

21.2.8. A description of the conditions imposed by the memorandum and articles of association statutes, charter or bylaw governing changes in the capital, where such conditions are more stringent than is required by law.

22. **MATERIAL CONTRACTS**

A summary of each material contract, other than contracts entered into in the ordinary course of business, to which the issuer or any member of the group is a party, for the two years immediately preceding publication of the registration document.

A summary of any other contract (not being a contract entered into in the ordinary course of business) entered into by any member of the group which contains any provision under which any member of the group has any obligation or entitlement which is material to the group as at the date of the registration document.

23. **THIRD PARTY INFORMATION AND STATEMENT BY EXPERTS AND DECLARATIONS OF ANY INTEREST**

23.1. Where a statement or report attributed to a person as an expert is included in the registration document, provide such person's name, business address, qualifications and material interest if any in the issuer. If the report has been produced at the issuer's request a statement to the effect that such statement or report is included, in the form and context in which it is included, with the consent of the person who has authorised the contents of that part of the registration document.

23.2. Where information has been sourced from a third party, provide a confirmation that this information has been accurately reproduced and that as far as the issuer is aware and is able to ascertain from information published by that third party, no facts have been omitted which would render the reproduced information inaccurate or misleading. In addition, identify the source(s) of the information.

24. **DOCUMENTS ON DISPLAY**

A statement that for the life of the registration document the following documents (or copies thereof), where applicable, may be inspected:

(a) the memorandum and articles of association of the issuer;

(b) all reports, letters, and other documents, historical financial information, valuations and statements prepared by any expert at the issuer's request any part of which is included or referred to in the registration document;

(c) the historical financial information of the issuer or, in the case of a group, the historical financial information for the issuer and its subsidiary undertakings for each of the two financial years preceding the publication of the registration document.

An indication of where the documents on display may be inspected, by physical or electronic means.

25. **INFORMATION ON HOLDINGS**

Information relating to the undertakings in which the issuer holds a proportion of the capital likely to have a significant effect on the assessment of its own assets and liabilities, financial position or profits and losses.

▼B

ANNEX II

Pro forma financial information building block

1. The pro forma information must include a description of the transaction, the businesses or entities involved and the period to which it refers, and must clearly state the following:

(a) the purpose to which it has been prepared;

(b) the fact that it has been prepared for illustrative purposes only;

(c) the fact that because of its nature, the pro forma financial information addresses a hypothetical situation and, therefore, does not represent the company's actual financial position or results.

2. In order to present pro forma financial information, a balance sheet and profit and loss account, and accompanying explanatory notes, depending on the circumstances may be included.

3. Pro forma financial information must normally be presented in columnar format, composed of:

(a) the historical unadjusted information;

(b) the pro forma adjustments;

and

(c) the resulting pro forma financial information in the final column.

The sources of the pro forma financial information have to be stated and, if applicable, the financial statements of the acquired businesses or entities must be included in the prospectus

4. The pro forma information must be prepared in a manner consistent with the accounting policies adopted by the issuer in its last or next financial statements and shall identify the following:

(a) the basis upon which it is prepared;

(b) the source of each item of information and adjustment.

5. Pro forma information may only be published in respect of:

(a) the current financial period;

(b) the most recently completed financial period;

and/or

(c) the most recent interim period for which relevant unadjusted information has been or will be published or is being published in the same document.

6. Pro forma adjustments related to the pro forma financial information must be:

(a) clearly shown and explained;

(b) directly attributable to the transaction;

(c) factually supportable.

In addition, in respect of a pro forma profit and loss or cash flow statement, they must be clearly identified as to those expected to have a continuing impact on the issuer and those which are not.

7. The report prepared by the independent accountants or auditors must state that in their opinion:

(a) the pro forma financial information has been properly compiled on the basis stated;

(b) that basis is consistent with the accounting policies of the issuer.

▼B

ANNEX III

Minimum disclosure requirements for the share securities note (schedule)

1. **PERSONS RESPONSIBLE**

1.1. All persons responsible for the information given in the prospectus and, as the case may be, for certain parts of it, with, in the latter case, an indication of such parts. In the case of natural persons including members of the issuer's administrative, management or supervisory bodies indicate the name and function of the person; in case of legal persons indicate the name and registered office.

1.2. A declaration by those responsible for the prospectus that, having taken all reasonable care to ensure that such is the case the information contained in the prospectus is, to the best of their knowledge, in accordance with the facts and contains no omission likely to affect its import. As the case may be, declaration by those responsible for certain parts of the prospectus that, having taken all reasonable care to ensure that such is the case the information contained in the part of the prospectus for which they are responsible is, to the best of their knowledge, in accordance with the facts and contains no omission likely to affect its import.

2. **RISK FACTORS**

Prominent disclosure of risk factors that are material to the securities being offered and/or admitted to trading in order to assess the market risk associated with these securities in a section headed 'Risk Factors'.

3. **KEY INFORMATION**

3.1. *Working capital Statement*

Statement by the issuer that, in its opinion, the working capital is sufficient for the issuer's present requirements or, if not, how it proposes to provide the additional working capital needed.

3.2. *Capitalisation and indebtedness*

A statement of capitalisation and indebtedness (distinguishing between guaranteed and unguaranteed, secured and unsecured indebtedness) as of a date no earlier than 90 days prior to the date of the document. Indebtedness also includes indirect and contingent indebtedness.

3.3. *Interest of natural and legal persons involved in the issue/offer*

A description of any interest, including conflicting ones that is material to the issue/offer, detailing the persons involved and the nature of the interest.

3.4. *Reasons for the offer and use of proceeds*

Reasons for the offer and, where applicable, the estimated net amount of the proceeds broken into each principal intended use and presented by order of priority of such uses. If the issuer is aware that the anticipated proceeds will not be sufficient to fund all the proposed uses, state the amount and sources of other funds needed. Details must be given with regard to the use of the proceeds, in particular when they are being used to acquire assets, other than in the ordinary course of business, to finance announced acquisitions of other business, or to discharge, reduce or retire indebtedness.

4. **INFORMATION CONCERNING THE SECURITIES TO BE OFFERED/ADMITTED TO TRADING**

4.1. A description of the type and the class of the securities being offered and/or admitted to trading, including the ISIN (international security identification number) or other such security identification code.

4.2. Legislation under which the securities have been created.

4.3. An indication whether the securities are in registered form or bearer form and whether the securities are in certificated form or book-entry form. In the latter case, name and address of the entity in charge of keeping the records.

4.4. Currency of the securities issue.

▼B

4.5. A description of the rights attached to the securities, including any limitations of those rights, and procedure for the exercise of those rights.

— Dividend rights:

— fixed date(s) on which the entitlement arises,

— time limit after which entitlement to dividend lapses and an indication of the person in whose favour the lapse operates,

— dividend restrictions and procedures for non-resident holders,

— rate of dividend or method of its calculation, periodicity and cumulative or non-cumulative nature of payments.

— Voting rights.

— Pre-emption rights in offers for subscription of securities of the same class.

— Right to share in the issuer's profits.

— Rights to share in any surplus in the event of liquidation.

— Redemption provisions.

— Conversion provisions.

4.6. In the case of new issues, a statement of the resolutions, authorisations and approvals by virtue of which the securities have been or will be created and/or issued.

4.7. In the case of new issues, the expected issue date of the securities.

4.8. A description of any restrictions on the free transferability of the securities.

4.9. An indication of the existence of any mandatory takeover bids and/or squeeze-out and sell-out rules in relation to the securities.

4.10. An indication of public takeover bids by third parties in respect of the issuer's equity, which have occurred during the last financial year and the current financial year. The price or exchange terms attaching to such offers and the outcome thereof must be stated.

4.11. In respect of the country of registered office of the issuer and the country(ies) where the offer is being made or admission to trading is being sought:

— information on taxes on the income from the securities withheld at source,

— indication as to whether the issuer assumes responsibility for the withholding of taxes at the source.

5. **TERMS AND CONDITIONS OF THE OFFER**

5.1. *Conditions, offer statistics, expected timetable and action required to apply for the offer*

5.1.1. Conditions to which the offer is subject.

5.1.2. Total amount of the issue/offer, distinguishing the securities offered for sale and those offered for subscription; if the amount is not fixed, description of the arrangements and time for announcing to the public the definitive amount of the offer.

5.1.3. The time period, including any possible amendments, during which the offer will be open and description of the application process.

5.1.4. An indication of when, and under which circumstances, the offer may be revoked or suspended and whether revocation can occur after dealing has begun.

5.1.5. A description of the possibility to reduce subscriptions and the manner for refunding excess amount paid by applicants.

5.1.6. Details of the minimum and/or maximum amount of application (whether in number of securities or aggregate amount to invest).

▼B

5.1.7. An indication of the period during which an application may be withdrawn, provided that investors are allowed to withdraw their subscription.

5.1.8. Method and time limits for paying up the securities and for delivery of the securities.

5.1.9. A full description of the manner and date in which results of the offer are to be made public.

5.1.10. The procedure for the exercise of any right of pre-emption, the negotiability of subscription rights and the treatment of subscription rights not exercised.

5.2. *Plan of distribution and allotment*

5.2.1. The various categories of potential investors to which the securities are offered. If the offer is being made simultaneously in the markets of two or more countries and if a tranche has been or is being reserved for certain of these, indicate any such tranche.

5.2.2. To the extent known to the issuer, an indication of whether major shareholders or members of the issuer's management, supervisory or administrative bodies intended to subscribe in the offer, or whether any person intends to subscribe for more than five per cent of the offer.

5.2.3. Pre-allotment disclosure:

(a) the division into tranches of the offer including the institutional, retail and issuer's employee tranches and any other tranches;

(b) the conditions under which the clawback may be used, the maximum size of such claw back and any applicable minimum percentages for individual tranches;

(c) the allotment method or methods to be used for the retail and issuer's employee tranche in the event of an over-subscription of these tranches;

(d) a description of any pre-determined preferential treatment to be accorded to certain classes of investors or certain affinity groups (including friends and family programmes) in the allotment, the percentage of the offer reserved for such preferential treatment and the criteria for inclusion in such classes or groups;

(e) whether the treatment of subscriptions or bids to subscribe in the allotment may be determined on the basis of which firm they are made through or by;

(f) a target minimum individual allotment if any within the retail tranche;

(g) the conditions for the closing of the offer as well as the date on which the offer may be closed at the earliest;

(h) whether or not multiple subscriptions are admitted, and where they are not, how any multiple subscriptions will be handled.

5.2.4. Process for notification to applicants of the amount allotted and indication whether dealing may begin before notification is made.

5.2.5. Over-allotment and 'green shoe':

(a) the existence and size of any over-allotment facility and/or 'green shoe'.

(b) the existence period of the over-allotment facility and/or 'green shoe'.

(c) any conditions for the use of the over-allotment facility or exercise of the 'green shoe'.

5.3. *Pricing*

5.3.1. An indication of the price at which the securities will be offered. If the price is not known or if there is no established and/or liquid market for the securities, indicate the method for determining the offer price, including a statement as to who has set the criteria or is formally responsible for the determination. Indication of the amount of any expenses and taxes specifically charged to the subscriber or purchaser.

▼B

5.3.2. Process for the disclosure of the offer price.

5.3.3. If the issuer's equity holders have pre-emptive purchase rights and this right is restricted or withdrawn, indication of the basis for the issue price if the issue is for cash, together with the reasons for and beneficiaries of such restriction or withdrawal.

5.3.4 Where there is or could be a material disparity between the public offer price and the effective cash cost to members of the administrative, management or supervisory bodies or senior management, or affiliated persons, of securities acquired by them in transactions during the past year, or which they have the right to acquire, include a comparison of the public contribution in the proposed public offer and the effective cash contributions of such persons.

5.4. *Placing and Underwriting*

5.4.1 Name and address of the coordinator(s) of the global offer and of single parts of the offer and, to the extend known to the issuer or to the offeror, of the placers in the various countries where the offer takes place.

5.4.2 Name and address of any paying agents and depository agents in each country.

5.4.3. Name and address of the entities agreeing to underwrite the issue on a firm commitment basis, and name and address of the entities agreeing to place the issue without a firm commitment or under 'best efforts' arrangements. Indication of the material features of the agreements, including the quotas. Where not all of the issue is underwritten, a statement of the portion not covered. Indication of the overall amount of the underwriting commission and of the placing commission.

5.4.4. When the underwriting agreement has been or will be reached.

6. **ADMISSION TO TRADING AND DEALING ARRANGEMENTS**

6.1. An indication as to whether the securities offered are or will be the object of an application for admission to trading, with a view to their distribution in a regulated market or other equivalent markets with indication of the markets in question. This circumstance must be mentioned, without creating the impression that the admission to trading will necessarily be approved. If known, the earliest dates on which the securities will be admitted to trading.

6.2. All the regulated markets or equivalent markets on which, to the knowledge of the issuer, securities of the same class of the securities to be offered or admitted to trading are already admitted to trading.

6.3. If simultaneously or almost simultaneously with the creation of the securities for which admission to a regulated market is being sought securities of the same class are subscribed for or placed privately or if securities of other classes are created for public or private placing, give details of the nature of such operations and of the number and characteristics of the securities to which they relate.

6.4. Details of the entities which have a firm commitment to act as intermediaries in secondary trading, providing liquidity through bid and offer rates and description of the main terms of their commitment.

6.5. *Stabilisation: where an issuer or a selling shareholder has granted an over-allotment option or it is otherwise proposed that price stabilising activities may be entered into in connection with an offer:*

6.5.1. The fact that stabilisation may be undertaken, that there is no assurance that it will be undertaken and that it may be stopped at any time,

6.5.2. The beginning and the end of the period during which stabilisation may occur,

6.5.3. The identity of the stabilisation manager for each relevant jurisdiction unless this is not known at the time of publication,

6.5.4. The fact that stabilisation transactions may result in a market price that is higher than would otherwise prevail.

▼B

7. **SELLING SECURITIES HOLDERS**

7.1. Name and business address of the person or entity offering to sell the securities, the nature of any position office or other material relationship that the selling persons has had within the past three years with the issuer or any of its predecessors or affiliates.

7.2. The number and class of securities being offered by each of the selling security holders.

7.3. Lock-up agreements

The parties involved.

Content and exceptions of the agreement.

Indication of the period of the lock up.

8. **EXPENSE OF THE ISSUE/OFFER**

8.1. The total net proceeds and an estimate of the total expenses of the issue/offer.

9. **DILUTION**

9.1. The amount and percentage of immediate dilution resulting from the offer.

9.2. In the case of a subscription offer to existing equity holders, the amount and percentage of immediate dilution if they do not subscribe to the new offer.

10. **ADDITIONAL INFORMATION**

10.1. If advisors connected with an issue are mentioned in the Securities Note, a statement of the capacity in which the advisors have acted.

10.2. An indication of other information in the Securities Note which has been audited or reviewed by statutory auditors and where auditors have produced a report. Reproduction of the report or, with permission of the competent authority, a summary of the report.

10.3. Where a statement or report attributed to a person as an expert is included in the Securities Note, provide such persons' name, business address, qualifications and material interest if any in the issuer. If the report has been produced at the issuer's request a statement to the effect that such statement or report is included, in the form and context in which it is included, with the consent of the person who has authorised the contents of that part of the Securities Note.

10.4. Where information has been sourced from a third party, provide a confirmation that this information has been accurately reproduced and that as far as the issuer is aware and is able to ascertain from information published by that third party, no facts have been omitted which would render the reproduced information inaccurate or misleading. In addition, identify the source(s) of the information.

▼B

ANNEX IV

Minimum disclosure requirements for the debt and derivative securities registration document (schedule)

(Debt and derivative securities with a denomination per unit of less than EUR 50 000)

1. **PERSONS RESPONSIBLE**

1.1. All persons responsible for the information given in the registration document and, as the case may be, for certain parts of it, with, in the latter case, an indication of such parts. In the case of natural persons including members of the issuer's administrative, management or supervisory bodies indicate the name and function of the person; in case of legal persons indicate the name and registered office.

1.2. A declaration by those responsible for the registration document that, having taken all reasonable care to ensure that such is the case the information contained in the registration document is, to the best of their knowledge, in accordance with the facts and contains no omission likely to affect its import. As the case may be, declaration by those responsible for certain parts of the registration document that, having taken all reasonable care to ensure that such is the case, the information contained in the part of the registration document for which they are responsible is, to the best of their knowledge, in accordance with the facts and contains no omission likely to affect its import.

2. **STATUTORY AUDITORS**

2.1. Names and addresses of the issuer's auditors for the period covered by the historical financial information (together with their membership in a professional body).

2.2. If auditors have resigned, been removed or not been re-appointed during the period covered by the historical financial information, details if material.

3. **SELECTED FINANCIAL INFORMATION**

3.1. Selected historical financial information regarding the issuer, presented, for each financial year for the period covered by the historical financial information, and any subsequent interim financial period, in the same currency as the financial information.

The selected historical financial information must provide key figures that summarise the financial condition of the issuer.

3.2. If selected financial information for interim periods is provided, comparative data from the same period in the prior financial year must also be provided, except that the requirement for comparative balance sheet data is satisfied by presenting the year end balance sheet information.

4. **RISK FACTORS**

Prominent disclosure of risk factors that may affect the issuer's ability to fulfil its obligations under the securities to investors in a section headed 'Risk Factors'.

5. **INFORMATION ABOUT THE ISSUER**

5.1. *History and development of the Issuer*

5.1.1. the legal and commercial name of the issuer;

5.1.2. the place of registration of the issuer and its registration number;

5.1.3. the date of incorporation and the length of life of the issuer, except where indefinite;

5.1.4. the domicile and legal form of the issuer, the legislation under which the issuer operates, its country of incorporation, and the address and telephone number of its registered office (or principal place of business if different from its registered office);

5.1.5. any recent events particular to the issuer which are to a material extent relevant to the evaluation of the issuer's solvency.

▼B

5.2. *Investments*

5.2.1. A description of the principal investments made since the date of the last published financial statements.

5.2.2. Information concerning the issuer's principal future investments, on which its management bodies have already made firm commitments.

5.2.3. Information regarding the anticipated sources of funds needed to fulfil commitments referred to in item 5.2.2.

6. **BUSINESS OVERVIEW**

6.1. *Principal activities*

6.1.1. A description of the issuer's principal activities stating the main categories of products sold and/or services performed;

and

6.1.2. an indication of any significant new products and/or activities.

6.2. *Principal markets*

A brief description of the principal markets in which the issuer competes.

6.3. The basis for any statements made by the issuer regarding its competitive position.

7. **ORGANISATIONAL STRUCTURE**

7.1. If the issuer is part of a group, a brief description of the group and of the issuer's position within it.

7.2. If the issuer is dependent upon other entities within the group, this must be clearly stated together with an explanation of this dependence.

8. **TREND INFORMATION**

8.1. Include a statement that there has been no material adverse change in the prospects of the issuer since the date of its last published audited financial statements.

In the event that the issuer is unable to make such a statement, provide details of this material adverse change.

8.2. Information on any known trends, uncertainties, demands, commitments or events that are reasonably likely to have a material effect on the issuer's prospects for at least the current financial year.

9. **PROFIT FORECASTS OR ESTIMATES**

If an issuer chooses to include a profit forecast or a profit estimate, the registration document must contain the information items 9.1 and 9.2:

9.1. A statement setting out the principal assumptions upon which the issuer has based its forecast, or estimate.

There must be a clear distinction between assumptions about factors which the members of the administrative, management or supervisory bodies can influence and assumptions about factors which are exclusively outside the influence of the members of the administrative, management or supervisory bodies; the assumptions must be readily understandable by investors, be specific and precise and not relate to the general accuracy of the estimates underlying the forecast.

9.2. A report prepared by independent accountants or auditors must be included stating that in the opinion of the independent accountants or auditors the forecast or estimate has been properly compiled on the basis stated and that the basis of accounting used for the profit forecast or estimate is consistent with the accounting policies of the issuer.

9.3. The profit forecast or estimate must be prepared on a basis comparable with the historical financial information.

10. **ADMINISTRATIVE, MANAGEMENT, AND SUPERVISORY BODIES**

10.1. Names, business addresses and functions in the issuer of the following persons, and an indication of the principal activities performed by them outside the issuer where these are significant with respect to that issuer:

▼B

(a) members of the administrative, management or supervisory bodies;

(b) partners with unlimited liability, in the case of a limited partnership with a share capital.

10.2. *Administrative, Management, and Supervisory bodies' conflicts of interests*

Potential conflicts of interests between any duties to the issuing entity of the persons referred to in item 10.1 and their private interests and or other duties must be clearly stated. In the event that there are no such conflicts, make a statement to that effect.

11. **BOARD PRACTICES**

11.1. Details relating to the issuer's audit committee, including the names of committee members and a summary of the terms of reference under which the committee operates.

11.2. A statement as to whether or not the issuer complies with its country's of incorporation corporate governance regime(s). In the event that the issuer does not comply with such a regime a statement to that effect must be included together with an explanation regarding why the issuer does not comply with such regime.

12. **MAJOR SHAREHOLDERS**

12.1. To the extent known to the issuer, state whether the issuer is directly or indirectly owned or controlled and by whom and describe the nature of such control, and describe the measures in place to ensure that such control is not abused.

12.2. A description of any arrangements, known to the issuer, the operation of which may at a subsequent date result in a change in control of the issuer.

13. **FINANCIAL INFORMATION CONCERNING THE ISSUER'S ASSETS AND LIABILITIES, FINANCIAL POSITION AND PROFITS AND LOSSES**

13.1. *Historical Financial Information*

Audited historical financial information covering the latest 2 financial years (or such shorter period that the issuer has been in operation), and the audit report in respect of each year. ►M2 If the issuer has changed its accounting reference date during the period for which historical financial information is required, the audited historical information shall cover at least 24 months, or the entire period for which the issuer has been in operation, whichever is the shorter. ◄ Such financial information must be prepared according to Regulation (EC) No 1606/2002, or if not applicable to a Member States national accounting standards for issuers from the Community. For third country issuers, such financial information must be prepared according to the international accounting standards adopted pursuant to the procedure of Article 3 of Regulation (EC) No 1606/2002 or to a third country's national accounting standards equivalent to these standards. If such financial information is not equivalent to these standards, it must be presented in the form of restated financial statements.

The most recent year's historical financial information must be presented and prepared in a form consistent with that which will be adopted in the issuer's next published annual financial statements having regard to accounting standards and policies and legislation applicable to such annual financial statements.

If the issuer has been operating in its current sphere of economic activity for less than one year, the audited historical financial information covering that period must be prepared in accordance with the standards applicable to annual financial statements under the Regulation (EC) No 1606/2002, or if not applicable to a Member States national accounting standards where the issuer is an issuer from the Community. For third country issuers, the historical financial information must be prepared according to the international accounting standards adopted pursuant to the procedure of Article 3 of Regulation (EC) No 1606/2002 or to a third country's national accounting standards equivalent to these standards. This historical financial information must be audited.

▼B

If the audited financial information is prepared according to national accounting standards, the financial information required under this heading must include at least:

(a) balance sheet;

(b) income statement;

(c) cash flow statement;

and

(d) accounting policies and explanatory notes

The historical annual financial information must have been independently audited or reported on as to whether or not, for the purposes of the registration document, it gives a true and fair view, in accordance with auditing standards applicable in a Member State or an equivalent standard.

13.2. *Financial statements*

If the issuer prepares both own and consolidated financial statements, include at least the consolidated financial statements in the registration document.

13.3. *Auditing of historical annual financial information*

13.3.1. A statement that the historical financial information has been audited. If audit reports on the historical financial information have been refused by the statutory auditors or if they contain qualifications or disclaimers, such refusal or such qualifications or disclaimers must be reproduced in full and the reasons given.

13.3.2. An indication of other information in the registration document which has been audited by the auditors.

13.3.3. Where financial data in the registration document is not extracted from the issuer's audited financial statements state the source of the data and state that the data is unaudited.

13.4. *Age of latest financial information*

13.4.1. The last year of audited financial information may not be older than 18 months from the date of the registration document.

13.5. *Interim and other financial information*

13.5.1. If the issuer has published quarterly or half yearly financial information since the date of its last audited financial statements, these must be included in the registration document. If the quarterly or half yearly financial information has been reviewed or audited the audit or review report must also be included. If the quarterly or half yearly financial information is unaudited or has not been reviewed state that fact.

13.5.2. If the registration document is dated more than nine months after the end of the last audited financial year, it must contain interim financial information, covering at least the first six months of the financial year. If the interim financial information is un-audited state that fact.

The interim financial information must include comparative statements for the same period in the prior financial year, except that the requirement for comparative balance sheet information may be satisfied by presenting the years end balance sheet.

13.6. *Legal and arbitration proceedings*

Information on any governmental, legal or arbitration proceedings (including any such proceedings which are pending or threatened of which the issuer is aware), during a period covering at least the previous 12 months which may have, or have had in the recent past, significant effects on the issuer and/or group's financial position or profitability, or provide an appropriate negative statement.

13.7. *Significant change in the issuer's financial or trading position*

A description of any significant change in the financial or trading position of the group which has occurred since the end of the last financial period for which either audited financial information or interim financial information have been published, or an appropriate negative statement.

▼B

14. **ADDITIONAL INFORMATION**

14.1. *Share Capital*

14.1.1. The amount of the issued capital, the number and classes of the shares of which it is composed with details of their principal characteristics, the part of the issued capital still to be paid up, with an indication of the number, or total nominal value, and the type of the shares not yet fully paid up, broken down where applicable according to the extent to which they have been paid up.

14.2. *Memorandum and Articles of Association*

14.2.1. The register and the entry number therein, if applicable, and a description of the issuer's objects and purposes and where they can be found in the memorandum and articles of association.

15. **MATERIAL CONTRACTS**

A brief summary of all material contracts that are not entered into in the ordinary course of the issuer's business, which could result in any group member being under an obligation or entitlement that is material to the issuer's ability to meet its obligation to security holders in respect of the securities being issued.

16. **THIRD PARTY INFORMATION AND STATEMENT BY EXPERTS AND DECLARATIONS OF ANY INTEREST**

16.1. Where a statement or report attributed to a person as an expert is included in the registration document, provide such person's name, business address, qualifications and material interest if any in the issuer. If the report has been produced at the issuer's request a statement to that effect that such statement or report is included, in the form and context in which it is included, with the consent of that person who has authorised the contents of that part of the registration document.

16.2. Where information has been sourced from a third party, provide a confirmation that this information has been accurately reproduced and that as far as the issuer is aware and is able to ascertain from information published by that third party, no facts have been omitted which would render the reproduced information inaccurate or misleading. In addition, the issuer shall identify the source(s) of the information.

17. **DOCUMENTS ON DISPLAY**

A statement that for the life of the registration document the following documents (or copies thereof), where applicable, may be inspected:

(a) the memorandum and articles of association of the issuer;

(b) all reports, letters, and other documents, historical financial information, valuations and statements prepared by any expert at the issuer's request any part of which is included or referred to in the registration document;

(c) the historical financial information of the issuer or, in the case of a group, the historical financial information of the issuer and its subsidiary undertakings for each of the two financial years preceding the publication of the registration document.

An indication of where the documents on display may be inspected, by physical or electronic means.

▼B

ANNEX V

Minimum disclosure requirements for the securities note related to debt securities (schedule)

(Debt securities with a denomination per unit of less than EUR 50 000)

1. **PERSONS RESPONSIBLE**

1.1. All persons responsible for the information given in the prospectus and, as the case may be, for certain parts of it, with, in the latter case, an indication of such parts. In the case of natural persons including members of the issuer's administrative, management or supervisory bodies indicate the name and function of the person; in case of legal persons indicate the name and registered office.

1.2. A declaration by those responsible for the prospectus that, having taken all reasonable care to ensure that such is the case, the information contained in the prospectus is, to the best of their knowledge, in accordance with the facts and contains no omission likely to affect its import. As the case may be, declaration by those responsible for certain parts of the prospectus that the information contained in the part of the prospectus for which they are responsible is, to the best of their knowledge, in accordance with the facts and contains no omission likely to affect its import.

2. **RISK FACTORS**

2.1. Prominent disclosure of risk factors that are material to the securities being offered and/or admitted to trading in order to assess the market risk associated with these securities in a section headed 'Risk Factors'.

3. **KEY INFORMATION**

3.1. *Interest of natural and legal persons involved in the issue/offer*

A description of any interest, including conflicting ones, that is material to the issue/offer, detailing the persons involved and the nature of the interest.

3.2. *Reasons for the offer and use of proceeds*

Reasons for the offer if different from making profit and/or hedging certain risks. Where applicable, disclosure of the estimated total expenses of the issue/offer and the estimated net amount of the proceeds. These expenses and proceeds shall be broken into each principal intended use and presented by order of priority of such uses. If the issuer is aware that the anticipated proceeds will not be sufficient to fund all the proposed uses, state the amount and sources of other funds needed.

4. **INFORMATION CONCERNING THE SECURITIES TO BE OFFERED/ADMITTED TO TRADING**

4.1. A description of the type and the class of the securities being offered and/or admitted to trading, including the ISIN (International Security Identification Number) or other such security identification code.

4.2. Legislation under which the securities have been created.

4.3. An indication of whether the securities are in registered form or bearer form and whether the securities are in certificated form or book-entry form. In the latter case, name and address of the entity in charge of keeping the records.

4.4. Currency of the securities issue.

4.5. Ranking of the securities being offered and/or admitted to trading, including summaries of any clauses that are intended to affect ranking or subordinate the security to any present or future liabilities of the issuer.

4.6. A description of the rights attached to the securities, including any limitations of those rights, and procedure for the exercise of those rights.

4.7. The nominal interest rate and provisions relating to interest payable.

▼B

— The date from which interest becomes payable and the due dates for interest

— The time limit on the validity of claims to interest and repayment of principal.

Where the rate is not fixed, description of the underlying on which it is based and of the method used to relate the two and an indication where information about the past and the further performance of the underlying and its volatility can be obtained.

— A description of any market disruption or settlement disruption events that affect the underlying

— Adjustment rules with relation to events concerning the underlying

— Name of the calculation agent.

If the security has a derivative component in the interest payment, provide a clear and comprehensive explanation to help investors understand how the value of their investment is affected by the value of the underlying instrument(s), especially under the circumstances when the risks are most evident.

4.8. Maturity date and arrangements for the amortisation of the loan, including the repayment procedures. Where advance amortisation is contemplated, on the initiative of the issuer or of the holder, it shall be described, stipulating amortisation terms and conditions.

4.9. An indication of yield. Describe the method whereby that yield is calculated in summary form.

4.10. Representation of debt security holders including an identification of the organisation representing the investors and provisions applying to such representation. Indication of where the public may have access to the contracts relating to these forms of representation.

4.11. In the case of new issues, a statement of the resolutions, authorisations and approvals by virtue of which the securities have been or will be created and/or issued.

4.12. In the case of new issues, the expected issue date of the securities.

4.13. A description of any restrictions on the free transferability of the securities.

4.14. In respect of the country of registered office of the issuer and the country(ies) where the offer being made or admission to trading is being sought:

— information on taxes on the income from the securities withheld at source;

— indication as to whether the issuer assumes responsibility for the withholding of taxes at the source.

5. **TERMS AND CONDITIONS OF THE OFFER**

5.1. *Conditions, offer statistics, expected timetable and action required to apply for the offer*

5.1.1. Conditions to which the offer is subject.

5.1.2. Total amount of the issue/offer; if the amount is not fixed, description of the arrangements and time for announcing to the public the definitive amount of the offer.

5.1.3. The time period, including any possible amendments, during which the offer will be open and description of the application process.

5.1.4. A description of the possibility to reduce subscriptions and the manner for refunding excess amount paid by applicants.

5.1.5. Details of the minimum and/or maximum amount of application, (whether in number of securities or aggregate amount to invest).

5.1.6. Method and time limits for paying up the securities and for delivery of the securities.

5.1.7. A full description of the manner and date in which results of the offer are to be made public.

▼B

5.1.8. The procedure for the exercise of any right of pre-emption, the negotiability of subscription rights and the treatment of subscription rights not exercised.

5.2. *Plan of distribution and allotment*

5.2.1. The various categories of potential investors to which the securities are offered. If the offer is being made simultaneously in the markets of two or more countries and if a tranche has been or is being reserved for certain of these, indicate any such tranche.

5.2.2. Process for notification to applicants of the amount allotted and indication whether dealing may begin before notification is made.

5.3. *Pricing*

5.3.1. An indication of the expected price at which the securities will be offered or the method of determining the price and the process for its disclosure. Indicate the amount of any expenses and taxes specifically charged to the subscriber or purchaser.

5.4. *Placing and Underwriting*

5.4.1. Name and address of the co-ordinator(s) of the global offer and of single parts of the offer and, to the extend known to the issuer or to the offeror, of the placers in the various countries where the offer takes place.

5.4.2. Name and address of any paying agents and depository agents in each country.

5.4.3. Name and address of the entities agreeing to underwrite the issue on a firm commitment basis, and name and address of the entities agreeing to place the issue without a firm commitment or under 'best efforts' arrangements. Indication of the material features of the agreements, including the quotas. Where not all of the issue is underwritten, a statement of the portion not covered. Indication of the overall amount of the underwriting commission and of the placing commission.

5.4.4. When the underwriting agreement has been or will be reached.

6. **ADMISSION TO TRADING AND DEALING ARRANGEMENTS**

6.1. An indication as to whether the securities offered are or will be the object of an application for admission to trading, with a view to their distribution in a regulated market or other equivalent markets with indication of the markets in question. This circumstance must be mentioned, without creating the impression that the admission to trading will necessarily be approved. If known, give the earliest dates on which the securities will be admitted to trading.

6.2. All the regulated markets or equivalent markets on which, to the knowledge of the issuer, securities of the same class of the securities to be offered or admitted to trading are already admitted to trading.

6.3. Name and address of the entities which have a firm commitment to act as intermediaries in secondary trading, providing liquidity through bid and offer rates and description of the main terms of their commitment.

7. **ADDITIONAL INFORMATION**

7.1. If advisors connected with an issue are mentioned in the Securities Note, a statement of the capacity in which the advisors have acted.

7.2. An indication of other information in the Securities Note which has been audited or reviewed by statutory auditors and where auditors have produced a report. Reproduction of the report or, with permission of the competent authority, a summary of the report.

7.3. Where a statement or report attributed to a person as an expert is included in the Securities Note, provide such persons' name, business address, qualifications and material interest if any in the issuer. If the report has been produced at the issuer's request a statement to that effect that such statement or report is included, in the form and context in which it is included, with the consent of that person who has authorised the contents of that part of the Securities Note.

7.4. Where information has been sourced from a third party, provide a confirmation that this information has been accurately reproduced and

▼B

that as far as the issuer is aware and is able to ascertain from information published by that third party, no facts have been omitted which would render the reproduced information inaccurate or misleading. In addition, identify the source(s) of the information.

7.5. Credit ratings assigned to an issuer or its debt securities at the request or with the co-operation of the issuer in the rating process. A brief explanation of the meaning of the ratings if this has previously been published by the rating provider.

▼B

ANNEX VI

Minimum disclosure requirements for guarantees

(Additional building block)

1. **Nature of the Guarantee**

A description of any arrangement intended to ensure that any obligation material to the issue will be duly serviced, whether in the form of guarantee, surety, Keep well Agreement, Mono-line Insurance policy or other equivalent commitment (hereafter referred to generically as 'guarantees' and their provider as 'guarantor' for convenience).

Without prejudice to the generality of the foregoing, such arrangements encompass commitments to ensure obligations to repay debt securities and/or the payment of interest and the description shall set out how the arrangement is intended to ensure that the guaranteed payments will be duly serviced.

2. **Scope of the Guarantee**

Details shall be disclosed about the terms and conditions and scope of the guarantee. Without prejudice to the generality of the foregoing, these details should cover any conditionality on the application of the guarantee in the event of any default under the terms of the security and the material terms of any mono-line insurance or keep well agreement between the issuer and the guarantor. Details must also be disclosed of any guarantor's power of veto in relation to changes to the security holder's rights, such as is often found in Mono-line Insurance.

3. **Information to be disclosed about the guarantor**

The guarantor must disclose information about itself as if it were the issuer of that same type of security that is the subject of the guarantee.

4. **Documents on display**

Indication of the places where the public may have access to the material contracts and other documents relating to the guarantee.

▼B

ANNEX VII

Minimum disclosure requirements for asset-backed securities registration document (schedule)

1. **PERSONS RESPONSIBLE**

1.1. All persons responsible for the information given in the registration document and, as the case may be, for certain parts of it, with, in the latter case, an indication of such parts. In the case of natural persons including members of the issuer's administrative, management or supervisory bodies indicate the name and function of the person; in case of legal persons indicate the name and registered office.

1.2. A declaration by those responsible for the registration document that, having taken all reasonable care to ensure that such is the case, the information given in the registration document is, to the best of their knowledge, in accordance with the facts and does not omit anything likely to affect its import. As the case may be, declaration by those responsible for certain parts of the registration document that having taken all reasonable care to ensure that such is the case, the information contained in that part of the registration document for which they are responsible is, to the best of their knowledge, in accordance with the facts and contains no omission likely to affect its import.

2. **STATUTORY AUDITORS**

2.1. Names and addresses of the issuer's auditors for the period covered by the historical financial information (together with any membership of any relevant professional body).

3. **RISK FACTORS**

3.1. The document must prominently disclose risk factors in a section headed 'Risk Factors' that are specific to the issuer and its industry.

4. **INFORMATION ABOUT THE ISSUER:**

4.1. A statement whether the issuer has been established as a special purpose vehicle or entity for the purpose of issuing asset backed securities;

4.2. The legal and commercial name of the issuer;

4.3. The place of registration of the issuer and its registration number;

4.4. The date of incorporation and the length of life of the issuer, except where indefinite;

4.5. The domicile and legal form of the issuer, the legislation under which the issuer operates its country of incorporation and the address and telephone number of its registered office (or principal place of business if different from its registered office).

4.6. Description of the amount of the issuer's authorised and issued capital and the amount of any capital agreed to be issued, the number and classes of the securities of which it is composed.

5. **BUSINESS OVERVIEW**

5.1. A brief description of the issuer's principal activities.

5.2. A global overview of the parties to the securitisation program including information on the direct or indirect ownership or control between those parties.

6. **ADMINISTRATIVE, MANAGEMENT AND SUPERVISORY BODIES**

6.1. Names, business addresses and functions in the issuer of the following persons, and an indication of the principal activities performed by them outside the issuer where these are significant with respect to that issuer:

(a) members of the administrative, management or supervisory bodies;

(b) partners with unlimited liability, in the case of a limited partnership with a share capital.

▼B

7. **MAJOR SHAREHOLDERS**

7.1. To the extent known to the issuer, state whether the issuer is directly or indirectly owned or controlled and by whom, and describe the nature of such control and describe the measures in place to ensure that such control is not abused.

8. **FINANCIAL INFORMATION CONCERNING THE ISSUER'S ASSETS AND LIABILITIES, FINANCIAL POSITION, AND PROFITS AND LOSSES**

8.1. Where, since the date of incorporation or establishment, an issuer has not commenced operations and no financial statements have been made up as at the date of the registration document, a statement to that effect shall be provided in the registration document.

8.2. *Historical Financial Information*

Where, since the date of incorporation or establishment, an issuer has commenced operations and financial statements have been made up, the registration document must contain audited historical financial information covering the latest 2 financial years (or shorter period that the issuer has been in operation) and the audit report in respect of each year. ►M2 If the issuer has changed its accounting reference date during the period for which historical financial information is required, the audited historical information shall cover at least 24 months, or the entire period for which the issuer has been in operation, whichever is the shorter. ◄Such financial information must be prepared according to Regulation (EC) No 1606/2002, or if not applicable to a Member's State national accounting standards for issuers from the Community. For third country issuers, such financial information must be prepared according to the international accounting standards adopted pursuant to the procedure of Article 3 of Regulation (EC) No 1606/2002 or to a third country's national accounting standards equivalent to these standards. If such financial information is not equivalent to these standards, it must be presented in the form of restated financial statements.

The most recent year's historical financial information must be presented and prepared in a form consistent with that which will be adopted in the issuer's next annual published financial statements having regard to accounting standards and policies and legislation applicable to such annual financial statements.

If the issuer has been operating in its current sphere of economic activity for less than one year, the audited historical financial information covering that period must be prepared in accordance with the standards applicable to annual financial statements under Regulation (EC) No 1606/2002, or if not applicable to a Member States national accounting standards where the issuer is from the Community. For third country issuers, the historical financial information must be prepared according to the international accounting standards adopted pursuant to the procedure of Article 3 of Regulation (EC) No 1606/2002 or to a third country's national accounting standards equivalent to these standards. This historical financial information must be audited.

If the audited financial information is prepared according to national accounting standards, the financial information required under this heading must include at least the following:

(a) the balance sheet;

(b) the income statement;

(c) the accounting policies and explanatory notes.

The historical annual financial information must be independently audited or reported on as to whether or not, for the purposes of the registration document, it gives a true and fair view, in accordance with auditing standards applicable in a Member State or an equivalent standard.

8.2a *This paragraph may be used only for issues of asset backed securities having a denomination per unit of at least EUR 50 000.*

Where, since the date of incorporation or establishment, an issuer has commenced operations and financial statements have been made up, the

▼B

registration document must contain audited historical financial information covering the latest 2 financial years (or shorter period that the issuer has been in operation) and the audit report in respect of each year. ►M2 If the issuer has changed its accounting reference date during the period for which historical financial information is required, the audited historical information shall cover at least 24 months, or the entire period for which the issuer has been in operation, whichever is the shorter. ◄ Such financial information must be prepared according to Regulation (EC) No 1606/2002 or, if not applicable, to a Member's State national accounting standards for issuers from the Community. For third country issuers, such financial information must be prepared according to the international accounting standards adopted pursuant to the procedure of Article 3 of Regulation (EC) No 1606/2002 or to a third country's national accounting standards equivalent to these standards. Otherwise, the following information must be included in the registration document:

(a) a prominent statement that the financial information included in the registration document has not been prepared in accordance with the international accounting standards adopted pursuant to the procedure of Article 3 of Regulation (EC) No 1606/2002 and that there may be material differences in the financial information had Regulation (EC) No 1606/2002 been applied to the historical financial information;

(b) immediately following the historical financial information a narrative description of the differences between the international accounting standards adopted pursuant to the procedure of Article 3 of Regulation (EC) No 1606/2002 and the accounting principles adopted by the issuer in preparing its annual financial statements.

The most recent year's historical financial information must be presented and prepared in a form consistent with that which will be adopted in the issuer's next annual financial statements having regard to accounting standards and policies and legislation applicable to such annual financial statements.

If the audited financial information is prepared according to national accounting standards, the financial information required under this heading must include at least the following:

(a) the balance sheet;

(b) the income statement;

(c) the accounting policies and explanatory notes.

The historical annual financial information must be independently audited or reported on as to whether or not, for the purposes of the registration document, it gives a true and fair view, in accordance with auditing standards applicable in a Member State or an equivalent standard. Otherwise, the following information must be included in the registration document:

(a) a prominent statement disclosing which auditing standards have been applied;

(b) an explanation of any significant departures from International Standards on Auditing.

8.3. *Legal and arbitration proceedings*

Information on any governmental, legal or arbitration proceedings (including any such proceedings which are pending or threatened of which the company is aware), during a period covering at least the previous 12 months, which may have, or have had in the recent past, significant effects on the issuer and/or group's financial position or profitability, or provide an appropriate negative statement.

8.4. *Material adverse change in the issuer's financial position*

Where an issuer has prepared financial statements, include a statement that there has been no material adverse change in the financial position or prospects of the issuer since the date of its last published audited financial statements. Where a material adverse change has occurred, this must be disclosed in the registration document.

▼B

9. THIRD PARTY INFORMATION AND STATEMENT BY EXPERTS AND DECLARATIONS OF ANY INTEREST

9.1. Where a statement or report attributed to a person as an expert is included in the registration document, provide such person's name, business address, qualifications and material interest if any in the issuer. If the report has been produced at the issuer's request a statement to that effect that such statement or report is included, in the form and context in which it is included, with the consent of that person who has authorised the contents of that part of the registration document.

9.2. Where information has been sourced from a third party, provide a confirmation that this information has been accurately reproduced and that as far as the issuer is aware and is able to ascertain from information published by that third party, no facts have been omitted which would render the reproduced information inaccurate or misleading In addition, the issuer shall identify the source(s) of the information.

10. DOCUMENTS ON DISPLAY

10.1. A statement that for the life of the registration document the following documents (or copies thereof), where applicable, may be inspected:

(a) the memorandum and articles of association of the issuer;

(b) all reports, letters, and other documents, historical financial information, valuations and statements prepared by any expert at the issuer's request any part of which is included or referred to in the registration document;

(c) the historical financial information of the issuer or, in the case of a group, the historical financial information of the issuer and its subsidiary undertakings for each of the two financial years preceding the publication of the registration document.

An indication of where the documents on display may be inspected, by physical or electronic means.

▼B

ANNEX VIII

Minimum disclosure requirements for the asset-backed securities additional building block

1. **THE SECURITIES**

1.1. The minimum denomination of an issue.

1.2. Where information is disclosed about an undertaking/obligor which is not involved in the issue, provide a confirmation that the information relating to the undertaking/obligor has been accurately reproduced from information published by the undertaking/obligor. So far as the issuer is aware and is able to ascertain from information published by the undertaking/obligor no facts have been omitted which would render the reproduced information misleading.

In addition, identify the source(s) of information in the Securities Note that has been reproduced from information published by an undertaking/obligor.

2. **THE UNDERLYING ASSETS**

2.1. Confirmation that the securitised assets backing the issue have characteristics that demonstrate capacity to produce funds to service any payments due and payable on the securities.

2.2. *In respect of a pool of discrete assets backing the issue:*

2.2.1. The legal jurisdiction by which the pool of assets is governed

2.2.2. (a) In the case of a small number of easily identifiable obligors, a general description of each obligor.

(b) In all other cases, a description of: the general characteristics of the obligors; and the economic environment, as well as global statistical data referred to the securitised assets.

2.2.3. the legal nature of the assets;

2.2.4. the expiry or maturity date(s) of the assets;

2.2.5. the amount of the assets;

2.2.6. loan to value ratio or level of collateralisation;

2.2.7. the method of origination or creation of the assets, and for loans and credit agreements, the principal lending criteria and an indication of any loans which do not meet these criteria and any rights or obligations to make further advances;

2.2.8. an indication of significant representations and collaterals given to the issuer relating to the assets;

2.2.9. any rights to substitute the assets and a description of the manner in which and the type of assets which may be so substituted; if there is any capacity to substitute assets with a different class or quality of assets a statement to that effect together with a description of the impact of such substitution;

2.2.10. a description of any relevant insurance policies relating to the assets. Any concentration with one insurer must be disclosed if it is material to the transaction.

2.2.11. Where the assets comprise obligations of 5 or fewer obligors which are legal persons or where an obligor accounts for 20 % or more of the assets, or where an obligor accounts for a material portion of the assets, so far as the issuer is aware and/or is able to ascertain from information published by the obligor(s) indicate either of the following:

(a) information relating to each obligor as if it were an issuer drafting a registration document for debt and derivative securities with an individual denomination of at least EUR 50 000;

(b) if an obligor or guarantor has securities already admitted to trading on a regulated or equivalent market or the obligations are guaranteed by an entity admitted to trading on a regulated or equivalent market, the name, address, country of incorporation, nature of

▼B

business and name of the market in which its securities are admitted.

2.2.12. If a relationship exists that is material to the issue, between the issuer, guarantor and obligor, details of the principal terms of that relationship.

2.2.13. Where the assets comprise obligations that are not traded on a regulated or equivalent market, a description of the principal terms and conditions of the obligations.

2.2.14. Where the assets comprise equity securities that are admitted to trading on a regulated or equivalent market indicate the following:

(a) a description of the securities;

(b) a description of the market on which they are traded including its date of establishment, how price information is published, an indication of daily trading volumes, information as to the standing of the market in the country and the name of the market's regulatory authority;

(c) the frequency with which prices of the relevant securities, are published.

2.2.15. Where more than ten (10) per cent of the assets comprise equity securities that are not traded on a regulated or equivalent market, a description of those equity securities and equivalent information to that contained in the schedule for share registration document in respect of each issuer of those securities.

2.2.16. Where a material portion of the assets are secured on or backed by real property, a valuation report relating to the property setting out both the valuation of the property and cash flow/income streams.

Compliance with this disclosure is not required if the issue is of securities backed by mortgage loans with property as security, where there has been no revaluation of the properties for the purpose of the issue, and it is clearly stated that the valuations quoted are as at the date of the original initial mortgage loan origination.

2.3. *In respect of an actively managed pool of assets backing the issue:*

2.3.1. equivalent information to that contained in items 2.1 and 2.2 to allow an assessment of the type, quality, sufficiency and liquidity of the asset types in the portfolio which will secure the issue;

2.3.2. the parameters within which investments can be made, the name and description of the entity responsible for such management including a description of that entity's expertise and experience, a summary of the provisions relating to the termination of the appointment of such entity and the appointment of an alternative management entity, and a description of that entity's relationship with any other parties to the issue.

2.4. Where an issuer proposes to issue further securities backed by the same assets, a prominent statement to that effect and unless those further securities are fungible with or are subordinated to those classes of existing debt, a description of how the holders of that class will be informed.

3. **STRUCTURE AND CASH FLOW**

3.1. Description of the structure of the transaction, including, if necessary, a structure diagram.

3.2. Description of the entities participating in the issue and description of the functions to be performed by them.

3.3. Description of the method and date of the sale, transfer, novation or assignment of the assets or of any rights and/or obligations in the assets to the issuer or, where applicable, the manner and time period in which the proceeds from the issue will be fully invested by the issuer.

3.4. *An explanation of the flow of funds including:*

3.4.1. how the cash flow from the assets will meet the issuer's obligations to holders of the securities, including, if necessary, a financial service table and a description of the assumptions used in developing the table;

▼B

3.4.2. information on any credit enhancements, an indication of where material potential liquidity shortfalls may occur and the availability of any liquidity supports and indication of provisions designed to cover interest/principal shortfall risks;

3.4.3. without prejudice to item 3.4.2, details of any subordinated debt finance;

3.4.4. an indication of any investment parameters for the investment of temporary liquidity surpluses and description of the parties responsible for such investment;

3.4.5. how payments are collected in respect of the assets;

3.4.6. the order of priority of payments made by the issuer to the holders of the class of securities in question;

3.4.7. details of any other arrangements upon which payments of interest and principal to investors are dependent;

3.5. the name, address and significant business activities of the originators of the securitised assets.

3.6. Where the return on, and/or repayment of the security is linked to the performance or credit of other assets which are not assets of the issuer, items 2.2 and 2.3 are necessary;

3.7. the name, address and significant business activities of the administrator, calculation agent or equivalent, together with a summary of the administrator's/calculation agents responsibilities, their relationship with the originator or the creator of the assets and a summary of the provisions relating to the termination of the appointment of the administrator/calculation agent and the appointment of an alternative administrator/calculation agent;

3.8. the names and addresses and brief description of:

(a) any swap counterparties and any providers of other material forms of credit/liquidity enhancement;

(b) the banks with which the main accounts relating to the transaction are held.

4. **POST ISSUANCE REPORTING**

4.1. Indication in the prospectus whether or not it intends to provide post-issuance transaction information regarding securities to be admitted to trading and the performance of the underlying collateral. Where the issuer has indicated that it intends to report such information, specify in the prospectus what information will be reported, where such information can be obtained, and the frequency with which such information will be reported.

▼B

ANNEX IX

Minimum disclosure requirements for the debt and derivative securities registration document (schedule)

(Debt and derivative securities with a denomination per unit of at least EUR 50 000)

1. **PERSONS RESPONSIBLE**

1.1. All persons responsible for the information given in the registration document and, as the case may be, for certain parts of it, with, in the latter case, an indication of such parts. In the case of natural persons including members of the issuer's administrative, management or supervisory bodies indicate the name and function of the person; in case of legal persons indicate the name and registered office.

1.2. A declaration by those responsible for the registration document that, having taken all reasonable care to ensure that such is the case, the information contained in the registration document is, to the best of their knowledge, in accordance with the facts and contains no omission likely to affect its import. As the case may be, declaration by those responsible for certain parts of the registration document that, having taken all reasonable care to ensure that such is the case, the information contained in the part of the registration document for which they are responsible is, to the best of their knowledge, in accordance with the facts and contains no omission likely to affect its import.

2. **STATUTORY AUDITORS**

2.1. Names and addresses of the issuer's auditors for the period covered by the historical financial information (together with their membership in a professional body).

2.2. If auditors have resigned, been removed or not been re-appointed during the period covered by the historical financial information, details if material.

3. **RISK FACTORS**

3.1. Prominent disclosure of risk factors that may affect the issuer's ability to fulfil its obligations under the securities to investors in a section headed 'Risk Factors'.

4. **INFORMATION ABOUT THE ISSUER**

4.1. *History and development of the Issuer*

4.1.1. the legal and commercial name of the issuer;

4.1.2. the place of registration of the issuer and its registration number;

4.1.3. the date of incorporation and the length of life of the issuer, except where indefinite;

4.1.4. the domicile and legal form of the issuer, the legislation under which the issuer operates, its country of incorporation, and the address and telephone number of its registered office (or principal place of business if different from its registered office;

4.1.5. any recent events particular to the issuer and which are to a material extent relevant to the evaluation of the issuer's solvency.

5. **BUSINESS OVERVIEW**

5.1. *Principal activities:*

5.1.1. A brief description of the issuer's principal activities stating the main categories of products sold and/or services performed;

5.1.2. The basis for any statements in the registration document made by the issuer regarding its competitive position.

6. **ORGANISATIONAL STRUCTURE**

6.1. If the issuer is part of a group, a brief description of the group and of the issuer's position within it.

▼B

6.2. If the issuer is dependent upon other entities within the group, this must be clearly stated together with an explanation of this dependence.

7. **TREND INFORMATION**

7.1. Include a statement that there has been no material adverse change in the prospects of the issuer since the date of its last published audited financial statements.

In the event that the issuer is unable to make such a statement, provide details of this material adverse change.

8. **PROFIT FORECASTS OR ESTIMATES**

If an issuer chooses to include a profit forecast or a profit estimate, the registration document must contain the information items 8.1 and 8.2 the following:

8.1. A statement setting out the principal assumptions upon which the issuer has based its forecast, or estimate.

There must be a clear distinction between assumptions about factors which the members of the administrative, management or supervisory bodies can influence and assumptions about factors which are exclusively outside the influence of the members of the administrative, management or supervisory bodies; be readily understandable by investors; be specific and precise; and not relate to the general accuracy of the estimates underlying the forecast.

8.2. Any profit forecast set out in the registration document must be accompanied by a statement confirming that the said forecast has been properly prepared on the basis stated and that the basis of accounting is consistent with the accounting policies of the issuer.

8.3. The profit forecast or estimate must be prepared on a basis comparable with the historical financial information.

9. **ADMINISTRATIVE, MANAGEMENT, AND SUPERVISORY BODIES**

9.1. Names, business addresses and functions in the issuer of the following persons, and an indication of the principal activities performed by them outside the issuer where these are significant with respect to that issuer:

(a) members of the administrative, management or supervisory bodies;

(b) partners with unlimited liability, in the case of a limited partnership with a share capital.

9.2. *Administrative, Management, and Supervisory bodies' conflicts of interests*

Potential conflicts of interests between any duties to the issuing entity of the persons referred to in item 9.1 and their private interests and or other duties must be clearly stated. In the event that there are no such conflicts, a statement to that effect.

10. **MAJOR SHAREHOLDERS**

10.1. To the extent known to the issuer, state whether the issuer is directly or indirectly owned or controlled and by whom, and describe the nature of such control, and describe the measures in place to ensure that such control is not abused.

10.2. A description of any arrangements, known to the issuer, the operation of which may at a subsequent date result in a change in control of the issuer.

11. **FINANCIAL INFORMATION CONCERNING THE ISSUER'S ASSETS AND LIABILITIES, FINANCIAL POSITION AND PROFITS AND LOSSES**

11.1. *Historical Financial Information*

Audited historical financial information covering the latest two financial years (or such shorter period that the issuer has been in operation), and the audit report in respect of each year. ►M2 If the issuer has changed its accounting reference date during the period for which historical financial information is required, the audited historical information shall cover at least 24 months, or the entire period for

▼B

which the issuer has been in operation, whichever is the shorter. ◄ Such financial information must be prepared according to Regulation (EC) No 1606/2002, or if not applicable to a Member's State national accounting standards for issuers from the Community. For third country issuers, such financial information must be prepared according to the international accounting standards adopted pursuant to the procedure of Article 3 of Regulation (EC) No 1606/2002 or to a third country's national accounting standards equivalent to these standards. Otherwise, the following information must be included in the registration document:

(a) a prominent statement that the financial information included in the registration document has not been prepared in accordance with the international accounting standards adopted pursuant to the procedure of Article 3 of Regulation (EC) No 1606/2002 and that there may be material differences in the financial information had Regulation (EC) No 1606/2002 been applied to the historical financial information.

(b) immediately following the historical financial information a narrative description of the differences between the international accounting standards adopted pursuant to the procedure of Article 3 of Regulation (EC) No 1606/2002 and the accounting principles adopted by the issuer in preparing its annual financial statements.

The most recent year's historical financial information must be presented and prepared in a form consistent with that which will be adopted in the issuer's next published annual financial statements having regard to accounting standards and policies and legislation applicable to such annual financial statements.

If the audited financial information is prepared according to national accounting standards, the financial information required under this heading must include at least the following:

(a) the balance sheet;

(b) the income statement;

(c) the accounting policies and explanatory notes.

The historical annual financial information must be independently audited or reported on as to whether or not, for the purposes of the registration document, it gives a true and fair view, in accordance with auditing standards applicable in a Member State or an equivalent standard. Otherwise, the following information must be included in the registration document:

(a) a prominent statement disclosing which auditing standards have been applied;

(b) an explanation of any significant departures from international standards on auditing.

11.2. *Financial statements*

If the issuer prepares both own and consolidated financial statements, include at least the consolidated financial statements in the registration document.

11.3. *Auditing of historical annual financial information*

11.3.1. A statement that the historical financial information has been audited. If audit reports on the historical financial information have been refused by the statutory auditors or if they contain qualifications or disclaimers, such refusal or such qualifications or disclaimers must be reproduced in full and the reasons given.

11.3.2. An indication of other information in the registration document which has been audited by the auditors.

11.3.3. Where financial data in the registration document is not extracted from the issuer's audited financial statements, state the source of the data and state that the data is unaudited.

▼B

11.4. *Age of latest financial information*

11.4.1. The last year of audited financial information may not be older than 18 months from the date of the registration document.

11.5. *Legal and arbitration proceedings*

Information on any governmental, legal or arbitration proceedings (including any such proceedings which are pending or threatened of which the issuer is aware), during a period covering at least the previous 12 months which may have, or have had in the recent past, significant effects on the issuer and/or group's financial position or profitability, or provide an appropriate negative statement.

11.6. *Significant change in the issuer's financial or trading position*

A description of any significant change in the financial or trading position of the group which has occurred since the end of the last financial period for which either audited financial information or interim financial information have been published, or an appropriate negative statement.

12. **MATERIAL CONTRACTS**

A brief summary of all material contracts that are not entered into in the ordinary course of the issuer's business, which could result in any group member being under an obligation or entitlement that is material to the issuer's ability to meet its obligation to security holders in respect of the securities being issued.

13. **THIRD PARTY INFORMATION AND STATEMENT BY EXPERTS AND DECLARATIONS OF ANY INTEREST**

13.1. Where a statement or report attributed to a person as an expert is included in the registration document, provide such person's name, business address, qualifications and material interest if any in the issuer. If the report has been produced at the issuer's request a statement to that effect that such statement or report is included, in the form and context in which it is included, with the consent of that person who has authorised the contents of that part of the registration document.

13.2. *Third party information*

Where information has been sourced from a third party, provide a confirmation that this information has been accurately reproduced and that as far as the issuer is aware and is able to ascertain from information published by that third party, no facts have been omitted which would render the reproduced information inaccurate or misleading; in addition, identify the source(s) of the information.

14. **DOCUMENTS ON DISPLAY**

A statement that for the life of the registration document the following documents (or copies thereof), where applicable, may be inspected:

(a) the memorandum and articles of association of the issuer;

(b) all reports, letters, and other documents, historical financial information, valuations and statements prepared by any expert at the issuer's request any part of which is included or referred to in the registration document;

(c) the historical financial information of the issuer or, in the case of a group, the historical financial information of the issuer and its subsidiary undertakings for each of the two financial years preceding the publication of the registration document.

An indication of where the documents on display may be inspected, by physical or electronic means.

▼B

ANNEX X

Minimum disclosure requirements for the depository receipts issued over shares (schedule)

INFORMATION ABOUT THE ISSUER OF THE UNDERLYING SHARES

1. **PERSONS RESPONSIBLE**

1.1. All persons responsible for the information given in the prospectus and, as the case may be, for certain parts of it, with, in the latter case, an indication of such parts. In the case of natural persons including members of the issuer's administrative, management or supervisory bodies indicate the name and function of the person; in case of legal persons indicate the name and registered office.

1.2. A declaration by those responsible for the prospectus that, having taken all reasonable care to ensure that such is the case, the information contained in the prospectus is, to the best of their knowledge, in accordance with the facts and contains no omission likely to affect its import. As the case may be, declaration by those responsible for certain parts of the prospectus that, having taken all reasonable care to ensure that such is the case, the information contained in the part of the prospectus for which they are responsible is, to the best of their knowledge, in accordance with the facts and contains no omission likely to affect its import.

2. **STATUTORY AUDITORS**

2.1. Names and addresses of the issuer's auditors for the period covered by the historical financial information (together with their membership in a professional body).

2.2. If auditors have resigned, been removed or not been re-appointed during the period covered by the historical financial information, indicate details if material.

3. **SELECTED FINANCIAL INFORMATION**

3.1. Selected historical financial information regarding the issuer, presented for each financial year for the period covered by the historical financial information, and any subsequent interim financial period, in the same currency as the financial information.

The selected historical financial information must provide the key figures that summarise the financial condition of the issuer.

3.2. If selected financial information for interim periods is provided, comparative data from the same period in the prior financial year shall also be provided, except that the requirement for comparative balance sheet information is satisfied by presenting the year end balance sheet information.

4. **RISK FACTORS**

Prominent disclosure of risk factors that are specific to the issuer or its industry in a section headed 'Risk Factors'.

5. **INFORMATION ABOUT THE ISSUER**

5.1. *History and development of the issuer*

5.1.1. the legal and commercial name of the issuer;

5.1.2. the place of registration of the issuer and its registration number;

5.1.3. the date of incorporation and the length of life of the issuer, except where indefinite;

5.1.4. the domicile and legal form of the issuer, the legislation under which the issuer operates, its country of incorporation, and the address and telephone number of its registered office (or principal place of business if different from its registered office);

5.1.5. the important events in the development of the issuer's business.

▼B

5.2. *Investments*

5.2.1. A description, (including the amount) of the issuer's principal investments for each financial year for the period covered by the historical financial information up to the date of the prospectus;

5.2.2. A description of the issuer's principal investments that are currently in progress, including the distribution of these investments geographically (home and abroad) and the method of financing (internal or external);

5.2.3. Information concerning the issuer's principal future investments on which its management bodies have already made firm commitments.

6. **BUSINESS OVERVIEW**

6.1. *Principal Activities*

6.1.1. A description of, and key factors relating to, the nature of the issuer's operations and its principal activities, stating the main categories of products sold and/or services performed for each financial year for the period covered by the historical financial information.

6.1.2. An indication of any significant new products and/or services that have been introduced and, to the extent the development of new products or services has been publicly disclosed, give the status of development.

6.2. *Principal Markets*

A description of the principal markets in which the issuer competes, including a breakdown of total revenues by category of activity and geographic market for each financial year for the period covered by the historical financial information.

6.3. Where the information given pursuant to items 6.1 and 6.2 has been influenced by exceptional factors, mention that fact.

6.4. If material to the issuer's business or profitability, disclose summary information regarding the extent to which the issuer is dependent, on patents or licences, industrial, commercial or financial contracts or new manufacturing processes.

6.5. The basis for any statements made by the issuer regarding its competitive position.

7. **ORGANISATIONAL STRUCTURE**

7.1. If the issuer is part of a group, a brief description of the group and the issuer's position within the group.

7.2. A list of the issuer's significant subsidiaries, including name, country of incorporation or residence, proportion of ownership interest and, if different, proportion of voting power held.

8. **PROPERTY, PLANTS AND EQUIPMENT**

8.1. Information regarding any existing or planned material tangible fixed assets, including leased properties, and any major encumbrances thereon.

8.2. A description of any environmental issues that may affect the issuer's utilisation of the tangible fixed assets.

9. **OPERATING AND FINANCIAL REVIEW**

9.1. *Financial condition*

To the extent not covered elsewhere in the prospectus, provide a description of the issuer's financial condition, changes in financial condition and results of operations for each year and interim period, for which historical financial information is required, including the causes of material changes from year to year in the financial information to the extent necessary for an understanding of the issuer's business as a whole.

9.2. *Operating results*

9.2.1. Information regarding significant factors, including unusual or infrequent events or new developments, materially affecting the issuer's income from operations, indicating the extent to which income was so affected.

▼B

9.2.2. Where the financial statements disclose material changes in net sales or revenues, provide a narrative discussion of the reasons for such changes.

9.2.3. Information regarding any governmental, economic, fiscal, monetary or political policies or factors that have materially affected, or could materially affect, directly or indirectly, the issuer's operations.

10. **CAPITAL RESOURCES**

10.1. Information concerning the issuer's capital resources (both short and long term).

10.2. An explanation of the sources and amounts of and a narrative description of the issuer's cash flows.

10.3. Information on the borrowing requirements and funding structure of the issuer.

10.4. Information regarding any restrictions on the use of capital resources that have materially affected, or could materially affect, directly or indirectly, the issuer's operations.

10.5. Information regarding the anticipated sources of funds needed to fulfil commitments referred to in items 5.2.3 and 8.1.

11. **RESEARCH AND DEVELOPMENT, PATENTS AND LICENCES**

Where material, provide a description of the issuer's research and development policies for each financial year for the period covered by the historical financial information, including the amount spent on issuer-sponsored research and development activities.

12. **TREND INFORMATION**

12.1. The most significant recent trends in production, sales and inventory, and costs and selling prices since the end of the last financial year to the date of the prospectus.

12.2. Information on any known trends, uncertainties, demands, commitments or events that are reasonably likely to have a material effect on the issuer's prospects for at least the current financial year.

13. **PROFIT FORECASTS OR ESTIMATES**

If an issuer chooses to include a profit forecast or a profit estimate the prospectus must contain the information items 13.1 and 13.2.

13.1. A statement setting out the principal assumptions upon which the issuer has based its forecast, or estimate.

There must be a clear distinction between assumptions about factors which the members of the administrative, management or supervisory bodies can influence and assumptions about factors which are exclusively outside the influence of the members of the administrative, management or supervisory bodies; the assumptions must be readily understandable by investors, be specific and precise and not relate to the general accuracy of the estimates underlying the forecast.

13.2. A report prepared by independent accountants or auditors stating that in the opinion of the independent accountants or auditors the forecast or estimate has been properly compiled on the basis stated and that the basis of accounting used for the profit forecast or estimate is consistent with the accounting policies of the issuer.

13.3. The profit forecast or estimate prepared on a basis comparable with the historical financial information.

13.4. If the issuer has published a profit forecast in a prospectus which is still outstanding, provide a statement setting out whether or not that forecast is still correct as at the time of the prospectus, and an explanation of why such forecast is no longer valid if that is the case.

14. **ADMINISTRATIVE, MANAGEMENT, AND SUPERVISORY BODIES AND SENIOR MANAGEMENT**

14.1. Names, business addresses and functions in the issuer of the following persons and an indication of the principal activities performed by them

▼B

outside that issuer where these are significant with respect to that issuer:

(a) members of the administrative, management or supervisory bodies;

(b) partners with unlimited liability, in the case of a limited partnership with a share capital;

(c) founders, if the issuer has been established for fewer than five years;

(d) any senior manager who is relevant to establishing that the issuer has the appropriate expertise and experience for the management of the issuer's business.

The nature of any family relationship between any of those persons.

In the case of each member of the administrative, management or supervisory bodies of the issuer and person described in points (b) and (d) of the first subparagraph, details of that person's relevant management expertise and experience and the following information:

(a) the names of all companies and partnerships of which such person has been a member of the administrative, management or supervisory bodies or partner at any time in the previous five years, indicating whether or not the individual is still a member of the administrative, management or supervisory bodies or partner. It is not necessary to list all the subsidiaries of an issuer of which the person is also a member of the administrative, management or supervisory bodies;

(b) any convictions in relation to fraudulent offences for at least the previous five years;

(c) details of any bankruptcies, receiverships or liquidations with which a person described in points (a) and (d) of the first subparagraph who was acting in the capacity of any of the positions set out in points (a) and (d) of the first subparagraph member of the administrative, management or supervisory bodies was associated for at least the previous five years;

(d) details of any official public incrimination and/or sanctions of such person by statutory or regulatory authorities (including designated professional bodies) and whether such person has ever been disqualified by a court from acting as a member of the administrative, management or supervisory bodies of an issuer or from acting in the management or conduct of the affairs of any issuer for at least the previous five years.

If there is no such information to be disclosed, a statement to that effect must be made.

14.2. *Administrative, Management, and Supervisory bodies' and Senior Management conflicts of interests*

Potential conflicts of interests between any duties to the issuer of the persons referred to in the first subparagraph of item 14.1 and their private interests and or other duties must be clearly stated. In the event that there are no such conflicts, make a statement to that effect.

Any arrangement or understanding with major shareholders, customers, suppliers or others, pursuant to which any person referred to in the first subparagraph of item 14.1 was selected as a member of the administrative, management or supervisory bodies or member of senior management.

15. **REMUNERATION AND BENEFITS**

In relation to the last full financial year for those persons referred to in points (a) and (d) of the first subparagraph of item 14.1:

15.1. The amount of remuneration paid (including any contingent or deferred compensation), and benefits in kind granted, to such persons by the issuer and its subsidiaries for services in all capacities to the issuer and its subsidiaries by any person.

This information must be provided on an individual basis unless individual disclosure is not required in the issuer's home country and is not otherwise publicly disclosed by the issuer.

▼B

15.2. The total amounts set aside or accrued by the issuer or its subsidiaries to provide pension, retirement or similar benefits.

16. **BOARD PRACTICES**

In relation to the issuer's last completed financial year, and unless otherwise specified, with respect to those persons referred to in point (a) of the first subparagraph of item 14.1:

16.1. Date of expiration of the current term of office, if applicable, and the period during which the person has served in that office.

16.2. Information about members of the administrative, management or supervisory bodies' service contracts with the issuer or any of its subsidiaries providing for benefits upon termination of employment, or an appropriate negative statement.

16.3. Information about the issuer's audit committee and remuneration committee, including the names of committee members and a summary of the terms of reference under which the committee operates.

16.4. A statement as to whether or not the issuer complies with its country's of incorporation corporate governance regime(s). In the event that the issuer does not comply with such a regime, a statement to that effect together with an explanation regarding why the issuer does not comply with such regime.

17. **EMPLOYEES**

17.1. Either the number of employees at the end of the period or the average for each financial year for the period covered by the historical financial information up to the date of the prospectus (and changes in such numbers, if material) and, if possible and material, a breakdown of persons employed by main category of activity and geographic location. If the issuer employs a significant number of temporary employees, include disclosure of the number of temporary employees on average during the most recent financial year.

17.2. Shareholdings and stock options

With respect to each person referred to in points (a) and (b) of the first subparagraph of item 14.1, provide information as to their share ownership and any options over such shares in the issuer as of the most recent practicable date.

17.3. Description of any arrangements for involving the employees in the capital of the issuer.

18. **MAJOR SHAREHOLDERS**

18.1. In so far as is known to the issuer, the name of any person other than a member of the administrative, management or supervisory bodies who, directly or indirectly, has an interest notifiable under the issuer's national law in the issuer's capital or voting rights, together with the amount of each such person's interest or, if there are no such persons, an appropriate negative statement.

18.2. Whether the issuer's major shareholders have different voting rights, or an appropriate negative statement.

18.3. To the extent known to the issuer, state whether the issuer is directly or indirectly owned or controlled and by whom and describe the nature of such control and describe the measures in place to ensure that such control is not abused.

18.4. A description of any arrangements, known to the issuer, the operation of which may at a subsequent date result in a change in control of the issuer.

19. **RELATED PARTY TRANSACTIONS**

Details of related party transactions (which for these purposes are those set out in the Standards adopted according to Regulation (EC) No 1606/2002), that the issuer has entered into during the period covered by the historical financial information and up to the date of the prospectus must be disclosed in accordance with the respective standard adopted according to Regulation (EC) No 1606/2002 if applicable.

▼B

If such standards do not apply to the issuer the following information must be disclosed:

(a) the nature and extent of any transactions which are - as a single transaction or in their entirety - material to the issuer. Where such related party transactions are not concluded at arm's length provide an explanation of why these transactions were not concluded at arms length. In the case of outstanding loans including guarantees of any kind indicate the amount outstanding;

(b) the amount or the percentage to which related party transactions form part of the turnover of the issuer.

20. **FINANCIAL INFORMATION CONCERNING THE ISSUER'S ASSETS AND LIABILITIES, FINANCIAL POSITION AND PROFITS AND LOSSES**

20.1. *Historical financial information*

Audited historical financial information covering the latest 3 financial years (or such shorter period that the issuer has been in operation), and the audit report in respect of each year. ►M2 If the issuer has changed its accounting reference date during the period for which historical financial information is required, the audited historical information shall cover at least 36 months, or the entire period for which the issuer has been in operation, whichever is the shorter. ◄ Such financial information must be prepared according to Regulation (EC) No 1606/2002, or if not applicable to a Member States national accounting standards for issuers from the Community. For third country issuers, such financial information must be prepared according to the international accounting standards adopted pursuant to the procedure of Article 3 of Regulation (EC) No 1606/2002 or to a third country's national accounting standards equivalent to these standards. If such financial information is not equivalent to these standards, it must be presented in the form of restated financial statements.

The last two years audited historical financial information must be presented and prepared in a form consistent with that which will be adopted in the issuer's next published annual financial statements having regard to accounting standards and policies and legislation applicable to such annual financial statements.

If the issuer has been operating in its current sphere of economic activity for less than one year, the audited historical financial information covering that period must be prepared in accordance with the standards applicable to annual financial statements under Regulation (EC) No 1606/2002, or if not applicable to a Member States national accounting standards where the issuer is an issuer from the Community. For third country issuers, the historical financial information must be prepared according to the international accounting standards adopted pursuant to the procedure of Article 3 of Regulation (EC) No 1606/2002 or to a third country's national accounting standards equivalent to these standards. This historical financial information must be audited.

If the audited financial information is prepared according to national accounting standards, the financial information required under this heading must include at least the following:

(a) the balance sheet;

(b) the income statement;

(c) a statement showing either all changes in equity or changes in equity other than those arising from capital transactions with owners and distributions to owners;

(d) the cash flow statement;

(e) the accounting policies and explanatory notes.

The historical annual financial information must be independently audited or reported on as to whether or not, for the purposes of the prospectus, it gives a true and fair view, in accordance with auditing standards applicable in a Member State or an equivalent standard.

▼B

20.1a *This paragraph may be used only for issues of depository receipts having a denomination per unit of at least EUR 50 000.*

Audited historical financial information covering the latest three financial years (or such shorter period that the issuer has been in operation), and the audit report in respect of each year. ►M2 If the issuer has changed its accounting reference date during the period for which historical financial information is required, the audited historical information shall cover at least 36 months, or the entire period for which the issuer has been in operation, whichever is the shorter. ◄ Such financial information must be prepared according to Regulation (EC) No 1606/2002, or if not applicable to a Member State's national accounting standards for issuers from the Community. For third country issuers, such financial information must be prepared according to the international accounting standards adopted pursuant to the procedure of Article 3 of Regulation (EC) No 1606/2002 or to a third country's national accounting standards equivalent to these standards. Otherwise, the following information must be included in the prospectus:

(a) a prominent statement that the financial information included in the registration document has not been prepared in accordance with the international accounting standards adopted pursuant to the procedure of Article 3 of Regulation (EC) No 1606/2002 and that there may be material differences in the financial information had Regulation (EC) No 1606/2002 been applied to the historical financial information;

(b) immediately following the historical financial information a narrative description of the differences between the international accounting standards adopted pursuant to the procedure of Article 3 of Regulation (EC) No 1606/2002 and the accounting principles adopted by the issuer in preparing its annual financial statements.

The last two years audited historical financial information must be presented and prepared in a form consistent with that which will be adopted in the issuer's next published annual financial statements having regard to accounting standards and policies and legislation applicable to such annual financial statements.

If the audited financial information is prepared according to national accounting standards, the financial information required under this heading must include at least the following:

(a) the balance sheet;

(b) the income statement;

(c) a statement showing either all changes in equity or changes in equity other than those arising from capital transactions with owners and distributions to owners;

(d) the cash flow statement;

(e) the accounting policies and explanatory notes.

The historical annual financial information must be independently audited or reported on as to whether or not, for the purposes of the prospectus, it gives a true and fair view, in accordance with auditing standards applicable in a Member State or an equivalent standard. Otherwise, the following information must be included in the prospectus:

(a) a prominent statement disclosing which auditing standards have been applied;

(b) an explanation of any significant departures from international standards on auditing.

20.2. *Financial statements*

If the issuer prepares both own and consolidated annual financial statements, include at least the consolidated annual financial statements in the prospectus.

▼B

20.3. *Auditing of historical annual financial information*

20.3.1. A statement that the historical financial information has been audited. If audit reports on the historical financial information have been refused by the statutory auditors or if they contain qualifications or disclaimers, such refusal or such qualifications or disclaimers must be reproduced in full and the reasons given.

20.3.2. Indication of other information in the prospectus which has been audited by the auditors.

20.3.3. Where financial data in the prospectus is not extracted from the issuer's audited financial statements state the source of the data and state that the data is unaudited.

20.4. *Age of latest financial information*

20.4.1. The last year of audited financial information may not be older than:

(a) 18 months from the date of the prospectus if the issuer includes audited interim financial statements in the prospectus;

(b) 15 months from the date of the prospectus if the issuer includes unaudited interim financial statements in the prospectus.

20.5. *Interim and other financial information*

20.5.1. If the issuer has published quarterly or half yearly financial information since the date of its last audited financial statements, these must be included in the prospectus. If the quarterly or half yearly financial information has been reviewed or audited the audit or review report must also be included. If the quarterly or half yearly financial information is unaudited or has not been reviewed, state that fact.

20.5.2. If the prospectus is dated more than nine months after the end of the last audited financial year, it must contain interim financial information, which may be unaudited (in which case that fact shall be stated) covering at least the first six months of the financial year.

The interim financial information must include comparative statements for the same period in the prior financial year, except that the requirement for comparative balance sheet information may be satisfied by presenting the years end balance sheet.

20.6. *Dividend policy*

A description of the issuer's policy on dividend distributions and any restrictions thereon.

20.6.1. The amount of the dividend per share for each financial year for the period covered by the historical financial information adjusted, where the number of shares in the issuer has changed, to make it comparable.

20.7. *Legal and arbitration proceedings*

Information on any governmental, legal or arbitration proceedings (including any such proceedings which are pending or threatened of which the issuer is aware), during a period covering at least the previous 12 months which may have, or have had in the recent past significant effects on the issuer and/or group's financial position or profitability, or provide an appropriate negative statement.

20.8. *Significant change in the issuer's financial or trading position*

A description of any significant change in the financial or trading position of the group which has occurred since the end of the last financial period for which either audited financial information or interim financial information have been published, or provide an appropriate negative statement.

21. **ADDITIONAL INFORMATION**

21.1. *Share capital*

The following information as of the date of the most recent balance sheet included in the historical financial information:

21.1.1. The amount of issued capital, and for each class of share capital:

(a) the number of shares authorised;

▼B

(b) the number of shares issued and fully paid and issued but not fully paid;

(c) the par value per share, or that the shares have no par value;

(d) a reconciliation of the number of shares outstanding at the beginning and end of the year. If more than 10 % of capital has been paid for with assets other than cash within the period covered by the historical financial information, state that fact.

21.1.2. If there are shares not representing capital, state the number and main characteristics of such shares.

21.1.3. The number, book value and face value of shares in the issuer held by or on behalf of the issuer itself or by subsidiaries of the issuer.

21.1.4. The amount of any convertible securities, exchangeable securities or securities with warrants, with an indication of the conditions governing and the procedures for conversion, exchange or subscription.

21.1.5. Information about and terms of any acquisition rights and or obligations over authorised but unissued capital or an undertaking to increase the capital.

21.1.6. Information about any capital of any member of the group which is under option or agreed conditionally or unconditionally to be put under option and details of such options including those persons to whom such options relate.

21.1.7. A history of share capital, highlighting information about any changes, for the period covered by the historical financial information.

21.2. *Memorandum and Articles of Association*

21.2.1. A description of the issuer's objects and purposes and where they can be found in the memorandum and articles of association.

21.2.2. A summary of any provisions of the issuer's articles of association, statutes or charter and bylaws with respect to the members of the administrative, management and supervisory bodies.

21.2.3. A description of the rights, preferences and restrictions attaching to each class of the existing shares.

21.2.4. A description of what action is necessary to change the rights of holders of the shares, indicating where the conditions are more significant than is required by law.

21.2.5. A description of the conditions governing the manner in which annual general meetings and extraordinary general meetings of shareholders are called including the conditions of admission.

21.2.6. A brief description of any provision of the issuer's articles of association, statutes, charter or bylaws that would have an effect of delaying, deferring or preventing a change in control of the issuer.

21.2.7. An indication of the articles of association, statutes, charter or bylaws provisions, if any, governing the ownership threshold above which shareholder ownership must be disclosed.

21.2.8. A description of the conditions imposed by the memorandum and articles of association statutes, charter or bylaws governing changes in the capital, where such conditions are more stringent than is required by law.

22. **MATERIAL CONTRACTS**

A summary of each material contract, other than contracts entered into in the ordinary course of business, to which the issuer or any member of the group is a party, for the two years immediately preceding publication of the prospectus.

A summary of any other contract (not being a contract entered into in the ordinary course of business) entered into by any member of the group which contains any provision under which any member of the group has any obligation or entitlement which is material to the group as at the date of the prospectus.

▼B

23. **THIRD PARTY INFORMATION, STATEMENT BY EXPERTS AND DECLARATIONS OF ANY INTEREST**

23.1. Where a statement or report attributed to a person as an expert is included in the prospectus provide such person's name, business address, qualifications and material interest if any in the issuer. If the report has been produced at the issuer's request a statement to that effect that such statement or report is included, in the form and context in which it is included, with the consent of that person who has authorised the contents of that part of the prospectus.

23.2. Where information has been sourced from a third party, provide a confirmation that this information has been accurately reproduced and that as far as the issuer is aware and is able to ascertain from information published by that third party, no facts have been omitted which would render the reproduced information inaccurate or misleading. In addition, the issuer shall identify the source(s) of the information.

24. **DOCUMENTS ON DISPLAY**

A statement that for the life of the prospectus the following documents (or copies thereof), where applicable, may be inspected:

(a) the memorandum and articles of association of the issuer;

(b) all reports, letters, and other documents, historical financial information, valuations and statements prepared by any expert at the issuer's request any part of which is included or referred to in the prospectus;

(c) the historical financial information of the issuer or, in the case of a group, the historical financial information for the issuer and its subsidiary undertakings for each of the two financial years preceding the publication of the prospectus.

An indication of where the documents on display may be inspected, by physical or electronic means.

25. **INFORMATION ON HOLDINGS**

25.1. Information relating to the undertakings in which the issuer holds a proportion of the capital likely to have a significant effect on the assessment of its own assets and liabilities, financial position or profits and losses.

26. **INFORMATION ABOUT THE ISSUER OF THE DEPOSITORY RECEIPTS**

26.1. Name, registered office and principal administrative establishment if different from the registered office.

26.2. Date of incorporation and length of life of the issuer, except where indefinite.

26.3. Legislation under which the issuer operates and legal form which it has adopted under that legislation.

27. **INFORMATION ABOUT THE UNDERLYING SHARES**

27.1. A description of the type and the class of the underlying shares, including the ISIN (International Security Identification Number) or other such security identification code.

27.2. Legislation under which the underlying shares have been created.

27.3. An indication whether the underlying shares are in registered form or bearer form and whether the underlying shares are in certificated form or book-entry form. In the latter case, name and address of the entity in charge of keeping the records.

27.4. Currency of the underlying shares.

27.5. A description of the rights, including any limitations of these, attached to the underlying shares and procedure for the exercise of said rights.

27.6. Dividend rights:

(a) fixed date(s) on which the entitlement arises;

(b) time limit after which entitlement to dividend lapses and an indication of the person in whose favour the lapse operates;

▼B

(c) dividend restrictions and procedures for non-resident holders;

(d) rate of dividend or method of its calculation, periodicity and cumulative or non-cumulative nature of payments.

27.7. Voting rights

Pre-emption rights in offers for subscription of securities of the same class

Right to share in the issuer's profits

Rights to share in any surplus in the event of liquidation

Redemption provisions

Conversion provisions.

27.8. The issue date of the underlying shares if new underlying shares are being created for the issue of the depository receipts and they are not in existence at the time of issue of the depository receipts.

27.9. If new underlying shares are being created for the issue of the depository receipts, state the resolutions, authorisations and approvals by virtue of which the new underlying shares have been or will be created and/or issued.

27.10. A description of any restrictions on the free transferability of the underlying shares.

27.11. In respect of the country of registered office of the issuer and the country(ies) where the offer is being made or admission to trading is being sought:

(a) information on taxes on the income from the underlying shares withheld at source;

(b) indication as to whether the issuer assumes responsibility for the withholding of taxes at the source.

27.12. An indication of the existence of any mandatory takeover bids and/or squeeze-out and sell-out rules in relation to the underlying shares.

27.13. An indication of public takeover bids by third parties in respect of the issuer's equity, which have occurred during the last financial year and the current financial year. The price or exchange terms attaching to such offers and the outcome thereof must be stated.

27.14. Lock up agreements:

— the parties involved,

— content and exceptions of the agreement,

— indication of the period of the lock up.

27.15. *Information about selling share holders if any*

27.15.1. Name and business address of the person or entity offering to sell the underlying shares, the nature of any position office or other material relationship that the selling persons has had within the past three years with the issuer of the underlying shares or any of its predecessors or affiliates.

27.16. *Dilution*

27.16.1. Amount and percentage of immediate dilution resulting from the offer of the depository receipts.

27.16.2. In the case of a subscription offer of the depository receipts to existing shareholders, disclose the amount and percentage of immediate dilutions if they do not subscribe to the offer of depository receipts.

27.17. *Additional information where there is a simultaneous or almost simultaneous offer or admission to trading of the same class of underlying shares as those underlying shares over which the depository receipts are being issued.*

27.17.1. If simultaneously or almost simultaneously with the creation of the depository receipts for which admission to a regulated market is being sought underlying shares of the same class as those over which the depository receipts are being issued are subscribed for or

▼B

placed privately, details are to be given of the nature of such operations and of the number and characteristics of the underlying shares to which they relate.

27.17.2. Disclose all regulated markets or equivalent markets on which, to the knowledge of the issuer of the depository receipts, underlying shares of the same class of those over which the depository receipts are being issued are offered or admitted to trading.

27.17.3. To the extent known to the issuer of the depository receipts, indicate whether major shareholders, members of the administrative, management or supervisory bodies intended to subscribe in the offer, or whether any person intends to subscribe for more than five per cent of the offer.

28. **INFORMATION REGARDING THE DEPOSITORY RECEIPTS**

28.1. A description of the type and class of depository receipts being offered and/or admitted to trading.

28.2. Legislation under which the depository receipts have been created.

28.3. An indication whether the depository receipts are in registered or bearer form and whether the depository receipts are in certificated or book-entry form. In the latter case, include the name and address of the entity in charge of keeping the records.

28.4. Currency of the depository receipts.

28.5. Describe the rights attaching to the depository receipts, including any limitations of these attached to the depository receipts and the procedure if any for the exercise of these rights.

28.6. If the dividend rights attaching to depository receipts are different from the dividend rights disclosed in relation to the underlying disclose the following about the dividend rights:

(a) fixed date(s) on which the entitlement arises;

(b) time limit after which entitlement to dividend lapses and an indication of the person in whose favour the lapse operates;

(c) dividend restrictions and procedures for non-resident holders;

(d) rate of dividend or method of its calculation, periodicity and cumulative or non-cumulative nature of payments.

28.7. If the voting rights attaching to the depository receipts are different from the voting rights disclosed in relation to the underlying shares disclose the following about those rights:

— Voting rights.

— Pre-emption rights in offers for subscription of securities of the same class.

— Right to share in the issuer's profits.

— Rights to share in any surplus in the event of liquidation.

— Redemption provisions.

— Conversion provisions.

28.8. Describe the exercise of and benefit from the rights attaching to the underlying shares, in particular voting rights, the conditions on which the issuer of the depository receipts may exercise such rights, and measures envisaged to obtain the instructions of the depository receipt holders - and the right to share in profits and any liquidation surplus which are not passed on to the holder of the depository receipt.

28.9. The expected issue date of the depository receipts.

28.10. A description of any restrictions on the free transferability of the depository receipts.

28.11. In respect of the country of registered office of the issuer and the country(ies) where the offer is being made or admission to trading is being sought:

(a) information on taxes on the income from the depository receipts withheld at source;

▼B

(b) indication as to whether the issuer assumes responsibility for the withholding of taxes at the source.

28.12. Bank or other guarantees attached to the depository receipts and intended to underwrite the issuer's obligations.

28.13. Possibility of obtaining the delivery of the depository receipts into original shares and procedure for such delivery.

29. **INFORMATION ABOUT THE TERMS AND CONDITIONS OF THE OFFER OF THE DEPOSITORY RECEIPTS**

29.1. *Conditions, offer statistics, expected timetable and action required to apply for the offer*

29.1.1. Total amount of the issue/offer, distinguishing the securities offered for sale and those offered for subscription; if the amount is not fixed, description of the arrangements and time for announcing to the public the definitive amount of the offer.

29.1.2. The time period, including any possible amendments, during which the offer will be open and description of the application process.

29.1.3. An indication of when, and under what circumstances, the offer may be revoked or suspended and whether revocation can occur after dealing has begun.

29.1.4. A description of the possibility to reduce subscriptions and the manner for refunding excess amount paid by applicants.

29.1.5. Details of the minimum and/or maximum amount of application (whether in number of securities or aggregate amount to invest).

29.1.6. An indication of the period during which an application may be withdrawn, provided that investors are allowed to withdraw their subscription.

29.1.7. Method and time limits for paying up the securities and for delivery of the securities.

29.1.8. A full description of the manner and date in which results of the offer are to be made public.

29.1.9. The procedure for the exercise of any right of pre-emption, the negotiability of subscription rights and the treatment of subscription rights not exercised.

29.2. *Plan of distribution and allotment*

29.2.1. The various categories of potential investors to which the securities are offered. If the offer is being made simultaneously in the markets of two or more countries and if a tranche has been or is being reserved for certain of these, indicate any such tranche.

29.2.2. To the extent known to the issuer, indicate whether major shareholders or members of the issuer's management, supervisory or administrative bodies intended to subscribe in the offer, or whether any person intends to subscribe for more than five per cent of the offer.

29.2.3. Pre-allotment Disclosure:

29.2.3.1. The division into tranches of the offer including the institutional, retail and issuer's employee tranches and any other tranches.

29.2.3.2. The conditions under which the claw-back may be used, the maximum size of such claw back and any applicable minimum percentages for individual tranches.

29.2.3.3. The allotment method or methods to be used for the retail and issuer's employee tranche in the event of an over-subscription of these tranches.

29.2.3.4. A description of any pre-determined preferential treatment to be accorded to certain classes of investors or certain affinity groups (including friends and family programmes) in the allotment, the percentage of the offer reserved for such preferential treatment and the criteria for inclusion in such classes or groups.

29.2.3.5. Whether the treatment of subscriptions or bids to subscribe in the allotment may be determined on the basis of which firm they are made through or by.

▼B

29.2.3.6. A target minimum individual allotment if any within the retail tranche.

29.2.3.7. The conditions for the closing of the offer as well as the date on which the offer may be closed at the earliest;

29.2.3.8. Whether or not multiple subscriptions are admitted, and where they are not, how any multiple subscriptions will be handled.

29.2.3.9. Process for notification to applicants of the amount allotted and indication whether dealing may begin before notification is made.

29.2.4. Over-allotment and 'green shoe':

29.2.4.1. The existence and size of any over-allotment facility and/or 'green shoe'.

29.2.4.2. The existence period of the over-allotment facility and/or 'green shoe'.

29.2.4.3. Any conditions for the use of the over-allotment facility or exercise of the 'green shoe'.

29.3. *Pricing*

29.3.1. An indication of the price at which the securities will be offered. When the price is not known or when there is not an established and/or liquid market for the securities, indicate the method for determination of the offer price, including who has set the criteria or is formally responsible for its determination. Indication of the amount of any expenses and taxes specifically charged to the subscriber or purchaser.

29.3.2. Process for the disclosure of the offer price.

29.3.3. Where there is or could be a material disparity between the public offer price and the effective cash cost to members of the administrative, management or supervisory bodies or senior management, or affiliated persons, of securities acquired by them in transactions during the past year, or which they have the right to acquire, include a comparison of the public contribution in the proposed public offer and the effective cash contributions of such persons.

29.4. *Placing and underwriting*

29.4.1. Name and address of the co-coordinator(s) of the global offer and of single parts of the offer and, to the extend known to the issuer, of the placers in the various countries where the offer takes place.

29.4.2. Name and address of any paying agents and depository agents in each country.

29.4.3. Name and address of the entities agreeing to underwrite the issue on a firm commitment basis, and name and address of the entities agreeing to place the issue without a firm commitment or under 'best efforts' arrangements. Indication of the material features of the agreements, including the quotas. Where not all of the issue is underwritten, a statement of the portion not covered. Indication of the overall amount of the underwriting commission and of the placing commission.

29.4.4. When the underwriting agreement has been or will be reached.

30. **ADMISSION TO TRADING AND DEALING ARRANGEMENTS IN THE DEPOSITORY RECEIPTS**

30.1. An indication as to whether the securities offered are or will be the object of an application for admission to trading, with a view to their distribution in a regulated market or other equivalent markets with indication of the markets in question. This circumstance must be mentioned, without creating the impression that the admission to trading necessarily will be approved. If known, the earliest dates on which the securities will be admitted to trading must be given.

30.2. All the regulated markets or equivalent markets on which, to the knowledge of the issuer, securities of the same class of the securities to be offered or admitted to trading are already admitted to trading.

30.3. If simultaneously or almost simultaneously with the creation of the securities for which admission to a regulated market is being sought securities of the same class are subscribed for or placed privately or if securities of other classes are created for public or private placing,

▼B

details must be given of the nature of such operations and of the number and characteristics of the securities to which they relate.

30.4. Name and address of the entities which have a firm commitment to act as intermediaries in secondary trading, providing liquidity through bid and offer rates and description of the main terms of their commitment.

30.5. Stabilisation: where an issuer or a selling shareholder has granted an over-allotment option or it is otherwise proposed that price stabilising activities may be entered into in connection with an offer:

30.6. The fact that stabilisation may be undertaken, that there is no assurance that it will be undertaken and that it may be stopped at any time.

30.7. The beginning and the end of the period during which stabilisation may occur.

30.8. The identity of the stabilisation manager for each relevant jurisdiction unless this is not known at the time of publication.

30.9. The fact that stabilisation transactions may result in a market price that is higher than would otherwise prevail.

31. **KEY INFORMATION ABOUT THE ISSUE OF THE DEPOSITORY RECEIPTS**

31.1. *Reasons for the offer and use of proceeds*

31.1.1. Reasons for the offer and, where applicable, the estimated net amount of the proceeds broken into each principal intended use and presented by order of priority of such uses. If the issuer is aware that the anticipated proceeds will not be sufficient to fund all the proposed uses, state the amount and sources of other funds needed. Details must be given with regard to the use of the proceeds, in particular when they are being used to acquire assets, other than in the ordinary course of business, to finance announced acquisitions of other business, or to discharge, reduce or retire indebtedness.

31.2. *Interest of natural and legal persons involved in the issue/offer*

31.2.1. A description of any interest, including conflicting ones, that is material to the issue/offer, detailing the persons involved and the nature of the interest.

31.3. *Risk factors*

31.3.1. Prominent disclosure of risk factors that are material to the securities being offered and/or admitted to trading in order to assess the market risk associated with these securities in a section headed 'Risk factors'.

32. **EXPENSE OF THE ISSUE/OFFER OF THE DEPOSITORY RECEIPTS**

32.1. The total net proceeds and an estimate of the total expenses of the issue/offer.

▼B

ANNEX XI

Minimum Disclosure Requirements for the Banks Registration Document (schedule)

1. **PERSONS RESPONSIBLE**

1.1. All persons responsible for the information given in the registration document and, as the case may be, for certain parts of it, with, in the latter case, an indication of such parts. In the case of natural persons including members of the issuer's administrative, management or supervisory bodies indicate the name and function of the person; in case of legal persons indicate the name and registered office.

1.2. A declaration by those responsible for the registration document that, having taken all reasonable care to ensure that such is the case, the information contained in the registration document is, to the best of their knowledge, in accordance with the facts and contains no omission likely to affect its import. As the case may be, declaration by those responsible for certain parts of the registration document that, having taken all reasonable care to ensure that such is the case, the information contained in the part of the registration document for which they are responsible is, to the best of their knowledge, in accordance with the facts and contains no omission likely to affect its import.

2. **STATUTORY AUDITORS**

2.1. Names and addresses of the issuer's auditors for the period covered by the historical financial information (together with their membership in a professional body).

2.2. If auditors have resigned, been removed or not been reappointed during the period covered by the historical financial information, details if material.

3. **RISK FACTORS**

3.1. Prominent disclosure of risk factors that may affect the issuer's ability to fulfil its obligations under the securities to investors in a section headed 'Risk factors'.

4. **INFORMATION ABOUT THE ISSUER**

4.1. *History and development of the Issuer*

4.1.1. the legal and commercial name of the issuer;

4.1.2. the place of registration of the issuer and its registration number;

4.1.3. the date of incorporation and the length of life of the issuer, except where indefinite;

4.1.4. the domicile and legal form of the issuer, the legislation under which the issuer operates, its country of incorporation, and the address and telephone number of its registered office (or principal place of business if different from its registered office);

4.1.5. any recent events particular to the issuer which are to a material extent relevant to the evaluation of the issuer's solvency.

5. **BUSINESS OVERVIEW**

5.1. *Principal activities:*

5.1.1. A brief description of the issuer's principal activities stating the main categories of products sold and/or services performed;

5.1.2. An indication of any significant new products and/or activities.

5.1.3. Principal markets

A brief description of the principal markets in which the issuer competes.

5.1.4. The basis for any statements in the registration document made by the issuer regarding its competitive position.

▼B

6. **ORGANISATIONAL STRUCTURE**

6.1. If the issuer is part of a group, a brief description of the group and of the issuer's position within it.

6.2. If the issuer is dependent upon other entities within the group, this must be clearly stated together with an explanation of this dependence.

7. **TREND INFORMATION**

7.1. Include a statement that there has been no material adverse change in the prospects of the issuer since the date of its last published audited financial statements.

In the event that the issuer is unable to make such a statement, provide details of this material adverse change.

7.2. Information on any known trends, uncertainties, demands, commitments or events that are reasonably likely to have a material effect on the issuer's prospects for at least the current financial year.

8. **PROFIT FORECASTS OR ESTIMATES**

If an issuer chooses to include a profit forecast or a profit estimate the registration document must contain the information items 8.1 and 8.2.

8.1. A statement setting out the principal assumptions upon which the issuer has based its forecast, or estimate.

There must be a clear distinction between assumptions about factors which the members of the administrative, management or supervisory bodies can influence and assumptions about factors which are exclusively outside the influence of the members of the administrative, management or supervisory bodies; be readily understandable by investors; be specific and precise; and not relate to the general accuracy of the estimates underlying the forecast.

8.2. A report prepared by independent accountants or auditors stating that in the opinion of the independent accountants or auditors the forecast or estimate has been properly compiled on the basis stated and that the basis of accounting used for the profit forecast or estimate is consistent with the accounting policies of the issuer.

8.3. The profit forecast or estimate must be prepared on a basis comparable with the historical financial information.

9. **ADMINISTRATIVE, MANAGEMENT, AND SUPERVISORY BODIES**

9.1. Names, business addresses and functions in the issuer of the following persons, and an indication of the principal activities performed by them outside the issuer where these are significant with respect to that issuer:

(a) members of the administrative, management or supervisory bodies;

(b) partners with unlimited liability, in the case of a limited partnership with a share capital.

9.2. *Administrative, Management, and Supervisory bodies conflicts of interests*

Potential conflicts of interests between any duties to the issuing entity of the persons referred to in item 9.1 and their private interests and or other duties must be clearly stated. In the event that there are no such conflicts, make a statement to that effect.

10. **MAJOR SHAREHOLDERS**

10.1. To the extent known to the issuer, state whether the issuer is directly or indirectly owned or controlled and by whom, and describe the nature of such control, and describe the measures in place to ensure that such control is not abused.

10.2. A description of any arrangements, known to the issuer, the operation of which may at a subsequent date result in a change in control of the issuer.

▼B

11. **FINANCIAL INFORMATION CONCERNING THE ISSUER'S ASSETS AND LIABILITIES, FINANCIAL POSITION AND PROFITS AND LOSSES**

11.1. *Historical Financial Information*

Audited historical financial information covering the latest two financial years (or such shorter period that the issuer has been in operation), and the audit report in respect of each year. ►M2 If the issuer has changed its accounting reference date during the period for which historical financial information is required, the audited historical information shall cover at least 24 months, or the entire period for which the issuer has been in operation, whichever is the shorter. ◄ Such financial information must be prepared according to Regulation (EC) No 1606/2002, or if not applicable to a Member State national accounting standards for issuers from the Community. For third country issuers, such financial information must be prepared according to the international accounting standards adopted pursuant to the procedure of Article 3 of Regulation (EC) No 1606/2002 or to a third country's national accounting standards equivalent to these standards. If such financial information is not equivalent to these standards, it must be presented in the form of restated financial statements.

The most recent year's audited historical financial information must be presented and prepared in a form consistent with that which will be adopted in the issuer's next published annual financial statements having regard to accounting standards and policies and legislation applicable to such annual financial statements.

If the issuer has been operating in its current sphere of economic activity for less than one year, the audited historical financial information covering that period must be prepared in accordance with the standards applicable to annual financial statements under Regulation (EC) No 1606/2002, or if not applicable to a Member State national accounting standards where the issuer is an issuer from the Community. For third country issuers, the historical financial information must be prepared according to the international accounting standards adopted pursuant to the procedure of Article 3 of Regulation (EC) No 1606/2002 or to a third country's national accounting standards equivalent to these standards. This historical financial information must be audited.

If the audited financial information is prepared according to national accounting standards, the financial information required under this heading must include at least the following:

(a) the balance sheet;

(b) the income statement;

(c) in the case of an admission of securities to trading on a regulated market only, a cash flow statement;

(d) the accounting policies and explanatory notes.

The historical annual financial information must be independently audited or reported on as to whether or not, for the purposes of the registration document, it gives a true and fair view, in accordance with auditing standards applicable in a Member State or an equivalent standard.

11.2. *Financial statements*

If the issuer prepares both own and consolidated financial statements, include at least the consolidated financial statements in the registration document.

11.3. *Auditing of historical annual financial information*

11.3.1. A statement that the historical financial information has been audited. If audit reports on the historical financial information have been refused by the statutory auditors or if they contain qualifications or disclaimers, such refusal or such qualifications or disclaimers must be reproduced in full and the reasons given.

11.3.2. An indication of other information in the registration document which has been audited by the auditors.

▼B

11.3.3. Where financial data in the registration document is not extracted from the issuer's audited financial statements state the source of the data and state that the data is un-audited.

11.4. *Age of latest financial information*

11.4.1. The last year of audited financial information may not be older than 18 months from the date of the registration document.

11.5. *Interim and other financial information*

11.5.1 If the issuer has published quarterly or half yearly financial information since the date of its last audited financial statements, these must be included in the registration document. If the quarterly or half yearly financial information has been reviewed or audited the audit or review report must also be included. If the quarterly or half yearly financial information is unaudited or has not been reviewed state that fact.

11.5.2. If the registration document is dated more than nine months after the end of the last audited financial year, it must contain interim financial information, covering at least the first six months of the financial year. If the interim financial information is un-audited state that fact.

The interim financial information must include comparative statements for the same period in the prior financial year, except that the requirement for comparative balance sheet information may be satisfied by presenting the years end balance sheet.

11.6. *Legal and arbitration proceedings*

Information on any governmental, legal or arbitration proceedings (including any such proceedings which are pending or threatened of which the issuer is aware), during a period covering at least the previous 12 months which may have, or have had in the recent past, significant effects on the issuer and/or group's financial position or profitability, or provide an appropriate negative statement.

11.7. *Significant change in the issuer's financial position*

A description of any significant change in the financial position of the group which has occurred since the end of the last financial period for which either audited financial information or interim financial information have been published, or an appropriate negative statement.

12. **MATERIAL CONTRACTS**

A brief summary of all material contracts that are not entered into in the ordinary course of the issuer's business, which could result in any group member being under an obligation or entitlement that is material to the issuer's ability to meet its obligation to security holders in respect of the securities being issued.

13. **THIRD PARTY INFORMATION AND STATEMENT BY EXPERTS AND DECLARATIONS OF ANY INTEREST**

13.1. Where a statement or report attributed to a person as an expert is included in the registration document, provide such person's name, business address, qualifications and material interest if any in the issuer. If the report has been produced at the issuer's request a statement to that effect that such statement or report is included, in the form and context in which it is included, with the consent of that person who has authorised the contents of that part of the registration document.

13.2. Where information has been sourced from a third party, provide a confirmation that this information has been accurately reproduced and that as far as the issuer is aware and is able to ascertain from information published by that third party, no facts have been omitted which would render the reproduced information inaccurate or misleading In addition, the issuer shall identify the source(s) of the information.

14. **DOCUMENTS ON DISPLAY**

A statement that for the life of the registration document the following documents (or copies thereof), where applicable, may be inspected:

(a) the memorandum and articles of association of the issuer;

(b) all reports, letters, and other documents, historical financial information, valuations and statements prepared by any expert at the

▼B

issuer's request any part of which is included or referred to in the registration document;

(c) the historical financial information of the issuer or, in the case of a group, the historical financial information of the issuer and its subsidiary undertakings for each of the two financial years preceding the publication of the registration document.

An indication of where the documents on display may be inspected, by physical or electronic means.

▼B

ANNEX XII

Minimum Disclosure Requirements for the Securities Note for derivative securities (schedule)

1. **PERSONS RESPONSIBLE**

1.1. All persons responsible for the information given in the prospectus and, as the case may be, for certain parts of it, with, in the latter case, an indication of such parts. In the case of natural persons including members of the issuer's administrative, management or supervisory bodies indicate the name and function of the person; in case of legal persons indicate the name and registered office.

1.2. A declaration by those responsible for the prospectus that, having taken all reasonable care to ensure that such is the case, the information contained in the prospectus is, to the best of their knowledge, in accordance with the facts and contains no omission likely to affect its import. As the case may be, declaration by those responsible for certain parts of the prospectus that, having taken all reasonable care to ensure that such is the case, the information contained in the part of the prospectus for which they are responsible is, to the best of their knowledge, in accordance with the facts and contains no omission likely to affect its import.

2. **RISK FACTORS**

Prominent disclosure of risk factors that are material to the securities being offered and/or admitted to trading in order to assess the market risk associated with these securities in a section headed 'risk factors'. This must include a risk warning to the effect that investors may lose the value of their entire investment or part of it, as the case may be, and/or, if the investor's liability is not limited to the value of his investment, a statement of that fact, together with a description of the circumstances in which such additional liability arises and the likely financial effect.

3. **KEY INFORMATION**

3.1. *Interest of natural and legal persons involved in the issue/offer*

A description of any interest, including conflicting ones that is material to the issue/offer, detailing the persons involved and the nature of the interest.

3.2. *Reasons for the offer and use of proceeds when different from making profit and/or hedging certain risks*

If reasons for the offer and use of proceeds are disclosed provide the total net proceeds and an estimate of the total expenses of the issue/offer.

4. **INFORMATION CONCERNING THE SECURITIES TO BE OFFERED/ADMITTED TO TRADING**

4.1. *Information concerning the securities*

4.1.1. A description of the type and the class of the securities being offered and/or admitted to trading, including the ISIN (International Security Identification Number) or other such security identification code.

4.1.2. A clear and comprehensive explanation to help investors understand how the value of their investment is affected by the value of the underlying instrument (s), especially under the circumstances when the risks are most evident unless the securities have a denomination per unit of at least EUR 50 000 or can only be acquired for at least EUR 50 000 per security.

4.1.3. Legislation under which the securities have been created.

4.1.4. An indication whether the securities are in registered form or bearer form and whether the securities are in certificated form or book-entry form. In the latter case, name and address of the entity in charge of keeping the records.

4.1.5. Currency of the securities issue.

▼B

4.1.6. Ranking of the securities being offered and/or admitted to trading, including summaries of any clauses that are intended to affect ranking or subordinate the security to any present or future liabilities of the issuer.

4.1.7. A description of the rights, including any limitations of these, attached to the securities and procedure for the exercise of said rights.

4.1.8. In the case of new issues, a statement of the resolutions, authorisations and approvals by virtue of which the securities have been or will be created and/or issued.

4.1.9. The issue date of the securities.

4.1.10. A description of any restrictions on the free transferability of the securities.

4.1.11. — The expiration or maturity date of the derivative securities.

— The exercise date or final reference date.

4.1.12. A description of the settlement procedure of the derivative securities.

4.1.13. A description of how any return on derivative securities takes place, the payment or delivery date, and the way it is calculated.

4.1.14. In respect of the country of registered office of the issuer and the country(ies) where the offer is being made or admission to trading is being sought:

(a) information on taxes on the income from the securities withheld at source;

(b) indication as to whether the issuer assumes responsibility for the withholding of taxes at the source.

4.2. *Information concerning the underlying*

4.2.1. The exercise price or the final reference price of the underlying.

4.2.2. A statement setting out the type of the underlying and details of where information on the underlying can be obtained:

— an indication where information about the past and the further performance of the underlying and its volatility can be obtained,

— where the underlying is a security,

  — the name of the issuer of the security,

  — the ISIN (international security identification number) or other such security identification code,

— where the underlying is an index,

  — the name of the index and a description of the index if it is composed by the issuer. If the index is not composed by the issuer, where information about the index can be obtained,

— where the underlying is an interest rate,

  — a description of the interest rate,

— others:

  — Where the underlying does not fall within the categories specified above the securities note shall contain equivalent information.

— where the underlying is a basket of underlyings,

  — disclosure of the relevant weightings of each underlying in the basket.

4.2.3. A description of any market disruption or settlement disruption events that affect the underlying.

4.2.4. Adjustment rules with relation to events concerning the underlying.

▼B

5. **TERMS AND CONDITIONS OF THE OFFER**

5.1. *Conditions, offer statistics, expected timetable and action required to apply for the offer*

5.1.1. Conditions to which the offer is subject.

5.1.2. Total amount of the issue/offer; if the amount is not fixed, description of the arrangements and time for announcing to the public the amount of the offer.

5.1.3. The time period, including any possible amendments, during which the offer will be open and description of the application process.

5.1.4. Details of the minimum and/or maximum amount of application, (whether in number of securities or aggregate amount to invest).

5.1.5. Method and time limits for paying up the securities and for delivery of the securities.

5.1.6. A full description of the manner and date in which results of the offer are to be made public.

5.2. *Plan of distribution and allotment*

5.2.1. The various categories of potential investors to which the securities are offered. If the offer is being made simultaneously in the markets of two or more countries and if a tranche has been or is being reserved for certain of these, indicate any such tranche.

5.2.2. Process for notification to applicants of the amount allotted and indication whether dealing may begin before notification is made.

5.3. *Pricing*

Indication of the expected price at which the securities will be offered or the method of determining the price and the process for its disclosure. Indicate the amount of any expenses and taxes specifically charged to the subscriber or purchaser.

5.4. *Placing and underwriting*

5.4.1. Name and address of the coordinator(s) of the global offer and of single parts of the offer and, to the extend known to the issuer or to the offeror, of the placers in the various countries where the offer takes place.

5.4.2. Name and address of any paying agents and depository agents in each country.

5.4.3. Entities agreeing to underwrite the issue on a firm commitment basis, and entities agreeing to place the issue without a firm commitment or under 'best efforts' arrangements. Where not all of the issue is underwritten, a statement of the portion not covered.

5.4.4. When the underwriting agreement has been or will be reached.

5.4.5. Name and address of a calculation agent.

6. **ADMISSION TO TRADING AND DEALING ARRANGEMENTS**

6.1. An indication as to whether the securities offered are or will be the object of an application for admission to trading, with a view to their distribution in a regulated market or other equivalent markets with indication of the markets in question. This circumstance shall be mentioned, without creating the impression that the admission to trading necessarily will be approved. If known, the earliest dates on which the securities will be admitted to trading shall be given.

6.2. All the regulated markets or equivalent markets on which, to the knowledge of the issuer, securities of the same class of the securities to be offered or admitted to trading are already admitted to trading.

6.3. Name and address of the entities which have a firm commitment to act as intermediaries in secondary trading, providing liquidity through bid and offer rates and description of the main terms of their commitment.

7. **ADDITIONAL INFORMATION**

7.1. If advisors connected with an issue are mentioned in the Securities Note, a statement of the capacity in which the advisors have acted.

▼B

7.2. An indication of other information in the Securities Note which has been audited or reviewed by statutory auditors and where auditors have produced a report. Reproduction of the report or, with permission of the competent authority, a summary of the report.

7.3. Where a statement or report attributed to a person as an expert is included in the Securities Note, provide such person's name, business address, qualifications and material interest, if any, in the issuer. If the report has been produced at the issuer's request a statement to that effect that such statement or report is included, in the form and context in which it is included, with the consent of that person who has authorised the contents of that part of the Securities Note.

7.4. Where information has been sourced from a third party, provide a confirmation that this information has been accurately reproduced and that as far as the issuer is aware and is able to ascertain from information published by that third party, no facts have been omitted which would render the reproduced information inaccurate or misleading. In addition, the issuer shall identify the source(s) of the information.

7.5. An indication in the prospectus whether or not the issuer intends to provide post-issuance information. Where the issuer has indicated that it intends to report such information, the issuer shall specify in the prospectus what information will be reported and where such information can be obtained.

▼B

ANNEX XIII

Minimum Disclosure Requirements for the Securities Note for debt securities with a denomination per unit of at least EUR 50 000 (Schedule)

1. **PERSONS RESPONSIBLE**

1.1. All persons responsible for the information given in the prospectus and, as the case may be, for certain parts of it, with, in the latter case, an indication of such parts. In case of natural persons including members of the issuer's administrative, management or supervisory bodies indicate the name and function of the person; in case of legal persons indicate the name and registered office.

1.2. A declaration by those responsible for the prospectus that, having taken all reasonable care to ensure that such is the case, the information contained in the prospectus is, to the best of their knowledge, in accordance with the facts and contains no omission likely to affect its import. As the case may be, declaration by those responsible for certain parts of the prospectus that the information contained in the part of the prospectus for which they are responsible is, to the best of their knowledge, in accordance with the facts and contains no omission likely to affect its import.

2. **RISK FACTORS**

Prominent disclosure of risk factors that are material to the securities admitted to trading in order to assess the market risk associated with these securities in a section headed 'Risk factors'.

3. **KEY INFORMATION**

Interest of natural and legal persons involved in the issue

A description of any interest, including conflicting ones, that is material to the issue, detailing the persons involved and the nature of the interest.

4. **INFORMATION CONCERNING THE SECURITIES TO BE ADMITTED TO TRADING**

4.1. Total amount of securities being admitted to trading.

4.2. A description of the type and the class of the securities being admitted to trading, including the ISIN (international security identification number) or other such security identification code.

4.3. Legislation under which the securities have been created.

4.4. An indication of whether the securities are in registered or bearer form and whether the securities are in certificated or book-entry form. In the latter case, name and address of the entity in charge of keeping the records.

4.5. Currency of the securities issue.

4.6. Ranking of the securities being admitted to trading, including summaries of any clauses that are intended to affect ranking or subordinate the security to any present or future liabilities of the issuer.

4.7. A description of the rights, including any limitations of these, attached to the securities and procedure for the exercise of said rights.

4.8. The nominal interest rate and provisions relating to interest payable:

— The date from which interest becomes payable and the due dates for interest.

— The time limit on the validity of claims to interest and repayment of principal.

Where the rate is not fixed, description of the underlying on which it is based and of the method used to relate the two:

— A description of any market disruption or settlement disruption events that affect the underlying.

— Adjustment rules with relation to events concerning the underlying.

▼B

— Name of the calculation agent.

4.9. Maturity date and arrangements for the amortisation of the loan, including the repayment procedures. Where advance amortisation is contemplated, on the initiative of the issuer or of the holder, it must be described, stipulating amortisation terms and conditions.

4.10. An indication of yield.

4.11. Representation of debt security holders including an identification of the organisation representing the investors and provisions applying to such representation. Indication of where investors may have access to the contracts relating to these forms of representation.

4.12. A statement of the resolutions, authorisations and approvals by virtue of which the securities have been created and/or issued.

4.13. The issue date of the securities.

4.14. A description of any restrictions on the free transferability of the securities.

5. **ADMISSION TO TRADING AND DEALING ARRANGEMENTS**

5.1. Indication of the market where the securities will be traded and for which prospectus has been published. If known, give the earliest dates on which the securities will be admitted to trading.

5.2. Name and address of any paying agents and depository agents in each country.

6. **EXPENSE OF THE ADMISSION TO TRADING**

An estimate of the total expenses related to the admission to trading.

7. **ADDITIONAL INFORMATION**

7.1. If advisors are mentioned in the Securities Note, a statement of the capacity in which the advisors have acted.

7.2. An indication of other information in the Securities Note which has been audited or reviewed by auditors and where auditors have produced a report. Reproduction of the report or, with permission of the competent authority, a summary of the report.

7.3. Where a statement or report attributed to a person as an expert is included in the Securities Note, provide such person's name, business address, qualifications and material interest if any in the issuer. If the report has been produced at the issuer's request a statement to that effect that such statement or report is included, in the form and context in which it is included, with the consent of that person who has authorised the contents of that part of the Securities Note.

7.4. Where information has been sourced from a third party, provide a confirmation that this information has been accurately reproduced and that as far as the issuer is aware and is able to ascertain from information published by that third party, no facts have been omitted which would render the reproduced information inaccurate or misleading. In addition, identify the source(s) of the information.

7.5. Credit ratings assigned to an issuer or its debt securities at the request or with the co-operation of the issuer in the rating process.

▼B

ANNEX XIV

Additional information building block on underlying share for some equity securities

1. Description of the underlying share

1.1. Describe the type and the class of the shares

1.2. Legislation under which the shares have been or will be created

1.3. Indication whether the securities are in registered form or bearer form and whether the securities are in certificated form or book-entry form. In the latter case, name and address of the entity in charge of keeping the records

1.4. Indication of the currency of the shares issue

1.5. A description of the rights, including any limitations of these, attached to the securities and procedure for the exercise of those rights:

- Dividend rights:
  - fixed date(s) on which the entitlement arises,
  - time limit after which entitlement to dividend lapses and an indication of the person in whose favour the lapse operates,
  - dividend restrictions and procedures for non resident holders,
  - rate of dividend or method of its calculation, periodicity and cumulative or non-cumulative nature of payments.
- Voting rights.
- Pre-emption rights in offers for subscription of securities of the same class.
- Right to share in the issuer's profits.
- Rights to share in any surplus in the event of liquidation.
- Redemption provisions.
- Conversion provisions.

1.6. In the case of new issues, a statement of the resolutions, authorisations and approvals by virtue of which the shares have been or will be created and/or issued and indication of the issue date.

1.7. Where and when the shares will be or have been admitted to trading.

1.8. Description of any restrictions on the free transferability of the shares.

1.9. Indication of the existence of any mandatory takeover bids/or squeeze-out and sell-out rules in relation to the shares.

1.10. Indication of public takeover bids by third parties in respect of the issuer's equity, which have occurred during the last financial year and the current financial year. The price or exchange terms attaching to such offers and the outcome thereof must be stated.

1.11. Impact on the issuer of the underlying share of the exercise of the right and potential dilution effect for the shareholders.

2. When the issuer of the underlying is an entity belonging to the same group, the information to provide on this issuer is the one required by the share registration document schedule.

▼B

ANNEX XV

Minimum disclosure requirements for the registration document for securities issued by collective investment undertakings of the closed-end type (schedule)

In addition to the information required in this schedule, the collective investment undertaking must provide the following information as required under paragraphs and items 1, 2, 3, 4, 5.1, 7, 9.1, 9.2.1, 9.2.3, 10.4, 13, 14, 15, 16, 17.2, 18, 19, 20, 21, 22, 23, 24, 25 in Annex I (minimum disclosure requirements for the share registration document schedule).

1. **Investment objective and policy**

1.1. A detailed description of the investment objective and policy which the collective investment undertaking will pursue and a description of how that investment objectives and policy may be varied including any circumstances in which such variation requires the approval of investors. A description of any techniques and instruments that may be used in the management of the collective investment undertaking.

1.2. The borrowing and/or leverage limits of the collective investment undertaking. If there are no such limits, include a statement to that effect.

1.3. The regulatory status of the collective investment undertaking together with the name of any regulator in its country of incorporation.

1.4. The profile of a typical investor for whom the collective investment undertaking is designed.

2. **Investment Restrictions**

2.1. A statement of the investment restrictions which apply to the collective investment undertaking, if any, and an indication of how the holders of securities will be informed of the actions that the investment manager will take in the event of a breach.

2.2. Where more than 20 % of the gross assets of any collective investment undertaking (except where items 2.3 or 2.5 apply) may be:

(a) invested in, either directly or indirectly, or lent to any single underlying issuer (including the underlying issuer's subsidiaries or affiliates);

or

(b) invested in one or more collective investment undertakings which may invest in excess of 20 % of its gross assets in other collective investment undertakings (open-end and/or closed-end type);

or

(c) exposed to the creditworthiness or solvency of any one counterparty (including its subsidiaries or affiliates);

the following information must be disclosed:

(i) information relating to each underlying issuer/collective investment undertaking/counterparty as if it were an issuer for the purposes of the minimum disclosure requirements for the share registration document schedule (in the case of (a)) or minimum disclosure requirements for the registration document schedule for securities issued by collective investment undertaking of the closed-end type (in the case of (b)) or the minimum disclosure requirements for the debt and derivative securities with an individual denomination per unit of at least EUR 50 000 registration document schedule (in the case of (c));

or

(ii) if the securities issued by the underlying issuer/collective investment undertaking/counterparty have already been admitted to trading on a regulated or equivalent market or the obligations are guaranteed by an entity admitted to trading on a regulated or equivalent market, the name, address, country of incorporation, nature of business and name of the market in which its securities are admitted.

▼B

This requirement shall not apply where the 20 % is exceeded due to appreciations or depreciations, changes in exchange rates, or by reason of the receipt of rights, bonuses, benefits in the nature of capital or by reason of any other action affecting every holder of that investment, provided the investment manager has regard to the threshold when considering changes in the investment portfolio.

2.3. Where a collective investment undertaking may invest in excess of 20 % of its gross assets in other collective investment undertakings (open ended and/or closed ended), a description of if and how risk is spread in relation to those investments. In addition, item 2.2 shall apply, in aggregate, to its underlying investments as if those investments had been made directly.

2.4. With reference to point (c) of item 2.2, if collateral is advanced to cover that portion of the exposure to any one counterparty in excess of 20 % of the gross assets of the collective investment undertaking, details of such collateral arrangements.

2.5. Where a collective investment undertaking may invest in excess of 40 % of its gross assets in another collective investment undertaking either of the following must be disclosed:

(a) information relating to each underlying collective investment undertaking as if it were an issuer under minimum disclosure requirements for the registration document schedule for securities issued by collective investment undertaking of the closed-end type;

(b) if securities issued by an underlying collective investment undertaking have already been admitted to trading on a regulated or equivalent market or the obligations are guaranteed by an entity admitted to trading on a regulated or equivalent market, the name, address, country of incorporation, nature of business and name of the market in which its securities are admitted.

2.6. *Physical Commodities*

Where a collective investment undertaking invests directly in physical commodities a disclosure of that fact and the percentage that will be so invested.

2.7. *Property Collective investment undertakings*

Where a collective investment undertaking is a property collective investment undertaking, disclosure of that fact, the percentage of the portfolio that is to be invested in the property, as well as a description of the property and any material costs relating to the acquisition and holding of such property. In addition, a valuation report relating to the properties must be included.

Disclosure of item 4.1. applies to:

(a) the valuation entity;

(b) any other entity responsible for the administration of the property.

2.8. *Derivatives Financial instruments/Money Market Instruments/ Currencies*

Where a collective investment undertaking invests in derivatives financial instruments, money market instruments or currencies other than for the purposes of efficient portfolio management (i.e. solely for the purpose of reducing, transferring or eliminating investment risk in the underlying investments of a collective investment undertaking, including any technique or instrument used to provide protection against exchange and credit risks), a statement whether those investments are used for hedging or for investment purposes, and a description of if and how risk is spread in relation to those investments.

2.9. Item 2.2 does not apply to investment in securities issued or guaranteed by a government, government agency or instrumentality of any Member State, its regional or local authorities, or OECD Member State.

2.10. Point (a) of item 2.2 does not apply to a collective investment undertaking whose investment objective is to track, without material modification, that of a broadly based and recognised published index. A description of the composition of the index must be provided.

▼B

3. **The applicant's service providers**

3.1. The actual or estimated maximum amount of all material fees payable directly or indirectly by the collective investment undertaking for any services under arrangements entered into on or prior to the date of the registration document and a description of how these fees are calculated.

3.2. A description of any fee payable directly or indirectly by the collective investment undertaking which cannot be quantified under item 3.1 and which is or may be material.

3.3. If any service provider to the collective investment undertaking is in receipt of any benefits from third parties (other than the collective investment undertaking) by virtue of providing any services to the collective investment undertaking, and those benefits may not accrue to the collective investment undertaking, a statement of that fact, the name of that third party, if available, and a description of the nature of the benefits.

3.4. The name of the service provider which is responsible for the determination and calculation of the net asset value of the collective investment undertaking.

3.5. A description of any material potential conflicts of interest which any of the service providers to the collective investment undertaking may have as between their duty to the collective investment undertaking and duties owed by them to third parties and their other interests. A description of any arrangements which are in place to address such potential conflicts.

4. **Investment Manager/Advisers**

4.1. In respect of any Investment Manager such information as is required to be disclosed under items 5.1.1 to 5.1.4 and, if material, under item 5.1.5 of Annex I together with a description of its regulatory status and experience.

4.2. In respect of any entity providing investment advice in relation to the assets of the collective investment undertaking, the name and a brief description of such entity.

5. **Custody**

5.1. A full description of how the assets of the collective investment undertaking will be held and by whom and any fiduciary or similar relationship between the collective investment undertaking and any third party in relation to custody:

Where a custodian, trustee, or other fiduciary is appointed:

(a) such information as is required to be disclosed under items 5.1.1 to 5.1.4 and, if material, under item 5.1.5 of Annex I;

(b) a description of the obligations of such party under the custody or similar agreement;

(c) any delegated custody arrangements;

(d) the regulatory status of such party and delegates.

5.2. Where any entity other than those entities mentioned in item 5.1, holds any assets of the collective investment undertaking, a description of how these assets are held together with a description of any additional risks.

6. **Valuation**

6.1. A description of how often, and the valuation principles and the method by which, the net asset value of the collective investment undertaking will be determined, distinguishing between categories of investments and a statement of how such net asset value will be communicated to investors.

6.2. Details of all circumstances in which valuations may be suspended and a statement of how such suspension will be communicated or made available to investors.

▼B

7. **Cross Liabilities**

7.1. In the case of an umbrella collective investment undertaking, a statement of any cross liability that may occur between classes or investments in other collective investment undertakings and any action taken to limit such liability.

8. **Financial Information**

8.1. Where, since the date of incorporation or establishment, a collective investment undertaking has not commenced operations and no financial statements have been made up as at the date of the registration document, a statement to that effect.

Where a collective investment undertaking has commenced operations, the provisions of item 20 of Annex I on the Minimum Disclosure Requirements for the share registration document apply.

8.2. A comprehensive and meaningful analysis of the collective investment undertaking's portfolio (if un-audited, clearly marked as such).

8.3. An indication of the most recent net asset value per security must be included in the securities note schedule (and, if un-audited, clearly marked as such).

▼B

ANNEX XVI

Minimum disclosure requirements for the registration document for securities issued by Member States, third countries and their regional and local authorities (schedule)

1. **PERSONS RESPONSIBLE**

1.1. All persons responsible for the information given in the registration document and, as the case may be, for certain parts of it, with, in the latter case, an indication of such parts. In the case of natural persons including members of the issuer's administrative, management or supervisory bodies indicate the name and function of the person; in case of legal persons indicate the name and registered office.

1.2. A declaration by those responsible for the registration document that, having taken all reasonable care to ensure that such is the case, the information contained in the registration document is, to the best of their knowledge in accordance with the facts and contains no omission likely to affect its import. As the case may be, declaration by those responsible for certain parts of the registration document that, having taken all reasonable care to ensure that such is the case the information contained in the part of the registration document for which they are responsible is, to the best of their knowledge, in accordance with the facts and contains no omission likely to affect its import.

2. **RISK FACTORS**

Prominent disclosure of risk factors that may affect the issuer's ability to fulfil its obligations under the securities to investors in a section headed 'Risk factors'.

3. **INFORMATION ABOUT THE ISSUER**

3.1. The legal name of the issuer and a brief description of the issuer's position within the national governmental framework.

3.2. The domicile or geographical location and legal form of the issuer and its contact address and telephone number.

3.3. Any recent events relevant to the evaluation of the issuer's solvency.

3.4. A description of the issuer's economy including:

(a) the structure of the economy with details of the main sectors of the economy;

(b) gross domestic product with a breakdown by the issuer's economic sectors over for the previous two fiscal years.

3.5. A general description of the issuer's political system and government including details of the governing body of the issuer.

4. **PUBLIC FINANCE AND TRADE**

Information on the following for the two fiscal years prior to the date of the registration document:

(a) the tax and budgetary systems;

(b) gross public debt including a summary of the debt, the maturity structure of outstanding debt (particularly noting debt with a residual maturity of less than one year) and debt payment record, and of the parts of debt denominated in the domestic currency of the issuer and in foreign currencies;

(c) foreign trade and balance of payment figures;

(d) foreign exchange reserves including any potential encumbrances to such foreign exchange reserves as forward contracts or derivatives;

(e) financial position and resources including liquid deposits available in domestic currency;

(f) income and expenditure figures.

Description of any auditing or independent review procedures on the accounts of the issuer.

▼B

5. **SIGNIFICANT CHANGE**

5.1. Details of any significant changes to the information provided pursuant to item 4 which have occurred since the end of the last fiscal year, or an appropriate negative statement.

6. **LEGAL AND ARBITRATION PROCEEDINGS**

Information on any governmental, legal or arbitration proceedings (including any such proceedings which are pending or threatened of which the issuer is aware), during a period covering at least the previous 12 months which may have, or have had in the recent past, significant effects on the issuer financial position, or provide an appropriate negative statement.

6.2. Information on any immunity the issuer may have from legal proceedings.

7. **STATEMENT BY EXPERTS AND DECLARATIONS OF ANY INTEREST**

Where a statement or report attributed to a person as an expert is included in the registration document, provide such person's name, business address and qualifications. If the report has been produced at the issuer's request a statement to that effect, that such statement or report is included, in the form and context in which it is included, with the consent of that person, who has authorised the contents of that part of the registration document.

To the extent known to the issuer, provide information in respect of any interest relating to such expert which may have an effect on the independence of the expert in the preparation of the report.

8. **DOCUMENTS ON DISPLAY**

A statement that for the life of the registration document the following documents (or copies thereof), where applicable, may be inspected:

(a) financial and audit reports for the issuer covering the last two fiscal years and the budget for the current fiscal year;

(b) all reports, letters, and other documents, valuations and statements prepared by any expert at the issuer's request any part of which is included or referred to in the registration document.

An indication of where the documents on display may be inspected, by physical or electronic means.

▼B

ANNEX XVII

Minimum disclosure requirements for the registration document for securities issued by public international bodies and for debt securities guaranteed by a Member State of the OECD (schedule)

1. **PERSONS RESPONSIBLE**

1.1. All persons responsible for the information given in the registration document and, as the case may be, for certain parts of it, with, in the latter case, an indication of such parts. In the case of natural persons including members of the issuer's administrative, management or supervisory bodies indicate the name and function of the person; in case of legal persons indicate the name and registered office.

1.2. A declaration by those responsible for the registration document, that, having taken all reasonable care to ensure that such is the case, the information contained in the registration document is, to the best of their knowledge, in accordance with the facts and contains no omission likely to materially affect its import. As the case may be, declaration by those responsible for certain parts of the registration document that, having taken all reasonable care to ensure that such is the case the information contained in the part of the registration document for which they are responsible is, to the best of their knowledge, in accordance with the facts and contains no omission likely to affect its import.

2. **RISK FACTORS**

Prominent disclosure of risk factors that may affect the issuer's ability to fulfil its obligations under the securities to investors in a section headed 'Risk factors'.

3. **INFORMATION ABOUT THE ISSUER**

3.1. The legal name of the issuer and a brief description of the issuer's legal status.

3.2. The location of the principal office and the legal form of the issuer and its contact address and telephone number.

3.3. Details of the governing body of the issuer and a description of its governance arrangements, if any.

3.4. A brief description of the issuer's purpose and functions.

3.5. The sources of funding, guarantees and other obligations owed to the issuer by its members.

3.6. Any recent events relevant to the evaluation of the issuer's solvency.

3.7. A list of the issuer's members.

4. **FINANCIAL INFORMATION**

4.1. The two most recently published audited annual financial statements prepared in accordance with the accounting and auditing principles adopted by the issuer, and a brief description of those accounting and auditing principles.

Details of any significant changes to the issuer's financial position which has occurred since the end of the latest published audited annual financial statement, or an appropriate negative statement.

5. **LEGAL AND ARBITRATION PROCEEDINGS**

5.1. Information on any governmental, legal or arbitration proceedings (including any such proceedings which are pending or threatened of which the issuer is aware), during a period covering at least the previous 12 months which are likely to have, or have had in the recent past, significant effects on the issuer's financial position, or provide an appropriate negative statement.

5.2. Information on any immunity the issuer may have from legal proceedings pursuant to its constituent document.

▼B

6. **STATEMENT BY EXPERTS AND DECLARATION OF ANY INTERESTS**

Where a statement or report attributed to a person as an expert is included in the registration document, provide such person's name, business address and qualifications. If the report has been produced at the issuer's request a statement to that effect, that such statement or report is included, in the form and context in which it is included, with the consent of that person.

To the extent known to the issuer, provide information in respect of any conflict of interests relating to such expert which may have an effect on the independence of the expert in the preparation of the report.

7. **DOCUMENT ON DISPLAY**

A statement that for the life of the registration document the following documents (or copies thereof), where applicable, will be made available on request:

(a) annual and audit reports of the issuer for each of the last two financial years prepared in accordance with the accounting and auditing principles adopted by the issuer;

(b) all reports, letters, and other documents, valuations and statements prepared by any expert at the issuer's request any part of which is included or referred to in the registration document;

(c) the issuer's constituent document.

An indication of where the documents on display may be inspected, by physical or electronic means.

▼B

ANNEX XVIII

Table of combinations

	REGISTRATION DOCUMENT					
	SCHEDULES					BUILDING BLOCK
TYPES OF SECURITIES	Share	Debt and derivative (< EUR 50 000)	Debt and derivative (> or = EUR 50 000)	Asset -backed securities	Banks debt and derivative	Pro forma information
Shares (preference shares, redeemable shares, shares with preferential subscription rights; etc.)						
Bonds (vanilla bonds, income bonds, structured bonds, etc.) with a denomination of less than EUR 50 000		or			or	
Bonds (vanilla bonds, income bonds, structured bonds, etc.) with a denomination of at least EUR 50 000			or		or	
Debt securities guaranteed by a third party		or	or		or	
Derivative securities guaranteed by a third party		or	or		or	
Asset-backed securities						
Bonds exchangeable or convertible into third-party shares or issuers' or group shares which are admitted on a regulated market		or	or		or	
Bonds exchangeable or convertible into the issuer's shares not admitted on a regulated market						

▼B

	REGISTRATION DOCUMENT					
	SCHEDULES					BUILDING BLOCK
TYPES OF SECURITIES	Share	Debt and derivative (< EUR 50 000)	Debt and derivative (> or = EUR 50 000)	Asset -backed securities	Banks debt and derivative	Pro forma information
Bonds exchangeable or convertible into group's shares not admitted on a regulated market		or	or		or	
Bonds with warrants to acquire the issuer's shares not admitted to trading on a regulated market						
Shares with warrants to acquire the issuer's shares not admitted to trading on a regulated market						
Derivatives securities giving the right to subscribe or to acquire the issuer's shares not admitted on a regulated market						
Derivatives securities giving the right to acquire group's shares not admitted on a regulated market		or	or		or	
Derivatives securities giving the right to subscribe or to acquire issuer's or group shares which are admitted on a regulated market and derivatives sec. linked to any other underlying than issuer's or group shares which are not admitted on a regulated market (including any derivatives sec. entitling to cash settlement)		or	or		or	

▼B

	REGISTRATION DOCUMENT		
	SCHEDULES		
TYPES OF SECURITIES	Collective investment undertaking of the closed-end type	States and their regional and local authorities	Public international bodies/Debt Securities guaranteed by a Member State of the OECD
Shares (preference shares, redeemable shares, shares with preferential subscription rights; etc.)			
Bonds (vanilla bonds, income bonds, structured bonds, etc with a denomination of less than EUR 50 000			
Bonds (vanilla bonds, income bonds, structured bonds, etc.) with a denomination of at least EUR 50 000			
Debt securities guaranteed by a third party			
Derivative securities guaranteed by a third party			
Asset-backed securities			
Bonds exchangeable or convertible into third party shares or issuers' or group shares which are admitted on a regulated market			
Bonds exchangeable or convertible into the issuer's shares not admitted on a regulated market			
Bonds exchangeable or convertible into group's shares not admitted on a regulated market			

▼B

	REGISTRATION DOCUMENT		
	SCHEDULES		
TYPES OF SECURITIES	Collective investment undertaking of the closed-end type	States and their regional and local authorities	Public international bodies/Debt Securities guaranteed by a Member State of the OECD
Bonds with warrants to acquire the issuer's shares not admitted to trading on a regulated market			
Shares with warrants to acquire the issuer's shares not admitted to trading on a regulated market			
Derivatives securities giving the right to subscribe or to acquire the issuer's shares not admitted on a regulated market			
Derivatives securities giving the right to acquire group's shares not admitted on a regulated market			
Derivatives securities giving the right to subscribe or to acquire issuer's or group shares which are admitted on a regulated market and derivatives sec. linked to any other underlying than issuer's or group shares which are not admitted on a regulated market (including any derivatives securities entitling to cash settlement)			

▼B

	SECURITIES NOTE						
	SCHEDULES				ADDITIONAL BUILDING BLOCKS		
TYPES OF SECURITIES	Share	Debt (<EUR 50 000)	Debt (> or = EUR 50 000)	Derivatives securities	Guarantees	Asset-backed securities	Underlying share
Shares (preference shares, redeemable shares, shares with preferential subscription rights; etc.)							
Bonds (vanilla bonds, income bonds, structured bonds, etc with a denomination of less than EUR 50 000							
Bonds (vanilla bonds, income bonds, structured bonds, etc) with a denomination of at least EUR 50 000							
Debt securities guaranteed by a third party		or	or				
Derivative securities guaranteed by a third party							
Asset-backed securities		or	or				
Bonds exchangeable or convertible into third party shares or issuers' or group shares which are admitted on a regulated market		or	or	Only point 4.2.2			
Bonds exchangeable or convertible into the issuer's shares not admitted on a regulated market		or	or				
Bonds exchangeable or convertible into group's shares not admitted on a regulated market		or	or				

▼B

	SECURITIES NOTE						
	SCHEDULES				ADDITIONAL BUILDING BLOCKS		
TYPES OF SECURITIES	Share	Debt (<EUR 50 000)	Debt (> or = EUR 50 000)	Derivatives securities	Guarantees	Asset-backed securities	Underlying share
Bonds with warrants to acquire the issuer's shares not admitted to trading on a regulated market		or	or	and except point 4.2.2			
Shares with warrants to acquire the issuer's shares not admitted to trading on a regulated market				and except point 4.2.2			
Derivatives securities giving the right to subscribe or to acquire the issuer's shares not admitted on a regulated market				except point 4.2.2			
Derivatives securities giving the right to acquire group's shares not admitted on a regulated market				except point 4.2.2			
Derivatives securities giving the right to subscribe or to acquire issuer's or group shares which are admitted on a regulated market and derivatives securities linked to any other underlying than issuer's or group shares which are not admitted on a regulated market (including any derivatives securities entitling to cash settlement)							

▼B

Annex XIX

List of specialist issuers

— Property companies

— Mineral companies

— Investment companies

— Scientific research based companies

— Companies with less than three years of existence (start-up companies)

— Shipping companies.

Annex III
List of national laws implementing the Directive

List of national laws implementing the Prospectus Directive

This Annex contains a list of the current national legislation implementing the Directive.

AUSTRIA

Bundesgesetz, mit dem das Kapitalmarktgesetz, das Börsegesetz, das Investmentfondsgesetz, das Wertpapieraufsichtsgesetz und das Finanzmarktaufsichtsbehördengesetz geändert werden

BELGIUM

Wet van 16 juni 2006 op de openbare aanbieding van beleggingsinstrumenten en de toelating van beleggingsinstrumenten tot de verhandeling op een gereglementeerde markt, *Belgisch Staatsblad* of 21 June 2006

Loi du 16 juin 2006 relative aux offres publiques d'instruments de placement et aux admissions d'instruments de placement à la négociation sur des marchés réglementés, *Moniteur belge* of 21 June 2006

CYPRUS

Ο περί Αξιών και Χρηματιστηρίου Αξιών (Τροποποιητικός) Νόμος του 2005
Ο περί Δημόσιας Προσφοράς και Ενημερωτικού Δελτίου Νόμος του 2005

CZECH REPUBLIC

Zákon č. 56/2006 Sb., kterým se mění zákon č. 256/2004 Sb., o podnikání na kapitálovém trhu, ve znění pozdějších předpisů, publicated on March 8, 2006, in the Collection of Acts of the Czech Republic

DENMARK

Lov nr. 1460 af 22 December 2004 om værdipapirhandel m.v.
Bekendtgørelse nr. 306/2005 om prospekter for værdipapirer, der optages til notering eller handel på et reguleret marked, og ved første offentlige udbud af værdipapirer over 2.500.000 euro

ESTONIA

Väärtpaberituru seaduse, Investeerimisfondide seaduse, Tagatisfondi seaduse ja asjaõigusseaduse muutmise seadus (RTI, 14.11.2005, 59, 464), adopted on 19 October 2005

FINLAND

Laki arvopaperimarkkinalain muuttamisesta
Laki Rahoitustarkastuksesta annetun lain muuttamisesta
Laki velkakirjalain muuttamisesta Laki korkotulon lähdeverosta annetun lain 3 §:n muuttamisesta
Valtiovarainministeriön asetus arvopaperimarkkinalain 2 luvussa tarkoitetusta esitteestä
Valtiovarainministeriön asetus eräistä arvopaperimarkkinalain 2 luvun 3 a §:ssä tarkoitetuista esitteistä (538/2005) (kumottu Valtiovarainministeriön asetuksella eräistä arvopaperimarkkinalain 2 luvun 3 a §:ssä ja kiinteistörahastolain 22 §:ssä tarkoitetuista esitteistä, 818/2007)

FRANCE

Loi No. 2005-842 du 26 juillet 2005 pour la confiance et la modernisation de l'économie

GERMANY

Gesetz zur Umsetzung der Richtlinie 2003/71/EG des Europäischen Parlaments und des Rates vom 4 November 2003 betreffend den Prospekt, der beim öffentlichen Angebot von Wertpapieren oder bei deren Zulassung zum Handel zu veröffentlichen ist, und zur Änderung der Richtlinie 2001/34/EG (Prospektrichtlinie-Umsetzungsgesetz)

GREECE

Ενημερωτικό δελτίο δημόσιας προσφοράς κινητών αξιών και εισαγωγής τους για διαπραγμάτευση (ΝΟΜΟΣ ΥΠ' ΑΡΙΘ. 3401/2005, ΦΕΚ Α' 257/17.10.2005)

HUNGARY

2005. évi LXII. törvény a tökepiacról szóló 2001. évi CXX. Törvény módosításáról

2004. évi CXL. törvény a közigazgatási hatósági eljárás és szolgáltatás általános szabályairól

2001. évi CXX. törvény a tőkepiacról

1999. évi CXXIV. törvény a Pénzügyi Szervezetek Állami Felügyeletéről

1995. évi LXVI. törvény a köziratokról, a közlevéltárakról és a magánlevéltári anyag védelméről.

1957. évi IV. törvény az államigazgatási eljárás általános szabályairól

IRELAND

Prospectus (Directive 2003/71/EC) Regulations 2005 (SI no. 324 of 2005)

LATVIA

Grozījumi Finanšu instrumentu tirgus likumā July 12, 2005
Publicēts: Vēstnesis 28.06.2005 Nr.99 (ZIŅTĀJS 28.07.2005 Nr.14)

LITHUANIA

Name of the legislation (in Lithuanian): Lietuvos Respublikos vertybinių popierių komisijos 2005 m. liepos 15 d. nutarimas Nr. 1K-21 dėl Vertybinių popierių prospekto rengimo ir tvirtinimo bei informacijos atskleidimo taisyklių patvirtinimo of 15 July 2005, *Valstybės Žinios*, 28 July 2005 (Nr. 91-3420), amended by Lietuvos Respublikos vertybinių popierių komisijos 2007 m. vasario 23 d. nutarimas Nr. 1K-8 Dėl Lietuvos Respublikos vertybinių popierių komisijos 2005 m. liepos 15 d. nutarimo Nr. 1K-21 „Dėl Vertybinių popierių prospekto rengimo ir tvirtinimo bei informacijos atskleidimo taisyklių patvirtinimo" pakeitimo, *Valstybės Žinios*, 1 March 2007 (Nr. 26-984)

Lietuvos Respublikos vertybinių popierių įstatymas (2007 m. sausio 18 d., Nr. X-1023), *Valstybės Žinios*, 8 February 2007 (Nr. 17-626)

LUXEMBOURG

Loi du 10 juillet 2005 relative aux prospectus pour valeurs mobilières et portant transposition de la directive 2003/71/CE du Parlement Européen et du Conseil du 4 novembre 2003 concernant le prospectus à publier en cas d'offre au public de valeurs mobilières ou en vue de l'admission de valeurs mobilières à la négociation, et modifiant la directive 2001/34/EC, Mémorial A, No. 98 du 12 juillet 2005

MALTA

Financial Markets Act (CAP. 345) Recognition of Approved Listing Particulars Regulations, 2004

NETHERLANDS

Wet van 28 september 2006 houdende regels met betrekking tot de financiële markten en het toezicht daarop (Wet op het financieel toezicht), *Staatsblad* 475

POLAND

Ustawa z dnia 29 lipca 2005 r. o obrocie instrumentami finansowymi (Dz. U. nr. 183 poz. 1538 z poź)
Ustawa z dnia 29 lipca 2005 r. o nadzorze nad rynkiem kapitałowym (Dz. U. nr. 183 poz. 1537)
Ustawa z dnia 29 lipca 2005 r. o ofercie publicznej i warunkach wprowadzania instrumentów finansowych do zorganizowanego systemu obrotu oraz o spółkach publicznych (Dz. U. nr. 183 poz. 1539)
Ustawa z dnia 21 lipca 2006 r. o nadzorze nad rynkiem finansowym (Dz. U. nr. 157 poz. 1119)

PORTUGAL

Decreto-Lei n.º 52/2006, de 15 de Março 2006, *Diário da República*, I Série A, n.º 53, 15 de Março de 2006 (págs. 1878 a 1909) (Diploma rectificado pela Declaração de Rectificação n.º 21/2006, de 30 de Março, emitida pela Presidência do Conselho de Ministros, publicado in *Diário da República* – I Série A, n.º 64 – 30 de Março, págs. 2330 a 2331)

SLOVAKIA

Zákon z 23. júna 2005 č. 336/2005 Z. z., ktorým sa mení a dopĺňa zákon č. 566/2001 Z. z. o cenných papieroch a investičných službách a o zmene a doplnení niektorných zákonov (zákon o cennných papieroch) v znení neskorších predpisov a o zmene a doplnení niektorých zákonov (Čiastka 141/2005 *Zbierky zákonov Slovenskej republiky*, dátum vydania 27.7.2005)

SLOVENIA

Zakon o spremembah in dopolnitvah Zakona o trgu vrednostnih papirjev of 1 April 2006

Zakon o trgu finančnih instrumentov (ZTFI), *Uradni list Republike Slovenije* št. 67/2007 of 27 July 2007

SPAIN

Real Decreto Ley 5/2005, de 11 de marzo 2005, de reformas urgentes para el impulso a la productividad y para la mejora de la contratación pública, *Boletín Oficial del Estado* nr. 62/2005, de 14 de marzo 2005

Real Decreto 1310/2005, de 4 de noviembre 2005, por el que se desarrolla parcialmente la Ley 24/1988, de 28 de julio, del Mercado de Valores, en materia de admisión a negociación de valores en mercados secundarios oficiales, de ofertas públicas de venta o suscripción y del folleto exigible a tales efectos, *Boletín Oficial del Estado* nr. 274/2005, de 16 de noviembre 2005

Orden EHA/3537/2005 (Ministerio de Economía y Hacienda), por la que se desarrolla el artículo 27.4 de la Ley 24/1988, de 28 de julio, del Mercado de Valores, *Boletín Oficial del Estado* nr. 274/2005, de 16 de noviembre 2005

SWEDEN

Lag (2005:833) om ändring i lagen (1991:980) om handel med finansiella instrument
Lag (2005:834) om ändring i lagen (1992:543) om börs- och clearingverksamhet
Lag (2004:46) om investeringsfonder
Lag (2005:380) om ändring i lagen (1992:543) om börs- och clearingverksamhet

UNITED KINGDOM

The Prospectus Regulations 2005 (SI 2005/1433) of 27 May 2005, published in the UK on 24 June 2005 by the Stationery Office Ltd (in accordance with the Office of Public Sector Information)

ICELAND

Lög um verðbréfaviðskipti nr. 33/2003, sbr. lög nr. 31/2005 og lög nr. 94/2006

Reglugerð um almenn útboð verðbréfa að verðmæti 210 millj. kr. eða meira og skráningu verðbréfa á skipulegan verðbréfamarkað. (242/2006)

Reglugerð um gildistöku reglugerðar framkvæmdastjórnarinnar nr. 809/2004 um framkvæmd tilskipunar Evrópuþingsins og ráðsins 2003/71/EB að því er varðar upplýsingar í lýsingum, svo og framsetningu þeirra, upplýsingar felldar inn með tilvísun, og birtingu lýsinganna, svo og dreifingu auglýsinga. (243/2006)

NORWAY

Verdipapirhandelloven of 19 June 1997
Verdipapirhandelloven of 29 June 2007

Index